PK19

FLEET HISTORY

OF

THAMES VALLEY TRACTION CO LTD

NEWBURY & DISTRICT MOTOR SERVICES LTD
SOUTH MIDLAND MOTOR SERVICES LTD

and their predecessors

PUBLISHED BY

THE PSV CIRCLE

AUGUST 2016

FOREWORD

The draft for this publication was prepared by Bob Howes and is based on publication PK4 (published in September 1960), updated from subsequent amendment and supplementary listings. The work of the late David Gray in producing an initial draft is acknowledged. Considerable help and other valued contributions have also come from Peter Bates, David Corke, Richard Gadsby, Tony Holdsworth, Paul Lacey, Colin Martin, Michael Plunkett, Mike Sutcliffe and Fred Ward. Reference was also made to a number of excellent publications which have helped immensely towards the accuracy of this Fleet History:

British Bus Systems number three – Thames Valley (Peter Holmes / TPC 1984)
Thames Valley – The British Years 1915-1920 (Paul Lacey 1990)
The History of the Thames Valley Traction Company 1920-1930 (Paul Lacey 1995)
The History of the Thames Valley Traction Company 1931-1945 (Paul Lacey 2003)
The History of the Thames Valley Traction Company 1946-1960 (Paul Lacey 2009)
Thames Valley – The final Decade 1961-1971 (Paul Lacey 2012)
A History of the Penn Bus Company 1920-1935 (Paul Lacey 1990)
The Newbury & District Motor Services Story (Paul Lacey 2011)
Thackray's Way – A Family in Road Transport (Paul Lacey 2001)
50 Years of South Midland (1921-1970) (David Flitton / Paul Lacey 2004)

This publication contains all material available in July 2016.

Photographs have kindly been supplied by Brush Coachworks, Chris Carter, John Clarke, Fraser Clayton, AB Cross, Derek Giles, John C Gilham, Peter Henson, JF Higham, Paul Lacey, Roy Marshall, John May (courtesy Mike Eyre), Geoffrey Morant (courtesy Richard Morant), Norris Collection, The Omnibus Society, JF Parke, RHG Simpson, Surfleet Photos, Mike Sutcliffe, Roger Warwick, SNJ White and Tony Wright.

Notes:
This is one of a range of publications produced by The PSV Circle primarily as a service to its members. The information contained herein has been taken from the range of sources indicated above; either from observation or other research, as well as the content of PSV Circle monthly news sheets and also includes information provided from other reputable sources. Considerable time and effort has been taken to ensure that the content of this publication is as complete and accurate as possible but no responsibility can be accepted for any errors or omissions.

Contents:

Any general comments on this publication may be sent to the Publications Manager, Crown House, Linton Road, Barking, IG11 8HG or via email to publications.manager@psvcircle.org.uk.

Details of how to join The PSV Circle and a list of all our publications can be obtained from The PSV Circle website - www.psv-circle.org.uk.

ISBN: 978-1-910767-12-2
Published by the PSV Circle.
© The PSV Circle August 2016

BRITISH AUTOMOBILE TRACTION CO LTD (THAMES VALLEY BRANCH)
THAMES VALLEY TRACTION CO LTD
NEWBURY & DISTRICT MOTOR SERVICES LTD
SOUTH MIDLAND MOTOR SERVICES LTD

This publication describes the activities of the Thames Valley branch of the **British Automobile Traction Co Ltd** from its launch in July 1915 to the formation of the **Thames Valley Traction Co Ltd** in July 1920. The history of Thames Valley is then tracked from 1920 through to 1 January 1972 when it was combined with the nearby Aldershot & District Traction Co Ltd to form Thames Valley & Aldershot Omnibus Co Ltd {Alder Valley}. Alder Valley itself was the subject of a previous fleet history (PK12) published in 1977.

In addition, two major associated companies are included:

Newbury & District Motor Services Ltd which was formed by a co-operative of local operators in 1932 and was later sold out to Red & White United Transport Ltd in 1943. Control passed to Thames Valley in 1950. This operation was quickly absorbed into the main Thames Valley fleet with most traces disappearing within a few years.

The South Midland company was originally an operation in the name of its founder, **WF Beesley** and then as **South Midland Touring & Transport Co Ltd** before assuming the title **South Midland Motor Services Ltd** in 1930. Like Newbury & District, it became part of the Red & White United Transport Ltd group in 1943 with control passing to Thames Valley in 1950. It did retain its identity however, being operated as a coaching subsidiary before control passed to City of Oxford Motor Services Ltd in on 1 January 1971.

BRITISH AUTOMOBILE TRACTION CO LTD (THAMES VALLEY BRANCH) (7/15-7/20)
THAMES VALLEY TRACTION CO LTD (7/20-12/71)

The origins of Thames Valley Traction Co Ltd are traced back to the early years of the 20th century with the formation of the British Automobile Development Co Ltd in 1905. This was set up by British Electric Traction Co Ltd (BET) in order to develop bus operations outside of urban areas. Its name was changed to British Automobile Traction Co Ltd (BAT) in 1912, by which time it had established operations in several other areas of the country.

By 1915, Sidney Garcke (son of BET's founder Emile Garcke) had recognised the potential for an operation in the Thames Valley area. Military requisitioning of bus chassis for use as lorries in World War 1 caused problems to most operators at the time and as a result, BAT's small operation in Banbury (Oxfordshire) was closed down and the staff of four was redeployed in Reading under the leadership of an engineer called T Graham Homer.

Premises with ample garage and yard space were obtained in Caversham Road, Reading and an order was placed with Thornycroft of Basingstoke for 20 of their J-type chassis. The whole of Thornycroft's production was however taken up with the military demand and it was not until 1919 that this order was eventually fulfilled. In the short term, the difficulty was resolved by obtaining five single-deck Leylands from the BAT-owned Barnsley & District Electric Traction Co Ltd.

After overhaul, two of these vehicles were ready in time for the 23½ mile inaugural service between Maidenhead and Streatley on 31 July 1915. This was a remarkable achievement at a time when bus services in the area were virtually unknown and even carriers' vehicles were largely horse-drawn. The recruitment of male drivers was hampered by the demands of the World War 1, with conductors being entirely female during the BAT years.

Reading Corporation had been running electric trams in the borough since 1903 and BAT had agreed early on to charge higher fares on journeys entirely within the borough boundaries. This was later extended to include routes that shared the same roads when the Corporation started running motor buses in 1919.

The unavailability of new vehicles during the War years were overcome by securing Belsize lorry chassis, with six arriving in September 1915 (fitted with second-hand bus bodies) followed by another 14 in the following year. These enabled expansion further up the River Thames to Wallingford and beyond to Abingdon as well as south to Swallowfield and east to Wokingham and Sunningdale – these routes all being established before the end of 1915.

In early 1916, a second base in Maidenhead was set up in the grounds of a large house called 'The Cedars' where a garage was built. From here, a route was established between Windsor and Cookham, part of which had been previously operated by the London General Omnibus Company but had been discontinued following the outbreak of the War.

Growing fuel shortages meant that some of the routes had to be curtailed. This deteriorating situation together with difficulties in recruiting drivers prompted the disposal of eight of the 14 Belsize chassis delivered in 1916 without them ever being fitted with bus bodies. Towards the end of 1917, coal gas was introduced as an alternative fuel and most of the fleet was quickly converted.

The first recorded double-deck vehicles arrived in 1918, these being a pair of Daimlers hired from BAT's Camden Town operation for the summer season. Following the end of the War, the long awaited Thornycrofts started to arrive from the beginning of 1919 which enabled the fleet to be quickly renewed and the network of services centred on Maidenhead and Reading quickly expanded. Also for the 1919 summer season, two second-hand charabanc type bodies were obtained and fitted to new Thornycroft chassis. These were used for excursions and tours of the Berkshire and Oxfordshire countryside as well as further afield to the south coast. Demand was such that at times, these had to be supplemented with ordinary saloons.

Due to difficulties at the Macclesfield branch, the staff at Reading were given the task of maintaining this operation, which at times involved towing vehicles south to work on. Disposals from the Macclesfield and Barrow-in-Furness fleets were also handled.

After the War ended, batches of former War Department AEC, Daimler and Thornycroft lorries were acquired via the War Department Disposals Board at Slough and taken to the nearby Maidenhead Garage. This became a centre for assessing them before onward travel to other BAT fleets. A number of the lorry bodies on these vehicles were fitted to outgoing Belsize chassis.

For the following year, despite the ready availability of new Thornycroft chassis from the nearby Basingstoke works, BAT's purchasing policy was switched to obtaining ex-War Department Thornycroft 3-ton lorries which were flooding the market in their thousands. These vehicles were then fitted with a variety of new and second-hand bodies and thus became the standard vehicle through the first half of the 1920s. These included second-hand LGOC double-deck bodies from 1922. These rugged chassis saw many years' service and were periodically updated by the fitting of new and refurbished bodies.

The Thames Valley branch of BAT had achieved its stated aims of establishing a bus network in the region and so a separate company was set up – Thames Valley Traction Co Ltd – which was incorporated on 10 July 1920 with a share capital of £75,000 (worth £1.5mn today). To assist with the rapid development of the new company, BAT had sought new investors and 14% of the new company was purchased by Thomas Tilling Ltd. The registered office was at Bridge Street, Maidenhead and the new company had control of 34 vehicles of Thornycroft manufacture. The Directors were Sidney Garcke and Leo Myers (from BAT) and Walter Wolsey (Tillings). The officers of the new company were T Graham Homer (General Manager), Basil Sutton (Engineer) and JW Dally (Company Secretary, later Traffic Manager). These three were to have long careers with Thames Valley, lasting into the 1950s. The route network encompassed 147 miles over 14 routes, which required 15 vehicles from Reading and eight from Maidenhead depot to operate:

Agreements with neighbouring companies were quickly established. A territorial agreement with Aldershot & District to the south of Thames Valley's operating area was established in November 1920 and a protective fares arrangement with Reading Corporation for travel wholly within the borough was agreed in the following May. By September 1921, an agreement with London General Omnibus Co was reached which enabled Thames Valley to operate in the Uxbridge area. This started in June 1922 with Thames Valley taking over two London General services on contract (to West Wycombe and Hounslow) plus a depot on Oxford Road, Denham. Three more services, to Windsor, Great Missenden and Watford were started although the latter two were short-lived. These were further extended in November 1922 with an agreement with National Omnibus & Transport Co to the area north of Uxbridge. Thames Valley's vehicles used in the Uxbridge were subject to Metropolitan Police regulations which were somewhat more stringent than those enforced elsewhere.

For the 1921 summer season, an ambitious programme of excursions to the south coast, race meetings, local tours and private hires was established which utilised six charabancs and in the following year, the company's head office was relocated to 60 St Mary's Butts, Reading – the central terminal for services in the town.

A programme of converting the standard normal control vehicles to forward control was put in place from early 1924. The main advantage of this was that more spacious bodies could be fitted with the driver sitting alongside the engine, rather than behind it.

In September 1924, an agreement with Dominion Motor Spirit Co for the haulage of petrol was established. A Thornycroft chassis was fitted with a tanker body and within a few years, four such vehicles were in use. Fuel haulage was to become a feature of Thames Valley's operations for over 30 years.

In October 1925, T Spragg Ltd's Progressive Bus Service was acquired eliminating significant competition between Reading and Ascot.

Share capital increased to £100,000 in January 1926 and in the following May, Thomas Tilling Ltd took another 5,000 shares and a further 20,000 in December 1927.

As the fleet strength passed 100 in 1926, further investment was made with the share capital increasing to £100,000. The first all new single-deck vehicles were ordered and given the Tilling influence, were unsurprisingly based on Tilling-Stevens chassis. Arrivals included both forward-control buses and a number of small batches of normal control coaches, the last of which was used on the Reading-London route.

1928 saw the first deliveries of Leyland vehicles which were to become the pre-war standard. In all, between that year and 1939, 172 models of that manufacture were delivered including 94 single-deck Tigers and 61 double-deck Titans.

Formal territorial agreements were struck with City of Oxford Motor Services in June 1927, but by the end of that year, London General had given notice that they were not renewing the Uxbridge agreement which ultimately expired 31 December 1928. After that date, the services and garage reverted to London General although all of the vehicles used there were retained by Thames Valley.

A new head office was built at Lower Thorn Street, fronting the premises at Somerset Place that had been established in 1922, and this was to remain the registered address of the company for the remaining 49 years of its existence (and was not ultimately closed until 1982). At the same time, a new company was formed – Tilling & British Automobile Traction Co Ltd (jointly owned by Thomas Tilling Ltd and BET), which became Thames Valley's parent company.

Negotiations were held with Marlow & District Motor Services through 1928 cumulating with the purchase of that business on 1 January 1929. The owner, Reginald Clayton was made a director of Thames Valley (remaining there until his death in 1938), whilst the operation continued to be run as a separate entity. Clayton was also a director of Karrier Motors and Marlow & District had become something of a testing ground for those products. When the business was later absorbed into the main fleet in May 1933, there were 12 operational vehicles, mostly of Karrier manufacture.

Competition on the Reading-London express route was intensified by the emergence of Ledbury Transport Co Ltd {Thackray's Way} of London W11 in September 1929, utilising a fleet of Gilfords. A site at Reading's Cemetery Junction was acquired and developed into the Colonnade Coach Station. This was used by other coach operators passing through the town who also took advantage of its garaging and servicing facilities.

In November 1930, agreement with Great Western Railway was struck for them to take a 35% stake in the company. In exchange, Thames Valley took over GWR bus services at Maidenhead, Twyford, Newbury and Windsor in the following year. Similarly, Southern Railway took a 15% stake although they ran no services in the area. Further discussions were held with GWR to take over Slough based services jointly with London General Country Services and control of these passed to Thames Valley in April 1932.

The fleet strength at the end of 1930 was 140 vehicles plus 14 in the Marlow & District fleet.

Following the 1930 Transport Act, Thames Valley, Reading Corporation and Ledbury Transport were all jockeying for position in Reading and although the status quo was largely maintained, Thames Valley did suffer reductions in the number of journeys on certain routes and had to relinquish using St Mary's Butts as a terminus which it had been since the start of operations in 1915. Some services started to use Reading Stations (Great Western and Southern Railway) which subsequently evolved into the main Reading terminus up to the end of operations in 1971. Reading Transport consolidated its position within the borough boundaries and the protective fare arrangement was formalised. The Act however also forced Thames Valley's many competitors to adhere to the same timetables, fares and vehicle maintenance standards. During the 1930s, several of these were taken over which brought numerous vehicles of different manufacture into the company. There was no clear policy over which vehicles were retained and which were disposed of, to an extent exacerbated by a general shortage of small capacity vehicles.

In 1931, Thames Valley together with a number of other interested coach companies, took shares in London Coastal Coaches Ltd, which was building a new coach station in Victoria, London. This became the terminus for the Reading-London express services thereafter.

The formation of London Passenger Transport Board on 1 July 1933 had given it statutory powers to gain control of services wholly within its area. This had only limited impact on Thames Valley and although it led to the surrender of the Windsor to Slough service together with two vehicles, there was significant financial compensation.

In May 1933, the Aylesbury Omnibus Co Ltd operations (owned by Premier Line Ltd of Shepherd's Bush) was acquired by Eastern National Omnibus Co Ltd. The services (and vehicles) were then divided up amongst the operators in the region including Amersham & District, City of Oxford Motor Services, London Passenger Transport Board and United Counties Omnibus Co as well as Thames Valley.

1934 saw vehicles on hire for evaluating oil (diesel) engines and from the following year, most new deliveries were so fitted. The cost savings were encouraging and a programme of converting older vehicles in the fleet was commenced from 1937.

Penn Bus Co of Tylers Green near High Wycombe was purchased in August 1935. The fleet of 23 vehicles, of Dennis and Gilford manufacture was acquired, but as part of the purchase agreement, seven of these (together with three services) were immediately passed to London Passenger Transport Board. At the end of the year, Ledbury Transport Co Ltd {Thackray's Way} was acquired by Tilling & British Automobile Traction Co Ltd and placed under Thames Valley control. Thames Valley operated it as a subsidiary (to ensure that the express licences were retained), replacing the fleet of Gilfords with vehicles from the main fleet. In reality, the Ledbury vehicles became indistinguishable (apart from legal lettering and a separate fleet numbering system) from vehicles in the main fleet and there was little effort to separate operations in practice. Nevertheless, Ledbury Transport Co Ltd was maintained as a separate legal entity until 1950.

Sidney Garcke, a BET man since the company's formation, retired in February 1936 and was replaced with George Cardwell from Tillings. After this, the influence of Tillings became more pronounced.

Following this, the Chiltern Bus Co Ltd of Lane End was acquired in May 1936. This business had a complicated history and was the amalgamation of a number of businesses that had merged together through the late 1920s and early 1930s. It came with seven operational vehicles of Bedford and AEC make together with a garage which was used up to the start of World War 2. This acquisition was followed by that of FH Crook in June 1937. As well as local services, this business came with a programme of excursions to the south coast and came together with ten vehicles.

The 1939 intake included ten Harrington bodied Leyland Tigers which marked a new level of design. To increase comfort, they were fitted with petrol engines removed from the earlier Leyland Titans, but the outbreak of war curtailed their use as front line coaches. The year also saw the introduction of the Bristol marque which became the standard for the remainder of the company's history.

At the outbreak of war in September 1939, some 24,000 children were evacuated to Thames Valley's territory and required conveying from railway stations to their new homes. This together with military call-ups and the need to conserve fuel led to a 30% reduction in normal mileage although the recruitment of women conductors relieved the staffing shortages to a certain extent.

June 1940, saw the introduction of The Emergency Powers (Defence) Acquisition & Disposal of Motor Vehicles Act which enabled the military to seize vehicles, during wartime. Coaches were favoured as their main role had been severely curtailed by the War. In all, 23 vehicles were impressed, mostly from the 1927 batch of TSMs and early 1930s Leyland Tiger coaches (the Harrington bodied Leyland Tigers delivered in 1939 had (perhaps), been kept discretely from view). The departed vehicles were replaced by a number hired in from other operators, notably East Kent and Westcliff-on-Sea. Seven of the impressed vehicles would later return to Thames Valley for further service and compensation of £11,152 was eventually paid in September 1947. During the War years, vehicles were dispersed at night away from their garages to avoid the risk bomb damage.

The large proportion of single-deck vehicles purchased in the 1930s led to capacity problems during wartime, so during 1941/42, most of the single-deck vehicles were converted to perimeter seating allowing, typically, for 30 seated and 30 standing passengers.

During the later stages of the war, in an effort to save fuel, bus companies were required to convert 10% of their fleet to producer gas propulsion. Thames Valley had been conducting tests from as early as 1939 and had established that towing the producer gas plant on a trailer was the best option. 18 vehicles were so converted over the 1943-45 period.

At the start of the war, manufacture of bus chassis had been frozen, but from 1941 under government control, a limited number of chassis were released for bodying. Nevertheless, Thames Valley was only able to obtain 14 Bristol and eight Guy double-deck vehicles over the War years, fitted with austere utility bodies.

In order to prolong the lives of the pre-war fleet, a major programme of body rebuilds and refurbishments was undertaken, utilising a variety of different outside body builders.

In September 1942, the Tilling / BET amalgamation was split up and a new company – Tilling Motor Services Ltd was formed which became the major shareholder of Thames Valley owning 48.7% of the shares. Great Western Railway had 34.1% and the Southern Railway 14.6%. The remaining 2.6% was in private hands.

By 1946, the fleet strength was 210. Mileage restrictions were lifted on private hire work, but the fleet was ageing and many vehicles badly in need of maintenance. As a result, restoration of services to pre-war levels was slow, but the first new post-war vehicles arrived steadily during 1946/47 and in large numbers from 1948 onwards.

Arctic weather in the early months of 1947 followed by flooding caused severe disruption. This was particularly bad in the Maidenhead area where army lorries were drafted in to help with passenger movements.

From 1 January 1948, the shares held by Tilling Group in Thames Valley were voluntarily passed to the new British Transport Commission (BTC) as part of the post-war Labour Government's nationalisation programme. One impact of this was that the products of the motor construction works of Bristol Tramways and the bodies built in Lowestoft by Eastern Coach Works, both Tilling owned, were now to be supplied only to state-owned operating companies.

Red & White United Transport Ltd of Chepstow in South Wales decided to follow the same route and, albeit not until 1950, it was decided that their subsidiaries South Midland Motor Services Ltd (of Oxford) and Newbury & District Motor Services Ltd, would come under Thames Valley control, effective from 10 February 1950. Their third subsidiary in the region, Venture Transport Ltd of Basingstoke, passed to Wilts & Dorset management. The Newbury & District operation was quickly absorbed into the main Thames Valley fleet and most traces of its separate identity had disappeared within a few years. South Midland on the other hand retained its distinct identity and continued to be operated as a separate concern.

In 1950, increased vehicle dimensions were permitted (8ft wide and 30ft long for single-deck, 27ft long for double-deck) although narrower 7ft 6in wide vehicles were still required for some rural services. Another innovation was the use of double-deck vehicles on the Reading-London express routes, fitted with semi-luxury seats, heaters, luggage racks and platform doors. In the following year, the first Bristol / ECW coaches arrived and in 1952, the first vehicles with underfloor horizontal engines were delivered. Deliveries of new vehicles continued in significant numbers through the 1950s and by 1955, the fleet strength peaked at 430 vehicles, covering over 16 million miles and carrying over 52 million passengers per annum.

One notable development in April / May 1954 was the introduction of joint workings with Aldershot & District on the newly created Reading to Guildford and Reading to Aldershot routes.

In late 1956, four elderly Bristol double-deck vehicles were acquired and converted to open-top for a route along the River Thames between Reading and Maidenhead, and later Windsor. One of these was quickly transferred to South Midland where it was used on a tour of Oxford colleges and Blenheim Palace. These services were not an unqualified success, largely due to the poor summers in this period, did not operate after 1959.

In the late 1950s, a programme of conversion of single-deck vehicles to one-man operation had commenced and from the early 1960s, vehicles arrived fitted as such from new. From 1959 through to the end of operations in 1971, numerous second-hand acquisitions arrived in an effort to maintain a serviceable fleet in a period when recruiting and maintaining workshop staff was becoming problematical. From the following year, a new generation of front entrance double-deckers started to arrive, including the first five of ten coaches for the Reading-London express routes. From 1961, new coaches for South Midland operations were of Bedford manufacture and these were used on less intensive routes.

At the start of 1961, the fleet strength (including Newbury & District and South Midland) was 376 comprising of 221 double-deck vehicles (all Bristol except seven Guy Arabs), 97 single-deck buses (all Bristol) and 58 coaches (all Bristol apart from one AEC Regal). Bodywork was just as standardised with the fleet being almost entirely ECW. The only exceptions were the Duple bodied Guy Arabs, one Brush bodied double-deck and one Windover bodied coach. These operated 95 routes plus two express services to London (South Midland in addition, operated another eight express services). Along the territorial boundaries, there were joint workings with other operators including London Transport (High Wycombe & Slough), City of Oxford (Abingdon & Oxford), Wilts & Dorset (Newbury & Basingstoke) and Aldershot & District (Aldershot & Guildford).

The BTC was replaced in 1962 by the Transport Holding Company (THC), although this had little visible change to policies.

Staff shortages continued to bite and some services had to be restricted for long periods of time, but vehicle developments continued to be innovative. 1963 had seen the permitted length of single-deck vehicles increased to 36ft and three of Bristol's new RE model were received in 1964 and put to use on the Reading-Oxford and Abingdon routes that were jointly operated with City of Oxford Motor Services.

From 1965 onwards, a programme of rebuilding Bristol LS and MW coaches to service buses was introduced which augmented numbers of the single-deck bus fleet.

In 1966 British Railways proposed that the Rail-Air link to Heathrow (which enabled rail passengers to reach the airport without travelling to London first) be extended west from Slough to Reading. The new service commenced in the following year using new Bedford coaches fitted with short-wave radios to keep them in touch with rail and air news.

In 1968, the THC purchased the bus operating companies of the BET Group and on 1 January 1969, the National Bus Company (NBC) came into being in order to integrate the operation of these companies with the existing former-Tilling companies within the THC. Part of the changes that ensued was the sale of the South Midland operations to City of Oxford Motor Services on 1 January 1971.

It was NBC's policy to organise its constituent companies into larger groups in the interests of economies of scale. Thus Thames Valley was coupled with Aldershot & District Traction Co Ltd and a new company formed – Thames Valley & Aldershot Omnibus Co Ltd which traded as 'Alder Valley'. This company came into being on 1 January 1972, acquiring 332 vehicles from Thames Valley (together with a similar number from Aldershot & District).

Today, all traces of the Thames Valley operation have disappeared. Protective fares within Reading were finally withdrawn in October 1975 when Reading Borough Transport (formerly Reading Corporation Transport) took over routes serving the Woodley and Twyford areas. The Thames Valley & Aldershot Omnibus Co lasted until 1986 when, in the run up to deregulation, it was split back into its original components. These were named Alder Valley North Ltd (covering the Thames Valley territory) and Alder Valley South Ltd (covering the Aldershot & District area). Following deregulation, Alder Valley North Ltd was sold to Q Drive Ltd in December 1987 and was renamed Berks Bucks Bus Co Ltd (trading as 'The Bee Line'). The business was then progressively broken up, with the High Wycombe operations passing to City of Oxford Motor Services in 1990 and the Reading and Newbury operations being sold to Reading Borough Transport in 1992. In 1993, Q Drive purchased the former London Country operations at Slough from Luton & District which led to the closure of the Maidenhead depot. In 1996, this operation together with the remaining depot at Bracknell was sold to CentreWest London Buses Ltd. In the following year, CentreWest was acquired by the First Group who in 1999, renamed the company First Bee Line Buses Ltd.

Liveries

The first single-deck vehicles were painted in BAT Saxon green livery with a white roof and gold fleet names. Double-deck vehicles had white window surrounds and these schemes were maintained into the early years of Thames Valley. The Ford Model T 'chasers' purchased at the end of 1922 were painted red and known as Scarlet Runners, but with no fleet names.

Red and white livery (with black lining out) was adopted from February 1924 with most of the existing vehicles repainted, but a few older vehicles retained their green livery but with added white window surrounds. Surplus stocks of green paint were used on buildings.

A black waist rail was incorporated in 1926 on the TSM B9As together with a modest amount of black lining out. All-weather coaches by London Lorries were black above the waist, as were the Leyland Tigers used on the London services. From the late 1920s the livery was standardised to red with cream bands and roof, black beading and lining out.

At the outbreak of the War, white and cream areas were overpainted brown and later grey. As the War progressed, vehicles were painted grey with red relief and some vehicles entered service in undercoat only. After the War, cream paintwork was reinstated although roofs generally became red. The Harrington bodied Leyland Tigers were repainted cream with green flashes.

From Tilling Group days, the livery layout was altered to the standard Tilling red, cream bands and black beading. Coaches became red with a small amount of cream relief and later, some wore the short-lived Tilling coach livery of cream with black mudguards and window surrounds. From 1958 coaches became maroon (lower panels) and cream (upper parts), with fleet names within a cream oblong on each side. Double-deck coaches on the Reading-London services were painted in a version of this in 1966, but reverted to a red and cream livery in 1968.

Premises
Garages with maintenance facilities

The original BAT Thames Valley branch garage was established at 113-115 Caversham Road, Reading during 1915. In the following year, a large house called 'The Cedars' in extensive grounds at Bridge Street Maidenhead was acquired which became the garage and original head office there. Upon formation of the new Thames Valley company in 1920, the registered address was located at 60 St Mary's Butts, Reading.

Land at Somerset Place, Reading was prepared at the end of 1920 and building work was competed in 1922. This became the depot and workshops and was gradually extended as surrounding properties in the adjacent Lower Thorn Street were purchased. These became in May 1928, the registered address of the company - 83 Lower Thorn Street. The premises progressively became larger as more of the surrounding houses and properties were acquired through the remainder of the 1920s and 1930s.

The take-over of services in the Uxbridge area from London General in June 1922 came with a garage in Oxford Road which remained operational until its return to London General with the services at the end of 1928.

An outstation had existed at Englemere Farm, Ascot during the early BAT days, and this was extended in 1922, but replaced with a new garage at Course Road in May 1924.

With the Marlow & District business in 1929 came, a small garage at Victoria Road which remained operational until 1937.

Land was purchased at London Road in nearby Wycombe Marsh in early 1924 which became the location of a new depot there which progressively was developed over the pre-War years, particularly after the acquisition of the Penn Motor Services business in 1935.

The Ledbury Transport business included the Crown Colonnade coach station situated at Reading's Cemetery Junction. This continued to be used after 1935 by coaches and later to store withdrawn vehicles. In 1953, workshops and a paint shop were built to alleviate pressure on the main depot.

The remaining garage in use pre-war was at Marlow Road, Lane End which was acquired with the Chiltern business in 1936, but only lasted in use until 1939.

After the War, in 1946 a new garage at Desborough Road, High Wycombe was opened to supplement the Wycombe Marsh garage. Both lasted until June 1970 when the new garage and bus station was opened at Newlands in June 1970.

The acquisition of the Newbury & District fleet in 1950 saw their much larger garage supersede the dormy shed that had been used by Thames Valley since 1927.

Discussions were first held in November 1954 regarding siting a garage in the new town of Bracknell. This was eventually opened in June 1960 in Market Street and housed 30 vehicles under cover. This saw the end of Ascot garage and Crowthorne dormy shed.

Summary (* passed to Alder Valley 1/1/72)

Ascot (Course Road)	1924-1960	
Bracknell (Market Street)	1960*	
High Wycombe (Desborough Road)	1946-1970	
High Wycombe (Newlands)	1971*	
Lane End (Marlow Road)	1936*	(former Chiltern Bus Co)
Maidenhead (Bridge Street)	1916*	
Marlow (Victoria Road)	1929-1937	(former Marlow & District)
Newbury (Mill Lane)	1950*	(former Newbury & District)
Reading (Caversham Road)	1915-1922	
Reading (Crown Colonnade)	1935*	(former Ledbury & District)
Reading (Somerset Place)	1922*	(extended to include the Lower Thorn Street head office and yard in Weldale Street)
Uxbridge (Oxford Road)	1922-1928	(former London General)
Wycombe Marsh (London Road)	1924-1970	

Dormy sheds

The first Thames Valley dormy shed was established at Tadley in 1923 (after the out-station at nearby Pamber Heath blew down in a gale). This was followed in 1924 by a shed at Yateley.

By 1928, further sheds had been established at Bucklebury, Crowthorne, Stoke Row and Mill Lane, Newbury. The latter was rented to Newbury & District Motor Services from 1932 with an agreement to allow Thames Valley to garage two vehicles there. In 1937 the acquisition of the Stokenchurch area services from City of Oxford Motor Services came with a small garage. The shed at Newbury was impressed by the Ministry of Supply during the World War 2 and vehicles used Newbury & District's garage during this period.

Summary

Baughurst	1960*	(Wilts & Dorset)
Bucklebury (Chapel Row)	1925-1937	
Crowthorne (Cambridge Road)	1926-1960	
Fingest (Turville Road)	1930*	
Newbury (Mill Lane)	1927-1949	(rented to Newbury & District 1932-1937 with Thames Valley garaging two vehicles there by agreement)
Odiham (Alton Road)	1932-1937	
Princes Risborough (Longwick Road)	1933*	
Stoke Row (Main Street)	1928-1939	
Stokenchurch (London Road)	1937*	(former City of Oxford)
Tadley (Fairlawn Road)	1923-1960	
Yateley (Reading Road)	1924-1942	

Outstations

There was numerous other parking areas established, as well as premises that were not owned by Thames Valley. These included locations at Ascot (1920-1924), Basingstoke (1932-1933), Bucklebury (1923-1925), Chilton Foliat (1950-1954), East Ilsley (1950-1956), Hungerford (1950-1962), Kingsclere (1950*), Lambourn (1950*), Lambourn Woodlands (1952), London (Samuelsons Garage) (1947-1971), Loudwater (1923-1924), Newbury (1920-1926), Pamber Heath (1921-1923), Princes Risborough (1928-1932), Sherfield-on-Loddon (1926-1927), Skirmett (1928-1930), Stoke Row (1925-1927), Wallingford (1920-1938), Wantage (1927-1942), West Ilsley (1950-1952) and Yateley (1921-1923).

Fleet numbering

BAT vehicles nationally were allocated a fleet number although none were recorded prior to the 1919 intake of Thornycrofts. In 1918, 'local' fleet numbers were introduced for the Belsizes, but what form they took is unknown. The 1919 Thornycrofts however carried local numbers T1 – T20.

From August 1920, the vehicles transferred from BAT were renumbered 1 to 34. Thereafter, a single sequential series was maintained, reaching 881 in 1963, although there was much gap-filling after 1959 with acquired double-deck vehicles, which led to particularly haphazard sequences.

The Marlow & District vehicles absorbed into the main fleet in May 1933 were numbered between 1 and 15 and the former Great Western Railway vehicles acquired in 1931/32 retained their (mostly) four-digit numbers.

Ledbury Transport Co vehicles acquired with that business in 1936 were numbered in a series up to 62, using even numbers only. This policy was maintained up to 1950 when only vehicles from the main Thames Valley fleet were transferred into this fleet. In order to avoid clashes this period, ancillary vehicles were given odd numbers only.

In 1950, the Newbury & District fleet (numbered between 94 and 172) and South Midland (numbered between 39 and 70) had no clashes with the Thames Valley system of the day (lowest number 179), so they retained their existing fleet numbers. South Midland acquisitions from 1958 onwards were numbered into the main Thames Valley scheme which had by then reached 800. Following a low-bridge accident in 1954, the highbridge Newbury & District Guy Arabs were numbered in a special series starting at H1.

In 1963, a new numbering system was started from D1 (for double-deckers, ultimately reaching D60), S301 (single-deckers, reaching S345) and C401 (coaches). In the final few years of operation, a further single-deck series in 1968 started at 200 and most of the surviving S300 series vehicles were renumbered into a new series in 1969 starting at 100. At this time, another double-deck series starting at 500 was established. The C prefix was dropped for coaches in early 1969.

Company body numbers

From October / November 1922 through to September 1935, the company allocated its own body numbers, numbered sequentially from 1 to 316. These are shown throughout in square brackets after the body builder.

BRITISH AUTOMOBILE TRACTION CO LTD (THAMES VALLEY BRANCH) (7/15-7/20)
THAMES VALLEY TRACTION CO LTD (7/20-12/71)

1915

New Vehicles:

DP 1655	Belsize 3 ton	?	Tilling	B26R	9/15	1-2/19
DP 1656	Belsize 3 ton	?	Tilling	B26R	9/15	1-2/19
DP 1657	Belsize 3 ton	?	Tilling	B26R	9/15	1-2/19
DP 1658	Belsize 3 ton	?	Tilling	B26R	9/15	1-2/19
DP 1659	Belsize 3 ton	?	Tilling	B26R	9/15	1-2/19
DP 1660	Belsize 3 ton	?	Tilling	B26R	9/15	1-2/19

Notes:

The Tilling bodies on these vehicles were acquired second-hand from elsewhere in the BAT Group. They were probably built c1913/4 and fitted to chassis that were later impressed by the War Department. Two spare bodies were also acquired which were subsequently fitted to DP 1756/7 of 1916. These eight bodies were subsequently fitted to Thornycrofts DP 2111-2118 of 1919 (order unknown).

The Belsize chassis were not traced further but some were probably fitted with the ex-War Department lorry bodies acquired in 1920 (on the Thornycroft chassis that became DP 2597-2600, DP 2602-2604 and DP 2606) and sold locally.

Vehicles acquired from Barnsley & District Electric Traction Co Ltd, Barnsley (WR) 6/15:

HE 8	Leyland S3.30.T	S210/955	Brush	B27F	5/13	11/16
HE 9	Leyland S3.30.T	S267/1036	Brush	B27F	5/13	11/16
HE 10	Leyland S3.30.T	(see note)	Brush	B27F	5/13	4/16
HE 11	Leyland S3.30.T	(see note)	Brush	B27F	5/13	4/16
HE 12	Leyland S3.30.T	S253/1020	Brush	B27F	5/13	11/16

Previous Histories:

HE 8-12: New to Barnsley & District Electric Traction Co Ltd, Barnsley (WR) 1-5.

Notes:

These vehicles were overhauled by Birch Bros Ltd before delivery to Thames Valley branch.
The inaugural service between Streatley and Maidenhead was operated by HE 11 & HE 12 on 31/7/15.

HE 8: Its chassis number is also recorded as S194/941
HE 10-11: Their chassis numbers were S249/995 and S256/1028 (order unknown).

Disposals:

HE 8: Barnsley & District Electric Traction Co Ltd, Barnsley (WR) 1 11/16; Barnsley & District Traction Co Ltd, Barnsley (WR) 1 8/19; Peterborough Electric Traction Co Ltd, Peterborough (SP) by 1/21 (but possibly on hire much earlier); AJ Gill, Godmanchester (HN) 1923; last licensed 9/26; scrapped 1931.

HE 9: Barnsley & District Electric Traction Co Ltd, Barnsley (WR) 2 11/16; Barnsley & District Traction Co Ltd, Barnsley (WR) 2 8/19; Peterborough Electric Traction Co Ltd, Peterborough (SP) by 1/21 (but possibly on hire much earlier); Richardson, Irthlingborough (NO) 1923; withdrawn 9/23; Hancock & Wibley, Saltford (?GSO) at an unknown date; scrapped 1933.

HE 10: No confirmed disposal, but it possibly became the vehicle re-registered FL 1561 by Peterborough Electric Traction Co Ltd, Peterborough (SP) A1 7/19; thereafter, this vehicle was rebodied B26F 1922; renumbered AB1 by 1929; Eastern Counties Omnibus Co Ltd, Norwich (NK) AB1 7/31; withdrawn 1931; F Ross (showman), Billericay at an unknown date; last licensed 12/35.

HE 11: No confirmed disposal, but it possibly became the vehicle re-registered FL 1562 by Peterborough Electric Traction Co Ltd, Peterborough (SP) A2 7/19; thereafter, this vehicle was rebodied B26F 1922; renumbered AB2 by 1929; Eastern Counties Omnibus Co Ltd, Norwich (NK) AB2 7/31; A Gilfrin, London SE15 (GLN) at an unknown date; last licensed 6/32.

HE 12: Barnsley & District Electric Traction Co Ltd, Barnsley (WR) 5 11/16 Barnsley & District Traction Co Ltd, Barnsley (WR) 5 8/19; converted to a breakdown vehicle 1924; E Emanuel (location / status unknown) 7/30; last licensed 8/30; W Lockwood, Huddersfield at an unknown date; later became as a static caravan and then built into a house (latterly owned by Blogg, Southwell); MA Sutcliffe, Totternhoe for preservation 5/97; restoration completed 2006.

1916

New Vehicles:

DP 1756	Belsize 3 ton	?	Tilling	B26R	3/16	1-2/19
DP 1757	Belsize 3 ton	?	Tilling	B26R	3/16	1-2/19
DP 1759	Belsize 3 ton	?	?	B---	c3/16	-/19
DP 1794	Belsize 3 ton	?	Brush	B26R	7/16	2/19
DP 1795	Belsize 3 ton	?	Brush	B26R	7/16	2/19
DP 1798	Belsize 3 ton	?	?	B---	8-10/16	-/19
DP 1801	Belsize 3 ton	?	?	B---	8-10/16	-/19
DP 1826	Belsize 3 ton	?	Brush	B26R	11/16	2/19
DP 1827	Belsize 3 ton	?	Brush	B26R	11/16	2/19

Notes:

The Tilling bodies on DP 1756-1757 were acquired second-hand from elsewhere in the BAT Group. They were probably built c1913/4 and fitted to chassis that were later impressed by the War Department. These together with those fitted to DP 1655-1660 (of 1915) were subsequently fitted to Thornycrofts DP 2111-2118 of 1919 (order unknown).

The Brush bodies were new. They were subsequently fitted to Thornycrofts DP 2119-2122 of 1919 (order unknown).

A further eight Belsize 3 ton chassis were obtained during 1916 but were later sold unused due to driver and petrol shortages, with two of them going to the British Red Cross in 12/16. A Belsize chassis was sold to Reading Corporation Transport for spares in 1921, but it is not known where this was sourced from.

Disposals - chassis only (unless otherwise indicated):

DP 1756-1757: No known disposals.

DP 1759: D Oglanby, Spennymoor (DM) 1/20.

DP 1794: Lipton Ltd, London EC (GLN) as a box van 12/20.

DP 1795: British Automobile Traction, Macclesfield branch by 7/19; returned to British Automobile Traction, Thames Valley branch 1/20 for resale; Ms AD Pugh, location unknown 1/20.

DP 1798: Lipton Ltd, London EC (GLN) as a box van 12/20.

DP 1801: G Phipps, location unknown (as a bus) 3/20.

DP 1826: Reading Corporation Transport (GBE) as a rail-grinding wagon c5/19.

DP 1827: Reading Corporation Transport (GBE) as a tower wagon c5/19.

1918

Vehicles acquired from War Department (GOV) 3/18-8/18:

DP 2032	Daimler Y	?	?	B---	3/18	-/19
DP 2033	Daimler Y	?	?	B---	3/18	-/19
DP 2064	Daimler Y	?	?	----	8/18	-/19

Notes:

These vehicles were three of four vehicles with chassis numbers 4006, 4046, 5621 and 7265 and were used as part of a small commercial lorry fleet that ran from 10/19 until the spring of 1920. Two of these four were fitted with the LGOC O18/16RO bodies removed from KN 2873 (311) and KN 3652 (310) (qv), but were not used as buses in this form. The identity of the fourth vehicle is unknown. All four passed to Southdown Motor Services Ltd, Brighton (ES) 1-3/20.

Vehicle on hire:

349	LF 9219	Daimler CC	? ?	O??/??RO -/10	7/18	c9/18

Notes:

This and another Daimler CC double-deck were on hire from BAT, Camden Town (LN) from 7/18 (and possibly earlier summers); they were returned by the autumn of 1918.

1919

New Vehicles:

244	DP 2111	Thornycroft J	7084	Tilling [3]	B26R	1/19	4/31
245	DP 2112	Thornycroft J	7052	Tilling [5]	B26R	1/19	8/28
246	DP 2113	Thornycroft J	7062	Tilling [4]	B26R	1/19	10/31
247	DP 2114 (1)	Thornycroft J	7074	Tilling [2]	B26R	1/19	11/28
248	DP 2115	Thornycroft J	7095	Tilling [1 or 8]	B26R	1/19	11/28

249	DP 2116	Thornycroft J	7097	Tilling [7]	B26R	2/19	12/28
250	DP 2117	Thornycroft J	7096	Tilling [1 or 8]	B26R	2/19	10/28
251	DP 2118	Thornycroft J	7120	Tilling [6]	B26R	2/19	10/29
252	DP 2119	Thornycroft J	7117	Brush [10]	B26R	2/19	5/23
253	DP 2120	Thornycroft J	7154	Brush [11]	B26R	2/19	6/23
254	DP 2121	Thornycroft J	7166	Brush [12]	B26R	2/19	5/23
255	DP 2122	Thornycroft J	7209	Brush [9]	B26R	2/19	12/28
259	DP 2123	Thornycroft J	7283	Birch [14]	B26R	4/19	8/28
260	DP 2124	Thornycroft J	7305	Birch [16]	B26R	4/19	12/28
261	DP 2125	Thornycroft J	7311	Birch [15]	B26R	4/19	11/28
262	DP 2126	Thornycroft J	7314	Birch [17]	B26R	4/19	10/28
283	DP 2127 (1)	AEC YC	14398	Birch [18]	B32R	5/19	7/19
263	DP 2127 (2)	Thornycroft J	7572	Birch [18]	B32R	7/19	10/29
290	DP 2128 (1)	AEC YC	14417	Birch [19]	B32R	5/19	7/19
275	DP 2128 (2)	Thornycroft J	7580	Birch [19]	B32R	7/19	12/28
276	DP 2129	Thornycroft J	7144	Bayley [13]	B24D	5/19	6/31
292	DP 2130 (1)	AEC YC	14419	Harrington [20]	Ch28	5/19	7/19
278	DP 2130 (2)	Thornycroft J	7583	Harrington [20]	Ch28	7/19	11/31
279	DP 2377	Thornycroft J	7647	Lorrybus [-]	B32R	7/19	c10/27
295	DP 2378	Thornycroft J	7652	Lorrybus [-]	B32R	8/19	7/29

Notes:

Before 1/1/21, there was no cross reference between the registration number and the chassis number. As a result, it was sometimes the practice for the registration to move with the body, so that chassis effectively exchanged identities. Those that were known to have been so affected were DP 2113 / DP 2130 and DP 2114 / DP 2605.

DP 2111-2130 also originally carried local fleetnumbers T1-20.

DP 2111-2118 (244-251): Fitted with the Tilling bodies from Belsizes DP 1655-1660 (of 1915) and DP 1756-1757 (of 1916) (order unknown).

DP 2119-2122 (252-255): Fitted with the Brush bodies from Belsizes DP 1794-1795 and DP 1826-1827 (of 1916) (order unknown).

DP 2377-2378 (279-280): Were high-bonneted military-type chassis probably intended for the War Department (GOV); their Lorrybus bodies were fitted with rear steps, wooden bench seats and a canvas hoods.

DP 2111 (244): Transferred to Thames Valley Traction Co Ltd 7/20 and renumbered 1 c8/20; converted to forward control layout and rebodied Brush (159) O28/26RO [133] 1/26-2/26; fitted with pneumatic tyres 4/28.

DP 2112 (245): Transferred to Thames Valley Traction Co Ltd 7/20 and renumbered 2 c8/20; fitted with the LGOC (1895) O18/16RO body [41] from Thornycroft DX 2175 (41) 3/23; rebuilt to forward control and rebodied Brush (216) O28/26RO [85] 4/24-5/24; fitted with the Dodson (9232) O26/24RO body [166] from Thornycroft XP 6422 (127) 12/27.

DP 2113 (246) (chassis 7062): Exchanged bodies with Thornycroft DP 2130 (278) 5/20, receiving the Harrington Ch28 body [20] and registration DP 2130 from that vehicle; transferred to Thames Valley Traction Co Ltd (as DP 2130) 7/20 and renumbered 3 c8/20; charabanc body removed c10/25; converted to forward control layout and rebodied Brush (156) O28/26RO [130] 1/26-2/26; fitted with pneumatic tyres 4/28.

DP 2114 (247) (chassis 7074): Rebodied Brush B32F [23], renumbered 298 and re-registered DP 2605 4/20 (its Tilling B26R body [2], still bearing the registration DP 2114, was fitted to a previously un-registered chassis 4/20 (qv)); transferred to Thames Valley Traction Co Ltd (as DP 2605) 7/20 and renumbered 4 c8/20; reseated to B29F 11/21 (its wooden slatted seats were re-spaced and converted to take cushions); fitted with pneumatic tyres 4/28.

DP 2115 (248): Rebodied Brush B32F [21] 4-6/20 (its Tilling body was fitted to either DP 2599 in 4/20 or DP 2606 in 7/20); transferred to Thames Valley Traction Co Ltd 7/20 and renumbered 5 c8/20; reseated to B29F 3/22 (its wooden slatted seats were re-spaced and converted to take cushions); fitted with pneumatic tyres 4/28.

DP 2116 (249): Transferred to Thames Valley Traction Co Ltd 7/20 and renumbered 6 c8/20; exchanged bodies with Thornycroft DP 2123 (14) 4/22, receiving the Birch B26R body [14] from that vehicle; reseated to B23R to meet Metropolitan Police requirements for Uxbridge town services 5/22; fitted with pneumatic tyres 7/28.

DP 2117 (250): Rebodied Brush B32F [28] 4-6/20 (its Tilling body was fitted to either DP 2599 in 4/20 or DP 2606 in 7/20); transferred to Thames Valley Traction Co Ltd 7/20 and renumbered 7 c8/20; reseated to B29F 3/22 (its wooden slatted seats were re-spaced and converted to take cushions); fitted with pneumatic tyres 1927.

DP 2118 (251): Transferred to Thames Valley Traction Co Ltd 7/20 and renumbered 8 c8/20; its roof was replaced with a detachable canvas top in 9/23; converted to forward control layout and rebodied Brush (283) O28/26RO [125] 5/25-7/25; fitted with pneumatic tyres 6/28.

DP 2119-2121 (252-254): Transferred to Thames Valley Traction Co Ltd 7/20 and renumbered 9-11 c8/20.

DP 2122 (255): Exchanged bodies with Thornycroft DP 2124 (260) by 7/20, receiving the Birch B26R body [16] from that vehicle (it is believed that the registration remained with its original chassis, so there was no identity swap); transferred to Thames Valley Traction Co Ltd 7/20 and renumbered 12 c8/20; its wooden anatomical (slatted) seats were converted to take cushions 1/22; reseated to B23R to meet Metropolitan Police requirements for Uxbridge town services 5/22; fitted with pneumatic tyres 7/28.

DP 2123 (259): Transferred to Thames Valley Traction Co Ltd 7/20 and renumbered 14 c8/20; its wooden anatomical (slatted) seats were converted to take cushions 1/22; exchanged bodies with Thornycroft DP 2116 (6) 4/22, receiving the Tilling B26R body [7] from that vehicle; fitted with the LGOC (2360) O18/16RO body from Thornycroft BL 9751 (44) 3/23; converted to forward control layout and rebodied Brush (222) O28/26RO [87] 4/24-5/24; Brush body removed 3/28; fitted with the Dodson (9233) O26/24RO body [167] from Thornycroft XP 9325 (128) 7/28.

DP 2124 (260): Exchanged bodies with Thornycroft DP 2124 (260) by 7/20, receiving the Brush B26R body [9] from that vehicle (it is believed that the registration remained with its original chassis, so there was no identity swap); transferred to Thames Valley Traction Co Ltd 7/20 and renumbered 15 c8/20; reseated to B22R to meet Metropolitan Police requirements for Uxbridge town services 5/22; fitted with pneumatic tyres 6/28.

DP 2125 (261): Fitted with a new Brush B32F [24] body in 4-6/20 (its Birch body was fitted to Thornycroft DP 2600 (316)); transferred to Thames Valley Traction Co Ltd 7/20 and renumbered 16 c8/20; reseated to B29F 2/22 (its wooden slatted seats were re-spaced and converted to take cushions); fitted with pneumatic tyres 4/28.

DP 2126 (262): Transferred to Thames Valley Traction Co Ltd 7/20 and renumbered 17 c8/20; its wooden anatomical (slatted) seats were probably converted to take cushions 1/22; reseated to B23R to meet Metropolitan Police requirements for Uxbridge town services c5/22.

DP 2127 (283): Obtained pending the delivery of Thornycroft 263 and was fitted with the Birch [18] B32R body that was subsequently transferred (together with the registration DP 2127) to that vehicle (for details, see the following entry).

DP 2127 (263): Ordered as a 26-seater, fitted with wooden slatted seats and extra 'drop-down' 'gangway' seats for evaluation purposes (this body was first fitted to AEC 283, above); transferred to Thames Valley Traction Co Ltd 7/20 and renumbered 19 c8/20; reseated to B26R by the removal of experimental tip-up gangway seats 1920/1; its wooden anatomical (slatted) seats were converted to take cushions 1/22; fitted with the Hora B28F body [52] from Thornycroft DX 2175 (41) 8/22 (its solid roof being replaced with a canvas one); converted to forward control layout and rebodied Brush (282) O28/26RO [121] 4/25-5/25; fitted with pneumatic tyres 7/28.

DP 2128 (290): Obtained pending the delivery of Thornycroft 275 and was fitted with the Birch [19] B32R body that was subsequently transferred (together with the registration DP 2128) to that vehicle (for details, see the following entry).

DP 2128 (275): Ordered as a 26-seater, fitted with cushioned seats and extra 'tip-up' 'gangway' seats for evaluation purposes (this body was first fitted to AEC 290, above); transferred to Thames Valley Traction Co Ltd 7/20 and renumbered 18 c8/20; reseated to B26R by the removal of experimental tip-up gangway seats 1920/1; its wooden anatomical (slatted) seats were probably converted to take cushions 1/22; reseated to B23R to meet Metropolitan Police requirements for Uxbridge town services 6/22; fitted with pneumatic tyres 9/28.

DP 2129 (276): Fitted with a second-hand Bayley body with two side doors, a fixed roof but no side glazing (possibly acquired from Southdown Motor Services Ltd, Brighton (ES) where it may have been mounted on a Daimler chassis); transferred to Thames Valley Traction Co Ltd 7/20 and renumbered 13 c8/20; following an accident, it was modified to a charabanc (as Ch28) by the fitting of a further three side doors and a cape cart hood 4/21; charabanc body removed c10/25; converted to forward control layout and rebodied Brush (157) O28/26RO [131] 1/26-2/26; fitted with pneumatic tyres 5/28.

DP 2130 (292): Obtained pending the delivery of Thornycroft 278 and was fitted with the Harrington [20] Ch28 body that was subsequently transferred (together with the registration DP 2130) to that vehicle (for details, see the following entry).

DP 2130 (278) (chassis 7583): Fitted with a second-hand Harrington charabanc body with a canvas hood (this body was first fitted to AEC 292, above); exchanged bodies with Thornycroft DP 2113 (246) 5/20, receiving the Tilling B26R body [4] and registration DP 2113 from that vehicle; transferred to Thames Valley Traction Co Ltd (as DP 2113) 7/20 and renumbered 20 c8/20; body removed 11/25; converted to forward control layout and rebodied Brush (162) O28/26RO [135] 1/26-2/26; fitted with pneumatic tyres 5/28.

DP 2377 (279): Rebodied Brush B32F [un-numbered] 4-6/20 (its Lorrybus body was sold to British Automobile Traction Macclesfield branch and mounted on a Daimler, either LF 9214 (339) or LP 8364 (255)); transferred to Thames Valley Traction Co Ltd 7/20 and renumbered 21 c8/20; its Brush body was removed 9/20 and it probably ran as a lorry from 9/20 to 3/21; rebodied Birch Ch28 [35] with a canvas roof 3/21; fitted with pneumatic tyres 4/26.

DP 2378 (280): Rebodied Brush B32F [26] 4-6/20 (its Lorrybus body was sold to British Automobile Traction Macclesfield branch and mounted on a Daimler, either LF 9214 (339) or LP 8364 (255)); transferred to Thames Valley Traction Co Ltd 7/20 and renumbered 22 c8/20; reseated to B29F 3/22 (its wooden slatted seats were re-spaced and converted to take cushions); fitted with pneumatic tyres 3/28.

Disposals - chassis only (unless otherwise indicated):

DP 2111 (1): AE Spears (dealer), London SW19 6/31; not licensed further.

DP 2112 (2): Riddell Bros, Coatbridge (GLK) 10/28; scrapped by 4/32.

DP 2113 (ex DP 2130) (20): AE Spears (dealer), London SW19 11/31; unidentified owner, Surrey (GSR) at an unknown date.

DP 2115 (5): Stanaway, Baynon & Johns, St Austell (GCO) 1/29.

DP 2116 (6): Jackson Manufacturing Co, Slough (GBK) 2/29; unidentified owner, London (GLN) at an unknown date; scrapped by 1937.

DP 2117 (7): Wilkinson Transport Co, Bury St Edmunds (GWF) (not licensed) 10/28; unidentified owner, Cheshire (GCH) 5/29; unidentified owner, Denbighshire (GDH) 4/30.

DP 2118 (8): AE Spears (dealer), London SW19 10/29; unidentified owner, London (GLN) 11/29; T & W Farmiloe Ltd, London (GLN) by 1934.

DP 2119 (9): Trent Motor Traction Co Ltd, Derby (DE) T160 5/23 (as a complete vehicle / B28R); reseated to B26R 1925; withdrawn 1927; unidentified operator / dealer 10/27.

DP 2120 (10): Trent Motor Traction Co Ltd, Derby (DE) T161 6/23 (as a complete vehicle / B28R); reseated to B26R 1925; withdrawn 1927; converted to lorry no. 2 by Trent and transferred to the ancillary fleet 1927; Newton's, Derby (GDE) 10/28.

DP 2121 (11): Trent Motor Traction Co Ltd, Derby (DE) T162 5/23 (as a complete vehicle / B28R); reseated to B26R 1925; withdrawn 1927; unidentified operator / dealer 10/27; unidentified owner, Ipswich (GEK) at an unknown date; unidentified owner, West Suffolk (GWF) 8/29.

DP 2122 (12): Lee Motor Works (dealer), Bournemouth 1/29; unidentified owner, Dorset (GDT) at an unknown date; unidentified owner, Middlesex (GMX) 1/32.

DP 2123 (14): AC Glaister, Preston (GLA) 8/28.

DP 2124 (15): J Cooke & Son {Greystone Lime Works}, Dorking (GSR) 2/29.

DP 2125 (16): G Wood, Birmingham (GWK?) (not licensed) 2/29.

DP 2126 (17): Dismantled for spares / scrap by Thames Valley 10/28.

DP 2127 (283): British Automobile Traction, Macclesfield (CH) 283 re-registered MA 2569 and fitted with Birch Ch30 body (also recorded as Ch28) 3/20; North Western Road Car Co Ltd, Stockport (CH) 283 5/23; renumbered 19 1927; Middlewood Brick Co, Middlewood (GCH) 1/29; Judson, Stockport 1929; last licensed 12/29; Blake's Motors (dealer), Manchester 2/30; Harrison & Blair (dealer), Farnworth 2/30.

DP 2127 (19): AE Spears (dealer), London SW19 10/29 (as a complete vehicle); not licensed further.

DP 2128 (290): British Automobile Traction, Macclesfield (CH) 290 re-registered MA 3128 and fitted with Birch Ch30 body 4/20; North Western Road Car Co Ltd, Stockport (CH) 290 5/23; renumbered 24 1928; withdrawn 1928; unidentified operator, Worcestershire 10/28; scrapped 1937.

DP 2128 (18): Lee Motor Works (dealer), Bournemouth 1/29; unidentified owner, Dorset (GDT) at an unknown date; unidentified owner, Middlesex (GMX) 9/30.

DP 2129 (13): AE Spears (dealer), London SW19 6/31; unidentified owner, Middlesex (GMX) (not licensed) 11/31.

DP 2130 (292): British Automobile Traction, Macclesfield (CH) 292 re-registered MA 2284 and fitted with Birch Ch30 body 2/20; North Western Road Car Co Ltd, Stockport (CH) 292 5/23; renumbered 25 1927; Phibbs (dealer), Knutsford 2/28; scrapped 10/28.

DP 2130 (ex DP 2113) (3): AE Spears (dealer), London SW19 10/31; unidentified owner, Surrey (GSR) 10/31.

DP 2377 (21): Dismantled for spares / scrap by Thames Valley 5/28 (as a complete vehicle).

DP 2378 (22): R Chapman & Son, Reading (GBE?) (not licensed) 8/29.

DP 2605 (ex DP 2114) (4): A Balchin & Son, Petworth (GWS) 3/29; licensed 6/29.

1920

New Vehicles:

247	DP 2114 (2)	Thornycroft J	7720	Tilling [2]	B26R	4/20	11/31
340	DP 2601	Thornycroft J	9003	Brush [22]	B32F	4/20	7/29

Notes:

DP 2114 (247) (chassis 7720): Was a high-bonneted military-type chassis probably intended for the War Department (GOV) (purchased in 8/19, but not bodied then); fitted with the Tilling body from the 1919 Thornycroft registered DP 2114 (chassis 7074) (the registration plates remaining affixed to that body) 4/20; transferred to Thames Valley Traction Co Ltd 7/20 and renumbered 23 c8/20; body removed 12/25; converted to forward control layout and rebodied Brush (160) O28/26RO [134] 1/25-2/26; fitted with pneumatic tyres 5/28.

DP 2601 (340): Its Brush body was referred to as a Pullman saloon with 11 of the 32 seats in a separate smoking compartment at the rear; transferred to Thames Valley Traction Co Ltd 7/20 and renumbered 29 c8/20; reseated to B29F 2/21 (its wooden slatted seats were re-spaced and converted to take cushions); fitted with pneumatic tyres 1927.

Disposals - chassis only:

DP 2114 (23): AE Spears (dealer), London SW19 11/31; unidentified owner, Kent (GKT) 7/32; Lodor Transport, Maidstone (GKT) by 1934.

DP 2601 (29): AJ Elvin, Wembley (GLN) 7/29.

Vehicles acquired from East Kent Road Car Co Ltd, Canterbury (KT) 1/20:

311	KN 2873	Thornycroft J	7117	LGOC [-]	O18/16RO	3/19	11/28
310	KN 3652	Thornycroft J	7329	LGOC [-]	O18/16RO	5/19	11/28

Previous histories:

KN 2873 (311): New to William Sayer & Sons, Margate (KT); East Kent Road Car Co Ltd (KT) 10/19.

KN 3652 (310): New to William Sayer & Sons, Margate (KT); East Kent Road Car Co Ltd (KT) 10/19.

Notes:

KN 2873 (311): Its LGOC body was second-hand, probably built c1913; rebodied Brush B32F [29] 6/20 (its LGOC body was sold to Southdown Motor Services Ltd, Brighton (ES) 1-3/20 mounted on a 1918 Daimler Y chassis (qv)); transferred to Thames Valley Traction Co Ltd 7/20 and renumbered 26 c8/20; reseated to B29F 10/21 (its wooden slatted seats were re-spaced and converted to take cushions); fitted with pneumatic tyres 3/28.

KN 3652 (310): Its LGOC body was second-hand, probably built c1913; rebodied Brush B32F [32] 6/20 (its LGOC body was sold to Southdown Motor Services Ltd, Brighton (ES) 1-3/20 mounted on a 1918 Daimler Y chassis (qv)); transferred to Thames Valley Traction Co Ltd 7/20 and renumbered 25 c8/20; reseated to B29F 10/21 (its wooden slatted seats were re-spaced and converted to take cushions).

Disposals - chassis only:

KN 2873 (26): Barnfield & Brenton, Fraddon (GCO?) 11/28.

KN 3652 (25): Nicholls Transport Co, Cornwall (GCO) 3/29.

Vehicles acquired from War Department (GOV) 4/20-7/20:

336	DP 2597	Thornycroft J	2992	Brush [25]	B32F	4/20	2/29
338	DP 2598	Thornycroft J	4157	Brush [27]	B32F	4/20	10/28
337	DP 2599	Thornycroft J	5063	Tilling [8]	B26R	4/20	6/23
316	DP 2600	Thornycroft J	6613	Birch [15]	B26R	4/20	12/28
339	DP 2602	Thornycroft J	3268	Brush [31]	B32F	4/20	2/29
341	DP 2603	Thornycroft J	4721	Brush [30]	B32F	4/20	3/29
352	DP 2604	Thornycroft J	6815	Brush [-]	B32F	4/20	c10/27
353	DP 2606	Thornycroft J	2871	Tilling [1]	B26R	7/20	6/28
354	------	Thornycroft J	2342	(chassis only)	----	----	

Notes:

These were ex-War Department (GOV) lorry chassis purchased through the War Department Disposals Board, Slough. Many of the lorry bodies removed from these vehicles were fitted to the earlier Belsize chassis from 1915/6 and sold locally.

The unregistered chassis (354) was intended to be registered DP 2606, but passed to Thames Valley Traction Co Ltd unused; it was eventually used in 1926 as the basis for MO 6842 (98) when it was allocated chassis no 2342 (qv).

The Brush bodies were referred to as Pullman saloons and 11 of the 32 seats were incorporated a smoking compartment at the rear.

DP 2597 (336): Its chassis was new in 1915, fitted with a new Brush body; transferred to Thames Valley Traction Co Ltd 7/20 and renumbered 28 c8/20; reseated to B29F 9/22 (its wooden slatted seats were re-spaced and converted to take cushions); fitted with pneumatic tyres 4/28.

DP 2598 (338): Its chassis was new in 1916, fitted with a new Brush body; transferred to Thames Valley Traction Co Ltd 7/20 and renumbered 30 c8/20; reseated to B29F 12/21 (its wooden slatted seats were re-spaced and converted to take cushions).

DP 2599 (337): Its chassis was new in 1917, fitted with a Tilling body dating from 1913/4 originally fitted to one of Belsize DP 1655-1660, DP 1756-1757 and later to one of Thornycrofts DP 2115 (248) or DP 2117 (250); transferred to Thames Valley Traction Co Ltd 7/20 and renumbered 27 c8/20.

DP 2600 (316): Its chassis was new in 1918, fitted with a Birch body previously fitted to Thornycroft DP 2125 (261); transferred to Thames Valley Traction Co Ltd 7/20 and renumbered 24 c8/20; its wooden anatomical (slatted) seats were probably converted to take cushions 1/22; reseated to B23R to meet Metropolitan Police requirements for Uxbridge town services 6/22.

DP 2602 (339): Its chassis was new in 1916, fitted with a new Brush body; transferred to Thames Valley Traction Co Ltd 7/20 and renumbered 31 c8/20; reseated to B29F 5/21 (its wooden slatted seats were re-spaced and converted to take cushions); fitted with pneumatic tyres 4/28.

DP 2603 (341): Its chassis was new in 1917, fitted with a new Brush body; transferred to Thames Valley Traction Co Ltd 7/20 and renumbered 32 c8/20; reseated to B29F 8/22 (its wooden slatted seats were re-spaced and converted to take cushions); fitted with pneumatic tyres 3/28.

DP 2604 (352): Its chassis was new in 1918, fitted with a new Brush body [un-numbered]); transferred to Thames Valley Traction Co Ltd 7/20 and renumbered 33 c8/20; its Brush body was removed 9/20 and it ran as a lorry from 9/20 to 3/21; rebodied Birch Ch28 [36] with a canvas roof 3/21; fitted with pneumatic tyres 4/26.

DP 2606 (353): Its chassis was new in 1915, fitted with a Tilling body dating from 1913/4 previously fitted to one of Belsize DP 1655-1660, DP 1756-1757 and later to one of Thornycrofts DP 2115 (248) or DP 2117 (250); transferred to Thames Valley Traction Co Ltd 7/20 and renumbered 34 c8/20; fitted with the LGOC (1763) O18/16RO [38] body from Thornycroft BL 9752 (38) 3/23; converted to forward control layout and rebodied Brush (221) O28/26RO [86] 4/24-5/24; fitted with the Dodson (9321 or 9326) O26/24RO body [169] from Thornycroft AN 6452 (130) 1/28; withdrawn after an accident 6/28.

Disposals - chassis only (unless otherwise indicated):

DP 2597 (28): Dawsons Motor Works (dealer?), Ashbourne 2/29; unidentified owner, Burton-on-Trent (GST) 5/31.

DP 2598 (30): JF Jeale, Dorking (GSR?) 10/28; unidentified owner, London (GLN) at an unknown date; unidentified owner, Essex (GEX) 4/30.

DP 2599 (27): Trent Motor Traction Co Ltd, Derby (DE) T163 6/23 (as a complete vehicle / B28R); reseated to B26R 1925; withdrawn 1927; converted to lorry no. 1 by Trent and transferred to the ancillary fleet 1927; unidentified operator / dealer 2/28; Thomas (showman), Nottingham 12/28; showman, Coventry 9/32.

DP 2600 (24): Nicholls Transport Co, Cornwall (GCO) 3/29.

DP 2602 (31): Nicholls Transport Co, Cornwall (GCO) 3/29.

DP 2603 (32): AJ Elvin, Wembley (GLN) 3/29; licensed 4/29.

DP 2604 (33): Dismantled for spares / scrap by Thames Valley 5/28 (as a complete vehicle).

DP 2606 (34): Dismantled for spares / scrap by Thames Valley 8/28.

Vehicle on hire:

An unidentified Daimler CK with a 'charabus' body seating around 20 was demonstrated in 11/20. It was fitted with experimental Dunlop pneumatic tyres which may have been the principal reason for the demonstration.

1921

Vehicles acquired from War Department (GOV) 3/21:

36	DP 3633	Thornycroft J	6419	Birch [34]		Ch28	3/21	c10/27
35	DP 3647	Thornycroft J	4914	Birch [33]		Ch28	3/21	c10/27

Notes:

These were ex-War Department (GOV) lorry chassis purchased through the War Department Disposals Board, Slough in 8/20.

DP 3633 (36): Its chassis was new in 1918, fitted with a new Birch charabanc body with a canvas roof; fitted with pneumatic tyres 3/26.

DP 3647 (35): Its chassis was new in 1917, fitted with a new Birch charabanc body with a canvas roof; fitted with pneumatic tyres 3/26.

Disposals – complete vehicles:

DP 3633 (36): Dismantled for spares / scrap by Thames Valley 5/28.

DP 3647 (35): Dismantled for spares / scrap by Thames Valley 5/28.

1922

New Vehicles:

54	MO 773	Ford T	6486788	Vincent [54]		B14F	12/22	4/24
55	MO 774	Ford T	6488073	Vincent [55]		B14F	12/22	12/23

Notes:

MO 773-774 (54-55): Were 'chaser' vehicles (known as 'Scarlet Runners') for use in competition with other operators. They were painted in an all-over red livery and did not carry fleet names.

Disposals:

MO 773 (54): Converted to a lorry and transferred to the service fleet 4/24 (qv).

MO 774 (55): FV Pritchard, Llanrug (CN) 12/23 (as a complete vehicle); last licensed 3/26.

Vehicles acquired from Eastern Counties Road Car Co Ltd, Ipswich (EK) 4/22:

42	DX 2173	Thornycroft J	7463	Hora [42]		B28F	10/19	11/29
40	DX 2174	Thornycroft J	7466	Hora [40]		B28F	10/19	10/29
41	DX 2175	Thornycroft J	7452	Hora [52]		B28F	10/19	9/26

Previous histories:

DX 2173 (42): New to Great Eastern Railway Co, London E15 (LN) (based at Ipswich); Eastern Counties Road Car Co Ltd (not operated) 4/22.

DX 2174-2175 (40-41): New to Great Eastern Railway Co, London E15 (LN) (based at Ipswich); Eastern Counties Road Car Co Ltd (not operated) 4/22.

Notes:

DX 2173 (42): Entered service with an enlarged front entrance 7/22; fitted with the LGOC (1760) O18/16RO body [37] from Thornycroft BL 9892 (37) 5/23; body wrecked after overturning between Sands and Lane End due to road subsidence 1/24; fitted with the LGOC O18/16RO body [51] from Thornycroft MO 1504 (58) 2/24; converted to forward control layout and rebodied Brush (155) O28/26RO [117] 3/25-4/25.

DX 2174 (40): Entered service with an enlarged front entrance 6/22; its saloon roof was replaced with a detachable top 8/23; converted to forward control layout and rebodied Brush (281) O28/26RO [120] 3/25-5/25.

DX 2175 (41): Rebodied LGOC (1895) O18/16RO [41] before entry into service 8/22; rebodied LGOC (1801) O18/16RO [56] 3/23; body removed 11/26.

Disposals - chassis only:

DX 2173 (42): AE Spears (dealer), London SW19 11/29; TC Grange, Wells-next-the-Sea (NK) for spares 12/29.

DX 2174 (40): AE Spears (dealer), London SW19 10/29; BPA Service Co, London N7 (GLN) at an unknown date; last licensed 3/36.

DX 2175 (41): Rebodied as a 1,000 gallon petrol tanker for the Dominion Motor Spirit Co Ltd haulage contract and transferred to the tanker fleet 3/27 (qv).

Vehicles acquired from War Department (GOV) 5/22-7/22:

44	BL 9751	Thornycroft J	5353	LGOC [44]	2360	O18/16RO	5/22	8/26
38	BL 9752	Thornycroft J	5370	LGOC [38]	1763	O18/16RO	5/22	5/26
37	BL 9892	Thornycroft J	5274	LGOC [37]	1760	O18/16RO	5/22	9/26
45	MO 51	Thornycroft J	6000	LGOC [45]	2714	O18/16RO	5/22	9/26
39	MO 52	Thornycroft J	4676	LGOC [39]	1810	O18/16RO	5/22	9/26

47	MO 62	Thornycroft J	4741	LGOC [47]	2915	O18/16RO	6/22	12/26
46	MO 128	Thornycroft J	4529	LGOC [46]	2848	O18/16RO	6/22	10/28
43	MO 129	Thornycroft J	5051	LGOC [43]	2057	O18/16RO	6/22	11/28
50	MO 150	Thornycroft J	4465	LGOC [50]	3264	O18/16RO	6/22	10/28
51	MO 151	Thornycroft J	4468	LGOC [51]	3631	O18/16RO	6/22	11/24
53	MO 158	Thornycroft J	2220	Birch [18]		B23R	7/22	9/28
48	MO 159	Thornycroft J	2580	LGOC [48]	3140	O18/16RO	6/22	11/29
49	MO 160	Thornycroft J	3145	LGOC [--]	3968	O18/16RO	6/22	8/28
52	MO 307	Thornycroft J	4749	LGOC [49]	3257	O18/16RO	7/22	2/30

Notes:

These were ex-War Department (GOV) lorry chassis purchased through the War Department Disposals Board, Slough.

BL 9751 (44): Its chassis was new in 1917, fitted with a second-hand LGOC body; rebodied LGOC O18/16RO [57] 3/23; body removed 5/24; fitted with the LGOC O18/16RO body [65] from Thornycroft MO 159 (48) 5/25.

BL 9752 (38): Its chassis was new in 1917, fitted with a second-hand LGOC body; rebodied LGOC O18/16RO [58] 3/23; rebodied LGOC (728) O18/16RO [112] 4/25.

BL 9892 (37): Its chassis was new in 1917, fitted with a second-hand LGOC body (this was the first double-deck vehicle purchased 'new' (in 4/22), although both chassis and body were second-hand); it was submitted to the Metropolitan Police for approval on Uxbridge area services; rebodied LGOC O18/16RO [62] 5/23; fitted with the LGOC (1763) O18/16RO [38] body from Thornycroft DP 2606 (34) 5/24; rebodied LGOC (3241) O18/16RO [113] 6/25.

MO 51 (45): Its chassis was new in 1918, fitted with a second-hand LGOC body; rebodied LGOC O18/16RO [61] 5/23; rebodied LGOC O18/16RO [114] 4/25.

MO 52 (39): Its chassis was new in 1917, fitted with a second-hand LGOC body; rebodied LGOC O18/16RO [63] 5/23.

MO 62 (47): Its chassis was new in 1917, fitted with a second-hand LGOC body; rebodied LGOC O18/16RO [60] 6/23; fitted with the LGOC O18/16RO body [57] 5/24 from Thornycroft BL 9751 (44); rebodied LGOC (3214) O18/16RO [115] 6/25; was used as a driver training vehicle and tree lopper c10/26-12/26.

MO 128 (46): Its chassis was new in 1917, fitted with a second-hand LGOC body; rebodied LGOC O18/16RO [66] 7/23; converted to forward control layout and rebodied Brush (280) O28/26RO [119] 4/25-5/25; fitted with pneumatic tyres 5/28.

MO 129 (43): Its chassis was new in 1917, fitted with a second-hand LGOC body; rebodied LGOC O18/16RO [67] 7/23; converted to forward control layout and rebodied Brush (152) O28/26RO [116] 2/25-4/25; fitted with pneumatic tyres 5/28.

MO 150 (50): Its chassis was new in 1917, fitted with a second-hand LGOC body; rebodied LGOC O18/16RO [68] 7/23; converted to forward control layout and rebodied Brush (285) O28/26RO [122] 5/25-6/25; fitted with pneumatic tyres 7/28.

MO 151 (51): Its chassis was new in 1917, fitted with a second-hand LGOC body; rebodied LGOC O18/16RO [71] 8/23.

MO 158 (53): Its chassis was new in 1915, fitted with the Birch body previously on Thornycroft DP 2127 (19).

MO 159 (48): Its chassis was new in 1915, fitted with a second-hand LGOC body; rebodied LGOC O18/16RO [65] 7/23; converted to forward control layout and rebodied Brush (284) O28/26RO [124] 5/25-6/25; fitted with pneumatic tyres 5/28.

MO 160 (49): Its chassis was new in 1916, fitted with a second-hand LGOC body (this was disposed of before the numbering system was introduced); body removed 9/22; fitted with a lorry body 11/22 and used in the ancillary fleet; rebodied LGOC (1810) O18/16RO [39] from MO 52 (39) 5/23; converted to forward control layout and rebodied Brush (224) O28/26RO [93] 4/24-5/24; fitted with the Dodson O26/24RO body [170] from Thornycroft XR 9847 (131) 11/27.

MO 307 (52): Its chassis was new in 1917, fitted with a second-hand LGOC body; rebodied LGOC O18/16RO [69] 8/23; converted to forward control layout and rebodied RSJ B32R [100] 12/24; fitted with pneumatic tyres over the winter of 1926/7.

Disposals - chassis only (unless otherwise indicated):

BL 9751 (44): Dismantled for spares / scrap by Thames Valley 11/26.
BL 9752 (38): Dismantled for spares / scrap by Thames Valley 10/26.
BL 9892 (37): Beckett, Basingstoke (GHA?) 10/26.
MO 51 (45): Dismantled for spares / scrap by Thames Valley 2/27.
MO 52 (39): Dismantled for spares / scrap by Thames Valley 11/26.

MO 62 (47): Rebodied as a 1,000 gallon petrol tanker for the Dominion Motor Spirit Co Ltd haulage contract and transferred to the tanker fleet 3/27 (qv).

MO 128 (46): Riddell Bros, Coatbridge (GLK) 10/28; Davies, Smith & Co, Airdrie (GLK) at an unknown date; last licensed 6/33.

MO 129 (43): HC Preater, Swindon (GWI?) 11/28; Mrs A Page {Pages}, Swindon (GWI) at an unknown date; last licensed 6/35.

MO 150 (50): Riddell Bros, Coatbridge (GLK) 10/28; scrapped by them 4/32.

MO 151 (51): Rebodied as a 1,000 gallon petrol tanker for the Dominion Motor Spirit Co Ltd haulage contract and transferred to the tanker fleet 11/24 (qv).

MO 158 (53): Wilkinson Transport Co, Bury St Edmunds (GWF) 10/28; Mrs E Marsh, Hawkedon, Bury St Edmunds (GWF) by 1933; last licensed 12/33.

MO 159 (48): AE Spears (dealer), London SW19 11/29; A Probyn & Co Ltd, London N1 (LN) (kept at Brighton) by 1938; last licensed 6/39.

MO 160 (49): AC Glaister, Preston (GLA) 8/28; last licensed 6/29.

MO 307 (52): AE Spears (dealer), London SW19 5/30; John Newman Ltd, London E13 (GLN) 5/31; last licensed 10/32.

1923

Vehicles acquired from War Department (GOV) 5/23-8/23:

57	MO 1503	Thornycroft J	4847	LGOC [45]	2714	O18/16RO	5/23	11/28
58	MO 1504	Thornycroft J	6591	LGOC [64]	?	O18/16RO	5/23	8/28
59	MO 1625	Thornycroft J	2307	LGOC [43]	2057	O18/16RO	7/23	11/28
61	MO 1626	Thornycroft J	4631	LGOC [64]	?	O18/16RO	6/23	11/28
60	MO 1627	Thornycroft J	2321	LGOC [46]	2848	O18/16RO	6/23	6/28
62	MO 1715	Thornycroft J	2277	LGOC [48]	3140	O18/16RO	7/23	10/28
63	MO 1716	Thornycroft J	2494	LGOC [72]	?	O18/16RO	8/23	8/28
64	MO 1717	Thornycroft J	4443	LGOC [50]	3264	O18/16RO	7/23	10/29
65	MO 1803	Thornycroft J	5055	LGOC [70]	?	O18/16RO	8/23	2/25

Notes:

These were ex-War Department (GOV) lorry chassis purchased through H Lane & Co Ltd (dealer), London SW10.

The missing LGOC body numbers were four from 1801, 1806, 1867, 2084, 2433, 2693, 3547, 3735, 4317, 4375, 4391, 4419, 4453, 4596, 4600 and 4615.

MO 1503 (57): Its chassis was new in 1916, fitted with the LGOC body from Thornycroft MO 51 (45); fitted with the LGOC (3257) O18/16RO body [49] from Thornycroft MO 307 (52) 10/23; fitted with the LGOC O16/18RO body [72] from Thornycroft MO 1716 (63) 5/24; converted to forward control layout and rebodied Brush (373) O28/26RO [96] 7/24; fitted with pneumatic tyres 7/28.

MO 1504 (58): Its chassis was new in 1918, fitted with a second-hand LGOC body; fitted with the LGOC (2915) O18/16RO body [47] from Thornycroft MO 62 (47) 6/23; fitted with the LGOC (3631) O18/16RO body [51] from Thornycroft MO 151 (51) 9/23; converted to forward control layout (the first such vehicle in the fleet) and rebodied Dodson O26/24RO [73] 2/24 (this body was purchased for evaluation for use on the Uxbridge routes as it was approved by the Metropolitan Police; it was also the first to be painted in red and white livery).

MO 1625 (59): Its chassis was new in 1915, fitted with the LGOC body from Thornycroft MO 129 (43); fitted with the LGOC O18/16RO body [60] from Thornycroft MO 62 (47) 6/24; converted to forward control layout and rebodied Brush (154) O28/26RO [118] 3/25-5/25; fitted with pneumatic tyres 5/28.

MO 1626 (61): Its chassis was new in 1916, fitted with the LGOC body from Thornycroft MO 1504 (58); converted to forward control layout and rebodied Brush (286) O28/26RO [123] 4/25-6/25; fitted with pneumatic tyres 8/28.

MO 1627 (60): Its chassis was new in 1914, fitted with the LGOC body from Thornycroft MO 128 (46); converted to forward control layout and rebodied Brush (225) O28/26RO [90] 3/24-5/24; fitted with the Dodson (9474) O26/24RO body [178] from Thornycroft MF 6914 (139) 2/28, retained for 'emergency work', but not operated in this form.

MO 1715 (62): Its chassis was new in 1915, fitted with the LGOC body [48] from Thornycroft MO 159 (48); converted to forward control layout and rebodied Brush (372) O28/26RO [97] 8/24; fitted with pneumatic tyres 7/28.

MO 1716 (63): Its chassis was new in 1915, fitted with a second-hand LGOC body; converted to forward control layout and rebodied Brush (223) O28/26RO [91] body 6/24; fitted with the Dodson (9193) O26/24RO body [163] from Thornycroft XP 5450 (124) 2/28.

MO 1717 (64): Its chassis was new in 1916, fitted with the LGOC body [50] from Thornycroft MO 150 (50); converted to forward control layout and rebodied Brush O54RO [92] 6/24; fitted with pneumatic tyres 7/28.

MO 1803 (65): Its chassis was new in 1916, fitted with a second-hand LGOC body.

Disposals - chassis only (unless otherwise indicated):

MO 1503 (57): JF Jeale, Dorking (GSR?) 6/29.

MO 1504 (58): A Honour, London W3 (GLN) 9/28; last licensed 6/31.

MO 1625 (59): A Mattia (dealer), Andover 3/29.

MO 1626 (61): AE Spears (dealer), London SW19 10/29; J Freeman (showman), Horley at an unknown date; last licensed 10/32.

MO 1627 (60): Dismantled for spares / scrap by Thames Valley 8/28.

MO 1715 (62): Riddell Bros, Coatbridge (GLK) 10/28; last licensed 11/31.

MO 1716 (63): A Honour, London W3 (GLN) 9/28.

MO 1717 (64): Thatcham Road Transport Co Ltd, Thatcham (BE) 10/29 (as a complete vehicle); licensed as a goods vehicle by 3/30; last licensed 6/30.

MO 1803 (65): Rebodied as a 1,000 gallon petrol tanker for the Dominion Motor Spirit Co Ltd haulage contract and transferred to the tanker fleet 3/25 (qv).

Vehicle acquired from F Simmonds, Reading (BE) 3/23:

56	DP 4400	Ford T		?	Russell & Paddick [59]	B14F	8/22	10/23

Previous history:

This vehicle was acquired with the Simmonds business; its previous history is detailed in the Vehicles of Acquired Operators section.

Notes:

DP 4400 (56): Used as a 'chaser' vehicle for use in competition with other operators

Disposal – complete vehicle:

DP 4400 (56): Yorkshire (Woollen District) Electric Traction Co Ltd, Dewsbury (WR) 10/23; possibly used as a goods vehicle on trade plates as it was never licensed in West Riding; unidentified owner, Leeds (GWR) 11/32.

1924
Vehicles acquired from War Department (GOV) 3/24-12/24:

66	MO 2610	Thornycroft J	4283	Birch [74]	482	B32R	3/24	1/30
67	MO 2611	Thornycroft J	4677	Brush [77]	213	O28/26RO	4/24	8/28
68	MO 2612	Thornycroft J	4654	Brush [80]	220	O28/26RO	5/24	8/28
69	MO 2613	Thornycroft J	2832	Brush [78]	215	O28/26RO	4/24	9/28
70	MO 2614	Thornycroft J	4955	Birch [84]	495	B32R	3/24	1/30
71	MO 2615	Thornycroft J	3055	Birch [76]	484	B32R	3/24	5/30
72	MO 2616	Thornycroft J	2681	Birch [88]	496	B32R	5/24	3/30
73	MO 2617	Thornycroft J	1918	Brush [81]	214	O28/26RO	5/24	9/28
74	MO 2618	Thornycroft J	2455	Birch [89]	497	B32R	5/24	3/30
75	MO 2619	Thornycroft J	2425	Brush [82]	218	O28/26RO	5/24	12/29
76	MO 2620	Thornycroft J	3640	Brush [79]	217	O28/26RO	4/24	10/29
77	MO 2621	Thornycroft J	3519	Brush [83]	219	O28/26RO	5/24	9/29
78	MO 2622	Thornycroft J	2893	Birch [75]	483	B32R	3/24	5/30
79	MO 3565	Thornycroft J	4081	Brush [94]	371	O28/26RO	7/24	9/29
80	MO 3566	Thornycroft J	4438	Brush [95]	370	O28/26RO	7/24	9/29
81	MO 4154	Thornycroft J	4042	RSJ [102]	?	B32R	12/24	1/30
82	MO 4155	Thornycroft J	4047	RSJ [101]	?	B32R	12/24	1/30
84	MO 4157	Thornycroft J	4489	RSJ [103]	382	B32R	12/24	1/30

Notes:

These were ex-War Department (GOV) lorry chassis purchased through H Lane & Co Ltd (dealer), London SW10; they were converted to forward control layout before receiving their bus bodies.

MO 2610 (66): Its chassis was new in 1917; re-registered MO 4610 9/24 (following the discovery that the registration MO 2610 had already been issued to a private Standard car); fitted with pneumatic tyres over the winter of 1926/7.

MO 2611 (67): Its chassis was new in 1917; fitted with the Dodson (9188) O26/24RO [156] body from Thornycroft XP 9081 (117) 10/27; withdrawn after an accident 8/28.

MO 2612 (68): Its chassis was new in 1917; fitted with the Dodson (9271) O26/24RO body [168] from Thornycroft XR 4559 (129) 10/27; withdrawn after an accident 8/28.

MO 2613 (69): Its chassis was new in 1915; fitted with the Dodson (9191) O26/24RO body [161] from Thornycroft XP 4705 (122) 3/28.

MO 2614 (70): Its chassis was new in 1917; fitted with pneumatic tyres 1/27.

MO 2615-2616 (71-72): Their chassis were new in 1915; fitted with pneumatic tyres over the winter of 1926/7.

MO 2617 (73): Its chassis was new in 1914; fitted with the Dodson (9192) O26/24RO body [162] from Thornycroft XP 5449 (123) 3/28.

MO 2618 (74): Its chassis was new in 1915; fitted with pneumatic tyres 1926.

MO 2619 (75): Its chassis was new in 1917; fitted with pneumatic tyres 7/28.

MO 2620 (76): Its chassis was new in 1916; fitted with pneumatic tyres 7/28.

MO 2621 (77): Its chassis was new in 1916; fitted with pneumatic tyres 8/28.

MO 2622 (78): Its chassis was new in 1915; fitted with pneumatic tyres over the winter of 1926/7.

MO 3565 (79): Its chassis was new in 1916; fitted with pneumatic tyres 7/28.

MO 3566 (80): Its chassis was new in 1917; fitted with pneumatic tyres 8/28.

MO 4154 (81): Its chassis was new in 1916; its RSJ body number was from the 379-384 batch; fitted with pneumatic tyres 10/26.

MO 4155 (82): Its chassis was new in 1916; its RSJ body number was from the 379-384 batch; fitted with pneumatic tyres over the winter of 1926/7.

MO 4157 (84): Its chassis was new in 1917; its RSJ body number was from the 379-384 batch; fitted with pneumatic tyres over the winter of 1926/7.

Disposals - chassis only:

MO 2611-2612 (67-68): Dismantled for spares / scrap by Thames Valley 8/28.

MO 2613 (69): A Honour, London W3 (GLN) 9/28; Maisie Rosier {Norfolk Roadways}, Hopton, Diss (GNK) at an unknown date; last licensed 6/31.

MO 2614 (70): AE Spears (dealer), London SW19 3/30; H Lane & Co Ltd & Sons Ltd, London SW10 (GLN) at an unknown date; last licensed 4/32.

MO 2615 (71): AE Spears (dealer), London SW19 5/30; E Fraser, London SW18 (GLN) by 1/31; last licensed 6/32.

MO 2616 (72): AE Spears (dealer), London SW19 4/30; TC Grange, Wells-next-the-Sea (GNK) at an unknown date; last licensed 2/33.

MO 2617 (73): EJ Messenger, London SW9 (GLN) 9/28; last licensed 6/32.

MO 2618 (74): AE Spears (dealer), London SW19 4/30; TC Grange, Wells-next-the-Sea (GNK) at an unknown date; last licensed 6/33.

MO 2619 (75): AE Spears (dealer), London SW19 12/29; JR Munday Ltd, London SW11 (GLN) at an unknown date; last licensed 9/33.

MO 2620 (76): AE Spears (dealer), London SW19 11/29; AJ White, North Wanborough (GHA) by 4/32; withdrawn 6/39; Hartley Wintney Rural District Council (GOV) as a dam-carrying lorry in connection with the Auxiliary Fire Service 2/41; Home Office (GOV) 8/41; Ministry of Home Security (GOV) at an unknown date; Ministry of Supply (GOV) 8/43.

MO 2621 (77): AE Spears (dealer), London SW19 9/29; T & W Farmiloe Ltd, London SW1 (GLN) at an unknown date; last licensed 12/33.

MO 2622 (78): AE Spears (dealer), London SW19 5/30; John Newman Ltd, London E13 (GLN?) 9/30; last licensed 1/33; scrapped 3/33.

MO 3565 (79): AE Spears (dealer), London SW19 9/29; H Abbott, Mendlesham (GWF?) at an unknown date; last licensed 10/33.

MO 3566 (80): AE Spears (dealer), London SW19 9/29; FJ Duckworth, Barford, Norwich (GNK?) at an unknown date; last licensed 2/31.

MO 4154 (81): AE Spears (dealer), London SW19 2/30; G Jose, Blackwater, Truro (GCO) 2/30; last licensed 9/30.

MO 4155 (82): AE Spears (dealer), London SW19 2/30; G Jose, Blackwater, Truro (GCO) 2/30; last licensed 6/32.

MO 4157 (84): AE Spears (dealer), London SW19 2/30; H Lane & Co Ltd & Sons Ltd, London SW10 (GLN) at an unknown date; last licensed 9/33.

MO 4610 (ex MO 2610) (66): AE Spears (dealer), London SW19 2/30; H Lane & Co Ltd & Sons Ltd, London SW10 (GLN) at an unknown date; last licensed 9/33.

Vehicles acquired from Southdown Motor Services Ltd, Brighton (ES) 12/24:

87	CD 5379	Thornycroft J	2697	Grimaldi [99]	Ch27	-/20	10/31
86	CD 6353	Thornycroft J	6065	Harrington [98]	Ch32	6/21	4/31

Previous histories:

CD 5379 (87): New as a War Department (GOV) lorry chassis 1915; WC Taylor {White Heather Motor Services}, Brighton (ES), fitted with a Harrington Ch27 body and registered CD 5379 1920; fitted with a second-hand (probably new in 1918) Grimaldi body 1920; Southdown Motor Services Ltd 31 8/21.

CD 6353 (86): New as a War Department (GOV) lorry chassis 1918; WC Taylor {White Heather Motor Services}, Brighton (ES), fitted with a Harrington body and registered CD 6353 6/21; Southdown Motor Services Ltd 30 8/21.

Notes:

CD 5379 (87): Charabanc body removed c10/25; converted to forward control layout and rebodied Brush (133) O28/26RO [137] 2/26-3/26; fitted with pneumatic tyres 6/28.

CD 6353 (86): Charabanc body removed c10/25; converted to forward control layout and rebodied Brush (158) O28/26RO [132] 1/26-2/26; fitted with pneumatic tyres 6/28; fitted with the JB type 50 hp BB4 engine from Thornycroft XP 5985 (126) (for disposal) by 4/31.

Disposals - chassis only:

CD 5379 (87): AE Spears (dealer), London SW19 10/31.

CD 6353 (86): AJ White, North Wanborough (GHA) (not licensed) 4/31; broken up (by Thames Valley) for spares 5/32.

1925

Vehicles acquired from War Department (GOV) 1/25-3/25:

83	MO 4156	Thornycroft J	4134	RSJ [105]	?	B32R	1/25	2/30
85	MO 4158	Thornycroft J	5086	RSJ [104]	?	B32R	1/25	2/30
88	MO 4306	Thornycroft J	4628	Brush [106]	147	O28/26RO	2/25	8/28
89	MO 4307	Thornycroft J	4718	Brush [107]	149	O28/26RO	2/25	11/29
90	MO 4308	Thornycroft J	4461	Brush [108]	153	O28/26RO	3/25	10/29
91	MO 4309	Thornycroft J	4826	Brush [109]	151	O28/26RO	3/25	11/29
92	MO 4310	Thornycroft J	4079	Brush [110]	150	O28/26RO	2/25	11/29
93	MO 4311	Thornycroft J	4873	Brush [111]	148	O28/26RO	2/25	10/29

Notes:

These were ex-War Department (GOV) lorry chassis purchased through H Lane & Co Ltd (dealer), London SW10; they were converted to forward control layout before receiving their bus bodies.

MO 4156 (83): Its chassis was new in 1916; its RSJ body number was from the 379-384 batch; fitted with pneumatic tyres over the winter of 1926/7.

MO 4158 (85): Its chassis was new in 1916; its RSJ body number was from the 379-384 batch; fitted with pneumatic tyres over the winter of 1926/7.

MO 4306 (88): Its chassis was new in 1917; fitted with the Dodson (9187) O26/24RO body [157] from Thornycroft XP 4051 (118) 11/27.

MO 4307-4308 (89-90): Their chassis were new in 1917; fitted with pneumatic tyres 7/28.

MO 4309 (91): Its chassis was new in 1917; fitted with pneumatic tyres 6/28.

MO 4310 (92): Its chassis was new in 1916; fitted with pneumatic tyres 6/28.

MO 4311 (93): Its chassis was new in 1917; fitted with pneumatic tyres 7/28.

Disposals - chassis only:

MO 4156 (83): AE Spears (dealer), London SW19 3/30.

MO 4158 (85): AE Spears (dealer), London SW19 3/30.

MO 4306 (88): R Knight, Kew (GSR?) 12/28.

MO 4307 (89): AE Spears (dealer), London SW19 11/29; H Lane & Co Ltd, London SW10 (GLN) 5/30; last licensed 12/33.

MO 4308 (90): AE Spears (dealer), London SW19 10/29; TC Grange, Wells-next-the-Sea (GNK) by 10/31; last licensed 12/33.

MO 4309 (91): AE Spears (dealer), London SW19 11/29; H Lane & Co Ltd, London SW10 (GLN) 2/30; last licensed 8/33.

MO 4310 (92): AE Spears (dealer), London SW19 11/29; A Probyn & Co Ltd, London N1 (GLN) at an unknown date; last licensed 12/30.

MO 4311 (93): AE Spears (dealer), London SW19 10/29; W Smith, Kirkton Holme, Boston (GHD?) at an unknown date; last licensed 6/33.

Vehicles acquired from T Spragg Ltd {Progressive Bus Service}, Bracknell (BE) 10/25:

95	MO 2213	Lancia Tetraiota	224E	Bartle [127]	B20F	10/23	4/26
94	MO 3530	Lancia Z	Z3394	Vincent / Manners [126]	B20F	7/24	4/26
96	MO 4648	Lancia Pentaiota	702	Strachan & Brown [128]	B25F	2/25	4/26
97	MO 5443	Lancia Pentaiota	846	Strachan & Brown [129]	B25F	5/25	4/26
	MO 6184	Dennis 2½ ton	45158	Strachan & Brown [-]	B30R	9/25	----

Previous histories:
These vehicles were acquired with the Spragg business; their previous histories are detailed in the Vehicles of Acquired Operators section.

Notes:
MO 6184: Not operated by Thames Valley.

Disposals – complete vehicles:
MO 2213 (95): GE Askew {GE Askew & Son}, Loughton (EX) 4/26; last licensed 9/28.
MO 3530 (94): GE Askew {GE Askew & Son}, Loughton (EX) 4/26; last licensed 9/29.
MO 4648 (96): GE Askew {GE Askew & Son}, Loughton (EX) 4/26; last licensed 9/29.
MO 5443 (97): GE Askew {GE Askew & Son}, Loughton (EX) 4/26; R Palmer, Great Massingham (NK) at an unknown date; last licensed 9/33.
MO 6184: Aldershot & District Traction Co Ltd, Aldershot (HA) D118 11/25; last licensed 12/30; chassis to Cow & Gate Ltd, Wincanton (GSO?) (not licensed) 9/31.

1926

New Vehicles:

98	MO 6842	Thornycroft J	2342	Brush [136]	161	O28/26RO	3/26	7/31
99	MO 6843	TSM B9A	4837	Tilling [138]		B32R	4/26	3/37
100	MO 6844	TSM B9A	4838	Tilling [140]		B32R	4/26	3/38
101	MO 6845	TSM B9A	4839	Tilling [141]		B32R	4/26	5/38
102	MO 6846	TSM B9A	4840	Tilling [139]		B32R	4/26	4/38
103	MO 6847	TSM B9A	4841	Birch [142]		B32R	4/26	3/38
104	MO 6848	TSM B9A	4842	Brush [143]		B32R	4/26	3/38
105	MO 6849	TSM B9A	4843	Brush [144]		B32R	6/26	2/38
106	MO 6850	TSM B9A	4844	Tilling [145]		B32R	5/26	7/37
107	MO 6851	TSM B9A	4845	Tilling [146]		B32R	5/26	8/37
108	MO 6852	TSM B9A	4846	Tilling [147]		B32R	6/26	9/33
109	MO 6853	TSM B9A	4847	Tilling [148]		B32R	6/26	4/38
110	MO 6854	TSM B9A	4848	Tilling [149]		B32R	6/26	3/37
111	MO 6855	TSM B9B	4849	London Lorries [150]		C29F	6/26	4/33
112	MO 6856	TSM B9B	4850	London Lorries [151]		C29F	6/26	4/33
113	MO 6857	TSM B9B	4851	London Lorries [152]		C29F	6/26	3/32
114	MO 6858	TSM B9B	4852	London Lorries [153]		C29F	6/26	9/33
132	MO 7942	TSM B9A	4915	Brush [171]	?	B32R	7/26	7/37
133	MO 7943	TSM B9A	4916	Brush [172]	?	B32R	7/26	3/37
134	MO 7944	TSM B9A	4917	Brush [173]	?	B32R	7/26	3/38
135	MO 7945	TSM B9A	4918	Brush [174]	?	B32R	7/26	3/38
136	MO 7946	TSM B9A	4919	Brush [175]	?	B32R	7/26	7/37

Notes:
It was originally intended to obtain eight new Brush bodies (to be mounted on Thornycroft JB chassis) suitable for operation in the Uxbridge area which came within the jurisdiction of the Metropolitan Police. Thornycroft J type units were to be modified from existing Thames Valley stock but before the programme could be implemented, suitable complete vehicles became available from Cambrian Coaching & Goods Transport Omnibus Co Ltd and 14 of these were acquired (115-28, qv). One vehicle however was constructed, built up from components in Thames Valley stock including chassis 2342 (which was a spare frame that had been in store since 1920), the engine from MO 158 (53), the gearbox from DP 2606 (34) and rear axle from DP 2115 (5). These were assembled with other parts into a new JB chassis by Thornycroft at their Basingstoke works.
MO 6843-6854 (99-110): Their bodies on these vehicles were shared by Birch, Brush and Tilling in order to meet delivery requirements; they were all built to the same Brush design; front destination boxes and entrance doors were fitted c1929.

MO 6855-6858 (111-114): Had London Lorries 'QP' (Quadruple Purpose) 'all-weather' bodies with a full length folding canvas hood (the windows wound down and pillars folded down into the waist rail). They were replacements for the charabancs.

MO 6842 (98): Fitted with pneumatic tyres 6/28.
MO 6843 (99): Hired to Marlow & District Motor Services Ltd c4/32.
MO 6851 (107): Converted to normal control layout during its conversion to a petrol tanker 9/33.
MO 6855 (111): Fitted with the London Lorries C30F body [180] from MO 9313 (141) 5/32.
MO 6856 (112): Fitted with the London Lorries C30F body [201] from RX 1398 (162) 5/32.
MO 6858 (114): Fitted with the London Lorries C30F body [202] from RX 1399 (163) 5/32.
MO 7942-7946 (132-136): Front destination boxes and entrance doors were fitted c1929

Disposals – complete vehicles (unless otherwise indicated):
MO 6842 (98): Chassis to AE Spears (dealer), London SW19 5/32; no further operator (body sold separately, qv).
MO 6843 (99): J Jones (dealer), London W3 for scrap 2/38.
MO 6844 (100): J Jones (dealer), London W3 for scrap 3/38.
MO 6845 (101): H Goodey (dealer), Twyford for scrap 5/38; still there until the 1950s at least.
MO 6846 (102): A Jones (dealer), Reading 4/38; no further operator.
MO 6847-6848 (103-104): J Jones (dealer), London W3 for scrap 3/38.
MO 6849 (105): J Jones (dealer), London W3 for scrap 2/38.
MO 6850 (106): A Jones (dealer), Reading 4/38; no further operator.
MO 6851 (107): Rebodied as a 1,000 gallon petrol tanker and transferred to the tanker fleet 9/33 (qv).
MO 6852 (108): J Jones (dealer), London W3 for scrap 2/38.
MO 6853 (109): A Jones (dealer), Reading 4/38; J Lawrence (showman), Surbiton 6/38 (fitted with a new body); not licensed 10/39 to 3/44; moved to St Austell and relicensed 4/44; last licensed 10/45.
MO 6854 (110): J Jones (dealer), London W3 for scrap 2/38.
MO 6855-6856 (111-112): Rebodied as 1,000 gallon petrol tankers and transferred to the tanker fleet 4/33 (qv).
MO 6857 (113): E Chapman (showman), London W1 3/32; last licensed 5/34.
MO 6858 (114): Rebodied as a 1,000 gallon petrol tanker and transferred to the tanker fleet 9/33 (qv).
MO 7942 (132): J Jones (dealer), London W3 for scrap 3/38.
MO 7943 (133): A Jones (dealer), Reading 4/38; no further operator.
MO 7944-7946 (134-136): J Jones (dealer), London W3 for scrap 3/38.

Vehicles acquired from London General Omnibus Co Ltd, London SW1 (LN) 4/26:

118	XP 4051	Thornycroft JB	10432	Dodson [157]	9187	O26/24RO	10/23	7/31
122	XP 4705	Thornycroft JB	10437	Dodson [161]	9191	O26/24RO	11/23	3/31
115	XP 4706	Thornycroft JB	10436	Dodson [154]	9185	O26/24RO	11/23	7/31
123	XP 5449	Thornycroft JB	10438	Dodson [162]	9192	O26/24RO	11/23	9/31
124	XP 5450	Thornycroft JB	10439	Dodson [163]	9193	O26/24RO	11/23	8/31
125	XP 5984	Thornycroft JB	10435	Dodson [164]	9194	O26/24RO	11/23	1/31
126	XP 5985	Thornycroft JB	10440	Dodson [165]	9195	O26/24RO	11/23	8/31
120	XP 6421	Thornycroft JB	10447	Dodson [159]	9189	O26/24RO	11/23	9/31
127	XP 6422	Thornycroft JB	10444	Dodson [166]	9232	O26/24RO	11/23	2/31
121	XP 9080	Thornycroft JB	10446	Dodson [160]	9190	O26/24RO	1/24	4/31
117	XP 9081	Thornycroft JB	10443	Dodson [156]	9188	O26/24RO	1/24	1/31
128	XP 9325	Thornycroft JB	10434	Dodson [167]	9233	O26/24RO	1/24	5/31
116	XP 9831	Thornycroft JB	10463	Dodson [155]	9184	O26/24RO	1/24	7/31
119	XU 2191	Thornycroft JB	10552	Dodson [158]	9186	O26/24RO	7/24	7/31

Previous histories:
XP 4051 (118): New to Cambrian Coaching & Goods Transport Omnibus Co Ltd {Cambrian}, London WC1 (LN) T101; London General Omnibus Co Ltd T101 1/26.
XP 4705 (122): New to Cambrian Coaching & Goods Transport Omnibus Co Ltd {Cambrian}, London WC1 (LN) T102; London General Omnibus Co Ltd T102 1/26.
XP 4706 (115): New to Cambrian Coaching & Goods Transport Omnibus Co Ltd {Cambrian}, London WC1 (LN) T103; London General Omnibus Co Ltd T103 1/26.
XP 5449-5450 (123-124): New to Cambrian Coaching & Goods Transport Omnibus Co Ltd {Cambrian}, London WC1 (LN) T104-T105; London General Omnibus Co Ltd T104-T105 1/26.
XP 5984-5985 (125-126): New to Cambrian Coaching & Goods Transport Omnibus Co Ltd {Cambrian}, London WC1 (LN) T106-T107; London General Omnibus Co Ltd T106-T107 1/26.
XP 6421 (120): New to Cambrian Coaching & Goods Transport Omnibus Co Ltd {Cambrian}, London WC1 (LN) T108; London General Omnibus Co Ltd T108 1/26.

XP 6422 (127): New to Cambrian Coaching & Goods Transport Omnibus Co Ltd {Cambrian}, London WC1 (LN) T109; London General Omnibus Co Ltd T109 1/26.

XP 9080 (121): New to Cambrian Coaching & Goods Transport Omnibus Co Ltd {Cambrian}, London WC1 (LN) T110; London General Omnibus Co Ltd T110 1/26.

XP 9081 (117): New to Cambrian Coaching & Goods Transport Omnibus Co Ltd {Cambrian}, London WC1 (LN) T111; London General Omnibus Co Ltd T111 1/26.

XP 9325 (128): New to Cambrian Coaching & Goods Transport Omnibus Co Ltd {Cambrian}, London WC1 (LN) T112; London General Omnibus Co Ltd T112 1/26.

XP 9831 (116): New to Cambrian Coaching & Goods Transport Omnibus Co Ltd {Cambrian}, London WC1 (LN) T113; London General Omnibus Co Ltd T113 1/26.

XU 2191 (119): New to Shamrock Traction Co Ltd {Shamrock}, London SW6 (LN); Cambrian Coaching & Goods Transport Omnibus Co Ltd {Cambrian}, London WC1 (LN) T114 4/25; London General Omnibus Co Ltd (LN) T114 1/26.

Notes:

XP 4051 (118): Fitted with the Brush (147) O28/26RO body [106] from Thornycroft MO 4306 (88) and pneumatic tyres 11/27.

XP 4705 (122): Fitted with a smaller 40 hp M4 engine (from a Thornycroft J type) 4/27-3/28 and 8/29-7/30; fitted with the Brush (215) O28/26RO body [78] from Thornycroft MO 2613 (69) and pneumatic tyres 3/28.

XP 4706 (115): Fitted with the Brush (285) O28/26RO body [122] from Thornycroft MO 150 (50) and pneumatic tyres 10/28.

XP 5449 (123): Fitted with the Brush (214) O28/26RO body [81] from Thornycroft MO 2617 (73) and pneumatic tyres 3/28.

XP 5450 (124): Fitted with the Brush (223) O28/26RO body [91] from MO 1716 (63) and pneumatic tyres 2/28; fitted with the RSJ B32R body [100] from Thornycroft MO 307 (52) 2/30.

XP 5984 (125): Fitted with the Brush (286) O28/26RO body [123] from Thornycroft MO 1626 (61) and pneumatic tyres 1/29.

XP 5985 (126): Fitted with the Brush (154) O28/26RO body [118] from Thornycroft MO 1625 (59) and pneumatic tyres 1/29; fitted with the J-type M4 engine from Thornycroft CD 6353 (86) by 4/31.

XP 6421 (120): Fitted with the Brush (280) O28/26RO body [119] from Thornycroft MO 128 (46) and pneumatic tyres 11/28.

XP 6422 (127): Fitted with the Brush (216) O28/26RO body [85] from Thornycroft DP 2112 (2) and pneumatic tyres 12/27.

XP 9080 (121): Fitted with the Brush (373) O28/26RO body [96] from Thornycroft MO 1503 (57) and pneumatic tyres 1/29.

XP 9081 (117): Fitted with the Brush (213) O28/26RO body [77] from Thornycroft MO 2611 (67) 10/27; fitted with pneumatic tyres 10/27 (believed to be the first double-deck vehicle so equipped).

XP 9325 (128): Fitted with the Brush (222) O28/26RO body [87] from Thornycroft DP 2123 (14) and pneumatic tyres 3/28; fitted with the RSJ B32R body [102] from Thornycroft MO 4154 (81) 2/30.

XP 9831 (116): Fitted with the Brush (372) O28/26RO body [97] from Thornycroft MO 1715 (62) and pneumatic tyres 12/28.

XU 2191 (119): Fitted with the Brush (152) O28/26RO body [116] from Thornycroft MO 129 (43) and pneumatic tyres 11/28.

Disposals - chassis only:

XP 4051 (118): AE Spears (dealer), London SW19 8/31; unidentified owner, Maidstone (GKT) 10/31.

XP 4705 (122): AE Spears (dealer), London SW19 3/31; unidentified owner (G??) at an unknown date.

XP 4706 (115): (?AE Spears (dealer), London SW19 by 4/32?); AJ White, North Wanborough (GHA) 4/32; unidentified owner 1/33; Auxiliary Fire Service (GOV) 5/41.

XP 5449 (123): Waterloo Motor Co (dealer), London SE1 2/32; Star Haulage Co, London (GLN) 1932.

XP 5450 (124): AE Spears (dealer), London SW19 10/31; unidentified owner (G??) 6/32.

XP 5984 (125): AE Spears (dealer), London SW19 1/31; unidentified owner (G??) 3/31.

XP 5985 (126): Last licensed 7/31; AE Spears (dealer), London SW19 5/32; no further operator.

XP 6421 (120): AE Spears (dealer), London SW19 11/31; unidentified owner (G??) 3/32.

XP 6422 (127): AE Spears (dealer), London SW19 3/31; unidentified owner (G??) 10/31.

XP 9080 (121): AE Spears (dealer), London SW19 4/31; unidentified owner (G??) 5/31.

XP 9081 (117): AE Spears (dealer), London SW19 1/31; AJ White, North Wanborough (GHA) by 1932; showman by 1942.

XP 9325 (128): AE Spears (dealer), London SW19 6/31; unidentified owner (G??) 6/31.

XP 9831 (116): Waterloo Motor Co (dealer), London SE1 2/32; unidentified owner (G??) 2/32 scrapped 10/32.

XU 2191 (119): AE Spears (dealer), London SW19 9/31; GF Jones, Maidstone (GKT) 11/31.

Vehicles acquired from London General Omnibus Co Ltd, London SW1 (LN) 5/26:

130	AN 6452	Thornycroft JB	10555	Dodson [169]	9321 or 9326	O26/24RO	7/24	2/31
129	XR 4559	Thornycroft JB	10517	Dodson [168]	9271	O26/24RO	3/24	7/31

Previous histories:

AN 6452 (130): New to Ubique Omnibus Co Ltd {Ubique}, London E12 (LN); London General Omnibus Co Ltd (not operated) 4/26.

XR 4559 (129): New to C Kurash {Diamond Omnibus Co}, London E3 (LN); J Kurash {Diamond Omnibus Co}, London E3 (LN) 4/24; Olympic Traction Co Ltd {Olympic}, London E3 (LN) 4/26; London General Omnibus Co Ltd (not operated) 4/26.

Notes:

AN 6452 (130): Fitted with the Brush (221) O28/26RO [86] body from Thornycroft DP 2606 (34) and pneumatic tyres 1/28; fitted with the RSJ B32R body [105] from Thornycroft MO 4156 (83) 2/30.

XR 4559 (129): Dodson body removed 10/27; fitted with the Brush (220) O28/26RO body [80] from Thornycroft MO 2612 (68) and pneumatic tyres 3/28; fitted with the RSJ B32R body [101] from Thornycroft MO 4155 (82) 2/30.

Disposals - chassis only:

AN 6452 (130): AE Spears (dealer), London SW19 3/31; unidentified owner (G??) 5/31.

XR 4559 (129): AE Spears (dealer), London SW19 3/32; Dock & General Transport Co, London EC1 (GLN) 6/32.

Vehicle acquired from Brailey Ltd {Fleur-de-Lys}, London SW2 (LN) 6/26:

131	XR 9847	Thornycroft JB	10531	Dodson [170]		O50RO	4/24	3/31

Previous history:

XR 9847 (131): New to Mrs FV Brailey {Magnet; Fleur-de-Lys c4/24}, London SW1 (LN); moved to London SW2 (LN) by 7/24; Brailey Ltd {Fleur-de-Lys} 1/26; JI Thornycroft & Co Ltd (dealer), Basingstoke c4/26, from whom it was acquired.

Notes:

XR 9847 (131): Fitted with the Brush (224) O28/26RO body [93] from Thornycroft MO 160 (49) and pneumatic tyres 11/27; fitted with the RSJ B32R body [103] from Thornycroft MO 4157 (84) 2/30.

Disposal - chassis only:

XR 9847 (131): AE Spears (dealer), London SW19 3/31.

Vehicle acquired from Grangewood Omnibus Co Ltd, London E6 (LN) 10/26:

137	XR 4694	Thornycroft JB	10508	Dodson [176]	?	O26/24RO	3/24	1/31

Previous history:

XR 4694 (137): New to L Myers {Lewis; later Essential}, London SE13 (LN); TW Lacey {Essential; later Grangewood}, London E6 (LN) 1/25; Grangewood Omnibus Co Ltd 3/26; HC Barratt (dealer?), Edmonton 9/26, from whom it was acquired.

Notes:

XR 4694 (137): Fitted with pneumatic tyres 2/28.

Disposal - chassis only:

XR 4694 (137): AE Spears (dealer), London SW19 2/31; Underhill Bros, Bexleyheath (GKT) 3/31.

Vehicle acquired from RE De Casagrande {Alma}, London N7 (LN) 10/26:

138	XR 999	Thornycroft JB	10485	Dodson [177]	?	O26/24RO	1/24	2/31

Previous history:

XR 999 (138): New to RE De Casagrande {Alma}, London SW11 (LN); moved to London N7 1925.

Notes:

XR 999 (138): Fitted with pneumatic tyres 1/28.

Disposal - chassis only:
> XR 999 (138): AE Spears (dealer), London SW19 2/31; unidentified owner (G??) by 1/32.

Vehicle acquired from London General Omnibus Co Ltd, London SW1 (LN) 11/26:

139	MF 6914	Thornycroft JB	10526	Dodson [178]		9474	O50RO	4/24	3/31

Previous history:
> MF 6914 (139): New to G Pauncefoot & Mrs V McReadie {Legion Omnibus Co}, London W12 (LN); Legion Omnibus Co Ltd {Legion}, London W12 (LN) 9/26; London General Omnibus Co Ltd 10/26.

Notes:
> MF 6914 (139): Fitted with the Brush (225) O28/26RO [90] body from Thornycroft MO 1627 (60) and pneumatic tyres 2/28; fitted with the RSJ B32R body [104] from Thornycroft MO 4158 (85) 2/30.

Disposal - chassis only:
> MF 6914 (139): AE Spears (dealer), London SW19 3/31; G Sullivan, London SW2 (GLN) at an unknown date; last licensed 7/37.

Vehicles acquired from SG Lovegrove {Lovegrove Bros}, Silchester (HA) 11/26:

	DP 4919	FIAT 15TER	?	(Vincent?)	B20F	7/23	----
	DP 5628	Dennis 2½ ton	?	(Vincent?)	B20F	6/24	----

Previous histories:
> These vehicles were new to SG Lovegrove {Lovegrove Bros}.

Notes:
> Thames Valley purchased Lovegrove's Reading to Silchester service (together with two vehicles, neither of which were operated) on 1 December 1926 for £1,100. Lovegrove continued with their garage business into the 1940s at least and ran coaches until 1959.

Disposals:
> DP 4919: Chassis to J Spratley {Blue Star Coaches}, Mortimer (BE) 5/27 (qv); body to WC, PB & NW Pocock {WC Pocock & Sons}, Cold Ash 5/27.
> DP 5628: S Ansell, London SE5 (LN) 12/26.

1927

New Vehicles:

140	MO 9312	TSM B9B	5268	London Lorries [179]		C30F	6/27	4/32
141	MO 9313	TSM B9B	5269	London Lorries [180]		C30F	6/27	4/32
142	MO 9314	TSM B9B	5270	London Lorries [181]		C30F	6/27	4/32
143	MO 9315	TSM B9B	5271	London Lorries [182]		C30F	6/27	4/32
144	MO 9316	TSM B9A	5272	Brush [183]	225	B35R	6/27	9/44
145	MO 9317	TSM B9A	5273	Brush [184]	224	B35R	5/27	7/40
146	MO 9318	TSM B9A	5274	Brush [185]	223	B35R	5/27	6/37
147	MO 9319	TSM B9A	5275	Brush [186]	230	B35R	6/27	7/40
148	MO 9320	TSM B9A	5276	Brush [187]	232	B35R	6/27	7/40
149	MO 9321	TSM B9A	5277	Brush [188]	234	B35R	6/27	9/44
150	MO 9322	TSM B9A	5278	Brush [189]	235	B35R	6/27	9/44
151	MO 9323	TSM B9A	5279	Brush [190]	233	B35R	6/27	7/40
152	MO 9324	TSM B9A	5280	Brush [191]	236	B35R	6/27	9/44
153	MO 9325	TSM B9A	5281	Brush [192]	227	B35R	6/27	9/44
154	MO 9326	TSM B9A	5282	Brush [193]	228	B35R	6/27	7/40
155	MO 9327	TSM B9A	5283	Brush [194]	231	B35R	6/27	7/40
156	MO 9328	TSM B9A	5284	Brush [195]	226	B35R	6/27	9/44
157	MO 9329	TSM B9A	5285	Brush [196]	229	B35R	6/27	7/40

Notes:
> The order of the Brush body numbers is uncertain.

> MO 9312-9315 (140-143): Had London Lorries 'QP' (Quadruple Purpose) 'all-weather' bodies with a full length folding canvas hood (the windows wound down and pillars folded down into the waist rail). They were charabanc replacements.

MO 9316 (144): Was licensed to Marlow & District Motor Services Ltd 4 4/32 to 5/33.
MO 9317-9318 (145-146): Fitted with roof ventilators and curtains when new for the Reading-London express service; reseated to B32R 1931.
MO 9319-9326 (147-154): Reseated to B32R 1931.
MO 9327 (155): Was licensed to Marlow & District Motor Services Ltd 5 4/32 to 5/33.

Disposals – complete vehicles (unless otherwise indicated):
MO 9312 (140): Chassis to Southdown Motor Services Ltd, Brighton (ES) 494 4/32; chassis shortened and fitted with a 1930 Park Royal C22R all-weather body from Dennis DB 2212 (Southdown 387) 6/32; reseated C20R 7/32; H Gilbert {Gilbert's Coaches}, Tunbridge Wells (KT) 3/36; last licensed 12/49.
MO 9313 (141): Chassis to Southdown Motor Services Ltd, Brighton (ES) 490 4/32; chassis shortened and fitted with a 1930 Park Royal C22R all-weather body from Dennis HC 5385 (Southdown 380) 6/32; SA Plumridge, Lowfield Heath (SR) 3/38; reseated C20R 6/38; BS Williams, Emsworth (HA) 7/50; withdrawn 9/51.
MO 9314 (142): Chassis to Southdown Motor Services Ltd, Brighton (ES) 491 4/32; chassis shortened and fitted with a 1930 Park Royal C26R all-weather body from Dennis HC 2349 (Southdown 373) 6/32; SW Bridge, Thundersley (EX) 1/36; Ardley Bros Ltd, London N17 (LN) 3/37; Stanway Coaches (Southend) Ltd {Royal Red}, Southend-on-Sea (EX) by 3/38 (as C26D); last licensed 3/38.
MO 9315 (143): Chassis to Southdown Motor Services Ltd, Brighton (ES) 495 4/32; chassis shortened and fitted with a 1930 Park Royal C22R all-weather body from Dennis DB 2210 (Southdown 386) 6/32; reseated to C20R 7/32; H Gilbert {Gilbert's Coaches}, Tunbridge Wells (KT) 3/37; withdrawn 12/49; W Jarvis (dealer?), Moulton at an unknown date.
MO 9316 (144): Showman, Middlesex as a living van 1/46; Mrs E Cohen, Bristol 3/48; last licensed 6/48.
MO 9317 (145): War Department (GOV) 7/40; used in Europe post-war transporting concentration camp survivors to hospitals; ultimately burnt as a health precaution.
MO 9318 (146): Unidentified operator / dealer 6/37; unidentified operator, Shropshire 2/42; D Ross {Rosaire's Circus} (showman), Twyford 4/45; last licensed 9/45; H Goodey (dealer), Twyford c1945 and scrapped 1957.
MO 9319 (147): War Department (GOV) 7/40; offered back to Thames Valley for re-purchase 7/42, but not taken up; unidentified operator, London 4/43; scrapped 4/54.
MO 9320 (148): War Department (GOV) 7/40; used in Europe post-war transporting concentration camp survivors to hospitals; ultimately burnt as a health precaution.
MO 9321 (149): S Hibbard, Tilehurst 12/45.
MO 9322 (150): S Pharo {showman}, Blackwater 1/46; ML Pharo (showman), Woking at an unknown date; last licensed 9/47; noted Farnborough 9/54.
MO 9323 (151): War Department (GOV) 7/40; used in Europe post-war transporting concentration camp survivors to hospitals; ultimately burnt as a health precaution.
MO 9324 (152): D Smith, Alton as a static caravan / store shed 2/46; preservation group, Hindhead c1971; M Plunkett, London for preservation 1972 restored back to 1930s condition; moved to Ashurst c1977; kept at Amberley Chalk Pits Museum by 9/85; Southdown Omnibus Trust for preservation c9/98; Thames Valley & Great Western Omnibus Trust for preservation c6/15 (still kept at Amberley).
MO 9325 (153): Showman, Buckinghamshire 1/46; showman (Yeates?), Middlesex 5/46; S Yeates (showman), Hayes End at an unknown date; last licensed 9/47.
MO 9326 (154): War Department (GOV) 7/40; used in Europe post-war transporting concentration camp survivors to hospitals; ultimately burnt as a health precaution.
MO 9327 (155): War Department (GOV) 7/40.
MO 9328 (156): Unidentified operator / dealer 1/46.
MO 9329 (157): War Department (GOV) 7/40; used in Europe post-war transporting concentration camp survivors to hospitals; ultimately burnt as a health precaution.

Vehicle on hire:

An unidentified Leyland TD1 double-deck was on demonstration during 12/27.

1928

New Vehicles:

159	RX 1394	TSM B9A		5375	Brush [198]	C28F	5/28	9/44
160	RX 1395	TSM B9A		5376	Brush [199]	C28F	5/28	9/44
161	RX 1396	TSM B9A		5377	Brush [200]	B35R	5/28	7/40
158	RX 1397	TSM B9A		5374	Brush [197]	B35R	5/28	7/40

162	RX 1398	TSM B9B	5335	London Lorries [201]	C30F	5/28	4/32
163	RX 1399	TSM B9B	5333	London Lorries [202]	C30F	5/28	4/32
164	RX 1753	Leyland TD1	70126	Leyland [203]	L24/24RO	5/28	9/49
165	RX 1754	Leyland TD1	70127	Leyland [204]	L24/24RO	5/28	10/49
166	RX 1755	Leyland TD1	70128	Leyland [205]	L24/24RO	5/28	10/49
167	RX 1756	Leyland TD1	70129	Leyland [206]	L24/24RO	5/28	9/49
168	RX 1757	Leyland TD1	70130	Leyland [207]	L24/24RO	6/28	5/49
169	RX 1758	Leyland TD1	70131	Leyland [208]	L24/24RO	6/28	9/49
170	RX 1759	Leyland TD1	70132	Leyland [209]	L24/24RO	6/28	11/49
171	RX 1760	Leyland TD1	70133	Leyland [210]	L24/24RO	6/28	7/50
172	RX 1761	Leyland TD1	70134	Leyland [211]	L24/24RO	7/28	11/49
173	RX 1762	Leyland TD1	70135	Short [212]	L24/24RO	7/28	9/49
174	RX 1763	Leyland TD1	70194	Short [213]	L24/24RO	7/28	9/49
175	RX 1764	Leyland TD1	70195	Short [214]	L24/24RO	7/28	10/49

Notes:

RX 1394 (159): Fitted with curtains when new for the Reading-London express service; reseated C30F 2/32; used as a temporary enquiry office at Reading over the winter of 1942/3.

RX 1395 (160): Fitted with curtains when new for the Reading-London express service; reseated C30F 2/32;

RX 1396 (161): Reseated B32R (probably in) 1930.

RX 1397 (158): Reseated B32R (probably in) 1930.

RX 1398-1399 (162-163): Were all-weather coaches.

RX 1754 (165): Fitted with a starter motor and converted for producer gas operation (equipment on a trailer) late 1943; reverted to petrol 10/44; body refurbished by TW Cawood & Son, Doncaster 3-7/48.

RX 1755 (166): Fitted with a starter motor and converted for producer gas operation (equipment on a trailer) late 1943; reverted to petrol 10/44; body refurbished by Thames Valley 7-11/47.

RX 1756 (167): Fitted with a starter motor and converted for producer gas operation (equipment on a trailer) late 1943; reverted to petrol 11/44.

RX 1757 (168): Fitted with a starter motor and converted for producer gas operation (equipment on a trailer) 4/43; reverted to petrol 10/44.

RX 1758 (169): Fitted with a starter motor and converted for producer gas operation (equipment on a trailer) 7/43; reverted to petrol 2/44; body refurbished by Thames Valley 7/49.

RX 1759 (170): Fitted with a starter motor and converted for producer gas operation (equipment on a trailer) 10/42; reverted to petrol 10/44; body refurbished by Thames Valley 7/47-2/48.

RX 1760 (171): Body refurbished and rebuilt by Thames Valley to L27/24R (to the same profile as ECW rebuilds) 12/44-7/45; hired to Westcliff-on-Sea Motor Services Ltd, Westcliff-on-Sea (EX) 9/49 to 2/50; it retained its petrol engine.

RX 1761 (172): Fitted with a starter motor and converted for producer gas operation (equipment on a trailer) 3/43; reverted to petrol 4/44; body refurbished by DR Hawkins, Stoke Row 11/47-5/48.

RX 1762 (173): Fitted with a starter motor and converted for producer gas operation (equipment on a trailer) 3/43; reverted to petrol 6/44.

RX 1763 (174): Retained its petrol engine (being allocated to Ascot, there may not have been a facility to use producer gas); fitted with a starter motor 6/44.

RX 1764 (175): Fitted with a starter motor and converted for producer gas operation (equipment on a trailer) late 1942; reverted to petrol 10/44.

Disposals – complete vehicles (unless otherwise indicated):

RX 1394 (159): F Ross {Rosaire's Circus} (showman), Twyford 12/45; noted at Billericay 3/47; last licensed 9/49.

RX 1395 (160): F Ross {Rosaire's Circus} (showman), Twyford 12/45; noted at Billericay 3/47; JE Foskett (showman), Ash Vale by 10/47; last licensed 12/47.

RX 1396 (161): War Department (GOV) 7/40; used in Europe post-war transporting concentration camp survivors to hospitals; ultimately burnt as a health precaution.

RX 1397 (158): War Department (GOV) 7/40; Cambridgeshire Agricultural Executive Committee (GOV) 2/42; Ministry of Supply (GOV) at an unknown date; scrapped 2/44.

RX 1398 (162): Chassis to Southdown Motor Services Ltd, Brighton (ES) 492 4/32; chassis shortened and fitted with a 1930 Park Royal C22R all-weather body from Dennis HC 2837 (Southdown 381) 6/32; SA Plumridge, Lowfield Heath (SR) 6/36; last licensed but retained for spares 12/39; Mackenzie (dealer), London W2 6/49.

RX 1399 (163): Chassis to Southdown Motor Services Ltd, Brighton (ES) 493 4/32; chassis shortened and fitted with a 1930 Park Royal C22R all-weather body from Dennis HC 2833 (Southdown 375) 6/32; A Bennett & Sons {Shirley Coaches}, Croydon (SR) 4/36; Bexleyheath Transport Co Ltd, Bexleyheath (KT) 1/39; last licensed 3/47 (as C20R).

RX 1753 (164): Shirley (dealer), Darby Green 10/49; no further operator.

RX 1754 (165): T Stirling (showman), Chesham 10/49; unidentified owner, Ashley Green, Chesham as a caravan 1/55.

RX 1755 (166): Speechley Garages (dealer), Colnbrook 10/49.

RX 1756 (167): Shirley (dealer), Darby Green 10/49; showman, Maidenhead (not licensed) 4/56.

RX 1757 (168): Shirley (dealer), Darby Green 10/49; no further operator.

RX 1758 (169): Converted to a route servicing vehicle (tree lopper) and transferred to the service fleet 9/49 (qv).

RX 1759 (170): AW Traylen (showman), Feltham 11/49; noted Staines (fitted with an AEC radiator and 'United Traction Co' inscription 6/52); noted Marlow 6/59; last licensed as a goods vehicle 9/59.

RX 1760 (171): S Ilott, Heckfield as a caravan 7/50; showman, noted Newhaven 8/56.

RX 1761 (172): AW Traylen (showman), Feltham 11/49; S Jones (showman), Kingston-upon-Thames as a goods vehicle 6/52; last licensed 9/52.

RX 1762-1763 (173-174): Shirley (dealer), Darby Green 10/49; no further operator.

RX 1764 (175): Gavin, Coventry 10/49 (delivered to Airedale, Castleford).

1929

New Vehicles:

176	RX 4338	TSM B10B2	5959	London Lorries [222]		C28D	6/29	4/35
177	RX 4339	TSM B10B2	5960	London Lorries [223]		C28D	6/29	4/35
178	RX 4340	TSM B10B2	5965	London Lorries [224]		C28D	6/29	4/35
179	RX 4341	Leyland TD1	70669	Leyland [225]		L27/24RO	6/29	4/50
180	RX 4342	Leyland TD1	70670	Leyland [226]		L27/24RO	6/29	9/52
181	RX 4343	Leyland TD1	70671	Leyland [227]		L27/24RO	6/29	4/50
182	RX 4344	Leyland TD1	70672	Leyland [228]		L27/24RO	6/29	8/52
183	RX 4345	Leyland TD1	70673	Leyland [229]		L27/24RO	6/29	8/52
184	RX 4346	Leyland TD1	70674	Leyland [230]		L27/24RO	6/29	7/52
185	RX 4347	Leyland TD1	70675	Leyland [231]		L27/24RO	6/29	5/52
186	RX 4348	Leyland TD1	70676	Leyland [232]		L27/24RO	6/29	7/52
187	RX 4349	Leyland TD1	70677	Leyland [233]		L27/24RO	6/29	9/52
188	RX 4350	Leyland TD1	70678	Leyland [234]		L27/24RO	7/29	7/33
189	RX 4351	Leyland TD1	70679	Leyland [235]		L27/24RO	7/29	7/33
190	RX 4352	Leyland TD1	70680	Leyland [236]		L27/24RO	7/29	9/52
191	RX 4353	Leyland TD1	70681	Leyland [237]		L27/24RO	7/29	4/39
199	RX 5561	Leyland TD1	70954	Leyland [238]		L27/24RO	10/29	10/51
200	RX 5562	Leyland TD1	70955	Leyland [239]		L27/24RO	10/29	8/50

Notes:

RX 4338-4340 (176-178): Were fitted with a 'plein azure' sliding roofs from new; were reseated C27D 1930.

RX 4338 (176): Fitted with a heating appliance 3/31.

RX 4339 (177): Fitted with a heating appliance 9/31.

RX 4341 (179): Fitted with a Gardner 5LW diesel engine 2/43; body refurbished and rebuilt by ECW to L27/24R 8-11/44.

RX 4342 (180): Fitted with a Gardner 5LW diesel engine 4/43; body refurbished and rebuilt by ECW to L27/24R 11/44-3/45.

RX 4343 (181): Fitted with an 8-litre Leyland diesel engine 8/33 (this was Thames Valley's first oil engine, fitted initially as a trial); body refurbished and rebuilt by Willowbrook to L27/24R 2-4/44.

RX 4344 (182): Fitted with a Gardner 5LW diesel engine 1/43; body refurbished and rebuilt by ECW to L27/24R 11/44-3/45.

RX 4345 (183): Fitted with a Gardner 5LW diesel engine 2/44; body refurbished and rebuilt by ECW to L27/24R 1-4/45.

RX 4346 (184): Fitted with a Gardner 5LW diesel engine 5/43; body refurbished and rebuilt by Beadle to L27/24R (after it being stolen and damaged) 9-12/44.

RX 4347 (185): Fitted with a Gardner 5LW diesel engine 7/43; body refurbished and rebuilt by ECW to L27/24R 10/44-1/45.

RX 4348-4349 (186-187): Fitted with Gardner 5LW diesel engines 4/43; bodies refurbished and rebuilt by ECW to L27/24R 8-11/44.

RX 4350-4351 (188-189): Following the formation of London Passenger Transport Board on 1 July 1933, these vehicles transferred to that operator with the Windsor to Staines route.

RX 4352 (190): Fitted with a Gardner 5LW diesel engine 2/43; body refurbished and rebuilt by ECW to L27/24R 6-9/44.

RX 4353 (191): Destroyed by fire following an accident at Wycombe Marsh 4/39.

RX 5561 (199): Fitted with a Gardner 5LW diesel engine 3/43; body refurbished and rebuilt by Beadle to L27/24R 6-9/44; overturned at Witheridge Hill, near Nettlebed 11/47 and further rebuilt by DR Hawkins, Stoke Row 11/47-c4/48.

RX 5562 (200): Fitted with a Gardner 5LW diesel engine 2/38; body refurbished and rebuilt by Beadle to L27/24R c3-6/44.

Disposals:

RX 4338 (176): FT Brook {White Heather Coaches}, Southsea (HA) 2 5/35; White Heather Transport Ltd, Southsea (HA) 2 12/43; withdrawn 4/45; no further operator.

RX 4339 (177): FT Brook {White Heather Coaches}, Southsea (HA) 5 5/35; withdrawn 6/40; no further operator.

RX 4340 (178): GJ Miller {GH Miller & Son}, Cirencester (GL) 5/35; last licensed 1/43; E Drew, Highworth (WI) 1/48 (as C26-).

RX 4341 (179): Newbury & District Motor Services Ltd 179 4/50 (qv).

RX 4342 (180): C Harries (showman), Hounslow 10/52; noted Reading 4/53 and High Wycombe 8/58; last licensed 9/60.

RX 4343 (181): Newbury & District Motor Services Ltd 181 4/50 (qv).

RX 4344 (182): C Phillips (dealer?), Writtle 8/52; noted in a field near Moreton, Ongar 8/52.

RX 4345 (183): C Phillips (dealer?), Writtle 8/52; noted in a scrapyard, Tooting 2/53.

RX 4346 (184): Dunning, Edgware (status unknown) 7/52; JE James (showman), Chertsey as a living van by 6/56; last licensed 9/57; scrapped 1/58; engine transferred to showman's lorry.

RX 4347 (185): J Remblance (dealer), Hornchurch 6/52; PH Remblance (showman), London E14 at an unknown date; last licensed 9/55.

RX 4348 (186): Dunning, Edgware 7/52; Rush Green Motors (dealer), Rush Green, Hitchin 7/52; JW Hardwick & Sons, West Ewell (not licensed) 7/52; showman, London SE15 by 1957; still in use 1959.

RX 4349 (187): E Tucker {Joyride Coaches}, Taunton (SO) (not licensed) 10/52.

RX 4350 (188): London Passenger Transport Board, London SW1 (LN) TD168 7/33; reseated L27/24RO 12/33; withdrawn 1936; PM Morrell (dealer), Leeds 7/38; R Shufflebotham (showman), Bradford 10/38; moved to Beverley 8/45; WG Watson (showman), Middlesbrough 8/48; moved to Kingston upon Hull 3/49; last licensed 11/53; noted London E8 8/54.

RX 4351 (189): London Passenger Transport Board, London SW1 (LN) TD169 7/33; reseated L27/24RO 12/33; withdrawn 1936; PM Morrell (dealer), Leeds 7/38; RA Jordan Ltd (dealer), Biggleswade 8/38; TS Madeley {Premier Bus Service}, Blaxton (WR) 4/40; withdrawn 5/46; showman (not operated) at an unknown date.

RX 4352 (190): Anderson, Butlins Amusement Park, Clacton-on-Sea (XEX) 10/52; showman (H Cheeseman?), Tooting 3/53; last licensed to H Cheeseman, London SW4 6/57; noted Tottenham 7/62 and London NW3 3/64.

RX 4353 (191): H Goodey (dealer), Twyford for scrap 6/39.

RX 5561 (199): F Cowley (dealer), Salford 10/51; scrapped by V Gregory, Derbyshire 1/52.

RX 5562 (200): AJ Curtis (dealer?), Didcot (minus engine) 9/50 (engine sold separately).

Vehicles acquired from Yorkshire Traction Co Ltd, Barnsley (WR) 5/29:

192	HE 2323	Leyland Z7	25131	RSJ [215]	B20F	6/25	11/31
193	HE 2325	Leyland Z7	25133	RSJ [216]	B20F	6/25	11/31
194	HE 2326	Leyland Z7	25134	RSJ [217]	B20F	6/25	11/31
195	HE 2327	Leyland Z7	25135	RSJ [218]	B20F	6/25	5/31
196	HE 2331	Leyland Z7	25139	RSJ [219]	B20F	6/25	11/31
197	HE 2336	Leyland Z7	25144	RSJ [220]	B20F	7/25	11/31
198	HE 2339	Leyland Z7	25147	RSJ [221]	B20F	7/25	5/31

Previous histories:

HE 2323 (192): New to Barnsley & District Traction Co Ltd, Barnsley 112 (WR); Yorkshire Traction Co Ltd, Barnsley (WR) 112 1/29.

HE 2325-2327 (193-195): New to Barnsley & District Traction Co Ltd, Barnsley 114-116 (WR); Yorkshire Traction Co Ltd, Barnsley (WR) 114-116 1/29.

HE 2331 (196): New to Barnsley & District Traction Co Ltd, Barnsley 120 (WR); Yorkshire Traction Co Ltd, Barnsley (WR) 120 1/29.

HE 2336 (197): New to Barnsley & District Traction Co Ltd, Barnsley 125 (WR); Yorkshire Traction Co Ltd, Barnsley (WR) 125 1/29.

HE 2339 (198): New to Barnsley & District Traction Co Ltd, Barnsley 128 (WR); Yorkshire Traction Co Ltd, Barnsley (WR) 128 1/29.

Notes:

These vehicles were ordered from Leyland as model Z7 (long wheelbase, 13ft 6in); they are recorded incorrectly as Z5 (12ft 6in wheelbase) in some records; they were unofficially referred to by Thames Valley as 'Leyland Pups' and had 4-cylinder engines developed from the Leyland Eight 40hp (half and eight). They had RSJ body numbers from the 421-40 batch; their 'bulkhead' entrance doors into the saloon were removed before entry into service.

Disposal - chassis only:

HE 2323 (192): AE Spears (dealer), London SW19 10/31; Sprakes, London W11 (GLN) at an unknown date.

HE 2325 (193): AE Spears (dealer), London SW19 10/31; Melton, Hillingdon (GMX) at an unknown date; last licensed 3/36.

HE 2326 (194): AE Spears (dealer), London SW19 10/31; Beldham, Edgware (GMX) at an unknown date; last licensed 9/33.

HE 2327 (195): AE Spears (dealer), London SW19 5/31; Allen, Ringwood (GHA) at an unknown date; last licensed 3/34.

HE 2331 (196): AE Spears (dealer), London SW19 10/31; Ward, Nottingham (GNG) at an unknown date; last licensed 12/33.

HE 2336 (197): AE Spears (dealer), London SW19 10/31; HP Rickards, Aylesbury (GBK) at an unknown date.

HE 2339 (198): AE Spears (dealer), London SW19 5/31; Colehall, Bagshot (GSR) at an unknown date; last licensed 7/33.

1930

New Vehicles:

No.	Reg.	Model	Body No.	Body	Type		
201	RX 5563	Leyland TD1	70956	Leyland [240]	L27/24RO	2/30	9/51
202	RX 5564	Leyland TD1	70957	Leyland [241]	L27/24RO	2/30	2/51
203	RX 5565	Leyland TD1	70958	Leyland [242]	L27/24RO	3/30	4/51
204	RX 5566	Leyland TD1	70959	Leyland [243]	L27/24RO	3/30	4/51
205	RX 5567	Leyland TD1	70960	Leyland [244]	L27/24RO	3/30	3/52
206	RX 5568	Leyland TD1	70961	Leyland [245]	L27/24RO	3/30	9/51
207	RX 5569	Leyland TD1	70962	Leyland [246]	L27/24RO	3/30	8/50
208	RX 5570	Leyland TD1	70963	Leyland [247]	L27/24RO	3/30	4/51
209	RX 5571	Leyland LT1	50770	Brush [248]	B32R	2/30	2/50
210	RX 5572	Leyland LT1	50771	Brush [249]	B32R	2/30	2/50
211	RX 5573	Leyland LT1	50772	Brush [250]	B32R	2/30	2/50
212	RX 5574	Leyland LT1	50773	Brush [251]	B32R	2/30	8/50
213	RX 5575	Leyland LT1	50774	Brush [252]	B32R	2/30	2/50
214	RX 5576	Leyland LT1	50775	Brush [253]	B32R	2/30	3/50
215	RX 5577	Leyland LT1	50776	Brush [254]	B32R	2/30	2/50
216	RX 5578	Leyland LT1	50777	Brush [255]	B32R	2/30	3/50
217	RX 5579	Leyland LT1	50778	Brush [256]	B32R	2/30	2/50
218	RX 5580	Leyland LT1	50779	Brush [257]	B32R	2/30	2/50
219	RX 6110	Leyland TD1	71323	Leyland [258]	L27/24RO	3/30	4/51
220	RX 6111	Leyland TD1	71324	Leyland [259]	L27/24RO	3/30	12/49
221	RX 6112	Leyland TD1	71372	Leyland [260]	L27/24RO	3/30	9/51
222	RX 6242	Leyland TD1	71435	Leyland [261]	L27/24RO	5/30	4/51
223	RX 6243	Leyland TD1	71436	Leyland [262]	L27/24RO	6/30	4/51
224	RX 6244	Leyland TD1	71437	Leyland [263]	L27/24RO	5/30	12/49
225	RX 6245	Leyland LT2	51208	Brush [264]	DP32R	7/30	9/51
226	RX 6246	Leyland LT2	51209	Brush [265]	DP32R	7/30	4/50
227	RX 6247	Leyland LT2	51210	Brush [266]	DP32R	7/30	7/50
228	RX 6248	Leyland LT2	51211	Brush [267]	DP32R	7/30	3/51
229	RX 6249	Leyland LT2	51212	Brush [268]	DP32R	7/30	1/50
230	RX 6250	Leyland TS3	61065	Brush [269]	C28D	8/30	7/40

Notes:

RX 5571-5580 (209-218): Reseated to DP29R with luxury seats; fitted with entrance doors by 12/30.

RX 6245-6249 (225-229): Reseated to DP29R with luxury seats and curtains; fitted with entrance doors by 12/30.

RX 5563 (201): Fitted with a Leyland diesel engine 9/37; body refurbished and rebuilt by Willowbrook to L27/24R 4-10/44.

RX 5564 (202): Fitted with a Leyland diesel engine 9/37; body refurbished and rebuilt by Willowbrook to L27/24R 7-12/43.

RX 5565 (203): Fitted with a Leyland diesel engine 9/37; body refurbished and rebuilt by Willowbrook to L27/24R 12/43-2/44.

RX 5566 (204): Fitted with a Leyland diesel engine 9/37; body refurbished and rebuilt by Willowbrook to L27/24R 2-4/44.

RX 5567 (205): Fitted with a Leyland diesel engine 8/37; body refurbished and rebuilt by ECW to L27/24R 4-6/44.

RX 5568 (206): Fitted with a Leyland diesel engine 11/37; body refurbished and rebuilt by Willowbrook to L27/24R 4-12/44.

RX 5569 (207): Fitted with a Leyland diesel engine 10/37; body refurbished and rebuilt by ECW to L27/24R 5-c10/44.

RX 5570 (208): Fitted with a Leyland diesel engine 8/37; body refurbished and rebuilt by Willowbrook to L27/24R 4-7/43.

RX 5571 (209): Licensed by Ledbury Transport Co Ltd 2 4/40 to 2/50; body refurbished by Beadle 10/44-2/45.

RX 5572 (210): Licensed by Ledbury Transport Co Ltd 4 4/40 to 2/50; body refurbished by Santus 11/44-3/45.

RX 5573 (211): Licensed by Ledbury Transport Co Ltd 6 4/40 to 2/50; body refurbished by Santus 5-8/45.

RX 5574 (212): Licensed by Ledbury Transport Co Ltd 8 4/40 to 2/50; body refurbished by Santus 3-6/45.

RX 5575 (213): Licensed by Ledbury Transport Co Ltd 10 4/40 to 7/50; body sent to Beadle for refurbishment 2-4/45, but the work was not proceeded with; body refurbished by Santus 12/45.

RX 5576 (214): Licensed by Ledbury Transport Co Ltd 12 4/40 to 2/50; body refurbished by Santus 11/44-5/45.

RX 5577 (215): Licensed by Ledbury Transport Co Ltd 20 11/38 to 2/50; reseated to B26F (perimeter) seats during World War 2; body refurbished by Beadle 3-5/44.

RX 5578 (216): Licensed by Ledbury Transport Co Ltd 22 11/38 to 2/50; reseated to B26F (perimeter) seats during World War 2; body refurbished by Beadle 1-2/44.

RX 5579 (217): Licensed by Ledbury Transport Co Ltd 38 11/38 to 2/50; body refurbished by Beadle 5-7/44.

RX 5580 (218): Licensed by Ledbury Transport Co Ltd 42 11/38 to 2/50; body refurbished by Santus 3-6/45.

RX 6110 (219): Fitted with a Gardner 5LW diesel engine 12/37; body refurbished and rebuilt by Willowbrook to L27/24R 7-11/43.

RX 6111 (220): Fitted with a Gardner 5LW diesel engine 12/37; body refurbished and rebuilt by Beadle to L27/24R 2-4/44.

RX 6112 (221): Fitted with a Leyland diesel engine 8/37; body refurbished and rebuilt by Willowbrook to L27/24R 12/43-2/44.

RX 6242 (222): Fitted with a Gardner 5LW diesel engine 2/38; body refurbished and rebuilt by ECW to L27/24R 2-5/44.

RX 6243 (223): Fitted with a Leyland diesel engine 10/37; body refurbished and rebuilt by ECW to L27/24R 1-4/44.

RX 6244 (224): Fitted with a Gardner 5LW diesel engine 12/37; body refurbished and rebuilt by Vincents to L27/24R 10/43-3/44.

RX 6245 (225): Licensed by Ledbury Transport Co Ltd 46 11/38 to 7/50; body refurbished by Santus 6-9/45; fitted with a Gardner 4LW diesel engine 11/46.

RX 6246 (226): Licensed by Ledbury Transport Co Ltd 50 11/38 to 4/50; body refurbished by Beadle 1-3/44; fitted with a Gardner 4LW diesel engine 10-11/46.

RX 6247 (227): Licensed by Ledbury Transport Co Ltd 52 11/38 to 7/50; body refurbished by Santus 3-7/44; fitted with a Gardner 4LW diesel engine 3/47.

RX 6248 (228): Licensed by Ledbury Transport Co Ltd 54 11/38 to 7/50; body refurbished by Santus c8-11/44; fitted with a Gardner 4LW diesel engine 11/46.

RX 6249 (229): Licensed by Ledbury Transport Co Ltd 14 4/40 to 7/50; body refurbished by Beadle 7-10/44; modified with straight side panels c1948/9.

RX 6250 (230): Fitted with a Leyland LT2 radiator and curtains from new; licensed by Ledbury Transport Co Ltd 62 4/40 to 7/40.

Disposals:

RX 5563 (201): AR Speechley (dealer), Hillingdon Heath (minus engine) 9/51.

RX 5564 (202): FA & RG Spratley {Spratley Bros / Victory Coaches}, Mortimer (BE) 2/51.

RX 5565-5566 (203-204): T Rowlands (dealer?), Reading 4/51.

RX 5567 (205): TJ Richardson & Sons (dealer), Oldbury 3/52.

RX 5568 (206): AR Speechley (dealer), Hillingdon Heath (minus engine) 9/51.

RX 5569 (207): T Rowlands (dealer?), Reading 4/51.

RX 5570 (208): J Smith (showman), Rickmansworth by 6/52; still in use 5/58.

RX 5571 (209): Hanslip (showman), Totton 2/50.

RX 5572 (210): Hanslip (showman), Totton 2/50; unidentified owner, Salisbury as a caravan by 10/51; Sparshatts Ltd (dealer), Southampton 7/52.

RX 5573 (211): Hanslip (showman), Totton 2/50.

RX 5574 (212): Hanslip (showman), Totton 2/50; unidentified owner, Marchwood as a caravan by 10/51,

RX 5575 (213): D Davis (dealer), South Mimms 8/50.

RX 5576 (214): Hanslip (showman), Totton 2/50; showman, Salisbury 3/52.

RX 5577 (215): Curtis, Upton 3/50; caravan, Crookham Common at an unknown date; P Pribik, Wokingham for preservation 9/79; moved to Winnersh by 1/01.

RX 5578 (216): Ingram, Woodcote (status unknown) 2/50.

RX 5579 (217): Fowler, Bracknell 3/50; Rush Green Motors, Stevenage (HT) at an unknown date; derelict by 12/59.

RX 5580 (218): Unidentified dealer 2/50; Sparshatts Ltd (dealer), Southampton 7/52; Rush Green Motors, Stevenage (HT) at an unknown date; derelict by 12/59.

RX 6110 (219): TJ Richardson & Sons (dealer), Oldbury 4/51; showman 6/52; noted Dudley 6/52 and London E10 4/56.

RX 6111 (220): D Davis (dealer), South Mimms 8/50.

RX 6112 (221): AR Speechley (dealer), Hillingdon Heath (minus engine) 9/51.

RX 6242 (222): TJ Richardson & Sons (dealer), Oldbury 4/51; dismantled for spares / scrap by J Charlton, Bolton 10/54.

RX 6243 (223): T Rowlands (dealer?), Reading 4/51; unidentified owner, Tilehurst as a caravan 4/51.

RX 6244 (224): VS Harper, Reading (minus engine) 7/50; later noted as a static caravan; H Goodey (dealer), Twyford 1953 to 1959 at least.

RX 6245 (225): Mrs W Wallis (showman), Hounslow (fitted with a Gardner 4-cylinder diesel engine) 9/51; noted Oxford 9/59 and Reading 7/60.

RX 6246 (226): Newbury & District Bus Services Ltd 50 4/50 (qv).

RX 6247 (227): Unidentified dealer 7/50; noted in a builders yard, Maidenhead 1950.

RX 6248 (228): S Whittle (showman), Blackwater 3/51.

RX 6249 (229): Green, Tilehurst (status unknown) 7/50.

RX 6250 (230): War Department (GOV) 7/40; offered back to Thames Valley 12/42 and re-acquired by them c4/43 (qv).

1931

New Vehicles:

231	RX 8164	Leyland TD1	71938	Leyland [270]	L27/24RO	3/31	3/40
232	RX 8165	Leyland TD1	71939	Leyland [271]	L27/24RO	3/31	10/51
233	RX 8166	Leyland TD1	71940	Leyland [272]	L27/24RO	3/31	12/49
234	RX 8167	Leyland TD1	71941	Leyland [273]	L27/24RO	3/31	9/51
235	RX 8168	Leyland TD1	71942	Leyland [274]	L27/24RO	3/31	10/52
236	RX 8169	Leyland TD1	71943	Leyland [275]	L27/24RO	3/31	8/50
237	RX 8170	Leyland TD1	71944	Leyland [276]	L27/24RO	3/31	4/51
239	RX 9307	Leyland TS4	100	Brush [278]	C28F	12/31	7/40

Notes:

RX 8164 (231): Fitted with a Gardner 5LW diesel engine 2/38; destroyed by an incendiary device at Reading depot on 1/3/40.

RX 8165 (232): Fitted with a Gardner 5LW diesel engine 9/37; body refurbished and rebuilt by Willowbrook to L27/24R 4-7/43.

RX 8166 (233): Fitted with a Gardner 5LW diesel engine 10/37; body refurbished and rebuilt by Willowbrook to L27/24R 2-4/43.

RX 8167 (234): Fitted with a Gardner 5LW diesel engine 3/37; body refurbished and rebuilt by Willowbrook to L27/24R 10/42-2/43; fitted with a petrol engine 1/44; fitted with a Leyland diesel engine 3/45.

RX 8168 (235): Fitted with a Gardner 5LW diesel engine 3/38; body refurbished and rebuilt by Willowbrook to L27/24R 2-4/43.

RX 8169 (236): Fitted with a Gardner 5LW diesel engine 3/38; body refurbished and rebuilt by Beadle to L27/24R 12/43-2/44.

RX 8170 (237): Fitted with a Gardner 5LW diesel engine 2/38; body refurbished and rebuilt by Willowbrook to L27/24R 10/42-2/43.

RX 9307 (239): Was the first Leyland Tiger TS4 and its chassis number was the first in a new series; it was exhibited at the Commercial Motor Show 11/31; internally reconditioned and refurbished by Weymann 5/38; hired to Aldershot & District Traction Co Ltd, Aldershot (HA) 5/39.

Disposals:

RX 8164 (231): Unidentified dealer for scrap 3/40.
RX 8165 (232): F Cowley (dealer), Salford 10/51; Morley Bros (Iron founders) Ltd, Hyde 10/51 and scrapped.
RX 8166 (233): H Remblance (dealer), Feltham 7/50.
RX 8167 (234): AR Speechley (dealer), Hillingdon Heath (minus engine) 9/51.
RX 8168 (235): Anderson, Butlins Amusement Park, Clacton-on-Sea (XEX) 10/52; noted Southend-on-Sea 9/57.
RX 8169 (236): D Davis (dealer), South Mimms 8/50.
RX 8170 (237): TJ Richardson & Sons (dealer), Oldbury 4/51.
RX 9307 (239): War Department (GOV) 7/40; Ministry of Supply (GOV) at an unknown date; offered back to Thames Valley but not taken up c1/43; Stanley Spencer's Tours Ltd, Sale (CH) 2/43; to service 7/43; rebodied Bellhouse Hartwell C33F 10/47; Sunbeam Coaches (Torquay) Ltd, Torquay (DN) 3/49; last licensed 8/55; chassis scrapped 11/57; body fitted to APC 421 (AEC Regal) of LA Arscott, Chagford (DN) 2/56; withdrawn 1960

Vehicles acquired from Great Western Railway Co, London W2 (LN) 1/31:

1238	UC 4865	Maudslay ML3	4242	Buckingham	B32R	3/28	9/31
1664	UU 5011	Morris Z2	1816Z	Buckingham	B14F	6/29	5/31
1655	UV 9121	Guy OND	OND9158	Guy	B18F	8/29	7/31
1657	UV 9413	Guy OND	OND9145	Guy	B18F	9/29	6/31
1659	UV 9414	Guy OND	OND9162	Guy	B18F	10/29	8/31
1285	YF 3921	Guy FBB	FBB22309	Buckingham	C32D	4/27	----
1225	YH 3797	Maudslay ML3A	4101	Buckingham	C32D	6/27	----
1228	YH 3800	Maudslay ML3A	4102	Buckingham	C32D	6/27	----
928	YK 3822	Thornycroft A1	11488	Vickers [281]	B19F	7/25	6/32
1202	YR 1089	Maudslay ML3	3939	Buckingham	B32R	9/26	5/32
1229	YW 1721	Maudslay ML3B	4177	Buckingham	C26D	5/28	3/31
1102	YW 5366	Morris Z2	5622	London Lorries	B12F	6/28	9/31

Previous histories:

These vehicles were all new to Great Western Railway Co, retaining their Great Western fleet numbers as shown above.

Notes:

These vehicles were acquired with the Great Western Railway operations from their bases at Maidenhead, Newbury, Twyford and Windsor. In exchange for the services, GWR took a 35% shareholding in Thames Valley plus £5,000 for the 12 vehicles (the Southern Railway also took a 15% shareholding although no vehicles or services were involved). Services continued largely unchanged until the railway staff could be redeployed elsewhere. The dates that Thames Valley assumed direct control were:

Twyford (Reading service)	31/1/31
Maidenhead (Twyford service)	31/1/31
Windsor	1/6/31
Maidenhead (Jealotts Hill service)	1/9/31
Newbury	16/9/31

YK 3822 (928): Renumbered 242 (and body number [281] allotted) 10/31.

Disposals:

UC 4865 (1238): H Lane & Co Ltd (dealer), London SW10 10/31; JB Perry, Rattlesden (EK) c10/31; last licensed 9/34.
UU 5011 (1664): H Lane & Co Ltd (dealer), London SW10 9/31; South Milton Garage, South Milton (DN) 1935; unidentified owner (G??) 1938.
UV 9121 (1655): H Lane & Co Ltd (dealer), London SW10 9/31; RG Martin & FM King {Nippy Bus Service}, Windsor (BE) 9/32; London Passenger Transport Board, London SW1 (LN) 2/34; AJ Maffey (dealer), Woodford 10/34; CAG Coffin {Pioneer / Ryde & District Motor Services}, Ryde (IW) (not operated) 4/35; Southern Vectis Omnibus Co Ltd, Newport (IW) (not operated) 3/37; scrapped 6/38.
UV 9413 (1657): Waterloo Motor Co (dealer), London SE1 9/31; CW Hutfield, Gosport (HA) 11/31; scrapped 5/35.
UV 9414 (1659): H Lane & Co Ltd (dealer), London SW10 9/31; EE Clarke, Swindon (WI) 4/32; EI Peake, Pontnewynydd (MH) 7/38; scrapped 1/39.

YF 3921 (1285): Waterloo Motor Co (dealer), London SE1 8/31; Burnell's Motors Ltd {Lorna Doone Coaches}, Weston-super-Mare (SO) 29 6/32; Bristol Tramways & Carriage Co Ltd, Bristol (GL) X164 7/33; dismantled for spares / scrap by Bristol Tramways 11/33.

YH 3797 (1225): Waterloo Motor Co (dealer), London SE1 8/31; P Owen & Sons Ltd, Abberley (WO) 13 12/31; withdrawn 12/36.

YH 3800 (1228): Waterloo Motor Co (dealer), London SE1 8/31; P Owen & Sons Ltd, Abberley (WO) 14 2/32; withdrawn 1/38; HF Taylor {Acton Beauchamp Transport}, Lower Tundridge (WO) at an unknown date.

YK 3822 (242): Body to an unidentified owner / dealer 2/33; chassis to Southern Railway, London SE1 8/33; converted to lorry 867M 11/33; scrapped 7/39.

YR 1089 (1202): GB Chapman, location unknown 5/32; showman 7/32.

YW 1721 (1229): Marlow & District Motor Services Ltd 3 3/31 (qv).

YW 5366 (1102): AJ Brown, Nettlebed (OX) 10/31.

Vehicle acquired from E & S Keep {Rambler Coaches}, Burghfield Common (BE) 3/31:

| 238 | RX 188 | Thornycroft A2 Long | 14060A | Challands Ross [277] | B20F | 5/27 | 1/38 |

Previous history:
RX 188 (238): New to E & S Keep {Rambler Coaches}.

Notes:
Thames Valley purchased the Reading to Mortimer service (together with one vehicle) on 21 March 1931 for £1,200 from E & S Keep who retained the coaching side of their business.

RX 188 (238): Licensed by Ledbury Transport Co Ltd 18 12/37 to 1/38.

Disposal:
RX 188 (18): H Goodey (dealer), Twyford for scrap c1/38 to the 1950s at least.

Vehicle acquired from RJ Robson {Premier Motor Omnibus Co}, Cookham Green (BE) 6/31:

| 239 | GU 7544 | Dennis 1½ ton | 54233 | ? | B14F | 4/29 | 10/31 |

Previous history:
This vehicle was acquired with the Robson business; its previous history is detailed in the Vehicles of Acquired Operators section.

Disposal:
GU 7544 (239): H Lane & Co Ltd (dealer), London SW10 10/31; A Howes {Howes' Brown Bus}, Englefield Green (SR) 10/31; London Passenger Transport Board, London SW1 (LN) 3/34; withdrawn 10/35; C & P Sales (dealer), London SW9 11/35; scrapped 11/37.

Vehicle acquired from AE Cowley {Lower Road Bus Service}, Cookham Rise (BE) 10/31:

| 243 | RX 3131 | Dennis 1½ ton | 53685 | Willmott [282] | B14F | 10/28 | 5/34 |

Previous history:
This vehicle was acquired with the Cowley business; its previous history is detailed in the Vehicles of Acquired Operators section.

Disposal:
RX 3131 (243): Unidentified operator / dealer 6/34; Hallamshire Coal Supplies Ltd, Sheffield (GWR) at an unknown date; last licensed 3/43.

1932

New Vehicles:

240	RX 9308	Leyland TS4	185	Brush [279]	C28F	1/32	7/40
241	RX 9309	Leyland TS4	186	Brush [280]	C28F	1/32	7/40
244	RX 9541	Leyland TS4	383	Brush [283]	C28F	3/32	7/40
245	RX 9699	Leyland TS4	585	Brush [284]	B32R	3/32	3/51
246	RX 9700	Leyland TS4	586	Brush [285]	B32R	3/32	4/50
247	RX 9701	Leyland TS4	587	Brush [286]	B32R	3/32	11/51
248	RX 9702	Leyland TS4	588	Brush [287]	B32R	3/32	8/52
249	RX 9703	Leyland TS4	589	Brush [288]	B32R	3/32	c5/53
250	RX 9704	Leyland TS4	590	Brush [289]	C28F	5/32	10/51

251	RX 9705	Leyland TS4	591	Brush [290]	C28F	5/32	7/40
252	RX 9706	Leyland TS4	592	Brush [291]	C28F	5/32	7/40
253	RX 9707	Leyland TS4	593	Brush [292]	C28F	5/32	7/40
254	RX 9708	Leyland TS4	594	Brush [293]	C28F	5/32	7/40
255	RX 9709	Leyland TS4	595	Brush [294]	C28F	5/32	7/40
256	RX 9710	Leyland TS4	596	Brush [295]	C28F	5/32	7/40

Notes:

RX 9704-9710 (250-256): Were fitted with sliding roofs from new.

RX 9308-9309 (240-241): Delivered 12/31, but were not licensed until 1/32; internally reconditioned and refurbished by Weymann 5/38; hired to Aldershot & District Traction Co Ltd, Aldershot (HA) 5/39.

RX 9541 (244): Internally reconditioned and refurbished by Weymann 6/38.

RX 9699 (245): Converted for producer gas operation (equipment on a trailer) late 1942; reverted to petrol 10/44; body refurbished by Santus 9-11/45; fitted with a Leyland 8.6 litre diesel engine 12/45; rebuilt by Thames Valley 1947.

RX 9700 (246): Converted for producer gas operation (equipment on a trailer) late 1942; reverted to petrol 12/44; body refurbished by Santus 9-10/45; fitted with a Leyland 8.6 litre diesel engine 12/45; rebuilt by Thames Valley 1947.

RX 9701 (247): Converted for producer gas operation (equipment on a trailer) late 1942; reverted to petrol 11/44; fitted with a Leyland 8.6 litre diesel engine 10/45; body refurbished by Santus 11/45-c1/46; rebuilt by Thames Valley 1947; used as a temporary waiting room at Maidenhead after withdrawal

RX 9702 (248): Converted for producer gas operation (equipment on a trailer) late 1942; reverted to petrol 11/44; fitted with a Leyland 8.6 litre diesel engine 10/45; body refurbished by Santus 10-12/45; rebuilt by Thames Valley 1947.

RX 9703 (249): Converted for producer gas operation (equipment on a trailer) late 1942; reverted to petrol 11/44; body refurbished by Santus 10-11/45; fitted with a Leyland 8.6 litre diesel engine 12/45; rebuilt by Thames Valley 1947; used as a temporary inspector's office at Maidenhead coach station c8/53.

RX 9704 (250): Internally reconditioned and refurbished by Weymann 6/38; converted for producer gas operation (equipment on a trailer) 9/42; reverted to petrol 10/44; body rebuilt and refurbished as a service bus (as B32R) by TW Cawood & Son, Doncaster 6-9/45; fitted with a Leyland 8.6 litre diesel engine 10/45; rebuilt and reseated to B28R by Thames Valley 1947.

RX 9705 (251): Internally reconditioned and refurbished by Weymann 6/38.

RX 9706 (252): Internally reconditioned and refurbished by Weymann 6/38; fitted with a larger front destination box post-War.

RX 9707 (253): Internally reconditioned and refurbished by Weymann 5/38; fitted with a larger front destination box post-War.

RX 9708 (254): Internally reconditioned and refurbished by Weymann 7/38.

RX 9709-9710 (255-256): Internally reconditioned and refurbished by Weymann 7/38; fitted with a larger front destination boxes post-War.

Disposals:

RX 9308 (240): War Department (GOV) 7/40; Ministry of Supply (GOV) for disposal at an unknown date; offered back to Thames Valley but not taken up 1/43; Tom Jackson (Chorley) Ltd, Chorley (LA) by 4/47 (probably 1/43); fitted with a Burlingham (2847) C32F body 4/47; Rossendale Division Carriage Co Ltd, Bacup (LA) 2/48; T Cunliffe, Heywood (LA) 2/48; withdrawn 6/50; AT Evans, Manchester (LA) (not licensed) at an unknown date; W Roan (dealer), Bury for scrap 12/53.

RX 9309 (241): War Department (GOV) 7/40; Ministry of Supply (GOV) for disposal at an unknown date; offered back to Thames Valley but not taken up c1/43; unidentified operator / dealer 2/43.

RX 9541 (244): War Department (GOV) 7/40; Ministry of Works and Buildings, London SE1 (GOV) 9/41; Ministry of Supply (GOV) for disposal 1946; returned to Thames Valley Traction Co Ltd c10/46 (qv).

RX 9699 (245): E Tucker {Joyride Coaches}, Taunton (SO) 3/51.

RX 9700 (246): Newbury & District Motor Services Ltd 246 4/50 (qv).

RX 9701 (247): R Springfield, Taplow 11/51.

RX 9702 (248): Unidentified operator / dealer 8/52; EJ Shaw (showman), Addlestone at an unknown date; noted Ripley 10/55 and Hawkhurst 9/57.

RX 9703 (249): WA Rendell, Bradfield (minus engine) 8/53.

RX 9704 (250): R Springfield, Taplow 11/51; unidentified owner (G??) at an unknown date.

RX 9705 (251): War Department (GOV) 7/40; Ministry of Supply (GOV) for disposal at an unknown date; noted at Royal Ordnance Corps vehicle park, Ash Vale 3/43, but not traced further.

RX 9706 (252): War Department (GOV) 7/40; Ministry of Supply (GOV) for disposal 11/42; offered back to Thames Valley 12/42; noted at Royal Ordnance Corps vehicle park, Ash Vale 2/43; returned to Thames Valley Traction Co Ltd c4/43 (qv).

RX 9707 (253): War Department (GOV) 7/40; later to Central Ordnance Depot, Chilwell; Ministry of Supply (GOV) for disposal and offered back to Thames Valley 12/42; at Royal Army Ordnance Corps Disposal Park, Leicester 2/43; returned to Thames Valley Traction Co Ltd c4/43 (qv).

RX 9708 (254): War Department (GOV) 7/40; re-registered GLU 645; Ministry of Supply (GOV) for disposal 9/42; unidentified operator at an unknown date; last licensed 6/64.

RX 9709 (255): War Department (GOV) 7/40; later to Central Ordnance Depot, Chilwell; Ministry of Supply (GOV) for disposal and offered back to Thames Valley 12/42; at Royal Army Ordnance Corps Disposal Park, Leicester 2/43; returned to Thames Valley Traction Co Ltd c4/43 (qv).

RX 9710 (256): War Department (GOV) 7/40; later to Central Ordnance Depot, Chilwell; Ministry of Supply (GOV) for disposal 10/42; at Command Vehicle Park, Castle Bromwich and offered back to Thames Valley 5/43; returned to Thames Valley Traction Co Ltd 6/43 (qv).

Vehicles acquired from Great Western Railway Co, London W2 (LN) 4/32:

1606	UV 4080	Thornycroft BC	18816	Vickers [296]	B26R	7/29	10/38
1269	YF 6815	Guy FBB	FBB22303	Vickers	B32R	4/27	----
1468	YX 5680	Thornycroft A1	15764	?	B18F	9/28	----

Previous histories:

These vehicles were all new to Great Western Railway Co, retaining their Great Western fleet numbers as shown above.

Notes:

These vehicles were acquired with the Great Western Railway operations from their base at Slough, jointly with London General County Services on 11/4/32. Thames Valley acquired the services to Taplow and Slough Trading Estate.

UV 4080 (1606): Renumbered 257 (and body number [296] allotted) 5-6/32; licensed by Ledbury Transport Co Ltd 56 3/38 to 10/38.

YF 6815 (1269): Not operated by Thames Valley.

YX 5680 (1468): Was one of a batch of 20 vehicles which were fitted (from new) with bodies from older vehicles (which were then rebodied as lorries). Bartle, GWR, London Lorries and Vickers bodies were involved but individual details are not known; it was not operated by Thames Valley.

Disposals:

UV 4080 (257): H Lane & Co Ltd (dealer), London SW10 10/38; scrapped 8/40.

YF 6815 (1269): Unidentified operator / dealer 6/34; Smith, Caversham 6/34.

YX 5680 (1468): Body to unidentified dealer 3/33; chassis to Southern Railway, London SE1 8/33 and converted to lorry 866M 11/33.

1933

Vehicle acquired from TE Ashby {Lane End & District Bus Service}, Lane End (BK) 3/33:

	KX 1523	Guy OND	OND8924	?	B20F	12/28	----

Previous history:

This vehicle was acquired with the Ashby business; its previous history is detailed in the Vehicles of Acquired Operators section.

Notes:

KX 1523: Not operated by Thames Valley.

Disposal:

KX 1523: Keeber & Oakley, Wellingborough (NO) 6/33; unidentified operator / dealer as a lorry by 1940.

Vehicles acquired from JH Harris {Pixey Bus}, Fifield (BK) 4/33:

	EF 3469	Chevrolet LM	16050	Strachan & Brown	B14-	4/27	----
	RM 3889	Chevrolet	15372	?	B14-	5/27	----
	RT 4952	Chevrolet LP	46367	?	B14F	10/28	----

RX 1162		Chevrolet LM	17081	?			B14F	11/27	4/33
TM 1258		Chevrolet	?	?			B14F	7/27	----
TW 8979		Chevrolet LM	15202	?			B14-	5/27	----
VF 3004		Chevrolet LO	40895	(chassis only)				3/28	----

Previous histories:
>These vehicles were acquired with the JH Harris business; their previous histories are detailed in the Vehicles of Acquired Operators section.

Notes:
>Apart from RX 1162 which was used in service for a few days only, none of these vehicles were used by Thames Valley Traction Co Ltd.

Disposals:
>EF 3469: Unidentified operator / dealer 9/33; W Hamblen, Marlborough (WI) at an unknown date; last licensed 3/36.
>RM 3889: Unidentified operator / dealer 9/33; Clark's Garage (dealer?), London SE1 at an unknown date; last licensed 6/34.
>RT 4952: RJ Smart {Ferring Omnibus Service}, Ferring (WS) 6/33.
>RX 1162: Last licensed 4/33; unidentified operator / dealer 9/33; scrapped by 5/34.
>TM 1258: Unidentified operator, East Sussex 9/33.
>TW 8979: Unidentified operator / dealer 9/33; unidentified operator, London 5/34; unidentified operator / dealer by 7/37.
>VF 3004: Unidentified operator / dealer 9/33 (chassis only); unidentified owner, Berkhamstead (presumably rebodied as a bus or a goods vehicle) at an unknown date; last licensed 10/35.

Vehicles acquired from Marlow & District Motor Services Ltd, Marlow (BK) 5/33:

9	KX 3638	Karrier CL4	35073	Ramsden			B24F	10/29	9/35
7	KX 3869	Karrier CL4	35072	Ramsden			B24F	12/29	9/35
8	KX 3870	Karrier CL4	35070	Ramsden			B24F	12/29	9/35
11	KX 3898	Karrier CL4	35076	Ramsden			B24F	12/29	9/35
12	KX 3899	Karrier CL4	35075	Ramsden			B24F	12/29	9/35
6	KX 3900	Karrier CL4	35069	Ramsden			B24F	12/29	9/35
10	KX 3901	Karrier CL4	35077	Ramsden			B24F	12/29	9/35
15	KX 8481	Karrier Coaster	35189	Weymann	W905	B24F	4/32	12/37
14	KX 8482	Karrier Coaster	35190	Weymann	W904	B24F	4/32	11/38
	PP 4107	Karrier CY	20847	?			B20F	5/25	----
1	PP 4388	Karrier WJ	?	?			Ch18	6/25	6/34
2	PP 5930	Morris T	9258T	Morris			B14F	4/26	6/34
	PP 6302	Karrier CL4	?	?			B26F	5/26	----
	PP 8371	Karrier CL4	35011	?			B20F	5/27	----
	RF 1625	Karrier CL4	?	(chassis only)				3/26	----
	RF 1708	Karrier CL4	?	Lawton			B28F	3/26	----
3	YW 1721	Maudslay ML3B	4177	Buckingham			C26D	5/28	6/34

Previous histories:
>These vehicles were acquired with the Marlow & District business; their previous histories are detailed in the Vehicles of Acquired Operators section.

Notes:
>KX 8481 (15): Licensed to Ledbury Transport Co Ltd 16 12/37 to 11/45 but remained in store throughout in a non-operational condition following a gearbox failure.
>PP 4107: Acquired as a withdrawn vehicle and not operated by Thames Valley.
>PP 6302: Acquired as a withdrawn vehicle and not operated by Thames Valley.
>PP 8371: Acquired as a withdrawn vehicle and not operated by Thames Valley.
>RF 1625: Acquired as a withdrawn chassis only and not operated by Thames Valley.
>RF 1708: Acquired as a withdrawn vehicle and not operated by Thames Valley.

Disposals:
>KX 3638 (9): Unidentified operator / dealer 9/35.
>KX 3869 (7): Unidentified operator / dealer 9/35; showman, Epsom noted 6/38 and 6/46.
>KX 3870 (8): Unidentified operator / dealer 9/35.
>KX 3898 (11): Unidentified operator / dealer 9/35.
>KX 3899 (12): Unidentified operator / dealer 9/35; H Davis, Neath (GG) at an unknown date.

KX 3900 (6): Unidentified operator / dealer 9/35.
KX 3901 (10): Unidentified operator / dealer 9/35.
KX 8481 (15): Unidentified owner, Tilehurst 11/45; converted to a caravan by 1949.
KX 8482 (14): Converted to a lorry 11-12/38 and transferred to the service fleet (qv).
PP 4107: Goldberg (dealer), London SW6 2/34.
PP 4388 (1): Unidentified operator / dealer 6/34.
PP 5930 (2): Body to an unidentified owner / dealer 6/34, chassis converted to a lorry and transferred to the service fleet 7/34 (qv).
PP 6302: Goldberg (dealer), London SW6 2/34.
PP 8371: Goldberg (dealer), London SW6 2/34.
RF 1625: Chassis to an unidentified operator / dealer, London 9/33; showman, Croydon 8/34.
RF 1708: Goldberg (dealer), London SW6 2/34; AJ Deeley, Maidenhead (GBE) 4/34; last licensed 10/38.
YW 1721 (3): Unidentified owner (G??) 6/34.

Vehicles acquired from CA Ranger & AW Simmonds {Reliance Motor Services}, Maidenhead (BK) 5/33:

GW 540	Dennis 1½ ton	55654	Willmott [300]	B14F	12/31	7/36
RX 8373	Dodge	8341677	Willmott	B14F	4/31	----
RX 8374	Dodge	8341607	Willmott	B14F	4/31	----
RX 8375	Dodge	8341784	Willmott	B14F	4/31	----

Previous histories:
These vehicles were acquired with the Ranger & Simmonds business; their previous histories are detailed in the Vehicles of Acquired Operators section.

Notes:
GW 540: Initially placed in store; numbered 261, body number [300] allotted and entered service 5/34.
RX 8373-8375: Not operated by Thames Valley.

Disposals:
GW 540 (261): RH Randall, New Forest Clinic, Windsor Forest (XBE) licensed as a private hospital bus 7/36; E Hyner & Co Ltd, Dersingham (NK) 1/43; withdrawn 12/44; last licensed 2/45.
RX 8373: Unidentified operator / dealer 6/34; EG Beech {Beech's Garage}, Liskeard (CO) by 1939; CA Gayton {Gayton's Coaches}, Ashburton (DN) at an unknown date; last licensed 12/42 and scrapped.
RX 8374: Unidentified operator / dealer 2/34; A Austin, Cold Ash (BE) by 1939; A Austin, Cold Ash (GBE) 3/40; last licensed 12/41.
RX 8375: WW & W Bulman {W Bulman & Sons}, Hook Heath (SR) 6/34; last licensed 5/39.

Vehicle acquired from Eastern National Omnibus Co Ltd, Chelmsford (EX) 9/33:

258	GN 5145	Leyland TS3	61810	Leyland [297]	C26R	5/31	10/49

Previous history:
GN 5145 (258): New to Premier Line Ltd, London W12 (LN); hired to Aylesbury Omnibus Co Ltd, Aylesbury (BK) 8/31 (under control of Premier Line Ltd); Eastern National Omnibus Co Ltd 5/33.

Notes:
Part of the operating area of Aylesbury Omnibus Co Ltd fell within Thames Valley territory. Following the acquisition of that operator by Eastern National Omnibus Co Ltd on 12 May 1933, Thames Valley contributed towards the purchase price in exchange for the Aylesbury-Princes Risborough-High Wycombe service together with one vehicle. The transfer took place on 30 September 1933 although the transaction was backdated to 12 May 1933.

GN 5145 (258): Refurbished and reseated to B31R 3/42; converted for producer gas operation (equipment on a trailer) 4/43; reverted to petrol 2/45; used as a static rest room at the Southern Railway yard, Reading 11/48 to 10/49.

Disposal:
GN 5145 (258): Lipinski, Whitchurch Hill (use unknown) 10/49.

1934

Vehicles acquired from London Passenger Transport Board, London SW1 (LN) 5/34:

259	GN 5139	Leyland TS3	61804	Leyland [298]	C26R	5/31	10/49
260	GN 5150	Leyland TS3	61671	Leyland [299]	C26R	7/31	12/40

Previous histories:

GN 5139 (259): New to Premier Line Ltd, London W12 (LN); London Passenger Transport Board 12/33.

GN 5150 (260): New to Premier Line Ltd, London W12 (LN); London Passenger Transport Board 12/33.

Notes:

London Transport had taken over Maidenhead to Slough workings from Premier Line Ltd in 12/33. Negotiations were held with Thames Valley, who took over the route on 26 May 1934 together with two vehicles.

GN 5139 (259): Refurbished and reseated to B31R 8/41; converted for producer gas operation (equipment on a trailer) 4/43; reverted to petrol 2/45.

Disposals:

GN 5139 (259): Duncan, Hurley 10/49.

GN 5150 (260): Crosville Motor Services Ltd, Chester (CH) K117 12/40; converted for producer gas operation 1942-1943; reseated to C30R 1945; fitted with a Leyland 8.6 litre diesel engine, the 1936 ECW (3940) B32F body from TSM VT 2653 (Crosville R35) and renumbered KA168 3/48; withdrawn 1953; J Williams, Liverpool (XLA) 3/53.

Vehicles on hire from Leyland Motors Ltd, Leyland:

TJ 1139	Leyland LT5		2213	Leyland		B35F	4/33	6/34	7/34
TJ 4511	Leyland TD3		3471	Weymann	M22	H24/24F	3/34	3/34	7/34

Notes:

TJ 1139: Fitted with a 4-cylinder diesel engine and was on hire for evaluation.

TJ 4511: Fitted with a diesel engine, painted in full Thames Valley livery and was on hire for evaluation; it was also recorded with 51 seats.

1935

New Vehicles:

262	JB 5841	Leyland TS7	7126	Duple [301]	5015	C32F	4/35	7/40
263	JB 5842	Leyland TS7	7127	Duple [302]	5014	C32F	4/35	7/40
264	JB 5843	Leyland TS7	7128	Duple [303]	5013	C32F	4/35	7/40
265	JB 5844	Leyland TS7	7135	Brush [304]		B32R	6/35	3/51
266	JB 5845	Leyland TS7	7136	Brush [305]		B32R	7/35	8/52
267	JB 5846	Leyland TS7	7137	Brush [306]		B32R	7/35	10/52
268	JB 5847	Leyland TS7	7138	Brush [307]		B32R	6/35	c3/51
269	JB 5848	Leyland TS7	7139	Brush [308]		B32R	7/35	3/51
270	JB 5849	Leyland TS7	7140	Brush [309]		B32R	6/35	c3/51
271	JB 5850	Leyland TS7	7141	Brush [310]		B32R	6/35	6/52
272	JB 5851	Leyland TD4	7129	Brush [311]		L24/24R	9/35	9/50
273	JB 5852	Leyland TD4	7130	Brush [312]		L24/24R	9/35	c8/53
274	JB 5853	Leyland TD4	7131	Brush [313]		L24/24R	9/35	c5/53
275	JB 5854	Leyland TD4	7132	Brush [314]		L24/24R	9/35	3/53
276	JB 5855	Leyland TD4	7133	Brush [315]		L24/24R	9/35	8/52
277	JB 5856	Leyland TD4	7134	Brush [316]		L24/24R	9/35	c5/53
294	JB 7494	Leyland TS7	8543	Brush		B32R	12/35	10/51
295	JB 7495	Leyland TS7	8544	Brush		B32R	12/35	8/52
296	JB 7496	Leyland TS7	8545	Brush		B32R	12/35	3/51
297	JB 7497	Leyland TS7	8546	Brush		B32R	12/35	7/50
298	JB 7498	Leyland TS7	8547	Brush		B32R	12/35	3/51
299	JB 7499	Leyland TS7	8548	Brush		B32R	12/35	2/51

Notes:

JB 5841-5843 (262-264): Had 'camel-back' roofs and petrol engines.

JB 5844-5850 (265-271): Were the first Thames Valley single-deck vehicles fitted with diesel engines from new.

JB 5844 (265): Converted for producer gas operation 6-9/39; its fuel tank was removed and the rear compartment (behind the passenger entrance) was boarded up (with a fire-proof wall) to house a Gohin-Poulenc gas filtration unit; it was reseated to B28R and ran in this form until 6/42 (no other vehicle in the Thames Valley fleet was converted in this way); tests were conducted in 5/42 using gas producer trailers and it is probable that this vehicle was used for that purpose; the built-in gas equipment was removed and the vehicle restored to diesel power

6/42, probably reverting to B32R at this time; reseated with perimeter seating during World War 2; it was reconverted for producer gas operation (equipment on a trailer) 8/44; converted to petrol 2/45; body refurbished by ECW 8-11/45.

JB 5845 (266): Body refurbished by ECW 7-11/45.

JB 5846 (267): Body refurbished by G & R Harding, Cookham 8-9/44; exchanged bodies with Leyland TS8 BBL 561 (375) c7/51, receiving the ECW (5666) B32R body from that vehicle; it was not used thereafter however.

JB 5847 (268): Body refurbished by Crimble, Staines 2-5/45.

JB 5848 (269): Body refurbished by Chamberlain & Sons, Aylesbury 4-8/44.

JB 5849 (270): Body refurbished by G & R Harding, Cookham 1-2/45.

JB 5850 (271): Fitted with a Leyland petrol engine 1/44; reverted to a Leyland diesel engine 3/45; body refurbished by ECW 9-12/45.

JB 5851-5856 (272-277): Were the first Thames Valley double-deck vehicles fitted with diesel engines from new.

JB 5851 (272): Badly damaged in a fire at Reading depot (resulting from an incendiary explosion) on 1/3/40; rebodied ECW (7227) L24/24R (with a plywood roof), returning to service 9/40; fitted with a petrol engine 1/44; overturned at Eversley whilst in service 9/50.

JB 5852 (273): Body refurbished by Santus 11/44-3/45.

JB 5853 (274): Body refurbished and rebuilt by Willowbrook 10/44-2/45.

JB 5854 (275): Body refurbished and rebuilt by Willowbrook 12/44-4/45.

JB 5855 (276): Body refurbished and rebuilt by Beadle 12/44-6/45.

JB 5856 (277): Body refurbished and rebuilt by ECW 1-5/45.

JB 7494 (294): Licensed by Ledbury Transport Co Ltd 18 5/38 to 7/50; was reseated to B29R (with perimeter seating) during World War 2; body refurbished by G & R Harding, Cookham 4-6/45.

JB 7495 (295): Body refurbished by Jones & Sons, Maidenhead 8-11/44.

JB 7496 (296): Body refurbished by Crimble, Staines 5-8/44.

JB 7497 (297): Body refurbished by Land Yachts, Egham 10/44-1/45.

JB 7498 (298): Reseated to B29R (with perimeter seating) during World War 2; body refurbished by G & R Harding, Cookham 2-3/45; body again refurbished by Lambourn Garages, Lambourn 11/47-1/48.

JB 7499 (299): Reseated to B29R (with perimeter seating) during World War 2; body refurbished by ECW 8-11/45.

Disposals:

JB 5841 (262): War Department (GOV) 7/40; Central Ordnance Depot, Chilwell (GOV) at an unknown date; Ministry of Supply (GOV) for disposal at an unknown date; at Royal Army Ordnance Corps Disposal Park, Leicester and offered back to Thames Valley 12/42; returned to Thames Valley Traction Co Ltd 3/43 (qv).

JB 5842 (263): War Department (GOV) 7/40; abandoned in North Africa by Italian forces.

JB 5843 (264): War Department (GOV) 7/40; Ministry of Supply (GOV) 2/43; Ministry of Works (GOV) 8/43; Ministry of Supply (GOV) for disposal 1948; returned to Thames Valley Traction Co Ltd 8/48 (qv).

JB 5844 (265): F Cowley (dealer), Salford 3/51; Tom Jackson (Chorley) Ltd, Chorley (LA) 4/51; rebodied Harrington C33F 4/54; unidentified operator, Leeds (WR) 2/56; J Shaw {G & A Shaw / Shaw's Tours}, Bolton (LA) 4/56; G Shaw, Bolton (LA) 7/60; withdrawn 8/61.

JB 5845 (266): M Cheeseman (showman), Tooting 8/52; noted Blackheath 8/54 and London SW19 9/59.

JB 5846 (267): C Phillips (dealer?), Writtle (minus engine) 10/52.

JB 5847 (268): Unidentified operator / dealer c3/51; EA Thomas {Edward Thomas}, West Ewell (SR) 10/51; showman, noted Preston 7/58.

JB 5848 (269): F Cowley (dealer), Salford 3/51; Tom Jackson (Chorley) Ltd, Chorley (LA) 7/51; rebodied Santus C33F at an unknown date; withdrawn 3/55; Mattinson Bros {Mattinson's Coaches}, Abbeytown (CU) 5/55; withdrawn 6/59.

JB 5849 (270): Connolly (showman), Chertsey c3/51; noted Yeovil 10/58.

JB 5850 (271): A East (showman), Perivale 6/52; noted Caversham 7/58; at Maidenhead (as a showman's winter quarters) 12/60.

JB 5851 (272): Mountain Transport Services Ltd, London SW10 (LN) in an accident damaged condition 9/50; dismantled for spares / scrap by Mountain Transport 1/52.

JB 5852 (273): D Davis (dealer), South Mimms 8/53.

JB 5853 (274): D Davis (dealer), South Mimms 8/53; converted to a pantechnicon by 4/54; WG Summersby, Sutton (GSR) by 3/55; last licensed 6/55; towing wagon, Selby (presumably on trade plates) by 5/56; later noted Hinckley.

JB 5854 (275): JG Sommerville (showman) London E6 3/53; noted Gillingham 7/59.

JB 5855 (276): Ayers (showman), London SW6 8/52; noted Hampstead Heath 4/53 and Hinckley 2/60.

JB 5856 (277): FG Hobbs {Watling Street Motors} (dealer), Redbourn 8/53; AMCC (dealer), London E15 12/53.

JB 7494 (294): W North Ltd (dealer), Leeds 10/51; derelict at North's Stourton premises 4/60.

JB 7495 (295): G Edwards (showman), Forest Gate 8/52.

JB 7496 (296): F Cowley (dealer), Salford 3/51; Tom Jackson (Chorley) Ltd, Chorley (LA) 7/51; rebodied Burlingham C33F 7/51; T Gledhill, Bolton (LA) 10/53; withdrawn 10/54; A Larkin, Farnworth (GLA?) (not operated) 12/55; T Townend (haulier), Farnworth (GLA?) (not operated) 1/56; scrapped by 4/56.

JB 7497 (297): FG Hobbs {Watling Street Motors} (dealer), Borehamwood / St Albans 7/50; Hillside Coaches Ltd, Markyate (HT) 22 3/51; fitted with a B34F body of unknown make; withdrawn 5/58.

JB 7498 (298): Mrs VM Jefford (showman), London E13 as a living van 2/51; moved to Brentwood 5/52; noted Blackheath 4/53.

JB 7499 (299): GE Hedges {Reliance Motor Services}, Brightwalton (BE) 27 2/51; Reliance Motor Services Ltd, Brightwalton (BE) 27 1/55; withdrawn 7/55; scrapped 3/57.

Vehicles acquired from Penn Bus Co Ltd, Tylers Green (BK) 8/35:

281	KX 498	Dennis 2½ ton	45542	Strachan & Brown	B25F	5/28	9/35
282	KX 1312	Dennis 2½ ton	45551	Strachan & Brown	B25F	10/28	9/35
	KX 1541	Dennis E	17614	Strachan	B32R	12/28	----
283	KX 1734	Dennis 2½ ton	45558	Strachan	B26F	1/29	9/35
284	KX 3484	Gilford 166OT	11070	Wycombe	B32F	9/29	9/35
285	KX 5733	Gilford 168OT	11312	Wycombe	B32F	9/30	9/35
286	KX 7382	Gilford 168OT	11967	Wycombe	B32F	7/31	9/35
	KX 7843	Gilford 168OT	12008	Wycombe	C32F	12/31	----
287	KX 8092	Dennis Lancet	170008	Wycombe	B32F	1/32	9/35
288	KX 8744	Dennis Lancet	170116	Dennis	B32R	6/32	9/35
	PP 2245	Dennis 2½ ton	30773	Wycombe	B26F	7/24	----
278	PP 4875	Dennis 2½ ton	31245	Wycombe	B26F	9/25	9/35
279	PP 5166	Dennis 2½ ton	31296	Wycombe	B26F	12/25	9/35
280	PP 9657	Leyland LSC1	46414	Strachan & Brown	B32F	1/28	9/35
	UV 7778	Gilford 166OT	11015	Wycombe	B32F	8/29	----
	ABH 350	Dennis Lancet	170390	Dennis	B32F	5/33	----
289	APP 271	Dennis Lancet	170657	Dennis	C32F	4/34	9/35
290	APP 272	Dennis Lancet	170652	Dennis	B32F	4/34	9/35
291	APP 273	Dennis Ace	200003	Dennis	B20F	4/34	9/35
	BBH 755	Dennis Mace	240028	Dennis	B26C	12/34	----
292	BKX 431	Dennis Lancet	170827	Dennis	C32C	3/35	9/35
	BKX 696	Dennis Lancet	170905	Dennis	C32C	4/35	----
293	BKX 898	Dennis Lancet	170904	Dennis	C32C	6/35	9/35

Previous histories:

These vehicles were acquired with the Penn Bus Co business; their previous histories are detailed in the Vehicles of Acquired Operators section.

Notes:

Seven vehicles were immediately transferred to London Passenger Transport Board, London SW1 (LN) as part of the purchase agreement and were not operated by Thames Valley Traction Co Ltd. These are detailed below.

Disposals:

KX 498 (281): Arlington Motor Co Ltd (dealer), London SW1 9/35; SJ Davies, Cardiff (GGG) 1936.

KX 1312 (282): Arlington Motor Co Ltd (dealer), London SW1 9/35; SJ Davies, Cardiff (GGG) 1936.

KX 1541: London Passenger Transport Board, London SW1 (LN) 8/35; GJ Dawson (Clapham) Ltd (dealer), London SW9 9/36; unidentified owner for conversion to a caravan 1936.

KX 1734 (283): Arlington Motor Co Ltd (dealer), London SW1 9/35; F Chalkley (showman), London NW5 7/36; still owned by a showman 4/45 at least.

KX 3484 (284): Arlington Motor Co Ltd (dealer), London SW1 9/35; Sir Alexander Gibb & Partners (contractor) (X) by 10/41; Ministry of Works & Buildings (GOV) at an unknown date; Ministry of Supply for disposal at an unknown date.

KX 5733 (285): Arlington Motor Co Ltd (dealer), London SW1 9/35; WJ Crisp, Northwold (NK) 12/35; withdrawn 3/39.

KX 7382 (286): Arlington Motor Co Ltd (dealer), London SW1 9/35; H Wright {Fram Coaches}, Addiscombe (SR) 4/36; EA Seager {Enterprise}, Sherborne (DT) 8/40; E Knight (showman), Farnham 5/53.

KX 7843: London Passenger Transport Board, London SW1 (LN) GF191 8/35; reseated to C31F 10/36; GJ Dawson (Clapham) Ltd (dealer), London SW9 12/37; B Ellis {Ideal Safety Coaches}, Barking (EX) 6/38; FG Driver, Barking (EX) 7/38; HC Simmons, Dover (KT) 6/39; AE Nicholls, Clare (WF) 3/43; unidentified operator / dealer 12/44; L Keeble, Bildeston (EK) (not operated) 3/45; WA Heritage {Binley Motor Co}, Coventry (WK) 7/45; EG Palmer {Fordham & District Motor Services}, Fordham (CM) by 11/45; withdrawn 6/50.

KX 8092 (287): Arlington Motor Co Ltd (dealer), London SW1 9/35; AS Varnham, Longfield Hill (KT) 8/36; F Davis {Davis Bros}, London SW18 (LN) 5/37; fitted with a Duple C32- body at an unknown date; WC Jones {Hanworth Acorn Coaches}, Hanworth (MX) 10/37; Acorn Coaches Ltd, Hanworth (MX) 47 10/46; to service 6/47; withdrawn 4/49; Corvedale Motor Co Ltd, Ludlow (SH) 1949; unidentified owner, Ludlow as a static caravan by 3/54.

KX 8744 (288): Arlington Motor Co Ltd (dealer), London SW1 9/35; GJ Dawson (Clapham) Ltd (dealer), London SW9 1/36; James & Mosley {Croft Motor Services}, Croft Spa (NR) 1 12/35 to 10/40 at least; MD Stapleton {Barningham Motor Services}, Newsham (NR) by 2/45 to 10/49 at least.

PP 2245: London Passenger Transport Board, London SW1 (LN) 8/35 (as B24F); GJ Dawson (Clapham) Ltd (dealer), London SW9 8/36; showman by 6/48.

PP 4875 (278): Arlington Motor Co Ltd (dealer), London SW1 9/35; showman by 11/39.

PP 5166 (279): Arlington Motor Co Ltd (dealer), London SW1 9/35; showman, Cambridge 5/36.

PP 9657 (280): Arlington Motor Co Ltd (dealer), London SW1 9/35; DC Lloyd, Neath (GG) at an unknown date.

UV 7778: London Passenger Transport Board, London SW1 (LN) GF192 8/35; GJ Dawson (Clapham) Ltd (dealer), London SW9 12/37; Lancashire Motor Traders (dealer), Salford 3/39.

ABH 350: London Passenger Transport Board, London SW1 (LN) DT8B 8/35; withdrawn 1937; Lancashire Motor Traders (dealer), Salford 5/38; Leighton Coach Co Ltd, Ilford (EX) 9/38; War Department (GOV) 8/40; Ministry of Supply (GOV) for disposal at an unknown date.

APP 271 (289): Arlington Motor Co Ltd (dealer), London SW1 9/35; AR Holder & Sons Ltd, London SE8 (LN) 12/35 (licensed 3/36); HR Grindle, Cinderford (GL) 4/40; possibly to War Department (GOV) 1940; Ministry of Supply (GOV) for disposal at an unknown date.

APP 272 (290): Arlington Motor Co Ltd (dealer), London SW1 9/35; GJ Dawson (Clapham) Ltd (dealer), London SW9 11/35; AW Berry & Son Ltd, Colchester (EX) 11/35; Eastern National Omnibus Co Ltd, Chelmsford (EX) 3695 2/37; last licensed 12/51; Road Haulage Executive (British Road Services), Colchester (for spares?) 4/52.

APP 273 (291): Arlington Motor Co Ltd (dealer), London SW1 11/35; B Emery, Blaenavon (MH) 1/36; South Wales Motor Traders (dealer), Newport 7/39; last licensed 12/39; Lancashire Motor Traders (dealer), Salford 1940; scrapped 6/40; reputedly as an agricultural merchant's showroom by 6/56, but not confirmed.

BBH 755: London Passenger Transport Board, London SW1 (LN) DC3B 8/35; withdrawn 1938; C Jordan (dealer), Biggleswade 9/38; C Wright, Cradley Heath (ST) by 6/42; withdrawn 5/49; A Crewe (showman), Bloxwich by 1/50; unidentified owner, Surrey at an unknown date; registration voided 12/60.

BKX 431 (292): Arlington Motor Co Ltd (dealer), London SW1 9/35 9/35; WA Pugh, Newport (MH) 2/36; Gorseinon & District Bus Co, Gowerton (GG) 4/37; WE Jones, Brynhyfryd (GG) 5/39; AE Olive, Billinghay (LI) 6/39; GG Pearce {Orient Coaches}, Kingswood (GL) 3/40; RB Pearce {G Pearce & Sons / Orient Coaches}, Kingswood (GL) 7/45; Orient Coaches Ltd, Bristol (GL) by 1/50; W Birch, Warmley, Gloucestershire (status unknown) 8/54.

BKX 696: London Passenger Transport Board, London SW1 (LN) DT9B 8/35; converted to a driver training vehicle at Chiswick Works 1936-7; GJ Dawson (Clapham) Ltd (dealer), London SW9 3/38; J Riley {Riley's Motor Tours}, Belper (DE) 5/38; rebodied Shearing B32C by 5/41; GH Austin & Sons {Happy Days}, Woodseaves (ST) 32 5/41; fitted with an AEC 7.7 litre diesel engine at an unknown date; withdrawn 9/54; still owned 2/55; registration voided 11/63.

BKX 898 (293): Arlington Motor Co Ltd (dealer), London SW1 9/35 by 10/35; JH Kingston {KW Services}, Blakesley (NO) 6 1935; KW Services Ltd, Blakesley (NO) 6 2/37; moved to Daventry (NO) 1/38; renumbered D1 by 10/44; withdrawn by 10/47; AH Bond, Kettering (NO) 5/49; P Freeman (showman), Cardiff as a van 12/55; last licensed 6/60.

1936

New Vehicles:

302	JB 8341	Leyland TS7	9394	Brush	DP32R	2/36	3/51
303	JB 8342	Leyland TS7	9395	Brush	DP32R	2/36	10/52
304	JB 8343	Leyland TS7	9396	Brush	DP32R	2/36	8/52
305	JB 8344	Leyland TS7	9397	Brush	DP32R	2/36	10/52
306	JB 8345	Leyland TS7	9398	Brush	DP32R	2/36	5/52
307	JB 8346	Leyland TS7	9399	Brush	DP32R	2/36	8/50

308	JB 8347	Leyland TS7	9400	Brush		DP32R	3/36	8/50
309	JB 8348	Leyland TS7	9401	Brush		B32R	2/36	9/52
310	JB 8349	Leyland TS7	9402	Brush		B32R	2/36	7/50
311	JB 8350	Leyland TS7	9403	Brush		B32R	2/36	8/51

Notes:

JB 8341-8347 (302-308): Fitted with sliding roofs and curtains from new; internally refurbished by Weymann 1938; possibly modified to DP31R replacing the two side-facing seats with two single forward-facing seats c1950.

JB 8348-8350 (309-311): Possibly modified to DP31R replacing the two side-facing seats with two single forward-facing seats c1950.

JB 8341 (302): Body refurbished by Crimble, Staines 5-9/45.

JB 8342 (303): Body refurbished by G & R Harding, Cookham 3-5/44.

JB 8343 (304): Displayed 'on hire to Ledbury Transport' plates for working Reading to London services during 1939; body refurbished by G & R Harding, Cookham 6-7/44.

JB 8344 (305): Displayed 'on hire to Ledbury Transport' plates for working Reading to London services during 1939; body refurbished by G & R Harding, Cookham 10-11/44; body again refurbished by Express Motor Bodies, Tooting 6-c8/47; reseated to B30R (with perimeter seating) during World War 2.

JB 8345 (306): Displayed 'on hire to Ledbury Transport' plates for working Reading to London services during 1939; body refurbished by ECW 12/45-5/46; reseated to B30R (with perimeter seating) during World War 2.

JB 8346 (307): Licensed by Ledbury Transport Co Ltd 22 12/37 to 5/38; displayed 'on hire to Ledbury Transport' plates for working Reading to London services during 1939; body refurbished by G & R Harding, Cookham 5-6/44.

JB 8347 (308): Body refurbished by G & R Harding, Cookham 4/45.

JB 8348 (309): Licensed by Ledbury Transport Co Ltd 24 12/37 to 7/50.

JB 8349 (310): Licensed by Ledbury Transport Co Ltd 26 12/37 to 7/50; body refurbished by G & R Harding, Cookham 12/44-1/45.

JB 8350 (311): Licensed by Ledbury Transport Co Ltd 28 12/37 to 7/50; body refurbished by G & R Harding, Cookham 11-12/44.

Disposals:

JB 8341 (302): F Cowley (dealer), Salford 3/51.

JB 8342 (303): Miss Jones (showman), Guildford 10/52; S Jones (showman), Kingston-upon-Thames (kept at Chertsey) by 7/54; J Matthews (showman?), Longford 3/55; unidentified dealer, Horton 9/56; derelict by 4/59.

JB 8343 (304): C Phillips (dealer?), Writtle 10/52; noted in a yard, Felsted 8/53.

JB 8344 (305): E Tucker {Joyride Coaches}, Taunton (SO) 10/52 to 1956 at least.

JB 8345 (306): Douai College, Woolhampton (minus engine and seats for use as a changing room) 5/52.

JB 8346 (307): Kents Luxury Coaches, Baughurst (HA) 11/50; showman 6/57.

JB 8347 (308): B Bolesworth (showman), Hanworth 9/50; noted London SW19 8/59.

JB 8348 (309): Anderson, Butlins Amusement Park, Clacton-on-Sea (XEX) 9/52; showman, Chingford 4/54; noted Hurstpierpoint 7/59.

JB 8349 (310): TC Drakeley (showman) 7/50; noted Tunbridge Wells 6/54.

JB 8350 (311): Davies (showman), Blackwater 8/51; noted Camberley 4/59 and East Worthing 7/60.

Vehicles acquired from G Jarvis & Son {Reading & District Motor Services}, Reading (BE) 1/36:

301	RD 3016	Star Flyer	D986	?		B26F	10/31	by-/40
300	RD 6270	Thornycroft Ardent FE	24776	?		B26F	12/34	10/38

Previous histories:

RD 3016: New to R Bragg & G Jarvis & Son, Reading (BE); G Jarvis & Son {Reading & District Motor Services} 11/33.

RD 6270: New to G Jarvis & Son {Reading & District Motor Services}.

Notes:

Thames Valley acquired G Jarvis & Son's Reading & District Motor Services business on 1 January 1936 (with the coaching side of that business passing to Smith's Coaches of Reading at the same time). Jarvis thereafter concentrated on his garage business.

RD 6270 (300): Licensed by Ledbury Transport Co Ltd 20 12/37 to 10/38.

Disposals:

RD 3016 (301): RW Toop, WJ Ironside & PW Davis {Bere Regis & District Motor Services}, Dorchester (DT) by 1940; withdrawn by 3/45; showman 6/48 to 9/51 at least.

RD 6270 (300): H Lane & Co Ltd (dealer), London SW10 10/38; RA Ford {A Ford & Son}, Silchester 10/38; Newbury & District Motor Services Ltd 26 10/38 (qv).

Vehicles acquired from BD Argrave {Vimmy Bus Service}, Winkfield (BE) 5/36:

313	RO 9027	Star Flyer VB3		B686	United	1248	B20F	2/28
312	VG 1631	Star Flyer VB4		VB949/C630	United	1792	C23F	7/29

Previous histories:

These vehicles were acquired with the Argrave business; their previous histories are detailed in the Vehicles of Acquired Operators section.

Disposals:

VG 1631 (312): No known disposal.

RO 9027 (313): HA Remblance, Ramsey (XHN) 1937; showman 1937.

Vehicles acquired from Chiltern Bus Co Ltd, Lane End (BK) 5/36:

316	GT 9199	Bedford WLB	108017	Willmott		B20F	8/31	8/36
315	GT 9324	Bedford WLB	108037	Willmott		B20F	9/31	8/36
322	KX 978	Graham Bros	GB4689	?		B20F	7/28	----
321	KX 2558	Graham Bros	D204010	?		B26F	5/29	----
317	KX 6094	AEC Regal	662599	Petty		B30R	12/30	10/38
314	KX 7157	AEC Regal	662644	Petty		C32F	6/31	8/38
319	MT 1330	AEC Reliance	660002	Hall Lewis		B31D	12/28	10/38
318	MY 639	AEC Reliance	660311	Short		B32F	7/29	9/38
320	UR 3767	AEC Reliance	660239	Craven		C31R	7/29	10/38

Previous histories:

These vehicles were acquired with the Chiltern Bus Co business; their previous histories are detailed in the Vehicles of Acquired Operators section.

Notes:

KX 978 (322): Probably did not operate for Thames Valley Traction Co Ltd (the fleet number was reused for the 1937 intake and was probably never carried by this vehicle).

KX 2558 (321): Probably did not operate for Thames Valley Traction Co Ltd (the fleet number was reused for the 1937 intake and was probably never carried by this vehicle).

KX 6094 (317): Licensed by Ledbury Transport Co Ltd 50 3/38 to 10/38.

KX 7157 (314): Licensed by Ledbury Transport Co Ltd 46 3/38 to 8/38.

MT 1330 (319): Licensed by Ledbury Transport Co Ltd 58 3/38 to 10/38.

MY 639 (318): Licensed by Ledbury Transport Co Ltd 54 3/38 to 10/38.

UR 3767 (320): Licensed by Ledbury Transport Co Ltd 60 3/38 to 10/38.

Disposals:

GT 9199 (316): Unidentified dealer for scrap 8/36.

GT 9324 (315): Unidentified dealer for scrap 8/36.

KX 978 (322): GC & TA Holland & CLW Payne {Hanworth & District Coaches}, Hanworth (MX) 7/36; TA Holland, Hanworth (MX) ?2/37?; showman by 10/45.

KX 2558 (321): Unidentified operator / dealer 9/36; showman at an unknown date; noted Southwick 9/60.

KX 6094 (317): H Lane & Co Ltd (dealer), London SW10 10/38; JJ Griffin {Centaur Coaches}, London NW2 (LN) 5/39; FH Bellham {Hanslope Direct Bus Service}, Hanslope (BK) 1940; War Department (GOV) 1940; Ministry of Supply for disposal by 1944; Mrs SJ Knight, Northampton (NO) by 6/44; JR Flatt & Sons Ltd {Yellow Bus Service}, Long Sutton (HD) by 8/46; WJ Grimer {Primrose Coaches}, Moulton (HD) 7/48; showman 1951.

KX 7157 (314): FA & RG Spratley {Spratley Bros / Victory Coaches}, Mortimer (BE) 8/38; rebodied Duple C32F body by 12/45; withdrawn 5/52.

MT 1330 (319): H Lane & Co Ltd (dealer), London SW10 10/38; showman by 9/45; last licensed 12/47.

MY 639 (318): Last licensed 9/38; H Lane & Co Ltd (dealer), London SW10 10/38; V Barsi, Penydarren (GG) (not operated) 1938; GC Cook (dealer), Lambeth 1938.

UR 3767 (320): H Lane & Co Ltd (dealer), London SW10 10/38.

1937

New Vehicles:

321	ABL 751	Leyland TS7	12599	ECW		4870	B32R	3/37	10/52
322	ABL 752	Leyland TS7	12600	ECW		4871	B32R	3/37	c5/53
323	ABL 753	Leyland TS7	12601	ECW		4872	B32R	3/37	c5/53
324	ABL 754	Leyland TS7	12602	ECW		4873	B32R	3/37	9/52
325	ABL 755	Leyland TS7	12603	ECW		4874	B32R	3/37	c5/53
326	ABL 756	Leyland TS7	12604	ECW		4875	B32R	3/37	9/52
327	ABL 757	Leyland TS7	12605	ECW		4876	B32R	3/37	3/51
328	ABL 758	Leyland TS7	12606	ECW		4877	B32R	3/37	c5/53
329	ABL 759	Leyland TS7	12607	ECW		4878	B32R	3/37	10/52
330	ABL 760	Leyland TS7	12608	ECW		4879	B32R	3/37	7/50
331	ABL 761	Leyland TS7	12609	ECW		4880	B32R	3/37	11/52
332	ABL 762	Leyland TS7	12610	ECW		4881	B32R	3/37	10/53
333	ABL 763	Leyland TS7	12611	ECW		4882	B32R	3/37	5/51
334	ABL 764	Leyland TS7	12612	ECW		4883	B32R	3/37	c5/53
335	ABL 765	Leyland TD4	12613	Brush			L26/26R	2/37	c8/53
336	ABL 766	Leyland TD4	12614	Brush			L26/26R	2/37	c8/53
337	ABL 767	Leyland KPZ2	6821	Brush			B24F	5/37	4/52
338	ABL 768	Leyland KPZ2	6822	Brush			B24F	5/37	4/52
339	AJB 811	Leyland TD5	14198	Brush			L26/26R	5/37	c8/53
340	AJB 812	Leyland TD5	14199	Brush			L26/26R	5/37	c8/53
341	AJB 813	Leyland TD5	14200	Brush			L26/26R	5/37	c5/53
342	AJB 814	Leyland TS8	14374	Brush			B32R	5/37	5/51
343	AJB 815	Leyland TS8	14375	Brush			B32R	5/37	5/51
344	AJB 816	Leyland TS8	14376	Brush			B32R	5/37	5/51
345	AJB 817	Leyland TS8	14377	Brush			B32R	5/37	11/53
346	AJB 818	Leyland TS8	14378	Brush			B32R	5/37	5/51
347	AJB 819	Leyland TS8	14379	Brush			B32R	5/37	5/51
348	AJB 820	Leyland TS8	14380	Brush			B32R	5/37	10/53

Notes:

ABL 751-764 (321-334): Reseated to B30R (with perimeter seating) during World War 2.
AJB 814-820 (342-348): Reseated to B30R (with perimeter seating) during World War 2.

ABL 751 (321): Licensed by Ledbury Transport Co Ltd 30 12/37 to 7/50; body refurbished by ECW 6-8/45.
ABL 752 (322): Licensed by Ledbury Transport Co Ltd 32 12/37 to 7/50; body refurbished by ECW 7-9/45.
ABL 753 (323): Licensed by Ledbury Transport Co Ltd 34 12/37 to 7/50; body refurbished by ECW 11/45-1/46.
ABL 754 (324): Licensed by Ledbury Transport Co Ltd 37 12/37 to 7/50; body refurbished by Thames Valley 9/45.
ABL 755 (325): Licensed by Ledbury Transport Co Ltd 40 12/37 to 7/50; body refurbished by ECW 4-7/45.
ABL 756 (326): Licensed by Ledbury Transport Co Ltd 44 12/37 to 7/50; body refurbished by ECW 5-8/45.
ABL 757 (327): Body refurbished by Land Yachts, Egham 1-6/45.
ABL 758 (328): Body refurbished by Thames Valley 8/46.
ABL 759 (329): Body refurbished by ECW 11/45-1/46.
ABL 760 (330): Body refurbished by Crimble, Staines 8/44-2/45.
ABL 761 (331): Licensed by Ledbury Transport Co Ltd 48 12/37 to 7/50; body refurbished by ECW 6-8/45.
ABL 762 (332): Body refurbished by ECW 8-11/45.
ABL 763 (333): Body refurbished by G & R Harding, Cookham 7-8/44; reseated to B35R post-1945.
ABL 764 (334): Body refurbished by ECW 1-4/45.
ABL 765-766 (335-336): Bodies refurbished and rebuilt by ECW 3-6/45.
ABL 767-768 (337-338): Purchased for the Marlow Bridge rote on which there was a five ton weight limit; bodies refurbished by Express Motor Bodies, Tooting 3-6/47.
AJB 811 (339): Body refurbished and rebuilt by Willowbrook 4-8/45.
AJB 812 (340): Body refurbished and rebuilt by ECW 4-7/45.
AJB 813 (341): Body refurbished and rebuilt by Willowbrook 2-6/45.
AJB 814-816 (342-344): Reseated to B35R post-1945.
AJB 817 (345): Body refurbished by BBW, Bristol and reseated to B35R 11/49-3/50.
AJB 818 (346): Body refurbished by G & R Harding, Cookham 9-10/44; reseated to B35R post-1945.
AJB 819 (347): Probably reseated to B35R post-1945.
AJB 820 (348): Body refurbished by ECW 11/45-1/46; probably reseated to B35R post-1945.

Disposals:

ABL 751 (321): G Moore (showman?), High Wycombe 10/52; showman, Enfield 3/53; noted Pewsey 9/59; noted Towcester 3/60; noted Southwick 9/60.

ABL 752 (322): EA Thomas {Edward Thomas}, West Ewell (SR) (not operated) 8/53: AMCC (dealer), London E15 8/54.

ABL 753 (323): Disposed of via London Horse & Motor Repository auction, Elephant & Castle 8/53; EA Thomas {Edward Thomas}, West Ewell (SR) (not operated) 8/53: AE Connorton Motors (dealer), London SW9 9/53; showman, Bedfont 6/54; noted Flackwell Heath 7/58.

ABL 754 (324): Anderson, Butlins Amusement Park, Clacton-on-Sea (XEX) 9/52; showman, Ipswich 4/57.

ABL 755 (325): EA Thomas {Edward Thomas}, West Ewell (SR) (not operated) 8/53.

ABL 756 (326): Anderson, Butlins Amusement Park, Clacton-on-Sea (XEX) 9/52; showman, Hastings 7/54; noted Christchurch 8/57.

ABL 757 (327): RA Ford {A Ford & Son}, Silchester (HA) 3/51; Reliance Motor Services Ltd, Newbury (BE) 35 1955; Edwards Showmens' Resting Grounds, London NW at an unknown date.

ABL 758 (328): EA Thomas {Edward Thomas}, West Ewell (SR) 8/53; unidentified owner, Abbey Wood as a caravan 7/55.

ABL 759 (329): Ross (showman), Lambourn 10/52; still with a showman by 7/58.

ABL 760 (330): Reliance Motor Services, Newbury (BE) 25 7/50; unidentified dealer for scrap 4/57.

ABL 761 (331): Anderson, Butlins Amusement Park, Clacton-on-Sea (XEX) 11/52.

ABL 762 (332): Cox, London SW11 10/53; showman, Woolwich 4/54; modified with a full-front by 8/57; noted Maidenhead 8/58.

ABL 763 (333): Newbury & District Motor Services Ltd 184 5/51 (qv).

ABL 764 (334): Disposed of via London Horse & Motor Repository auction, Elephant & Castle 7/53; Bolesworth (showman), West Ham 10/53; noted as a pantechnicon, South Woodford 6/57 and as a lorry 9/58.

ABL 765 (335): D Davis (dealer), South Mimms 8/53; showman, Richmond 4/57.

ABL 766 (336): D Davis (dealer), South Mimms 8/53; K Swain, Finchley as a mobile caravan (fitted with platform doors and hauling a boat trailer) 1953; Green, Reading for preservation 7/66; derelict at Chazey Heath by 11/74 to 6/98 at least, but still in existence at least to 7/05.

ABL 767 (337): Edwards (dealer), Barnet 9/52.

ABL 768 (338): Edwards (dealer), Barnet 9/52; greengrocer's van, Staines 4/53.

AJB 811 (339): D Davis (dealer), South Mimms 8/53

AJB 812 (340): Bolesworth (showman), West Ham 8/53; noted London E10 9/53; cut-down by 5/56 and at Stevenage 9/59;

AJB 813 (341): J Mattia (dealer), Nether Wallop 7/53.

AJB 814 (342): Newbury & District Motor Services Ltd 179 5/51 (qv).

AJB 815 (343): Newbury & District Motor Services Ltd 185 5/51 (qv).

AJB 816 (344): Newbury & District Motor Services Ltd 180 5/51 (qv).

AJB 817 (345): Schwartz {Baker Street Trading Co} (dealer), London SW7 10/54; exported to Yugoslavia (probably operated for Belgrade City Transport, Belgrade (O-YU)).

AJB 818 (346): Newbury & District Motor Services Ltd 182 5/51 (qv).

AJB 819 (347): F Cowley (dealer), Salford 5/51; Tom Jackson (Chorley) Ltd, Chorley (LA) 5/51.

AJB 820 (348): Unidentified dealer 10/53; showman, Dundee 4/54; Circus Rosaire (showman), Bath 1954.

Vehicles acquired from FH Crook, Booker (BK) 6/37:

354	GC 9901	Reo FB (Gold Crown)	FB1144	Wray		B20F	2/30	7/37
355	KX 6376	AJS Pilot n/c	210	Petty		C24F	2/31	10/38
356	KX 7575	AJS Commodore	5048	Petty		B32F	10/31	10/38
357	KX 8533	Bedford WLB	108479	Duple	2727	B20F	5/32	2/38
353	UU 5749	Reo Sprinter Long FAX	FAX10410	Wray		C20F	6/29	5/38
352	VX 6549	Reo Pullman GE	GE193	?		B20F	7/30	5/38
358	YT 5420	Reo Sprinter 6	145268	Wray		C20D	8/27	----
349	BMG 703	Albion PK115	25001H	Duple	4272	B26F	6/34	9/44
350	BPP 141	Albion PW69	16404A	Duple	5133	DP32F	5/35	9/44
351	CPP 80	Albion PK115	25009E	Duple	6933	C31F	5/36	9/44

Previous histories:

These vehicles were new to FH Crook, with the exception of:

GC 9901 (354): Probably registered by a dealer / agent (as were many of Crook's vehicles) and used initially as a demonstrator; FH Crook 4/30.

VX 6549 (352): New to A Akers {Bird Motor Services}, Halstead (EX) 7; Eastern National Omnibus Co Ltd, Chelmsford (EX) 3509 12/33; unidentified operator / dealer 10/35; FH Crook by 1937.

Notes:

Thames Valley purchased the bus operations together with ten vehicles with Crook concentrating thereafter on his coaching business which continued through to the 1960s. The service was described as 'The Booker Bus' in literature although this did not appear on vehicles as a fleet name. The nearest thing to a fleet name may have been 'Advance' as this appeared within a painting on the sides of the buses.

GC 9901 (354): This Reo did not have a model name but was frequently referred to as the 'Gold Crown'; which was the name given to the new Reo engine which was fitted to their various models.

VX 6549 (352): Licensed by Ledbury Transport Co Ltd 52 12/37 to 5/38.

YT 5420 (358): Not operated by Thames Valley.

BMG 703 (349): Prepared for conversion to an ambulance 6/39 (probably based at King Edward Hospital, Windsor for a period), but remained available for use as a bus; was stored from 10/42 to summer 1945 following mechanical failure.

BPP 141 (350): Prepared for conversion to an ambulance 6/39 (probably based at King Edward Hospital, Windsor for a period), but remained available for use as a bus; it was stored out of use by 4/42; reinstated to receive wounded troops returning from the Continent 6/44; converted back to a bus 9/44 but only used as a towing vehicle.

CPP 80 (351): Prepared for conversion to an ambulance 6/39 (probably based at King Edward Hospital, Windsor for a period), but remained available for use as a bus; it was stored out of use by 4/42; reinstated to receive wounded troops returning from the Continent 6/44; converted back to a bus 9/44 but only used as a towing vehicle.

Disposals:

GC 9901 (354): Last licensed 7/37; unidentified dealer, Banstead for scrap 5/38.

KX 6376 (355): H Lane & Co Ltd (dealer), London SW10 10/38.

KX 7575 (356): H Lane & Co Ltd (dealer), London SW10 10/38; AJ Pearle {Rose Coaches}, London N7 (LN) 4/39; withdrawn 10/46; Glider & Blue Motor Services Ltd, Bishops Waltham (HA) 1946; withdrawn 10/51.

KX 8533 (357): Unidentified operator / dealer 2/38; R Knapp, Shrivenham (BE) by 1/40; showman by 4/46.

UU 5749 (353): RA Ford {A Ford & Son}, Silchester (HA) 5/38; GE Costin, Dunstable (BD) 1/41; RG & T Wesley, Stoke Goldington (BK) 7/41; showman 8/50.

VX 6549 (352): RA Ford {A Ford & Son}, Silchester (HA) 5/38; A Perdue {Chiltonian Motors}, Chilton Foliat (BE) 7/47 (as B24F); last licensed 10/48; G Smart, Bedminster (SO) 8/49;

YT 5420 (358): No known disposal.

BMG 703 (349): United Nations Refugee Rehabilitation Agency (UNRRA) (for use in Germany) 7/45.

BPP 141 (350): United Nations Refugee Rehabilitation Agency (UNRRA) (for use in Germany) 6/45.

CPP 80 (351): United Nations Refugee Rehabilitation Agency (UNRRA) (for use in Germany) 6/45.

1938

New Vehicles:

359	ARX 981	Leyland TS8	16986	ECW	5508	B32R	2/38	7/50
360	ARX 982	Leyland TS8	16987	ECW	5509	B32R	2/38	7/50
361	ARX 983	Leyland TS8	16988	ECW	5510	B32R	3/38	10/53
362	ARX 984	Leyland TS8	16989	ECW	5511	B32R	3/38	9/52
363	ARX 985	Leyland TS8	16990	ECW	5512	B32R	2/38	10/54
364	ARX 986	Leyland TS8	16991	ECW	5513	B32R	2/38	7/50
365	ARX 987	Leyland TS8	16992	ECW	5514	B32R	3/38	9/50
366	ARX 988	Leyland TS8	16993	ECW	5515	B32R	3/38	10/54
367	ARX 989	Leyland TS8	16994	ECW	5516	B32R	3/38	9/50
368	ARX 990	Leyland TS8	16995	ECW	5517	B32R	3/38	5/51
369	ARX 991	Leyland TD5	17183	ECW	5518	L24/24R	5/38	5/53
370	ARX 992	Leyland TD5	17184	ECW	5519	L24/24R	5/38	10/53
371	BBL 557	Leyland TS8	300218	ECW	5662	B32R	6/38	5/54
372	BBL 558	Leyland TS8	300219	ECW	5663	B32R	6/38	5/51
373	BBL 559	Leyland TS8	300220	ECW	5664	B32R	6/38	10/53
374	BBL 560	Leyland TS8	300221	ECW	5665	B32R	6/38	3/54
375	BBL 561	Leyland TS8	300222	ECW	5666	B32R	6/38	11/53
376	BBL 562	Leyland TS8	300223	ECW	5667	B32R	6/38	7/50
377	BBL 563	Leyland TS8	300224	ECW	5668	B32R	6/38	3/51
378	BBL 564	Leyland TS8	300225	ECW	5669	B32R	6/38	6/53
379	BBL 565	Leyland TS8	300226	ECW	5670	B32R	6/38	5/51
380	BBL 566	Leyland TS8	300227	ECW	5671	B32R	6/38	3/54

Notes:

BBL 557-566 (371-380): Reseated to B30R (with perimeter seating) during World War 2.

ARX 984 (362): Reseated to B35R post-1945.
ARX 985 (363): Body refurbished by BBW, Bristol and reseated to B35R 2-5/50.
ARX 986-987 (364-365): Reseated to B35R post-1945.
ARX 988 (366): Body refurbished by BBW, Bristol and reseated to B35R 2-5/50.
ARX 989 (367): Reseated to B35R post-1945.
ARX 990 (368): Reseated to B35R post-1945; body refurbished by Lambourn Garages, Lambourn 2-c4/48.
ARX 991-992 (369-370): Fitted with Gardner 5LW diesel engines 1950.
BBL 557 (371): Displayed 'on hire to Ledbury Transport' plates for working Reading to London services during 1939; body refurbished by BBW, Bristol and reseated to B35R 11/49-3/50.
BBL 558 (372): Displayed 'on hire to Ledbury Transport' plates for working Reading to London services during 1939; body refurbished by BBW and reseated to B35R 11/49-c1/50.
BBL 561 (375): Exchanged bodies with Leyland TS7 JB 5846 (267) c7/51, receiving the Brush B32R body from that vehicle.
BBL 565 (379): Reseated to B35R post-1945.
BBL 566 (380): Probably reseated to B35R post-1945.

Disposals:

ARX 981 (359): Plant (showman), Newbury 7/50; noted Barnet 7/51 and Gravesend 10/59.
ARX 982 (360): Mayne (showman), Farnborough 7/50; noted Epsom 5/55, Burghfield 5/58 and Elstead 5/59; EJ Baker & Co (Dorking) Ltd (dealer), Farnham 1962; in a field (probably showman's winter quarters) near Farnborough 6/62; derelict by 8/63.
ARX 983 (361): Token Construction Co Ltd (contractor), London (XLN) 12/53.
ARX 984 (362): Ross (showman), Lambourn 9/52; noted Reading 5/53, Marlborough 10/59 and Lower Rainham 3/61.
ARX 985 (363): Schwartz {Baker Street Trading Co} (dealer), London SW7 10/54; Belgrade City Transport, Belgrade (O-YU) 8/55; registered C6212.
ARX 986 (364): RA Ford {A Ford & Son}, Silchester (HA) 7/50; Lovegrove & Lovegrove Ltd, Silchester (HA) 5/56; EJ Baker & Co (Dorking) Ltd (dealer), Farnham 9/59; showman, Elstead by 1960.
ARX 987 (365): Edwards (showman), Barnet 9/50; noted Reading 1951; noted Peckham Rye 6/55.
ARX 988 (366): Schwartz {Baker Street Trading Co} (dealer), London SW7 10/54; Belgrade City Transport, Belgrade (O-YU) 8/55; registered C6213.
ARX 989 (367): Edwards (showman), Barnet 9/50; noted Maidenhead 1951 and Brackley 9/59.
ARX 990 (368): Newbury & District Motor Services Ltd 186 5/51 (qv).
ARX 991 (369): F Pelham (showman), Hurst 5/53 to 10/57 at least.
ARX 992 (370): Angle & Poulton (contractor), Bracknell (XBE) 5/54.
BBL 557 (371): Schwartz {Baker Street Trading Co} (dealer), London SW7 10/54; exported to Yugoslavia (probably operated for Belgrade City Transport, Belgrade (O-YU)).
BBL 558 (372): Newbury & District Motor Services Ltd 181 5/51 (qv).
BBL 559 (373): Smith (showman), Farnborough 3/54; noted near Lymington 7/54, Grays 9/58, Tottenham 7/62 and Chichester 10/64; in a scrapyard alongside the A31 7/65.
BBL 560 (374): Hanslip (showman), Southampton 3/54; noted Salisbury 9/55.
BBL 561 (375): Shufflebottom, Billericay (minus engine) 11/53; Circus Rosaire (showman), Bath 1954.
BBL 562 (376): T Rowland (showman) 7/50; noted Mitcham 1951; noted Horsham 8/58.
BBL 563 (377): Stevens (showman), London SW6 3/51; noted Hampton Court 5/51.
BBL 564 (378): Ayres (showman), Southampton 6/53; noted Rickmansworth 6/54 and Mitcham 8/59.
BBL 565 (379): Newbury & District Motor Services Ltd 183 5/51 (qv).
BBL 566 (380): Keeble (showman), London E11 3/54; noted Mitcham 8/59.

1939

New Vehicles:

381	BMO 980	Leyland TS8	301936	Harrington	C32F	6/39	10/54
382	BMO 981	Leyland TS8	301937	Harrington	C32F	6/39	4/54
383	BMO 982	Leyland TS8	301938	Harrington	C32F	6/39	10/54
384	BMO 983	Leyland TS8	301939	Harrington	C32F	6/39	10/54
385	BMO 984	Leyland TS8	301940	Harrington	C32F	6/39	4/54
386	BMO 985	Leyland TS8	301941	Harrington	C32F	6/39	10/54
387	BMO 986	Leyland TS8	301942	Harrington	C32F	6/39	10/54
388	BMO 987	Leyland TS8	301943	Harrington	C32F	7/39	10/54
389	BMO 988	Leyland TS8	301944	Harrington	C32F	7/39	10/54
390	BMO 989	Leyland TS8	301945	Harrington	C32F	7/39	10/54

391	BRX 656	Bristol K5G	51.094	ECW		6562	L24/24R	6/39	9/55
392	BRX 908	Bristol K5G	53.003	ECW		6353	L24/24R	9/39	5/56
393	BRX 909	Bristol K5G	53.004	ECW		6354	L24/24R	9/39	9/54
394	BRX 910	Bristol K5G	53.005	ECW		6355	L24/24R	9/39	5/56
395	BRX 911	Bristol K5G	53.006	ECW		6356	L24/24R	9/39	10/53
396	BRX 912	Bristol K5G	53.007	ECW		6357	L24/24R	9/39	10/53
397	BRX 913	Bristol K5G	53.008	ECW		6358	L24/24R	9/39	9/54
398	BRX 914	Bristol K5G	53.009	ECW		6359	L24/24R	10/39	10/53
399	BRX 915	Bristol K5G	53.010	ECW		6360	L24/24R	10/39	4/54
400	BRX 916	Bristol K5G	53.011	ECW		6361	L24/24R	10/39	5/56
401	BRX 917	Bristol K5G	53.012	ECW		6368	L24/24R	10/39	10/54
402	BRX 918	Bristol K5G	53.013	ECW		6362	L24/24R	10/39	5/56
403	BRX 919	Bristol K5G	53.014	ECW		6363	L24/24R	10/39	10/53
404	BRX 920	Bristol K5G	53.015	ECW		6364	L24/24R	10/39	9/54
405	BRX 921	Bristol K5G	53.016	ECW		6365	L24/24R	10/39	9/56
406	BRX 922	Bristol K5G	53.017	ECW		6366	L24/24R	10/39	9/54
407	BRX 923	Bristol K5G	53.018	ECW		6367	L24/24R	10/39	9/54
408	BRX 924	Bristol K5G	53.019	ECW		6369	L24/24R	10/39	10/53
409	BRX 925	Bristol K5G	53.020	ECW		6370	L24/24R	10/39	10/54

Notes:

BMO 980-989 (381-390): Fitted from new with petrol engines removed from re-engined Leyland TD1s of 1929-31; fitted with Leyland diesel engines 1951.

BMO 980 (381): Body refurbished by TW Cawood & Son, Doncaster 3-5/47; body again refurbished by Associated Deliveries, Reading and reseated to C33F 1-3/50.

BMO 981 (382): Body refurbished by TW Cawood & Son, Doncaster 10-11/47; body again refurbished by Associated Deliveries, Reading and reseated to C33F 2-c4/50; refurbished by Hants & Dorset Motor Services Ltd at Southampton 5/52.

BMO 982 (383): Body refurbished by TW Cawood & Son, Doncaster 2/47; body again refurbished by Associated Deliveries, Reading and reseated to C33F 12/49-2/50.

BMO 983 (384): Body refurbished by TW Cawood & Son, Doncaster 3-4/47; body again refurbished by Associated Deliveries, Reading and reseated to C33F 2-4/50; refurbished by Hants & Dorset Motor Services Ltd at Southampton 5/52.

BMO 984 (385): Body refurbished by TW Cawood & Son, Doncaster 2-4/47; body again refurbished by Associated Deliveries, Reading and reseated to C33F 12/49-2/50; refurbished by Hants & Dorset Motor Services Ltd at Southampton 5/52.

BMO 985 (386): Body refurbished by TW Cawood & Son, Doncaster 11-12/47; body again refurbished by Associated Deliveries, Reading and reseated to C33F 2-4/50; refurbished by Hants & Dorset Motor Services Ltd at Southampton 5/52.

BMO 986 (387): Body refurbished by TW Cawood & Son, Doncaster 11-12/47; body again refurbished by Associated Deliveries, Reading and reseated to C33F 12/49-2/50.

BMO 987 (388): Body refurbished by TW Cawood & Son, Doncaster 4-5/47; body again refurbished by Associated Deliveries, Reading and reseated to C33F 12/49-2/50; refurbished by Hants & Dorset Motor Services Ltd at Southampton 5/52.

BMO 988 (389): Body refurbished by TW Cawood & Son, Doncaster 2-3/47; body again refurbished by Associated Deliveries, Reading and reseated to C33F 1-3/50; refurbished by Hants & Dorset Motor Services Ltd at Southampton 5/52.

BMO 989 (390): Body refurbished by TW Cawood & Son, Doncaster 5-6/47; body again refurbished by Associated Deliveries, Reading and reseated to C33F 3-4/50.

BRX 656 (391): Was a replacement for RX 4353 (191) which was destroyed in an accident 4/39; body refurbished by TW Cawood & Son, Doncaster 2-6/48.

BRX 909 (393): Body damaged in a fire 3/40; rebuilt by ECW 8/40; body refurbished by Thames Valley over the winter of 1949/50; rebuilt to L27/24R at an unknown date.

BRX 910 (394): Badly damaged in a fire at Reading depot on 1/3/40; rebuilt by ECW and fitted with a plywood roof, returning to service 9/40.

BRX 911 (395): Fitted with a chrome-plated radiator for the 1939 Commercial Motor Show (which in the event was cancelled following the outbreak of World War 2); body refurbished by TW Cawood & Son, Doncaster 10-11/48.

BRX 912 (396): Body refurbished by TW Cawood & Son, Doncaster 11/48-2/49.

BRX 913 (397): Body refurbished by Thames Valley over the winter of 1949/50; rebuilt to L27/24R at an unknown date.

BRX 914 (398): Body refurbished by TW Cawood & Son, Doncaster 7-10/48.

BRX 916-918 (400-402): Bodies refurbished by Thames Valley over the winter of 1949/50; rebuilt to L27/24R at unknown dates.

BRX 920-921 (404-405): Bodies refurbished by Thames Valley over the winter of 1949/50; rebuilt to L27/24R at unknown dates.

BRX 925 (409): Body refurbished by Thames Valley over the winter of 1949/50; rebuilt to L27/24R at an unknown date.

Disposals:

BMO 980 (381): Schwartz {Baker Street Trading Co} (dealer), London SW7 10/54; exported to Yugoslavia (probably operated for Belgrade City Transport, Belgrade (O-YU)).

BMO 981 (382): AMCC (dealer), London E15 4/54.

BMO 982-983 (383-384): Schwartz {Baker Street Trading Co} (dealer), London SW7 10/54; exported to Yugoslavia (probably operated for Belgrade City Transport, Belgrade (O-YU)).

BMO 984 (385): AMCC (dealer), London E15 4/54; Jopling Bros, Birtley (DM) by 8/55.

BMO 985-989 (386-390): Schwartz {Baker Street Trading Co} (dealer), London SW7 10/54; exported to Yugoslavia (probably operated for Belgrade City Transport, Belgrade (O-YU)).

BRX 656 (391): AE Connorton Motors (dealer), London SW9 9/55; showman, Willesden 4/56; noted Barking 9/58 and London N22 9/63.

BRX 908 (392): Chassis broken up by Thames Valley 5/56; body to Curtis (dealer), Stokenchurch for scrap 5/56.

BRX 909 (393): FG Hobbs {Watling Street Motors} (dealer), Redbourn 9/54; Butlins Ltd, Clacton-on-Sea (XEX) 9/54; showman, Chelmsford 4/57; noted Long Melford 5/58.

BRX 910 (394): Chassis broken up by Thames Valley 5/56; body to Curtis (dealer), Stokenchurch for scrap 5/56.

BRX 911 (395): Eastern National Omnibus Co Ltd, Chelmsford (EX) 1002 4/54; AMCC (dealer), London E15 6/58.

BRX 912 (396): Eastern National Omnibus Co Ltd, Chelmsford (EX) 1003 4/54; AMCC (dealer), London E15 11/56.

BRX 913 (397): FG Hobbs {Watling Street Motors} (dealer), St Albans 9/54; K & R Russell {Robert Russell Developments} (contractor), Rickmansworth (XHT) by 10/55 to 6/57 at least.

BRX 914 (398): Eastern National Omnibus Co Ltd, Chelmsford (EX) 1004 4/54; returned to Thames Valley Traction Co Ltd for resale 3/59, but not traced further.

BRX 915 (399): Eastern National Omnibus Co Ltd, Chelmsford (EX) 1005 4/54; returned to Thames Valley Traction Co Ltd for resale 12/57; Jones (showman), Chertsey 4/58; noted Epsom 6/58, Hampton Court 9/60 and London SW15 4/64.

BRX 916 (400): Chassis broken up by Thames Valley 5/56; body to J Mattia (dealer), Nether Wallop for scrap 5/56.

BRX 917 (401): FG Hobbs {Watling Street Motors} (dealer), Redbourn 10/54; Simmonds & Hawker, Feltham (XMX) 10/54; noted Maidstone 12/55 and Feltham 10/56; unidentified owner, Stanford-le-Hope as a mobile caravan 7/60.

BRX 918 (402): AMCC (dealer), London E15 5/56 and exported.

BRX 919 (403): Eastern National Omnibus Co Ltd, Chelmsford (EX) 1006 4/54; returned to Thames Valley Traction Co Ltd for resale 12/57; J Deacon (dealer), Dorchester-on-Thames 6/58; showman, Southend-on-Sea cut down to single deck 8/62.

BRX 920 (404): FG Hobbs {Watling Street Motors} (dealer), Redbourn 9/54; Buckmaster, Leighton Buzzard (BD) (not operated – vehicle was sold on condition it was not subsequently resold for PSV work) at an unknown date; showman, London E18 (cut down to single-deck) 4/57; noted London E6 9/57.

BRX 921 (405): Converted for use as a tree-lopper and transferred to the service fleet 9/56 (qv).

BRX 922 (406): FG Hobbs {Watling Street Motors} (dealer), Redbourn 9/54; showman, Ipswich 7/55 and Chelmsford 5/60; Halfway Autos (dealer), East Horndon by 1961.

BRX 923 (407): FG Hobbs {Watling Street Motors} (dealer), Redbourn 9/54; McAlpine (contractor), Luton (XBD) at an unknown date; Halfway Autos (dealer), East Horndon by 1961.

BRX 924 (408): Eastern National Omnibus Co Ltd, Chelmsford (EX) 1007 4/54; AMCC (dealer), London E15 9/58; showman, Luton 5/59; noted Harpenden 9/64 and Finchley 7/67.

BRX 925 (409): FG Hobbs {Watling Street Motors} (dealer), Redbourn 10/54; McAlpine (contractor), Luton (XBD) at an unknown date; Halfway Autos (dealer), East Horndon by 1961.

1940

New Vehicle:

410	CJB 131	Bristol K5G	55.101	ECW		7262	L24/24R	12/40

Notes:

CJB 131 (410): Rebuilt to L27/24R at an unknown date.

Disposal:

CJB 131 (410): Barber (showman), Mexborough 10/54.

Vehicle acquired from Crosville Motor Services Ltd, Chester (CH) 12/40:

411	FM 7455	Leyland KP3		969	Brush		B24F	12/32	4/52

Previous history:

FM 7455 (411): New to Crosville Motor Services Ltd (CH) 728 (as B20F) [renumbered N45 1935].

Notes:

FM 7455 (411): Acquired for the Marlow Bridge route on which there was a five ton weight limit; body refurbished by Express Motor Bodies, Tooting (work also being carried out at Leyland Motors Ltd, Kingston works) 8/47-1/48;

Disposal:

FM 7455 (411): Phillips (dealer?), Chelmsford 9/52.

Vehicles on hire from Westcliff-on-Sea Motor Services Ltd, Westcliff-on-Sea (EX):

106	JN 9541	Bristol K5G	42.25	ECW	5344	L27/28R	10/37	12/40	12/41
107	JN 9542	Bristol K5G	42.26	ECW	5345	L27/28R	10/37	11/40	2/42
108	JN 9543	Bristol K5G	42.27	ECW	5346	L27/28R	10/37	11/40	2/42
101	AHJ 401	Bristol K5G	45.20	ECW	5449	L27/28R	5/38	12/40	2/42
102	AHJ 402	Bristol K5G	45.21	ECW	5450	L27/28R	5/38	12/40	12/41
103	AHJ 403	Bristol K5G	45.22	ECW	5451	L27/28R	5/38	12/40	12/41
104	BHJ 532	Bristol K5G	53.087	ECW	6698	L27/28R	11/39	11/40	1/42
105	BHJ 533	Bristol K5G	53.088	ECW	6699	L27/28R	11/39	11/40	1/42

Vehicles on hire from East Kent Road Car Co Ltd, Canterbury (KT):

	FN 9001	TSM B10C2	5628	Park Royal	?	C32R	-/28	-/40	-/41
	FN 9009	TSM B10C2	5636	Park Royal	B3467	C32R	4/28	-/40	-/41
	FN 9011	TSM B10C2	5638	Park Royal	?	C32R	4/28	-/40	-/41
	JG 1417	TSM B49C2	7070	Brush		C32R	4/31	-/40	-/41
	JG 1431	TSM B49C2	7084	Brush		C32R	6/31	-/40	-/41
	JG 1447	TSM B49C2	7100	Hoyal		C32R	-/31	-/40	-/41
	JG 1451	TSM B49C2	7104	Hoyal		C32R	-/31	-/40	-/41
	JG 1624	Leyland TD1	72318	Leyland		L27/24R	-/31	-/40	-/41
	JG 7010	Leyland TD4	9495	Brush		L27/26R	4/36	12/40	3/41
	JG 8979	Leyland TS8	14674	Park Royal	B4822	C32R	-/37	12/40	3/41
	JG 9933	Leyland TS8	16589	Park Royal	B4897	C32R	-/38	-/40	-/41
	JG 9939	Leyland TS8	16628	Park Royal	B4903	C32R	-/38	-/40	-/41
	JG 9940	Leyland TS8	16629	Park Royal	B4904	C32R	-/38	-/40	-/41
	JG 9942	Leyland TS8	16631	Park Royal	B4906	C32R	-/38	-/40	-/41
	JG 9943	Leyland TS8	16632	Park Royal	B4907	C32R	-/38	-/40	-/41
	JG 9944	Leyland TS8	17134	Park Royal	?	C32R	-/38	-/40	-/41
	JG 9946	Leyland TS8	17136	Park Royal	B4998	C32R	-/38	-/40	-/41
	JG 9948	Leyland TS8	17138	Park Royal	B5000	C32R	-/38	-/40	-/41
	JG 9949	Leyland TS8	17139	Park Royal	B5001	C32R	-/38	-/40	-/41
	JG 9964	Leyland TS8	17154	Park Royal	B5016	C32R	-/38	-/40	-/41
	CYL 243	Leyland TS7	9584	Duple	7292	C33R	-/36	-/40	-/41
	DXV 741	Leyland TS7	13145	Duple	8807	C33R	6/37	-/40	-/41

Notes:

These vehicles were operated for varying periods between 9/40 and the early months of 1941. Possibly not all were used and some may have been merely passing through en-route to other operators. In addition, East Kent FN 9002-9008, FN 9010, JG 1438, JG 1441, JG 1448 and JG 1452 were also recorded at Reading depot, but were probably not operated by Thames Valley.

JG 9944: Its Park Royal body number was from the B4034-41 batch.

FN 9001: Its Park Royal body was new in 4/33 with its body number from the B3552-7 batch; its original body was Beadle (4603) B37R.

FN 9009: Its Park Royal body was new in 2/34; its original body was Brush B37R.

FN 9011: Its Park Royal body was new in 2/34 with its body number from the B3465-9 batch; its original body was Brush B37R.

CYL 243: New to MT Co (Motor Coaches) Ltd, London SE14 (LN) T18, passing to East Kent 5/37.

DXV 741: New to MT Co (Motor Coaches) Ltd, London SE14 (LN) T24, passing to East Kent 5/37.

Vehicle on hire from S Dryer {Dryers Coaches}, London E8 (LN):

EXF 878	Dennis Lancet II	175538	Dennis		C35F	4/38	-/40	-/40

Vehicle on hire from W Marshall & Sons, Blackpool (LA):

FV 8971	Leyland TS7	13772	Burlingham		C32R	4/37	-/40	-/40

1941

Vehicle acquired from W Alexander & Sons Ltd, Falkirk (SN) 6/41:

412	HF 6041	Leyland TD1	70687	Leyland		L27/24RO	6/29	5/52

Previous history:

HF 6041 (412): New to Wallasey Corporation (CH) 54; E & N Sanderson {Millburn Garage} (dealer), Glasgow 5/37; W Alexander & Sons Ltd R174 6/37; fitted with a Leyland 8.6 litre diesel engine 10/40; E & N Sanderson {Millburn Garage} (dealer), Glasgow 4/41, from whom it was acquired.

Notes:

HF 6041 (412): Entered service after overhaul with a petrol engine 10/41; fitted with a Gardner 5LW diesel engine 4/43; body refurbished and rebuilt by ECW to L27/24R 9/44-1/45.

Disposal:

HF 6041 (412): H Botton (showman), Croydon 5/52; withdrawn 10/55.

Vehicles on hire from East Kent Road Car Co Ltd, Canterbury (KT):

109	JG 8205	Leyland TD4	11601	Park Royal	B4425	L27/26R	-/36	2/41	8/42
110	JG 8206	Leyland TD4	11602	Park Royal	B4426	L27/26R	-/36	2/41	8/42
111	JG 8207	Leyland TD4	11603	Park Royal	B4427	L27/26R	-/36	3/41	8/42
112	JG 8208	Leyland TD4	11604	Park Royal	B4428	L27/26R	-/36	3/41	8/42
113	JG 8209	Leyland TD4	11605	Park Royal	B4429	L27/26R	-/36	3/41	7/42
114	JG 8210	Leyland TD4	11606	Park Royal	B4430	L27/26R	-/36	4/41	8/42

1942

New Vehicles:

413	CJB 132	Bristol K5G	57.017	ECW		7263	L27/28R	5/42	9/55
414	CJB 133	Bristol K5G	57.018	ECW		7264	L27/28R	4/42	9/55
415	CJB 134	Bristol K5G	57.019	ECW		7265	L27/28R	4/42	5/56
416	CJB 135	Bristol K5G	57.031	ECW		7266	L27/28R	5/42	5/56
417	CJB 136	Bristol K5G	57.076	Duple		31657	L27/28R	11/42	5/56
418	CJB 137	Guy Arab 1	FD25486	Duple		31632	L27/28R	12/42	8/55
419	CJB 138	Guy Arab 1	FD25508	Duple		31633	L27/28R	12/42	8/55

Notes:

CJB 132-136 (413-417): Were 'unfrozen' chassis, fitted with plywood roofs.

CJB 132 (413): Hired to City of Oxford Motor Services Ltd, Oxford (OX) in 7/50.

CJB 137-138 (418-419): Fitted with Gardner 5LW engines and delivered with the upstairs rear windows panelled over and fitted with wooden slatted seats; glass from withdrawn Leyland TD1s was fitted to some c1950.

Disposals:

CJB 132 (413): AE Connorton Motors (dealer), London SW9 9/55; showman, Gillingham (with a cut-down body) 1956; noted Reading 1956 and Rye 6/59.

CJB 133 (414): AE Connorton Motors (dealer), London SW9 9/55; FC Moore Ltd {Viceroy Coaches}, Saffron Walden (EX) by 11/55.

CJB 134 (415): Herbert (showman?), Southampton 5/56; showman, Christchurch 8/57; noted Salisbury 10/59 and Christchurch 8/60.

CJB 135 (416): Simmonds & Hawker, Feltham (XMX) 5/56; unidentified owner; Leicester as a caravan 5/57; unidentified owner, Rhondda as a furniture demonstration van 5/58; showman, Bath 7/59.

CJB 136 (417): AE Connorton Motors (dealer), London SW9 5/56 and exported.

CJB 137-138 (418-419): Guy Motors Ltd (dealer), Wolverhampton 8/55; REICOM (O-IC) 1/56.

1943

New Vehicles:

420	CJB 139	Guy Arab I	FD25546	Strachan	L27/28R	1/43	5/51
421	CJB 140	Guy Arab I	FD25597	Strachan	L27/28R	2/43	5/56
422	CJB 141	Guy Arab I	FD25825	Brush	L27/28R	2/43	6/56
423	CMO 653	Guy Arab I	FD25828	Brush	L27/28R	4/43	5/56
424	CMO 654	Guy Arab I	FD25855	Brush	L27/28R	4/43	10/55
425	CMO 655	Guy Arab I	FD25935	Brush	L27/28R	4/43	5/56

Notes:

These vehicles were fitted with Gardner 5LW engines and were delivered with upstairs rear windows panelled over; glass from withdrawn Leyland TD1s was fitted c1950.

CJB 139 (420): Rebuilt and reseated to L27/26R by Strachan following an accident at an unknown date.

CJB 140 (421): Overturned in an accident at Windsor 2/44; rebuilt by Santus 7-11/44.

Disposals:

CJB 139 (420): Newbury & District Motor Services Ltd 187 5/51.

CJB 140 (421): J Mattia (dealer), Nether Wallop for scrap 5/56.

CJB 141 (422): Day (showman), Farnborough 6/56; noted Epsom 9/57 and Winchester 10/59.

CMO 653 (423): J Mattia (dealer), Nether Wallop for scrap 5/56

CMO 654 (424): J Shewring, Norwich (NK) 10/55.

CMO 655 (425): J Mattia (dealer), Nether Wallop for scrap 5/56

Vehicles re-acquired from the War Department (GOV) c4-6/43:

262	JB 5841	Leyland TS7	7126	Duple	5015	C32F	4/35	4/50
230	RX 6250	Leyland TS3	61065	Brush		DP29R	7/30	7/50
252	RX 9706	Leyland TS4	592	Brush		C28F	4/32	10/51
253	RX 9707	Leyland TS4	593	Brush		C28F	5/32	9/52
255	RX 9709	Leyland TS4	595	Brush		C28F	5/32	4/50
256	RX 9710	Leyland TS4	596	Brush		C28F	5/32	11/51

Previous histories:

JB 5841 (262): New to Thames Valley Traction Co Ltd 262; War Department (GOV) 7/40; re-acquired 3/43.

RX 6250 (230): New to Thames Valley Traction Co Ltd 230; Ledbury Transport Co Ltd {Thackray's Way}, Reading (BE) 62 4/40; War Department (GOV) 7/40; re-acquired c4/43.

RX 9706-9707 (252-253): New to Thames Valley Traction Co Ltd 252-253; War Department (GOV) 7/40; re-acquired c4/43.

RX 9709 (255): New to Thames Valley Traction Co Ltd 255; War Department (GOV) 7/40; re-acquired c4/43.

RX 9710 (256): New to Thames Valley Traction Co Ltd 256; War Department (GOV) 7/40; re-acquired 6/43.

Notes:

These vehicles were re-acquired in poor condition and were initially placed in store until they could be made fit for further service.

JB 5841 (262): Body rebuilt and refurbished by TW Cawood & Son, Doncaster 8/46-1/47; body again refurbished by Associated Deliveries, Reading and reseated to C33F 2-3/50.

RX 6250 (230): Body rebuilt and refurbished as a service bus (as B29R) by TW Cawood & Son, Doncaster 1-7/45; fitted with a Gardner 4LW diesel engine 2/48.

RX 9706 (252): Body rebuilt and refurbished as a service bus (as B29R) by TW Cawood & Son, Doncaster 7/44-1/45; fitted with a Leyland 8.6 litre diesel engine 10/45.

RX 9707 (253): Body rebuilt and refurbished as a service bus (as B29R) by TW Cawood & Son, Doncaster 12/44-3/45; fitted with a Leyland 8.6 litre diesel engine 12/45.

RX 9709 (255): Body rebuilt and refurbished as a service bus (as B29R) by H Markham Ltd, Reading 3-7/44; fitted with a Leyland 8.6 litre diesel engine 11/45.

RX 9710 (256): Body rebuilt and refurbished as a service bus (as B31R) by TW Cawood & Son, Doncaster 7-12/44; fitted with a Leyland 8.6 litre diesel engine 10/45.

Disposals:

JB 5841 (262): Newbury & District Motor Services Ltd 262 4/50 (qv).
RX 6250 (230): GE Hedges {Reliance Motor Services}, Brightwalton (BE) 22 for spares 7/50.
RX 9706 (252): R Springfield, Taplow 10/51; converted to a mobile crane by 5/57; noted Potters Bar 1959.
RX 9707 (253): Unidentified operator / dealer 9/52.
RX 9709 (255): Newbury & District Motor Services Ltd 255 4/50 (qv).
RX 9710 (256): Unidentified operator / dealer 11/51.

1945

New Vehicles:

426	CRX 196	Bristol K6A	W1.034	Strachan		L27/28R	1/45	12/57
427	CRX 197	Bristol K6A	W1.070	Strachan		L27/28R	3/45	9/57
428	CRX 198	Bristol K6A	W1.120	Strachan		L27/28R	6/45	10/57
429	CRX 540	Bristol K6A	W1.150	Strachan		L27/28R	7/45	10/57
430	CRX 541	Bristol K6A	W2.001	Strachan		L27/28R	8/45	2/57
431	CRX 542	Bristol K6A	W2.005	Strachan		L27/28R	8/45	2/57
432	CRX 543	Bristol K6A	W2.006	Strachan		L27/28R	9/45	c6/57
433	CRX 544	Bristol K6A	W2.058	Strachan		L27/28R	10/45	12/57
434	CRX 545	Bristol K6A	W2.059	Strachan		L27/28R	11/45	2/57
437	CRX 546	Bedford OB	11097	Duple	41504	B26F	12/45	12/56
438	CRX 547	Bedford OB	12005	Duple	41523	B26F	12/45	6/57

Notes:

CRX 196 (426): Fitted with wooden slatted seats; fitted with 5 speed gearboxes 5/45; reseated to L27/24R with upholstered seats late 1946.

CRX 197 (427): Fitted with wooden slatted seats; fitted with 5 speed gearboxes 5/45; reseated to L27/24R with upholstered seats late 1946; fitted with a Gardner engine c1954; reverted to an AEC engine at an unknown date.

CRX 198 (428): Built to relaxed utility specifications with upholstered seats; reseated to L27/24R by 10/46.

CRX 540-545 (429-434): Built to relaxed utility specifications with upholstered seats.

CRX 546-547 (437-438): Purchased for the Marlow Bridge route on which there was a five ton weight limit, entering service 1/46.

Disposals:

CRX 196 (426): GH Groves (dealer), London SW19 Abbey 12/57.

CRX 197 (427): Reynolds News as a mobile showroom 9/57 to 10/60 at least; mobile showroom for Sunday Citizen by 9/63; publicity vehicle for 'International Co-operation Year', Nottingham 8/65; RG Searle (dealer), London E17 for scrap by 1/67.

CRX 198 (428): PD Sleeman (dealer), London W5 10/57; Kyle Stewart (contractor), London NW6 (XLN) by 2/58.

CRX 540 (429): AE Connorton Motors (dealer), London SW9 10/57; R Taylor & Son, London SE1 (LN) 1957; hired to EB Martell & B Goddard (Peoples League for the Defence of Freedom), London SW9 (XLN) during the London Bus Strike 5/58 to 6/58.

CRX 541-542 (430-431): AMCC (dealer), London E15 2/57.

CRX 543 (432): AE Connorton Motors (dealer), London SW9 c7/57; R Taylor & Son, London SE1 (LN) 1957; hired to EB Martell & B Goddard (Peoples League for the Defence of Freedom), London SW9 (XLN) during the London Bus Strike 5/58 to 6/58.

CRX 544 (433): FG Hobbs {Watling Street Motors} (dealer), St Albans 12/57; Dunning (dealer), Edgware 4/58.

CRX 545 (434): J Mattia (dealer), Nether Wallop 2/57; showman, Christchurch 8/57; noted Salisbury 10/59 and 10/60 and Titchfield 11/62.

CRX 546 (437): AMCC (dealer), London E15 12/56; Eileen Hurren Blind Fund & G Hitchen (Pearly King of the City of London) by 7/57.

CRX 547 (438): Converted by Thames Valley for use as an ambulance; some seats were removed, a space created for stretchers and a toilet fitted; Mrs G Legge (later Lady Lewisham), London W1 6/57; presented to Hendon Old Peoples' Welfare Committee (XLN); named 'Polly'; Queen Mary's Hospital, Carshalton (XSR) at an unknown date; mobile shop, Borehamwood 1/66.

Vehicles acquired from Plymouth City Transport (DN) 3/45:

435	DR 9636	Leyland TD2	283	Mumford		L24/24R	3/32	3/53
436	DR 9846	Leyland TD2	1265	Mumford		L24/24R	6/32	10/52

Previous histories:
DR 9636 (435): New to Plymouth City Transport 137.
DR 9846 (436): New to Plymouth City Transport 57.

Notes:
DR 9636 (435): Rebuilt and refurbished by Vincents 4/45-1/46; fitted with a Leyland diesel engine 5/45.
DR 9846 (436): Rebuilt and refurbished by Vincents 7/45-2/46; fitted with a Leyland diesel engine by 2/46.

Disposals:
DR 9636 (435): Crowe (showman}, March by 6/53.
DR 9846 (436): F Pelham (showman), Hurst by 4/53; noted London E11 4/58; D Reynolds (dealer), Takeley for scrap 9/59.

1946

New Vehicles:

439	CRX 548	Bristol K6A	W3.111	ECW	1111	L27/28R	5/46	3/64
440	CRX 549	Bristol K6A	W3.112	ECW	1110	L27/28R	5/46	12/63
441	CRX 550	Bristol K6A	W3.132	ECW	1127	L27/28R	6/46	1/66
442	CRX 551	Bristol K6A	W3.133	ECW	1126	L27/28R	6/46	10/62
443	DBL 151	Bristol K6A	62.005	ECW	1168	L27/28R	9/46	4/63
444	DBL 152	Bristol K6A	62.006	ECW	1172	L27/28R	9/46	10/62
445	DBL 153	Bristol K6A	62.007	ECW	1173	L27/28R	9/46	4/63
446	DBL 154	Bristol K6A	62.014	ECW	1180	L27/28R	10/46	2/65
447	DBL 155	Bristol K6A	62.015	ECW	1181	L27/28R	10/46	7/65
448	DBL 156	Bristol K6A	62.028	ECW	1186	L27/28R	11/46	5/65
449	DBL 157	Bristol K6A	62.041	ECW	1189	L27/28R	12/46	10/62
450	DBL 158	Bristol K6A	62.042	ECW	1190	L27/28R	12/46	10/65
451	DBL 159	Bristol K6A	62.044	ECW	1192	L27/28R	12/46	10/62
452	DBL 160	Bristol K6A	62.045	ECW	1193	L27/28R	12/46	1/66

Notes:
CRX 548 (439): Rebuilt by Thames Valley 4/62.
CRX 549 (440): Rebuilt by Thames Valley 10/61.
CRX 550 (441): Rebuilt by Thames Valley 11/61.
DBL 154 (446): Rebuilt by Thames Valley 1/62; withdrawn following a collision with a mobile crane 2/65.
DBL 155 (447): Rebuilt by Thames Valley 5/61.
DBL 156 (448): Rebuilt by Thames Valley 10/61.
DBL 158 (450): Rebuilt by Thames Valley 3/62.
DBL 160 (452): Rebuilt by Thames Valley 10/61.

Disposals:
CRX 548 (439): Liss & District Omnibus Co Ltd, Liss (HA) 3/64; P Jeffreys {Liss & District}, Grayshott (HA) 4/64; James (dealer), Hedge End 11/66.
CRX 549 (440): W Norths (PV) Ltd (dealer), Sherburn in Elmet 12/63; unidentified dealer for scrap 1/64.
CRX 550 (441): W Norths (PV) Ltd (dealer), Sherburn in Elmet 1/66; unidentified dealer for scrap 10/66.
CRX 551 (442): Passenger Vehicle Disposals Ltd (dealer), Dunchurch 10/62; Costain (contractor), London (X) 7/62.
DBL 151 (443): W Norths (PV) Ltd (dealer), Sherburn in Elmet 4/63; unidentified dealer for scrap 7/63.
DBL 152 (444): Passenger Vehicle Disposals Ltd (dealer), Dunchurch 10/62.
DBL 153 (445): W Norths (PV) Ltd (dealer), Sherburn in Elmet 4/63; unidentified dealer for scrap 1/64.
DBL 154 (446): Rossmore Bus Co Ltd, Sandbanks (DT) 3/65; Ward Jones, High Wycombe for preservation 1/72; Thames Valley & Great Western Omnibus Trust, Fifield for preservation 10/14.
DBL 155 (447): TD Alexander {Greyhound Luxury Coaches}, Sheffield (WR) 8/65.
DBL 156 (448): W Norths (PV) Ltd (dealer), Sherburn in Elmet 5/65; Parker (dealer), Bradford for scrap 9/66.
DBL 157 (449): Passenger Vehicle Disposals Ltd (dealer), Dunchurch 10/62.
DBL 158 (450): Unidentified operator / dealer 10/65.
DBL 159 (451): Passenger Vehicle Disposals Ltd (dealer), Dunchurch 10/62.
DBL 160 (452): W Norths (PV) Ltd (dealer), Sherburn in Elmet 1/66; Parker (dealer), Bradford for scrap 9/66.

Vehicle re-acquired from the War Department (GOV) c10/46:

244	RX 9541	Leyland TS4	383	Brush		C28F	2/32	c5/53

Previous history:

RX 9541 (244): New to Thames Valley Traction Co Ltd 244; War Department (GOV) 7/40; Ministry of Works and Buildings (GOV) (probably as a dealer) 7/45, from whom it was re-acquired.

Notes:

RX 9541 (244): Body rebuilt and refurbished as a service bus (as B31R) by TW Cawood & Son, Doncaster 11/46-7/47; fitted with a Leyland 8.6 litre diesel engine by 5/48; used as a temporary inspector's office at Maidenhead coach station c8/53.

Disposal:

RX 9541 (244): Unidentified operator / dealer (minus engine) 7/53.

Vehicle on hire from Eastern National Omnibus Co Ltd, Chelmsford (EX):

JVW 430	Bristol K5G	57.087	ECW	8062	L27/28R	2/44	3/46	3/46

Notes:

JVW 430: Was numbered 3885 in the Eastern National fleet and was on hire for evaluation.

1947

New Vehicles:

453	DBL 161	Bristol K6B	62.051	ECW	1196	L27/28R	1/47	2/63
454	DBL 162	Bristol K6B	62.057	ECW	1197	L27/28R	4/47	10/65
455	DBL 163	Bristol L6A	61.066	ECW	1262	DP35R	1/47	7/58
456	DBL 164	Bristol L6A	61.085	ECW	1271	DP35R	1/47	9/58
456	DBL 165	Bristol L6A	61.086	ECW	1272	DP35R	1/47	7/58
458	DBL 166	Bristol L6A	61.103	ECW	1279	DP35R	1/47	7/58
459	DBL 167	Bristol L6A	63.026	ECW	1331	DP35R	5/47	9/58
460	DMO 664	Bristol L6B	63.127	Windover	6663	C32F	9/47	3/67
462	DMO 666	Bristol L6B	63.178	Windover	6664	C32F	9/47	8/67
463	DMO 667	Bristol L6B	63.179	Windover	6665	C32F	10/47	3/67
465	DMO 669	Bristol L6B	65.018	Windover	6666	C32F	10/47	11/66
466	DMO 670	Bristol K6A	64.067	ECW	1725	L27/28R	11/47	10/62
467	DMO 671	Bristol K6A	64.068	ECW	1726	L27/28R	12/47	10/62

Notes:

DMO 664 (460): Reseated to C33F over the winter of 1951/2; withdrawn 7/57; its Windover body was removed and broken up 9/57; chassis rebuilt to 30ft long and fitted with a Gardner 5LW engine (to LL5G specification); rebodied ECW (10736) FB39F (one-man-operated); renumbered 794 6/58; re-entered service 8/58.

DMO 666 (462): Reseated to C33F over the winter of 1951/2; withdrawn 7/57; its Windover body was removed and broken up 9/57; chassis rebuilt to 30ft long and fitted with a Gardner 5LW engine (to LL5G specification); rebodied ECW (10733) FB39F (one-man-operated); renumbered 796 5/58; re-entered service 6/58.

DMO 667 (463): Reseated to C33F over the winter of 1951/2; withdrawn 7/57; its Windover body was removed and broken up 9/57; chassis rebuilt to 30ft long and fitted with a Gardner 5LW engine (to LL5G specification); rebodied ECW (10734) FB39F (one-man-operated); renumbered 797 5/58; re-entered service 8/58; was intended to be sold to United Welsh Services Ltd, Swansea (GG) 4/67, but the sale was not completed.

DMO 669 (465): Reseated to C33F over the winter of 1951/2; withdrawn 7/57; its Windover body was removed and broken up 9/57; chassis rebuilt to 30ft long and fitted with a Gardner 5LW engine (to LL5G specification); rebodied ECW (10737) FB39F (one-man-operated); renumbered 799 5/58; re-entered service 8/58.

Disposals:

DBL 161 (453): W Norths (PV) Ltd (dealer), Sherburn in Elmet 2/63; unidentified dealer for scrap 5/63.

DBL 162 (454): Unidentified operator / dealer 10/65.

DBL 163 (455): Passenger Vehicle Disposals Ltd (dealer), Dunchurch 7/58; TD Alexander {Greyhound Luxury Coaches}, Sheffield (WR) 70 11/58; withdrawn 11/64; unidentified dealer for scrap 1964/5.

DBL 164 (456): Fleet Car (Sales) Ltd (dealer), Dunchurch 1/59; unidentified owner, London 3/60; Gee, Walker & Slater (contractor), Derby (XDE) 62 6/61; unidentified owner, Middlesex 3/62; Jenkins Garage, Bridgend (GG) at an unknown date; last licensed 12/63.

DBL 165 (457): Passenger Vehicle Disposals Ltd (dealer), Dunchurch 7/58; unidentified dealer, Monmouth shire 12/58; Derek Crouch (Contractor) Ltd (contractor), Birtley (XDM) 4/59; moved to Eye (XSP) 9/59; last licensed 12/63; but still owned 5/65.

DBL 166 (458): Passenger Vehicle Disposals Ltd (dealer), Dunchurch 7/58; TD Alexander {Greyhound Luxury Coaches}, Sheffield (WR) 72 12/58; W Norths (PV) Ltd (dealer), Sherburn in Elmet 6/63; B Johnson (dealer), Goldthorpe for scrap 1963.

DBL 167 (459): Passenger Vehicle Disposals Ltd (dealer), Dunchurch 12/58; Derek Crouch (Contractor) Ltd (contractor), Birtley (XDM) 4/59; moved to Eye (XSP) 9/59; last licensed 12/63.

DMO 664 (794): G Percy Trentham (contractor), Pangbourne (XBE) 4/67; Mills {Wallington Commercials} (dealer), Fareham for scrap 4/70.

DMO 666 (796): W Norths (PV) Ltd (dealer), Sherburn in Elmet 9/67; Blanch-Lely, Crudwell (XWI) 9/67.

DMO 667 (797): G Percy Trentham (contractor), Pangbourne (XBE) 4/67.

DMO 669 (799): A Moore & Sons {Imperial Bus Service}, Windsor (BE) 12/66.

DMO 670 (466): Berkshire County Council, Reading and converted to a grit spreader (cut down to chassis and cab) 10/62; scrapped 3/69.

DMO 671 (467): Berkshire County Council, Reading and converted to a grit spreader (cut down to chassis and cab) 10/62; at Basingstoke minus engine and gearbox by 8/68; scrapped 3/69.

1948

New Vehicles:

461	DMO 665	Bristol L6B	63.149	Vincent		C32F	2/48	1/67
464	DMO 668	Bristol L6B	63.165	Vincent		C32F	3/48	11/66
468	DMO 672	Bristol K6B	64.155	ECW	1727	L27/28R	3/48	3/65
469	DMO 673	Bristol K6B	64.156	ECW	1728	L27/28R	3/48	10/66
470	DMO 674	Bristol K6B	64.195	ECW	1729	L27/28R	4/48	4/63
471	DMO 675	Bristol K6B	64.196	ECW	1730	L27/28R	4/48	5/66
472	DMO 676	Bristol L6A	65.198	ECW	2001	DP31R	1/48	7/58
473	DMO 677	Bristol L6A	65.199	ECW	2002	DP31R	1/48	4/59
474	DMO 678	Bristol L6A	67.020	ECW	2003	DP31R	1/48	7/58
475	DMO 679	Bristol L6A	67.021	ECW	2004	DP31R	1/48	4/59
476	DMO 680	Bristol L6A	67.063	ECW	2005	DP31R	1/48	7/58
477	DMO 681	Bristol L6A	67.064	ECW	2006	DP31R	1/48	7/58
478	DMO 682	Bristol L6A	67.079	ECW	2007	DP31R	3/48	9/58
479	DMO 683	Bristol L6A	67.080	ECW	2008	DP31R	3/48	9/58
480	DMO 684	Bristol L6A	67.081	ECW	2009	DP31R	3/48	9/58
481	DMO 685	Bristol L6A	67.093	ECW	2010	DP31R	3/48	7/58
482	DMO 686	Bristol L6A	67.094	ECW	2011	DP31R	3/48	7/58
483	DMO 687	Bristol L6A	67.109	ECW	2012	DP31R	3/48	7/58
484	DMO 688	Bristol L6A	67.110	ECW	2013	DP31R	3/48	7/58
485	DMO 689	Bristol L6A	67.163	ECW	2014	DP31R	4/48	7/58
486	DMO 690	Bristol L6A	67.164	ECW	2015	DP31R	5/48	7/58
487	EJB 209	Bristol L6B	67.188	Windover	6839	C32F	9/48	10/57
488	EJB 210	Bristol L6B	67.189	Windover	6840	C32F	9/48	10/57
489	EJB 211	Bristol L6B	67.190	Windover	6841	C32F	9/48	10/57
490	EJB 212	Bristol L6B	67.191	Windover	6842	C32F	9/48	10/57
491	EJB 213	Bristol L6B	67.192	Windover	6843	C32F	9/48	10/57
492	EJB 214	Bristol K6B	68.091	ECW	2643	L27/28R	11/48	12/63
493	EJB 215	Bristol K6B	68.092	ECW	2644	L27/28R	12/48	8/65
494	EJB 216	Bristol K6B	68.093	ECW	2645	L27/28R	12/48	8/65
495	EJB 217	Bristol K6B	68.094	ECW	2646	L27/28R	12/48	8/65
496	EJB 218	Bristol K6B	68.095	ECW	2647	L27/28R	12/48	7/65
499	EJB 221	Bristol K6B	68.164	ECW	2650	L27/28R	12/48	3/66

Notes:

DMO 665 (461): Reseated to C33F over the winter of 1951/2; withdrawn 7/57; its Vincents body was removed and broken up 9/57; chassis rebuilt to 30ft long and fitted with a Gardner 5LW engine (to LL5G specification); rebodied ECW (10732) FB39F (one-man-operated); renumbered 795 5/58; re-entered service 6/58.

DMO 668 (464): Reseated to C33F over the winter of 1951/2; withdrawn 7/57; its Vincents body was removed and broken up 9/57; chassis rebuilt to 30ft long and fitted with a Gardner 5LW engine(to LL5G specification); rebodied ECW (10735) FB39F (one-man-operated); renumbered 798 6/58; re-entered service 8/58.

DMO 673 (469): Rebuilt by Thames Valley 12/62; was intended to be sold to United Welsh Services Ltd, Swansea (GG) 11/66, but the sale was not completed.

DMO 675 (471): Collided with a low bridge 4/62; rebuilt and returned to service 10/62.

DMO 676-677 (472-473): Reseated to DP35R 12/50.

DMO 678-679 (474-475): Reseated to DP35R 11/50.

DMO 680 (476): Reseated to DP35R 10/50.

DMO 681 (477): Reseated to DP35R 11/50.

DMO 682-684 (478-480): Reseated to DP35R 12/50.

DMO 685 (481): Reseated to DP35R 11/50.

DMO 686-687 (482-483): Reseated to DP35R 12/50.

DMO 688-689 (484-485): Reseated to DP35R 11/50.

DMO 689 (485): Reseated to DP35R 11/50.

DMO 690 (486): Reseated to DP35R 10/50.

EJB 209-213 (487-491): Reseated to C33F 1951.

Disposals:

DMO 665 (795): A Moore & Sons {Imperial Bus Service}, Windsor (BE) 1/67; withdrawn 7/73.

DMO 668 (798): A Moore & Sons {Imperial Bus Service}, Windsor (BE) 12/66; Ward Jones (dealer), High Wycombe 4/74; Kingswood Middle School, High Wycombe (XBK) 9/74; CF Booth Ltd (dealer), Rotherham for scrap 8/78.

DMO 672 (468): TD Alexander {Greyhound Luxury Coaches}, Sheffield (WR) 6/65; working at Teesport 3/67; unidentified dealer for scrap 5/68.

DMO 673 (469): W Norths (PV) Ltd (dealer), Sherburn in Elmet for scrap 11/66.

DMO 674 (470): W Norths (PV) Ltd (dealer), Sherburn in Elmet 4/63; unidentified dealer for scrap 5/63.

DMO 675 (471): W Norths (PV) Ltd (dealer), Sherburn in Elmet 5/66; unidentified dealer for scrap 1/67.

DMO 676 (472): Passenger Vehicle Disposals Ltd (dealer), Dunchurch 7/58; Colbro Ltd (dealer), Rothwell 7/58; TD Alexander {Greyhound Luxury Coaches}, Sheffield (WR) 74 12/58; withdrawn 5/65; Dennis Higgs & Son Ltd (dealer), Monk Bretton for scrap 5/65.

DMO 677 (473): Passenger Vehicle Disposals Ltd (dealer), Dunchurch 6/59; AGH Jordan, Blaenavon (MH) 6/59; withdrawn (engine removed) by 5/62 and scrapped.

DMO 678 (474): Passenger Vehicle Disposals Ltd (dealer), Dunchurch 7/58; Colbro Ltd (dealer), Rothwell 7/58; TD Alexander {Greyhound Luxury Coaches}, Sheffield (WR) 68 11/58; withdrawn 4/65.

DMO 679 (475): Passenger Vehicle Disposals Ltd (dealer), Dunchurch 6/59; Unidentified owner, London 11/59; Gee, Walker & Slater (contractor), Derby (XDE) by 3/60; moved to Middlesex 10/62; Hardwick, Driffield (EY) at an unknown date; FC Construction Co Ltd, Derby (XDE) 8/64; last licensed 7/65.

DMO 680 (476): Passenger Vehicle Disposals Ltd (dealer), Dunchurch 7/58; Colbro Ltd (dealer), Rothwell 7/58; TD Alexander {Greyhound Luxury Coaches}, Sheffield (WR) 67 11/58; withdrawn 6/65; Dennis Higgs & Son Ltd (dealer), Monk Bretton for scrap 6/65.

DMO 681 (477): Passenger Vehicle Disposals Ltd (dealer), Dunchurch 7/58; Colbro Ltd (dealer), Rothwell 7/58; TD Alexander {Greyhound Luxury Coaches}, Sheffield (WR) 71 12/58; withdrawn 6/65; Dennis Higgs & Son Ltd (dealer), Monk Bretton for scrap 6/65.

DMO 682 (478): Passenger Vehicle Disposals Ltd (dealer), Dunchurch 12/58; AGH Jordan, Blaenavon (MH) 2/59; last licensed 10/61; (Minoley?) (dealer), Barnsley for scrap by 7/63.

DMO 683 (479): Passenger Vehicle Disposals Ltd (dealer), Dunchurch 12/58; Derek Crouch (Contractor) Ltd (contractor), Birtley (XDM) 4/59; moved to Eye (SP) 9/59; last licensed 11/63.

DMO 684 (480): Fleet Car (Sales) Ltd (dealer), Dunchurch 1/59; AGH Jordan, Blaenavon (MH) 2/59; last licensed 12/61; still owned (engine removed) by 5/62 and scrapped.

DMO 685 (481): Passenger Vehicle Disposals Ltd (dealer), Dunchurch 7/58; Colbro Ltd (dealer), Rothwell 7/58; G Blenkinsopp {Scarlet Band Motor Services}, West Cornforth (DM) 41 8/58; F Cowley (dealer), Salford 3/60; Simon Carves (contractor), Stockport (XCH) 6/60; last licensed 12/61; BJ Donaghue (dealer), Shaw for scrap 1962.

DMO 686 (482): Passenger Vehicle Disposals Ltd (dealer), Dunchurch 7/58; Colbro Ltd (dealer), Rothwell 7/58; TD Alexander {Greyhound Luxury Coaches}, Sheffield (WR) 60 9/58; withdrawn 10/64.

DMO 687 (483): Passenger Vehicle Disposals Ltd (dealer), Dunchurch 7/58; Colbro Ltd (dealer), Rothwell 7/58; TD Alexander {Greyhound Luxury Coaches}, Sheffield (WR) 59 9/58; unidentified operator, Llanwern (MH) 6/61 to 5/62; C Davies, Pontlottyn (GG) 11/62; last licensed 7/63.

DMO 688 (484): Passenger Vehicle Disposals Ltd (dealer), Dunchurch 7/58; Colbro Ltd (dealer), Rothwell 7/58; TD Alexander {Greyhound Luxury Coaches}, Sheffield (WR) 58 9/58; withdrawn 2/65; last licensed 1/66.

DMO 689 (485): Passenger Vehicle Disposals Ltd (dealer), Dunchurch 7/58; Colbro Ltd (dealer), Rothwell 7/58; TD Alexander {Greyhound Luxury Coaches}, Sheffield (WR) 56 9/58; last licensed 6/66.

DMO 690 (486): Passenger Vehicle Disposals Ltd (dealer), Dunchurch 7/58; Colbro Ltd (dealer), Rothwell 7/58; TD Alexander {Greyhound Luxury Coaches}, Sheffield (WR) 57 9/58; last licensed 12/59.

EJB 209 (487): AE Connorton Motors (dealer), London SW9 10/57; S Gaskin {Cabin Coaches}, Hayes (MX) 10/57; Young's Coach & Bus Co Ltd, Hornchurch (EX) 3/58; Regional & Finance Securities Ltd, London SW1 at an unknown date; last licensed 6/59; reportedly stolen 10/59.

EJB 210 (488): AE Connorton Motors (dealer), London SW9 10/57; WL Thurgood (Coachbuilders) Ltd (dealer), Ware 10/57; Young's International Cars Ltd, Loughton (EX) 1/58 and fitted with a Gardner 5LW engine; last licensed 12/58.

EJB 211 (489): AE Connorton Motors (dealer), London SW9 10/57; HF Cheek {Elms Coaches}, Kenton (MX) 10/57; last licensed 8/61; disposed of via Goddard, Davison & Smith (auctioneers), Putney Bridge by 6/62; Eastbourne Coachways Ltd, Eastbourne (ES) (not operated) by 6/62; withdrawn by 6/62.

EJB 212 (490): AE Connorton Motors (dealer), London SW9 10/57; R Taylor (Coaches) Ltd, London SE1 9/57; last licensed 6/60; unidentified dealer 1961.

EJB 213 (491): AE Connorton Motors (dealer), London SW9 10/57; WL Thurgood (Coachbuilders) Ltd (dealer), Ware 10/57; Young's International Cars Ltd, Loughton (EX) 2/58 and fitted with a Gardner 5LW engine; last licensed 6/59; disposed of via Goddard, Davison & Smith (auctioneers), Putney Bridge 9/59.

EJB 214 (492): W Norths (PV) Ltd (dealer), Sherburn in Elmet 12/63; unidentified dealer for scrap 1/64.

EJB 215-217 (493-495): Unidentified operators / dealers 8/65.

EJB 218 (496): TD Alexander {Greyhound Luxury Coaches}, Sheffield (WR) 8/65; W Norths (PV) Ltd (dealer), Sherburn in Elmet by 6/66.

EJB 221 (499): W Norths (PV) Ltd (dealer), Sherburn in Elmet 3/66; Parker (dealer), Bradford for scrap by 8/66.

Vehicle re-acquired from the War Department (GOV) 8/48:

264	JB 5843	Leyland TS7	7128	Duple		5013	C32F	4/35	4/50

Previous history:
JB 5843 (264): New to Thames Valley Traction Co Ltd 264; War Department (GOV) 7/40; discovered at a sale of former War Department vehicles, from where it was re-acquired.

Notes:
JB 5843 (264): Body rebuilt and refurbished by Lambourn Garages, Lambourn 12/48-4/49; fitted with a diesel engine by 4/49.

Disposal:
JB 5843 (264): Newbury & District Motor Services Ltd 264 4/50 (qv).

1949

New Vehicles:

497	EJB 219	Bristol K6B	68.162	ECW	2648	L27/28R	1/49	7/66
498	EJB 220	Bristol K6B	68.163	ECW	2649	L27/28R	1/49	7/65
500	EJB 222	Bristol K6B	68.165	ECW	2651	L27/28R	1/49	7/65
501	EJB 223	Bristol K6B	68.166	ECW	2652	L27/28R	1/49	12/63
502	EJB 224	Bristol K6B	72.004	ECW	2653	L27/28R	1/49	7/65
503	EJB 225	Bristol K6B	72.005	ECW	2654	L27/28R	1/49	7/65
504	EJB 226	Bristol K6B	72.006	ECW	2655	L27/28R	1/49	7/66
505	EJB 227	Bristol K6B	72.007	ECW	2656	L27/28R	1/49	8/66
506	EJB 228	Bristol K6B	72.008	ECW	2657	L27/28R	1/49	8/66
507	EJB 229	Bristol K6B	72.092	ECW	2658	L27/28R	7/49	11/66
508	EJB 230	Bristol K6B	72.093	ECW	2659	L27/28R	7/49	8/66
509	EJB 231	Bristol K6B	72.094	ECW	2660	L27/28R	7/49	3/66
510	EJB 232	Bedford OB	106266	Beadle	C155	DP26F	6/49	6/57
511	EJB 233	Bedford OB	106343	Beadle	C156	DP26F	6/49	6/57
512	EJB 234	Bedford OB	103848	Beadle	C153	DP26F	5/49	6/57
513	EJB 235	Bristol K6B	74.092	ECW	2661	L27/28R	7/49	1/67
514	EJB 236	Bristol K6B	74.093	ECW	2662	L27/28R	8/49	7/65
515	EJB 237	Bristol K6B	74.116	ECW	2663	L27/28R	8/49	2/66
516	EJB 238	Bristol K6B	74.117	ECW	2665	L27/28R	8/49	8/66
517	EJB 239	Bristol K6B	74.118	ECW	2664	L27/28R	8/49	7/66

518	EJB 240	Bristol K6B	74.161	ECW	2666	L27/28R	8/49	7/66
519	EJB 241	Bristol K6B	74.162	ECW	2667	L27/28R	8/49	7/66
520	EJB 242	Bedford OB	104017	Beadle	C154	DP26F	5/49	8/58
521	FBL 23	Bristol L6B	73.037	ECW	4095	B35R	10/49	4/59
522	FBL 24	Bristol L6B	73.036	ECW	4096	B35R	11/49	4/59
523	FBL 25	Bristol L6B	73.058	ECW	4097	B35R	11/49	4/59
524	FBL 26	Bristol K6B	76.166	ECW	3632	L27/28R	11/49	10/66
525	FBL 27	Bristol K6B	76.167	ECW	3633	L27/28R	12/49	7/66
534	FMO 9	Bristol L6B	73.059	ECW	4098	B35R	12/49	3/60

Notes:

EJB 232-234 (510-512): Purchased for the Marlow Bridge route on which there was a five ton weight limit, but delays in the delivery of new coaches saw these used initially on private hires and excursions until 10/50; they were fitted with luggage lockers and more luxurious seats; reseated to B27F at an unknown date.

EJB 242 (520): Purchased for the Marlow Bridge route; fitted with luggage lockers and more luxurious seats; reseated to B27F at an unknown date; equipped for one-man-operation 6/57.

Disposals:

EJB 219 (497): W Norths (PV) Ltd (dealer), Sherburn in Elmet for scrap 11/66.

EJB 220 (498): TD Alexander {Greyhound Luxury Coaches}, Sheffield (WR) 8/65; W Norths (PV) Ltd (dealer), Sherburn in Elmet by 7/66.

EJB 222 (500): W Norths (PV) Ltd (dealer), Sherburn in Elmet 8/66; unidentified dealer for scrap 12/66.

EJB 223 (501): W Norths (PV) Ltd (dealer), Sherburn in Elmet 12/63; unidentified dealer for scrap 1/64.

EJB 224 (502): W Norths (PV) Ltd (dealer), Sherburn in Elmet 3/66; Parker (dealer), Bradford for scrap by 8/66.

EJB 225 (503): W Norths (PV) Ltd (dealer), Sherburn in Elmet 9/65.

EJB 226 (504): W Norths (PV) Ltd (dealer), Sherburn in Elmet for scrap 8/66.

EJB 227 (505): W Norths (PV) Ltd (dealer), Sherburn in Elmet 3/66; Parker (dealer), Bradford for scrap by 8/66.

EJB 228 (506): W Norths (PV) Ltd (dealer), Sherburn in Elmet for scrap 11/66.

EJB 229-230 (507-508): W Norths (PV) Ltd (dealer), Sherburn in Elmet for scrap 11/66.

EJB 231 (509): W Norths (PV) Ltd (dealer), Sherburn in Elmet 3/66; Parker (dealer), Bradford for scrap by 8/66.

EJB 232 (510): AMCC (dealer), London E15 7/57; Ellinas, Nicosia (O-CY) registered TAH 911 9/57; Georghiou, Aglandjia (O-CY) 4/62; Kaimakli Bus Co, Kaimakli (O-CY) 7/70; rebodied BAK FB39F 7/70; Nicosia Buses Ltd, Nicosia (O-CY) 1/71; withdrawn 8/83.

EJB 233 (511): AMCC (dealer), London E15 7/57; Georghiou, Psimolophou (O-CY) registered TAH 310 8/57; Kamenos, Tembria (O-CY) 12/62; Kourris, Psimolophou (O-CY) 11/64; Iordanous, Lythrodhonda (O-CY) 11/70, rebodied Arsiotis FB36F 7/71, withdrawn 3/80.

EJB 234 (512): AMCC (dealer), London E15 7/57; Ellinas, Nicosia (O-CY) 8/57; Koumbaris, Limnia (O-CY) registered TAH 666 8/57; rebodied FB31F 4/65; Limnia Transport Co Ltd, Limnia (O-CY) 6/67; Yiallouros, Limnia (O-CY) 3/69; Colocassides, Nicosia (O-CY) 9/72; Themistocleous, Avgorou (O-CY) 4/73; Apollo 11 Bus Co Ltd, Larnaca (O-CY) 11/76; Karcanis, Kandou (O-CY) 8/77; Ioannou, Potamiou (O-CY) 10/78; Panayi, Kato, Polemidia (O-CY) (not operated) 3/80.

EJB 235 (513): W Norths (PV) Ltd (dealer), Sherburn in Elmet 3/67; B Johnson (dealer), South Elmsall for scrap 4/67.

EJB 236 (514): W Norths (PV) Ltd (dealer), Sherburn in Elmet 1/67; B Johnson (dealer), South Elmsall for scrap 4/67.

EJB 237 (515): W Norths (PV) Ltd (dealer), Sherburn in Elmet 3/66; Parker (dealer), Bradford for scrap by 8/66.

EJB 238 (516): W Griffiths, Earley, Reading (use unknown) 9/66; Bird's Commercial Metals Ltd (dealer), Stratford-on-Avon 7/67.

EJB 239 (517): W Norths (PV) Ltd (dealer), Sherburn in Elmet for scrap 11/66.

EJB 240 (518): W Norths (PV) Ltd (dealer), Sherburn in Elmet 9/66; unidentified dealer for scrap 11/66.

EJB 241 (519): Hounslow Evangelical Church, Isleworth (XLN) 8/66; Come & See Club, Hounslow (XLN) 1/70.

EJB 242 (520): Glacier Foods Ltd, Maidenhead (XBE) 8/58; unidentified owner, High Wycombe as a mobile shop 3/61.

FBL 23 (521): Fleet Car Sales (dealer), Dunchurch 10/59; C Davies, Pontlottyn (GG) 5/60; WA Way & Sons (dealer), Cardiff 10/63; Jones (dealer), Cardiff Docks for scrap by 4/64.

FBL 24 (522): Fleet Car Sales (dealer), Dunchurch 10/59; T Johnsey, Newport (MH) 2/60; RR Adams {Domino Coaches}, Fairwater (GG) 3/62; last licensed 5/62; parked on waste land at Llanwern 9/62.

FBL 25 (523): Fleet Car Sales (dealer), Dunchurch 10/59; AGH Jordan, Blaenavon (MH) 1/60; last licensed
     9/62.
FBL 26 (524): W Norths (PV) Ltd (dealer), Sherburn in Elmet for scrap 11/66.
FBL 27 (525): W Norths (PV) Ltd (dealer), Sherburn in Elmet for scrap 8/66.
FMO   9 (534): United Welsh Omnibus Co Ltd, Swansea (GG) 534 3/60; withdrawn 1965; Sir Lindsay
     Parkinson (contractor), London SW15 (X) 6/66 to 1/68 at least; unidentified owner, Birkenhead
     11/72.

1950

New Vehicles:

526	FBL 28	Bristol K6B	78.050	ECW	3634	L27/28R	1/50	1/67
527	FBL 29	Bristol K6B	78.051	ECW	3635	L27/28R	2/50	1/67
528	FBL 30	Bristol K6B	78.052	ECW	3636	L27/28R	2/50	1/67
529	FBL 31	Bristol K6B	78.105	ECW	3637	L27/28R	3/50	3/67
530	FBL 32	Bristol K6B	78.106	ECW	3638	L27/28R	4/50	11/66
531	FBL 33	Bristol K6B	78.126	ECW	3639	L27/28R	4/50	3/67
532	FMO 7	Bristol K6B	78.127	ECW	3640	L27/28R	4/50	5/67
533	FMO 8	Bristol K6B	78.128	ECW	3641	L27/28R	4/50	5/67
535	FMO 10	Bristol L6B	73.092	ECW	4099	B35R	1/50	3/60
536	FMO 11	Bristol L6B	73.093	ECW	4100	B35R	2/50	3/60
537	FMO 12	Bristol L6B	73.113	ECW	4102	B35R	3/50	3/60
538	FMO 13	Bristol L6B	79.027	ECW	4101	B35R	3/50	5/60
539	FMO 14	Bristol L6B	79.057	ECW	4103	B35R	3/50	9/60
540	FMO 15	Bristol L6B	73.118	ECW	4105	B35R	5/50	5/60
541	FMO 16	Bristol L6B	73.119	ECW	4104	B35R	5/50	9/60
542	FMO 17	Bristol L6B	79.147	ECW	4106	B35R	5/50	5/60
543	FMO 18	Bristol L6B	79.148	ECW	4107	B35R	5/50	3/60
544	FMO 19	Bristol L6B	79.149	ECW	4108	B35R	6/50	3/60
545	FMO 20	Bristol L6B	79.058	Windover	6844	C33F	3/50	5/60
546	FMO 21	Bristol L6B	79.089	Windover	6845	C33F	3/50	7/68
547	FMO 22	Bristol L6B	79.090	Windover	6846	C33F	3/50	6/68
548	FMO 23	Bristol L6B	79.116	Windover	6857	C33F	3/50	1/55
549	FMO 24	Bristol L6B	79.117	Windover	6858	C33F	3/50	3/68
550	FMO 25	Bristol L6B	81.068	Windover	6906	C33F	6/50	7/60
551	FMO 26	Bristol L6B	81.069	Windover	6907	C33F	6/50	5/60
552	FMO 934	Bristol L6B	81.070	Windover	6908	C33F	6/50	3/60
553	FMO 935	Bristol L6B	81.071	Windover	6909	C33F	7/50	1/55
554	FMO 936	Bristol L6B	81.072	Windover	6910	C33F	7/50	5/60
555	FMO 937	Bristol L6B	81.120	Windover	6911	C33F	7/50	5/60
556	FMO 938	Bristol LL6B	81.121	ECW	4711	B39R	8/50	9/60
557	FMO 939	Bristol LL6B	81.122	ECW	4712	B39R	8/50	9/60
558	FMO 940	Bristol LL6B	81.123	ECW	4713	B39R	8/50	9/60
559	FMO 941	Bristol LL6B	81.124	ECW	4714	B39R	8/50	3/67
560	FMO 942	Bristol LL6B	83.093	ECW	4715	B39R	11/50	4/68
561	FMO 943	Bristol LL6B	83.094	ECW	4716	B39R	11/50	9/60
562	FMO 944	Bristol LL6B	83.095	ECW	4717	B39R	11/50	12/60
563	FMO 945	Bristol LL6B	83.096	ECW	4718	B39R	11/50	12/60
564	FMO 946	Bristol LL6B	83.097	ECW	4719	B39R	11/50	5/67
565	FMO 947	Bristol LL6B	83.128	ECW	4720	B39R	12/50	8/68
566	FMO 948	Bristol LL6B	83.129	ECW	4721	B39R	12/50	6/68
567	FMO 949	Bristol LL6B	83.130	ECW	4722	B39R	12/50	8/68
568	FMO 950	Bristol LL6B	83.173	ECW	4723	B39R	12/50	8/68
569	FMO 951	Bristol LL6B	83.174	ECW	4724	B39R	12/50	5/68
586	FMO 968	Bristol KS6B	80.085	ECW	4367	L27/28R	8/50	4/68
587	FMO 969	Bristol KS6B	80.086	ECW	4368	L27/28R	9/50	9/68
588	FMO 970	Bristol KS6B	80.087	ECW	4369	L27/28R	9/50	7/68
589	FMO 971	Bristol KS6B	82.009	ECW	4370	L27/28R	11/50	5/68
590	FMO 972	Bristol KS6B	82.012	ECW	4371	L27/28R	11/50	8/68
591	FMO 973	Bristol KS6B	82.013	ECW	4372	L27/28R	11/50	2/68
592	FMO 974	Bristol KS6B	82.014	ECW	4373	L27/28R	11/50	8/68
593	FMO 975	Bristol KS6B	82.021	ECW	4374	L27/28R	11/50	8/68
594	FMO 976	Bristol KS6B	82.022	ECW	4375	L27/28R	11/50	10/68

601	FMO 983	Bristol KSW6B	80.117	ECW	4382	L27/28R	12/50	4/69
602	FMO 984	Bristol KSW6B	80.118	ECW	4383	L27/28R	12/50	9/69
603	FMO 985	Bristol KSW6B	80.119	ECW	4384	L27/28R	12/50	10/68
604	FRX 313	Bedford OB	139390	Duple	56127	C29F	5/50	12/56
605	FRX 314	Bedford OB	140822	Duple	56128	C29F	5/50	12/56
606	FRX 315	Bedford OB	142021	Duple	56129	C29F	5/50	12/56

Notes:

FMO 938-951 (556-569) were the first 30ft long single-deck vehicles new to Thames Valley.

FMO 968-976 (586-594) were the first 27ft long double-deck vehicles new to Thames Valley.

FMO 983-985 (601-603) were the first 8ft wide double-deck vehicles new to Thames Valley (these were distinguished by white steering wheels as certain routes had restrictions on their use).

FMO 21 (546): Withdrawn 7/58; its Windover body was removed and broken up 10/58; chassis rebuilt to 30ft long and fitted with a Gardner 5LW engine (to LL5G specification); rebodied ECW (11402) FB39F (one-man-operated); renumbered 817 2/59; re-entered service 4/59.

FMO 22 (547): Withdrawn 8/58; its Windover body was removed and broken up 10/58; chassis rebuilt to 30ft long and fitted with a Gardner 5LW engine (to LL5G specification); rebodied ECW (11400) FB39F (one-man-operated); renumbered 818 2/59; re-entered service 4/59.

FMO 24 (549): Withdrawn 8/58; its Windover body was removed and broken up 10/58; chassis rebuilt to 30ft long and fitted with a Gardner 5LW engine (to LL5G specification); rebodied ECW (11401) FB39F (one-man-operated); renumbered 820 2/59; re-entered service 4/59.

FMO 25 (550): Fitted out as a mobile travelling enquiry and booking office, decorated with red, white and blue lamps 11/50; toured the company's area in connection with the Festival of Britain until c3/51.

FMO 946 (564): Rebuilt to B39F and equipped for one man operation by ECW 8/58-1/59.

FMO 947 (565): Rebuilt to B39F and equipped for one man operation by ECW 8/58-1/59; used as a towing vehicle from c6/60.

FMO 948-950 (566-568): Rebuilt to B39F and equipped for one man operation by ECW 8/58-1/59.

FMO 969 (587): Decapitated in a low bridge accident in Reading 2/56.

FRX 313-315 (604-606): Fitted with petrol engines and incorrectly carried fleet numbers TV604-TV606 when new.

Disposals:

FBL 28 (526): DL Morgan, Swaythling, Southampton (dealer?) 2/67; Sidford Car Sales (dealer), Southampton 3/67; Southampton University Shelter Group (XHA) (driven to Turkey and back on a student holiday) 1967; noted Sheffield 7/68, Cheshire 5/69 and Southampton 11/69; T Jefferis (dealer), Hedge End 7/70; Mills {Wallington Commercials} (dealer), Fareham for scrap 9/70.

FBL 29-30 (527-528): W Norths (PV) Ltd (dealer), Sherburn in Elmet 3/67; B Johnson (dealer), South Elmsall for scrap 4/67.

FBL 31 (529): S Englander & Sons Ltd, Weybridge (XSR) as a mobile upholstery showroom 5/67 to 4/70 at least.

FBL 32 (530): W Norths (PV) Ltd (dealer), Sherburn in Elmet for scrap 11/66.

FBL 33 (531): W Norths (PV) Ltd (dealer), Sherburn in Elmet 3/67; B Johnson (dealer), South Elmsall for scrap 4/67.

FMO 7 (532): Don's Coaches (Hale Bros) Ltd, Bishops Stortford (HT) 10/67.

FMO 8 (533): Elm Park Coaches Ltd, Romford (LN) 9/67; withdrawn by 6/71.

FMO 10 (535): United Welsh Omnibus Co Ltd, Swansea (GG) 535 3/60; withdrawn 1965; Commando Industrial Cleaners, Warwick (XWK), Sparkhill (XWK) and Oxford (XOX) 8/65; withdrawn 1972.

FMO 11 (536): United Welsh Omnibus Co Ltd, Swansea (GG) 536 3/60; withdrawn 1965; Sir Lindsay Parkinson (contractor), London SW15 (X) 7/66.

FMO 12 (537): United Welsh Omnibus Co Ltd, Swansea (GG) 537 3/60; withdrawn 1965; WS Edwards & Son (Builders) Ltd (contractor), Port Talbot (XGG) 9/65; unidentified owner, Huntingdonshire & Peterborough 11/67.

FMO 13 (538): United Welsh Omnibus Co Ltd, Swansea (GG) 538 5/60; withdrawn 1965; Thomas & James Garage, Felinfoel (CR) (not operated) 7/65; unidentified owner (Commando Industrial Cleaners?), Warwick (XWK) 8/65.

FMO 14 (539): United Welsh Omnibus Co Ltd, Swansea (GG) 539 9/60; withdrawn 1965; unidentified owner, Huntingdonshire & Peterborough 7/66.

FMO 15 (540): United Welsh Omnibus Co Ltd, Swansea (GG) 540 5/60; withdrawn 1965; unidentified owner, Huntingdonshire & Peterborough 7/66.

FMO 16 (541): United Welsh Omnibus Co Ltd, Swansea (GG) 541 9/60; withdrawn 1965; T Williams {Tudor Williams Bros / Pioneer}, Laugharne (CR) 2/66; Baker, Saundersfoot (PE or XPE?) by 1/74; West of England Transport Collection, Winkleigh for preservation spares 10/76; CF Booth Ltd (dealer), Rotherham for scrap 7/79.

FMO 17 (542): United Welsh Omnibus Co Ltd, Swansea (GG) 542 5/60; withdrawn 1965; Sir Lindsay Parkinson (contractor), London SW15 (X) SLP4550 2/66.

FMO 18 (543): United Welsh Omnibus Co Ltd, Swansea (GG) 543 3/60; withdrawn 1965; Sir Lindsay Parkinson (contractor), London SW15 (X) 2/66.

FMO 19 (544): United Welsh Omnibus Co Ltd, Swansea (GG) 544 3/60; withdrawn 1965; WS Edwards & Son (Builders) Ltd (contractor), Port Talbot (XGG) 7/65; scrapped 9/65.

FMO 20 (545): South Midland Motor Services Ltd 545 5/60 (qv).

FMO 21 (817): Elm Park Coaches Ltd, Romford (LN) 7/68; Continental Pioneer School Holidays Ltd, Richmond (SR) 8/68; numbered 7 4/70; withdrawn 3/73.

FMO 22 (818): Rossmore Bus Co Ltd, Sandbanks (DT) 6/68; withdrawn by 9/72.

FMO 23 (548): South Midland Motor Services Ltd 548 1/55 (qv).

FMO 24 (820): FG Wilder & Son Ltd {Golden Miller}, Feltham (LN) 3/68; W Norths (PV) Ltd (dealer), Sherburn in Elmet 12/71; Andrews, Leeds (XWR) 4/72; W Norths (PV) Ltd (dealer), Sherburn in Elmet 3/75.

FMO 25 (550): South Midland Motor Services Ltd 550 7/60 (qv).

FMO 26 (551): South Midland Motor Services Ltd 551 5/60 (qv).

FMO 934 (552): South Midland Motor Services Ltd 552 3/60 (qv).

FMO 935 (553): South Midland Motor Services Ltd 553 1/55 (qv).

FMO 936-937 (554-555): South Midland Motor Services Ltd 554-555 5/60 (qv).

FMO 938 (556): United Welsh Omnibus Co Ltd, Swansea (GG) 556 9/60; withdrawn 1966; Precelley Motors, Clynderwen (CR) 10/66; AT Jones {Jones Motor Services}, Login (PE) 9/68; Ward, Bishop Auckland for preservation c5/78; Ward Jones, High Wycombe for preservation by 9/82; JA Belson, Partridge Green for preservation 1983; I Yates, Mansfield for preservation 1-2/91; R Pratt, Clifton-on-Teme for preservation by 1/93; G Tyler, Warndon for preservation by 4/97; still owned 3/12.

FMO 939 (557): United Welsh Omnibus Co Ltd, Swansea (GG) 557 12/60; withdrawn 1965; T Williams {Tudor Williams Bros / Pioneer}, Laugharne (CR) 12/65; unidentified dealer, Cinderford by 9/71.

FMO 940 (558): United Welsh Omnibus Co Ltd, Swansea (GG) 558 9/60; withdrawn 1966.

FMO 941 (559): W Norths (PV) Ltd (dealer), Sherburn in Elmet 3/67; JJ Elms, Blaenavon (MH) 5/67; unidentified owner, Carmarthenshire 5/67.

FMO 942 (560): Elm Park Coaches Ltd, Romford (LN) 5/68; Cedric Garages (Wivenhoe) Ltd, Wivenhoe (EX) 12/69; Bridge Motors (dealer), Cattawade for scrap 11/72.

FMO 943 (561): United Welsh Omnibus Co Ltd, Swansea (GG) 561 9/60; withdrawn 1965; W Norths (PV) Ltd (dealer), Sherburn in Elmet by 6/66; Derek Crouch (Contractor) Ltd (contractor), Birtley (XDM) 11/66; noted Huntingdonshire & Peterborough 11/66.

FMO 944 (562): United Welsh Omnibus Co Ltd, Swansea (GG) 562 12/60; withdrawn 1965; W Norths (PV) Ltd (dealer), Sherburn in Elmet by 6/66; Leggatt (contractor), noted Garelochhead 6/66 and Huntingdonshire & Peterborough 7/66; Derek Crouch (Contractor) Ltd (contractor), Billingham (XDM) 7/67; W Norths (PV) Ltd (dealer), Sherburn in Elmet by 2/71.

FMO 945 (563): United Welsh Omnibus Co Ltd, Swansea (GG) 556 12/60; withdrawn 1965; W Norths (PV) Ltd (dealer), Sherburn in Elmet by 6/66; Dew (contractor), Oldham (XLA) 8/66 to 7/71; Lister (PVS) Bolton Ltd (dealer), Bolton 9/72; D Rollinson (Bus Centre) Ltd (dealer), Carlton 11/72.

FMO 946 (564): Elm Park Coaches Ltd, Romford (LN) 9/67; Continental Pioneer School Holidays Ltd, Richmond (SR) 4/68; numbered 6 (not carried) 4/70; licensed 5/72.

FMO 947 (565): TD Alexander {Greyhound Luxury Coaches}, Arbroath (AS) 8/68; withdrawn 4/70; unidentified dealer, Barnsley for scrap 1971.

FMO 948 (566): Drake & Scull Engineering Ltd, Croydon (XSR) 6/68.

FMO 949 (567): TD Alexander {Greyhound Luxury Coaches}, Sheffield (WR) 8/68; TD Alexander {Greyhound Luxury Coaches}, Arbroath (AS) 10/68; withdrawn by 4/71; unidentified dealer, Barnsley 1971; W Ritchie, Glasgow for preservation by 6/95; A Hopkins, Kirk Sandall for preservation 11/95; D Hoare, Chepstow for preservation by 10/96; Rexquote Ltd, Bishops Lydeard (SO) for preservation by 9/97; moved to Norton Fitzwarren (SO) by 6/02; Quantock Motor Services Ltd, Wiveliscombe (SO) for preservation 3/04; R Rampton, Reading for preservation by 9/04.

FMO 950 (568): TD Alexander {Greyhound Luxury Coaches}, Arbroath (AS) 8/68; unidentified dealer, Barnsley for scrap 1971.

FMO 951 (569): Rev B Green, British Council of Protestant Christian Church, London SW6 (XLN) 9/68; unidentified owner, Co Down, Northern Ireland 8/69.

FMO 968 (586): Rev B Green, British Council of Protestant Christian Church, London SW6 (XLN) 4/68.

FMO 969 (587): TD Alexander {Greyhound Luxury Coaches}, Arbroath (AS) 9/68; withdrawn 1969; Hartwood Finance Ltd (dealer), Birdwell for scrap 2/70.

FMO 970 (588): Rev B Green, British Council of Protestant Christian Church, London SW6 (XLN) 7/68.

FMO 971 (589): Winlon Autos Ltd, Harrow (LN) 6/68.

FMO 972 (590): TD Alexander {Greyhound Luxury Coaches}, Arbroath (AS) 8/68; withdrawn 1969; Hartwood Finance Ltd (dealer), Birdwell for scrap 2/70.

FMO 973 (591): Twickenham Baptist Church, Twickenham (XLN) 2/68; Continental Pioneer School Holidays Ltd, Richmond (SR) 9/73; Continental Pioneer Ltd, Richmond (SR) 4/74; Chessington Play Group, Chessington (XLN) as a play bus 7/74; burnt out by vandals 8/74.

FMO 974 (592): TD Alexander {Greyhound Luxury Coaches}, Arbroath (AS) 8/68; TD Alexander {Greyhound Luxury Coaches}, Sheffield (WR) 1/70; TD Alexander {Greyhound Luxury Coaches}, Arbroath (AS) 4/71.

FMO 975 (593): Rev B Green, British Council of Protestant Christian Churches, London SW6 (XLN) 8/68; Coopers Seafood House, Pittston, Pennsylvania (O-USA) by 1999; Greaves, Guilford, Connecticut (O-USA) for preservation by 12/08.

FMO 976 (594): Elm Park Coaches Ltd, Romford (LN) 10/68; British Radio Corporation, London WC2 (XLN) 11/69.

FMO 983 (601): Elm Park Coaches Ltd, Romford (LN) 5/69; Bee-Line Coaches (Brentwood) Ltd, Brentwood (EX) 12/69; withdrawn 12/70; Denyer Bros, Stondon Massey (EX) 7/77 (possibly since 12/70); R Rampton, Reading for preservation 1/01.

FMO 984 (602): W Norths (PV) Ltd (dealer), Sherburn in Elmet 9/69; J Dreelan {Langley Coach Co}, Slough (BK) 3 9/69; Langley Coach Co Ltd, Langley (BK) 3 1971; Lewis (dealer), Maidenhead for scrap 11/74.

FMO 985 (603): W Norths (PV) Ltd (dealer), Sherburn in Elmet 11/68.

FRX 313 (604): AMCC (dealer), London E15 12/56; Lefkaritis Bros Ltd, Larnaca (O-CY) registered TAE 49 4/57; withdrawn 2/70; derelict 10/72 to 4/81; probably destroyed by fire 7/84.

FRX 314 (605): AMCC (dealer), London E15 12/56; Lefkaritis Bros Ltd, Larnaca (O-CY) registered TAH 815 9/57; withdrawn 4/68; derelict 10/72 to 4/81; probably destroyed by fire 7/84.

FRX 315 (606): AMCC (dealer), London E15 12/56; Lefkaritis Bros Ltd, Larnaca (O-CY) registered TAH 813 12/56; Savva, Lysi (O-CY) 1/58; Paschali, Agios Georgois (O-CY) 3/58; Spyrou, Trikomo (O-CY) 7/59; Jafer, Famagusta (O-CY) 1/61; scrapped by 1971.

Vehicles acquired from Newbury & District Motor Services Ltd 4/50:

164	LJO 756	Bedford OB	54661	Duple	46745	C29F	7/47	12/56
165	LJO 757	Bedford OB	61338	Duple	46751	C29F	3/48	12/56

Previous histories:

LJO 756-757 (164-165): New to South Midland Motor Services Ltd 43-44; Newbury & District Motor Services Ltd 164-165 1/50.

Disposals:

LJO 756 (164): AMCC (dealer), London E15 12/56; Vasili, Trikomo (O-CY) registered TAD 821 3/57; Spyrou, Trikomo (O-CY) 7/59; Potamitis, Strovolos (O-CY) 1/62; Kombos Transport Co Ltd, Limassol (O-CY) 1/63; withdrawn 9/72.

LJO 757 (165): AMCC (dealer), London E15 12/56; Lefkaritis Bros Ltd, Larnaca (O-CY) registered TAH 288 8/57; withdrawn 7/67 [the registration LJO 757 was transferred or re-issued in the UK to GBL 200 (Bedford OB / Duple) 11/83].

1951

New Vehicles:

570	FMO 952	Bristol LL6B	83.175	ECW	4725	B39R	1/51	10/61
571	FMO 953	Bristol LL6B	83.176	ECW	4726	B39R	1/51	12/67
572	FMO 954	Bristol LL6B	83.177	ECW	4727	B39R	2/51	1/61
573	FMO 955	Bristol LL6B	83.190	ECW	4728	B39R	1/51	10/61
574	FMO 956	Bristol LL6B	83.191	ECW	4729	B39R	1/51	8/68
575	FMO 957	Bristol LL6B	83.192	ECW	4730	B39R	1/51	10/61
576	FMO 958	Bristol LL6B	83.193	ECW	4731	B39R	2/51	10/61
577	FMO 959	Bristol LWL6B	83.272	ECW	4732	B39R	3/51	4/62
578	FMO 960	Bristol LWL6B	83.273	ECW	4733	B39R	3/51	4/62
579	FMO 961	Bristol LWL6B	83.274	ECW	4734	B39R	3/51	4/62
580	FMO 962	Bristol LWL6B	85.014	ECW	4735	B39R	3/51	4/62
581	FMO 963	Bristol LWL6B	85.015	ECW	4736	B39R	3/51	2/62
582	FMO 964	Bristol LWL6B	85.016	ECW	4737	B39R	3/51	3/66

583	FMO 965	Bristol LWL6B	85.017	ECW	4738	B39R	3/51	4/62
584	FMO 966	Bristol LWL6B	85.018	ECW	4739	B39R	3/51	9/62
585	FMO 967	Bristol LWL6B	85.019	ECW	4740	B39R	3/51	2/62
595	FMO 977	Bristol KS6B	82.023	ECW	4376	CL27/26RD	1/51	12/68
596	FMO 978	Bristol KS6B	82.024	ECW	4377	CL27/26RD	1/51	4/69
597	FMO 979	Bristol KS6B	82.038	ECW	4378	CL27/26RD	1/51	10/68
598	FMO 980	Bristol KS6B	82.039	ECW	4379	CL27/26RD	1/51	4/69
599	FMO 981	Bristol KS6B	82.040	ECW	4380	CL27/26RD	1/51	4/69
600	FMO 982	Bristol KS6B	82.041	ECW	4381	CL27/26RD	1/51	10/68
607	GBL 871	Bristol LWL6B	85.108	ECW	5434	FC37F	7/51	12/63
608	GBL 872	Bristol LWL6B	85.109	ECW	5435	FC37F	7/51	7/60
609	GBL 873	Bristol LWL6B	85.110	ECW	5436	FC37F	8/51	7/60
610	GBL 874	Bristol LWL6B	85.111	ECW	5437	FC37F	8/51	2/62
611	GBL 875	Bristol LWL6B	85.112	ECW	5438	FC37F	8/51	12/63
612	GBL 876	Bristol LWL6B	85.113	ECW	5439	FC37F	8/51	5/62
613	GJB 251	Bristol LWL6B	85.042	ECW	5360	B39R	10/51	4/68
614	GJB 252	Bristol LWL6B	85.043	ECW	5361	B39R	10/51	8/64
634	GJB 272	Bristol KSW6B	82.095	ECW	5074	L27/28R	6/51	12/68
635	GJB 273	Bristol KSW6B	82.096	ECW	5075	L27/28R	7/51	3/69
636	GJB 274	Bristol KSW6B	82.097	ECW	5076	L27/28R	7/51	3/69
637	GJB 275	Bristol KSW6B	84.016	ECW	5077	CL27/26RD	10/51	9/69
638	GJB 276	Bristol KSW6B	84.017	ECW	5078	CL27/26RD	10/51	4/69
639	GJB 277	Bristol KSW6B	84.018	ECW	5079	CL27/26RD	10/51	4/69
640	GJB 278	Bristol KSW6B	84.045	ECW	5080	L27/28R	10/51	4/69
641	GJB 279	Bristol KSW6B	84.046	ECW	5081	L27/28R	10/51	5/69
642	GJB 280	Bristol KSW6B	84.047	ECW	5082	L27/28R	10/51	5/69
643	GJB 281	Bristol KSW6B	84.110	ECW	5083	L27/28R	11/51	5/69
644	GJB 282	Bristol KSW6B	84.111	ECW	5084	L27/28R	11/51	5/69
645	GJB 283	Bristol KSW6B	84.112	ECW	5085	L27/28R	11/51	6/69
646	GJB 284	Bristol KSW6B	84.113	ECW	5086	L27/28R	11/51	6/69
647	GJB 285	Bristol KSW6B	84.119	ECW	5087	L27/28R	11/51	5/69

Notes:

FMO 977-982 (595-600): Had luxury type bodies built for the Limited Stop services between Reading and London; fitted with semi-luxury seats, luggage racks, heaters and platform doors, the first of this type constructed by ECW.

GJB 275-277 (639-641): Also had luxury type bodies built for the Limited Stop services between Reading and London.

FMO 977 (595): Luggage racks removed and coach seats cut down to bus-style (as L27/26RD) 3/64.

FMO 978 (596): Luggage racks removed and coach seats cut down to bus-style (as L27/26RD) 4/65.

FMO 979 (597): Luggage racks removed and coach seats cut down to bus-style (as L27/26RD) 6/64.

FMO 980 (598): Luggage racks removed and coach seats cut down to bus-style (as L27/26RD) 9/65.

FMO 981 (599): Luggage racks removed and coach seats cut down to bus-style (as L27/26RD) 2/66.

FMO 982 (600): Luggage racks removed and coach seats cut down to bus-style (as L27/26RD) 7/65.

GJB 274 (636): Used as a driver training vehicle 12/68-3/69.

GJB 275 (637): Rebuilt by Thames Valley 7/63; luggage racks removed and coach seats cut down to bus-style (as L27/26RD) 1/64.

GJB 276 (638): Luggage racks removed and coach seats cut down to bus-style (as L27/26RD) 2/65.

GJB 277 (639): Exhibited at the Modern Coach Exhibition, Victoria during 1/52; luggage racks removed and coach seats cut down to bus-style (as L27/26RD) 3/65.

Disposals:

FMO 952 (570): United Welsh Omnibus Co Ltd, Swansea (GG) 570 10/61; withdrawn 1/66.

FMO 953 (571): TD Alexander {Greyhound Luxury Coaches}, Sheffield (WR) 2/68; TD Alexander {Greyhound Luxury Coaches}, Arbroath (AS) 6/68; withdrawn 1969; burnt out 12/69.

FMO 954 (572): United Welsh Omnibus Co Ltd, Swansea (GG) 572 1/61; withdrawn 1965; W Norths (PV) Ltd (dealer), Sherburn in Elmet by 6/66; W Thompson (contractor), Northallerton (XNR) 11/66.

FMO 955 (573): United Welsh Omnibus Co Ltd, Swansea (GG) 573 10/61; withdrawn 1966; W Norths (PV) Ltd (dealer), Sherburn in Elmet 7/66; C Payne (contractor), Marske-by-the-sea (XNR) 7/66; W Norths (PV) Ltd (dealer), Sherburn in Elmet 5/68; B Johnson (dealer), South Elmsall for scrap 7/70.

FMO 956 (574): TD Alexander {Greyhound Luxury Coaches}, Arbroath (AS) 8/68; TD Alexander {Greyhound Luxury Coaches}, Sheffield (WR) 8/70; unidentified dealer, Barnsley for scrap 1971.

FMO 957 (575): United Welsh Omnibus Co Ltd, Swansea (GG) 575 10/61; withdrawn 1965; W Norths (PV) Ltd (dealer), Sherburn in Elmet by 6/66; P Devine, Ossett (WR) 9/66.

FMO 958 (576): United Welsh Omnibus Co Ltd, Swansea (GG) 576 10/61; withdrawn 1966; AT Jones {Jones Motor Services}, Login (PE) 9/66; withdrawn 6/68.

FMO 959 (577): Passenger Vehicle Disposals Ltd (dealer), Dunchurch 4/62; W Davies {Marino Coaches}, Ferryhill (DM) 6/62; JF Nicholson {Rough Lea Coaches}, Hunwick (DM) 11/63; W Norths (PV) Ltd (dealer), Sherburn in Elmet for scrap 3/64.

FMO 960 (578): Passenger Vehicle Disposals Ltd (dealer), Dunchurch 4/62; F Rendell & Sons (contractor), Devizes (XWI) by 1/64 to 8/70 at least.

FMO 961 (579): Passenger Vehicle Disposals Ltd (dealer), Dunchurch 4/62; Platman Motors, London SW15 5/62 to 2/64 at least; Sir Lindsay Parkinson (contractor), London SW15 (X) SLP3883 by 8/65; last licensed 7/66.

FMO 962 (580): Passenger Vehicle Disposals Ltd (dealer), Dunchurch 4/62; S Blenkinsopp {Scarlet Band Motor Services}, West Cornforth (DM) 56 5/62; last licensed 12/65.

FMO 963 (581): Rossmore Bus Co Ltd, Sandbanks (DT) 2/62 and rebuilt to front-entrance (as B39F); unidentified owner, Plymouth 2/72.

FMO 964 (582): TD Alexander {Greyhound Luxury Coaches}, Sheffield (WR) 12/66; withdrawn 12/68; unidentified dealer for scrap 2/69.

FMO 965 (583): Passenger Vehicle Disposals Ltd (dealer), Dunchurch 4/62; DS Edwards, Llangeinor (GG) 9/62; withdrawn by 5/64; last licensed 11/64.

FMO 966 (584): Passenger Vehicle Disposals Ltd (dealer), Dunchurch 9/62; Bedlington & District Luxury Coaches Ltd, Ashington (ND) 9/62; Hancock & Turner (dealer), Lynemouth 1965; last licensed 8/65.

FMO 967 (585): Rossmore Bus Co Ltd, Sandbanks (DT) 2/62 and rebuilt to front-entrance (as B39F); unidentified dealer for scrap 9/71.

FMO 977 (595): W Norths (PV) Ltd (dealer), Sherburn in Elmet 1/69; B Johnson (dealer), Goldthorpe for scrap 12/69.

FMO 978 (596): W Norths (PV) Ltd (dealer), Sherburn in Elmet 4/69; TD Alexander {Greyhound Luxury Coaches}, Arbroath (AS) 5/69; withdrawn by 11/70.

FMO 979 (597): W Norths (PV) Ltd (dealer), Sherburn in Elmet 11/68.

FMO 980 (598): W Norths (PV) Ltd (dealer), Sherburn in Elmet 4/69; TD Alexander {Greyhound Luxury Coaches}, Arbroath (AS) 5/69; exported to USA possibly with a church or other religious organisation c1969; noted at Cape Canaveral, Florida (O-USA) in poor condition by 10/86.

FMO 981 (599): W Norths (PV) Ltd (dealer), Sherburn in Elmet 4/69; TD Alexander {Greyhound Luxury Coaches}, Arbroath (AS) (not operated) 4/69; TD Alexander {Greyhound Luxury Coaches}, Sheffield (WR) 4/70; P Sykes (dealer), Barnsley 7/71.

FMO 982 (600): W Norths (PV) Ltd (dealer), Sherburn in Elmet 10/68; Lewis (dealer), Maidenhead 12/75.

GBL 871 (607): TD Alexander {Greyhound Luxury Coaches}, Arbroath (AS) 12/63; TD Alexander {Greyhound Luxury Coaches}, Sheffield (WR) 12/64; withdrawn 5/66.

GBL 872-873 (608-609): South Midland Motor Services Ltd 608-609 7/60 (qv).

GBL 874 (610): South Midland Motor Services Ltd 610 2/62 (qv).

GBL 875 (611): TD Alexander {Greyhound Luxury Coaches}, Arbroath (AS) 12/63; TD Alexander {Greyhound Luxury Coaches}, Sheffield (WR) 12/64; withdrawn 1/66; Kirk, Bamford, Derbyshire 2/66.

GBL 876 (612): Alexander & Walker (dealer), Bretforton 5/62; TD Alexander {Greyhound Luxury Coaches}, Arbroath (AS) 5/62; TD Alexander {Greyhound Luxury Coaches}, Sheffield (WR) 12/64 (licensed 9/65); withdrawn 1/66.

GJB 251 (613): New Horizon School Camps, Kingston-on-Thames (SR) 4/68; withdrawn 1/70; unidentified owner, Norfolk 2/70; stored at Chazey Heath 1973; stored at West of England Transport Collection, Winkleigh late 1998, but not traced further.

GJB 252 (614): Rossmore Bus Co Ltd, Sandbanks (DT) 8/64; withdrawn 10/66; unidentified dealer by 9/71.

GJB 272 (634): W Norths (PV) Ltd (dealer), Sherburn in Elmet 12/68.

GJB 273 (635): TD Alexander {Greyhound Luxury Coaches}, Arbroath (AS) 4/69; TD Alexander {Greyhound Luxury Coaches}, Sheffield (WR) 4/69.

GJB 274 (636): W Norths (PV) Ltd (dealer), Sherburn in Elmet 3/69; M King (dealer?), Pelham St Mary, Diss 3/69; Omnibus Promotions Ltd (dealer), London EC1 1969; British Promotions (dealer), Massachusetts, USA (O-USA) 1969; Marine Zoo, San Diego, California (O-USA) c1970; Economy Imports, San Jose (O-USA) by 1990; registered 302 TNH; Heafner Tire, San Jose (O-USA) by 6/01.

GJB 275 (637): W Norths (PV) Ltd (dealer), Sherburn in Elmet 10/69; Glevum Coaches Ltd, Gloucester (GL) 10/69; Omnibus Promotions Ltd (dealer), London EC1 after 2/73; British Promotions (dealer), Massachusetts, USA after 2/73; National Equipment Co, Cupertuo, California (O-USA) after 2/73; Presidential Limousines, San Diego, California (O-USA) 1984; unidentified operator / dealer by 3/92.

GJB 276 (638): W Norths (PV) Ltd (dealer), Sherburn in Elmet 4/69; TD Alexander {Greyhound Luxury Coaches}, Arbroath (AS) 5/69.

GJB 277 (639): W Norths (PV) Ltd (dealer), Sherburn in Elmet 4/69; TD Alexander {Greyhound Luxury Coaches}, Arbroath (AS) 5/69; withdrawn 1969.

GJB 278 (640): W Norths (PV) Ltd (dealer), Sherburn in Elmet 4/69.

GJB 279 (641): Rev RWA West, Betchworth (XSR) 6/69; Chiltern Omnibus Group (dealer), High Wycombe 5/75; 14th Aylesbury Scout Group, Aylesbury (XBK) 7/75; Wacton Trading / Coach Sales (dealer), Bromyard 9/82; J Karlberg, New Ferry for preservation 1/83; still in existence 6/11.

GJB 280 (642): W Norths (PV) Ltd (dealer), Sherburn in Elmet 5/69; Arnold, Coburg, Ontario (O-CDN) at an unknown date; Jules Mansion, Toronto (O-CDN) by 9/71; Levys Auto Parts (dealer), Toronto by 8/80; Campus Transportation Ltd {Hiawathaland Tours}, Sault Ste Marie, Ontario (O-CDN) registered BB8-170 8/80; Andrews (dealer?), Sault Ste Marie, Ontario 6/01 and scrapped.

GJB 281 (643): W Norths (PV) Ltd (dealer), Sherburn in Elmet 5/69; Leeds University Students' Rag Committee (XWR) 10/69; W Norths (PV) Ltd (dealer), Sherburn in Elmet for scrap 1/70.

GJB 282 (644): W Norths (PV) Ltd (dealer), Sherburn in Elmet 5/69; Seghill Construction Co (contractor), Seaton Delaval (XND) 10/69; unidentified dealer, Carlton for scrap 1/75.

GJB 283 (645): W Norths (PV) Ltd (dealer), Sherburn in Elmet 6/69; TD Alexander {Greyhound Luxury Coaches}, Arbroath (AS) 6/69; unidentified dealer, Barnsley for scrap 12/69.

GJB 284 (646): W Norths (PV) Ltd (dealer), Sherburn in Elmet 6/69; TD Alexander {Greyhound Luxury Coaches}, Arbroath (AS) 6/69; Hartwood Finance Ltd (dealer), Birdwell for scrap 3/70.

GJB 285 (647): Elm Park Coaches Ltd, Romford (LN) 5/69; Bee-Line Coaches (Brentwood) Ltd, Brentwood (EX) 12/69; Passenger Vehicle Sales (London) Ltd (dealer), Silver End 7/71; A Barraclough (dealer), Carlton for scrap 8/71.

Vehicles acquired from RE Jackson {Crescent Coaches}, Windsor (BE) 6/51:

JB 7289	Bedford WLB	110131	Duple	5849	C20F	10/35	----
JB 9860	Bedford WTB	110787	Duple	8227	B26F	8/36	----
BJB 580	Bedford WTB	4563	Duple	5435/2	C20F	10/38	----
CRX 333	Bedford OWB	23487	Duple	39005	B26F	1/45	----
EBL 967	Bedford OB	67260	Mulliner	T182	B32F	1/48	----

Previous histories:
JB 7289: New to JA Perry {Crescent Coaches}, Windsor (BE); RE Jackson {Crescent Coaches} 8/50.

JB 9860: New to Frowen & Hill Ltd {Borough Bus Services}, Windsor (BE); RE Jackson {Crescent Coaches} 8/50.

BJB 580: New to JA Perry {Crescent Coaches}, Windsor (BE); RE Jackson {Crescent Coaches} 8/50.

CRX 333: New to JA Perry {Crescent Coaches}, Windsor (BE) (as B32F); reseated to B26F at an unknown date; RE Jackson {Crescent Coaches} 8/50.

EBL 967: New to JA Perry {Crescent Coaches}, Windsor (BE); (as B32F); reseated to B30F at an unknown date; RE Jackson {Crescent Coaches} 8/50.

Notes:
In a joint venture with London Transport Executive, Jackson's Crescent Coaches local services were acquired on 1 June 1951. London Transport took the Windsor to Slough service whilst Thames Valley acquired the Slough to Cippenham route together with five vehicles (none of which were operated). Thames Valley's share of the purchase was £6,750. Jackson subsequently continued operating a coaching business.

Disposals:
JB 7289: Disposals Ltd {Horton Motor Works} (dealer), Northampton 7/51; unidentified dealer, Walsall 7/51.

JB 9860: T Baker & Sons (Compton) Ltd, Compton (XBE) 7/51; Foundry & Engineers (Compton) Ltd, Compton (XBE) at an unknown date; last licensed 12/54.

BJB 580: AE Bengry {Primrose Motor Services}, Kingsland (HR) 7/51; last licensed 5/58; Staples, Leominster (HR) for spares 10/58.

CRX 333: AE Bengry {Primrose Motor Services}, Kingsland (HR) 7/51; unidentified dealer 8/59; last licensed 9/59; scrapped by 10/61.

EBL 967: Lucas Ltd, London SW2 (XLN) 10/51.

Vehicle on hire from Bristol Tramways & Carriage Co Ltd, Bristol (GL):

LHY 949	Bristol LDX6B	LDX001	ECW	3852	H33/25R	10/49 3/51	3/51

Notes:

LHY 949: Was numbered C5000 in the Bristol Tramways & Carriage Co Ltd fleet and was on hire for evaluation.

1952

New Vehicles:

615	GJB 253	Bristol LWL6B	85.167	ECW	5362	B39R	1/52	8/68
616	GJB 254	Bristol LWL6B	85.168	ECW	5363	B39R	1/52	7/65
617	GJB 255	Bristol LWL6B	85.169	ECW	5364	B39R	1/52	2/65
618	GJB 256	Bristol LWL6B	85.170	ECW	5365	B39R	1/52	2/65
619	GJB 257	Bristol LWL6B	85.184	ECW	5366	B39R	1/52	7/66
620	GJB 258	Bristol LWL6B	85.185	ECW	5367	B39R	1/52	12/68
621	GJB 259	Bristol LWL6B	85.186	ECW	5368	B39R	1/52	5/70
622	GJB 260	Bristol LWL6B	87.002	ECW	5369	B39R	2/52	3/65
623	GJB 261	Bristol LWL6B	87.003	ECW	5370	B39R	2/52	5/64
624	GJB 262	Bristol LWL6B	87.015	ECW	5371	B39R	2/52	4/68
625	GJB 263	Bristol LWL6B	87.016	ECW	5372	B39R	2/52	6/70
626	GJB 264	Bristol LWL6B	87.017	ECW	5373	B39R	2/52	4/68
627	GJB 265	Bristol LWL6B	87.018	ECW	5374	B39R	2/52	4/71
628	GJB 266	Bristol LWL6B	87.019	ECW	5375	B39R	3/52	11/68
629	GJB 267	Bristol LWL6B	87.030	ECW	5376	B39R	4/52	6/70
630	GJB 268	Bristol LWL6B	87.031	ECW	5377	B39R	3/52	12/68
631	GJB 269	Bristol LWL6B	87.032	ECW	5378	B39R	3/52	5/70
632	GJB 270	Bristol LWL6B	87.054	ECW	5379	B39R	4/52	10/68
633	GJB 271	Bristol LWL6B	87.055	ECW	5380	B39R	4/52	11/68
648	GJB 286	Bristol KSW6B	84.193	ECW	5088	L27/28R	1/52	11/69
649	GJB 287	Bristol KSW6B	84.194	ECW	5089	L27/28R	1/52	5/69
650	GJB 288	Bristol KSW6B	84.195	ECW	5090	L27/28R	1/52	3/70
651	HBL 53	Bristol KSW6B	90.054	ECW	5900	L27/28R	7/52	3/70
652	HBL 54	Bristol KSW6B	90.055	ECW	5901	L27/28R	7/52	3/70
653	HBL 55	Bristol KSW6B	92.043	ECW	5902	L27/28R	8/52	11/69
654	HBL 56	Bristol KSW6B	92.044	ECW	5903	L27/28R	9/52	7/70
655	HBL 57	Bristol KSW6B	92.045	ECW	5904	L27/28R	9/52	7/70
656	HBL 58	Bristol KSW6B	92.046	ECW	5905	L27/28R	9/52	11/69
657	HBL 59	Bristol KSW6B	92.065	ECW	5906	L27/28R	9/52	5/70
658	HBL 60	Bristol KSW6B	92.066	ECW	5907	L27/28R	9/52	8/70
659	HBL 61	Bristol KSW6B	92.109	ECW	5908	L27/28R	11/52	9/69
660	HBL 62	Bristol KSW6B	92.110	ECW	5909	L27/28R	11/52	9/69
661	HBL 63	Bristol KSW6B	92.111	ECW	5910	L27/28R	11/52	9/69
662	HBL 64	Bristol KSW6B	92.122	ECW	5911	L27/28R	11/52	6/70
671	HBL 73	Bristol LS6G	89.036	ECW	6210	C39F	6/52	2/62
672	HBL 74	Bristol LS6G	89.037	ECW	6211	C39F	7/52	4/65
673	HBL 75	Bristol LS6G	89.087	ECW	6212	C39F	7/52	12/61
674	HBL 76	Bristol LS6G	89.109	ECW	6213	C39F	10/52	7/64
675	HBL 77	Bristol LS6G	89.110	ECW	6214	C39F	10/52	12/66
676	HBL 78	Bristol LS6G	89.111	ECW	6215	C39F	10/52	7/68
677	HBL 79	Bristol LS6G	89.127	ECW	5699	B45F	11/52	7/71
678	HBL 80	Bristol LS6G	89.128	ECW	5700	B45F	11/52	9/71

Notes:

GJB 254 (616): Converted to a Supervisor's Office, Maidenhead Coach Station with stools and desks replacing the seats 7/65; later used as an enquiry office and then a driver training vehicle 7/66; withdrawn 4/69 fitted with coach seats (as DP35R) before disposal.

GJB 259 (621): Renumbered 259 4/70.

GJB 260 (622): Withdrawn following an accident 3/65; cannibalised for spares; chassis only by 6/65.

GJB 263 (625): Renumbered 263 1/70.

GJB 265 (627): Renumbered 265 10/69.

GJB 267 (629): Renumbered 267 4/70.

GJB 269 (631): Renumbered 269 4/70.

GJB 270 (632): Used on light oils trials with Esso Petroleum at FVDRE, Chobham 11/52 to 12/52.

HBL 60 (658): Used as a driver training vehicle from 8/70.

HBL 79-80 (677-678): Equipped for one-man-operation and reseated to B41F 4/69; renumbered 100-101 8/69.

Disposals:

GJB 253 (615): TD Alexander {Greyhound Luxury Coaches}, Sheffield (WR) 8/68; withdrawn 8/70.

GJB 254 (616): C Hills {Sussex Rural Rides Association}, Lindfield (XWS) 4/69; EJ Baker & Co (Dorking), Ltd (dealer), Bordon 1/71; Coalporters Amateur Rowing Club, Southampton (fitted with a boat rack on its roof) 1/71; EJ Baker & Co (Dorking), Ltd (dealer), Bordon 4/74; RA Milton (dealer), Haslemere 5/74; Haslemere Scout Group, Haslemere (XSR) 5/74; group of hippies 9/74; Egham Bus Group, Egham for preservation 12/74; platform doors fitted and reseated to B39RD 9/75; R Matthews & A Wheatley, Staines for preservation 1983; Davies, Castle Cary for preservation by 12/93; CJ Hallett, Trowbridge for preservation 1/94; MD Shaw, Farmoor for preservation 2/95 (kept at Oxford Bus Museum); platform doors removed by 3/99 (probably much earlier); 616 Preservation Group, Luton for preservation 9/08.

GJB 255 (617): TD Alexander {Greyhound Luxury Coaches}, Sheffield (WR) 3/65; withdrawn 3/67.

GJB 256 (618): TD Alexander {Greyhound Luxury Coaches}, Sheffield (WR) 3/65; withdrawn 3/67.

GJB 257 (619): EA Bicknell & Sons Ltd (contractor), Bristol (XGL) 9/66 to 4/70 at least.

GJB 258 (620): Rev B Green, British Council of Protestant Christian Church, London SW6 (XLN) 12/68; Martyrs Memorial Church, Belfast (XAM) 1/69; Magherafelt Parish Church, Magherafelt (XLY) by 1973; withdrawn by 6/91.

GJB 259 (259): W Norths (PV) Ltd (dealer), Sherburn in Elmet 6/70; Derek Crouch (Contractor) Ltd (contractor), Eye (SP) 7/70; moved to Seghill (XND) by 1971.

GJB 260 (622): Dismantled for spares / scrap by Thames Valley 5-6/65.

GJB 261 (623): Rossmore Bus Co Ltd, Sandbanks (DT) 5/64 and rebuilt to front-entrance (as B39F); scrapped on the premises by 7/71.

GJB 262 (624): The Princess Margaret Royal Free School, Windsor (XBE) 4/68; T Wigley (dealer), Carlton 4/89.

GJB 263 (263): W Norths (PV) Ltd (dealer), Sherburn in Elmet 9/70; Filmcraft Catering Services, New Maldon (XSR) 12/70; E Beckett (dealer), Carlton 2/77.

GJB 264 (626): Elm Park Coaches Ltd, Romford (LN) 4/68; Cedric Garages (Wivenhoe) Ltd, Wivenhoe (EX) 7/71; scrapped on the premises 12/75.

GJB 265 (265): The Princess Margaret Royal Free School, Windsor (XBE) 4/71; G Bilbe, G Green & R Rampton, Reading for preservation 6/94; still in existence 6/12.

GJB 266 (628): W Norths (PV) Ltd (dealer), Sherburn in Elmet 12/68; Sadler Bros (contractor), Newcastle upon Tyne (XND) 3/69; withdrawn 1971.

GJB 267 (267): Elm Park Coaches Ltd, Romford (LN) 9/70; Cedric Garages (Wivenhoe) Ltd, Wivenhoe (EX) 7/71; Hillside Autos (dealer), Great Yeldham 7/75; cannibalised for spares by Egham Bus Group and scrapped by Hillside 9/75.

GJB 268 (630): W Norths (PV) Ltd (dealer), Sherburn in Elmet 1/69; Dowsett (contractor), London (X) 3/69.

GJB 269 (269): W Norths (PV) Ltd (dealer), Sherburn in Elmet 6/70; Evans, Sunderland (DM) 8/70; W Norths (PV) Ltd (dealer), Sherburn in Elmet 4/73; unidentified dealer for scrap 5/74.

GJB 270 (632): W Norths (PV) Ltd (dealer), Sherburn in Elmet 11/68; Drury, Huddersfield (XWR) 11/68.

GJB 271 (633): W Norths (PV) Ltd (dealer), Sherburn in Elmet 11/68; Dew (contractor), Oldham (XLA) 12/68; G Jameson {Dunscroft Commercials} (dealer), Dunscroft 3/74.

GJB 286 (648): Elm Park Coaches Ltd, Romford (LN) (not operated) 11/69; Liss & District Omnibus Co Ltd, Grayshott (HA) 11/69; ESG Vane-Hunt, Headley for preservation 11/70; withdrawn by 1/78; P Hughes, Hartley for preservation by 1982; G Ledger (dealer), Northampton 5/84; D Rollinson (Bus Centre) Ltd (dealer), Carlton for scrap 5/84.

GJB 287 (649): W Norths (PV) Ltd (dealer), Sherburn in Elmet 6/69; J Dreelan {Langley Coach Co}, Langley (BK) 9/70; Lewis (dealer), Maidenhead 1/71; Elm Park Coaches Ltd, Romford (LN) (not operated) 7/71; Lewis (dealer), Maidenhead 7/71 to 12/75 at least.

GJB 288 (650): J Dreelan {Langley Coach Co}, Langley (BK) 2 4/70; Langley Coach Co Ltd, Langley (BK) 2 1971; withdrawn 6/72.

HBL 53 (651): Unidentified dealer 3/70; F Showler {British Double Deck Hire}, Oakville, Ontario (O-CDN) 7/70; Africa Lion Safari Game Farm, Rockton, Ontario (O-CDN) 1970; Wodsworth, Genesco, New York State (O-USA) 4/87; Arnold (dealer), Coburg, Ontario by 7/87; National War Plane Museum, New York State (O-USA) 7/87.

HBL 54 (652): W Norths (PV) Ltd (dealer), Sherburn in Elmet 7/70; Harvey (peace movement), Southampton 4/71; unidentified owner(s) in Somerset 12/73, Cornwall 5/74; Worcestershire 10/79, Redditch (fitted with platform doors) 10/84.

HBL 55 (653): W Norths (PV) Ltd (dealer), Sherburn in Elmet 11/69; Filmcraft Catering Services, New Maldon (XSR) 11/69; unidentified dealer, Carlton 3/77.

HBL 56 (654): W Norths (PV) Ltd (dealer), Sherburn in Elmet 8/70; Armoride Ltd, Earby (XWR) 9/70; Ambermarle (Skipton) Ltd, Skipton (XWR) 8/71; W Norths (PV) Ltd (dealer), Sherburn in Elmet 9/72.

HBL 57 (655): W Norths (PV) Ltd (dealer), Sherburn in Elmet 9/70; British Radio Corporation {Ultra}, Gosport (XHA) 11/70.

Leylands HE 11 & HE 12 are posed outside BAT's Caversham Road premises in Reading before the start of the inaugural service in July 1915. They were new in 1913 and were fitted with Brush bodies. HE 12 spent many later years built into a house, but is now restored to its original condition (Paul Lacey & Mike Sutcliffe collections)

DP 1657 was amongst a batch of 'new' vehicles received in 1915. Its Tilling body on a Belsize chassis, was second-hand and was later reused on one of the 1919 Thornycrofts. It is pictured at Sonning Halt on the Reading to Maidenhead service on what is now the busy A4. (Mike Sutcliffe collection)

Due to demand for military vehicles, BAT's Thornycroft order was not fulfilled until 1919. DP 2113 (246) and DP 2115 (248) (the latter with boards for retaining a gas bag) were fitted with Tilling bodies previously mounted on the 1915/16 Belsizes. They are pictured in the original Reading terminus at St Mary's Butts. (Paul Lacey collection)

Day trips in the early days of bus operation were extremely popular and Thames Valley maintained a small fleet of charabancs for excursions to the countryside and the south coast. Thornycrofts DP 2129 (29) (Bayley body) and DP 3633 (36) (Birch) are seen here fully laden on a sunny day in the early 1920s. (Roger Warwick collection)

The chassis of DP 2606 (34) previously saw service as a War Department lorry and during its eight years with Thames Valley, was fitted with four different bodies. This one, its third, was manufactured by Brush and seated 54. It is seen here at Mortimer in the summer of 1925. (Paul Lacey & Mike Sutcliffe collections)

1926 saw the arrival of the first TSM chassis which were the first all-new full-sized vehicles to be received by Thames Valley. MO 6849 (105) in Bridge Avenue, Maidenhead, was fitted with a Brush 32-seat bus body, others in the batch were completed (to the same design) by Tilling and Birch. (Omnibus Society, XLM collection)

The 20 former London General Thornycroft JB double-deckers obtained in 1926 were more powerful than the incumbent J-types and were particularly needed at Uxbridge where they met the more stringent Metropolitan Police licensing requirements. Typical of these is Dodson bodied XP 5985 (126) seen here in Wycombe High Street. (Norris Collection, Omnibus Society)

Leylands arrived in 1928 in the form of a batch of TD1s with open-staircase bodywork. Most of these were converted to producer gas operation during WW2 and RX 1761 (172) pictured here at Reading Southern Railway Station (with name boards covered), was so fitted for a year between 1943 and 1944. (Derek Giles collection, Omnibus Society)

The Marlow & District fleet came into Thames Valley ownership in 1929. It comprised mainly of Karriers and was used by that company as a test bed for their products. A typical vehicle was KX 3901 (10), a Karrier CL4 with Ramsden 26-seat body, seen outside the Crown Hotel, Marlow. (JF Parke, Omnibus Society)

KX 8481 (15) was one of a pair of Karrier Coasters acquired in 1932 by Marlow & District for use on the Marlow to Maidenhead route. It did not operate after 1937 having been stored following a gearbox failure but was sold after the War for further use as a caravan. (JF Higham, Omnibus Society)

Leyland TD1 RX 5566 (204) is seen in a busy and atmospheric early 1930s street scene complete with a Reading Corporation tram in the background. It is emerging from Forbury Road, Reading where Thames Valley was trying at the time to demonstrate that this road was wide enough for buses to pass. (Fraser Clayton collection)

The Leyland LT1 'Lion' / Brush model as typified by RX 5572 (210) arrived in 1930 and is seen here outside Slough station. Other than a second batch received later in that year, no further examples were ordered, but all enjoyed long careers with Thames Valley, surviving until the early 1950s. (JF Higham, Omnibus Society).

RX 6250 (230) was a solitary Leyland TS3 purchased in 1930 and was unusual in that it was a Tiger fitted with a Lion radiator at Thames Valley's special request in order for it to receive the company nameplate. It was ordered for evaluation on the Reading - Ascot - London express service. (Brush Coachworks)

Numerous examples of both bus and coach seated Leyland Tigers arrived 1930-1939. Typical of the earlier deliveries is RX 9708 (254), a TS4 model with Brush bodywork, one of seven coach seated examples delivered in 1932. This, like some of the others in the batch, was impressed by the War Department in 1940. (Norris Collection, Omnibus Society)

The Penn Bus Co fleet acquired in 1935 comprised mostly of Gilford and Dennis models. APP 273 (291) was a Dennis Ace with Dennis 20-seat bodywork. Like the others in the fleet, this neat little vehicle did not last long with Thames Valley, but saw further service in South Wales. (Norris Collection, Omnibus Society)

The largest of the Dennis saloons with Penn Bus was KX 8092, a Lancet delivered in 1932 with a Wycombe body, which became Thames Valley 287 at the takeover. It is seen here at Frogmoor, High Wycombe bus terminus. (JF Higham, The Omnibus Society)

Ledbury & District GF 6677 (52) is seen in Maidenhead garage in 1937, shortly before withdrawal, by which time it had received Thames Valley fleet names. It was a Gilford 168SD with 26-seat Duple bodywork. It saw further use elsewhere including with Newbury & District where it was later used as a source of spares. (Omnibus Society, XLM collection)

In contrast to the previous view, GP 5140 (4) was the more modern Gilford 168OT forward control model with Wycombe bodywork, constructed at the same works. It is seen at work in Maidenhead on the former Ledbury service to Henley with an 'on hire to Thames Valley' notice in the front. (Norris Collection, Omnibus Society)

Petrol-engined JB 5844 (265) was a Leyland TS7 dating from 1935. It was used as a test vehicle in 1939 for producer gas operation long before this type of wartime propulsion became mandatory. It also ran with a diesel engine for a time and survived with Thames Valley until 1951. (Norris Collection, Omnibus Society)

JB 5856 (277) was one of six Leyland TD4 with Brush 48 seat bodywork received in 1935. These were notable for being the first vehicles to enter service from new with diesel engines. They were thoroughly rebuilt and refurbished during the war years which ensured that they enjoyed long lives with Thames Valley. (Surfleet Photos, Omnibus Society)

KX 6094 (317) was a 1932 Petty bodied AEC Regal which was new to Pioneer Bus Service before passing to Chiltern Bus Co in 1936 and is seen here in High Wycombe. It was disposed of after little over two years, but survived elsewhere until 1951. (Norris Collection, Omnibus Society)

ABL 768 (338) was one of a pair of petrol-engined Leyland KPZ2 'Cubs' with Brush bodywork, purchased for the service over Marlow Bridge which had a 5-ton weight limit. It was the first of several different types acquired specifically for this over the years and is seen post-war at Maidenhead Bus Station. (AB Cross, The Omnibus Society)

BMG 703 (349) was one of three Albions with Duple bodywork, which were acquired with the business of FH Crook in 1937. It is seen shortly after acquisition, still in Crook's green livery and wearing their 'Advance' logos, outside London Transport's High Wycombe depot which was used at the time for some local services. (Mike Sutcliffe collection, Omnibus Society)

The first Bristols arrive in 1939 as Tillings began to influence vehicle policy. These covered the trunk routes out of Reading for many years but BRX 922 (406) it seen on a shorter working to Tidmarsh. It had ECW 48-seat bodywork which was outwardly similar to that bodied on the Leyland Titans of the previous year. (Omnibus Society, XLM collection)

Shortages during WW2 saw a number of vehicles arriving on loan. JG 8206 (110) was a 1936 Leyland TD4 with Park Royal bodywork, borrowed from East Kent for about 18 months during 1941/2. It retained East Kent's dark red and grey livery, but had Thames Valley fleetnames. (JF Parke, Omnibus Society)

New vehicles in Wartime were, through necessity, manufactured to lower standards, as exemplified by CJB 136 (417). This was a one-off Bristol K5G delivered in 1942 with a Duple utility body which included a plywood roof. It is seen at the Radnage terminus on one of the Stokenchurch routes taken over from City of Oxford in 1937. (Mike Sutcliffe collection)

In contrast to the Duple bodied example, Bristol K5G CJB 134 (415) was also delivered in 1942 but with an ECW body. This was much closer to ECW's pre-war design, but also had a plywood roof. Nevertheless, it lasted until 1956 after which it enjoyed a second career with a showman. (Roy Marshall collection, Omnibus Society)

DMO 665 (461) was a 1948 Bristol L6B with a Vincents coach body. It was one of ten rebodied by ECW as service buses in 1957/8 in which form it lasted until 1967. After withdrawal, it saw another six years in Thames Valley territory with Moore {Imperial Bus Service} of Windsor. (Omnibus Society, XLM collection)

DMO 682 (478) was a dual-purpose Bristol L6A with ECW bodywork delivered in 1948. It is seen at High Wycombe Station working service 36 to Lane End, the bus being garaged at Fingest dormy shed. The model was superseded by the longer LL6B and wider LWL6B models. (Norris Collection, Omnibus Society)

In order to carry traffic for the 1950 Royal Agricultural Show, City of Oxford Motor Services hired in a number of double-deckers from Thames Valley. EJB 216 (494) was a 1946 Bristol K6B with ECW bodywork and is seen at Gloucester Green in Oxford on those duties. (RHG Simpson, The Omnibus Society)

After the pre-war Leyland Cubs, Thames Valley turned to Bedford OBs in the immediate post-war period for the Marlow Bridge service where a weight limit of 5-tons was imposed. EJB 233 (511) was a 1949 delivery with Beadle bodywork. It is on the stand at Bridge Avenue, Maidenhead (RHG Simpson, The Omnibus Society)

FMO 21 (546) was amongst the third batch of Bristol L6B coaches, seen here with its original Windover 33-seat body. This was another coach that was rebodied by ECW in 1958/9 in which form it lasted until 1968. An example of the rebuilt form is depicted by FMO 24 on the front cover. (Tony Wright, Omnibus Society)

HBL 58 (656): Elm Park Coaches Ltd, Romford (LN) 12/69; unidentified owner, West Sussex 3/71.
HBL 59 (657): W Norths (PV) Ltd (dealer), Sherburn in Elmet 6/70; Liss & District, Grayshott (HA) by 8/70; P
        Jeffreys {Liss & District}, Grayshott (HA) 11/70; Tillingbourne Valley Services Ltd, Guildford
        (SR) 5/72; Tillingbourne Valley Bus Co Ltd, Guildford (SR) 12/72.
HBL 60 (658): W Norths (PV) Ltd (dealer), Sherburn in Elmet 8/70; Riverway Enterprises (Harlow) Ltd
        {Riverway Coaches}, Harlow (EX) 8/70; destroyed in a depot fire 12/71.
HBL 61 (659): Elm Park Coaches Ltd, Romford (LN) 10/69.
HBL 62 (660): Elm Park Coaches Ltd, Romford (LN) 10/69; Bee-Line Coaches (Brentwood) Ltd, Brentwood
        (EX) 2/70; withdrawn 3/72.
HBL 63 (661): Elm Park Coaches Ltd, Romford (LN) 10/69; withdrawn 12/71.
HBL 64 (662): W Norths (PV) Ltd (dealer), Sherburn in Elmet 6/70; Beyer, Hoofddorp (O-NL) registered
        ZV-78-22 9/70; believed current 7/79, but not traced further.
HBL 73 (671): South Midland Motor Services Ltd 671 2/62 (qv).
HBL 74 (672): South Midland Motor Services Ltd 672 4/65 (qv).
HBL 75 (673): South Midland Motor Services Ltd 673 12/61 (qv).
HBL 76 (674): South Midland Motor Services Ltd 674 7/64 (qv).
HBL 77 (675): South Midland Motor Services Ltd 675 12/66 (qv).
HBL 78 (676): W Norths (PV) Ltd (dealer), Sherburn in Elmet 7/68; Elm Park Coaches Ltd, Romford (EX)
        8/68; withdrawn by 7/69.
HBL 79-80 (100-101): TD Alexander {Greyhound Luxury Coaches}, Sheffield (WR) (minus engines) 10/71.

1953

New Vehicles:

663	HBL 65	Bristol KSW6B	92.123	ECW	5912	L27/28R	1/53	11/70
664	HBL 66	Bristol KSW6B	94.053	ECW	5913	L27/28R	5/53	7/70
665	HBL 67	Bristol KSW6B	94.054	ECW	5914	L27/28R	5/53	2/71
666	HBL 68	Bristol KSW6B	94.055	ECW	5915	L27/28R	5/53	2/71
667	HBL 69	Bristol KSW6B	94.063	ECW	5916	L27/28R	6/53	4/71
668	HBL 70	Bristol KSW6B	94.064	ECW	5917	L27/28R	6/53	11/70
669	HBL 71	Bristol KSW6B	98.039	ECW	5918	L27/28R	6/53	5/70
670	HBL 72	Bristol KSW6B	98.040	ECW	5919	L27/28R	6/53	11/70
679	HBL 81	Bristol LS6G	93.020	ECW	5701	B45F	2/53	8/71
680	HBL 82	Bristol LS6G	93.021	ECW	5703	B45F	3/53	3/69
681	HBL 83	Bristol LS6G	93.032	ECW	5702	B45F	2/53	12/71
682	HBL 84	Bristol LS6G	93.033	ECW	6117	B45F	3/53	12/71
683	HBL 85	Bristol LS6G	93.034	ECW	6118	B45F	4/53	12/71
684	HBL 86	Bristol LS6G	93.064	ECW	6119	B45F	5/53	3/71
685	HBL 87	Bristol LS6G	93.065	ECW	6120	B45F	5/53	12/71
686	HBL 88	Bristol LS5G	93.081	ECW	6121	B45F	6/53	10/68
687	HBL 89	Bristol LS5G	93.082	ECW	6122	B45F	8/53	11/68
688	HMO 834	Bristol LS6B	97.067	ECW	6981	C39F	10/53	12/61
689	HMO 835	Bristol LS6B	97.068	ECW	6982	C39F	10/53	6/58
690	HMO 836	Bristol LS6B	97.069	ECW	6983	C39F	10/53	6/58
694	HMO 840	Bristol KSW6B	98.075	ECW	6496	L27/28R	7/53	11/70
695	HMO 841	Bristol KSW6B	98.076	ECW	6497	L27/28R	7/53	6/71
696	HMO 842	Bristol KSW6B	98.096	ECW	6498	L27/28R	9/53	5/71
697	HMO 843	Bristol KSW6B	98.097	ECW	6499	L27/28R	9/53	8/70
698	HMO 844	Bristol KSW6B	98.098	ECW	6500	L27/28R	9/53	3/71
699	HMO 845	Bristol KSW6B	98.131	ECW	6501	L27/28R	10/53	11/70
700	HMO 846	Bristol KSW6B	98.132	ECW	6502	L27/28R	10/53	6/70
701	HMO 847	Bristol KSW6B	98.148	ECW	6503	L27/28R	10/53	3/71
702	HMO 848	Bristol KSW6B	98.149	ECW	6504	L27/28R	10/53	1/71
703	HMO 849	Bristol KSW6B	102.007	ECW	6505	L27/28R	12/53	11/70
704	HMO 850	Bristol KSW6B	102.008	ECW	6506	L27/28R	12/53	1/71
706	HMO 852	Bristol LS5G	97.098	ECW	6749	B45F	10/53	3/71
707	HMO 853	Bristol LS5G	97.099	ECW	6750	B45F	10/53	11/69
708	HMO 854	Bristol LS5G	97.125	ECW	6751	B45F	11/53	2/71
709	HMO 855	Bristol LS5G	97.126	ECW	6752	B45F	12/53	2/71
710	HMO 856	Bristol LS6B	97.127	ECW	6753	B45F	11/53	11/68

Notes:

HBL 72 (670): Used as a driver training vehicle 6/69 to c10/69.
HBL 81 (679): Equipped for one-man-operation and reseated to B41F 4/68; renumbered 102 8/69.

HBL 82 (680): Equipped for one-man-operation and reseated to B41F 8/68.
HBL 83 (681): Equipped for one-man-operation and reseated to B41F 8/68; renumbered 103 11/69.
HBL 84 (682): Equipped for one-man-operation and reseated to B41F 11/63; renumbered 104 8/69.
HBL 85 (683): Equipped for one-man-operation and reseated to B41F 5/61; renumbered 105 8/69.
HBL 86 (684): Equipped for one-man-operation and reseated to B41F by 7/64; renumbered 106 4/70; being cannibalised by 3/71.
HBL 87 (685): Equipped for one-man-operation and reseated to B41F 12/56; reverted to crew operation and B45F 2/58; re-equipped for one-man-operation and reseated to B41F 10/63; renumbered 107 4/70.
HBL 88 (686): Equipped for one-man-operation and reseated to B41F 1956; reverted to crew operation and B45F 1958; re-equipped for one-man-operation and reseated to B41F 1/60.
HBL 89 (687): Equipped for one-man-operation and reseated to B41F 1956; reverted to crew operation and B45F 1958; re-equipped for one-man-operation and reseated to B41F 1/60.
HMO 834-836 (688-690): Did not enter service until 5/54.
HMO 840-841 (694-695): Fitted with staggered seating on the upper deck.
HMO 849-850 (703-704): Fitted with staggered seating on the upper deck.
HMO 852 (706): Equipped for one-man-operation and reseated to B41F 1/57; renumbered 108 11/69.
HMO 853 (707): Equipped for one-man-operation and reseated to B41F 1/57; fitted with a Bristol AVW diesel engine (to LS6B specification) 9/69; allocated 109 in the 1969 renumbering scheme, but not carried.
HMO 854 (708): Equipped for one-man-operation and reseated to B41F 1/57; reverted to crew operation and B45F mid-1958; renumbered 110 10/69.
HMO 855 (709): Equipped for one-man-operation and reseated to B41F 1/57; reverted to crew operation and B45F mid-1958; re-equipped for one-man-operation and reseated to B41F 1/60; renumbered 111 7/69.
HMO 856 (710): Equipped for one-man-operation and reseated to B41F by 7/64.

Disposals:

HBL 65 (663): W Norths (PV) Ltd (dealer), Sherburn in Elmet 12/70.
HBL 66 (664): W Norths (PV) Ltd (dealer), Sherburn in Elmet 8/70.
HBL 67 (665): W Norths (PV) Ltd (dealer), Sherburn in Elmet 2/71; unidentified owner, West Riding 2/72.
HBL 68 (666): W Norths (PV) Ltd (dealer), Sherburn in Elmet 2/71; WH & L Fowler {WH Fowler & Sons}, Holbeach (HD) 5/71; retained for preservation by 6/73; Escrick Bus & Coach Preservation Group (N Halliday & I Hunter), Escrick for preservation by 12/14.
HBL 69 (667): W Norths (PV) Ltd (dealer), Sherburn in Elmet 5/71; Langley Coach Co Ltd, Langley (BK) 2/72; Thames Valley Preservation Society for preservation 7/72; Omnibus Promotions Ltd (dealer), London EC1 7/73; exported to San Francisco, California, USA 8/73; Winery Restaurant, San Francisco (O-USA) by 7/75; Bedayn, Lafayette, California (O-USA) as a caravan c1992 to prior to 9/09.
HBL 70 (668): Tillingbourne Valley Services Ltd, Guildford (SR) 12/70; Harrimonde, Brighton (ES) (not licensed) 4/71.
HBL 71 (669): W Norths (PV) Ltd (dealer), Sherburn in Elmet 6/70.
HBL 72 (670): W Norths (PV) Ltd (dealer), Sherburn in Elmet 7/70.
HBL 81 (102): WR Alexander {Alexander Coaches}, Sheffield (WR) (minus mechanical units) 9/71.
HBL 82 (680): W Norths (PV) Ltd (dealer), Sherburn in Elmet 3/69.
HBL 83 (103): Thames Valley & Aldershot Omnibus Co Ltd {Alder Valley}, Reading (BE) 201 1/72; W Norths (PV) Ltd (dealer), Sherburn in Elmet 12/73; Hills Pharmaceuticals Ltd, Nelson (XLA) 1/74; unidentified dealer (probably W Norths (PV) Ltd, Sherburn in Elmet) for scrap by 9/76.
HBL 84 (104): Thames Valley & Aldershot Omnibus Co Ltd {Alder Valley}, Reading (BE) 202 1/72; W Norths (PV) Ltd (dealer), Sherburn in Elmet for scrap 6/72.
HBL 85 (105): Thames Valley & Aldershot Omnibus Co Ltd {Alder Valley}, Reading (BE) 203 1/72; W Norths (PV) Ltd (dealer), Sherburn in Elmet for scrap 12/73.
HBL 86 (106): GJ Page Ltd, Maidenhead 6/71.
HBL 87 (107): Thames Valley & Aldershot Omnibus Co Ltd {Alder Valley}, Reading (BE) 204 1/72; Paul Sykes Organisation Ltd (dealer), Barnsley for scrap 2/75.
HBL 88 (686): W Norths (PV) Ltd (dealer), Sherburn in Elmet 11/68; HFJ Cheek {Starline Coaches; Starline Elms Coaches from 3/70}, Kenton (LN) 12/68; withdrawn 6/71; BJP Cheek {Elm Tree Transport}, Wealdstone (LN) 10/71; Country Carpet Warehouses Ltd, Walton-on-Thames (XSR) as a mobile demonstration unit 3/72; Cedric Garages (Wivenhoe) Ltd (contract fleet), Wivenhoe (EX) 12/73; Whiting Bros (dealer), Featherstone for scrap 12/74.
HBL 89 (687): W Norths (PV) Ltd (dealer), Sherburn in Elmet 12/68; HFJ Cheek {Starline Coaches; Starline Elms Coaches from 3/70}, Kenton (LN) 1/69; P Sykes (dealer), Barnsley for scrap 8/71.
HMO 834 (688): South Midland Motor Services Ltd 688 12/61 (qv).
HMO 835 (689): South Midland Motor Services Ltd 689 6/58 (qv).

HMO 836 (690): South Midland Motor Services Ltd 690 6/58 (qv).
HMO 840 (694): W Norths (PV) Ltd (dealer), Sherburn in Elmet 12/70.
HMO 841 (695): W Norths (PV) Ltd (dealer), Sherburn in Elmet 7/71.
HMO 842 (696): TD Alexander {Greyhound Luxury Coaches}, Arbroath (AS) 6/71; TD Alexander {Greyhound Luxury Coaches}, Sheffield (WR) 7/71; TD Alexander {Greyhound Luxury Coaches}, Arbroath (AS) 2/72; withdrawn by 12/72.
HMO 843 (697): W Norths (PV) Ltd (dealer), Sherburn in Elmet 9/70; Beyer, Hoofddorp (O-NL) registered VN-36-51 12/70; last seen 9/74 (the registration VN-36-51 was later carried by Bristol FS6B 683 AAM of Streamline, Ijsselstein (O-NL).
HMO 844 (698): W Norths (PV) Ltd (dealer), Sherburn in Elmet 5/71.
HMO 845 (699): W Norths (PV) Ltd (dealer), Sherburn in Elmet 12/70.
HMO 846 (700): W Norths (PV) Ltd (dealer), Sherburn in Elmet 6/70.
HMO 847 (701): W Norths (PV) Ltd (dealer), Sherburn in Elmet 5/71; Langley Coach Co Ltd, Langley (BK) 5/71; HFJ Cheek {Starline Elms Coaches} (dealer), Kenton 6/72.
HMO 848 (702): W Norths (PV) Ltd (dealer), Sherburn in Elmet (minus running units) 1/71.
HMO 849-850 (703-704): W Norths (PV) Ltd (dealer), Sherburn in Elmet 1/71.
HMO 852 (108): Elm Park Coaches Ltd, Romford (LN) 6/71; HJ Plastow {Collett's Garage}, Wheatley (OX) 7/71; scrapped by 5/85.
HMO 853 (707): Elm Park Coaches Ltd, Romford (LN) 3/70; Bee-Line Coaches (Brentwood) Ltd, Brentwood (EX) for spares 12/70.
HMO 854 (110): WR Alexander {Alexander Coaches}, Sheffield (WR) 6/71.
HMO 855 (111): W Norths (PV) Ltd (dealer), Sherburn in Elmet 2/71; Langley Coach Co Ltd, Langley (BK) 5/71; withdrawn 3/72; Thames Valley Preservation Society for preservation 1972; unidentified operator / dealer by 1/85.
HMO 856 (710): W Norths (PV) Ltd (dealer), Sherburn in Elmet 12/68; T Ward, Kirkburton (WR) 2/69; unidentified dealer for scrap 5/70.

Vehicles transferred from South Midland Motor Services Ltd 1/53:

71	EBD 234	Bristol L6B	71.023	ECW		2963	DP31R	9/48	9/59
72	EBD 235	Bristol L6B	71.024	ECW		2964	DP31R	9/48	11/59

Previous histories:

EBD 234-235 (71-72): New to United Counties Omnibus Co Ltd 107-108; renumbered 807-808 2/50 and 71-72 3/52; South Midland Motor Services Ltd 71-72 5/52.

Notes:

EBD 235 (72): Rebuilt to B35F 5/57.

Disposals:

EBD 234 (71): Fleet Car (Sales) Ltd (dealer), Dunchurch 10/59; Misses AR & R Jordan, Blaenavon (MH) 10/59; withdrawn (engine removed) 5/62.
EBD 235 (72): Fleet Car (Sales) Ltd (dealer), Dunchurch 11/59; Misses AR & R Jordan, Blaenavon (MH) 11/59; withdrawn (engine removed) 4/62.

Vehicle on hire from Western National Omnibus Co Ltd, Exeter (DN):

OTT 2	Bristol LD6B	100.006	ECW		7179	H33/25R	5/53	6/53	6/53

Notes:

OTT 2: Was numbered 1863 in the Western National fleet and was on hire for evaluation.

1954

New Vehicles:

691	HMO 837	Bristol LS6B	101.061	ECW	6984	C39F	3/54	1/62
692	HMO 838	Bristol LS6B	101.062	ECW	6985	C39F	3/54	6/58
693	HMO 839	Bristol LS6B	101.063	ECW	6986	C39F	3/54	6/58
705	HMO 851	Bristol KSW6B	102.009	ECW	6507	L27/28R	2/54	3/71
711	HMO 857	Bristol LS6B	97.164	ECW	6754	B45F	2/54	5/70
712	HMO 858	Bristol LS6B	97.165	ECW	6755	B45F	2/54	12/71
713	HMO 859	Bristol LS6B	97.166	ECW	6756	B45F	2/54	5/70
714	HMO 860	Bristol LS6B	97.167	ECW	6757	B45F	2/54	7/70
715	HMO 861	Bristol LS6B	97.184	ECW	6758	B45F	5/54	10/65
716	HMO 862	Bristol LS6B	97.185	ECW	6759	B45F	5/54	3/69
717	HMO 863	Bristol LS6B	101.015	ECW	6760	B45F	6/54	12/71

718	HMO 864	Bristol LS6B	101.016	ECW	6761	B45F	6/54	9/70
719	HMO 865	Bristol LS6B	105.023	ECW	6762	B45F	11/54	1/71
720	HMO 866	Bristol LS6B	105.024	ECW	6763	B45F	11/54	11/69
721	HMO 867	Bristol LS6B	105.025	ECW	6764	B45F	11/54	11/69
722	HMO 868	Bristol LS6B	105.113	ECW	6765	B45F	12/54	12/71
726	JRX 801	Bristol KSW6B	102.020	ECW	7204	L27/28R	8/54	6/71
727	JRX 802	Bristol KSW6B	102.021	ECW	7205	L27/28R	8/54	2/71
728	JRX 803	Bristol KSW6B	102.055	ECW	7206	L27/28R	9/54	2/71
729	JRX 804	Bristol KSW6B	102.056	ECW	7207	L27/28R	8/54	3/71
730	JRX 805	Bristol KSW6B	102.057	ECW	7208	L27/28R	9/54	3/71
731	JRX 806	Bristol KSW6B	102.058	ECW	7209	L27/28R	9/54	2/71
732	JRX 807	Bristol KSW6B	102.059	ECW	7210	L27/28R	9/54	2/71
733	JRX 808	Bristol KSW6B	102.060	ECW	7211	L27/28R	9/54	12/71
734	JRX 809	Bristol KSW6B	102.061	ECW	7212	L27/28R	9/54	3/71
735	JRX 810	Bristol KSW6B	102.062	ECW	7213	L27/28R	9/54	2/71
736	JRX 811	Bristol KSW6B	102.070	ECW	7214	L27/28R	9/54	2/71
737	JRX 812	Bristol KSW6B	102.071	ECW	7215	L27/28R	9/54	2/71
738	JRX 813	Bristol KSW6B	102.072	ECW	7466	CL27/26RD	9/54	9/70
739	JRX 814	Bristol KSW6B	102.073	ECW	7467	CL27/26RD	9/54	6/71
740	JRX 815	Bristol KSW6B	102.074	ECW	7468	CL27/26RD	9/54	6/71
741	JRX 816	Bristol KSW6B	102.075	ECW	7469	CL27/26RD	9/54	7/71
742	JRX 817	Bristol KSW6B	102.076	ECW	7470	CL27/26RD	9/54	3/71
743	JRX 818	Bristol KSW6B	102.077	ECW	7471	CL27/26RD	9/54	7/71
744	JRX 819	Bristol KSW6B	102.078	ECW	7472	CL27/26RD	10/54	2/71

Notes:

HMO 837-839 (691-693): Did not enter service until 5/54.

HMO 851 (705): Fitted with staggered seating on the upper deck; fitted with modified front ventilators and put to wind tunnel tests at FVDRE, Chobham 2/53.

HMO 857 (711): Equipped for one-man-operation and reseated to B41F 11/60; renumbered 117 8/69.

HMO 858 (712): Equipped for one-man-operation and reseated to B41F 10/56; renumbered 118 1/70; fitted with a Gardner 6HLW engine (to LS6G specification) 7/71.

HMO 859 (713): Equipped for one-man-operation and reseated to B41F 8/57; renumbered 119 8/69.

HMO 860 (714): Equipped for one-man-operation and reseated to B41F 4/56; reverted to crew operation and B45F by 6/60; re-equipped for one-man-operation and reseated to B41F by 12/63; renumbered 120 8/69.

HMO 861 (715): Equipped for one-man-operation and reseated to B41F 4/56; reverted to crew operation and B45F by 6/60; destroyed by fire at Maidenhead depot 31/10/65 and cannibalised for spares.

HMO 862 (716): Equipped for one-man-operation and reseated to B41F by 7/64.

HMO 863 (717): Experimentally fitted with a Clayton-Oetiker exhaust brake 3-4/55; equipped for one-man-operation and reseated to B41F 9/61; renumbered 121 4/69; fitted with a Gardner 6HLW engine (to LS6G specification) 10/71.

HMO 864 (718): Equipped for one-man-operation and reseated to B41F 9/61; renumbered 122 8/69; cannibalised for spares 9/70.

HMO 865 (719): Did not enter service until 5/55; equipped for one-man-operation and reseated to B41F 9/61; renumbered 123 10/69.

HMO 866 (720): Did not enter service until 5/55; equipped for one-man-operation and reseated to B41F 4/62; allocated 144 in the 1969 renumbering scheme, but not carried.

HMO 867 (721): Did not enter service until 5/55; equipped for one-man-operation and reseated to B41F 4/56; allocated 145 in the 1969 renumbering scheme, but not carried.

HMO 868 (722): Did not enter service until 5/55; equipped for one-man-operation and reseated to B41F 3/57; fitted with a Gardner 6HLW engine (to LS6G specification) 6/68; renumbered 146 4/70.

JRX 801-807 (726-732): Fitted with staggered seating on the upper deck.

JRX 808 (733): Fitted with staggered seating on the upper deck; used as a driver training vehicle from 6/71.

JRX 809-812 (734-737): Fitted with staggered seating on the upper deck.

JRX 813 (738): Body refurbished, luggage racks removed and coach seats cut down to bus-style (as L27/26RD) 6/66.

JRX 814 (739): Body refurbished, luggage racks removed and coach seats cut down to bus-style (as L27/26RD) 10/66.

JRX 815 (740): Body refurbished, luggage racks removed and coach seats cut down to bus-style (as L27/26RD) 4/67.

JRX 817 (742): Body refurbished, luggage racks removed and coach seats cut down to bus-style (as L27/26RD) 3/67.

JRX 819 (744): Fitted with staggered seating on the upper deck.

Disposals:

HMO 837 (691): South Midland Motor Services Ltd 690 1/62 (qv).

HMO 838-839 (692-693): South Midland Motor Services Ltd 692-693 6/58 (qv).

HMO 851 (705): W Norths (PV) Ltd (dealer), Sherburn in Elmet 5/71.

HMO 857 (117): Jordans Motor Services Ltd, Blaenavon (MH) 5/70; P Sykes (dealer), Barnsley 1971; J Sykes (dealer), Carlton 3/74.

HMO 858 (118): Thames Valley & Aldershot Omnibus Co Ltd {Alder Valley}, Reading (BE) 208 1/72; Paul Sykes Organisation Ltd (dealer), Barnsley for scrap 2/74.

HMO 859 (119): Jordans Motor Services Ltd, Blaenavon (MH) 5/70; unidentified dealer 1971.

HMO 860 (120): W Norths (PV) Ltd (dealer), Sherburn in Elmet 8/70; unidentified dealer for scrap 7/76.

HMO 861 (715): Dismantled for spares / scrap by Thames Valley 2/66.

HMO 862 (716): W Norths (PV) Ltd (dealer), Sherburn in Elmet 3/69; Margo's Luxury Coaches (Streatham) Ltd, London SW16 (LN) 3/69; moved to Thornton Heath (SR) by 11/71; withdrawn by 3/71.

HMO 863 (121): Thames Valley & Aldershot Omnibus Co Ltd {Alder Valley}, Reading (BE) 211 1/72; Main Motors (dealer), Ewelme for scrap 4/75.

HMO 864 (122): W Norths (PV) Ltd (dealer), Sherburn in Elmet 10/70.

HMO 865 (123): Elm Park Coaches Ltd, Romford (LN) 2/71; scrapped on the premises 2/72.

HMO 866 (720): Elm Park Coaches Ltd, Romford (LN) 12/69; EJ Baker & Co (Dorking), Ltd (dealer), Bordon 7/70; Ipswich Coach Co Ltd, Ipswich (EK) 9/70; cannibalised for spares 9/71; Bridge Motors (dealer), Cattawade for scrap 9/73.

HMO 867 (721): Elm Park Coaches Ltd, Romford (LN) 12/69; RE Debnam {RD Motors}, Canvey Island (EX) 9/70; DW Parsons {A1 Coachways}, London N22 (LN) by 11/72.

HMO 868 (146): Thames Valley & Aldershot Omnibus Co Ltd {Alder Valley}, Reading (BE) 227 1/72; Martins Bus & Coach Sales Ltd (dealer), Middlewich for scrap 5/75.

JRX 801 (726): W Norths (PV) Ltd (dealer), Sherburn in Elmet 7/71; Beyer, Hoofddorp (O-NL) 1971/2); noted with the incorrect registration ZV-78-22 1974; registered 81-79-DB 1/78; T & GM de Greef {de Greef Bros}, Echteld (O-NL) 2/93.

JRX 802 (727): W Norths (PV) Ltd (dealer), Sherburn in Elmet 2/71; Beyer, Hoofddorp (O-NL) registered 47-45-FB c1971/2; re-registered BK-19-FV 4/75; Hotel de Witte Brug, Lekkerkerk (O-NL) by 5/97 (possibly by 4/75); fitted with a Scania engine by 4/98; Delta Tours, Wapenfeld (O-NL) 8/06 (carrying UK registration RHN 948F); HM Asselbergs, Bellingwolde (O-NL) 2/08; GJ van den Bor, Baarn (O-NL) 8/09.

JRX 803 (728): W Norths (PV) Ltd (dealer), Sherburn in Elmet 11/71.

JRX 804 (729): TD Alexander {Greyhound Luxury Coaches}, Sheffield (WR) 6/71; TD Alexander {Greyhound Luxury Coaches}, Arbroath (AS) 10/71; withdrawn 12/72.

JRX 805 (730): W Norths (PV) Ltd (dealer), Sherburn in Elmet 5/71.

JRX 806 (731): W Norths (PV) Ltd (dealer), Sherburn in Elmet 2/71; P Blatchly {Contractus}, Stevenage (HT) 6/71; withdrawn 10/72.

JRX 807 (732): W Norths (PV) Ltd (dealer), Sherburn in Elmet 5/71.

JRX 808 (733): Thames Valley & Aldershot Omnibus Co Ltd {Alder Valley}, Reading (BE) 27 as a permanent driver training vehicle 1/72 (still licensed as a PSV); Martyrs Memorial Church, Belfast (XAM) at an unknown date; T Wigley (dealer), Carlton for scrap 2/86.

JRX 809 (734): TD Alexander {Greyhound Luxury Coaches}, Arbroath (AS) 4/71; P Sykes (dealer), Carlton by 10/71.

JRX 810-811 (735-736): TD Alexander {Greyhound Luxury Coaches}, Arbroath (AS) 4/71; P Sykes (dealer), Carlton by 8/71.

JRX 812 (737): W Norths (PV) Ltd (dealer), Sherburn in Elmet 2/71.

JRX 813 (738): W Norths (PV) Ltd (dealer), Sherburn in Elmet 10/70; TD Alexander {Greyhound Luxury Coaches}, Arbroath (AS) 4/71.

JRX 814 (739): W Norths (PV) Ltd (dealer), Sherburn in Elmet 7/71; Treaty Road Evangelical Church, Hounslow (XLN) 7/71; Lister (PVS) Bolton Ltd (dealer), Bolton c3/76; Omnibus Promotions Ltd (dealer), London EC1 by 5/76; exported to Germany 8/76.

JRX 815 (740): W Norths (PV) Ltd (dealer), Sherburn in Elmet 7/71.

JRX 816 (741): W Norths (PV) Ltd (dealer), Sherburn in Elmet 8/71; Twickenham Baptist Church, Twickenham (XLN) 8/71; Lister (PVS) Bolton Ltd (dealer), Bolton 5/75; Omnibus Promotions Ltd (dealer), London EC1 5/75; exported to Germany 6/75.

JRX 817 (742): TD Alexander {Greyhound Luxury Coaches}, Arbroath (AS) 4/71; AA Ford, Althorne (EX) 5/71; Clark, Beazley End (XEX) as a caravan for a tour of Canada and USA 7/73; Roy (dealer), Detroit 5/74; N Higgs, Adolphustown, Ontario (O-CDN) 1974; still owned 1/08 registered 553 KFL.

JRX 818 (743): D Fereday Glenn, Alton (HA) 8/71; withdrawn 8/73; Omnibus Promotions Ltd (dealer), London EC1 1/74; unidentified operator, New York (O-USA) 2/74.

JRX 819 (744): TD Alexander {Greyhound Luxury Coaches}, Arbroath (AS) 4/71; P Sykes (dealer), Carlton by 8/71.

1955

New Vehicles:

723	HMO 869	Bristol LS6B	107.079	ECW	6766	B45F	6/55	11/68
724	HMO 870	Bristol LS6B	107.080	ECW	6767	B45F	6/55	12/71
725	HMO 871	Bristol LS6B	107.082	ECW	6768	B45F	6/55	11/68
745	JRX 820	Bristol KSW6B	106.023	ECW	7473	L27/28R	9/55	12/71
746	JRX 821	Bristol KSW6B	106.024	ECW	7474	L27/28R	9/55	6/71
747	JRX 822	Bristol KSW6B	106.025	ECW	7475	L27/28R	9/55	3/71
748	JRX 823	Bristol KSW6B	106.026	ECW	7476	L27/28R	9/55	12/71
749	JRX 824	Bristol KSW6B	106.027	ECW	7477	L27/28R	9/55	6/71

Notes:

JRX 820-824 (745-749): Fitted with staggered seating on the upper deck.

HMO 869 (723): Equipped for one-man-operation and reseated to DP41F (with seats from MBL 842/3 (761/2)) c10/56.

HMO 870 (724): Experimentally fitted with a Clayton-Oetiker exhaust brake 11/55; equipped for one-man-operation and reseated to B41F 10/56; renumbered 147 7/69; fitted with a Gardner 6HLW engine (to LS6G specification) 4/71.

HMO 871 (725): Equipped for one-man-operation and reseated to DP41F (with seats from MBL 842/3 (761/2)) c10/56.

JRX 820 (745): Fitted with a heater 6/61; used as a driver training vehicle from 5/71.

JRX 821 (746): Fitted with a heater 8/61.

JRX 822 (747): Fitted with a heater 7/61.

JRX 823 (748): Fitted with a heater 10/61; used as a driver training vehicle from 6/71.

JRX 824 (749): Fitted with a heater 1961.

Disposals:

HMO 869 (723): W Norths (PV) Ltd (dealer), Sherburn in Elmet 12/68; HEP Sherriff {Star Tours}, Gainsborough (LI) 2/69; withdrawn 6/72.

HMO 870 (147): Thames Valley & Aldershot Omnibus Co Ltd {Alder Valley}, Reading (BE) 228 1/72; Main Motors (dealer), Ewelme 4/75; scrapped by 10/75.

HMO 871 (725): W Norths (PV) Ltd (dealer), Sherburn in Elmet 12/68; EJ Arnold (printers), Leeds (XWR) 1/69; W Norths (PV) Ltd (dealer), Sherburn in Elmet 12/71.

JRX 820 (745): Thames Valley & Aldershot Omnibus Co Ltd {Alder Valley}, Reading (BE) 28 as a permanent driver training vehicle 1/72 (still licensed as a PSV); W Norths (PV) Ltd (dealer), Sherburn in Elmet 6/72; at a house at Spencers Wood as a store by 1/75; N Trump, Knaphill for preservation (kept at the Castle Point Transport Museum) by 10/89; burnt out by vandals by 2/93.

JRX 821 (746): W Norths (PV) Ltd (dealer), Sherburn in Elmet 7/71; unidentified dealer, Barnsley 8/71; The Wakefield Shirt Co Ltd {Double Two Shirts}, Wakefield (XWR) 6/72; E Beckett (dealer), Carlton 12/76.

JRX 822 (747): W Norths (PV) Ltd (dealer), Sherburn in Elmet 5/71; RW Denyer {Denyer Bros}, Stondon Massey (EX) 6/71; Colosia, Los Angeles, California (O-USA) 9/79; Presidential Limousines, San Diego, California (O-USA) by 5/85; Cerritos Ford, Cerritos, California (O-USA) by 2/91; Roscoe Auto Sales (dealer), Panorama City, California 3/92; registered 2K35325; Red Bus Music & Video, Murrieta, California (O-USA) by 5/96; K Adey {Television Video Music Recording Institute}, Murrieta, California (O-USA) as a promotional vehicle c1998; re-registered 382E; T McAbee, Birmingham, Alabama (O-USA) for preservation 6/07.

JRX 823 (748): Thames Valley & Aldershot Omnibus Co Ltd {Alder Valley}, Reading (BE) 29 as a permanent driver training vehicle 1/72 (still licensed as a PSV); PF Wilks et al, High Wycombe for preservation 12/74; P Pribik, Wokingham for preservation by 12/83; moved to Winnersh by 1/01; still owned 6/11.

JRX 824 (749): W Norths (PV) Ltd (dealer), Sherburn in Elmet 7/71; Beyer, Hoofddorp (O-NL) by 7/76 (probably c1971/2) to 8/79 at least.

Vehicle on hire from Eastern National Omnibus Co Ltd, Chelmsford (EX):

724 APU	Bristol SCX4G	SCX001	ECW	7801	B35F	10/54	1/55	1/55

Notes:

724 APU: Was numbered 395 in the Eastern National fleet and was on hire for evaluation.

1956

New Vehicles:

750	MBL 831	Bristol LD6G	116.104	ECW	8804	CH31/25RD	3/56	12/71
751	MBL 832	Bristol LD6G	116.105	ECW	8805	CH31/25RD	3/56	12/71
752	MBL 833	Bristol LD6G	116.108	ECW	8806	CH31/25RD	3/56	12/71
753	MBL 834	Bristol LD6G	116.109	ECW	8807	CH31/25RD	3/56	12/71
754	MBL 835	Bristol LD6G	116.110	ECW	8808	CH31/25RD	3/56	12/71
755	MBL 836	Bristol LD6B	116.111	ECW	8814	H33/27R	3/56	12/71
756	MBL 837	Bristol LD6B	116.112	ECW	8815	H33/27R	3/56	12/71
757	MBL 838	Bristol LD6B	116.113	ECW	8816	H33/27R	3/56	12/71
758	MBL 839	Bristol LD6G	116.114	ECW	8817	H33/27R	5/56	12/71
759	MBL 840	Bristol LD6G	116.115	ECW	8818	H33/27R	6/56	12/71
760	MBL 841	Bristol LD6G	116.158	ECW	8809	CH31/25RD	6/56	12/71
761	MBL 842	Bristol LD6G	116.159	ECW	8810	CH31/25RD	5/56	12/71
762	MBL 843	Bristol LD6G	116.165	ECW	8811	CH31/25RD	6/56	12/71
763	MBL 844	Bristol LD6G	116.166	ECW	8812	CH31/25RD	5/56	12/71
764	MBL 845	Bristol LD6G	116.175	ECW	8813	CH31/25RD	6/56	12/71
765	MBL 846	Bristol LD5G	120.023	ECW	8819	H33/27R	7/56	12/71
766	MBL 847	Bristol LD5G	120.024	ECW	8820	H33/27R	7/56	12/71
767	MBL 848	Bristol LD5G	120.027	ECW	8821	H33/27R	7/56	12/71
768	MBL 849	Bristol LD5G	120.032	ECW	8822	H33/27R	7/56	12/71
769	MBL 850	Bristol LD5G	120.033	ECW	8823	H33/27R	7/56	12/71
774	NBL 731	Bristol SC4LK	113.072	ECW	8784	B35F	12/56	12/69
775	NBL 732	Bristol SC4LK	113.073	ECW	8785	B35F	12/56	12/69
776	NBL 733	Bristol SC4LK	113.074	ECW	8786	B35F	12/56	12/69

Notes:

MBL 831-835 (750-754): Fitted with heaters and semi-luxury seats; originally carried fleet numbers TV750-754 in error.

MBL 841-845 (760-764): Fitted with heaters and semi-luxury seats.

MBL 831 (750): Reseated to CH31/24RD (with a luggage pen) 8/56; reseated to H33/27RD 2/69.

MBL 832 (751): Reseated to CH31/24RD (with a luggage pen) 9/56; reseated to H33/27RD 2/70.

MBL 833 (752): Reseated to CH31/24RD (with a luggage pen) 7/56; fitted with experimental black on white registration plates 4/64; reseated to H33/27RD 6/69.

MBL 834 (753): Reseated to CH31/24RD (with a luggage pen) 9/56; fitted with experimental black on white registration plates 4/64; reseated to H33/27RD 10/69.

MBL 835 (754): Reseated to CH31/24RD (with a luggage pen) 12/56;

MBL 836-837 (755-756): Originally carried fleet numbers TV755-756 in error; fitted with platform doors by ECW as H33/27RD (rebuild nos. R920-921) 4/68.

MBL 838 (757): Originally carried fleet number TV757 in error; fitted with platform doors by ECW as H33/27RD (rebuild no. R923) 5/68.

MBL 839-840 (758-759): Fitted with platform doors by ECW as H33/27RD (rebuild nos. R925-926) 6/68.

MBL 841 (760): Reseated to CH31/24RD (with a luggage pen) 11/56; reseated to H33/27RD 10/69.

MBL 842 (761): Reseated to H33/27RD 9/56.

MBL 843 (762): Reseated to H33/27RD 11/56.

MBL 844 (763): Reseated to H33/27RD 5/71.

MBL 845 (764): Reseated to H33/27RD 4/71.

MBL 846 (765): Fitted with a Gardner 6LW diesel engine (to LD6G specification) 4/67; fitted with platform doors by ECW as H33/27RD (rebuild no. R924) 5/68.

MBL 847 (766): Fitted with a Bristol AVW diesel engine (to LD6B specification) 4/67; fitted with platform doors by ECW as H33/27RD (rebuild no. R928) 6/68.

MBL 848 (767): Fitted with a Bristol AVW diesel engine (to LD6B specification) 1/67; fitted with platform doors by ECW as H33/27RD (rebuild no. R922) 4/68.

MBL 849 (768): Fitted with a Bristol AVW diesel engine (to LD6B specification) 2/67; fitted with platform doors by ECW as H33/27RD (rebuild no. R927) 6/68.

MBL 850 (769): Fitted with a Bristol AVW diesel engine (to LD6B specification) 3/67; fitted with platform doors by ECW as H33/27RD (rebuild no. R941) 10/68.

NBL 731-733 (774-776): Purchased for the Marlow Bridge route on which there was a five ton weight limit.

NBL 731 (774): Renumbered S301 9/66; renumbered 155 10/69.

NBL 732 (775): Renumbered S302 9/66; renumbered 156 11/69.

NBL 733 (776): Renumbered S303 9/66; renumbered 157 10/69.

Disposals:

MBL 831 (750): Thames Valley & Aldershot Omnibus Co Ltd {Alder Valley}, Reading (BE) 523 1/72; Paul Sykes Organisation Ltd (dealer), Barnsley 2/75; Martins Bus & Coach Sales Ltd (dealer), Middlewich by 4/75; Petercars Ltd, Peterborough (XCM) as a publicity vehicle 4/75; E Beckett (dealer), Carlton 1/79; S Twell (dealer), Ingham for scrap by 3/86.

MBL 832 (751): Thames Valley & Aldershot Omnibus Co Ltd {Alder Valley}, Reading (BE) 524 1/72; Martins Bus & Coach Sales Ltd (dealer), Middlewich 5/75; exported to the Netherlands 6/75, but not traced further.

MBL 833 (752): Thames Valley & Aldershot Omnibus Co Ltd {Alder Valley}, Reading (BE) 525 1/72; renumbered 546 in 7/75; D Rollinson (Bus Centre) Ltd (dealer), Carlton for scrap 9/76.

MBL 834 (753): Thames Valley & Aldershot Omnibus Co Ltd {Alder Valley}, Reading (BE) 526 1/72; Main Motors (dealer), Ewelme for scrap 5/74.

MBL 835 (754): Thames Valley & Aldershot Omnibus Co Ltd {Alder Valley}, Reading (BE) 527 1/72; reseated to H33/26RD 6/72; Martins Bus & Coach Sales Ltd (dealer), Middlewich 5/75; Chester-Barrie Ltd, Crewe (XCH) by 8/75; Martins Bus & Coach Sales Ltd (dealer), Middlewich 7/78; T Goodwin (dealer), Carlton for scrap 9/78.

MBL 836 (755): Thames Valley & Aldershot Omnibus Co Ltd {Alder Valley}, Reading (BE) 528 1/72; W Norths (PV) Ltd (dealer), Sherburn in Elmet 6/72; HFJ Cheek {Starline Elms Coaches}, Kenton (LN) 9/72; Starline-Elms Coaches (Kenton) Ltd, Kenton (LN) 11/73; W Norths (PV) Ltd (dealer), Sherburn in Elmet for scrap 10/77.

MBL 837 (756): Thames Valley & Aldershot Omnibus Co Ltd {Alder Valley}, Reading (BE) 529 1/72; Paul Sykes Organisation Ltd (dealer), Barnsley for scrap 2/74.

MBL 838 (757): Thames Valley & Aldershot Omnibus Co Ltd {Alder Valley}, Reading (BE) 530 1/72; Hardwick & Jones (dealer), Carlton for scrap 6/73.

MBL 839 (758): Thames Valley & Aldershot Omnibus Co Ltd {Alder Valley}, Reading (BE) 531 1/72; Paul Sykes Organisation Ltd (dealer), Barnsley for scrap 2/75.

MBL 840 (759): Thames Valley & Aldershot Omnibus Co Ltd {Alder Valley}, Reading (BE) 532 1/72; Paul Sykes Organisation Ltd (dealer), Barnsley for scrap 2/74.

MBL 841 (760): Thames Valley & Aldershot Omnibus Co Ltd {Alder Valley}, Reading (BE) 533 1/72; reseated to H33/27RD in 6/72; Paul Sykes Organisation Ltd (dealer), Barnsley for scrap 2/75.

MBL 842 (761): Thames Valley & Aldershot Omnibus Co Ltd {Alder Valley}, Reading (BE) 534 1/72; Paul Sykes Organisation Ltd (dealer), Barnsley for scrap 2/75.

MBL 843 (762): Thames Valley & Aldershot Omnibus Co Ltd {Alder Valley}, Reading (BE) 535 1/72; renumbered 547 7/75; D Rollinson (Bus Centre) Ltd (dealer), Carlton for scrap 9/76.

MBL 844 (763): Thames Valley & Aldershot Omnibus Co Ltd {Alder Valley}, Reading (BE) 536 1/72; converted to a driver training vehicle no 31 2/75 and transferred to the service fleet; renumbered 14 3/75 and 1103 6/78; D Rollinson (Bus Centre) Ltd (dealer), Carlton for scrap 6/81.

MBL 845 (764): Thames Valley & Aldershot Omnibus Co Ltd {Alder Valley}, Reading (BE) 537 1/72; Martins Bus & Coach Sales Ltd (dealer), Middlewich 6/75; J Moffat, Cardenden (FE) 10/75; Moffat & Williamson Ltd, Gauldry (FE) 8/78; RW Dunsmore (dealer), Larkhall for scrap c10/78.

MBL 846 (765): Thames Valley & Aldershot Omnibus Co Ltd {Alder Valley}, Reading (BE) 538 1/72; renumbered 548 7/75; D Rollinson (Bus Centre) Ltd (dealer), Carlton for scrap 9/76.

MBL 847 (766): Thames Valley & Aldershot Omnibus Co Ltd {Alder Valley}, Reading (BE) 539 1/72; Hardwick & Jones (dealer), Carlton for scrap 5/73.

MBL 848 (767): Thames Valley & Aldershot Omnibus Co Ltd {Alder Valley}, Reading (BE) 540 1/72; Main Motors (dealer), Ewelme for scrap 5/74.

MBL 849 (768): Thames Valley & Aldershot Omnibus Co Ltd {Alder Valley}, Reading (BE) 541 1/72; Paul Sykes Organisation Ltd (dealer), Barnsley for scrap 2/75.

MBL 850 (769): Thames Valley & Aldershot Omnibus Co Ltd {Alder Valley}, Reading (BE) 542 1/72; W Norths (PV) Ltd (dealer), Sherburn in Elmet 5/73; J Laverty {Eagle Coaches} Neilston (SC) 7/73; Wilson (contractor), Stonehouse (XSC) by 10/75.

NBL 731 (155): R Hughes Jones {Express Motors}, Rhostryfan (CN) 2/70; RS Brown {Shaftsbury & District Motor Services}, Motcombe (DT) 2/77; Lister (PVS) Bolton Ltd (dealer), Bolton for scrap 7/77.

NBL 732 (156): R Hughes Jones {Express Motors}, Rhostryfan (CN) 2/70; EW Thomas {Silver Star}, Upper Llandwrog (CN) 10/70; withdrawn by 2/82.

NBL 733 (157): ER Pritchard, TH & ER Davies & M Williams {Purple Motors}, Bethesda (CN) 2/70; T Hollis, Queensferry (CL) 2/75.

Vehicles acquired from Brighton, Hove & District Omnibus Co Ltd, Brighton (ES) 11/56:

771	CAP 132	Bristol K5G	55.071	ECW		6923	O30/26R	7/40	7/60
772	CAP 176	Bristol K5G	55.072	ECW		6924	H30/26R	8/40	7/60
770	CAP 206	Bristol K5G	55.070	ECW		6932	O30/26R	9/40	8/57
773	CAP 211	Bristol K5G	55.073	ECW		6933	O30/26R	9/40	6/60

Previous histories:

CAP 132 (771): New to Brighton, Hove & District Omnibus Co Ltd 6354 (as H30/26R; renumbered 354 1955; converted to open top immediately prior to acquisition]; entering service 5/57.

CAP 176 (772): New to Brighton, Hove & District Omnibus Co Ltd 6355 (as H30/26R; renumbered 355 1955].

CAP 206 (770): New to Brighton, Hove & District Omnibus Co Ltd 6353 (as H30/26R; renumbered 353 1955; converted to open top immediately prior to acquisition]; entering service 5/57.

CAP 211 (773): New to Brighton, Hove & District Omnibus Co Ltd 6356 (as H30/26R; renumbered 356 1956; converted to open top immediately prior to acquisition]; entering service 5/57.

Notes:

These vehicles were acquired for a 'Riverside Express' service along the River Thames between Reading, Henley-on-Thames, Marlow and Maidenhead. The three acquired already converted to open top entered service 5/57.

CAP 176 (772): Converted to open-top as O30/26R 5/57, entering service 6/57.

Disposals:

CAP 132 (771): Passenger Vehicle Disposals Ltd (dealer), Dunchurch 7/60; Colbro Ltd (dealer), Rothwell 8/60.

CAP 176 (772): Passenger Vehicle Disposals Ltd (dealer), Dunchurch 7/60; Colbro Ltd (dealer), Rothwell 8/60.

CAP 206 (770): South Midland Motor Services Ltd 770 8/57 (qv).

CAP 211 (773): Red & White Services Ltd, Chepstow (MH) as a tree-lopper 6/60; Critchcraft (dealer), Chepstow 3/68; Dart Valley Railway Association, Buckfastleigh for preservation 8/68; Ashburton Carnival Committee, Ashburton (XDN) 1972; N Dawson-Smith, Romford for preservation by 9/73; exported possibly to Netherlands or Belgium by 12/98, but not traced further.

1957

New Vehicles:

777	NBL 734	Bristol SC4LK	113.075	ECW	8787	B35F	1/57	12/69
778	NBL 735	Bristol SC4LK	113.076	ECW	8788	B35F	1/57	7/63
779	NBL 736	Bristol LDL6G	134.128	ECW	9520	H37/33R	11/57	12/71
780	NBL 737	Bristol LD5G	134.020	ECW	9521	H33/27R	6/57	12/71
781	NBL 738	Bristol LD5G	134.027	ECW	9522	H33/27R	6/57	12/71
782	NBL 739	Bristol LD5G	134.033	ECW	9523	H33/27R	8/57	12/71
783	NBL 740	Bristol LD5G	134.157	ECW	9524	H33/27R	10/57	12/71
784	NBL 741	Bristol LD5G	134.175	ECW	9525	H33/27R	11/57	12/71
785	NBL 742	Bristol LD5G	134.176	ECW	9526	H33/27R	11/57	12/71
786	NBL 743	Bristol LD6G	134.211	ECW	9527	H33/27R	12/57	12/71

Notes:

NBL 734-735 (777-778): Purchased for the Marlow Bridge route on which there was a five ton weight limit.
NBL 737-742 (780-785): Fitted new with reconditioned engines from withdrawn Newbury & District Guys.

NBL 734 (777): Renumbered S304 9/66; renumbered 158 8/69.
NBL 735 (778): Dut did not enter service until 6/57.
NBL 736 (779): Originally intended for Southern Vectis Omnibus Co Ltd, Newport (IW); fitted from new with air pressure braking; converted to an air hydraulic system by Bristol Commercial Vehicles 8/60; collided with a low bridge 8/62, returning to service 12/62; fitted with platform doors by ECW as H37/33RD (rebuild R898) 9/67.
NBL 737 (780): Fitted with a Bristol AVW diesel engine (to LD6B specification) 4/67; fitted with platform doors by ECW as H33/27RD (rebuild R912) 12/67.
NBL 738 (781): Fitted with a Bristol AVW diesel engine (to LD6B specification) 2/67; fitted with platform doors by ECW as H33/27RD (rebuild R911) 11/67.
NBL 739 (782): Fitted with a Bristol AVW diesel engine (to LD6B specification) 11/66; fitted with platform doors by ECW as H33/27RD (rebuild R909) 11/67.
NBL 740 (783): Fitted with a Bristol AVW diesel engine (to LD6B specification) 5/67; fitted with platform doors by ECW as H33/27RD (rebuild R905) 10/67.
NBL 741 (784): Fitted with a Bristol AVW diesel engine (to LD6B specification) 12/66; fitted with platform doors by ECW as H33/27RD (rebuild R907) 11/67.

NBL 742 (785): Fitted with a Bristol AVW diesel engine (to LD6B specification) 4/67; fitted with platform doors by ECW as H33/27RD (rebuild R910) 11/67.

NBL 743 (786): Fitted with platform doors by ECW as H33/27RD (rebuild R903) 10/67.

Disposals:

NBL 734 (158): W Norths (PV) Ltd (dealer), Sherburn in Elmet 7/70; Costain Civil Engineering Ltd (contractor), Maidenhead (XBE) 8/70; hired to Westminster Plant Ltd (contractor), Boston Spa (XWY) 8/70; withdrawn 1/76.

NBL 735 (778): Liss & District Omnibus Co Ltd, Liss (HA) 7/63; P Jeffreys {Liss & District}, Grayshott (HA) 4/64; withdrawn and stored mid-1965; James (dealer), Hedge End 11/66.

NBL 736 (779): Thames Valley & Aldershot Omnibus Co Ltd {Alder Valley}, Reading (BE) 548 1/72; withdrawn after a low-bridge accident on 20/6/73; WR Alexander {Alexander Coaches}, Sheffield (WR) (minus mechanical units) 8/73.

NBL 737 (780): Thames Valley & Aldershot Omnibus Co Ltd {Alder Valley}, Reading (BE) 549 1/72; Paul Sykes Organisation Ltd (dealer), Barnsley for scrap 11/75.

NBL 738 (781): Thames Valley & Aldershot Omnibus Co Ltd {Alder Valley}, Reading (BE) 550 1/72; withdrawn after being destroyed by fire at Reading depot on 16/7/76; D Rollinson (Bus Centre) Ltd (dealer), Carlton for scrap 9/76.

NBL 739 (782): Thames Valley & Aldershot Omnibus Co Ltd {Alder Valley}, Reading (BE) 551 1/72; withdrawn after fire damage at Reading depot on 7/7/73; WR Alexander {Alexander Coaches}, Sheffield (WR) (minus mechanical units) 9/73.

NBL 740 (783): Thames Valley & Aldershot Omnibus Co Ltd {Alder Valley}, Reading (BE) 552 1/72; Main Motors (dealer), Ewelme for scrap 5/74.

NBL 741 (784): Thames Valley & Aldershot Omnibus Co Ltd {Alder Valley}, Reading (BE) 553 1/72; Main Motors (dealer), Ewelme for scrap 5/74.

NBL 742 (785): Thames Valley & Aldershot Omnibus Co Ltd {Alder Valley}, Reading (BE) 554 1/72; Paul Sykes Organisation Ltd (dealer), Barnsley 11/75; J & J Car Dismantlers (dealer), Carlton for scrap 12/75.

NBL 743 (786): Thames Valley & Aldershot Omnibus Co Ltd {Alder Valley}, Reading (BE) 555 1/72; Passenger Vehicle Spares (Barnsley) Ltd (dealer), Carlton for scrap 11/76.

1958

New Vehicles:

787	NBL 744	Bristol LD6G	134.212	ECW	9528	H33/27R	1/58	12/71
788	NBL 745	Bristol LD6G	134.213	ECW	9529	H33/27R	1/58	12/71
789	NBL 746	Bristol LD5G	138.006	ECW	9530	H33/27R	2/58	12/71
790	NBL 747	Bristol LD6G	138.007	ECW	9531	H33/27R	2/58	12/71
791	NBL 748	Bristol LD5G	138.023	ECW	9532	H33/27R	3/58	12/71
792	NBL 749	Bristol LD6G	138.174	ECW	9533	H33/27R	9/58	12/71
793	NBL 750	Bristol LD6G	138.175	ECW	9534	H33/27R	9/58	12/71
808	PRX 926	Bristol LD6G	138.190	ECW	10313	H33/27RD	10/58	12/71
809	PRX 927	Bristol LD6G	138.191	ECW	10314	H33/27RD	10/58	12/71

Notes:

NBL 744 (787): Fitted with platform doors by ECW as H33/27RD (rebuild R908) 11/67.

NBL 745 (788): Fitted with platform doors by ECW as H33/27RD (rebuild R906) 11/67.

NBL 746 (789): Fitted new with a reconditioned engine from a withdrawn Newbury & District Guy; fitted with a Bristol AVW diesel engine (to LD6B specification) 2/67; fitted with platform doors by ECW as H33/27RD (rebuild R904) 10/67.

NBL 747 (790): Fitted with platform doors by ECW as H33/27RD (rebuild R901) 10/67.

NBL 748 (791): Fitted new with a reconditioned engine from a withdrawn Newbury & District Guy; fitted with a Bristol AVW diesel engine (to LD6B specification) 12/66; fitted with platform doors by ECW as H33/27RD (rebuild R902) 10/67.

NBL 749-750 (792-793): Were the last new double-deck vehicles to be delivered without platform doors and heaters; fitted with platform doors by ECW as H33/27RD (rebuild R899-R900) 9/67.

PRX 926-927 (808-809): Were the first bus-seated double-deck vehicles to be fitted with heaters and platform doors from new.

Disposals:

NBL 744 (787): Thames Valley & Aldershot Omnibus Co Ltd {Alder Valley}, Reading (BE) 556 1/72; D Rollinson (Bus Centre) Ltd (dealer), Carlton for scrap 9/76.

NBL 745 (788): Thames Valley & Aldershot Omnibus Co Ltd {Alder Valley}, Reading (BE) 557 1/72; Passenger Vehicle Spares (Barnsley) Ltd (dealer), Carlton for scrap 11/76.

NBL 746 (789): Thames Valley & Aldershot Omnibus Co Ltd {Alder Valley}, Reading (BE) 558 1/72; Passenger Vehicle Spares (Barnsley) Ltd (dealer), Carlton for scrap 11/76.

NBL 747 (790): Thames Valley & Aldershot Omnibus Co Ltd {Alder Valley}, Reading (BE) 559 1/72; Passenger Vehicle Spares (Barnsley) Ltd (dealer), Carlton for scrap 11/76.

NBL 748 (791): Thames Valley & Aldershot Omnibus Co Ltd {Alder Valley}, Reading (BE) 560 1/72; D Rollinson (Bus Centre) Ltd (dealer), Carlton for scrap 9/76.

NBL 749 (792): Thames Valley & Aldershot Omnibus Co Ltd {Alder Valley}, Reading (BE) 561 1/72; Passenger Vehicle Spares (Barnsley) Ltd (dealer), Carlton for scrap 11/76.

NBL 750 (793): Thames Valley & Aldershot Omnibus Co Ltd {Alder Valley}, Reading (BE) 562 1/72; D Rollinson (Bus Centre) Ltd (dealer), Carlton for scrap 9/76.

PRX 926 (808): Thames Valley & Aldershot Omnibus Co Ltd {Alder Valley}, Reading (BE) 563 1/72; D Rollinson (Bus Centre) Ltd (dealer), Carlton for scrap 9/76.

PRX 927 (809): Thames Valley & Aldershot Omnibus Co Ltd {Alder Valley}, Reading (BE) 564 1/72; Passenger Vehicle Spares (Barnsley) Ltd (dealer), Carlton for scrap 11/76.

Vehicle transferred from South Midland Motor Services Ltd 10/58:

548	FMO 23	Bristol L6B	79.116	Windover	6857	C33F	3/50	5/68

Previous history:

FMO 23 (548): New to Thames Valley Traction Co Ltd 548; South Midland Motor Services 548 1/55.

Notes:

FMO 23 (548): Upon its return from South Midland Motor Services Ltd, its Windover body was removed and broken up 10/58; chassis rebuilt to 30ft long and fitted with a Gardner 5LW engine (to LL5G specification); rebodied ECW (11403) FB39F (one-man-operated); renumbered 819 2/59; entered service 4/59.

Disposal:

FMO 23 (819): R Hughes Jones {Express Motors}, Rhostryfan (CN) 5/68; EW Thomas {Silver Star}, Upper Llandwrog (CN) 10/70; Paul Sykes Organisation Ltd (dealer), Barnsley for scrap 3/75.

1959

New Vehicles:

810	PRX 928	Bristol LD6B	150.008	ECW	10315	H33/27RD	1/59	12/71
811	PRX 929	Bristol LD6B	150.009	ECW	10316	H33/27RD	1/59	12/71
812	SMO 78	Bristol LD6G	150.163	ECW	11021	H33/27RD	6/59	12/71
813	SMO 79	Bristol LD6G	150.189	ECW	11022	H33/27RD	6/59	12/71
814	SMO 80	Bristol LD6G	150.190	ECW	11023	H33/27RD	6/59	12/71
815	SMO 81	Bristol LD6B	150.210	ECW	11024	H33/27RD	7/59	12/71
816	SMO 82	Bristol LD6B	150.211	ECW	11025	H33/27RD	7/59	12/71

Notes:

PRX 928 (810): Fitted with a reconditioned engine from a Bristol L6B; fitted with a Gardner 6LW diesel engine (to LD6G specification) 8/71.

PRX 929 (811): Fitted with a reconditioned engine from a Bristol L6B.

Disposals:

PRX 928 (810): Thames Valley & Aldershot Omnibus Co Ltd {Alder Valley}, Reading (BE) 565 1/72; D Rollinson (Bus Centre) Ltd (dealer), Carlton for scrap 9/76.

PRX 929 (811): Thames Valley & Aldershot Omnibus Co Ltd {Alder Valley}, Reading (BE) 566 1/72; D Rollinson (Bus Centre) Ltd (dealer), Carlton for scrap 9/76.

SMO 78 (812): Thames Valley & Aldershot Omnibus Co Ltd {Alder Valley}, Reading (BE) 567 1/72; Martins Bus & Coach Sales Ltd (dealer), Middlewich for scrap 2/76.

SMO 79 (813): Thames Valley & Aldershot Omnibus Co Ltd {Alder Valley}, Reading (BE) 568 1/72; Passenger Vehicle Spares (Barnsley) Ltd (dealer), Carlton for scrap 11/76.

SMO 80 (814): Thames Valley & Aldershot Omnibus Co Ltd {Alder Valley}, Reading (BE) 569 1/72; D Rollinson (Bus Centre) Ltd (dealer), Carlton for scrap 9/76.

SMO 81 (815): Thames Valley & Aldershot Omnibus Co Ltd {Alder Valley}, Reading (BE) 570 1/72; Paul Sykes Organisation Ltd (dealer), Barnsley for scrap 11/75.

SMO 82 (816): Thames Valley & Aldershot Omnibus Co Ltd {Alder Valley}, Reading (BE) 571 1/72; Martins Bus & Coach Sales Ltd (dealer), Middlewich 5/75; AA & O Lloyd, Bagillt (CL) 6/75; K Askin (dealer), Barnsley for scrap 4/80.

Vehicles acquired from United Counties Omnibus Co Ltd, Northampton (NO) 1/59:

828	FRP 843	Bristol LL6B	83.147	ECW	4950	FC37F	5/51	10/61
829	FRP 844	Bristol LL6B	83.148	ECW	4951	FC37F	3/51	10/61

Previous histories:
FRP 843 (828): New to United Counties Omnibus Co Ltd 843 [built with an 8ft wide body on a 7ft 6in chassis; fitted with wider axles 1952; renumbered 378 3/52]; entering service 6/59.
FRP 844 (829): New to United Counties Omnibus Co Ltd 844 [built with an 8ft wide body on a 7ft 6in chassis; fitted with wider axles 1952; renumbered 379 3/52]; entering service service 4/59.

Disposals:
FRP 843 (828): Parlanes (Aldershot) Ltd, Bordon (HA) 11/61; unidentified dealer, Birmingham for scrap 4/66.
FRP 844 (829): Creamline Motor Services Ltd, Bordon (HA) 10/61; withdrawn 9/64.

Vehicles acquired from Bristol Omnibus Co Ltd, Bristol (GL) 6/59:

438	HTT 980	Bristol K5G	62.019	ECW	1183	L27/28R	10/46	5/62
437	KHU 601	Bristol K6B	62.121	ECW	1597	L27/28R	9/47	12/63
436	KHU 624	Bristol K5G	64.028	ECW	1591	L27/28R	9/47	7/66

Previous histories:
HTT 980 (438): New to Western National Omnibus Co Ltd, Exeter (DN) 809; Bristol Tramways & Carriage Co Ltd, Bristol (GL) L4130 5/50; Bristol Omnibus Co Ltd L4130 6/57; entering service 9/59.
KHU 601 (437): New to Bristol Tramways & Carriage Co Ltd, Bristol (GL) L4104; Bristol Omnibus Co Ltd L4104 6/57; enetering service 9/59.
KHU 624 (436): New to Bristol Tramways & Carriage Co Ltd, Bristol (GL) L4103; fitted with a Bristol AVW diesel engine (to K6B specification) 3/53; Bristol Omnibus Co Ltd L4103 6/57; entering service 8/59.

Notes:
HTT 980 (438): Fitted with a Bristol AVW diesel engine (to K6B specification) before entry into service.

Disposals:
HTT 980 (438): Passenger Vehicle Disposals Ltd (dealer), Dunchurch 5/62.
KHU 601 (437): W Norths (PV) Ltd (dealer), Sherburn in Elmet 12/63; unidentified dealer for scrap 1/64.
KHU 624 (436): F Showler {British Double Deck Hire}, Oakville, Ontario (O-CDN) 4361 8/66; Piccadilly Bus Tours, Ottawa (O-CDN) 7/73; Campus Transportation Ltd {Hiawathaland Tours}, Sault Ste Marie (O-CDN) c6/74; registered BB8 171 by 12/80; in use as a booking office by 1990; W King & Son Salvage (dealer), Sault Ste Marie (O-CDN) by 6/01; P Cook, Exeter for preservation 2002; shipped back to the UK 6/04; being restored at Winkleigh by 2006-8.

Vehicles acquired from Bath Tramways Motor Co Ltd, Bath (SO) 11/59:

455	KHU 604	Bristol K6B	64.006	ECW	1599	L27/28R	10/47	12/63
457	KHU 605	Bristol K6A	64.029	ECW	1593	L27/28R	9/47	2/65
458	KHU 606	Bristol K6A	64.030	ECW	1594	L27/28R	9/47	4/63
456	KHW 633	Bristol K5G	64.071	ECW	1605	L27/28R	11/47	3/63

Previous histories:
KHU 604 (455): New to Bath Tramways Motor Co Ltd L3900 [it was intended for the Bristol Tramways & Carriage Co Ltd, Bristol (GL) L4107]; entering service 12/59.
KHU 605 (457): New to Bristol Tramways & Carriage Co Ltd, Bristol (GL) L4108; Bath Tramways Motor Co Ltd L3904; entering service 5/60.
KHU 606 (458): New to Bristol Tramways & Carriage Co Ltd, Bristol (GL) L4109; Bath Tramways Motor Co Ltd L3905; entering service 2/60.
KHW 633 (456): New to Bath Tramways Motor Co Ltd L3901 [it was intended for the Bristol Tramways & Carriage Co Ltd, Bristol (GL) L4115]; entering service 1/60.

Disposals:
KHU 604 (455): W Norths (PV) Ltd (dealer), Sherburn in Elmet 12/63; unidentified dealer for scrap 1/64.
KHU 605 (457): P Jeffreys {Liss & District}, Grayshott (HA) 4/65; unidentified operator / dealer by 8/70.
KHU 606 (458): W Norths (PV) Ltd (dealer), Sherburn in Elmet 4/63; Jackson (dealer), Bradford for scrap 7/63.
KHW 633 (456): W Norths (PV) Ltd (dealer), Sherburn in Elmet 3/63; Jackson (dealer), Bradford for scrap 9/63.

Vehicle acquired from Bristol Omnibus Co Ltd, Bristol (GL) 11/59:

459	KHU 622	Bristol K5G	64.026	ECW	1592	L27/28R	9/47	2/65

Previous histories:

KHU 622 (459): New to Bristol Tramways & Carriage Co Ltd, Bristol (GL) L4101; fitted with an AEC 7.7 litre diesel engine (to K6A specification) 9/51; Bristol Omnibus Co Ltd L4101 6/57; entering service 3/60.

Disposals:

KHU 622 (459): Chris Hoyle & Son Ltd (dealer), Wombwell for scrap 2/65.

Vehicles acquired from United Counties Omnibus Co Ltd, Northampton (NO) 11/59:

461	FPU 509	Bristol K5G	42.52	ECW	5652	L27/28R	11/37	8/65
460	FPU 510	Bristol K5G	42.53	ECW	5648	L27/28R	11/37	9/64
462	FPU 515	Bristol K5G	42.58	ECW	5653	L27/28R	12/37	1/65
463	FPU 517	Bristol K5G	42.60	ECW	5649	L27/28R	12/37	2/66

Previous histories:

FPU 509 (461): New to Eastern National Omnibus Co Ltd, Chelmsford (EX) 3729 (with an ECW (4955) L26/24R 8ft wide body; reseated to L24/24R before entry into service); rebodied (8ft wide) 2/52; United Counties Omnibus Co Ltd 610 5/52; entering service 12/59.

FPU 510 (460): New to Eastern National Omnibus Co Ltd, Chelmsford (EX) 3730 (with an ECW (4956) L26/24R 8ft wide body; reseated to L24/24R before entry into service); rebodied (8ft wide) 12/51; United Counties Omnibus Co Ltd 611 5/52; entering service 12/59.

FPU 515 (462): New to Eastern National Omnibus Co Ltd, Chelmsford (EX) 3735 (with an ECW (4961) L26/24R 8ft wide body; reseated to L24/24R before entry into service); rebodied (8ft wide) 2/52; United Counties Omnibus Co Ltd 617 5/52.

FPU 517 (463): New to Eastern National Omnibus Co Ltd, Chelmsford (EX) 3737 (with an ECW (4964) L26/24R 8ft wide body; reseated to L24/24R before entry into service); rebodied (8ft wide) 12/51; United Counties Omnibus Co Ltd 612 5/52.

Notes:

FPU 515 (462): Withdrawn following an accident 1/65.

Disposals:

FPU 509 (461): W Norths (PV) Ltd (dealer), Sherburn in Elmet 8/65; TD Alexander {Greyhound Luxury Coaches}, Sheffield (WR) 8/65.

FPU 510 (460): Converted to a route servicing vehicle (tree lopper) ED53 11/64 and transferred to the service fleet (qv).

FPU 515 (462): Chris Hoyle & Son Ltd (dealer), Wombwell for scrap 2/65.

FPU 517 (463): Zoar Baptist Church, Hounslow (XMX) 2/66.

1960

New Vehicles:

834	UJB 200	Bristol FLF6B	156.006	ECW	11418	CH37/28F	7/60	12/71
835	UJB 201	Bristol FLF6G	169.006	ECW	11419	CH37/28F	11/60	12/71
836	UJB 202	Bristol FLF6G	169.007	ECW	11420	CH37/28F	11/60	12/71
837	UJB 203	Bristol FLF6G	169.008	ECW	11421	CH37/28F	11/60	12/71
838	UJB 204	Bristol FLF6G	169.009	ECW	11422	CH37/28F	11/60	12/71
852	VJB 943	Bristol MW6G	164.079	ECW	11856	DP41F	7/60	12/71
853	VJB 944	Bristol MW6G	164.080	ECW	11857	DP41F	8/60	12/71
854	VJB 945	Bristol MW6G	164.132	ECW	11858	B41F	11/60	12/71
855	VJB 946	Bristol MW6G	164.133	ECW	11859	B41F	11/60	12/71
856	VJB 947	Bristol MW6G	164.144	ECW	11860	B41F	12/60	12/71
857	VJB 948	Bristol MW6G	164.145	ECW	11861	B41F	12/60	12/71

Notes:

UJB 200 (834): Fitted with a Gardner 6LW diesel engine (to FLF6G specification) 10/65; reseated to H38/32F 4/70.

UJB 201 (835): Luggage pen removed and reseated to CH37/30F 3/70; reseated to H38/32F 10/71.

UJB 202 (836): Luggage pen removed and reseated to CH37/30F 6/70; reseated to H38/32F (retaining coach seats in the lower saloon) 8/71.

UJB 203 (837): Luggage pen removed and reseated to CH37/30F 6/70.
UJB 204 (838): Luggage pen removed and reseated to CH37/30F 4/70.
VJB 943 (852): Renumbered 179 10/69.
VJB 944 (853): Renumbered 180 9/69.
VJB 945 (854): Renumbered 181 12/69.
VJB 946 (855): Renumbered 182 9/69.
VJB 947 (856): Did not enter service until 1/61; renumbered 183 8/69.
VJB 948 (857): Did not enter service until 1/61; renumbered 184 10/69.

Disposals:
UJB 200 (834): Thames Valley & Aldershot Omnibus Co Ltd {Alder Valley}, Reading (BE) 601 1/72; D Rollinson (Bus Centre) Ltd (dealer), Carlton for scrap 11/77.
UJB 201 (835): Thames Valley & Aldershot Omnibus Co Ltd {Alder Valley}, Reading (BE) 602 1/72; Paul Sykes Organisation Ltd (dealer), Barnsley for scrap 3/78.
UJB 202 (836): Thames Valley & Aldershot Omnibus Co Ltd {Alder Valley}, Reading (BE) 603 1/72; Paul Sykes Organisation Ltd (dealer), Barnsley 3/78; A Barraclough (dealer), Carlton for scrap 4/78.
UJB 203 (837): Thames Valley & Aldershot Omnibus Co Ltd {Alder Valley}, Reading (BE) 604 1/72; reseated to H38/30F retaining its coach seats in the lower saloon in 3/72; D Rollinson (Bus Centre) Ltd (dealer), Carlton for scrap 11/77.
UJB 204 (838): Thames Valley & Aldershot Omnibus Co Ltd {Alder Valley}, Reading (BE) 605 1/72; reseated to H38/30F retaining its coach seats in the lower saloon in 4/72; Martins Bus & Coach Sales Ltd (dealer), Middlewich 9/75.
VJB 943 (179): Thames Valley & Aldershot Omnibus Co Ltd {Alder Valley}, Reading (BE) 251 1/72; reseated to B41F, probably in 4/72; Main Motors (dealer), Ewelme for scrap 5/74.
VJB 944 (180): Thames Valley & Aldershot Omnibus Co Ltd {Alder Valley}, Reading (BE) 252 1/72; reseated to B41F at an unknown date; Paul Sykes Organisation Ltd (dealer), Barnsley for scrap 11/75.
VJB 945 (181): Thames Valley & Aldershot Omnibus Co Ltd {Alder Valley}, Reading (BE) 253 1/72; Paul Sykes Organisation Ltd (dealer), Barnsley for scrap 11/75.
VJB 946 (182): Thames Valley & Aldershot Omnibus Co Ltd {Alder Valley}, Reading (BE) 254 1/72; Paul Sykes Organisation Ltd (dealer), Barnsley for scrap 11/75.
VJB 947 (183): Thames Valley & Aldershot Omnibus Co Ltd {Alder Valley}, Reading (BE) 255 1/72; Martins Bus & Coach Sales Ltd (dealer), Middlewich for scrap 2/76.
VJB 948 (184): Thames Valley & Aldershot Omnibus Co Ltd {Alder Valley}, Reading (BE) 256 1/72; Egham Bus Group, Egham for preservation 8/76; stolen and wrecked c1991; GP Ripley (dealer), Carlton for scrap 1991.

Vehicles acquired from United Counties Omnibus Co Ltd, Northampton (NO) 1/60:

464	FPU 511	Bristol K5G	42.54	ECW	5646	L27/28R	12/37	5/65
465	FPU 513	Bristol K5G	42.56	ECW	1621	L27/28R	12/37	10/62

Previous histories:
FPU 511 (464): New to Eastern National Omnibus Co Ltd, Chelmsford (EX) 3731 (with an ECW (4957) L26/24R 8ft wide body; reseated to L24/24R before entry into service); rebodied (8ft wide) 12/51; United Counties Omnibus Co Ltd 615 5/52
FPU 513 (465): New to Eastern National Omnibus Co Ltd, Chelmsford (EX) 3733 (with an ECW (4959) L26/24R 8ft wide body; reseated to L24/24R before entry into service); rebodied ECW (5650) L27/28R (8ft wide) 2/52; United Counties Omnibus Co Ltd 620 5/52 [fitted with a 1948 ECW (7ft 6in wide) body from MPU 11 (727) immediately prior to disposal]; entering service 3/60.

Disposals:
FPU 511 (464): TD Alexander {Greyhound Luxury Coaches}, Sheffield (WR) (not operated) 6/65; W Norths (PV) Ltd (dealer), Sherburn in Elmet by 8/65.
FPU 513 (465): TD Alexander {Greyhound Luxury Coaches}, Arbroath (AS) 10/62; TD Alexander {Greyhound Luxury Coaches}, Sheffield (WR) 1962; S Johnson (dealer), Worksop for scrap by 4/64.

Vehicles acquired from Hants & Dorset Motor Services Ltd, Bournemouth (DT) 3/60:

472	JT 9354	Bristol K5G	45.87	ECW	3416	L27/28R	5/38	3/64
473	JT 9355	Bristol K5G	45.88	ECW	3415	L27/28R	7/38	3/64
474	JT 9360	Bristol K5G	45.93	ECW	3419	L27/28R	7/38	9/64
475	FLJ 978	Bristol K5G	57.014	Brush		L28/26R	4/42	11/64

Previous histories:

JT 9354 (472): New to Hants & Dorset Motor Services Ltd TD646 with a Brush L28/26R body [rebodied 6/49; renumbered 1026 1/50]; entering service 5/60.

JT 9355 (473): New to Hants & Dorset Motor Services Ltd TD648 with a Brush L28/26R body [rebodied 6/49; renumbered 1027 1/50]; entering service 5/60.

JT 9360 (474): New to Hants & Dorset Motor Services Ltd TD658 with a Brush L28/26R body [rebodied 7/49; renumbered 1032 1/50]; entering service 5/60.

FLJ 978 (475): New to Hants & Dorset Motor Services Ltd TD670 with a Strachan L27/28R body [fitted with the 1938 Brush body from JT 9358 (1030) in 1/54 (this had been rebuilt by Hants & Dorset in 1950); renumbered 1095 1/50]; entering service 5/60.

Disposals:

JT 9354 (472): Liss & District Omnibus Co Ltd, Liss (HA) 3/64; P Jeffreys {Liss & District}, Grayshott (HA) 4/64; James (dealer), Hedge End 11/66 (collected 1/67).

JT 9355 (473): Creamline Motor Services Ltd, Bordon (HA) 3/64; withdrawn 8/67.

JT 9360 (474): Wolchovers Ltd (hardware merchants), London E2 (XLN) 9/64; unidentified dealer, London E2 12/64; scrapped 6/65.

FLJ 978 (475): FC Construction (contractor), Derby (XDE) 11/64; W Norths (PV) Ltd (dealer), Sherburn in Elmet 2/65; Chris Hoyle & Son Ltd (dealer), Wombwell for scrap by 6/65.

Vehicles acquired from United Counties Omnibus Co Ltd, Northampton (NO) 4/60:

476	GNO 688	Bristol K5G	45.137	ECW		1626	L27/28R	7/38	4/63
477	GNO 698	Bristol K5G	45.147	ECW		1623	L27/28R	8/38	10/62

Previous histories:

GNO 688 (476): New to Eastern National Omnibus Co Ltd, Chelmsford (EX) 3744 (with an ECW (5762) L26/24R 8ft wide body; reseated to L24/24R before entry into service); rebodied ECW (5656) L27/28R (8ft wide) 5/52; United Counties Omnibus Co Ltd 624 5/52 [fitted with a 1948 ECW (7ft 6in wide) body from MPU 16 (733) immediately prior to disposal]; entering service 6/60.

GNO 698 (477): New to Eastern National Omnibus Co Ltd, Chelmsford (EX) 3754 (with an ECW (5772) L26/24R 8ft wide body; reseated to L24/24R before entry into service); rebodied ECW (5651) L27/28R (8ft wide) 2/52; United Counties Omnibus Co Ltd 632 5/52 [fitted with a 1948 ECW (7ft 6in wide) body from MPU 13 (732) immediately prior to disposal]; entering service 6/60.

Disposals:

GNO 688 (476): W Norths (PV) Ltd (dealer), Sherburn in Elmet 4/63; unidentified dealer for scrap 7/63.

GNO 698 (477): TD Alexander {Greyhound Luxury Coaches}, Arbroath (AS) 30 10/62; withdrawn 12/64.

1961

New Vehicles:

839	WJB 223	Bristol FLF6G	169.056	ECW	12078	H38/32F	1/61	12/71
840	WJB 224	Bristol FLF6G	169.057	ECW	12079	H38/32F	1/61	12/71
841	WJB 225	Bristol FLF6G	169.058	ECW	12080	H38/32F	1/61	12/71
842	WJB 226	Bristol FLF6G	169.059	ECW	12081	H38/32F	1/61	12/71
843	WJB 227	Bristol FLF6G	169.060	ECW	12082	H38/32F	1/61	12/71
844	WJB 228	Bristol FLF6G	181.004	ECW	12083	H38/32F	7/61	12/71
845	WJB 229	Bristol FLF6G	181.005	ECW	12084	H38/32F	7/61	12/71
846	WJB 230	Bristol FLF6G	181.006	ECW	12085	H38/32F	7/61	12/71
847	WJB 231	Bristol FLF6G	181.007	ECW	12086	H38/32F	7/61	12/71
848	WJB 232	Bristol FLF6G	181.012	ECW	12087	H38/32F	7/61	12/71
849	WJB 233	Bristol FLF6G	181.049	ECW	12088	H38/32F	12/61	12/71
850	WJB 234	Bristol FLF6G	181.050	ECW	12089	H38/32F	12/61	12/71
851	WJB 235	Bristol FLF6G	181.051	ECW	12090	H38/32F	12/61	12/71

Notes:

WJB 228-235 (844-851): Fitted with an offside illuminated advertising panels; some of these were removed in 1971.

Disposals:

WJB 223 (839): Thames Valley & Aldershot Omnibus Co Ltd {Alder Valley}, Reading (BE) 606 1/72; Martins Bus & Coach Sales Ltd (dealer), Middlewich 9/75; J Moffat, Cardenden (FE) 1/76; Moffat & Williamson Ltd, Gauldry (FE) 8/78; K Askin (dealer), Barnsley 6/81; Kirkby Central (dealer), Thurcroft by 2/83; exported to USA 2/83; unknown owner, Ozark Mountain area (O-USA) c1983; Holiday Inn, Dallas-Fort Worth Airport, Irving, Texas (O-USA) c1987; registered T 3522; Grayline, Dallas, Texas (O-USA) by 5/00; converted to open-top 2000; Dallas Bus Co, Dallas, Texas (O-USA) by 4/02.

WJB 224 (840): Thames Valley & Aldershot Omnibus Co Ltd {Alder Valley}, Reading (BE) 607 1/72; D Rollinson (Bus Centre) Ltd (dealer), Carlton for scrap 11/77.

WJB 225 (841): Thames Valley & Aldershot Omnibus Co Ltd {Alder Valley}, Reading (BE) 608 1/72; Paul Sykes Organisation Ltd (dealer), Barnsley 3/78; A Barraclough (dealer), Carlton for scrap 4/78.

WJB 226-227 (842-843): Thames Valley & Aldershot Omnibus Co Ltd {Alder Valley}, Reading (BE) 609-610 1/72; Paul Sykes Organisation Ltd (dealer), Barnsley for scrap 3/78.

WJB 228 (844): Thames Valley & Aldershot Omnibus Co Ltd {Alder Valley}, Reading (BE) 611 1/72; Passenger Vehicle Spares (Barnsley) Ltd (dealer), Carlton for scrap 6/78.

WJB 229 (845): Thames Valley & Aldershot Omnibus Co Ltd {Alder Valley}, Reading (BE) 612 1/72; Paul Sykes Organisation Ltd (dealer), Barnsley for scrap 3/78.

WJB 230 (846): Thames Valley & Aldershot Omnibus Co Ltd {Alder Valley}, Reading (BE) 613 1/72; Passenger Vehicle Spares (Barnsley) Ltd (dealer), Carlton 6/78; T Wigley (dealer), Carlton for scrap 6/78.

WJB 231 (847): Thames Valley & Aldershot Omnibus Co Ltd {Alder Valley}, Reading (BE) 614 1/72; Passenger Vehicle Spares (Barnsley) Ltd (dealer), Carlton for scrap 6/78.

WJB 232 (848): Thames Valley & Aldershot Omnibus Co Ltd {Alder Valley}, Reading (BE) 615 1/72; cannibalised from 12/75; Martins Bus & Coach Sales Ltd (dealer), Middlewich for scrap 2/76.

WJB 233-234 (849-850): Thames Valley & Aldershot Omnibus Co Ltd {Alder Valley}, Reading (BE) 616-617 1/72; Passenger Vehicle Spares (Barnsley) Ltd (dealer), Carlton for scrap 6/78.

WJB 235 (851): Thames Valley & Aldershot Omnibus Co Ltd {Alder Valley}, Reading (BE) 618 1/72; Passenger Vehicle Spares (Barnsley) Ltd (dealer), Carlton 6/78; T Wigley (dealer), Carlton for scrap 6/78.

1962

New Vehicles:

866	520 ABL	Bristol MW6G	195.008	ECW	12839	C39F	5/62	12/71
868	536 BBL	Bristol FLF6B	199.108	ECW	13188	H38/32F	9/62	12/71
869	537 BBL	Bristol FLF6B	199.109	ECW	13189	H38/32F	9/62	12/71
870	538 BBL	Bristol FLF6B	199.141	ECW	13190	H38/32F	9/62	12/71
871	539 BBL	Bristol FLF6B	199.142	ECW	13191	H38/32F	9/62	12/71
872	540 BBL	Bristol FLF6B	199.151	ECW	13192	H38/32F	9/62	12/71
873	541 BBL	Bristol FLF6B	199.152	ECW	13193	H38/32F	9/62	12/71
874	542 BBL	Bristol FLF6B	199.153	ECW	13194	H38/32F	9/62	12/71

Notes:

536-540 BBL (868-872): Fitted with an offside illuminated advertising panels; some of these were removed in 1971.

Disposals:

520 ABL (866): South Midland Motor Services Ltd 866 5/66 (qv).

536 BBL (868): Thames Valley & Aldershot Omnibus Co Ltd {Alder Valley}, Reading (BE) 619 1/72; fitted with a Gardner 6LW engine in 11/72; Passenger Vehicle Spares (Barnsley) Ltd (dealer), Carlton for scrap 6/78.

537-538 BBL (869-870): Thames Valley & Aldershot Omnibus Co Ltd {Alder Valley}, Reading (BE) 620-621 1/72; fitted with Gardner 6LW engines 4/74-5/74; Passenger Vehicle Spares (Barnsley) Ltd (dealer), Carlton for scrap 11/78.

539 BBL (871): Thames Valley & Aldershot Omnibus Co Ltd {Alder Valley}, Reading (BE) 622 1/72; fitted with a Gardner 6LW engine in 6/74; Passenger Vehicle Spares (Barnsley) Ltd (dealer), Carlton for scrap 11/78.

540 BBL (872): Thames Valley & Aldershot Omnibus Co Ltd {Alder Valley}, Reading (BE) 623 1/72; fitted with a Gardner 6LW engine in 7/74; Passenger Vehicle Spares (Barnsley) Ltd (dealer), Carlton 11/78; T Wigley (dealer), Carlton for scrap 12/78.

541 BBL (873): Thames Valley & Aldershot Omnibus Co Ltd {Alder Valley}, Reading (BE) 624 1/72; fitted with a Gardner 6LW engine in 4/74; Passenger Vehicle Spares (Barnsley) Ltd (dealer), Carlton for scrap 6/78.

542 BBL (874): Thames Valley & Aldershot Omnibus Co Ltd {Alder Valley}, Reading (BE) 625 1/72; fitted with a Gardner 6LW engine in 2/75; Passenger Vehicle Spares (Barnsley) Ltd (dealer), Carlton for scrap 11/78.

1963

New Vehicles:

875	543 BBL	Bristol FLF6G	208.001	ECW	13195	H38/32F	1/63	12/71
876	544 BBL	Bristol FLF6G	208.002	ECW	13196	H38/32F	1/63	12/71
877	545 BBL	Bristol FLF6G	208.037	ECW	13197	H38/32F	2/63	12/71
878	546 BBL	Bristol FLF6G	208.038	ECW	13198	H38/32F	2/63	12/71
879	547 BBL	Bristol FLF6G	208.039	ECW	13199	H38/32F	3/63	12/71
880	548 BBL	Bristol FLF6G	210.027	ECW	13200	H38/32F	3/63	12/71
881	549 BBL	Bristol FLF6G	210.059	ECW	13201	H38/32F	4/63	12/71
D1	839 CRX	Bristol FLF6G	217.020	ECW	13995	H38/32F	10/63	12/71
D2	840 CRX	Bristol FLF6G	217.021	ECW	13996	H38/32F	10/63	12/71
D3	841 CRX	Bristol FLF6G	217.022	ECW	13997	H38/32F	10/63	12/71

Notes:

839-841 CRX (D1-3): Fitted with a Cave-Browne-Cave heating system (as were all subsequent Bristol FLFs up to 1967).

839 CRX (D1): Fitted with an offside illuminated advertising panel.
840 CRX (D2): Fitted with an offside illuminated advertising panel; this was removed 7/71.

Disposals:

543 BBL (875): Thames Valley & Aldershot Omnibus Co Ltd {Alder Valley}, Reading (BE) 626 1/72; Passenger Vehicle Spares (Barnsley) Ltd (dealer), Carlton for scrap 11/78.

544 BBL (876): Thames Valley & Aldershot Omnibus Co Ltd {Alder Valley}, Reading (BE) 627 1/72; Passenger Vehicle Spares (Barnsley) Ltd (dealer), Carlton 11/78; T Wigley (dealer), Carlton for scrap 12/78.

545-546 BBL (877-878): Thames Valley & Aldershot Omnibus Co Ltd {Alder Valley}, Reading (BE) 628-629 1/72; Paul Sykes Organisation Ltd (dealer), Barnsley 3/78; A Barraclough (dealer), Carlton for scrap 4/78.

547 BBL (879): Thames Valley & Aldershot Omnibus Co Ltd {Alder Valley}, Reading (BE) 630 1/72; Paul Sykes Organisation Ltd (dealer), Barnsley for scrap 7/80.

548-549 BBL (880-881): Thames Valley & Aldershot Omnibus Co Ltd {Alder Valley}, Reading (BE) 631-632 1/72; Passenger Vehicle Spares (Barnsley) Ltd (dealer), Carlton 6/78; K Askin (dealer), Barnsley for scrap 8/80.

839 CRX (D1): Thames Valley & Aldershot Omnibus Co Ltd {Alder Valley}, Reading (BE) 633 1/72; Paul Sykes Organisation Ltd (dealer), Barnsley 7/80; K Askin (dealer), Carlton for scrap 7/80.

840 CRX (D2): Thames Valley & Aldershot Omnibus Co Ltd {Alder Valley}, Reading (BE) 634 1/72; Passenger Vehicle Spares (Barnsley) Ltd (dealer), Carlton 6/78; T Wigley (dealer), Carlton for scrap 6/78.

841 CRX (D3): Thames Valley & Aldershot Omnibus Co Ltd {Alder Valley}, Reading (BE) 635 1/72; Paul Sykes Organisation Ltd (dealer), Barnsley for scrap 7/80.

Vehicles acquired from Crosville Motor Services Ltd, Chester (CH) 5/63:

S301	GFM 881	Bristol L6A	67.103	ECW	1945	B35F	3/48	11/64
S302	GFM 882	Bristol L6A	67.115	ECW	1946	B35F	4/48	3/65
S303	GFM 884	Bristol L6A	67.116	ECW	1948	B35F	4/48	11/64
S304	GFM 887	Bristol L6A	67.106	ECW	1951	B35F	5/48	2/65
S305	GFM 888	Bristol L6A	67.132	ECW	1952	B35F	4/48	12/66

Previous histories:

GFM 881 (S301): New to Crosville Motor Services Ltd, Chester (CH) KB72 (with a B35R body) [rebuilt to B35F by Crosville 1958 and renumbered SLA72 5/58]; entering service 7/63.

GFM 882 (S302): New to Crosville Motor Services Ltd, Chester (CH) KB73 (with a B35R body) [rebuilt to B35F by Crosville 1958 and renumbered SLA73 5/58].

GFM 884 (S303): New to Crosville Motor Services Ltd, Chester (CH) KB75 (with a B35R body) [rebuilt to B35F by Crosville 1958 and renumbered SLA75 5/58]; entering service 6/63.

GFM 887 (S304): New to Crosville Motor Services Ltd, Chester (CH) KB78 (with a B35R body) [rebuilt to B35F by Crosville 1958 and renumbered SLA78 5/58]; entering service 4/64.

GFM 888 (S305): New to Crosville Motor Services Ltd, Chester (CH) KB79 (with a B35R body) [rebuilt to B35F by Crosville 1958 and renumbered SLA79 5/58].

Disposals:

GFM 881 (S301): Collier & Catley (Plant) Ltd (contractor), Reading (XBE) 11/64.

GFM 882 (S302): Rossmore Bus Co Ltd, Sandbanks (DT) 7/65; withdrawn by 12/71; JP Hypher & JM Judge, Poole for preservation 1/72; R McLoughlin, Addlestone for preservation 6/78; Rowe, Port Dinorwic for preservation 9/87; JM, AF & DP Philp {Allison's Coaches}, Dunfermline (FE) 8/89; JN MacEwan {MacEwan's Coach Services}, Dumfries (DG) for preservation 8/90; Quantock Motor Services Ltd, Bishops Lydeard (SO) for preservation 11/14; moved to Wiveliscombe (SO) for preservation by 1/15.

GFM 884 (S303): Collier & Catley (Plant) Ltd (contractor), Reading (XBE) 11/64.

GFM 887 (S304): TD Alexander {Greyhound Luxury Coaches}, Arbroath (AS) 71 2/65 (operated at Teesport by 3/67); unidentified dealer 2/68.

GFM 888 (S305): W Norths (PV) Ltd (dealer), Sherburn in Elmet 12/66; Marshall (contractor), Elland (XWR) as a site office 1/67.

1964

New Vehicles:

C406	836 CRX	Bedford SB13	93524	Duple	1170/155	C37F	1/64	12/69
D4	ABL 116B	Bristol FLF6B	217.084	ECW	13998	CH37/28F	2/64	12/71
D5	ABL 117B	Bristol FLF6B	217.085	ECW	13999	CH37/28F	2/64	12/71
D6	ABL 118B	Bristol FLF6B	217.086	ECW	14000	CH37/28F	2/64	12/71
D7	ABL 119B	Bristol FLF6B	217.087	ECW	14001	CH37/28F	2/64	12/71
D8	BRX 141B	Bristol FLF6B	224.027	ECW	14002	CH37/28F	8/64	12/71
D9	BRX 142B	Bristol FLF6B	224.028	ECW	14003	H38/32F	8/64	12/71
S306	CBL 355B	Bristol RELL6G	222.028	ECW	14186	B54F	9/64	12/71
S307	CBL 356B	Bristol RELL6G	222.029	ECW	14187	B54F	9/64	12/71
S308	CBL 357B	Bristol RELL6G	222.030	ECW	14188	B54F	9/64	12/71
D10	CMO 833B	Bristol FLF6G	224.065	ECW	14610	H38/32F	11/64	12/71
D11	CMO 834B	Bristol FLF6G	224.066	ECW	14611	H38/32F	11/64	12/71
D12	CMO 835B	Bristol FLF6G	224.076	ECW	14612	H38/32F	11/64	12/71
D13	CMO 836B	Bristol FLF6G	224.090	ECW	14613	H38/32F	11/64	12/71

Notes:

ABL 116-119B (D4-7): Were originally intended to be registered 842-845 CRX; fitted with experimental black on white registration plates 4/64.

BRX 141-142B (D8-9): Were originally intended to be registered 846-847 CRX.

836 CRX (C406): Did not enter service until 3/64; was fitted with a two-way radio c3/67 for the new Rail-air service between Reading and Heathrow Airport; renumbered 406 2/69.

ABL 116B (D4): Luggage pen removed and reseated to CH37/30F in 10/70.

ABL 117B (D5): Luggage pen removed and reseated to CH37/30F in 12/70.

ABL 118B (D6): Luggage pen removed and reseated to CH37/30F in 9/70.

ABL 119B (D7): Luggage pen removed and reseated to CH37/30F in 11/70.

BRX 141B (D8): Luggage pen removed and reseated to CH37/30F in 9/70.

CBL 355B (401): Equipped for one-man-operation, reseated to B51F and fitted with a luggage pen 12/68; renumbered 185 8/69.

CBL 356B (402): Equipped for one-man-operation, reseated to B51F and fitted with a luggage pen 10/68; renumbered 186 9/69.

CBL 357B (403): Equipped for one-man-operation, reseated to B51F and fitted with a luggage pen 11/68; renumbered 187 9/69.

Disposals:

836 CRX (406): FJ Miller (Bristol) Ltd (dealer), Bristol 11/69; Carlton Homes, Bristol (XGL) as a mobile exhibition unit by 1/70; Ingal, Preston 7/73; Radio Victory, Portsmouth (XHA) 1/76; donated to the 'Raise the Mary Rose' project, Portsmouth (XHA) as an exhibition unit by 10/82; Elizabeth Foundation for Deaf Children, Cosham (XHA) 6/90; P Quinn, Portsmouth as a mobile caravan 1992; last licensed 11/96.

ABL 116B (D4): Thames Valley & Aldershot Omnibus Co Ltd {Alder Valley}, Reading (BE) 636 1/72; destroyed by fire at Reading depot on 7/7/73; WR Alexander {Alexander Coaches}, Sheffield (WR) 9/73; Paul Sykes Organisation Ltd (dealer), Barnsley 1974; scrapped by 12/74.

ABL 117B (D5): Thames Valley & Aldershot Omnibus Co Ltd {Alder Valley}, Reading (BE) 637 1/72; fitted with a Gardner 6LW engine in 7/73; converted to a driver training vehicle no 1111 4/79 and transferred to the service fleet; Amalgamated Passenger Transport Ltd (dealer), Bracebridge Heath 2/83; Passenger Vehicle Spares (Barnsley) Ltd (dealer), Carlton for scrap 3/83.

ABL 118B (D6): Thames Valley & Aldershot Omnibus Co Ltd {Alder Valley}, Reading (BE) 638 1/72; fitted with a Gardner 6LW engine in 11/73; converted to a driver training vehicle no 1110 11/78 and transferred to the service fleet; Amalgamated Passenger Transport Ltd (dealer), Bracebridge Heath 7/84; Passenger Vehicle Spares (Barnsley) Ltd (dealer), Carlton for scrap 7/84.

ABL 119B (D7): Thames Valley & Aldershot Omnibus Co Ltd {Alder Valley}, Reading (BE) 639 1/72; fitted with a Gardner 6LW engine in 12/74; converted to a driver training vehicle no 1114 2/80 and transferred to the service fleet; Amalgamated Passenger Transport Ltd (dealer), Bracebridge Heath 2/83; Passenger Vehicle Spares (Barnsley) Ltd (dealer), Carlton for scrap 3/83.

BRX 141B (D8): Thames Valley & Aldershot Omnibus Co Ltd {Alder Valley}, Reading (BE) 640 1/72; converted to a driver training vehicle no 1112 4/79 and transferred to the service fleet; Amalgamated Passenger Transport Ltd (dealer), Bracebridge Heath 2/83; Passenger Vehicle Spares (Barnsley) Ltd (dealer), Carlton for scrap 3/83.

BRX 142B (D9): Thames Valley & Aldershot Omnibus Co Ltd {Alder Valley}, Reading (BE) 641 1/72; withdrawn after a low-bridge accident in 10/75; Southern Vectis Omnibus Co Ltd, Newport (IW) OT6 2/76 as O38/32F; withdrawn 9/78; CF Booth Ltd (dealer), Rotherham 11/79; exported to USA 4/80; The Pointe Resort Hotel, Phoenix, Arizona (O-USA) by 3/91; registered 3ZJ750 3/92; Rodriguez, Phoenix, Arizona (O-USA) by 12/98; re-registered 3ZN547.

CBL 355B (185): Thames Valley & Aldershot Omnibus Co Ltd {Alder Valley}, Reading (BE) 401 1/72; Passenger Vehicle Spares (Barnsley) Ltd (dealer), Carlton 6/78; North Cornwall Cars, Langdon Cross (CO) 12 10/78; J Sykes (dealer), Carlton for scrap 4/82.

CBL 356B (186): Thames Valley & Aldershot Omnibus Co Ltd {Alder Valley}, Reading (BE) 402 1/72; Passenger Vehicle Spares (Barnsley) Ltd (dealer), Carlton for scrap 6/78.

CBL 357B (187): Thames Valley & Aldershot Omnibus Co Ltd {Alder Valley}, Reading (BE) 403 1/72; D Rollinson (Bus Centre) Ltd (dealer), Carlton for scrap 11/77.

CMO 833B (D10): Thames Valley & Aldershot Omnibus Co Ltd {Alder Valley}, Reading (BE) 642 1/72; Paul Sykes Organisation Ltd (dealer), Barnsley 7/80; K Askin (dealer), Barnsley for scrap 8/80.

CMO 834B (D11): Thames Valley & Aldershot Omnibus Co Ltd {Alder Valley}, Reading (BE) 643 1/72; Paul Sykes Organisation Ltd (dealer), Barnsley 7/80; K Askin (dealer), Barnsley 8/80; G Jones {Carlton Metals} (dealer), Carlton for scrap 10/80.

CMO 835B (D12): Thames Valley & Aldershot Omnibus Co Ltd {Alder Valley}, Reading (BE) 644 1/72; Paul Sykes Organisation Ltd (dealer), Barnsley for scrap 2/80.

CMO 836B (D13): Thames Valley & Aldershot Omnibus Co Ltd {Alder Valley}, Reading (BE) 645 1/72; Passenger Vehicle Spares (Barnsley) Ltd (dealer), Carlton 6/78; T Wigley (dealer), Carlton for scrap 6/78.

Vehicles transferred from South Midland Motor Services Ltd 4/64:

S309	HMO 835	Bristol LS6B	97.068	ECW		6982 DP41F	10/53	11/68
S310	HMO 836	Bristol LS6B	97.069	ECW		6983 DP41F	10/53	1/71
S311	HMO 837	Bristol LS6B	101.061	ECW		6984 DP41F	3/54	9/69

Previous histories:

HMO 835 (S309): New to Thames Valley Traction Co Ltd 689; South Midland Motor Services Ltd 689 [reseated to C37F from c5/59 to 11/59; reverted to C39F by 4/60; delicensed 11/63, equipped for one-man-operation, reseated to DP41F and renumbered S309 4/64].

HMO 836 (S310): New to Thames Valley Traction Co Ltd 690; South Midland Motor Services Ltd 690 [reseated to C37F from c3/59 to 8/59; delicensed 11/63, equipped for one-man-operation, reseated to DP41F and renumbered S310 4/64].

HMO 837 (S311): New to Thames Valley Traction Co Ltd 691; South Midland Motor Services Ltd 691 1/62 [delicensed 11/63, equipped for one-man-operation, reseated to DP41F and renumbered S311 4/64].

Notes:

HMO 836 (S310): Fitted with a Gardner 6LHW diesel engine (to LS6G specification) 5/68; renumbered 124 8/69; wrecked in an accident at Hermitage 1/71; cannibalised 1-6/71.

HMO 837 (S311): Renumbered 125 8/69.

Disposals:

HMO 835 (S309): Margo's Luxury Coaches (Streatham) Ltd, London SW16 (LN) 1/69; withdrawn by 2/71.

HMO 836 (S310): WR Alexander {Alexander Coaches}, Sheffield (WR) (minus mechanical units) 7/71.

HMO 837 (125): W Norths (PV) Ltd (dealer), Sherburn in Elmet (minus engine) for scrap 10/69.

1965

New Vehicles:

D14	DJB 529C	Bristol FLF6G	224.124	ECW	15001	H38/32F	1/65	12/71
D15	DJB 530C	Bristol FLF6G	224.125	ECW	15002	H38/32F	1/65	12/71
D16	DRX 120C	Bristol FLF6G	224.149	ECW	15003	H38/32F	2/65	12/71
D17	DRX 121C	Bristol FLF6G	224.150	ECW	15004	H38/32F	2/65	12/71
D18	DRX 122C	Bristol FLF6G	224.162	ECW	15005	H38/32F	3/65	12/71
D19	FBL 483C	Bristol FLF6G	229.070	ECW	15006	H38/32F	6/65	12/71
D20	FBL 484C	Bristol FLF6G	229.076	ECW	15007	H38/32F	6/65	12/71
D21	FBL 485C	Bristol FLF6G	229.077	ECW	15008	H38/32F	6/65	12/71
D22	FJB 738C	Bristol FLF6G	229.150	ECW	15009	H38/32F	8/65	12/71
D23	FJB 739C	Bristol FLF6G	229.151	ECW	15010	H38/32F	8/65	12/71
D24	FJB 740C	Bristol FLF6G	229.157	ECW	15011	H38/32F	9/65	12/71
D25	GBL 907C	Bristol FLF6G	229.209	ECW	15012	H38/32F	11/65	12/71
D26	GJB 874C	Bristol FLF6G	229.232	ECW	15013	H38/32F	11/65	12/71
D27	GMO 827C	Bristol FLF6G	229.245	ECW	15014	H38/32F	12/65	12/71
D28	GMO 828C	Bristol FLF6G	229.246	ECW	15015	H38/32F	12/65	12/71

Disposals:

DJB 529C (D14): Thames Valley & Aldershot Omnibus Co Ltd {Alder Valley}, Reading (BE) 646 1/72; converted to a driver training vehicle no 1113 4/79 and transferred to the service fleet; Whiting Bros (dealer), Carlton for scrap 6/81.

DJB 530C (D15): Thames Valley & Aldershot Omnibus Co Ltd {Alder Valley}, Reading (BE) 647 1/72; Paul Sykes Organisation Ltd (dealer), Barnsley 7/80; K Askin (dealer), Barnsley for scrap 7/80.

DRX 120C (D16): Thames Valley & Aldershot Omnibus Co Ltd {Alder Valley}, Reading (BE) 648 1/72; Paul Sykes Organisation Ltd (dealer), Barnsley for scrap 7/80.

DRX 121C (D17): Thames Valley & Aldershot Omnibus Co Ltd {Alder Valley}, Reading (BE) 649 1/72; Paul Sykes Organisation Ltd (dealer), Barnsley 7/80; K Askin (dealer), Barnsley 7/80; J Sykes (dealer), Carlton for scrap 9/80.

DRX 122C (D18): Thames Valley & Aldershot Omnibus Co Ltd {Alder Valley}, Reading (BE) 650 1/72; converted to a driver training vehicle no 1084 4/79 and transferred to the service fleet; renumbered 62 9/82; W Norths (PV) Ltd (dealer), Sherburn in Elmet 8/85; Jorvik Tour Bus Ltd, Market Weighton (NY) 11/85; rebuilt to PO33/8F 9/88; named 'Eric the Centurion' by 8/90; withdrawn 10/92; M Stadie & D Turner {Viking Tours}, Acaster Malbis (NY) 12/92; reseated to PO33/27F by 10/93; last licensed 10/93; C Ireland (dealer), Kingston upon Hull for spares c8/94; extensively stripped by 1/03; scrapped on site 2007.

FBL 483-484C (D19-20): Thames Valley & Aldershot Omnibus Co Ltd {Alder Valley}, Reading (BE) 651-652 1/72; Paul Sykes Organisation Ltd (dealer), Barnsley 7/80; K Askin (dealer), Barnsley for scrap 7/80.

FBL 485C (D21): Thames Valley & Aldershot Omnibus Co Ltd {Alder Valley}, Reading (BE) 653 1/72; Paul Sykes Organisation Ltd (dealer), Barnsley 7/80; K Askin (dealer), Barnsley for scrap 8/80.

FJB 738C (D22): Thames Valley & Aldershot Omnibus Co Ltd {Alder Valley}, Reading (BE) 654 1/72; Paul Sykes Organisation Ltd (dealer), Barnsley 8/80; Chiltern Omnibus Group, High Wycombe for preservation 9/80; Upstairs Downstairs Travel, Oxford (XOX) 9/84; JP Atiyah {Upstairs Downstairs Travel}, Oxford (OX) c9/85; Stagecoach Ltd, Perth (TE) 12/86 (as H--/--F); converted to a driver training vehicle and numbered 703 by 5/90; Seventh Day Adventist Church, location unknown (Scotland) by 6/94; C Ireland (dealer), Kingston upon Hull by 1997; Stairway Promotions, Assen (O-NL) 4/97; registered BE-28-29 4/97; Delta Tours, Wapenveld (O-NL) by 8/02; Party on Wheels BV, Ulvenhout (O-NL) 8/05; JJ Krijnen, Huizen (O-NL) 1/10; D-J Baan, Sliedrecht (O-NL) by 11/12 (seating 50 or 55); moved to Alblasserdam (O-NL) and trading as Alblas Events by 3/15.

FJB 739C (D23): Thames Valley & Aldershot Omnibus Co Ltd {Alder Valley}, Reading (BE) 655 1/72; Paul Sykes Organisation Ltd (dealer), Barnsley 8/80; Abingdon Coaches (A & C) Ltd, Abingdon (OX) 10/80; Percival's Motors (Oxford) Ltd, Oxford (OX) 97 12/84; Tourex Ltd {Tourex / Nostalgia Travel}, Oxford (OX) 15 11/87; moved to North Hinksey (OX) 11/89; The School Bus Co (Oxford) Ltd {Nostalgia Travel}, Kinston Bagpuize (OX) 8/05.

FJB 740C (D24): Thames Valley & Aldershot Omnibus Co Ltd {Alder Valley}, Reading (BE) 656 1/72; Paul Sykes Organisation Ltd (dealer), Barnsley 7/80; K Askin (dealer), Barnsley for scrap 7/80.

GBL 907C (D25): Thames Valley & Aldershot Omnibus Co Ltd {Alder Valley}, Reading (BE) 657 1/72; W Norths (PV) Ltd (dealer), Sherburn in Elmet for scrap 4/79.

GJB 874C (D26): Thames Valley & Aldershot Omnibus Co Ltd {Alder Valley}, Reading (BE) 658 1/72; Paul Sykes Organisation Ltd (dealer), Barnsley 7/80; K Askin (dealer), Barnsley for scrap 7/80.

GMO 827C (D27): Thames Valley & Aldershot Omnibus Co Ltd {Alder Valley}, Reading (BE) 659 1/72; Paul Sykes Organisation Ltd (dealer), Barnsley for scrap 7/80.

GMO 828C (D28): Thames Valley & Aldershot Omnibus Co Ltd {Alder Valley}, Reading (BE) 660 1/72; Paul Sykes Organisation Ltd (dealer), Barnsley 7/80; K Askin (dealer), Barnsley 7/80; G Jones {Carlton Metals} (dealer), Carlton for scrap 10/80.

Vehicles transferred from South Midland Motor Services Ltd 2-7/65:

S314	HMO 834	Bristol LS6B	97.067	ECW	6981	DP41F	10/53	11/68
S312	HMO 838	Bristol LS6B	101.062	ECW	6985	DP39F	3/54	1/70
S313	HMO 839	Bristol LS6B	101.063	ECW	6986	DP39F	3/54	10/68
862	516 ABL	Bedford SB8	88965	Duple	1145/233	C37F	5/62	4/68
863	517 ABL	Bedford SB8	89057	Duple	1145/234	C37F	5/62	6/68

Previous histories:

HMO 834 (S314): New to Thames Valley Traction Co Ltd 688; South Midland Motor Services Ltd 688 12/61 [delicensed 10/64, equipped for one-man-operation, reseated to DP41F and renumbered S314 7/65]; transferred 7/65.

HMO 838 (S312): New to Thames Valley Traction Co Ltd 692; South Midland Motor Services Ltd 692 [reseated to C37F from c1/59 to c8/60; delicensed 12/64, equipped for one-man-operation, reseated to DP39F and renumbered S312 3/65]; transferred 3/65.

HMO 839 (S313): New to Thames Valley Traction Co Ltd 692; South Midland Motor Services Ltd 692 [reseated to C34F and fitted with a luggage rack in place of the rear five seats (for American tourist work) 5/58 to late 1958; delicensed 11/64, equipped for one-man-operation, reseated to DP39F and renumbered S313 2/65]; transferred 2/65.

516-517 ABL (862-863): New to South Midland Motor Services Ltd 862-863; transferred 4/65.

Notes:

HMO 838 (S312): Allocated fleet number 126 in the 1969 renumbering scheme, but not carried.

Disposals:

HMO 834 (S314): I & B Margo {Margo's Europa Coaches}, London SE19 (LN) 11/68; Commando Industrial Cleaners, Warwick (XWK) 10/70; Army Cadet Force, Solihull (XST) 3/71.

HMO 838 (S312): W Norths (PV) Ltd (dealer), Sherburn in Elmet 1/70; Elm Park Coaches Ltd, Romford (LN) 5/70; Bee-Line Coaches (Brentwood) Ltd, Brentwood (EX) 7/70; withdrawn 8/71; unidentified dealer, Willingale 5/73; reduced to chassis only 1988.

HMO 839 (S313): W Norths (PV) Ltd (dealer), Sherburn in Elmet 11/68; Trevor Ward & Son (1968) Ltd, Kirkburton (WR) 11/68; withdrawn 4/72.

516 ABL (862): Shamrock & Rambler (THC) Ltd, Bournemouth (HA) 5/68 (as C29F); Southern Vectis Omnibus Co Ltd, Newport (IW) 109 5/69; withdrawn 10/75.

517 ABL (863): Shamrock & Rambler (THC) Ltd, Bournemouth (HA) 5/68 (as C41F); Southern Vectis Omnibus Co Ltd, Newport (IW) 110 5/69; withdrawn 8/76.

Vehicle acquired from United Welsh Services Ltd, Swansea (GG) c4/65:

DWN 379	Guy Arab II		FD26810	(chassis only)	7/44	----

Previous history:

DWN 379: New to United Welsh Services Ltd 677 (with a Strachan H30/26R body); rebodied BBW H30/26R 1953; withdrawn 1963.

Notes:

The identity of this vehicle is not confirmed, but was probably DWN 379 (although DWN 328 which had passed to Contract Bus Services Ltd, Caerwent (MH) by 3/64 and withdrawn 6/64 is a possibility); it was acquired in chassis form only for spares for the surviving Newbury & District Guy Arabs.

Disposal (chassis only):

DWN 379: No known disposal.

1966

New Vehicles:

D29	GRX 129D	Bristol FLF6G	231.022	ECW	15647	H38/32F	1/66	12/71
D30	GRX 130D	Bristol FLF6G	231.030	ECW	15648	H38/32F	1/66	12/71
D31	GRX 131D	Bristol FLF6G	231.031	ECW	15649	H38/32F	1/66	12/71

D32	GRX 132D	Bristol FLF6G	231.068	ECW	15650	H38/32F	2/66	12/71
D33	GRX 133D	Bristol FLF6G	231.069	ECW	15651	H38/32F	2/66	12/71
D34	GRX 134D	Bristol FLF6G	231.152	ECW	15652	H38/32F	6/66	12/71
D35	GRX 135D	Bristol FLF6G	231.153	ECW	15653	H38/32F	6/66	12/71
D36	GRX 136D	Bristol FLF6G	231.154	ECW	15654	H38/32F	6/66	12/71
D37	GRX 137D	Bristol FLF6G	231.184	ECW	15655	H38/32F	8/66	12/71
D38	GRX 138D	Bristol FLF6G	231.185	ECW	15656	H38/32F	8/66	12/71
D39	GRX 139D	Bristol FLF6G	231.232	ECW	15657	H38/32F	9/66	12/71
D40	GRX 140D	Bristol FLF6G	231.233	ECW	15658	H38/32F	9/66	12/71
D41	GRX 141D	Bristol FLF6G	231.234	ECW	15659	H38/32F	9/66	12/71
D42	GRX 142D	Bristol FLF6G	231.296	ECW	15660	H38/32F	10/66	12/71
D43	GRX 143D	Bristol FLF6G	231.297	ECW	15661	H38/32F	10/66	12/71
D44	GRX 144D	Bristol FLF6G	231.306	ECW	15662	H38/32F	10/66	12/71
D45	GRX 145D	Bristol FLF6G	231.314	ECW	15663	H38/32F	11/66	12/71
D46	GRX 146D	Bristol FLF6G	231.315	ECW	15664	H38/32F	12/66	12/71

Disposals:
GRX 129D (D29): Thames Valley & Aldershot Omnibus Co Ltd {Alder Valley}, Reading (BE) 661 1/72; Paul Sykes Organisation Ltd (dealer), Barnsley 7/80; AJ & RA Morris {Morris Bros}, Swansea (GG) 4 8/80; JD Cleverly Ltd, Cwmbran (MH) 5/84; GP Ripley (dealer), Carlton 2/87; Stagecoach Ltd, Perth (TE) 3/87; withdrawn 12/87; Magicbus (Scotland) Ltd, Glasgow (SC) 075 8/88; renumbered 654 3/92; last licensed 11/92; C Ireland (dealer), Kingston upon Hull for export to Germany 5/94.

GRX 130D (D30): Thames Valley & Aldershot Omnibus Co Ltd {Alder Valley}, Reading (BE) 662 1/72; Paul Sykes Organisation Ltd (dealer), Barnsley 7/80; J Sykes (dealer), Carlton for scrap 8/80.

GRX 131D (D31): Thames Valley & Aldershot Omnibus Co Ltd {Alder Valley}, Reading (BE) 663 1/72; Paul Sykes Organisation Ltd (dealer), Barnsley 7/80; AJ & RA Morris {Morris Bros}, Swansea (GG) 6 8/80; JD Cleverly Ltd, Cwmbran (MH) 6 5/84; Stagecoach Ltd, Perth (TE) 3/87; withdrawn 12/87; Magicbus (Scotland) Ltd, Glasgow (SC) 076 8/88; renumbered 655 3/92; probably to C Ireland (dealer), Kingston upon Hull c5/94; exported to Germany 5/94; last licensed 10/94.

GRX 132D (D32): Thames Valley & Aldershot Omnibus Co Ltd {Alder Valley}, Reading (BE) 664 1/72; Paul Sykes Organisation Ltd (dealer), Barnsley 7/80; AJ & RA Morris {Morris Bros}, Swansea (GG) 7 8/80; JD Cleverly Ltd, Cwmbran (MH) 7 5/84; Stagecoach Ltd, Perth (TE) 3/87; withdrawn 12/87; Magicbus (Scotland) Ltd, Glasgow (SC) 077 8/88; renumbered 656 3/92; last licensed 11/92; C Ireland (dealer), Kingston upon Hull for export 5/94; noted at the Eros Centre, Rostock as a nightclub (O-D) by 12/04; O Zilberg {Café Big Bus}, Kotlas as a static bar and café (O-RUS) by 6/13; Café-Bus 1966, Pyatigorsk (O-RUS) by 5/15.

GRX 133D (D33): Thames Valley & Aldershot Omnibus Co Ltd {Alder Valley}, Reading (BE) 665 1/72; Paul Sykes Organisation Ltd (dealer), Barnsley 7/80; AJ & RA Morris {Morris Bros}, Swansea (GG) 8 8/80; JD Cleverly Ltd, Cwmbran (MH) 8 5/84; last licensed 8/85; Omnibus Promotions Ltd (dealer), London EC1 11/85; exported to USA 8/86; unidentified owner, Fort Myers, Florida (O-USA) as a restaurant by 1996; Overcash {Great Knight Tours}, Atlanta, Georgia (O-USA) 101 registered KPF 1930 1996; re-registered 1136A 2001.

GRX 134D (D34): Thames Valley & Aldershot Omnibus Co Ltd {Alder Valley}, Reading (BE) 666 1/72; Paul Sykes Organisation Ltd (dealer), Barnsley 7/80; AJ & RA Morris {Morris Bros}, Swansea (GG) 9 8/80; JD Cleverly Ltd, Cwmbran (MH) 9 5/84; last licensed 8/85; Omnibus Promotions Ltd (dealer), London W10 11/85; exported to USA 8/86; Windjammer Cruises, Honolulu, Hawaii (O-USA) 11 registered CVB 385 by 6/89; cannibalised for spares by 2/93.

GRX 135D (D35): Thames Valley & Aldershot Omnibus Co Ltd {Alder Valley}, Reading (BE) 667 1/72; Paul Sykes Organisation Ltd (dealer), Barnsley 7/80; AJ & RA Morris {Morris Bros}, Swansea (GG) 10 9/80; JD Cleverly Ltd, Cwmbran (MH) 10 5/84; last licensed 7/86; GP Ripley (dealer), Carlton for scrap 2/87.

GRX 136-138D (D36-38): Thames Valley & Aldershot Omnibus Co Ltd {Alder Valley}, Reading (BE) 668-670 1/72; Paul Sykes Organisation Ltd (dealer), Barnsley 7/80; J Sykes (dealer), Carlton for scrap 8/80.

GRX 139D (D39): Thames Valley & Aldershot Omnibus Co Ltd {Alder Valley}, Reading (BE) 671 1/72; withdrawn after fire damage at Reading depot on 7/7/73; WR Alexander {Alexander Coaches}, Sheffield (WR) 9/73; Paul Sykes Organisation Ltd (dealer), Barnsley for scrap by 12/74.

GRX 140D (D40): Thames Valley & Aldershot Omnibus Co Ltd {Alder Valley}, Reading (BE) 672 1/72; Paul Sykes Organisation Ltd (dealer), Barnsley 7/80; AJ & RA Morris {Morris Bros}, Swansea (GG) 11 9/80; JD Cleverly Ltd, Cwmbran (MH) 11 5/84; D40 Preservation Group, Bracknell for preservation 12/86; R Rampton, Reading for preservation 1997; still in existence 11/11.

GRX 141D (D41): Thames Valley & Aldershot Omnibus Co Ltd {Alder Valley}, Reading (BE) 673 1/72; Paul Sykes Organisation Ltd (dealer), Barnsley 7/80; J Sykes (dealer), Carlton 8/80; Omnibus Promotions Ltd (dealer), London EC1 probably for export 10/88.

GRX 142D (D42): Thames Valley & Aldershot Omnibus Co Ltd {Alder Valley}, Reading (BE) 674 1/72; cannibalised after serious accident in 6/77; Paul Sykes Organisation Ltd (dealer), Barnsley for scrap 3/78.

GRX 143-144D (D43-44): Thames Valley & Aldershot Omnibus Co Ltd {Alder Valley}, Reading (BE) 675-676 1/72; Paul Sykes Organisation Ltd (dealer), Barnsley 7/80; J Sykes (dealer), Carlton for scrap 8/80.

GRX 145D (D45): Thames Valley & Aldershot Omnibus Co Ltd {Alder Valley}, Reading (BE) 677 1/72; Paul Sykes Organisation Ltd (dealer), Barnsley 7/80; AJ & RA Morris {Morris Bros}, Swansea (GG) 12 8/80; JD Cleverly Ltd, Cwmbran (MH) 12 5/84; last licensed 8/85; Omnibus Promotions Ltd (dealer), London EC1 11/85; exported to USA 8/86; Big Ben's of London, Columbus, Ohio (O-USA) registered B377 BAB by 5/92.

GRX 146D (D46): Thames Valley & Aldershot Omnibus Co Ltd {Alder Valley}, Reading (BE) 678 1/72; Paul Sykes Organisation Ltd (dealer), Barnsley 7/80; AJ & RA Morris {Morris Bros}, Swansea (GG) 13 8/80; JD Cleverly Ltd, Cwmbran (MH) 13 5/84; last licensed 8/85; Omnibus Promotions Ltd, London EC1 by 11/88; exported to USA 11/88; Windjammer Cruises, Honolulu, Hawaii (O-USA) 17 registered DFG 544 by 2/93.

Vehicles transferred from South Midland Motor Services Ltd 2-7/66:

S315	TWL 55	Bristol LS6B	97.017	ECW	6975	DP41F	6/53	5/69
S316	TWL 56	Bristol LS6B	97.018	ECW	6976	DP39F	6/53	3/69
S317	TWL 57	Bristol LS6B	97.019	ECW	6977	DP39F	6/53	3/69
S318	TWL 58	Bristol LS6B	97.020	ECW	6978	DP39F	7/53	9/70

Previous histories:

TWL 55 (S315): New to South Midland Motor Services Ltd 90 (as C37F) [reseated to C39F 2/62; delicensed 10/65, reseated to DP41F; equipped for one-man-operation and renumbered S315 2/66]; transferred 2/66.

TWL 56 (S316): New to South Midland Motor Services Ltd 91 (as C37F) [reseated to C39F 7/62; delicensed 11/65, reseated to DP39F; equipped for one-man-operation and renumbered S316 5/66]; transferred 5/66.

TWL 57 (S317): New to South Midland Motor Services Ltd 92 (as C37F) [reseated to C39F 2/62; delicensed 2/66, reseated to DP39F; equipped for one-man-operation and renumbered S317 7/66]; transferred 7/66.

TWL 58 (S318): New to South Midland Motor Services Ltd 93 (as C37F) [reseated to C39F 5/62; delicensed 2/66, reseated to DP39F; equipped for one-man-operation and renumbered S318 7/66]; transferred 7/66.

Notes:

TWL 55 (S315): Cannibalised for spares from 5/69.

TWL 58 (S318): Fitted with a Gardner 6HLW diesel engine (to LS6G specification) 3/69 allocated 113 in the 1969 renumbering scheme, but not carried; cannibalised for spares 9/70.

Disposals:

TWL 55 (S315): W Norths (PV) Ltd (dealer), Sherburn in Elmet (minus engine) for scrap 10/69.

TWL 56 (S316): W Norths (PV) Ltd (dealer), Sherburn in Elmet 3/69; Business Vehicles, York (XYK) 3/69; W Norths (PV) Ltd (dealer), Sherburn in Elmet for scrap by 7/70.

TWL 57 (S317): W Norths (PV) Ltd (dealer), Sherburn in Elmet 3/69; Holloway Coaches Ltd, Scunthorpe (LI) 3/69; Margo's Luxury Coaches (Streatham) Ltd, London SW16 (LN) 9/69; cannibalised for spares from 11/69.

TWL 58 (S318): W Norths (PV) Ltd (dealer), Sherburn in Elmet (minus engine) for scrap 2/71.

Vehicles acquired from United Welsh Services Ltd, Swansea (GG) 5-7/66:

S321	KWN 794	Bristol LS6B	105.114	ECW	7498	B44F	1/55	12/71
S322	KWN 795	Bristol LS6B	105.115	ECW	7499	B45F	2/55	12/71
S323	KWN 796	Bristol LS6B	107.095	ECW	7500	B45F	7/55	6/70
S324	KWN 797	Bristol LS6B	107.096	ECW	7501	B45F	7/55	6/70
772	LWN 48	Bristol LD6B	104.071	ECW	7376	H33/25R	5/55	10/71
773	LWN 49	Bristol LD6B	104.072	ECW	7377	H33/27R	5/55	12/71
774	LWN 50	Bristol LD6B	104.073	ECW	7378	H33/27R	7/55	10/71
775	LWN 51	Bristol LD6B	104.074	ECW	7379	H33/27R	6/55	10/71

770	LWN 52	Bristol LD6B	104.129	ECW	7380	H33/27RD	7/55	10/71
771	LWN 53	Bristol LD6B	104.130	ECW	7381	H33/27RD	7/55	10/71
S325	MCY 39	Bristol LS6B	107.112	ECW	8171	B45F	7/55	6/70

Previous histories:

KWN 794 (S321): New to United Welsh Services Ltd, Swansea (GG) 1263 (as B54F with 3+2 seating and a central rear emergency door) [reseated to B41F 10/59; reseated to B44F 12/63]; acquired in 5/66, entering service 6/66.

KWN 795 (S322): New to United Welsh Services Ltd, Swansea (GG) 1264; acquired 5/66, entering service 6/66.

KWN 796-797 (S323-S324): New to United Welsh Services Ltd, Swansea (GG) 1265-1266; acquired 7/66, entering service 8/66.

LWN 48 (772): New to United Welsh Services Ltd, Swansea (GG) 1257; acquired in 7/66, entering service 8/66.

LWN 49 (773): New to United Welsh Services Ltd, Swansea (GG) 1258 [as H33/25R, altered to H33/27R before disposal]; acquired in 7/66, entering service 9/66.

LWN 50-51 (774-775): New to United Welsh Services Ltd, Swansea (GG) 1253-1254 [as H33/25R, altered to H33/27R before disposal]; acquired in 7/66, entering service 9/66.

LWN 52 (770): New to United Welsh Services Ltd, Swansea (GG) 1255 [as H33/25R - fitted with platform doors, as H33/27RD, before disposal]; acquired and entering service 6/66.

LWN 53 (771): New to United Welsh Services Ltd, Swansea (GG) 1256 [as H33/25R - fitted with platform doors, as H33/27RD, before disposal]; acquired in 6/66, entering service 8/66.

MCY 39 (S325): New to United Welsh Services Ltd, Swansea (GG) 1267; acquired in 7/66, entering service 8/66.

Notes:

KWN 794 (S321): Equipped for one-man-operation and reseated to B40F, before entering service; renumbered 148 8/69; fitted with a Gardner 6HLW engine (to LS6G specification) 1/71.

KWN 795 (S322): Equipped for one-man-operation and reseated to B41F, before entering service; renumbered 149 9/69; fitted with a Gardner 6HLW engine (to LS6G specification) 6/71.

KWN 796 (S323): Equipped for one-man-operation and reseated to B41F, before entering service; renumbered 150 9/69.

KWN 797 (S324): Equipped for one-man-operation and reseated to B41F, before entering service; renumbered 151 10/69.

LWN 48 (772): Fitted with platform doors by ECW as H33/27RD by 7/70.

LWN 49 (773): Fitted with platform doors by ECW as H33/27RD (rebuild R1046) 4/70.

LWN 50-51 (774-775): Fitted with platform doors by ECW as H33/27RD by 7/70.

MCY 39 (S325): Equipped for one-man-operation and reseated to B41F, before entering service; renumbered 152 9/69.

Disposals:

KWN 794-795 (148-149): Thames Valley & Aldershot Omnibus Co Ltd {Alder Valley}, Reading (BE) 223-224 1/72; Paul Sykes Organisation Ltd (dealer), Barnsley for scrap 2/75.

KWN 796-797 (150-151): W Norths (PV) Ltd (dealer), Sherburn in Elmet for scrap 6/70.

LWN 48 (772): W Norths (PV) Ltd (dealer), Sherburn in Elmet 11/71; Blue Line Coaches Ltd, Upminster (LN) 5/72; withdrawn 5/73.

LWN 49 (773): Thames Valley & Aldershot Omnibus Co Ltd {Alder Valley}, Reading (BE) 512 1/72; W Norths (PV) Ltd (dealer), Sherburn in Elmet 6/72; Don's Coaches {Hale Bros}, Dunmow (EX) 1/73; W Norths (PV) Ltd (dealer), Sherburn in Elmet 12/73; exported 1/74; Koller Reisen, Paderborn (O-D) by 8/76; Alga Mobiles Hafrzeugmuseum, Sittensen (O-D) as a hospitality unit by 9/06; still owned 8/13.

LWN 50-51 (774-775): W Norths (PV) Ltd (dealer), Sherburn in Elmet 11/71; Blue Line Coaches Ltd, Upminster (LN) 12/71; W Norths (PV) Ltd (dealer), Sherburn in Elmet for scrap 6/73.

LWN 52 (770): W Norths (PV) Ltd (dealer), Sherburn in Elmet 11/71; P Jeffreys {Liss & District}, Grayshott (HA) 11/72.

LWN 53 (771): W Norths (PV) Ltd (dealer), Sherburn in Elmet 11/71; J Laverty {Eagle Coaches}, Neilston (RW) 5/72; RW Dunsmore (dealer), Larkhall for scrap 12/74.

MCY 39 (152): W Norths (PV) Ltd (dealer), Sherburn in Elmet 7/70; Port of Liverpool Stevedoring Co (XLA) 8/70.

Vehicles acquired from United Welsh Services Ltd, Swansea (GG) 11/66:

672	JCY 989	Bristol KSW6G	98.043	ECW	6543	L27/28R	7/53	11/70
673	JCY 990	Bristol KSW6G	98.044	ECW	6544	L27/28R	7/53	7/70
S326	JCY 997	Bristol LS5G	97.171	ECW	6929	B45F	12/53	12/70

S327	OCY 947	Bristol LS6G	119.122	ECW		9848	B45F	8/57	12/71
S328	OCY 948	Bristol LS6G	119.127	ECW		9843	B45F	9/57	12/71

Previous histories:

JCY 989-990 (672-673): New to United Welsh Services Ltd, Swansea (GG) 1242-1243; entering service 12/66.

JCY 997 (S326): New to United Welsh Services Ltd, Swansea (GG) 1250 [allotted fleet number 94 in the 11/66 scheme, but not carried]; entering service 12/66.

OCY 947 (S327): New to United Welsh Services Ltd, Swansea (GG) 107 [equipped for one-man operation 1/64]; entering service 12/66.

OCY 948 (S328): New to United Welsh Services Ltd, Swansea (GG) 108 [equipped for one-man operation 2/64]; entering service 12/66.

Notes:

JCY 989-990 (672-673): Fitted with Bristol AVW diesel engines (to KSW6B specification), before entering service.

JCY 997 (S326): Reseated to B41F, before entering service; renumbered 116 8/69.

OCY 947 (S327): Reseated to B41F, before entering service; renumbered 153 9/69; fitted with a Gardner 6HLW engine (to LS6G specification) 8/71.

OCY 948 (S328): Reseated to B41F, before entering service; fitted with a Gardner 6HLW engine (to LS6G specification) 4/69; renumbered 154 8/69.

Disposals:

JCY 989 (672): W Norths (PV) Ltd (dealer), Sherburn in Elmet 11/70; Riverway Enterprises (Harlow) Ltd {Riverway Coaches}, Harlow (EX) 11/70; withdrawn 9/71.

JCY 990 (673): W Norths (PV) Ltd (dealer), Sherburn in Elmet 8/70; Riverway Enterprises (Harlow) Ltd {Riverway Coaches}, Harlow (EX) 8/70; destroyed in a depot fire 12/71.

JCY 997 (116): W Norths (PV) Ltd (dealer), Sherburn in Elmet for scrap 1/71.

OCY 947 (153): Thames Valley & Aldershot Omnibus Co Ltd {Alder Valley}, Reading (BE) 240 1/72; Paul Sykes Organisation Ltd (dealer), Barnsley 2/75; K Askin (dealer), Barnsley for scrap 7/75.

OCY 948 (154): Thames Valley & Aldershot Omnibus Co Ltd {Alder Valley}, Reading (BE) 241 1/72; Main Motors (dealer), Ewelme 5/74; unidentified dealer, Carlton for scrap 10/76.

Vehicle transferred from South Midland Motor Services Ltd 12/66:

866	520 ABL	Bristol MW6G	195.008	ECW		12839	C39F	5/62	12/71

Previous history:

520 ABL (866): New to Thames Valley Traction Co Ltd 866; South Midland Motor Services Ltd 866 5/66.

Notes:

520 ABL (866): Fitted with a two-way radio c3/67 for the new rail-air service between Reading and Heathrow Airport.

Disposal:

520 ABL (866): Thames Valley & Aldershot Omnibus Co Ltd {Alder Valley}, Reading (BE) 31 1/72; Paul Sykes Organisation Ltd (dealer), Barnsley for scrap 11/75.

1967

New Vehicles:

D47	LBL 847E	Bristol FLF6G	236.057	ECW		16215	H38/32F	1/67	12/71
D48	LBL 848E	Bristol FLF6G	236.058	ECW		16216	H38/32F	1/67	12/71
D49	LBL 849E	Bristol FLF6G	236.086	ECW		16217	H38/32F	2/67	12/71
D50	LBL 850E	Bristol FLF6G	236.087	ECW		16218	H38/32F	2/67	12/71
D51	LBL 851E	Bristol FLF6G	236.088	ECW		16219	H38/32F	3/67	12/71
D52	LBL 852E	Bristol FLF6G	236.089	ECW		16220	H38/32F	3/67	12/71
D53	LBL 853E	Bristol FLF6G	236.140	ECW		16221	H38/32F	6/67	12/71
C417	LJB 417E	Bedford VAM14	6875393	Duple		1208/159	C41F	1/67	5/68
C418	LJB 418E	Bedford VAM14	6875051	Duple		1208/160	C41F	1/67	5/68
C419	LJB 419E	Bedford VAM14	6875402	Duple		1208/161	C41F	1/67	12/71
C420	LJB 420E	Bedford VAM14	6875041	Duple		1208/162	C41F	1/67	12/71
S331	LJB 331F	Bristol RESL6G	5/122	ECW		16387	B38D	9/67	12/71
S332	LJB 332F	Bristol RESL6G	5/123	ECW		16388	B38D	9/67	12/71
S333	LJB 333F	Bristol RESL6G	5/124	ECW		16389	B38D	10/67	12/71

S334 LJB 334F	Bristol RESL6G	5/125	ECW	16390 B38D	10/67	12/71
S335 LJB 335F	Bristol RESL6G	5/126	ECW	16391 B38D	10/67	12/71
S336 LJB 336F	Bristol RESL6G	5/127	ECW	16392 B38D	10/67	12/71
S337 LJB 337F	Bristol RESL6G	5/128	ECW	16393 B38D	10/67	12/71
S338 LJB 338F	Bristol RESL6G	5/129	ECW	16394 B38D	10/67	12/71

Notes:

LJB 331-338F (S331-S338): Were delivered registered LJB 331-338E, but not licensed; they were built as B38D (with provision for 27 standing passengers) but following Union discussions, they were placed in store before being reseated to B40D (with provision for 8 standing passengers) in 2/68; entering service 3/68 as LJB 331-338F.

LJB 417-420E (C417-C420): Did not enter service until 4/67 when the new rail-air service between Reading and Heathrow Airport began; they were fitted with two-way radios.

LBL 848E (D48): Reseated to H38/30F with an additional luggage pen fitted 2/69; luggage pen removed and reverted to H38/32F 5/69.

LBL 849E (D49): Reseated to H38/30F with an additional luggage pen fitted 1/69; luggage pen removed and reverted to H38/32F 5/69.

LBL 850E (D50): Reseated to H38/30F with an additional luggage pen fitted 1/69; luggage pen removed and reverted to H38/32F 7/71.

LBL 852E (D52): Reseated to H38/30F with an additional luggage pen fitted 1-2/69; luggage pen removed and reverted to H38/32F 5/69.

LBL 853E (D53): Fitted with a Gardner 6LW engine (the others of this batch were Gardner 6LX).

LJB 419-420E (C419-420): Renumbered 419-420 2/69.

LJB 331F (S331): Renumbered 188 9/69.

LJB 332F (S332): Renumbered 189 3/69.

LJB 333F (S333): Renumbered 190 9/69.

LJB 334F (S334): Renumbered 191 10/69.

LJB 335F (S335): Renumbered 192 9/69.

LJB 336F (S336): Renumbered 193 8/69.

LJB 337F (S337): Renumbered 194 6/69.

LJB 338F (S338): Renumbered 195 7/69.

Disposals:

LBL 847E (D47): Thames Valley & Aldershot Omnibus Co Ltd {Alder Valley}, Reading (BE) 679 1/72; Scottish Omnibuses Ltd {Eastern Scottish}, Edinburgh (MN) AA973 11/73; withdrawn 7/82; J Locke (dealer), Edinburgh 7/82; Hartwood Exports (Machinery) Ltd (dealer), Birdwell 8/82; R Thornton (dealer), Cundy Cross for scrap 2/83.

LBL 848E (D48): Thames Valley & Aldershot Omnibus Co Ltd {Alder Valley}, Reading (BE) 680 1/72; Scottish Omnibuses Ltd {Eastern Scottish}, Edinburgh (MN) AA974 11/73; withdrawn 12/81; Thomas Muir (Metals) Ltd (dealer), Kirkcaldy 1/82; T Wigley (dealer), Carlton for scrap 6/82.

LBL 849E (D49): Thames Valley & Aldershot Omnibus Co Ltd {Alder Valley}, Reading (BE) 681 1/72; Central SMT Co Ltd, Motherwell (LK) BE360 9/73; withdrawn 1/79; T Wigley (dealer), Carlton for scrap 3/79.

LBL 850E (D50): Thames Valley & Aldershot Omnibus Co Ltd {Alder Valley}, Reading (BE) 682 1/72; Central SMT Co Ltd, Motherwell (LK) BE358 4/73; withdrawn 2/79; broken up for spares.

LBL 851E (D51): Thames Valley & Aldershot Omnibus Co Ltd {Alder Valley}, Reading (BE) 683 1/72; Central SMT Co Ltd, Motherwell (LK) BE359 9/73; withdrawn 3/79; R Irvine {Tiger Coaches} (dealer), Salsburgh for scrap 7/79.

LBL 852E (D52): Thames Valley & Aldershot Omnibus Co Ltd {Alder Valley}, Reading (BE) 684 1/72; Central SMT Co Ltd, Motherwell (LK) BE361 7/73; broken up for spares 9/79.

LBL 853E (D53): Thames Valley & Aldershot Omnibus Co Ltd {Alder Valley}, Reading (BE) 685 1/72; Western SMT Co Ltd, Kilmarnock (AR) B2419 6/73; withdrawn 8/79; Ensign Bus Co Ltd (dealer), Purfleet 12/79; Justin Jacobs, San Francisco, California (O-USA) 3/80.

LJB 417-418E (C417-418): South Midland Motor Services Ltd C417-418 5/68 (qv).

LJB 419E (419): Thames Valley & Aldershot Omnibus Co Ltd {Alder Valley}, Reading (BE) 34 1/72; Martins Bus & Coach Sales Ltd (dealer), Middlewich 8/76; J Shennan, Drongan (SC) 9/76; Ralph Loney (Trucks), Portadown (AH) by 3/77.

LJB 420E (420): Thames Valley & Aldershot Omnibus Co Ltd {Alder Valley}, Reading (BE) 35 1/72; Martins Bus & Coach Sales Ltd (dealer), Middlewich 8/76; RP Prentice & Sons, West Calder (LO) 9/76; withdrawn by 10/79.

LJB 331F (188): Thames Valley & Aldershot Omnibus Co Ltd {Alder Valley}, Reading (BE) 404 1/72; Passenger Vehicle Spares (Barnsley) Ltd (dealer), Carlton 6/78; T Wigley (dealer), Carlton for scrap 5/79.

LJB 332F (189): Thames Valley & Aldershot Omnibus Co Ltd {Alder Valley}, Reading (BE) 405 1/72;
converted to a traffic survey vehicle no 1082 10/78 and transferred to the service fleet;
renumbered 27 9/82; Alder Valley South Ltd, Aldershot 67 as a mobile office 1/86; W Norths
(PV) Ltd (dealer), Sherburn in Elmet for scrap 8/86.
LJB 333F (190): Thames Valley & Aldershot Omnibus Co Ltd {Alder Valley}, Reading (BE) 406 1/72;
Passenger Vehicle Spares (Barnsley) Ltd (dealer), Carlton 12/78; T Wigley (dealer), Carlton
for scrap 12/78.
LJB 334F (191): Thames Valley & Aldershot Omnibus Co Ltd {Alder Valley}, Reading (BE) 407 1/72; W
Norths (PV) Ltd (dealer), Sherburn in Elmet 4/79; Whiting Bros (dealer), Carlton for scrap 4/79.
LJB 335F (192): Thames Valley & Aldershot Omnibus Co Ltd {Alder Valley}, Reading (BE) 408 1/72;
Passenger Vehicle Spares (Barnsley) Ltd (dealer), Carlton for scrap 6/78.
LJB 336-338F (193-195): Thames Valley & Aldershot Omnibus Co Ltd {Alder Valley}, Reading (BE) 409-411
1/72; Passenger Vehicle Spares (Barnsley) Ltd (dealer), Carlton for scrap 12/78.

Vehicles transferred from South Midland Motor Services Ltd 1-6/67:

S319	TWL 59	Bristol LS6B	97.041	ECW		6979	DP39F	8/53	12/68
S320	TWL 60	Bristol LS6B	97.042	ECW		6980	DP39F	10/53	3/69

Previous histories:
TWL 59 (S319): New to South Midland Motor Services Ltd 94 (as C37F) [reseated to C39F 1/64; delicensed
12/66, reseated to DP39F; equipped for one-man-operation and renumbered S319 6/67];
transferred 6/67.
TWL 60 (S320): New to South Midland Motor Services Ltd 95 (as C37F) [reseated to C39F 1/64; delicensed
4/66, reseated to DP39F; equipped for one-man-operation and renumbered S320 1/67];
transferred 1/67.

Disposals:
TWL 59 (S319): W Norths (PV) Ltd (dealer), Sherburn in Elmet 1/69; DR MacGregor {Hedingham & District
Omnibuses}, Sible Hedingham (EX) L54 2/69; Ipswich Coach Co Ltd, Ipswich (EK) 11/71; D
Boughton (dealer?), Ipswich by 3/76 to 10/77 at least.
TWL 60 (S320): W Norths (PV) Ltd (dealer), Sherburn in Elmet 3/69; Holloway Coaches Ltd, Scunthorpe (LI)
3/69; Margo's Luxury Coaches (Streatham) Ltd, London SW16 (LN) 9/69; scrapped 2/71.

Vehicles acquired from United Welsh Services Ltd, Swansea (GG) 2/67:

S329	JCY 995	Bristol LS6G	97.107	ECW		6927	B45F	12/53	9/71
S330	JCY 996	Bristol LS6G	97.108	ECW		6928	B45F	12/53	12/71

Previous histories:
JCY 995-996 (S329-S330): New to United Welsh Services Ltd, Swansea (GG) 1248-1249 [allotted fleet
numbers 92-93 in the 11/66 scheme, but not carried]; entering service 3/67.

Notes:
JCY 995 (S329): Reseated to B41F, before entering service; renumbered 114 8/69.
JCY 996 (S330): Reseated to B41F, before entering service; renumbered 115 4/70.

Disposals:
JCY 995 (114): W Norths (PV) Ltd (dealer), Sherburn in Elmet 11/71; Kellogg International (contractor),
London W1 (XLN) 3/72.
JCY 996 (115): Thames Valley & Aldershot Omnibus Co Ltd {Alder Valley}, Reading (BE) 206 1/72; Paul
Sykes Organisation Ltd (dealer), Barnsley for scrap 2/74.

Vehicles acquired from United Welsh Services Ltd, Swansea (GG) 6/67:

776	JCY 993	Bristol LD6G	100.067	ECW		6652	H33/25R	6/54	12/71
777	JCY 994	Bristol LD6G	100.169	ECW		6653	H33/25R	12/54	10/71

Previous histories:
JCY 993-994 (776-777): New to United Welsh Services Ltd, Swansea (GG) 1246-1247 [renumbered 299-
300 1/67].

Notes:
JCY 993 (776): Fitted with platform doors by ECW as H33/25RD (rebuild R1043) 6/70.
JCY 994 (777): Fitted with platform doors by ECW as H33/25RD (rebuild R1044) 7/70.

Disposals:
JCY 993 (776): Thames Valley & Aldershot Omnibus Co Ltd {Alder Valley}, Reading (BE) 504 1/72; converted to a driver training vehicle 27 6/72 and transferred to the service fleet; renumbered 1101 6/78; unidentified dealer for scrap post 6/81.
JCY 994 (777): W Norths (PV) Ltd (dealer), Sherburn in Elmet 11/71; J Laverty {Eagle Coaches}, Neilston (RW) 5/72.

Vehicles acquired from United Welsh Services Ltd, Swansea (GG) 12/67:

778	JCY 991	Bristol LD6G	100.013	ECW		6650	H33/25RD	3/54	8/71
794	JCY 992	Bristol LD6G	100.029	ECW		6651	H33/25RD	3/54	12/71

Previous histories:
JCY 991 (778): New to United Welsh Services Ltd, Swansea (GG) 1244 (as H33/25R - fitted with platform doors before disposal) [renumbered 297 11/66].
JCY 992 (794): New to United Welsh Services Ltd, Swansea (GG) 1245 (as H33/25R - fitted with platform doors before disposal) [renumbered 298 11/66].

Disposals:
JCY 991 (778): W Norths (PV) Ltd (dealer), Sherburn in Elmet (minus running units) for scrap 9/71.
JCY 992 (794): Thames Valley & Aldershot Omnibus Co Ltd {Alder Valley}, Reading (BE) 505 1/72; converted to a driver training vehicle 28 6/72 and transferred to the service fleet; D Rollinson (Bus Centre) Ltd (dealer), Carlton for scrap 9/76.

1968

New Vehicles:

D54	PBL 53F	Bristol FLF6G	236.311	ECW		17007	H38/32F	2/68	12/71
D55	PBL 55F	Bristol FLF6G	236.312	ECW		17008	H38/32F	2/68	12/71
D56	PBL 56F	Bristol FLF6G	236.313	ECW		17009	H38/32F	2/68	12/71
D57	PBL 57F	Bristol FLF6G	236.314	ECW		17010	H38/32F	2/68	12/71
D58	PBL 58F	Bristol FLF6G	236.315	ECW		17011	H38/32F	2/68	12/71
D59	PBL 59F	Bristol FLF6G	236.316	ECW		17012	H38/32F	2/68	12/71
D60	PBL 60F	Bristol FLF6G	236.317	ECW		17013	H38/32F	2/68	12/71
C424	RJB 424F	Bristol RELH6G	4/155	Duple Northern	190/6	C49F	4/68	6/70
C425	RJB 425F	Bristol RELH6G	4/156	Duple Northern	190/7	C49F	4/68	12/71
C426	RJB 426F	Bristol RELH6G	4/157	Duple Northern	190/8	C49F	4/68	12/71
C427	RJB 427F	Bristol RELH6G	4/158	Duple Northern	190/9	C49F	4/68	12/71
200	RRX 991G	Bristol LH6L	LH-167	ECW		17360	B45F	10/68	12/71
201	RRX 992G	Bristol LH6L	LH-168	ECW		17361	B45F	10/68	12/71
202	RRX 993G	Bristol LH6L	LH-169	ECW		17362	B45F	10/68	12/71
203	RRX 994G	Bristol LH6L	LH-170	ECW		17363	B45F	10/68	12/71
204	RRX 995G	Bristol LH6L	LH-171	ECW		17364	B45F	10/68	12/71
205	RRX 996G	Bristol LH6L	LH-172	ECW		17365	B45F	10/68	12/71
206	RRX 997G	Bristol LH6L	LH-173	ECW		17366	B45F	10/68	12/71
207	RRX 998G	Bristol LH6L	LH-174	ECW		17367	B45F	10/68	12/71
501	SRX 945G	Bristol VRT/SL6G	115	ECW		17270	H41/29F	12/68	12/71

Notes:
PBL 53F (D54): Fitted with a Clayton Dewandre heating system and a Gardner 6LX diesel engine.
PBL 55-60F (D55-60): Fitted with Clayton Dewandre heating systems and Gardner 6LX diesel engines.
RJB 424-427F (C424-427): Fitted with Gardner 6HLX diesel engines.
RRX 991-998G (200-207): Did not enter service until 12/68; reseated to B41F, before entering service; some were fitted with tow bars for use as towing vehicles.

PBL 53F (D54): Reseated to H38/30F with an additional luggage pen fitted 1/69; luggage pen removed and reverted to H38/32F 7/71.
PBL 57F (D57): Reseated to H38/30F with an additional luggage pen fitted 1/69.
PBL 60F (D60): Reseated to H38/30F with an additional luggage pen fitted 1/69.
RJB 424F (C424): Named 'Western Pegasus'; renumbered 424 2/69; burnt out whilst on service near Littlewick Green 17/6/70.
RJB 425F (C425): Named 'Western Mercury'; renumbered 425 2/69; name removed 1971.
RJB 426F (C426): Named 'Western Eros'; renumbered 426 2/69; name removed 1971.
RJB 427F (C427): Named 'Western Hermes'; renumbered 427 2/69; name removed 1971.
SRX 945G (501): Did not enter service until 2/69.

Disposals:

PBL   53F (D54): Thames Valley & Aldershot Omnibus Co Ltd {Alder Valley}, Reading (BE) 686 1/72; Western SMT Co Ltd, Kilmarnock (AR) 2413 4/73; Ensign Bus Co Ltd (dealer), Purfleet 12/79; Piccadilly Promotions, Galveston, Texas (O-USA) 3/80; Continental Air Transport, Chicago, Illinois (O-USA) 03 by 10/84; Chicago Motor Coach Co, Chicago, Illinois (O-USA) 539 registered 7946 H 7/90; scrapped by 7/98.

PBL   55F (D55): Thames Valley & Aldershot Omnibus Co Ltd {Alder Valley}, Reading (BE) 687 1/72; Western SMT Co Ltd, Kilmarnock (AR) 2434 3/74; Ensign Bus Co Ltd (dealer), Purfleet 3/80; Central Garage (Southborough) Ltd, Tonbridge (XKT) as a 'Jean Bus' mobile showroom 6/80; last licensed 5/81; noted with Countrywide Markets, Worcester (XHW) 8/83.

PBL   56F (D56): Thames Valley & Aldershot Omnibus Co Ltd {Alder Valley}, Reading (BE) 688 1/72; Western SMT Co Ltd, Kilmarnock (AR) 2437 4/74; withdrawn 4/80; Mrs P Papadopolous, Listleigh for conversion to a caravan for a trip to Australia (but not converted) 5/80; stored at West of England Transport Collection, Winkleigh 11/80; T Wigley (dealer), Carlton for scrap 11/81.

PBL   57F (D57): Thames Valley & Aldershot Omnibus Co Ltd {Alder Valley}, Reading (BE) 689 1/72; Western SMT Co Ltd, Kilmarnock (AR) 2432 1/74; withdrawn by 8/80; converted to a driver training vehicle no DW1064 8/80; last licensed 2/92; GP Ripley (dealer), Carlton 8/93; C Ireland (dealer), Kingston upon Hull for export 5/94; unidentified owner, Germany at an unknown date; unidentified owner as a mobile classroom, Wien (O-A) by 6/13.

PBL   58F (D58): Thames Valley & Aldershot Omnibus Co Ltd {Alder Valley}, Reading (BE) 690 1/72; Western SMT Co Ltd, Kilmarnock (AR) 2439 4/74; withdrawn by 2/80; Gordon (dealer), Elderslie 3/80; G Jameson {Dunscroft Commercials} (dealer), Dunscroft 3/80; T Wigley (dealer), Carlton for scrap 4/80.

PBL   59F (D59): Thames Valley & Aldershot Omnibus Co Ltd {Alder Valley}, Reading (BE) 691 1/72; Western SMT Co Ltd, Kilmarnock (AR) 2440 4/74; withdrawn by 2/80; Ensign Bus Co Ltd (dealer), Purfleet 7/80; Association Pont de la Unite, Carazel (O-F) 8/80.

PBL   60F (D60): Thames Valley & Aldershot Omnibus Co Ltd {Alder Valley}, Reading (BE) 692 1/72; Western SMT Co Ltd, Kilmarnock (AR) 2433 2/74; withdrawn by 8/80; Ensign Bus Co Ltd (dealer), Purfleet 11/80; Tillingbourne Valley Bus Co Ltd, Green Street Green (LN) 3/83; W Norths (PV) Ltd (dealer), Sherburn in Elmet 2/85; Top Deck Travel Ltd, Edgware (LN) 9/85; reseated to H12/16F, fitted with a stove, bunks etc for overland travel and named 'Drought Breaker'; moved to Horsell (SR) 4/89; last licensed 8/92; Passenger Vehicle Spares (Barnsley) Ltd (dealer), Carlton for scrap by 3/96.

RJB 424F (424): Dismantled for spares / scrap by Thames Valley 11/70.

RJB 425-427F (425-427): Thames Valley & Aldershot Omnibus Co Ltd {Alder Valley}, Reading (BE) 56-58 1/72; D Rollinson (Bus Centre) Ltd (dealer), Carlton for scrap 11/77.

RRX 991-992G (200-201): Thames Valley & Aldershot Omnibus Co Ltd {Alder Valley}, Reading (BE) 257-258 1/72; renumbered 511-512 8/75; United Automobile Services Ltd, Darlington (DM) 1492 2/77; withdrawn 10/78; NBC Eastern Region Disposal Centre (dealer), Bracebridge Heath for scrap 10-12/78.

RRX 993G (202): Thames Valley & Aldershot Omnibus Co Ltd {Alder Valley}, Reading (BE) 259 1/72; renumbered 513 8/75; United Automobile Services Ltd, Darlington (DM) 1494 2/77; withdrawn 10/78; CF Booth Ltd (dealer), Rotherham 10/79; Fr DJ Green (dealer), Weymouth by 11/79; David List Ltd, Debenham (SK) 11/79; Felixstowe Omnibuses Ltd, Ipswich (SK) 5 and named 'Jupiter' 6/86; last licensed 5/88; Tyne & Wear Omnibus Co Ltd, Gateshead (TW) for spares 8/88; North Eastern Bus Breakers (dealer), Craghead for scrap 11/89.

RRX 994G (203): Thames Valley & Aldershot Omnibus Co Ltd {Alder Valley}, Reading (BE) 260 1/72; renumbered 514 8/75; United Automobile Services Ltd, Darlington (DM) 1495 2/77; withdrawn 10/78; NBC Eastern Region Disposal Centre (dealer), Bracebridge Heath for scrap 10-12/78.

RRX 995G (204): Thames Valley & Aldershot Omnibus Co Ltd {Alder Valley}, Reading (BE) 261 1/72; renumbered 515 8/75; S Twell (dealer), Ingham for scrap 1/77.

RRX 996G (205): Thames Valley & Aldershot Omnibus Co Ltd {Alder Valley}, Reading (BE) 262 1/72; renumbered 516 8/75; United Automobile Services Ltd, Darlington (DM) 1496 2/77; withdrawn 10/78; CF Booth Ltd (dealer), Rotherham for scrap 10/79.

RRX 997G (206): Thames Valley & Aldershot Omnibus Co Ltd {Alder Valley}, Reading (BE) 263 1/72; renumbered 517 8/75; S Twell (dealer), Ingham 1/77; Parton & Allen (dealer), Carlton for scrap 6/84.

RRX 998G (207): Thames Valley & Aldershot Omnibus Co Ltd {Alder Valley}, Reading (BE) 264 1/72; renumbered 518 8/75; Passenger Vehicle Spares (Barnsley) Ltd (dealer), Carlton 6/78; C & J Bannister {Isle Coaches}, Owston Ferry (LI) (not operated) 1978; derelict by 4/93; scrapped on site by 3/97.

SRX 945G (501): Thames Valley & Aldershot Omnibus Co Ltd {Alder Valley}, Reading (BE) 902 1/72; Alder Valley North Ltd, Reading (BE) 902 1/86; The Berks Bucks Bus Co Ltd {The Bee Line}, Reading (BE) 902 1/87; renumbered 502 10/87; City of Oxford Motor Services Ltd, Oxford (OX) 1502 11/90; last licensed 2/91; Passenger Vehicle Spares (Barnsley) Ltd (dealer), Carlton 3/91 for scrap.

Vehicles acquired from United Automobile Services Ltd, Darlington (DM) 1/68:

691	PHN 819	Bristol KSW5G	90.056	ECW	6094	L27/28R	6/52	1/71
690	PHN 821	Bristol KSW5G	90.058	ECW	6096	L27/28R	7/52	1/71
688	PHN 828	Bristol KSW6B	90.070	ECW	6100	L27/28R	6/52	2/71
689	PHN 829	Bristol KSW6B	90.071	ECW	6101	L27/28R	7/52	9/70

Previous histories:

PHN 819 (691): New to United Automobile Services Ltd, Darlington (DM) BGL76 [fitted with a Bristol AVW diesel engine and renumbered BBL74 11/59]; entering service 3/68.

PHN 821 (690): New to United Automobile Services Ltd, Darlington (DM) BGL78 [fitted with a Bristol AVW diesel engine and renumbered BBL68 1/61]; entering service 3/68.

PHN 828 (688): New to United Automobile Services Ltd, Darlington (DM) BBL66; entering service 5/68.

PHN 829 (689): New to United Automobile Services Ltd, Darlington (DM) BBL67; entering service 4/68.

Disposals:

PHN 819 (691): W Norths (PV) Ltd (dealer), Sherburn in Elmet for scrap 3/71.

PHN 821 (690): W Norths (PV) Ltd (dealer), Sherburn in Elmet 3/71; Uncle Bobby Ash, Toronto, Ontario (O-CDN) 11/71; Campus Transportation Ltd {Hiawathaland Tours}, Sault Ste Marie, Ontario (O-CDN) registered BC5 941 by 7/82; re-registered BJ8 228 by 1998; Bickell, Sault Ste Marie, Ontario (O-CDN) by 2005; scrapped by 2005.

PHN 828 (688): W Norths (PV) Ltd (dealer), Sherburn in Elmet for scrap 3/71.

PHN 829 (689): W Norths (PV) Ltd (dealer), Sherburn in Elmet 10/70; Cheltenham Motor Club, Cheltenham (XGL) 12/70; R Kell, Durham for preservation c12/84; J Purvis, Seaburn for preservation c6/85; A Dolan, Crook for preservation by 9/88; Lister (PVS) Bolton Ltd (dealer), Bolton 2/94; E Brakell (dealer), Cheam 2/94; Londag, Wadenswil (O-CH) 2/94; moved to Bassersdorf (O-CH) 2/96; H Gerspach, Murghammer (O-D) 3/98; registered WT GB 244; A Dolan, Crook for preservation c12/10.

Vehicles acquired from United Automobile Services Ltd, Darlington (DM) 2/68:

S339	SHN 728	Bristol LS5G	97.130	ECW	6776	B45F	1/54	12/71
S340	SHN 729	Bristol LS5G	97.145	ECW	6777	B45F	1/54	5/71
S341	SHN 730	Bristol LS5G	97.146	ECW	6778	B45F	1/54	4/71

Previous histories:

SHN 728-730 (S339-S341): New to United Automobile Services Ltd, Darlington (DM) BU38-BU40 [renumbered U38-U40 11/64]; entering service 6/68.

Notes:

SHN 728 (S339): Reseated to B41F, before entering service; renumbered 127 11/69.

SHN 729 (S340): Reseated to B41F, before entering service; renumbered 128 9/69; being cannibalised from 5/71.

SHN 730 (S341): Reseated to B41F, before entering service; renumbered 129 9/69.

Disposals:

SHN 728 (127): Thames Valley & Aldershot Omnibus Co Ltd {Alder Valley}, Reading (BE) 207 1/72; W Norths (PV) Ltd (dealer), Sherburn in Elmet 5/73; Thorn Electronics, Gosport (XHA) 1/74; W Norths (PV) Ltd (dealer), Sherburn in Elmet 4/75; Companhia de Autocarros Fok Lei Lda (O-MAC) LS139 registered M-11-43 5/75.

SHN 729 (128): WR Alexander {Alexander Coaches}, Sheffield (WR) (minus mechanical units) 10/71.

SHN 730 (129): Unidentified operator / dealer 7/71.

Vehicles acquired from Bristol Omnibus Co Ltd, Bristol (GL) 3/68:

S342	PHW 929	Bristol LS5G	97.176	ECW	6839	B45F	6/54	3/69
S343	PHW 930	Bristol LS5G	97.177	ECW	6840	B45F	6/54	12/71
S344	PHW 931	Bristol LS5G	97.178	ECW	6841	B45F	6/54	9/71
S345	PHW 932	Bristol LS5G	97.179	ECW	6842	B45F	6/54	11/69

Previous histories:
    PHW 929-930 (S342-S343): New to Bristol Tramways & Carriage Co Ltd, Bristol (GL) 2839-2840; Bristol Omnibus Co Ltd, Bristol (GL) 2839-2840 6/57; entering service 5/68.
    PHW 931-932 (S344-S345): New to Bristol Tramways & Carriage Co Ltd, Bristol (GL) 2841-2842; Bristol Omnibus Co Ltd, Bristol (GL) 2841-2842 6/57; entering service 6/68.

Notes:
    PHW 929 (S342): Reseated to B41F, before entering service.
    PHW 930 (S343): Reseated to B41F, before entering service; renumbered 130 10/69.
    PHW 931 (S344): Reseated to B41F, before entering service; renumbered 131 9/69.
    PHW 932 (S345): Reseated to B41F, before entering service; allocated 132 in the 1969 renumbering scheme, but not carried.

Disposals:
    PHW 929 (S342): Margo's Luxury Coaches (Streatham) Ltd, London SW16 (LN) 3/69; withdrawn by 3/71.
    PHW 930 (130): Thames Valley & Aldershot Omnibus Co Ltd {Alder Valley}, Reading (BE) 210 1/72; fitted with a Gardner 6HLW engine 7/72; Egham Bus Group, Egham for preservation 4/75; unidentified operator / dealer probably soon after being advertised for sale 9/76.
    PHW 931 (131): Tillingbourne Valley Services Ltd, Guildford (SR) 10/71; scrapped 12/71.
    PHW 932 (S345): Elm Park Coaches Ltd, Romford (LN) 8/70; Lister (PVS) Bolton Ltd (dealer), Bolton by 1/75; Glen Tours, Baildon (WY) 1/75; Beaumont Heating, Ashton-under-Lyne (XGM) 9/75; unidentified dealer, Barnsley for scrap 5/78.

Vehicles acquired from United Welsh Services Ltd, Swansea (GG) 4/68:

795	NCY 634	Bristol LD6G	120.031	ECW	8646	H33/27R	8/56	12/71
796	NCY 635	Bristol LD6G	120.034	ECW	8647	H33/27R	8/56	12/71
797	NCY 636	Bristol LD6G	130.025	ECW	8648	H33/27R	12/56	12/71
798	OCY 953	Bristol LD6G	130.101	ECW	9565	H33/27R	2/57	12/71

Previous histories:
    NCY 634-635 (795-796): New to United Welsh Services Ltd, Swansea (GG) 301-302; entering service 5/68.
    NCY 636 (797): New to United Welsh Services Ltd, Swansea (GG) 303; entering service 7/68.
    OCY 953 (798): New to United Welsh Services Ltd, Swansea (GG) 306; entering service 7/68.

Notes:
    NCY 634 (795): Fitted with platform doors by ECW as H33/27RD (rebuild R943) 11/68.
    NCY 635 (796): Fitted with platform doors by ECW as H33/27RD (rebuild R942) 10/68.
    NCY 636 (797): Fitted with platform doors by ECW as H33/27RD (rebuild R929) 7/68.
    OCY 953 (798): Fitted with platform doors by ECW as H33/27RD (rebuild R944) 11/68.

Disposals:
    NCY 634 (795): Thames Valley & Aldershot Omnibus Co Ltd {Alder Valley}, Reading (BE) 519 1/72; Paul Sykes Organisation Ltd (dealer), Barnsley for scrap 2/75.
    NCY 635 (796): Thames Valley & Aldershot Omnibus Co Ltd {Alder Valley}, Reading (BE) 520 1/72; Main Motors (dealer), Ewelme for scrap 5/74.
    NCY 636 (797): Thames Valley & Aldershot Omnibus Co Ltd {Alder Valley}, Reading (BE) 521 1/72; converted to a driver training vehicle no 29 2/75 and transferred to the service fleet; renumbered 1104 6/78; W Norths (PV) Ltd (dealer), Sherburn in Elmet 4/79; Whiting Bros (dealer), Carlton 5/79; D Rollinson (Bus Centre) Ltd (dealer), Carlton for scrap 6/81.
    OCY 953 (798): Thames Valley & Aldershot Omnibus Co Ltd {Alder Valley}, Reading (BE) 522 1/72; Martins Bus & Coach Sales Ltd (dealer), Middlewich 5/75; unidentified owner, Billington as a mobile caravan 6/76.

Vehicles acquired from United Welsh Services Ltd, Swansea (GG) 10/68:

| 623 | NCY 637 | Bristol LD6G | 130.026 | ECW | 8649 | H33/27R | 12/56 | 12/71 |
| 624 | NCY 638 | Bristol LD6G | 130.027 | ECW | 8650 | H33/27R | 12/56 | 12/71 |

Previous histories:
    NCY 637-638 (623-624): New to United Welsh Services Ltd, Swansea (GG) 304-305; entering service 12/68.

Notes:
    NCY 637 (623): Fitted with platform doors by ECW as H33/27RD (rebuild R1049) 4/70.
    NCY 638 (624): Fitted with platform doors by ECW as H33/27RD (rebuild R1050) 6/70.

Disposals:

NCY 637 (623): Thames Valley & Aldershot Omnibus Co Ltd {Alder Valley}, Reading (BE) 517 1/72; Main Motors (dealer), Ewelme for scrap 5/74.

NCY 638 (624): Thames Valley & Aldershot Omnibus Co Ltd {Alder Valley}, Reading (BE) 518 1/72; Hardwick & Jones (dealer), Carlton (minus engine) for scrap 5/73.

Vehicles acquired from Red & White Services Ltd, Chepstow (MH) 10-11/68:

346	MAX 116	Bristol LS6G	105.001	ECW	6913	B45F	8/54	12/71
347	MAX 117	Bristol LS6G	105.010	ECW	6914	B45F	8/54	12/71
348	MAX 118	Bristol LS6G	105.011	ECW	6915	B45F	8/54	12/71
349	MAX 119	Bristol LS6G	105.012	ECW	6916	B45F	8/54	12/71
354	MAX 121	Bristol LS6G	105.033	ECW	6918	B45F	9/54	12/71
350	MAX 122	Bristol LS6G	105.034	ECW	6919	B45F	10/54	12/71
351	MAX 123	Bristol LS6G	105.035	ECW	6920	B45F	10/54	12/71
355	MAX 125	Bristol LS6G	105.049	ECW	6922	B45F	11/54	12/71
352	MAX 126	Bristol LS6G	105.050	ECW	6923	B45F	11/54	12/71
353	MAX 127	Bristol LS6G	105.054	ECW	6924	B45F	12/54	12/71
356	MAX 128	Bristol LS6G	105.057	ECW	6925	B45F	11/54	12/71

Previous histories:

MAX 116-118 (346-348): New to Red & White Services Ltd, Chepstow (MH) U1654-U1854; acquired 10/68, entering service 11/68.

MAX 119 (349): New to Red & White Services Ltd, Chepstow (MH) U1954; acquired 10/68, entering service 12/68.

MAX 121 (354): New to Red & White Services Ltd, Chepstow (MH) U2154; acquired 11/68, entering service 1/69.

MAX 122 (350): New to Red & White Services Ltd, Chepstow (MH) U2254; acquired 10/68, entering service 12/68.

MAX 123 (351): New to Red & White Services Ltd, Chepstow (MH) U2354; acquired 10/68, entering service 11/68.

MAX 125 (355): New to Red & White Services Ltd, Chepstow (MH) U2554; acquired 11/68, entering service 1/69.

MAX 126-127 (352-353): New to Red & White Services Ltd, Chepstow (MH) U2654-U2754; acquired 10/68, entering service 12/68.

MAX 128 (356): New to Red & White Services Ltd, Chepstow (MH) U2854; acquired in 11/68, entering service 1/69.

Notes:

MAX 116 (346): Reseated to B41F, before entering service; renumbered 133 7/69.

MAX 117 (347): Reseated to B41F, before entering service; renumbered 134 6/69.

MAX 118 (348): Reseated to B41F, before entering service; renumbered 135 8/69.

MAX 119 (349): Reseated to B41F, before entering service; renumbered 136 6/69.

MAX 121 (354): Reseated to B41F, before entering service; renumbered 141 7/69.

MAX 122 (350): Reseated to B41F, before entering service; renumbered 137 10/69.

MAX 123 (351): Reseated to B41F, before entering service; renumbered 138 8/69.

MAX 125 (355): Reseated to B41F, before entering service; renumbered 142 7/69.

MAX 126 (352): Reseated to B41F, before entering service; renumbered 139 8/69.

MAX 127 (353): Reseated to B41F, before entering service; renumbered 140 9/69.

MAX 128 (356): Reseated to B41F, before entering service; renumbered 143 7/69.

Disposals:

MAX 116 (133): Thames Valley & Aldershot Omnibus Co Ltd {Alder Valley}, Reading (BE) 212 1/72; Main Motors (dealer), Ewelme for scrap 5/74.

MAX 117 (134): Thames Valley & Aldershot Omnibus Co Ltd {Alder Valley}, Reading (BE) 213 1/72; Paul Sykes Organisation Ltd (dealer), Barnsley 2/74; WG & CS Peake, Pontypool (MH) 1/75.

MAX 118-119 (135-136): Thames Valley & Aldershot Omnibus Co Ltd {Alder Valley}, Reading (BE) 214-215 1/72; Paul Sykes Organisation Ltd (dealer), Barnsley for scrap 2/74.

MAX 121 (141): Thames Valley & Aldershot Omnibus Co Ltd {Alder Valley}, Reading (BE) 216 1/72; Paul Sykes Organisation Ltd (dealer), Barnsley for scrap 2/75.

MAX 122 (137): Thames Valley & Aldershot Omnibus Co Ltd {Alder Valley}, Reading (BE) 217 1/72; W Norths (PV) Ltd (dealer), Sherburn in Elmet for scrap 12/73.

MAX 123 (138): Thames Valley & Aldershot Omnibus Co Ltd {Alder Valley}, Reading (BE) 218 1/72; converted for use as a temporary rest room at Farnham Road Bus Station, Guildford 10/73; transferred to Maidenhead garage for use as a training room 7/75; W Norths (PV) Ltd (dealer), Sherburn in Elmet 4/79; Cooper (dealer), Carlton for scrap 4/79.

MAX 125 (142): Thames Valley & Aldershot Omnibus Co Ltd {Alder Valley}, Reading (BE) 219 1/72; W Norths (PV) Ltd (dealer), Sherburn in Elmet for scrap 12/73.

MAX 126 (139): Thames Valley & Aldershot Omnibus Co Ltd {Alder Valley}, Reading (BE) 220 1/72; W Norths (PV) Ltd (dealer), Sherburn in Elmet for scrap 12/73.

MAX 127 (140): Thames Valley & Aldershot Omnibus Co Ltd {Alder Valley}, Reading (BE) 221 1/72; W Norths (PV) Ltd (dealer), Sherburn in Elmet 12/73; Hills Pharmaceuticals Ltd, Nelson (XLA) 1/74; unidentified dealer (probably W Norths (PV) Ltd, Sherburn in Elmet) for scrap 4/78.

MAX 128 (143): Thames Valley & Aldershot Omnibus Co Ltd {Alder Valley}, Reading (BE) 222 1/72; W Norths (PV) Ltd (dealer), Sherburn in Elmet for scrap 12/73.

1969

New Vehicles:

500	SRX 944G	Bristol VRT/SL6G	114	ECW	17269	H41/29F	1/69	12/71
502	UBL 243G	Bristol VRT/SL6G	195	ECW	17789	H39/31F	4/69	12/71
503	UBL 244G	Bristol VRT/SL6G	196	ECW	17790	H39/31F	4/69	12/71
504	UBL 245G	Bristol VRT/SL6G	197	ECW	17791	H39/31F	4/69	12/71
505	UBL 246G	Bristol VRT/SL6G	210	ECW	17792	H39/31F	5/69	12/71
506	UBL 247G	Bristol VRT/SL6G	211	ECW	17793	H39/31F	5/69	12/71
507	UBL 248G	Bristol VRT/SL6G	212	ECW	17794	H39/31F	5/69	12/71
508	VMO 223H	Bristol VRT/SL6G	266	ECW	17795	H39/31F	7/69	12/71
509	VMO 224H	Bristol VRT/SL6G	267	ECW	17796	H39/31F	8/69	12/71
208	VMO 225H	Bristol LH6L	LH-311	ECW	17929	B45F	8/69	12/71
209	VMO 226H	Bristol LH6L	LH-312	ECW	17930	B45F	8/69	12/71
210	VMO 227H	Bristol LH6L	LH-313	ECW	17931	B45F	8/69	12/71
211	VMO 228H	Bristol LH6L	LH-314	ECW	17932	B45F	8/69	12/71
510	VMO 229H	Bristol VRT/SL6G	299	ECW	17797	H39/31F	9/69	12/71
511	VMO 230H	Bristol VRT/SL6G	300	ECW	17798	H39/31F	10/69	12/71
512	VMO 231H	Bristol VRT/SL6G	301	ECW	17799	H39/31F	11/69	12/71
212	VMO 232H	Bristol LH6L	LH-354	ECW	17933	B45F	11/69	12/71
213	VMO 233H	Bristol LH6L	LH-355	ECW	17934	B45F	11/69	12/71
214	VMO 234H	Bristol LH6L	LH-357	ECW	17935	B45F	11/69	12/71
215	VMO 235H	Bristol LH6L	LH-358	ECW	17936	B45F	11/69	12/71

Notes:

UBL 243-248G (502-507): Were not equipped for one-man operation when new (unlike all other Bristol VRs).

UBL 244G (503): Equipped for one-man operation 2/71.
UBL 245G (504): Equipped for one-man operation 5/71.
UBL 246G (505): Equipped for one-man operation 12/70.
UBL 248G (507): Equipped for one-man operation c11/70.
VMO 225-228H (208-211): Reseated to B41F before entering service.
VMO 232-235H (212-215): Reseated to B41F before entering service.

Disposals:

SRX 944G (500): Thames Valley & Aldershot Omnibus Co Ltd {Alder Valley}, Reading (BE) 901 1/72; Amalgamated Passenger Transport Ltd (dealer), Bracebridge Heath 1/82; Passenger Vehicle Spares (Barnsley) Ltd (dealer), Carlton for scrap 2/82.

UBL 243G (502): Thames Valley & Aldershot Omnibus Co Ltd {Alder Valley}, Reading (BE) 903 1/72; equipped for one-man operation 5/72; Amalgamated Passenger Transport Ltd (dealer), Bracebridge Heath 2/83; Passenger Vehicle Spares (Barnsley) Ltd (dealer), Carlton for scrap 3/83.

UBL 244G (503): Thames Valley & Aldershot Omnibus Co Ltd {Alder Valley}, Reading (BE) 904 1/72; Amalgamated Passenger Transport Ltd (dealer), Bracebridge Heath for scrap 2/83.

UBL 245G (504): Thames Valley & Aldershot Omnibus Co Ltd {Alder Valley}, Reading (BE) 905 1/72; Amalgamated Passenger Transport Ltd (dealer), Bracebridge Heath 1/82; W Norths (PV) Ltd (dealer), Sherburn in Elmet 3/82; Corlett & Brown {Sundekkers}, San Diego, California (O-USA) 8/82; British Bus Co, Spring Valley, California (O-USA) c1990; broken up at Spring Valley c1990.

UBL 246G (505): Thames Valley & Aldershot Omnibus Co Ltd {Alder Valley}, Reading (BE) 906 1/72; fitted with a Gardner 6LXB engine in 4/74; Amalgamated Passenger Transport Ltd (dealer), Bracebridge Heath 2/83; Passenger Vehicle Spares (Barnsley) Ltd (dealer), Carlton for scrap 2/83.

UBL 247G (506): Thames Valley & Aldershot Omnibus Co Ltd {Alder Valley}, Reading (BE) 907 1/72; Equipped for one-man operation 5/72; Alder Valley North Ltd, Reading (BE) 907 1/86; The Berks Bucks Bus Co Ltd {The Bee Line}, Reading (BE) 907 1/87; renumbered 503 10/87; City of Oxford Motor Services Ltd, Oxford (OX) 1503 11/90; last licensed 6/91; Passenger Vehicle Spares (Barnsley) Ltd (dealer), Carlton for scrap 9/91.

UBL 248G (507): Thames Valley & Aldershot Omnibus Co Ltd {Alder Valley}, Reading (BE) 908 1/72; Amalgamated Passenger Transport Ltd (dealer), Bracebridge Heath 1/82; W Norths (PV) Ltd (dealer), Sherburn in Elmet for scrap 3/82.

VMO 223H (508): Thames Valley & Aldershot Omnibus Co Ltd {Alder Valley}, Reading (BE) 909 1/72; Amalgamated Passenger Transport Ltd (dealer), Bracebridge Heath 2/83; Passenger Vehicle Spares (Barnsley) Ltd (dealer), Carlton for scrap 2/83.

VMO 224H (509): Thames Valley & Aldershot Omnibus Co Ltd {Alder Valley}, Reading (BE) 910 1/72; Amalgamated Passenger Transport Ltd (dealer), Bracebridge Heath for scrap 12/83.

VMO 225H (208): Thames Valley & Aldershot Omnibus Co Ltd {Alder Valley}, Reading (BE) 265 1/72; renumbered 519 8/75; S Twell (dealer), Ingham 1/77; HR Jarvis, Maltby (SY) 4/77; Dickinson & Shippey (dealer), Monk Bretton for scrap 11/79.

VMO 226H (209): Thames Valley & Aldershot Omnibus Co Ltd {Alder Valley}, Reading (BE) 266 1/72; renumbered 520 8/75; S Twell (dealer), Ingham 1/77; B Marfleet, Binbrook (LI) 5/77; withdrawn 4/82; last licensed 11/88.

VMO 227H (210): Thames Valley & Aldershot Omnibus Co Ltd {Alder Valley}, Reading (BE) 266 1/72; renumbered 521 8/75; Bristol Omnibus Co Ltd, Bristol (GL) 346 2/77; withdrawn 9/79; Ensign Bus Co Ltd (dealer), Purfleet 8/80; Pullman Kellogg Ltd, Wembley (XLN) 11/80; last licensed 11/81; noted at British Car Auctions, Blackbushe Airport 4/85.

VMO 228H (211): Thames Valley & Aldershot Omnibus Co Ltd {Alder Valley}, Reading (BE) 268 1/72; renumbered 522 8/75; S Twell (dealer), Ingham 1/77; Marshall (farmer), Butterwick (XHD) 10/77; S Twell (dealer), Ingham by 3/98; R Rampton, Reading for preservation by 1/01.

VMO 229H (510): Thames Valley & Aldershot Omnibus Co Ltd {Alder Valley}, Reading (BE) 911 1/72; last licensed 8/83; Top Deck Travel Ltd, Edgware (LN) (not operated) 7/84.

VMO 230H (511): Thames Valley & Aldershot Omnibus Co Ltd {Alder Valley}, Reading (BE) 912 1/72; Amalgamated Passenger Transport Ltd (dealer), Bracebridge Heath 2/83; Passenger Vehicle Spares (Barnsley) Ltd (dealer), Carlton 2/83.

VMO 231H (512): Thames Valley & Aldershot Omnibus Co Ltd {Alder Valley}, Reading (BE) 913 1/72; last licensed 1/84; Top Deck Travel Ltd, Edgware (LN) (not operated) 7/84.

VMO 232H (212): Thames Valley & Aldershot Omnibus Co Ltd {Alder Valley}, Reading (BE) 269 1/72; renumbered 523 8/75; S Twell (dealer), Ingham for scrap 1/77.

VMO 233H (213): Thames Valley & Aldershot Omnibus Co Ltd {Alder Valley}, Reading (BE) 270 1/72; renumbered 524 8/75; S Twell (dealer), Ingham 1/77; RJ & RH Eaglen {Eagre}, Morton (LI) 6/77; Robinson (farmer), Brigg (XLI) 9/77; K Askin (dealer), Barnsley 10/81; Barrys Coaches Ltd {Interbus}, Weymouth (DT) 9/82; Stanbridge & Crichel Bus Co Ltd, Stanbridge (DT) 12/87; TC Greenslade, Blandford Forum (DT) by 1/90; last licensed 3/91; United Provincial Services Ltd {Pennine Blue}, Dukinfield (GM) 9033 (not operated) 12/91; scrapped 1996.

VMO 234H (214): Thames Valley & Aldershot Omnibus Co Ltd {Alder Valley}, Reading (BE) 271 1/72; renumbered 525 8/75; S Twell (dealer), Ingham 1/77; Marshall (farmer), Butterwick (XHD) 10/77; S Twell (dealer), Ingham by 3/98; Robertson, Biggleswade for preservation 7/98; N Halliday & I Hunter, Shipley for preservation 9/14.

VMO 235H (215): Thames Valley & Aldershot Omnibus Co Ltd {Alder Valley}, Reading (BE) 272 1/72; renumbered 526 8/75; S Twell (dealer), Ingham 1/77; HR Jarvis, Maltby (SY) 4/77; Dickinson & Shippey (dealer), Monk Bretton 11/79.

Vehicles transferred from South Midland Motor Services Ltd 3-7/69:

159	ORX 631	Bristol MW6G	135.069	ECW	10652	DP41F	3/58	12/71
160	ORX 632	Bristol MW6G	135.074	ECW	10653	DP41F	3/58	12/71
161	ORX 633	Bristol MW6G	135.075	ECW	10654	DP41F	4/58	12/71
162	ORX 634	Bristol MW6G	135.089	ECW	10655	DP41F	4/58	12/71

Previous histories:

ORX 631 (159): New to South Midland Motor Services Ltd 800 (as C34F) [reseated to C38F 1/63; delicensed 12/68, reseated to DP41F with folding doors, altered front dome, fitted for one-man-operation and renumbered 159 3/69]; transferred 3/69.

ORX 632 (160): New to South Midland Motor Services Ltd 801 (as C34F) [reseated to C38F 1/63; delicensed 3/69, reseated to DP41F with folding doors, altered front dome, fitted for one-man-operation and renumbered 160 7/69]; transferred 7/69.

ORX 633 (161): New to South Midland Motor Services Ltd 802 (as C34F) [reseated to C38F 1/64; delicensed 3/69, reseated to DP41F with folding doors, altered front dome, fitted for one-man-operation and renumbered 161 6/69]; transferred 6/69.

ORX 634 (162): New to South Midland Motor Services Ltd 803 (as C32F) [reseated to C34F 10/58 and C38F 11/62; delicensed 12/68, reseated to DP41F with folding doors, altered front dome, fitted for one-man-operation and renumbered 162 4/69]; transferred 4/69.

Disposals:

ORX 631 (159): Thames Valley & Aldershot Omnibus Co Ltd {Alder Valley}, Reading (BE) 243 1/72; Paul Sykes Organisation Ltd (dealer), Barnsley for scrap 2/75.

ORX 632 (160): Thames Valley & Aldershot Omnibus Co Ltd {Alder Valley}, Reading (BE) 245 1/72; converted to a mobile employment office 30 8/74; renumbered 1051 6/78; last licensed 8/82; renumbered 26 9/82 (possibly not carried); unidentified dealer for scrap c1982.

ORX 633 (161): Thames Valley & Aldershot Omnibus Co Ltd {Alder Valley}, Reading (BE) 244 1/72; Paul Sykes Organisation Ltd (dealer), Barnsley 11/75; JM Normington {Orpington & District}, Orpington (KT) 2/76; Transport (Passenger Equipment) Ltd (dealer), Macclesfield 11/77; Passenger Vehicle Spares (Barnsley) Ltd (dealer), Carlton for scrap 12/77.

ORX 634 (162): Thames Valley & Aldershot Omnibus Co Ltd {Alder Valley}, Reading (BE) 242 1/72; Paul Sykes Organisation Ltd (dealer), Barnsley 2/75; J Sykes (dealer), Carlton for scrap by 10/76.

Vehicles acquired from United Welsh Services Ltd, Swansea (GG) 5-8/69:

632	OCY 954	Bristol LD6G	130.112	ECW	9566	H33/27R	3/57	12/71
620	OCY 955	Bristol LD6G	130.113	ECW	9567	H33/27R	3/57	12/71
633	OCY 956	Bristol LD6G	130.114	ECW	9568	H33/27R	2/57	12/71
622	OCY 957	Bristol LD6G	134.007	ECW	9569	H33/27R	6/57	12/71

Previous histories:

OCY 954 (632): New to United Welsh Services Ltd, Swansea (GG) 307; acquired 5/69, entering service 6/69.

OCY 955 (620): New to United Welsh Services Ltd, Swansea (GG) 308; acquired 8/69, entering service 9/69.

OCY 956 (633): New to United Welsh Services Ltd, Swansea (GG) 309; acquired 5/69, entering service 6/69.

OCY 957 (622): New to United Welsh Services Ltd, Swansea (GG) 310; acquired in 8/69, entering service 9/69.

Notes:

OCY 954 (632): Fitted with platform doors by ECW as H33/27RD (rebuild R1054) 5/70.

OCY 955 (620): Fitted with platform doors by ECW as H33/27RD (rebuild R1051) 4/70.

OCY 956 (633): Fitted with platform doors by ECW as H33/27RD (rebuild R1052) 4/70.

OCY 957 (622): Fitted with platform doors by ECW as H33/27RD (rebuild R1053) 5/70.

Disposals:

OCY 954 (632): Thames Valley & Aldershot Omnibus Co Ltd {Alder Valley}, Reading (BE) 546 1/72; Paul Sykes Organisation Ltd (dealer), Barnsley for scrap 5/75.

OCY 955 (620): Thames Valley & Aldershot Omnibus Co Ltd {Alder Valley}, Reading (BE) 543 1/72; Rev RWA West, Brockham Green (XSR) 5/75; 22nd Dorking (Brockham) Scout Group, Betchworth (XSR) 5/86; still in use 1/15.

OCY 956 (633): Thames Valley & Aldershot Omnibus Co Ltd {Alder Valley}, Reading (BE) 547 1/72; Paul Sykes Organisation Ltd (dealer), Barnsley 5/75; M Lewis, Morriston (GG) 11/75; unidentified dealer for scrap by 7/76.

OCY 957 (622): Thames Valley & Aldershot Omnibus Co Ltd {Alder Valley}, Reading (BE) 544 1/72; Martins Bus & Coach Sales Ltd (dealer), Middlewich 5/75; J Jenkins & Sons (Skewen) Ltd, Skewen (GG) by 6/75; withdrawn by 9/76; A Barraclough (dealer), Carlton for scrap 12/77.

Vehicles transferred from South Midland Motor Services Ltd 9-12/69:

163	PRX 930	Bristol MW6G	139.256	ECW	11316	DP41F	3/59	12/71
164	PRX 931	Bristol MW6G	139.257	ECW	11317	DP41F	4/59	12/71
165	PRX 932	Bristol MW6G	139.258	ECW	11318	DP41F	4/59	12/71
418	LJB 418E	Bedford VAM14	6875051	Duple	1208/160	C41F	3/67	12/71

Previous histories:

PRX 930 (163): New to South Midland Motor Services Ltd 804 (as C34F) [reseated to C38F 11/62; delicensed 10/69, reseated to DP41F with folding doors, altered front dome fitted for one-man-operation and renumbered 163 11/69]; transferred 11/69.

PRX 931 (164): New to South Midland Motor Services Ltd 805 (as C34F) [reseated to C38F 2/66; delicensed 10/69, reseated to DP41F with folding doors, altered front dome, fitted for one-man-operation and renumbered 164 12/69]; transferred 12/69.

PRX 932 (165): New to South Midland Motor Services Ltd 806 (as C34F) [reseated to C38F 4/63; delicensed 8/69, reseated to DP41F with folding doors, altered front dome, fitted for one-man-operation and renumbered 165 10/69]; transferred 10/69.

LJB 418E (418): New to Thames Valley Traction Co Ltd C418; South Midland Motor Services Ltd C418 [renumbered 418 2/69]; transferred 9/69.

Disposals:

PRX 930 (163): Thames Valley & Aldershot Omnibus Co Ltd {Alder Valley}, Reading (BE) 246 1/72; Paul Sykes Organisation Ltd (dealer), Barnsley for scrap 2/75.

PRX 931 (164): Thames Valley & Aldershot Omnibus Co Ltd {Alder Valley}, Reading (BE) 247 1/72; Main Motors (dealer), Ewelme for scrap 5/74.

PRX 932 (165): Thames Valley & Aldershot Omnibus Co Ltd {Alder Valley}, Reading (BE) 248 1/72; Paul Sykes Organisation Ltd (dealer), Barnsley for scrap 11/75.

LJB 418E (418): Thames Valley & Aldershot Omnibus Co Ltd {Alder Valley}, Reading (BE) 33 1/72; Martins Bus & Coach Sales Ltd (dealer), Middlewich 8/76; JD Ogden, Haydock (MY) at an unknown date; car transporter 9/81.

Vehicles hired (and later transferred) from United Welsh Services Ltd, Swansea (GG) 11-12/69:

626	OCY 958	Bristol LD6G	134.008	ECW	9570	H33/27R	6/57	12/71
634	OCY 960	Bristol LD6G	134.217	ECW	9572	H33/27R	2/58	12/71
635	OCY 961	Bristol LD6G	138.027	ECW	9573	H33/27R	3/58	12/71
628	OCY 962	Bristol LD6G	138.030	ECW	9574	H33/27R	3/58	12/71

Previous histories:

OCY 958 (626): New to United Welsh Services Ltd, Swansea (GG) 311; acquired initially on hire 12/69 and permanently from 1/70.

OCY 960-961 (634-635): New to United Welsh Services Ltd, Swansea (GG) 313-314; acquired initially on hire 11/69 and permanently from 5/70.

OCY 962 (628): New to United Welsh Services Ltd, Swansea (GG) 315; acquired initially on hire 11/69 and permanently from 1/70.

Notes:

OCY 958 (626): Fitted with platform doors by ECW as H33/27RD (rebuild R1056) 6/70.

OCY 960 (634): Fitted with platform doors by ECW as H33/27RD (rebuild R1090) 1/71.

OCY 961 (635): Fitted with platform doors by ECW as H33/27RD (rebuild R1091) 3/71.

OCY 962 (628): Fitted with platform doors by ECW as H33/27RD (rebuild R1055) 5/70.

Disposals:

OCY 958 (626): Thames Valley & Aldershot Omnibus Co Ltd {Alder Valley}, Reading (BE) 545 1/72; Martins Bus & Coach Sales Ltd (dealer), Middlewich for scrap 6/75.

OCY 960 (634): Thames Valley & Aldershot Omnibus Co Ltd {Alder Valley}, Reading (BE) 573 1/72; Main Motors (dealer), Ewelme for scrap 5/74.

OCY 961 (635): Thames Valley & Aldershot Omnibus Co Ltd {Alder Valley}, Reading (BE) 574 1/72; Martins Bus & Coach Sales Ltd (dealer), Middlewich for scrap 2/76.

OCY 962 (628): Thames Valley & Aldershot Omnibus Co Ltd {Alder Valley}, Reading (BE) 572 1/72; Martins Bus & Coach Sales Ltd (dealer), Middlewich for scrap 2/76.

Vehicle acquired from Bristol Omnibus Co Ltd, Bristol (GL) 12/69:

198	844 THY	Bristol SUS4A	218.013	ECW	14218	B30F	9/63	12/71

Previous history:

844 THY (198): New to Bath Tramways Motor Co Ltd, Bath (SO) 304; Bristol Omnibus Co Ltd 304 12/69.

Disposal:

844 THY (198): Thames Valley & Aldershot Omnibus Co Ltd {Alder Valley}, Reading (BE) 497 1/72; Paul Sykes Organisation Ltd (dealer), Barnsley for scrap 2/75.

Vehicle on hire from Bristol Omnibus Co Ltd, Bristol (GL):

AHW 227B	Bristol SUS4A		226.002	ECW	14552	B30F	12/64	11/69	1/70

Notes:

AHW 227B: Was numbered 308 in the Bristol Omnibus fleet and was on hire for evaluation.

1970

New Vehicles:

513	XMO 541H	Bristol VRT/SL6G	2/121	ECW	18210	H39/31F	5/70	12/71
514	XMO 542H	Bristol VRT/SL6G	2/122	ECW	18211	H39/31F	5/70	12/71
216	XRX 819H	Bristol LH6L	LH-456	ECW	18734	B45F	5/70	12/71
217	XRX 820H	Bristol LH6L	LH-457	ECW	18735	B45F	5/70	12/71
224	YJB 521H	Bristol RELL6G	3/1093	ECW	18532	B49F	7/70	12/71
225	YJB 522H	Bristol RELL6G	3/1094	ECW	18533	B49F	7/70	12/71
226	YJB 523H	Bristol RELL6G	3/1095	ECW	18534	B49F	7/70	12/71
218	ABL 121J	Bristol LH6L	LH-486	ECW	18736	B45F	8/70	12/71
219	ABL 122J	Bristol LH6L	LH-487	ECW	18737	B45F	8/70	12/71
227	AMO 233J	Bristol RELL6G	3/1232	ECW	18535	B49F	11/70	12/71
228	AMO 234J	Bristol RELL6G	3/1233	ECW	18536	B49F	11/70	12/71
220	AMO 235J	Bristol LH6L	LH-520	ECW	18738	B45F	11/70	12/71
221	AMO 236J	Bristol LH6L	LH-521	ECW	18739	B45F	11/70	12/71
222	AMO 237J	Bristol LH6L	LH-522	ECW	18740	B45F	11/70	12/71
223	AMO 238J	Bristol LH6L	LH-523	ECW	18741	B45F	12/70	12/71

Notes:

XRX 819-820H (216-217): Reseated to B41F, before entering service.
ABL 121-122J (218-219): Reseated to B41F, before entering service.
AMO 235-238J (220-223): Reseated to B41F, before entering service.

Disposals:

XMO 541H (513): Thames Valley & Aldershot Omnibus Co Ltd {Alder Valley}, Reading (BE) 914 1/72; Alder Valley North Ltd, Reading (BE) 914 1/86; The Berks Bucks Bus Co Ltd {The Bee Line}, Reading (BE) 914 1/87; renumbered 504 10/87; withdrawn 3/92; Northern Bus Co Ltd, Anston (SY) 3041 10/92; named 'Constable Knapweed' by 6/93; last licensed 5/95; Passenger Vehicle Spares (Barnsley) Ltd (dealer), Carlton for scrap 10/95.

XMO 542H (514): Thames Valley & Aldershot Omnibus Co Ltd {Alder Valley}, Reading (BE) 915 1/72; last licensed 12/83; unidentified dealer for scrap 12/83.

XRX 819H (216): Thames Valley & Aldershot Omnibus Co Ltd {Alder Valley}, Reading (BE) 273 1/72; renumbered 527 8/75; Bristol Omnibus Co Ltd, Bristol (AV) 347 2/77; withdrawn 9/79; Ensign Bus Co Ltd (dealer), Purfleet 8/80; Pullman, Pullman Kellogg, Wembley (XLN) 11/80; unidentified operator / dealer by 1987.

XRX 820H (217): Thames Valley & Aldershot Omnibus Co Ltd {Alder Valley}, Reading (BE) 274 1/72; renumbered 528 8/75; Bristol Omnibus Co Ltd, Bristol (AV) 348 2/77; withdrawn 11/79; Ensign Bus Co Ltd (dealer), Purfleet 8/80; Transport Supplies (dealer) (O-HK) by 2/81; City Bus Ltd (O-HK) 103 as a recovery vehicle (chassis shortened to Bristol LHS length) 2/81.

YJB 521H (224): Thames Valley & Aldershot Omnibus Co Ltd {Alder Valley}, Reading (BE) 412 1/72; Eastern Counties Omnibus Co Ltd, Norwich (NK) RL689 6/81; last licensed 3/84; cannibalised for spares 1984; Hartwood Exports (Machinery) Ltd (dealer), Birdwell for scrap 7/84.

YJB 522H (225): Thames Valley & Aldershot Omnibus Co Ltd {Alder Valley}, Reading (BE) 413 1/72; Wombwell Diesels Ltd (dealer), Wombwell for scrap 6/81.

YJB 523H (226): Thames Valley & Aldershot Omnibus Co Ltd {Alder Valley}, Reading (BE) 414 1/72; Eastern Counties Omnibus Co Ltd, Norwich (NK) RL690 6/81; Fr DJ Green (dealer), Weymouth 7/83; MJ Evans {Primrose Coaches / Bedminster Coaches}, Bristol (AV) by 3/84; Edmunds Omnibus Services Ltd, Rassau (GT) 2/86; burnt out whilst in service 7/87; last licensed 8/88; Wacton Trading / Coach Sales (dealer), Bromyard for scrap 1/89.

ABL 121J (218): Thames Valley & Aldershot Omnibus Co Ltd {Alder Valley}, Reading (BE) 275 1/72; renumbered 529 8/75; United Automobile Services Ltd, Darlington (DM) 1497 9/76; W Norths (PV) Ltd (dealer), Sherburn in Elmet 9/80; Parton & Allen (dealer), Carlton for scrap 7/82.

ABL 122J (219): Thames Valley & Aldershot Omnibus Co Ltd {Alder Valley}, Reading (BE) 276 1/72; renumbered 530 8/75; United Automobile Services Ltd, Darlington (DM) 1498 9/76; W Norths (PV) Ltd (dealer), Sherburn in Elmet for scrap 9/80.

AMO 233J (227): Thames Valley & Aldershot Omnibus Co Ltd {Alder Valley}, Reading (BE) 415 1/72; W Norths (PV) Ltd (dealer), Sherburn in Elmet for scrap 10/82.

AMO 234J (228): Thames Valley & Aldershot Omnibus Co Ltd {Alder Valley}, Reading (BE) 416 1/72; Amalgamated Passenger Transport Ltd (dealer), Bracebridge Heath 2/83; Passenger Vehicle Spares (Barnsley) Ltd (dealer), Carlton for scrap 3/83.

AMO 235J (220): Thames Valley & Aldershot Omnibus Co Ltd {Alder Valley}, Reading (BE) 277 1/72; renumbered 531 8/75; United Automobile Services Ltd, Darlington (DM) 1499 9/76; converted to a uniform store no 63 11/80; last licensed 6/84.

AMO 236J (221): Thames Valley & Aldershot Omnibus Co Ltd {Alder Valley}, Reading (BE) 278 1/72; renumbered 532 8/75; Bristol Omnibus Co Ltd, Bristol (AV) 349 2/77; last licensed 11/79; Ensign Bus Co Ltd (dealer), Purfleet 8/80; NBC Eastern Region Disposal Centre (dealer), Bracebridge Heath for scrap 11/80.

AMO 237J (222): Thames Valley & Aldershot Omnibus Co Ltd {Alder Valley}, Reading (BE) 279 1/72; renumbered 533 8/75; United Automobile Services Ltd, Darlington (DM) 1500 9/76; withdrawn 8/80.

AMO 238J (223): Thames Valley & Aldershot Omnibus Co Ltd {Alder Valley}, Reading (BE) 280 1/72; renumbered 534 8/75; Bristol Omnibus Co Ltd, Bristol (AV) 350 2/77; withdrawn 11/79; Ensign Bus Co Ltd (dealer), Purfleet 8/80; Griffiths, Bodorgan (GD) 4/81; AH Lewis, Llanerchymedd (GD) 10/86; AH & RM Lewis, Llanerchymedd (GD) 10/88; last licensed 11/90; unidentified dealer for scrap 9/92.

Vehicles acquired from Western National Omnibus Co Ltd, Exeter (DN) 1/70:

| 196 | 668 COD | Bristol SUS4A | 157.010 | ECW | 11387 | B30F | 3/60 | 12/71 |
| 197 | 669 COD | Bristol SUS4A | 157.011 | ECW | 11388 | B30F | 3/60 | 12/71 |

Previous histories:

668-669 COD (196-197): New to Southern National Omnibus Co Ltd, Exeter (DN) 612-613; Western National Omnibus Co Ltd (DN) 612-613 11/69.

Disposals:

668-669 COD (196-197): Thames Valley & Aldershot Omnibus Co Ltd {Alder Valley}, Reading (BE) 495-496 1/72; Main Motors (dealer), Ewelme for scrap 5/74.

Vehicles acquired from Bristol Omnibus Co Ltd, Bristol (GL) 1-2/70:

| 158 | 845 THY | Bristol SUS4A | 218.014 | ECW | 14219 | B30F | 9/63 | 12/71 |
| 199 | 846 THY | Bristol SUS4A | 218.015 | ECW | 14220 | B30F | 9/63 | 12/71 |

Previous histories:

845 THY (158): New to Bristol Omnibus Co Ltd, Bristol (GL) 305; acquired 2/70.
846 THY (199): New to Bristol Omnibus Co Ltd, Bristol (GL) 306; acquired 1/70.

Disposals:

845 THY (158): Thames Valley & Aldershot Omnibus Co Ltd {Alder Valley}, Reading (BE) 499 1/72; Paul Sykes Organisation Ltd (dealer), Barnsley for scrap 2/75.
846 THY (199): Thames Valley & Aldershot Omnibus Co Ltd {Alder Valley}, Reading (BE) 498 1/72; Paul Sykes Organisation Ltd (dealer), Barnsley for scrap 2/75.

Vehicles transferred from South Midland Motor Services Ltd 2/70:

| 166 | PRX 933 | Bristol MW6G | 139.259 | ECW | 11319 | DP41F | 3/59 | 12/71 |

Previous histories:

PRX 933 (166): New to South Midland Motor Services Ltd 807 (as C34F) [reseated to C38F 2/66; delicensed 12/69, reseated to DP41F with folding doors, altered front dome, fitted for one-man-operation, and renumbered 166 2/70].

Disposals:

PRX 933 (166): Thames Valley & Aldershot Omnibus Co Ltd {Alder Valley}, Reading (BE) 249 1/72; Martins Bus & Coach Sales Ltd (dealer), Middlewich 6/75; J Jenkins & Sons (Skewen) Ltd, Skewen (GG) by 7/75; withdrawn by 9/76; A Barraclough (dealer), Carlton for scrap 1/78.

Vehicles acquired from Lincolnshire Road Car Co Ltd, Lincoln (LI) 3/70:

605	LFW 329	Bristol LD6B	104.124	ECW	7348	H33/25RD	5/55	11/71
606	NBE 129	Bristol LD6B	108.137	ECW	8036	H33/27R	10/55	8/71
607	NBE 133	Bristol LD6B	108.172	ECW	8040	H33/27R	11/55	8/71

Previous histories:

LFW 329 (605): New to Lincolnshire Road Car Co Ltd (LI) 2321; entering service 5/70.
NBE 129 (606): New to Lincolnshire Road Car Co Ltd (LI) 2326; entering service 5/70.
NBE 133 (607): New to Lincolnshire Road Car Co Ltd (LI) 2330; entering service 5/70.

Notes:

NBE 129 (606): Fitted with platform doors by ECW as H33/27RD (rebuild R1089) 2/71.
NBE 133 (607): Fitted with platform doors by ECW as H33/27RD (rebuild R1088) 12/70.

Disposals:

LFW 329 (605): W Norths (PV) Ltd (dealer), Sherburn in Elmet 11/71; Elm Park Coaches Ltd, Romford (LN)
1/72; Elm Park Coaches (Romford) Ltd 2/76; withdrawn 8/77.
NBE 129 (606): W Norths (PV) Ltd (dealer), Sherburn in Elmet for scrap 9/71.
NBE 133 (607): W Norths (PV) Ltd (dealer), Sherburn in Elmet 9/71; unidentified operator 10/71; S Twell
(dealer), Ingham by 11/73; Bernard Matthews Ltd, Great Witchingham (XNK) 1/74.

Vehicles acquired from Crosville Motor Services Ltd, Chester (CH) 3-4/70:

600	VFM 607	Bristol LD6B	104.110	ECW	7285	H33/27R	6/55	9/71
601	XFM 187	Bristol LD6B	108.102	ECW	7918	H33/27RD	9/55	8/71
602	XFM 190	Bristol LD6B	108.105	ECW	7921	H33/27RD	10/55	9/71
603	XFM 192	Bristol LD6B	108.114	ECW	7923	H33/27RD	3/56	12/71
604	XFM 195	Bristol LD6B	108.131	ECW	7926	H33/27RD	3/56	12/71

Previous histories:

VFM 607 (600): New to Crosville Motor Services Ltd (CH) ML742 as H33/27R [renumbered DLB742 1958];
acquired 4/70, entering service 7/70.
XFM 187 (601): New to Crosville Motor Services Ltd (CH) ML776 as H33/27R [fitted with platform doors
1956; renumbered DLB776 1958]; acquired 3/70, entering service 4/70.
XFM 190 (602): New to Crosville Motor Services Ltd (CH) ML779 as H33/27R [fitted with platform doors
1956; renumbered DLB779 1958]; acquired 4/70, entering service 5/70.
XFM 192 (603): New to Crosville Motor Services Ltd (CH) ML781 as H33/27R [fitted with platform doors
1956; renumbered DLB781 1958]; acquired 3/70, entering service 4/70.
XFM 195 (604): New to Crosville Motor Services Ltd (CH) ML784 as H33/27R [fitted with platform doors
1956; renumbered DLB784 1958]; acquired 4/70, entering service 7/70.

Notes:

VFM 607 (600): Fitted with platform doors by ECW as H33/27RD 7/70.

Disposals:

VFM 607 (600): W Norths (PV) Ltd (dealer), Sherburn in Elmet 9/71; J Laverty {Eagle Coaches}, Neilston
(RW) 11/71; Kilwinning Round Table, Kilwinning (XAR) as a play bus (based at Kerelaw
School) by 7/74; Whitevale Motors (dealer), Stepps for scrap by 5/80.
XFM 187 (601): W Norths (PV) Ltd (dealer), Sherburn in Elmet 9/71; F Knowles, Oulton (WR) 10/71; Mrs E
Brooksbank {Blue Line Coaches}, Featherstone (WR) 2/73; Paul Sykes Organisation Ltd
(dealer), Carlton for scrap 8/74.
XFM 190 (602): W Norths (PV) Ltd (dealer), Sherburn in Elmet 9/71; Cobholm Hire Services Ltd, Great
Yarmouth (NK) 12/71; unidentified dealer, Bungay for scrap 1/77.
XFM 192 (603): Thames Valley & Aldershot Omnibus Co Ltd {Alder Valley}, Reading (BE) 513 1/72; W
Norths (PV) Ltd (dealer), Sherburn in Elmet 6/72; The Wakefield Shirt Co Ltd {Double Two
Shirts}, Wakefield (XWY) by 1/75; unidentified dealer, Barnsley for scrap by 2/76.
XFM 195 (604): Thames Valley & Aldershot Omnibus Co Ltd {Alder Valley}, Reading (BE) 514 1/72; W
Norths (PV) Ltd (dealer), Sherburn in Elmet 6/72; Armoride Ltd, Earby (XWR) c1972; W
Norths (PV) Ltd (dealer), Sherburn in Elmet 10/75.

Vehicles acquired from Midland General Omnibus Co Ltd, Langley Mill (DE) 5-6/70:

145	956 ARA	Bristol LS6G	117.022	ECW	8933	B43F	5/56	12/71
144	959 ARA	Bristol LS6G	117.026	ECW	9049	B43F	5/56	12/71
150	961 ARA	Bristol LS6G	117.044	ECW	9051	B43F	7/56	12/71

Previous histories:
956 ARA (145): New to Midland General Omnibus Co Ltd, Langley Mill (DE) 242 (as DP43F) [reseated to B43F 1968]; acquired 6/70, entering service 7/70.
959 ARA (144): New to Midland General Omnibus Co Ltd, Langley Mill (DE) 245 (as DP43F) [reseated to B43F 1968]; acquired and entering service 5/70.
961 ARA (150): New to Midland General Omnibus Co Ltd, Langley Mill (DE) 247 (as DP43F) [reseated to B43F 1968]; acquired 6/70, entering service 7/70.

Notes:
956 ARA (145): Reseated to B41F, before entering service
959 ARA (144): Reseated to B41F, before entering service
961 ARA (150): Reseated to B41F, before entering service

Disposals:
956 ARA (145): Thames Valley & Aldershot Omnibus Co Ltd {Alder Valley}, Reading (BE) 230 1/72; Main Motors (dealer), Ewelme for scrap 5/74.
959 ARA (144): Thames Valley & Aldershot Omnibus Co Ltd {Alder Valley}, Reading (BE) 229 1/72; Paul Sykes Organisation Ltd (dealer), Barnsley for scrap 2/75.
961 ARA (150): Thames Valley & Aldershot Omnibus Co Ltd {Alder Valley}, Reading (BE) 237 1/72; Main Motors (dealer), Ewelme 5/74; unidentified dealer, Carlton for scrap 10/76.

Vehicle transferred from South Midland Motor Services Ltd 6/70:

408	838 CRX	Bedford SB13	93607	Duple	1170/157	C37F	4/64	9/70

Previous history:
838 CRX (408): New to South Midland Motor Services Ltd C408.

Notes:
838 CRX (408): Transferred to Thames Valley Traction Co Ltd as a replacement for fire-victim RJB 424F (C424).

Disposal:
838 CRX (408): FJ Miller (Bristol) Ltd (dealer), Bristol 10/70; AW & MK Spiller {Arleen Coach Tours}, Peasedown St John (SO) 2/71; D Lansdown {CH Lansdown & Sons}, Tockington (AV) 1/74; PI & Mrs IL Ford {Watson's Coaches / Tamar Valley}, Gunnislake (CO) 4/78; FR Guscott, Halwill (DN) 1/80; unidentified owner as a caravan by 6/84; last licensed 2/88.

Vehicles acquired from Crosville Motor Services Ltd, Chester (CH) 7-8/70:

608	VFM 611	Bristol LD6B	104.119	ECW	7289	H33/27R	7/55	10/71
611	VFM 617	Bristol LD6B	104.141	ECW	7295	H33/27RD	7/55	12/71
609	VFM 618	Bristol LD6B	104.142	ECW	7296	H33/27RD	7/55	9/71
610	VFM 622	Bristol LD6B	104.150	ECW	7300	H33/27RD	7/55	12/71
613	XFM 193	Bristol LD6B	108.129	ECW	7924	H33/27RD	3/56	12/71
614	XFM 196	Bristol LD6B	108.132	ECW	7927	H33/27RD	5/56	12/71

Previous histories:
VFM 611 (608): New to Crosville Motor Services Ltd (CH) ML746 as H33/27R [renumbered DLB746 1958]; acquired 8/70, entering service 1/71.
VFM 617 (611): New to Crosville Motor Services Ltd (CH) ML752 as H33/27R [fitted with platform doors 1956; renumbered DLB752 1958]; acquired in 8/70, entering service 8/71.
VFM 618 (609): New to Crosville Motor Services Ltd (CH) ML753 as H33/27R [fitted with platform doors 1956; renumbered DLB753 1958]; acquired 7/70, entering service 8/70.
VFM 622 (610): New to Crosville Motor Services Ltd (CH) ML757 as H33/27R [fitted with platform doors 1956; renumbered DLB757 1958]; acquired 7/70, entering service 8/70.
XFM 193 (613): New to Crosville Motor Services Ltd (CH) ML782 as H33/27R [fitted with platform doors 1956; renumbered DLB782 1958]; acquired 8/70, entering service 11/70.
XFM 196 (614): New to Crosville Motor Services Ltd (CH) ML785 as H33/27R [fitted with platform doors 1956; renumbered DLB785 1958]; acquired 7/70, entering service 12/70.

Notes:
VFM 611 (608): Fitted with platform doors by ECW as H33/27RD 11/70.

Disposals:

VFM 611 (608): W Norths (PV) Ltd (dealer), Sherburn in Elmet 11/71; Blue Line Coaches Ltd, Upminster (LN) 12/71; SJ Mott, Upton (BK) 9/73; withdrawn by 4/75; G Jameson {Dunscroft Commercials} (dealer), Dunscroft for scrap 12/77.

VFM 617 (611): Thames Valley & Aldershot Omnibus Co Ltd {Alder Valley}, Reading (BE) 508 1/72; W Norths (PV) Ltd (dealer), Sherburn in Elmet 6/72; Shaw Bros, Byers Green (DM) 11/72; RI Davies & Son, Tredegar (MH) 2/75; John Anderson (Caravans) Ltd, Iver (XLN) by 3/76.

VFM 618 (609): W Norths (PV) Ltd (dealer), Sherburn in Elmet 9/71; J Laverty {Eagle Coaches}, Neilston (RW) 11/71; RW Dunsmore (dealer), Larkhall for scrap 12/74.

VFM 622 (610): Thames Valley & Aldershot Omnibus Co Ltd {Alder Valley}, Reading (BE) 507 1/72; W Norths (PV) Ltd (dealer), Sherburn in Elmet 6/72; Northern Roadways Ltd, Glasgow (LK) 9/72; unidentified dealer (Codona?) between Baillieston and Uddingston 6/74.

XFM 193 (613): Thames Valley & Aldershot Omnibus Co Ltd {Alder Valley}, Reading (BE) 515 1/72; W Norths (PV) Ltd (dealer), Sherburn in Elmet 6/72; Northern Roadways Ltd, Glasgow (LK) 9/72; unidentified dealer (Codona?) between Baillieston and Uddingston 6/74.

XFM 196 (614): Thames Valley & Aldershot Omnibus Co Ltd {Alder Valley}, Reading (BE) 516 1/72; W Norths (PV) Ltd (dealer), Sherburn in Elmet 6/72; Northern Roadways Ltd, Glasgow (LK) 9/72.

Vehicles acquired from Lincolnshire Road Car Co Ltd, Lincoln (LI) 8/70:

615	LFW 322	Bristol LD6B	104.002	ECW	7341	H33/25RD	3/55	10/71
616	LFW 324	Bristol LD6G	104.062	ECW	7343	H33/25RD	5/55	7/71
617	NBE 130	Bristol LD6B	108.138	ECW	8037	H33/27R	11/55	9/71

Previous histories:

LFW 322 (615): New to Lincolnshire Road Car Co Ltd (LI) 2314; entering service 10/70.

LFW 324 (616): New to Lincolnshire Road Car Co Ltd (LI) 2316; entering service 10/70.

NBE 130 (617): New to Lincolnshire Road Car Co Ltd (LI) 2327.

Notes:

NBE 130 (617): Not operated by Thames Valley; cannibalised for spares 7/71.

Disposals:

LFW 322 (615): W Norths (PV) Ltd (dealer), Sherburn in Elmet 11/71; Langley Coach Co Ltd, Langley (BK) 2/72; HFJ Cheek {Starline Elms Coaches}, Kenton (LN) 7/72; Starline Elms Coaches (Kenton) Ltd, Kenton (LN) 11/73; withdrawn 11/75.

LFW 324 (616): W Norths (PV) Ltd (dealer), Sherburn in Elmet 11/71; Martyrs Memorial Church, Belfast (XAM) 12/71.

NBE 130 (617): W Norths (PV) Ltd (dealer), Sherburn in Elmet for scrap 9/71.

Vehicle acquired from Crosville Motor Services Ltd, Chester (CH) 11/70:

612	XFM 186	Bristol LD6B	108.096	ECW	7917	H33/27RD	9/55	9/71

Previous history:

XFM 186 (612): New to Crosville Motor Services Ltd (CH) ML775 as H33/27R [fitted with platform doors 1956; renumbered DLB775 1958].

Notes:

XFM 186 (612): Not operated by Thames Valley.

Disposal:

XFM 186 (612): W Norths (PV) Ltd (dealer), Sherburn in Elmet 9/71; Blue Line Coaches Ltd, Upminster (LN) 5/72; W Norths (PV) Ltd (dealer), Sherburn in Elmet 5/73; unidentified dealer, Carlton for scrap 6/73.

Vehicle acquired from Nottinghamshire & Derbyshire Traction Co Ltd, Langley Mill (DE) 11/70:

636	14 DRB	Bristol LD6G	134.166	ECW	9445	H33/25RD	1/58	12/71

Previous history:

14 DRB (636): New to Nottinghamshire & Derbyshire Traction Co Ltd, Langley Mill (DE) 465 (as H33/25R) [fitted with platform doors 6/64]; entering service 12/70.

Disposal:
14 DRB (636): Thames Valley & Aldershot Omnibus Co Ltd {Alder Valley}, Reading (BE) 575 1/72; Passenger Vehicle Spares (Barnsley) Ltd (dealer), Carlton for scrap 11/76.

Vehicles transferred from South Midland Motor Services Ltd 11/70:

167	UJB 196	Bristol MW6G	164.001	ECW	11949	DP41F	3/60	12/71
417	LJB 417E	Bedford VAM14	6875393	Duple	1208/159	C41F	3/67	12/71

Previous histories:
UJB 196 (167): New to South Midland Motor Services Ltd 830 (as C34F) [reseated to C38F c3/66; delicensed 9/70, reseated to DP41F with folding doors, altered front dome, fitted for one-man-operation and renumbered 167 11/70].
LJB 417E (417): New to Thames Valley Traction Co Ltd C417; South Midland Motor Services Ltd C417 [renumbered 417 2/69].

Disposals:
UJB 196 (167): Thames Valley & Aldershot Omnibus Co Ltd {Alder Valley}, Reading (BE) 250 1/72; Paul Sykes Organisation Ltd (dealer), Barnsley for scrap 11/75.
LJB 417E (417): Thames Valley & Aldershot Omnibus Co Ltd {Alder Valley}, Reading (BE) 32 1/72; Martins Bus & Coach Sales Ltd (dealer), Middlewich 8/76; RP Prentice & Sons, West Calder (LO) 9/76; withdrawn by 10/79.

Vehicles acquired from Midland General Omnibus Co Ltd, Langley Mill (DE) 11-12/70:

151	957 ARA	Bristol LS6G	117.023	ECW	8934	B43F	5/56	12/71
152	958 ARA	Bristol LS6G	117.025	ECW	9048	B43F	5/56	12/71
156	960 ARA	Bristol LS6G	117.027	ECW	9050	DP43F	5/56	12/71
155	962 ARA	Bristol LS6G	117.045	ECW	9052	B43F	7/56	12/71
157	963 ARA	Bristol LS6G	117.046	ECW	9053	DP43F	7/56	12/71

Previous histories:
957-958 ARA (151-152): New to Midland General Omnibus Co Ltd, Langley Mill (DE) 243-244 (as DP43F) [reseated to B43F 1968]; acquired 11/70, entering service 12/70.
960 ARA (156): New to Midland General Omnibus Co Ltd, Langley Mill (DE) 246; acquired and entering service 12/70.
962 ARA (155): New to Midland General Omnibus Co Ltd, Langley Mill (DE) 248 (as DP43F) [reseated to B43F 1968]; acquired 11/70, entering service 12/70.
963 ARA (157): New to Midland General Omnibus Co Ltd, Langley Mill (DE) 249; acquired and entering service 12/70.

Notes:
957-958 ARA (151-152): Reseated to B41F, before entering service
960 ARA (156): Reseated to DP41F, before entering service
962 ARA (155): Reseated to B41F, before entering service
963 ARA (157): Reseated to DP41F, before entering service

Disposals:
957-958 ARA (151-152): Thames Valley & Aldershot Omnibus Co Ltd {Alder Valley}, Reading (BE) 231-232 1/72; Paul Sykes Organisation Ltd (dealer), Barnsley for scrap 2/75; R Askin (dealer), Barnsley for scrap c2/75.
960 ARA (156): Thames Valley & Aldershot Omnibus Co Ltd {Alder Valley}, Reading (BE) 233 1/72; Martins Bus & Coach Sales Ltd (dealer), Middlewich for scrap 5/75.
962 ARA (155): Thames Valley & Aldershot Omnibus Co Ltd {Alder Valley}, Reading (BE) 238 1/72; Paul Sykes Organisation Ltd (dealer), Barnsley for scrap 2/75.
963 ARA (157): Thames Valley & Aldershot Omnibus Co Ltd {Alder Valley}, Reading (BE) 239 1/72; Main Motors (dealer), Ewelme 5/74; unidentified dealer, Carlton for scrap 9/76.

Vehicles acquired from Bristol Omnibus Co Ltd, Bristol (GL) 12/70:

621	THW 742	Bristol LD6B	104.050	ECW	7236	H33/25RD	3/55	10/71
625	THW 743	Bristol LD6B	104.051	ECW	7237	H33/25RD	3/55	10/71
627	THW 744	Bristol LD6B	104.052	ECW	7238	H33/25RD	3/55	12/71
629	THW 745	Bristol LD6B	104.053	ECW	7239	H33/25RD	3/55	12/71
630	THW 750	Bristol LD6B	104.103	ECW	7244	H33/25RD	6/55	12/71

Previous histories:

THW 742 (621): New to Bristol Tramways & Carriage Co Ltd, Bristol (GL) L8252; Bristol Omnibus Co Ltd, Bristol (GL) L8252 6/57; entering service 2/71.

THW 743 (625): New to Bristol Tramways & Carriage Co Ltd, Bristol (GL) L8253; Bristol Omnibus Co Ltd, Bristol (GL) L8253 6/57; entering service 2/71.

THW 744 (627): New to Bristol Tramways & Carriage Co Ltd, Bristol (GL) L8254; Bristol Omnibus Co Ltd, Bristol (GL) L8254 6/57; entering service 1/71.

THW 745 (629): New to Bristol Tramways & Carriage Co Ltd, Bristol (GL) L8255; Bristol Omnibus Co Ltd, Bristol (GL) L8255 6/57; entering service 1/71.

THW 750 (630): New to Bristol Tramways & Carriage Co Ltd, Bristol (GL) L8260; Bristol Omnibus Co Ltd, Bristol (GL) L8260 6/57; entering service 1/71.

Disposals:

THW 742 (621): W Norths (PV) Ltd (dealer), Sherburn in Elmet 11/71; WG Anderton {Andy's Coaches}, Birmingham (WK) 12/71; Andy's of Birmingham Ltd, Birmingham (WK) 7/72; W Norths (PV) Ltd (dealer), Sherburn in Elmet for scrap 9/76.

THW 743 (625): W Norths (PV) Ltd (dealer), Sherburn in Elmet 11/71; Shephardson's Coaches Ltd, Barton-on-Humber (LI) 11/71; John Anderson (Caravans) Ltd, Iver (XLN) by 3/76.

THW 744 (627): Thames Valley & Aldershot Omnibus Co Ltd {Alder Valley}, Reading (BE) 509 1/72; W Norths (PV) Ltd (dealer), Sherburn in Elmet 6/72; HWT Pressings Ltd, Redditch (XWO) by 10/72; scrapped at Brierley Hill 1/76.

THW 745 (629): Thames Valley & Aldershot Omnibus Co Ltd {Alder Valley}, Reading (BE) 510 (not operated) 1/72; W Norths (PV) Ltd (dealer), Sherburn in Elmet 6/72; Northern Roadways Ltd, Glasgow (LK) 2/73; Codona (dealer), Baillieston for scrap by 2/75.

THW 750 (630): Thames Valley & Aldershot Omnibus Co Ltd {Alder Valley}, Reading (BE) 511 1/72; W Norths (PV) Ltd (dealer), Sherburn in Elmet 6/72; H Wray & Sons {Ideal Service}, Hoyle Mill (WR) 1/73; K Askin (dealer), Barnsley for scrap c4/74.

Vehicles acquired from Lincolnshire Road Car Co Ltd, Lincoln (LI) 12/70:

618	LFW 317	Bristol LD6B	100.143	ECW		7336	H33/25RD	12/54	7/71
619	LFW 318	Bristol LD6B	100.167	ECW		7337	H33/25RD	12/54	7/71

Previous histories:

LFW 317-318 (618-619): New to Lincolnshire Road Car Co Ltd (LI) 2309-2310; entering service 1/71.

Disposals:

LFW 317-318 (618-619): W Norths (PV) Ltd (dealer), Sherburn in Elmet for scrap 9/71.

1971

New Vehicles:

400	BJB 883J	Bristol RELH6G	4/346	Plaxton	713375	C51F	4/71	12/71
401	BJB 884J	Bristol RELH6G	4/347	Plaxton	713376	C51F	4/71	12/71
402	CJB 587J	Bristol RELH6G	4/400	Plaxton	713377	C51F	7/71	12/71
403	CJB 588J	Bristol RELH6G	4/401	Plaxton	713378	C51F	7/71	12/71
404	CJB 589J	Bristol RELH6G	4/402	Plaxton	713379	C51F	7/71	12/71
405	CJB 590J	Bristol RELH6G	4/403	Plaxton	713380	C51F	7/71	12/71
229	CMO 647J	Bristol RELL6G	3/1479	ECW	19354	B49F	5/71	12/71
230	CMO 648J	Bristol RELL6G	3/1480	ECW	19355	B49F	5/71	12/71
231	CMO 649J	Bristol RELL6G	3/1481	ECW	19356	B49F	5/71	12/71
515	DRX 101K	Bristol VRT/SL6G	2/211	ECW	18922	H39/31F	8/71	12/71
516	DRX 102K	Bristol VRT/SL6G	2/212	ECW	18923	H39/31F	8/71	12/71
517	DRX 103K	Bristol VRT/SL6G	2/213	ECW	18924	H39/31F	8/71	12/71
518	DRX 104K	Bristol VRT/SL6G	2/214	ECW	18925	H39/31F	8/71	12/71
232	DRX 625K	Bristol RELL6G	3/1556	ECW	19357	B49F	9/71	12/71
233	DRX 626K	Bristol RELL6G	3/1558	ECW	19358	B49F	9/71	12/71
234	DRX 627K	Bristol RELL6G	3/1559	ECW	19359	B49F	9/71	12/71
241	EBL 390K	Bristol RELL6L	3/1569	ECW	19369	B50F	9/71	12/71
242	EBL 437K	Bristol RELL6L	3/1570	ECW	19370	B50F	9/71	12/71
243	EBL 438K	Bristol RELL6L	3/1575	ECW	19371	B50F	9/71	12/71
920	FBL 112K	Bristol VRT/SL6G	2/249	ECW	18926	H39/31F	12/71	12/71
921	FBL 113K	Bristol VRT/SL6G	2/250	ECW	18927	H39/31F	12/71	12/71
922	FBL 114K	Bristol VRT/SL6G	2/251	ECW	18928	H39/31F	12/71	12/71

Notes:

CJB 587-588J (402-403): Did not enter service until 8/71.

CJB 589-590J (404-405): Did not enter service until 9/71.

DRX 625-627K (232-234): Part of a larger order with the balance delivered in 1972 to Thames Valley & Aldershot Omnibus Co Ltd {Alder Valley} registered DRX 628-633K.

EBL 390K (241): Part of a diverted order from Southdown Motor Services Ltd, Brighton (ES) where it was intended to be no. 604.

EBL 437-438K (242-243): Part of a diverted order from Southdown Motor Services Ltd, Brighton (ES) where they were intended to be nos. 605-606. The balance of these diverted orders (intended to be Southdown 607-610) were delivered in 1972 to Thames Valley & Aldershot Omnibus Co Ltd {Alder Valley} registered EBL 439-441K, EBL 461K.

FBL 112-114K (920-922): Did not enter service until 1/72 (with Thames Valley & Aldershot Omnibus Co Ltd {Alder Valley}), their fleet numbers being in the Alder Valley scheme. Further vehicles to complete the order were delivered to Alder Valley in 1972 and registered FBL 115-117K (923-925).

Disposals:

BJB 883J (400): Thames Valley & Aldershot Omnibus Co Ltd {Alder Valley}, Reading (BE) 59 1/72; renumbered 1059 in 9/82; Alder Valley South Ltd, Aldershot (HA) 1059 1/86; last licensed 3/86; W Norths (PV) Ltd (dealer), Sherburn in Elmet for scrap 8/86.

BJB 884J (401): Thames Valley & Aldershot Omnibus Co Ltd {Alder Valley}, Reading (BE) 60 1/72; hired to South Wales Transport Co Ltd, Swansea (GG) 9/81; renumbered 1060 in 9/82; withdrawn 12/85; Alder Valley South Ltd, Aldershot (HA) (not operated) 1059 1/86; J Sykes (dealer), Carlton 6/86; Carcroft Happy Wanderers Majorettes Band, Carcroft (XSY) by 11/88; last licensed 11/95.

CJB 587J (402): Thames Valley & Aldershot Omnibus Co Ltd {Alder Valley}, Reading (BE) 61 1/72; renumbered 1061 in 9/82; Alder Valley South Ltd, Aldershot (HA) 1061 1/86; W Norths (PV) Ltd (dealer), Sherburn in Elmet 9/86; Athelstan Coaches Ltd {Overland & County}, Malmesbury (WI) 11/86; Fr DJ Green (dealer), Weymouth by 8/88; Parfitts Motor Services Ltd, Rhymney Bridge (MG) 6/89; DH Stolzenberg, Maesteg (MG) 9/89; AE & FR Brewer Ltd, Caerau (MG) (not operated) 5/90; Treboeth Gospel Hall, Swansea (XWG) 11/90; unidentified dealer for scrap by 10/99; last licensed 10/99.

CJB 588J (403): Thames Valley & Aldershot Omnibus Co Ltd {Alder Valley}, Reading (BE) 62 1/72; renumbered 1062 in 9/82; last licensed 7/85; Alder Valley South Ltd, Aldershot (HA) 1062 (not operated) 1/86; J Sykes (dealer), Carlton (minus seats) for scrap 3/86.

CJB 589J (404): Thames Valley & Aldershot Omnibus Co Ltd {Alder Valley}, Reading (BE) 63 1/72; hired to South Wales Transport Co Ltd, Swansea (GG) 9/81; renumbered 1063 in 9/82; hired to South Wales Transport Co Ltd, Swansea (GG) 3/84; Alder Valley North Ltd, Reading (BE) 1063 1/86; The Berks Bucks Bus Co Ltd {The Bee Line}, Reading (BE) 1063 1/87; last licensed 3/87; W Norths (PV) Ltd (dealer), Sherburn in Elmet for scrap by 11/87.

CJB 590J (405): Thames Valley & Aldershot Omnibus Co Ltd {Alder Valley}, Reading (BE) 64 1/72; hired to South Wales Transport Co Ltd, Swansea (GG) 9/81; renumbered 1064 in 9/82; Alder Valley South Ltd, Aldershot (HA) 1064 1/86; W Norths (PV) Ltd (dealer), Sherburn in Elmet 10/86; Athelstan Coaches Ltd {Overland & County}, Malmesbury (WI) 11/86; Fr DJ Green (dealer), Weymouth by 6/89; Parfitts Motor Services Ltd, Rhymney Bridge (MG) 6/89; DH Stolzenberg, Maesteg (MG) 9/89; AE & FR Brewer Ltd, Caerau (MG) for spares 5/90; last licensed 9/90.

CMO 647J (229): Thames Valley & Aldershot Omnibus Co Ltd {Alder Valley}, Reading (BE) 471 1/72; Eastern Counties Omnibus Co Ltd, Norwich (NK) RL691 6/81; last licensed 1/84; cannibalised for spares 1984; Hartwood Exports (Machinery) Ltd (dealer), Birdwell 7/84; GP Ripley (dealer), Carlton for scrap 7/84.

CMO 648J (230): Thames Valley & Aldershot Omnibus Co Ltd {Alder Valley}, Reading (BE) 472 1/72; W Norths (PV) Ltd (dealer), Sherburn in Elmet for scrap 10/82.

CMO 649J (231): Thames Valley & Aldershot Omnibus Co Ltd {Alder Valley}, Reading (BE) 473 1/72; Eastern Counties Omnibus Co Ltd, Norwich (NK) RL692 6/81; last licensed 5/86; T Wigley (dealer), Carlton for scrap 1/87.

DRX 101K (515): Thames Valley & Aldershot Omnibus Co Ltd {Alder Valley}, Reading (BE) 916 1/72; Amalgamated Passenger Transport Ltd (dealer), Bracebridge Heath 2/83; Passenger Vehicle Spares (Barnsley) Ltd (dealer), Carlton 3/83; Whiting Bros (dealer), Carlton for scrap 9/87.

DRX 102K (516): Thames Valley & Aldershot Omnibus Co Ltd {Alder Valley}, Reading (BE) 917 1/72; converted to a tree lopper 3/85 and transferred to the service fleet; Alder Valley South Ltd, Aldershot (HA) TL61 as a tree lopper 1/86; Alder Valley Ltd, Aldershot (HA) TL61 as a tree lopper 1/89; last licensed 5/91; W Norths (PV) Ltd (dealer), Sherburn in Elmet for scrap 7/92.

DRX 103K (517): Thames Valley & Aldershot Omnibus Co Ltd {Alder Valley}, Reading (BE) 918 1/72;
Amalgamated Passenger Transport Ltd (dealer), Bracebridge Heath 2/83; Passenger Vehicle
Spares (Barnsley) Ltd (dealer), Carlton for scrap 3/83.

DRX 104K (518): Thames Valley & Aldershot Omnibus Co Ltd {Alder Valley}, Reading (BE) 919 1/72; Alder
Valley North Ltd, Reading (BE) 919 1/86; The Berks Bucks Bus Co Ltd {The Bee Line},
Reading (BE) 919 1/87; renumbered 505 10/87; City of Oxford Motor Services Ltd, Oxford
(OX) 1505 11/90; last licensed 2/91; Lister PVS (Bolton) Ltd (dealer), Bolton 3/91; Passenger
Vehicle Spares (Barnsley) Ltd (dealer), Carlton 4/91; Whiting Bros (dealer), Pontefract for
scrap 9/91.

DRX 625K (232): Thames Valley & Aldershot Omnibus Co Ltd {Alder Valley}, Reading (BE) 474 1/72; Paul
Sykes Organisation Ltd (dealer), Barnsley 7/80; K Askin (dealer), Barnsley 7/80; K Boon Ltd,
Standish (GM) 6/81; Barrys Coaches Ltd {Interbus}, Weymouth (DT) 9/82; North East Bus
Services Ltd {North Eastern}, Gateshead (TW) 3/88; last licensed 1/89; North Eastern Bus
Breakers (dealer), Craghead 8/89; Parton & Allen (dealer), Carlton for scrap 8/89.

DRX 626K (233): Thames Valley & Aldershot Omnibus Co Ltd {Alder Valley}, Reading (BE) 475 1/72;
Eastern Counties Omnibus Co Ltd, Norwich (NK) RL693 6/81; last licensed 4/84; Hartwood
Exports (Machinery) Ltd (dealer), Birdwell for scrap 7/84.

DRX 627K (234): Thames Valley & Aldershot Omnibus Co Ltd {Alder Valley}, Reading (BE) 476 1/72; Paul
Sykes Organisation Ltd (dealer), Barnsley 7/80; K Askin (dealer), Barnsley for scrap 8/80.

EBL 390K (241): Thames Valley & Aldershot Omnibus Co Ltd {Alder Valley}, Reading (BE) 477 1/72; W
Norths (PV) Ltd (dealer), Sherburn in Elmet 3/82; R & JM Barwick {Jaronda Travel}, Barlow
(NY) by 4/83; W Norths (PV) Ltd (dealer), Sherburn in Elmet 8/85; J Leask {J Leask & Son},
Lerwick (SD) 9/85; PR & AJN Leask & GR Silver {John Leask & Son}, Lerwick (SD) by 12/86;
unidentified owner, Cunnister, Yell as an immobile store shed 2/86 (last licensed 10/86) to
5/08 at least.

EBL 437K (242): Thames Valley & Aldershot Omnibus Co Ltd {Alder Valley}, Reading (BE) 478 1/72; Paul
Sykes Organisation Ltd (dealer), Barnsley 7/80; K Askin (dealer), Barnsley 7/80; G Jones
{Carlton Metals} (dealer), Carlton for scrap 6/81.

EBL 438K (243): Thames Valley & Aldershot Omnibus Co Ltd {Alder Valley}, Reading (BE) 479 1/72;
unidentified dealer for scrap by 5/85.

FBL 112K (920): Thames Valley & Aldershot Omnibus Co Ltd {Alder Valley}, Reading (BE) 920 1/72; loaned
to City of Oxford Motor Services Ltd, Oxford (OX) 3-4/77; Alder Valley South Ltd, Aldershot
(HA) 920 1/86; withdrawn 1/87; W Norths (PV) Ltd (dealer), Sherburn in Elmet 5/87; S
Pemberton & FMG Elkins {Redline}, Lickey End (HW) 9/87; last licensed 8/89; GP Ripley
(dealer), Carlton for scrap 8/89.

FBL 113K (921): Thames Valley & Aldershot Omnibus Co Ltd {Alder Valley}, Reading (BE) 921 1/72; Alder
Valley South Ltd, Aldershot (HA) 921 1/86; withdrawn 1/87; W Norths (PV) Ltd (dealer),
Sherburn in Elmet 5/87; K Rodham {Calvary Coaches}, Washington (TW) 8/87; W Norths (PV)
Ltd (dealer), Sherburn in Elmet 9/87; Excelsior Coaches (Telford) Ltd, Wellington (SH) 11/87;
last licensed 4/88; W Norths (PV) Ltd (dealer), Sherburn in Elmet by 12/88; Passenger Vehicle
Spares (Barnsley) Ltd (dealer), Carlton for scrap 11/89.

FBL 114K (922): Thames Valley & Aldershot Omnibus Co Ltd {Alder Valley}, Reading (BE) 922 1/72; last
licensed 11/85; Alder Valley South Ltd, Aldershot (HA) 922 (not operated) 1/86; W Norths (PV)
Ltd (dealer), Sherburn in Elmet 8/86; Parton & Allen (dealer), Carlton for scrap 6/87.

Vehicles acquired from Nottinghamshire & Derbyshire Traction Co Ltd, Langley Mill (DE) 1-3/71:

637	16 DRB	Bristol LD6G	134.218	ECW		9447	H33/25RD	2/58	12/71
638	17 DRB	Bristol LD6G	134.246	ECW		9448	H33/25RD	3/58	12/71
639	18 DRB	Bristol LD6G	138.004	ECW		9449	H33/25RD	3/58	12/71
640	19 DRB	Bristol LD6G	138.005	ECW		9450	H33/25RD	3/58	12/71
641	20 DRB	Bristol LD6G	138.171	ECW		9451	H33/25RD	9/58	12/71

Previous histories:
16 DRB (637): New to Nottinghamshire & Derbyshire Traction Co Ltd, Langley Mill (DE) 467 (as H33/25R)
[fitted with platform doors 2/64]; acquired 1/71, entering service 5/71.

17 DRB (638): New to Nottinghamshire & Derbyshire Traction Co Ltd, Langley Mill (DE) 468 (as H33/25R)
[fitted with platform doors 7/64]; acquired 1/71, entering service 3/71.

18 DRB (639): New to Nottinghamshire & Derbyshire Traction Co Ltd, Langley Mill (DE) 469 (as H33/25R)
[fitted with platform doors 4/64]; acquired 1/71, entering service 7/71.

19 DRB (640): New to Nottinghamshire & Derbyshire Traction Co Ltd, Langley Mill (DE) 470 (as H33/25R)
[fitted with platform doors 4/64]; acquired 1/71, entering service 3/71.

20 DRB (641): New to Nottinghamshire & Derbyshire Traction Co Ltd, Langley Mill (DE) 471 (as H33/25R)
[fitted with platform doors 5/64]; acquired 3/71, entering service 7/71.

Disposals:
>16-17 DRB (637-638): Thames Valley & Aldershot Omnibus Co Ltd {Alder Valley}, Reading (BE) 576-577 1/72; Passenger Vehicle Spares (Barnsley) Ltd (dealer), Carlton for scrap 11/76.
>18-20 DRB (639-641): Thames Valley & Aldershot Omnibus Co Ltd {Alder Valley}, Reading (BE) 578-580 1/72; D Rollinson (Bus Centre) Ltd (dealer), Carlton for scrap 9/76.

Vehicles acquired from Midland General Omnibus Co Ltd, Langley Mill (DE) 2/71:

125	964 ARA	Bristol LS6G	117.047	ECW		9054	B43F	7/56	12/71
126	966 ARA	Bristol LS6G	117.052	ECW		9056	B43F	7/56	12/71
132	967 ARA	Bristol LS6G	117.058	ECW		9057	B43F	7/56	12/71

Previous histories:
>964 ARA (125): New to Midland General Omnibus Co Ltd, Langley Mill (DE) 250 (as DP43F) [reseated to B43F 1968]; entering service 3/71.
>966 ARA (126): New to Midland General Omnibus Co Ltd, Langley Mill (DE) 252 (as DP43F) [reseated to B43F 1968]; entering service 3/71.
>967 ARA (132): New to Midland General Omnibus Co Ltd, Langley Mill (DE) 253 (as DP43F) [reseated to B43F 1968]; entering service 3/71.

Notes:
>964 ARA (125): Reseated to B41F, before entering service.
>966 ARA (126): Reseated to B41F, before entering service.
>967 ARA (132): Reseated to B41F, before entering service.

Disposals:
>964 ARA (125): Thames Valley & Aldershot Omnibus Co Ltd {Alder Valley}, Reading (BE) 234 1/72; Paul Sykes Organisation Ltd (dealer), Barnsley for scrap 2/75.
>966 ARA (126): Thames Valley & Aldershot Omnibus Co Ltd {Alder Valley}, Reading (BE) 235 1/72; Paul Sykes Organisation Ltd (dealer), Barnsley for scrap 2/75.
>967 ARA (132): Thames Valley & Aldershot Omnibus Co Ltd {Alder Valley}, Reading (BE) 236 1/72; Paul Sykes Organisation Ltd (dealer), Barnsley for scrap 2/75.

Vehicles acquired from Mansfield District Traction Co Ltd, Mansfield (NG) 2-3/71:

119	PNN 769	Bristol LS6G	101.080	ECW		7559	DP41F	4/54	12/71
642	WAL 440	Bristol LD6G	134.210	ECW		9436	H33/25RD	1/58	12/71
643	213 ANN	Bristol LD6G	138.188	ECW		10302	H33/25RD	11/58	12/71
644	214 ANN	Bristol LD6G	138.189	ECW		10303	H33/25RD	11/58	12/71

Previous histories:
>PNN 769 (119): New to Mansfield District Traction Co Ltd 200 (as C39F) [reseated to DP41F 7/67]; acquired 2/71, entering service 3/71.
>WAL 440 (642): New to Mansfield District Traction Co Ltd 513 (as H33/25R) [fitted with platform doors 1964]; acquired 2/71, entering service 5/71.
>213 ANN (643): New to Mansfield District Traction Co Ltd 516; acquired in 2/71, entering service 5/71.
>214 ANN (644): New to Mansfield District Traction Co Ltd 517; acquired 3/71, entering service 7/71.

Notes:
>PNN 769 (119): Reseated to DP39F 7/71.

Disposals:
>PNN 769 (119): Thames Valley & Aldershot Omnibus Co Ltd {Alder Valley}, Reading (BE) 209 1/72; Paul Sykes Organisation Ltd (dealer), Barnsley for scrap 2/75.
>WAL 440 (642): Thames Valley & Aldershot Omnibus Co Ltd {Alder Valley}, Reading (BE) 581 1/72; destroyed by fire at Reading depot on 26/5/76; D Rollinson (Bus Centre) Ltd (dealer), Carlton for scrap 9/76.
>213 ANN (643): Thames Valley & Aldershot Omnibus Co Ltd {Alder Valley}, Reading (BE) 582 1/72; D Rollinson (Bus Centre) Ltd (dealer), Carlton for scrap 9/76.
>214 ANN (644): Thames Valley & Aldershot Omnibus Co Ltd {Alder Valley}, Reading (BE) 583 1/72; converted to a driver training vehicle no 28 9/76 and transferred to the service fleet; renumbered 1102 6/78; Passenger Vehicle Spares (Barnsley) Ltd (dealer), Carlton for scrap 11/78.

Vehicle acquired from Midland General Omnibus Co Ltd, Langley Mill (DE) 8/71:

647	515 JRA	Bristol LD6G	150.177	ECW		10993	H33/25RD	7/59	12/71

Previous history:

515 JRA (647): New to Midland General Omnibus Co Ltd, Langley Mill (DE) 477; entering service 9/71.

Disposal:

515 JRA (647): Thames Valley & Aldershot Omnibus Co Ltd {Alder Valley}, Reading (BE) 586 1/72; Main Motors (dealer), Ewelme for scrap 5/74.

Vehicles acquired from Mansfield District Traction Co Ltd, Mansfield (NG) 8-11/71:

645	215 ANN	Bristol LD6G	138.273	ECW	10304	H33/25RD	12/58	12/71
646	216 ANN	Bristol LD6G	138.274	ECW	10305	H33/25RD	12/58	12/71
648	191 BRR	Bristol LD6G	150.230	ECW	10988	H33/25RD	8/59	12/71
588	566 ERR	Bristol FS6G	155.060	ECW	11640	H33/27RD	6/60	12/71

Previous histories:

215 ANN (645): New to Mansfield District Traction Co Ltd 518; acquired 9/71, entering service 11/71.
216 ANN (646): New to Mansfield District Traction Co Ltd 519; acquired 10/71, entering service 11/71.
191 BRR (648): New to Mansfield District Traction Co Ltd 520; acquired 8/71, entering service 10/71.
566 ERR (588): New to Mansfield District Traction Co Ltd 530; acquired 11/71, entering service 12/71.

Notes:

566 ERR (588): Was numbered in the Thames Valley & Aldershot Omnibus Co Ltd {Alder Valley} scheme.

Disposals:

215 ANN (645): Thames Valley & Aldershot Omnibus Co Ltd {Alder Valley}, Reading (BE) 584 1/72; Passenger Vehicle Spares (Barnsley) Ltd (dealer), Carlton for scrap 11/76.
216 ANN (646): Thames Valley & Aldershot Omnibus Co Ltd {Alder Valley}, Reading (BE) 585 1/72; D Rollinson (Bus Centre) Ltd (dealer), Carlton for scrap 9/76.
191 BRR (648): Thames Valley & Aldershot Omnibus Co Ltd {Alder Valley}, Reading (BE) 587 1/72; Martins Bus & Coach Sales Ltd (dealer), Middlewich for scrap 2/76.
566 ERR (588): Thames Valley & Aldershot Omnibus Co Ltd {Alder Valley}, Reading (BE) 588 1/72; D Rollinson (Bus Centre) Ltd (dealer), Carlton for scrap 11/77.

Vehicles acquired from East Midland Motor Services Ltd, Chesterfield (DE) 9/71:

123	XNU 415	Bristol LS6G	107.048	ECW	8208	B43F	5/55	12/71
124	XNU 416	Bristol LS6G	107.049	ECW	8209	B43F	5/55	12/71

Previous histories:

XNU 415 (123): New to Midland General Omnibus Co Ltd, Langley Mill (DE) 234 (as DP43F); East Midland Motor Services Ltd, Chesterfield (DE) R315 1/70 [reseated to B43F and equipped for one-man-operation 3/70]; entering service 10/71.
XNU 416 (124): New to Midland General Omnibus Co Ltd, Langley Mill (DE) 235 (as DP43F); East Midland Motor Services Ltd, Chesterfield (DE) R316 1/70 [reseated to B43F and equipped for one-man-operation 2/70]; entering service 10/71.

Notes:

XNU 415-416 (123-124): Reseated to B41F, before entering service.

Disposals:

XNU 415 (123): Thames Valley & Aldershot Omnibus Co Ltd {Alder Valley}, Reading (BE) 225 1/72; Main Motors (dealer), Ewelme for scrap 5/74.
XNU 416 (124): Thames Valley & Aldershot Omnibus Co Ltd {Alder Valley}, Reading (BE) 226 1/72; Paul Sykes Organisation Ltd (dealer), Barnsley for scrap 2/75.

ANCILLARY VEHICLES

New & acquired vehicles:

	?	Ford model T	van	-/--	7/19	-/--
21	DP 2377	Thornycroft J	lorry	7/19	9/20	3/21
30	DP 2604	Thornycroft J	lorry	4/20	9/20	3/21
49	MO 160	Thornycroft J	lorry	6/22	11/22	5/23
54	MO 773	Ford T	lorry	12/22	4/24	10/27
	MO 5537	Morris (Z?) 25 cwt	lorry	6/25	6/25	9/27
3	DP 7413	Morris (Z?) 25 cwt	lorry	3/26	3/26	10/49
4	DP 7414	Morris (Z?) 25 cwt	lorry	3/26	3/26	10/49
5	DP 7415	Morris (Z?) 25 cwt	lorry	3/26	3/26	8/40
	PP 2822	?	lorry	11/24	5/33	9/33
2	PP 5930	Morris T	lorry	4/26	7/34	10/49
6	RX 3755	Austin 7 hp	van	2/29	-/36	4/51
14	KX 8482	Karrier Coaster	lorry	4/32	c11/38	6/39
1	WO 9157	Leyland Cub	lorry	2/35	6/40	9/54
8	JB 4217	Austin 7 hp	van	5/34	1/42	11/51
15	DJB 914	Bedford 10/12 cwt	van	11/46	11/46	2/60
17	DJB 943	Ford (Canada) V8 FWD	recovery vehicle	-/--	11/46	2/60
19	trade plates	Ford (Canada) V8 FWD	recovery vehicle	-/--	11/46	12/71
21	trade plates	Dodge (US) 6-wheel	recovery vehicle	-/--	11/46	12/57
23	EBL 533	Bedford 10/12 cwt	van	9/47	9/47	9/60
25	JGF 406	Commer Q4 3 ton	breakdown lorry	-/46	9/48	10/57
27	FJB 99	Bedford 10/12 cwt	van	7/49	7/49	7/56
29	RX 1758	Leyland TD1	route servicing vehicle	6/28	9/49	10/56
	CMO 963	Bedford OW 3 ton	lorry	11/43	1/50	1/58
31	GJB 552	Bedford 10/12 cwt	van	2/51	2/51	10/65
33	GMO 943	Austin A40	van	10/51	10/51	11/66
35	KBL 963	Ford 3 ton	dropside lorry	10/54	10/54	11/66
37	MRX 113	Commer Cob	van	7/56	7/56	5/68
39	MRX 114	Commer Cob	van	7/56	7/56	4/67
41	MRX 115	Bedford CA5	van	7/56	7/56	10/65
43	BRX 921	Bristol K5G	route servicing vehicle	11/39	10/56	11/64
RV1	trade plates	AEC Matador	recovery vehicle	-/--	1/60	12/71
45	UJB 298	Bedford CAV	van	2/60	2/60	11/68
47	UJB 299	Bedford CAV	van	2/60	2/60	3/69
49	765 BJB	Ford 307E 7 cwt	van	7/62	7/62	5/68
51	32 GBL	Ford 307E 7 cwt	van	2/64	2/64	7/69
ED53	FPU 510	Bristol K5G	route servicing vehicle	4/37	12/64	3/71
55	FMO 831C	Leyland 15 cwt	van	7/65	7/65	7/70
57	GBL 760C	Leyland 15 cwt	van	10/65	10/65	12/71
61	KRX 261D	Bedford CALV30	van	10/66	10/66	12/71
63	KRX 563D	Bedford KDLC1	dropside lorry	10/66	10/66	12/71
65	LRX 865E	Bedford CALV30	van	3/67	3/67	12/71
67	MMO 367E	Bedford CALV30	van	5/67	5/67	12/71
49	PJB 349F	Ford 7 cwt	van	2/68	2/68	12/71
37	RJB 37F	Bedford CAV 10/12 cwt	van	5/68	5/68	12/71
45	RJB 45F	Bedford CAV 15/17 cwt	van	5/68	5/68	12/71
69	VBL 838H	Ford Escort	van	8/69	8/69	12/71
71	SRD 167H	Bedford CAV	van	1/70	1/70	12/71
73	SRD 168H	Bedford CAV	van	1/70	1/70	12/71

Notes:

An unidentified Morris van was also acquired from Penn Bus Co Ltd, Tylers Green (BK) 8/35; it passed to London Passenger Transport Board, London SW1 (LN) 8/35.

Unidentified Ford T: Was referred to as an inspection car with the British Automobile Traction (Thames Valley branch), but was fitted with a box body and numbered 257 (it is not known whether it was new or second-hand); transferred to Thames Valley Traction Co Ltd 7/20.

19: Was a Canadian Ford V8 model C290 four-wheel drive gun tractor; it was acquired via a Ministry of Supply (GOV) auction at Dorchester in 11/46 and was a former War Department vehicle.

21: Was a three-axle vehicle carrying an overhead crane; it was acquired via a Ministry of Supply (GOV) auction at Dorchester in 11/46 and was a former War Department vehicle.

RV1: Purchased from Ministry of Supply, Ruddington (GOV) in 9/58; its chassis was overhauled and Thames Valley constructed a new body between 4/59 and 11/59 to which recovery equipment was fitted; it entered service in 1/60.

DP 2377 (21): Numbered 21 in the PSV fleet; it was fitted with a Lorrybus B32R body from new; rebodied Brush B32F 4-6/20; body removed 9/20 and it was probably fitted with a lorry body; rebodied Birch Ch28 3/21 and returned to the PSV fleet.

DP 2604 (33): Numbered 33 in the PSV fleet; it was fitted with a B32F from new; body removed 9/20 and it was fitted with a lorry body 9/20; rebodied Birch Ch28 3/21 and returned to the PSV fleet.

DP 7415 (2): Appears to have been renumbered 5 in 1929.

JB 4217 (8): Converted from a staff car 1/42; it was fitted with a new van body.

KX 8482 (14): Previously numbered 14 in the PSV fleet with a Weymann B24F body; was converted to a lorry for the specific purpose of transporting engines removed from withdrawn Leyland TD1s to Leyland Vehicles Ltd at Leyland; these were fitted to new Leyland TS8 coaches BMO 980-989 (381-390) (qv).

MO 160 (49): Numbered 49 in the PSV fleet; it was fitted with an LGOC O18/16RO body from new; body removed 9/22; fitted with a lorry body 11/22; rebodied LGOC O18/16RO 5/23 and returned to the PSV fleet.

MO 773 (54): Numbered 54 in the PSV fleet with a Vincent B14F body.

PP 2822: Acquired with the Marlow & District Motor Services Ltd, Marlow (BK) business in 5/33.

PP 5930 (2): Numbered 2 in the PSV fleet with a Morris B14F body.

RX 1758 (29): Numbered 169 in the PSV fleet; was converted for use as a route servicing vehicle (tree lopper); fitted with a Gardner 5LW diesel engine by 9/50.

RX 3755 (6): Converted from a staff car; used for the maintenance of producer gas trailers during the War; used for publicity purposes from 3/45.

WO 9157 (1): Acquired from Praills (dealer), Hereford; it operated on trade plates 031 MO.

AKX 590: Acquired with the Penn Bus Co Ltd, Tylers Green (BK) business in 8/35.

BBH 364: Acquired with the Penn Bus Co Ltd, Tylers Green (BK) business in 8/35.

BRX 921 (43): Numbered 405 in the PSV fleet; was converted for use as a route servicing vehicle (tree lopper).

CMO 963: Acquired with the Newbury & District Motor Services Ltd 1/50.

DJB 943 (17): Was a Canadian Ford V8 model C290 four-wheel drive gun tractor; it was acquired via a Ministry of Supply (GOV) auction at Dorchester in 11/46 and was a former War Department vehicle; it was converted for use as a recovery vehicle and subsequently operated on trade plates 533 MO from 1956/7.

FPU 510 (ED53): Numbered 460 in the PSV fleet; was converted for use as a route servicing vehicle (tree lopper) 11/64; wrecked in an accident near Mortimer 3/71.

JGF 406 (25): Purchased at a Ministry of Supply (GOV) auction in 9/48; the vehicle was said to have been new in 1946, probably first registered in 5/47.

Disposals:

Only the following disposals are known:

19: Thames Valley & Aldershot Omnibus Co Ltd {Alder Valley}, Reading (BE) 1/1/72; Tillingbourne Valley Services Ltd, Guildford (SR) 1/72; Tillingbourne Valley Bus Co Ltd, Guildford (SR) 12/72.

RV1: Thames Valley & Aldershot Omnibus Co Ltd {Alder Valley}, Reading (BE) 15 1/1/72; renumbered 1050 6/78

DP 7413 (3-4): Shirley (dealer), Darby Green for scrap 10/49.

KX 8482 (M16): Unidentified operator / dealer 6/39.

MO 160 (49): Returned to the PSV fleet 3/23.

MO 773 (54): B Toms (dealer), Reading 10/27.

MO 5537: North Western Road Car Co Ltd, Stockport (CH) 9/27; last licensed 12/29.

PP 5930 (2): Shirley (dealer), Darby Green for scrap 10/49.

RX 1758 (29): Thomas, Reading (GBE) 10/56.

WO 9157 (1): H Goodey, Twyford 10/54.

BRX 921 (43): Broken up by Thames Valley 11/64.

FPU 510 (ED53): WR Alexander {Alexander Coaches}, Sheffield (WR) 9/71.

GBL 760C (57): Thames Valley & Aldershot Omnibus Co Ltd {Alder Valley}, Reading (BE) 16 1/1/72; Main Motors (dealer), Ewelme 5/74.

HBL 297D: Thames Valley & Aldershot Omnibus Co Ltd {Alder Valley}, Reading (BE) 1/1/72.

KRX 261D (61): Thames Valley & Aldershot Omnibus Co Ltd {Alder Valley}, Reading (BE) 17 1/1/72; renumbered 16 2/73; Eric White Group {Timms of Bracknell}, Binfield 9/75.

KRX 563D (63): Thames Valley & Aldershot Omnibus Co Ltd {Alder Valley}, Reading (BE) 18 1/1/72; renumbered 1054 6/78; unidentified owner / dealer 12/79.

LRX 865E (65): Thames Valley & Aldershot Omnibus Co Ltd {Alder Valley}, Reading (BE) 20 1/1/72; Main Motors (dealer), Ewelme 5/74.

MMO 367E (67): Thames Valley & Aldershot Omnibus Co Ltd {Alder Valley}, Reading (BE) 19 1/1/72; Elliott Metal Co, Reading 1/76.

PJB 349F (49): Thames Valley & Aldershot Omnibus Co Ltd {Alder Valley}, Reading (BE) 21 1/1/72; B Coney, Thatcham 10/73.

RJB 37F (37): Thames Valley & Aldershot Omnibus Co Ltd {Alder Valley}, Reading (BE) 23 1/1/72; unidentified owner / dealer 5/77.

RJB 45F (45): Thames Valley & Aldershot Omnibus Co Ltd {Alder Valley}, Reading (BE) 22 1/1/72; renumbered 1056 6/78; Merlin Motors, Uxbridge 10/78.

SRD 167H (71): Thames Valley & Aldershot Omnibus Co Ltd {Alder Valley}, Reading (BE) 25 1/1/72; Eric White Group {Timms of Bracknell}, Binfield 9/75.

SRD 168H (73): Thames Valley & Aldershot Omnibus Co Ltd {Alder Valley}, Reading (BE) 26 1/1/72; D Wilkinson, Aldershot 1/77.

VBL 838H (69): Thames Valley & Aldershot Omnibus Co Ltd {Alder Valley}, Reading (BE) 24 1/1/72; M Cook, Hambledon 8/76.

TANK WAGONS

The tank wagons constituted a separate commercial operation by Thames Valley. They were on contract to oil companies and delivered to many other outlets as well as to Thames Valley's own depots. In return for a commitment to purchase fuel from the oil company at a favourable rate, Thames Valley was guaranteed a basic weekly contract mileage. Other bus companies enjoyed similar arrangements.

The initial fleet was on contract to Dominion Motor Spirit Co Ltd and from late 1924, was built up to four vehicles each of which was fitted with a 1,000 gallon tank mounted on a Thornycroft chassis, previously used for buses. The tanks were owned by Dominion until the expiry of the contract in October 1930, when they were purchased by Thames Valley and a new contract was established with Russian Oil Products Ltd.

The contract was again renewed in April 1933 when it passed to Trinidad Leaseholds Ltd (trading as Regent). The Thornycrofts were by this time the only such vehicles left in the fleet, so they were replaced with four seven-year old TSM chassis, again taken from the PSV fleet. From 1934, two vehicles were based at Reading and two in London, at West Ham (pre-war) and Barking (post-war). The London-based vehicles were maintained by the Maidenhead depot.

In 1936, the fleet was again renewed with the purchase of four new Leyland Beaver lorries which were fitted with new 1,500 gallon drums. As these entered service at the start of 1937, the TSMs were at first used as mobile fuel stores during the rebuilding of Reading garage. After the outbreak of hostilities, they were discretely dispersed around Thames Valley's dormy sheds at Crowthorne and probably Fingest, Stoke Row, Stokenchurch or Yateley where they were used to store emergency stocks of oil for the duration of World War 2.

Under wartime regulations, the contract came under the control of the Petroleum Board, before reverting to Regent (by now Regent Oil Co Ltd) in January 1948.

Efforts were made to divest the contract to the Road Haulage Executive in 1950, but this failed and operations continued until 1956 by which time, the Leyland Beavers were approaching the end of their working lives. The contract was eventually terminated at the end of September 1956.

New & acquired vehicles:

51	MO 151	Thornycroft J	4468	1,000 gallon oil tank	6/22	10/24	4/33
65	MO 1803	Thornycroft J	5055	1,000 gallon oil tank	8/23	3/25	9/33
41	DX 2175	Thornycroft J	7452	1,000 gallon oil tank	10/19	3/27	4/33
47	MO 62	Thornycroft J	4741	1,000 gallon oil tank	6/22	3/27	9/33
111	MO 6855	TSM B9B	4849	1,000 gallon oil tank	6/26	4/33	12/36
112	MO 6856	TSM B9B	4850	1,000 gallon oil tank	6/26	4/33	12/36
107	MO 6851	TSM B9A n/c	4845	1,000 gallon oil tank	5/26	9/33	12/36
114	MO 6858	TSM B9B	4852	1,000 gallon oil tank	6/26	9/33	12/36
5	ABL 769	Leyland Beaver TSC8	12428	1,500 gallon oil tank	1/37	1/37	9/56
7	ABL 770	Leyland Beaver TSC8	12429	1,500 gallon oil tank	1/37	1/37	9/56
9	ABL 771	Leyland Beaver TSC8	12430	1,500 gallon oil tank	1/37	1/37	9/56
11	ABL 772	Leyland Beaver TSC8	12431	1,500 gallon oil tank	1/37	1/37	9/56

Notes:

The TSM tankers (107, 111, 112 and 114) received their 1,000 gallon oil tanks transferred from the Thornycrofts (41, 47, 51 and 65) (order unknown).

DX 2175 (41): Previously numbered 41 in the PSV fleet, it retained this number in the tanker fleet; it was presumed to also carry 'No. 3 or No. 4 Petrol Tank Wagon'; its cab was built by Thames Valley at its Reading works.

MO 62 (47): Previously numbered 47 in the PSV fleet, it retained this number in the tanker fleet; it was presumed to also carry 'No. 3 or No. 4 Petrol Tank Wagon'; its cab was built by Thames Valley at its Reading works.

MO 151 (51): Previously numbered 51 in the PSV fleet, it retained this number in the tanker fleet; it was presumed to also carry 'No. 1 Petrol Tank Wagon'; its cab was constructed from an ex-War Department lorry body.

MO 1803 (65): Previously numbered 65 in the PSV fleet, it retained this number in the tanker fleet; it also carried 'No. 2 Petrol Tank Wagon'; its cab was built by Thames Valley at its Reading works.

MO 6851 (107): Previously numbered 107 in the PSV fleet, it retained this number in the tanker fleet; it also carried 'No. 2 Petrol Tank Wagon'; it had been converted to normal control prior to being bodied as a petrol tanker.

MO 6855 (111): Previously numbered 107 in the PSV fleet, it retained this number in the tanker fleet; it also carried 'No. 1 Petrol Tank Wagon'.

MO 6856 (112): Previously numbered 112 in the PSV fleet, it retained this number in the tanker fleet; it also carried 'No. 3 Petrol Tank Wagon'.

MO 6858 (114): Previously numbered 114 in the PSV fleet, it retained this number in the tanker fleet; it also carried 'No. 4 Petrol Tank Wagon'.

Disposals:

DX 2175 (41): Phillips Mills & Co Ltd (dealer), London SW1 for scrap 6/33 (chassis only).

MO 62 (47): Chassis broken up 8/34.

MO 151 (51): Unidentified operator / dealer 6/33 (chassis only).

MO 1803 (65): Unidentified operator / dealer 9/33 (chassis only).

MO 6851 (107): London & Suburban Commercial Vehicles Ltd, London 6/45.

MO 6855 (111): London & Suburban Commercial Vehicles Ltd, London 6/45.

MO 6856 (112): London & Suburban Commercial Vehicles Ltd, London 6/45.

MO 6858 (114): London & Suburban Commercial Vehicles Ltd, London 7/45.

ABL 769 (5): Regent Oil Co Ltd, London 10/56; Stuart Oil & Chemical Co, Liverpool; last licensed 9/57.

ABL 770 (7): Regent Oil Co Ltd, London 10/56; unidentified owner, London 10/56; licensed until the late-1960s.

ABL 771 (9): Regent Oil Co Ltd, London 10/56; W & C French Ltd, Loughton 5/57; last licensed 7/60; probably scrapped 3/61.

ABL 772 (11): Regent Oil Co Ltd, London 10/56; unidentified owner (Penford?), Dorset 12/56; TC Penford, Stoford by 7/63; last licensed 7/63; JD Jessop (dealer?), Cleckmoor, Broadstone and scrapped 3/67.

PRODUCER GAS TRAILER UNITS

Tests for running buses on producer gas had begun as early as the summer of 1939 when JB 5844 (265) had its fuel tank removed and its rear compartment (behind the passenger entrance) boarded up with a fire-proof wall up to house a Gohin-Poulenc gas filtration unit. The trial was not a complete success as the vehicle suffered a number of engine problems caused by (amongst other things) the abrasive nature of the coal dust which required more frequent maintenance interventions and overhauls. It was restored to diesel power in June 1942, although it was later re-converted to gas using a trailer.

Ten trailer units were ordered from Bristol Tramways in June 1942, but with stricter enforcement of the Wartime regulations that required companies to convert 10% of their fleets, a further ten trailers were ordered in the following November.

The trailers were delivered between September 1942 and December 1943. Tests elsewhere had found that the most suitable vehicles for conversion were 6-cylinder petrol engines and so the earlier Leyland TD1 and TS4 models were selected. The first two conversions (single deck RX 9704 (250) and double-deck RX 1759 (170)) re-entered service in November 1942.

The converted vehicles were restricted to Reading and Maidenhead depots but were unpopular with the crews as they entailed considerably more work to prepare them for service and keep them maintained. As a result, it was often not possible to keep more than four vehicles on the road at any one time. Complaints that the gas fumes were causing sickness were also common.

A further two trailers were received in September 1944 from an unknown source, shortly before the requirement to operate on producer gas was withdrawn. There followed a swift programme of decommissioning the trailers, with the vehicles all converted back to petrol (including JB 5844 which as a result, had operated with all three means of propulsion – petrol, diesel and producer gas).

Thames Valley is known to have converted a total of 18 vehicles over 1942-1944 – it is presumed that the other four trailers were retained as spares:

GN 5139 (259)	Leyland TS3	Leyland	4/43 – 2/45
GN 5145 (258)	Leyland TS3	Leyland	4/43 – 2/45
JB 5844 (265)	Leyland TS7	Brush	8/44 – 2/45
RX 1754 (165)	Leyland TD1	Leyland	late 1943 – 10/44
RX 1755 (166)	Leyland TD1	Leyland	late 1943 – 10/44
RX 1756 (167)	Leyland TD1	Leyland	late 1943 – 10/44
RX 1757 (168)	Leyland TD1	Leyland	4/43 – 10/44
RX 1758 (169)	Leyland TD1	Leyland	7/43 – 2/44
RX 1759 (170)	Leyland TD1	Leyland	10/42 – 10/44
RX 1761 (172)	Leyland TD1	Leyland	3/43 – 4/44
RX 1762 (173)	Leyland TD1	Short	3/43 – 4/44
RX 1764 (175)	Leyland TD1	Short	late 1942 – 10/44
RX 9699 (245)	Leyland TS4	Brush	late 1942 – 10/44
RX 9700 (246)	Leyland TS4	Brush	late 1942 – 12/44
RX 9701 (247)	Leyland TS4	Brush	late 1942 – 11/44
RX 9702 (248)	Leyland TS4	Brush	late 1942 – 11/44
RX 9703 (249)	Leyland TS4	Brush	late 1942 – 11/44
RX 9704 (250)	Leyland TS4	Brush	9/42 – 10/44

The 22 trailer units were sold in March 1945 for £12 each (having cost £92 each when new) to J Deacon of Dorchester-on-Thames whose principal interest was in acquiring the tyres.

COMPANY BODY NUMBERS

From late 1922 to September 1935, the company allocated its own body numbers. Up to 1930, bodies were frequently swapped between chassis and disposed of as separate units. The list below is a cross-reference of the bodies and the chassis on which they were mounted together with their final disposals. Seats and stairs were removed and the vehicles driven to their final destination where the body was demounted from the chassis. These were subsequently put to many different uses; for example, the numerous bodies sold to WM Peto were used as chicken huts (complete with anthracite stoves) and those to WC Pocock & Sons and Reffell Bros became greenhouses. Others were put to use as garden sheds, offices, pavilions, summer houses or simply for firewood.

Body numbers 1-32 (plus two un-numbered) were those fitted to the 34 vehicles transferred to Thames Valley from British Automobile Traction in July 1920. For clarity, only Thames Valley fleet numbers are shown here even though the first 34 bodies dated from the BAT era.

The bodies shown as LGOC were mainly constructed by the London General Omnibus Co Ltd at one of their coachworks. Some bodies described as LGOC however, were constructed by others (notably Hora and Dodson), but no records remain to indicate which these were.

Tilling rear-entrance, single-deck (c1913/4, origins unknown)
The first known chassis that these bodies were fitted to were DP 1655-60 of 9/15 and DP 1756/7 of 3/16. Thereafter they were fitted to:

1 Either DP 2115 (15) or DP 2117 (17) 1-2/19; DP 2606 (34) 7/20; Tynemouth & District Electric Traction Co Ltd 3/23 (fitted to a Daimler B chassis – one of J 2551 (1), J 2682 (5) or J 2685 (3)).
2 DP 2114 (14) (chassis 7074) 1/19; DP 2114 (23) (chassis 7720) 4/20; to Maidenhead garage for use as a cycle shed 12/25; T Hilton, Uxbridge 5/26.
3 DP 2111 (1) 1/19; to Maidenhead garage for use as a cycle shed 12/25; Hind & Pettifer, Stokenchurch 6/27.
4 DP 2113 (3) (chassis 7062) 1/19; DP 2113 (20) (chassis 7583) 5/20; to Wycombe garage for use as a cycle shed 12/25; AJ Vine, Newbury 6/27.
5 DP 2112 (2) 1/19; Tynemouth & District Electric Traction Co Ltd 3/23 (fitted to a Daimler B chassis – one of J 2551 (1), J 2682 (5) or J 2685 (3)).
6 DP 2118 (8) 2/19; to Maidenhead garage as a store 12/25; AJ Vine, Newbury 6/27.
7 DP 2116 (6) 2/19; DP 2123 (14) 4/22; Tynemouth & District Electric Traction Co Ltd 3/23 (fitted to a Daimler B chassis – one of J 2551 (1), J 2682 (5) or J 2685 (3)).
8 Either DP 2115 (15) or DP 2117 (17) 1-2/19; DP 2599 (27) 2/20; Trent Motor Traction Co Ltd, Derby (DE) (sold as a complete vehicle) 6/23.

Brush rear-entrance, single-deck (1916)
These were first fitted to DP 1794/5 of 7/16 and DP 1826/7 of 11/16. Thereafter they were fitted to:

9 DP 2122 (22) 2/19; DP 2124 (15) by 7/20; BE Channell, Slough 12/28.
10 DP 2119 (9) 2/19; Trent Motor Traction Co Ltd, Derby (DE) (sold as a complete vehicle) 5/23.
11 DP 2120 (10) 2/19; Trent Motor Traction Co Ltd, Derby (DE) (sold as a complete vehicle) 6/23.
12 DP 2121 (11) 2/19; Trent Motor Traction Co Ltd, Derby (DE) (sold as a complete vehicle) 5/23.

Bayley dual front-entrance, single deck (origins unknown)
13 Fitted to DP 2129 (13) 5/19; B Toms, Reading for scrap 12/25.

Birch rear-entrance, single-deck (1919)
14 Fitted to DP 2123 (14) 4/19; DP 2116 4/22; A McConnachie, Wokingham 12/28.
15 Fitted to DP 2125 (16) 4/19; DP 2600 (24) 4/20; A McConnachie, Wokingham 12/28.
16 Fitted to DP 2124 (15) 4/19; DP 2122 (12) by 7/20; A McConnachie, Wokingham 12/28.
17 Fitted to DP 2126 (17) 4/19; Lambourn, Farley Hill 10/28.
18 Fitted to DP 2127 (AEC) 5/19; DP 2127 (Thornycroft) (19) 7/19; MO 158 (53) 7/22; WM Peto, Furze Platt 12/28.
19 Fitted to DP 2128 (AEC) 5/19; DP 2128 (Thornycroft) (18) 7/19; A McConnachie, Wokingham 12/28.

Harrington charabanc (origin unknown, possibly Southdown Motor Services)
20 Fitted to DP 2130 (AEC) 5/19; DP 2130 (3) (Thornycroft chassis 7583) 7/19; DP 2130 (3) (Thornycroft chassis 7062) 5/20; B Toms, Reading 11/25.

Brush front-entrance, single-deck (1920)

(including two bodies disposed of before company body numbers were introduced)

21	Fitted to DP 2115 (5) 4-6/20; WM Peto, Furze Platt 12/28.
22	Fitted to DP 2601 (29) 4/20; Miss Hunsdon, Reading 7/29.
23	Fitted to DP 2605 (4) 4/20; WM Peto, Furze Platt 12/28.
24	Fitted to DP 2125 (16) 4-6/20; WM Peto, Furze Platt 12/28.
25	Fitted to DP 2597 (28) 4/20; Reffell Bros, Wraysbury 2/29.
26	Fitted to DP 2378 (22) 4-6/20; AW Chivers, Reading 7/29.
27	Fitted to DP 2598 (30) 4/20; WM Peto, Furze Platt 12/28.
28	Fitted to DP 2117 (7) 4-6/20; To & Fro Cycle Co, Maidenhead 10/28.
29	Fitted to KN 2873 (26) 6/20; WM Peto, Furze Platt 12/28.
30	Fitted to DP 2603 (32) 4/20; WM Peto, Furze Platt 12/28.
31	Fitted to DP 2602 (31) 4/20; Reffell Bros, Wraysbury 2/29.
32	Fitted to KN 3652 (25) 6/20; WM Peto, Furze Platt 12/28.
--	Fitted to DP 2377 (21) 4-6/20; Potteries Electric Traction Co Ltd, Stoke-on-Trent (ST) 9/20.
--	Fitted to DP 2604 (33) 4/20; Potteries Electric Traction Co Ltd, Stoke-on-Trent (ST) 9/20.

Birch charabanc (1921)

33	Fitted to DP 3647 (35) 3/21; dismantled for spares / scrap by Thames Valley (as a complete vehicle) 5/28.
34	Fitted to DP 3633 (36) 3/21; dismantled for spares / scrap by Thames Valley (as a complete vehicle) 5/28.
35	Fitted to DP 2377 (21) 3/21; dismantled for spares / scrap by Thames Valley (as a complete vehicle) 5/28.
36	Fitted to DP 2604 (33) 3/21; dismantled for spares / scrap by Thames Valley (as a complete vehicle) 5/28.

LGOC double-deck (O18/16RO) (acquired second-hand in 1922)

(including two bodies disposed of before company body numbers were introduced).

37	Fitted to BL 9892 (37) 4/22; DX 2173 (42) 5/23; wrecked between Sands and Lane End when the vehicle overturned due to road subsidence 1/24 and scrapped.
38	Fitted to BL 9752 (38) 5/22; DP 2606 (34) 3/23; BL 9892 (37) 5/24; Mrs Watson, Maidenhead 5/25.
39	Fitted to MO 52 (39) 5/22; MO 160 (49) 5/23; Cocks, Reading 6/24.
40	see next section below.
41	Fitted to DX 2175 (41) 8/22; DP 2112 (2) 3/23; retained as a spare body 5/24; S Evans, Courthouse Lane Tennis Club, Maidenhead 10/24.
42	see next section below.
43	Fitted to MO 129 (43) 7/22; MO 1625 (59) 6/23; G Sinderbury, Arborfield 7/24.
44	Fitted to BL 9751 (44) 5/22; DP 2123 (14) 3/23; Richards, Tooting 8/25.
45	Fitted to MO 51 (45) 5/22; MO 1503 (57) 5/23; Dixon, Loudwater 10/23.
46	Fitted to MO 128 (46) 6/22; MO 1627 (60) 6/23; retained as a spare body 5/24; Mrs Armstrong, Bradfield 8/24 (also recorded a L Hofland 6/24)
47	Fitted to MO 62 (47) 6/22; MO 1504 (58) 6/23; JL Polack, Maidenhead 9/23.
48	Fitted to MO 159 (48) 7/22; MO 1715 (62) 7/23; G Sinderbury, Arborfield 7/24.
49	Fitted to MO 307 (52) 7/22; MO 1503 (57) 10/23; retained as a spare body 5/24; Mrs Armstrong, Bradfield 8/24 (also recorded L Hofland 6/24).
50	Fitted to MO 150 (50) 7/22; MO 1717 (64) 7/23; Cocks, Reading 6/24.
51	Fitted to MO 151 (51) 6/22; MO 1504 (58) 9/23; DX 2173 (42) 2/24; Baker, Tilehurst 3/25.
52	see next section below.
--	spare body not used; unidentified owner / dealer 5/22.
--	probably fitted to MO 160 (49) 6/22; unidentified owner / dealer 10/22.

Lorry body (ex War Department 3 ton body)

53	used on various J-type chassis as an inter-depot lorry: T Wigmore, Wokingham 9/25.

Hora single-deck (B28F) (ex-Eastern Counties in 1922)

40	As acquired on DX 2174 (40) 4/22; J Anderton, Newbury 4/25.
42	As acquired on DX 2173 (42) 4/22; Chivers & Sons, Histon, Cambridge 4/23.
52	As acquired on DX 2175 (41) 4/22; DP 2127 (19) 8/22; J Anderton, Newbury 4/25.

Vincent single-deck (B14F) (new in 1922)

54	As built on MO 773 (54) 12/22; FV Pritchard, Llanrug (CN) c4/24 (body only).
55	As built on MO 774 (55) 12/22; FV Pritchard, Llanrug (CN) 12/23 (as a complete vehicle).

LGOC double-deck (O18/16RO) (acquired second-hand in 1923)
56   Fitted to DX 2175 (41) 3/23; WC, PB & NW Pocock {WC Pocock & Sons}, Cold Ash 10/26.
57   Fitted to BL 9751 (44) 3/23; MO   62 (47) 5/24; J Anderton, Newbury 6/25.
58   Fitted to BL 9752 (38) 3/23; J Anderton, Newbury 6/25.
59   see next section below
60   Fitted to MO   62 (47) 6/23; MO 1625 (59) 6/24; Miss Reeves, Twyford 3/25.
61   Fitted to MO   51 (45) 6/23; Barkus, Reading 2/26.
62   Fitted to BL 9892 (37) 5/23; Smith, Maidenhead 5/24.
63   Fitted to MO   52 (39) 5/23; WC, PB & NW Pocock {WC Pocock & Sons}, Cold Ash 10/26.
64   Fitted to MO 1504 (58) 6/23; MO 1626 (61) 6/23; Mrs Moss, Hythe, Staines 4/25.
65   Fitted to MO   159 (48) 7/23; BL 9751 (44) 5/25; Hayman, Maidenhead 9/26.
66   Fitted to MO   128 (46) 7/23; Nash, Reading (delivered to Bucklebury Common) 3/25.
67   Fitted to MO   129 (43) 7/23; Stransom, Emmer Green 3/25.
68   Fitted to MO   150 (50) 7/23; Miss Reeves, Twyford 7/25.
69   Fitted to MO   307 (52) 8/23; Pope, Maidenhead 11/24.
70   Fitted to MO 1803 (65) 8/23; Nash, Reading (delivered to Bucklebury Common) 1/25.
71   Fitted to MO   151 (51) 8/23; A Tucker (Tuckin?), Stoke Row 11/24.
72   Fitted to MO 1716 (63) 8/23; MO 1503 (57) 5/24; A Ball (Bull?), Tilehurst 7/24.

Russell & Paddick single-deck (B14-) (ex-Simmonds in 1923)
59   Acquired on DP 4400 (56) 3/23; Yorkshire (Woollen District) Electric Traction Co Ltd, Dewsbury (WR) 10/23.

Dodson double-deck (O26/24RO) (1924)
73   Fitted to MO 1504 (58) 2/24; G Cooper, Earley 6/28.

Birch single-deck (B32R) (1924)
74   Fitted to MO 2610 (66) 3/24; Geary, Reading 3/30.
75   Fitted to MO 2622 (78) 3/24; WM Peto, Furze Platt 4/30.
76   Fitted to MO 2615 (71) 5/24; Geary, Reading 3/30.

Brush 'S' type double-deck (O28/26RO) (1924)
77   Fitted to MO 2611 (67) 4/24; XP 9081 (117) 10/27; AE Portlock, Upton 3/31.
78   Fitted to MO 2613 (69) 4/24; XP 4705 (122) 3/28; Bird, Watlington 3/31.
79   Fitted to MO 2620 (76) 4/24; Abbott, Stokenchurch 10/29.
80   Fitted to MO 2612 (68) 5/24; XR 4559 (129) 3/28; Mrs GW Stevenson, Newbury 4/30.
81   Fitted to MO 2617 (73) 5/24; XP 5449 (123) 3/28; Dicker (Dicks?), Wooburn Green 9/31.
82   Fitted to MO 2619 (75) 5/24; Pike, Pamber 2/30.
83   Fitted to MO 2621 (77) 5/24; AG Bint (Burt?), Harwell 12/29.
84   see next section below.
85   Fitted to DP 2112 (2) 5/24; XP 6422 (127) 12/27; Eden, Mortimer 3/31.
86   Fitted to DP 2606 (34) 5/24; AN 6452 (130) 1/28; Mrs Wells, Maidenhead 5/30.
87   Fitted to DP 2123 (14) 5/24; XP 9325 (128) 3/28; Gibbs, Burghfield 3/30.

Birch single-deck (B32R) (1924)
84   Fitted to MO 2614 (70) 5/24; Sheppard, Burghfield 3/30.
88   Fitted to MO 2616 (72) 5/24 Geary, Reading 3/30.
89   Fitted to MO 2618 (74) 5/24 Cotton, Iver 3/30.

Brush 'S' type double-deck (O28/26RO) (1924)
90   Fitted to MO 1627 (60) 5/24; MF 6914 (139) 2/28; West, Pamber 3/30.
91   Fitted to MO 1716 (63) 6/24; XP 5450 (124) 1/28; A Cooper, Crowthorne 5/30.
92   Fitted to MO 1717 (64) 6/24; Thatcham Road Transport Co Ltd, Thatcham (BE) 10/29 (as a complete vehicle).
93   Fitted to MO   160 (49) 5/24; XR 9847 (131) 11/27; Mrs Wells, Maidenhead 5/30.
94   Fitted to MO 3565 (79) 7/24; AG Bint (Burt?), Harwell 12/29.
95   Fitted to MO 3566 (80) 7/24; AG Bint (Burt?), Harwell 12/29.
96   Fitted to MO 1503 (57) 7/24; XP 9080 (121) 1/29; Mrs L Clifton, High Wycombe 5/31.
97   Fitted to MO 1715 (62) 8/24; XP 9831 (116) 12/28; Nash, Mortimer 8/31.

Harrington charabanc (ex-Southdown in 1924)
98   As acquired on CD 6353 (86) 12/24; B Toms, Reading for scrap 12/25.

Grimaldi charabanc (ex-Southdown in 1924)
99   As acquired on CD 5379 (87) 12/24; B Toms, Reading for scrap 12/25.

RSJ single-deck (B32R) (1924/5)
100 Fitted to MO 307 (52) 12/24; XP 5450 (124) 2/30; WM Peto, Furze Platt 8/31.
101 Fitted to MO 4155 (82) 12/24; XR 4559 (129) 2/30; WM Peto, Furze Platt 8/31.
102 Fitted to MO 4154 (81) 12/24; XP 9325 (128) 2/30; WM Peto, Furze Platt 8/31.
103 Fitted to MO 4157 (84) 12/24; XR 9847 (131) 2/30; WM Peto, Furze Platt 3/31.
104 Fitted to MO 4158 (85) 1/25; MF 6914 (139) 2/30; WM Peto, Furze Platt 3/31.
105 Fitted to MO 4156 (83) 1/25; AN 6452 (130) 2/30; WM Peto, Furze Platt 3/31.

Brush 'S' type double-deck (O28/26RO) (1925)
106 Fitted to MO 4306 (88) 2/25; XP 4051 (118) 11/27; White, Spencers Wood 7/31.
107 Fitted to MO 4307 (89) 2/25; WM Peto, Furze Platt 12/29.
108 Fitted to MO 4308 (90) 3/25; WM Peto, Furze Platt 12/29.
109 Fitted to MO 4309 (91) 3/25; WM Peto, Furze Platt 12/29.
110 Fitted to MO 4310 (92) 2/25; WM Peto, Furze Platt 12/29.
111 Fitted to MO 4311 (93) 2/25; WM Peto, Furze Platt 12/29.

LGOC double-deck (O18/16RO) (acquired second-hand in 1925)
112 Fitted to BL 9752 (38) 4/25; AV Price, Newbury 6/26.
113 Fitted to BL 9892 (37) 6/25; WC, PB & NW Pocock {WC Pocock & Sons}, Cold Ash 10/26.
114 Fitted to MO 51 (45) 4/25; Mrs Gyles, Caversham 10/26.
115 Fitted to MO 62 (47) 6/25; F Noble, Reading 12/26.

Brush 'S' type double-deck (O28/26RO) (1925)
116 Fitted to MO 129 (43) 4/25; XU 2191 (119) 11/28; Dicker (Dicks?), Wooburn Green 9/31.
117 Fitted to DX 2173 (42) 4/25; WM Peto, Furze Platt 12/29.
118 Fitted to MO 1625 (59) 5/25; XP 5985 (126) 1/29; E Wilson, Reading 8/31.
119 Fitted to MO 128 (46) 5/25; XP 6421 (120) 11/28; Chapman, Crowthorne 9/31.
120 Fitted to DX 2174 (40) 5/25; WM Peto, Furze Platt 12/29.
121 Fitted to DP 2127 (19) 5/25; AE Spears (dealer), London SW19 (sold as a complete vehicle) 10/29.
122 Fitted to MO 150 (50) 6/25; XP 4706 (115) 10/28; Holmes, Bradfield 8/31.
123 Fitted to MO 1626 (61) 6/25; XP 5984 (125) 1/29; Eynsham Estate Co, Eynsham Hall 4/31.
124 Fitted to MO 159 (49) 6/25; WM Peto, Furze Platt 12/29.
125 Fitted to DP 2118 (8) 7/25; Brean, Arborfield 10/29.

Various – on Lancia chassis (ex T Spragg Ltd in 1925)
126 As acquired on MO 3530 (95) 10/25; GE Askew, Loughton (EX) 4/26) (as a complete vehicle).
127 As acquired on MO 2213 (94) 10/25; GE Askew, Loughton (EX) 4/26) (as a complete vehicle).
128 As acquired on MO 4648 (96) 10/25; GE Askew, Loughton (EX) 4/26) (as a complete vehicle).
129 As acquired on MO 5443 (97) 10/25; GE Askew, Loughton (EX) 4/26) (as a complete vehicle).

Brush 'S' type double-deck (O28/26RO) (1926)
130 Fitted to DP 2130 (3) 2/26; Bird, Watlington 5/31.
131 Fitted to DP 2129 (13) 2/26; Eden, Mortimer 2/31.
132 Fitted to CD 6353 (86) 2/26; WM Peto, Furze Platt 11/31.
133 Fitted to DP 2111 (1) 2/26; Bird, Watlington 5/31.
134 Fitted to DP 2114 (23) 2/26; Dicker (Dicks?), Wooburn Green 9/31.
135 Fitted to DP 2113 (20) 2/26; E Wilson, Reading 8/31.
136 Fitted to MO 6842 (98) 3/26; E Wilson, Reading 8/31.
137 Fitted to CD 5379 (87) 3/26; Eynsham Estate Co, Eynsham Hall 4/31.

Birch / Brush / Tilling single-deck (B32R) (1926)
138 Fitted to MO 6843 (99) 4/26; J Jones (dealer), London W3 2/38 (as a complete vehicle).
139 Fitted to MO 6846 (102) 4/26; A Jones (dealer), Reading 4/38 (as a complete vehicle).
140 Fitted to MO 6844 (100) 4/26; J Jones (dealer), London W3 3/38 (as a complete vehicle).
141 Fitted to MO 6845 (101) 4/26; H Goodey (dealer), Twyford 5/38 (as a complete vehicle).
142 Fitted to MO 6847 (103) 4/26; J Jones (dealer), London W3 3/38 (as a complete vehicle).
143 Fitted to MO 6848 (104) 4/26; J Jones (dealer), London W3 3/38 (as a complete vehicle).
144 Fitted to MO 6849 (105) 6/26; J Jones (dealer), London W3 2/38 (as a complete vehicle).
145 Fitted to MO 6850 (106) 6/26; A Jones (dealer), Reading 4/38 (as a complete vehicle).
146 Fitted to MO 6851 (107) 5/26; not sold, presumed dismantled for spares / scrap by Thames Valley.
147 Fitted to MO 6852 (108) 6/26; J Jones (dealer), London W3 2/38 (as a complete vehicle).
148 Fitted to MO 6853 (109) 6/26; A Jones (dealer), Reading 4/38 (as a complete vehicle).
149 Fitted to MO 6854 (110) 6/26; J Jones (dealer), London W3 2/38 (as a complete vehicle).

London Lorries single-deck (C29F) (1926)
150   Fitted to MO 6855 (111) 6/26; Holmes, Bradfield 6/32.
151   Fitted to MO 6856 (112) 6/26; H Tutte, Wokingham 11/32.
152   Fitted to MO 6857 (113) 6/26; E Chapman (showman), London W1 3/32 (as a complete vehicle).
153   Fitted to MO 6858 (114) 6/26; H Tutte, Wokingham 9/32.

Dodson double-deck (O26/24RO) (ex-various London operators in 1926)
154   As acquired on XP 4706 (115) 4/26; Dorrell, London 12/28.
155   As acquired on XP 9831 (116) 4/26; Green, Finchampstead 12/28.
156   As acquired on XP 9081 (117) 4/26; MO 2611 (67) 10/27; AW Chivers, Reading 8/28.
157   As acquired on XP 4051 (118) 4/26; MO 4306 (88) 11/27; Mrs White, Wokingham 8/28.
158   As acquired on XU 2191 (119) 4/26; Reffell Bros, Wraysbury 2/29.
159   As acquired on XP 6421 (120) 4/26; Reffell Bros, Wraysbury 2/29.
160   As acquired on XP 9080 (121) 4/26; Reffell Bros, Wraysbury 2/29.
161   As acquired on XP 4705 (122) 4/26; MO 2613 (69) 3/28; Mrs White, Wokingham 9/28.
162   As acquired on XP 5449 (123) 4/26; MO 2617 (73) 3/28; Mrs White, Wokingham 9/28.
163   As acquired on XP 5450 (124) 4/26; MO 1716 (63) 2/28; AW Chivers, Reading 8/28.
164   As acquired on XP 5984 (125) 4/26; Reffell Bros, Wraysbury 2/29.
165   As acquired on XP 5985 (126) 4/26; Reffell Bros, Wraysbury 2/29.
166   As acquired on XP 6422 (127) 4/26; DP 2112 (2) 12/27; Mrs White, Wokingham 8/28.
167   As acquired on XP 9325 (128) 4/26; DP 2123 (14) 7/28; WM & FG Pocock, Reading 8/28.
168   As acquired on XR 4559 (129) 5/26; MO 2612 (68) 10/27; AW Chivers, Reading 6/28.
169   As acquired on AN 6452 (130) 5/26; DP 2606 1/28; Lewis, Winnersh 7/28.
170   As acquired on XR 9847 (131) 5/26; MO 160 (49) 11/27; Lewis, Winnersh 7/28.

Brush single-deck (B32R) (1926)
171   Fitted to MO 7942 (132) 7/26; J Jones (dealer), London W3 3/38 (as a complete vehicle).
172   Fitted to MO 7943 (133) 7/26; A Jones (dealer), Reading 4/38 (as a complete vehicle).
173   Fitted to MO 7944 (134) 7/26; J Jones (dealer), London W3 3/38 (as a complete vehicle).
174   Fitted to MO 7945 (135) 7/26; J Jones (dealer), London W3 3/38 (as a complete vehicle).
175   Fitted to MO 7946 (136) 7/26; J Jones (dealer), London W3 3/38 (as a complete vehicle).

Dodson double-deck (O28/24RO) (ex-various London operators in 1926)
176   As acquired on XR 4694 (137) 10/26; Bird, Watlington 3/31.
177   As acquired on XR 999 (138) 11/26; Eynsham Estate Co, Eynsham Hall 4/31.
178   As acquired on MF 6914 (139) 11/26; MO 1627 (60) 2/28; G Cooper, Earley 6/28.

London Lorries single-deck (C30F) (1927)
179   Fitted to MO 9312 (140) 6/27; H Tutte, Wokingham 9/32.
180   Fitted to MO 9313 (141) 6/27; MO 6855 (111) 5/32; H Tutte, Wokingham 11/32.
181   Fitted to MO 9314 (142) 6/27; H Tutte, Wokingham 6/32.
182   Fitted to MO 9315 (143) 6/27; H Tutte, Wokingham 11/32.

Brush single-deck (1927/8)
183-200 Fitted to MO 9316-29 (144-57), RX 1397/4-6 (158-61); all sold as complete vehicles.

London Lorries single-deck (C30F) (1928)
201   Fitted to RX 1398 (162) 4/28; MO 6856 (112) 5/32; H Tutte, Wokingham 11/32.
202   Fitted to RX 1399 (163) 4/28; MO 6858 (114) 5/32; H Tutte, Wokingham 11/32.

Leyland double-deck (L24/24RO) (1928)
203-211 Fitted to RX 1753-61 (164-72); all sold as complete vehicles.

Short double-deck (L24/24RO) (1928)
212-214 Fitted to RX 1762-4 (173-5); all sold as complete vehicles.

RSJ single-deck (B20F) (ex-Yorkshire Traction in 1926)
215   As acquired on HE 2323 (192) 5/29; WM Peto, Furze Platt 11/31.
216   As acquired on HE 2325 (193) 5/29; WM Peto, Furze Platt 11/31.
217   As acquired on HE 2326 (194) 5/29; WM Peto, Furze Platt 11/31.
218   As acquired on HE 2327 (195) 5/29; WM Peto, Furze Platt 4/31.
219   As acquired on HE 2331 (196) 5/29; WM Peto, Furze Platt 11/31.
220   As acquired on HE 2336 (197) 5/29; WM Peto, Furze Platt 11/31.
221   As acquired on HE 2339 (198) 5/29; WM Peto, Furze Platt 4/31.

London Lorries single-deck (C28D) (1929)
222-224 Fitted to RX 4338-40 (176-8); all sold as complete vehicles.

Leyland double-deck (L27/24RO) (1929/30)
225-237 Fitted to RX 4341-53 (179-91); all sold as complete vehicles.
238-247 Fitted to RX 5561-70 (199-208); all sold as complete vehicles.

Brush single-deck (B32R) (1930)
248-257 Fitted to RX 5571-80 (209-18); all sold as complete vehicles.

Leyland double-deck (L27/24RO) (1930)
258-263 Fitted to RX 6110-2 (219-21), RX 6242-4 (222-4); all sold as complete vehicles.

Brush single-deck (DP32R) (1930)
264-268 Fitted to RX 6245-9 (225-9); all sold as complete vehicles.

Brush single-deck (C28D) (1930)
269   Fitted to RX 6250 (230); sold as a complete vehicle.

Leyland double-deck (L27/24RO) (1931)
270-276 Fitted to RX 8164-70 (231-7); all sold as complete vehicles.

Challands Ross (B20F) (ex Keep in 1931)
277   As acquired on RX 188 (238); sold as a complete vehicle.

Brush single-deck (C28F) (1931/2)
278-80 Fitted to RX 9307-9 (239-41); all sold as complete vehicles.
283   Fitted to RX 9541 (244); sold as a complete vehicle.

Vickers single-deck (B19F) (ex-Great Western Railway in 1931)
281   As acquired on YK 3822 (242); sold as a complete vehicle.

Willmott (B14F) (ex Cowley in 1931)
282   As acquired on RX 3131 (243); sold as a complete vehicle.

Brush single-deck (B32R) (1932)
284-295 Fitted to RX 9699-710 (245-56); all sold as complete vehicles.

Vickers single-deck (B26R) (ex-Great Western Railway in 1932)
296   As acquired on UV 4080 (257); sold as a complete vehicle.

London Lorries single-deck (C26R) (ex-various 1933/4)
297   Fitted to GN 5145 (258); sold as a complete vehicle.
298   Fitted to GN 5139 (259); sold as a complete vehicle.
299   Fitted to GN 5150 (260); sold as a complete vehicle.

Strachan & Brown single-deck (B14F) (ex Ranger & Simmonds in 1933)
300   As acquired on GW 540 (261); sold as a complete vehicle.

Duple single-deck (C32F) (1935)
301-303 Fitted to JB 5841-3 (262-4); all sold as complete vehicles.

Brush single-deck (B32R) (1935)
304-316 Fitted to JB 5844-5 (265-6); all sold as complete vehicles.
306   Fitted to JB 5846 (267); BBL 561 (375) 1951 (vehicles exchanged bodies).
307-316 Fitted to JB 5847-56 (268-77); all sold as complete vehicles.

OPERATORS ACQUIRED BY THAMES VALLEY

Thames Valley acquired interests in many small independent concerns between 1923 and 1969. The nature of these acquisitions varied considerably, but most simply involved Thames Valley taking over a service or services, some with and some without vehicles being included in the deal. In one or two cases, these were joint acquisitions with neighbouring operators.

The two Red & White United Transport Ltd subsidiaries (Newbury & District Motor Services Ltd and South Midland Motor Services Ltd) that were transferred to Thames Valley control on 10 February 1950 are included in separate sections later in this publication.

The following operators were acquired in their entirety (where no vehicles were taken into Thames Valley stock, operators are marked *). Details of these can be found in this section:

3/23	F Simmonds, Reading (BE)
10/25	T Spragg Ltd {Progressive Bus Service}, Bracknell (BE)
1/29	Marlow & District Motor Services Ltd, Marlow (BK) (operated as a subsidiary to 5/33)
6/31	RJ Robson {Premier Motor Omnibus Co}, Cookham Green (BK)
10/31	AE Cowley {Lower Road Bus Service}, Cookham Rise (BE)
3/33	TE Ashby {Lane End & District Bus Service}, Lane End (BK)
4/33	JH Harris {Pixey Bus}, Fifield (BE)
5/33	CA Ranger & AW Simmonds {Reliance Omnibus Co}, Maidenhead (BE)
8/35	Penn Bus Co Ltd, Tylers Green (BK)
1/36	Ledbury Transport Co Ltd {Thackray's Way}, Reading (BE) (operated as a subsidiary to 7/50)
5/36	B Argrave {Vimmy Bus Service}, Winkfield (BE)
5/36	Chiltern Bus Co Ltd, Lane End (BK)
3/49	*HD Farmer {Gem Bus Service}, Monks Risborough (BK)
1/50	Newbury & District Motor Services Ltd, Newbury (BE) (gradually absorbed in the early 1950s)
1/50	South Midland Motor Services Ltd, Oxford (OX) (always operated as a subsidiary)

In addition, certain assets and / or services of the following operators were acquired. In many cases, these continued operating a residual business independently. Details of vehicles acquired can be found in the main Thames Valley section (where no vehicles were acquired, operators are marked *).

6/22	*London General Omnibus Co Ltd, London (LN)
5/26	*J & A Povey {Povey Bros}, Sonning (BE)
12/26	SG Lovegrove {Lovegrove Bros}, Silchester (HA)
4/28	*F Baylis & Mr Poat, Barkham (BE)
4/28	*EG Venn-Brown {The Venture}, Henley-on-Thames (OX)
1/31	Great Western Railway Co, London W2 (LN) (Maidenhead, Newbury, Twyford & Windsor services)
3/31	E & S Keep {Rambler Coaches}, Burghfield Common (BE)
7/31	*J & J Franks {Shamrock Saloon Coaches}, Steeple Aston (OX)
4/32	Great Western Railway Co, London W2 (LN) (Slough services)
5/32	*FJ Lintott {Direct Bus Service}, Basingstoke (HA)
4/33	*B Keene {Cody Bus}, Popeswood (BE)
9/33	Aylesbury Omnibus Co Ltd, Aylesbury (BK)
9/33	*JC Chastell & DG Gray {Dean Bus Service}, Cookham Dean (BE)
9/33	*CW Fuller & AW Pomroy {Beta Bus Service}, Maidenhead (BE)
5/34	London Passenger Transport Board, London SW1 (LN)
1/36	G Jarvis & Son {Reading & District Motor Services}, Reading (BE)
4/36	*AE Warwick, Farnham Common (BK)
5/36	*WR Jeatt {White Bus Service}, Winkfield (BE)
6/37	FH Crook, Booker (BK)
7/37	*City of Oxford Motor Services Ltd, Oxford (OX)
11/37	*J & EJ Spratley {Blue Star Coaches}, Mortimer (BE)
4/40	*PH Keep {B & M Bus Service}, Maidenhead (BE)
6/51	RE Jackson {Crescent Coaches}, Windsor (BE)
5/52	United Counties Omnibus Co Ltd, Northampton (NO) (for South Midland)
12/54	*Frowen & Hill Ltd {Borough Bus Service}, Windsor (BE)
6/66	*A Cole {Blue Bus Services}, Maidenhead (BE)
6/66	*Reliance Motor Services Ltd, Newbury (BE)
10/69	*R Cole {Blue Bus Services}, Maidenhead (BE)

VEHICLES OF ACQUIRED OPERATORS

Bruce Douglas ARGRAVE {Vimmy Bus Service}   **3 Jassimaine Cottage, WINKFIELD (BE)**

Cannon Garage, SUNNINGDALE (SR)

Argrave's business was purchased on 13 May 1936 and included a service between Windsor and Ascot (via Winkfield) and an express licence for Ascot Races.

FG 4104	Reo	FB462	?		B14-	6/28	-/--	-/--
UR 644	Reo	FAX5722	?		B20-	7/28	5/31	-/--
VG 1631	Star Flyer VB4	VB949/C630	United	1792	C23F	7/29	11/33	*
RO 9027	Star Flyer VB3	B686	United	1248	B20F	2/28	1/35	*

Previous histories:
FG 4104:   Its origins are unknown; it originally was B20-.
RO 9027:   New to AR Blowers {Express Motor Service}, St Albans (HT) 3; London Passenger Transport Board, London SW1 (LN) 1/34; C & P Sales (dealer), London SW9 10/34, from whom it was acquired.
UR 644:   New C Aston, Watford (HT), from whom it was acquired.
VG 1631:   New to Harrison & Ives Ltd {Eastern Motorways}, Norwich (NK) (as C23F); United Automobile Services Ltd, York (YK) B94 10/30; Eastern Counties Omnibus Co Ltd, Norwich (NK) T1 7/31, from whom it was acquired.

Disposals:
FG 4104:   Last licensed 12/33; British Motor Trust Co Ltd, London SW1 at an unknown date and scrapped.
UR 644:   No known disposal.

The following vehicles marked with an asterisk above, transferred to Thames Valley 5/36 (qv):
RO 9027 (313), VG 1631 (312).

Thomas E ASHBY {Lane End & District Bus Service}   LANE END (BK)

Ashby had commenced operations in 1924 with a Lane End to High Wycombe service. This together with Ashby's solitary vehicle was purchased on 25 March 1933 for £575.

KX 1523	Guy OND	OND8924	?		B20F	12/28	12/28	*

Notes:
Ashby operated another vehicle between 10/24 and 12/28 – no details are known.

The following vehicle marked with an asterisk above, transferred to Thames Valley 3/33 (qv):
KX 1523.

LANE END & WYCOMBE SERVICES Ltd (10/33)
CHILTERN BUS Co Ltd (9/34)   Marlow Road, LANE END (BK)

Lane End & Wycombe Services Ltd was formed in October 1933 from the merger of two businesses: G Bishop {Bishop's Bus Services} and Jesty & Tudor {Wycombe & District Bus Co}. The latter business had been purchased from F & T Brown {Brown Bros / Lane End & District Motor Services} in March 1930 who in turn had acquired it from C Wilkinson {Wilkinson's Bus Service} in May 1929.

Lane End & Wycombe Services Ltd was renamed Chiltern Bus Co Ltd in September 1934 and then merged with another local operator, Pioneer Bus Service Ltd, in March 1935. The Pioneer company was incorporated in February 1933, prior to which the business was in the name of its owner, C Holland.

Thames Valley made an offer of £11,750 for the Chiltern Bus Co business and this took effect from 23 May 1936.

The history of these operators is complicated and their antecedents stretch as far back as World War 1. The following breaks the operations into their component parts in order to simplify.

GT 9199	Bedford WLB	108017	Willmott		B20F	8/31	10/33	*
GT 9324	Bedford WLB	108037	Willmott		B20F	9/31	10/33	*
GC 8783	Federal 3F6	66043	?		C18-	3/30	7/34	by5/36
KX 978	Graham Bros	GB4689	?		B20F	7/28	3/35	*
KX 2558	Graham Bros	D204010	?		B26F	5/29	3/35	*

MY 639	AEC Reliance	660311	Short	B32F	7/29	3/35	*
KX 6094	AEC Regal	662599	Petty	B30R	12/30	3/35	*
KX 7157	AEC Regal	662644	Petty	C32F	6/31	3/35	*
UR 3767	AEC Reliance	660239	Craven	C31R	7/29	-/35	*
MT 1330	AEC Reliance	660002	Hall Lewis	B31D	12/28	-/36	*

Previous histories:

GC 8783: New to F Newman {Medway District Bus Owners Association}, Rochester (KT); Maidstone & District Motor Services Ltd, Maidstone (KT) 8/31; Leyland Motors Ltd (dealer), Leyland 1/32, from whom it was acquired.

GT 9199: New to G Bishop {Bishop's Bus Service}, Lane End (BK), from whom it was acquired.

GT 9324: New to G Bishop {Bishop's Bus Service}, Lane End (BK), from whom it was acquired.

KX 978: New to C Holland {Pioneer}, Lane End (BK); Pioneer Bus Service Ltd, Lane End (BK) 2/33, from whom it was acquired.

KX 2558: New to C Holland {Pioneer}, Lane End (BK); Pioneer Bus Service Ltd, Lane End (BK) 2/33, from whom it was acquired.

KX 6094: New to C Holland {Pioneer}, Lane End (BK); Pioneer Bus Service Ltd, Lane End (BK) 2/33, from whom it was acquired.

KX 7157: New to C Holland {Pioneer}, Lane End (BK); Pioneer Bus Service Ltd, Lane End (BK) 2/33, from whom it was acquired.

MT 1330: New as a demonstrator with AEC Ltd, Southall; HJ, MK, EG & JH Brown {Brown Bros}, Sapcote (LE) at an unknown date, from whom it was acquired.

MY 639: New as a demonstrator with AEC Ltd, Southall; C Holland {Pioneer}, Lane End (BK) 10/29; Pioneer Bus Service Ltd, Lane End (BK) 2/33, from whom it was acquired.

UR 3767: New to London Midland & Scottish Railway, Watford (HT) 51F; Sheffield Joint Omnibus Committee, Sheffield (WR) 'C' fleet 4/30; numbered 209 (probably not carried) c1932; withdrawn 1935; Leyland Motors Ltd (dealer), Leyland 9/35; William R Wintour & Co (dealer), London W1, from whom it was acquired.

Disposals:

GC 8783: Davies (dealer), London NW5 for scrap 9/37.

The following vehicles marked with an asterisk above, transferred to Thames Valley 5/36 (qv):

GT 9199 (316), GT 9324 (315), KX 978 (322), KX 2558 (321), KX 6094 (317), KX 7157 (314), MT 1330 (319), MY 639 (318), UR 3767 (320).

ADDITIONAL VEHICLES OF PREDECESSORS TO LANE END & WYCOMBE SERVICES Ltd
W BISHOP {Bishop's Bus Services} to G BISHOP {Bishop's Bus Services} (-/28)

LC 5373	Daimler	?	?	B10R	-/--	6/19	-/24
?	Garford	?	?	B14R	-/--	-/24	-/--
?	Bean	?	?	B14F	-/28	-/28	12/30
YV 5053	Chevrolet LM	18192	Willmott	B14F	4/28	4/28	11/31
XV 5867	Bean model 11	1027/11	?	B20F	12/28	12/28	6/31
VF 1381	Chevrolet LM	17193	Waveney	B14F	8/27	6/29	-/--
TX 1965	Lancia Pentaiota	1409	Hall Lewis	B20D	11/26	10/29	-/--
VX 6462	ADC 416	416601	Duple	B32-	6/30	3/31	-/--

Previous histories:

? (Bean): Its origins are unknown.

? (Garford): Was originally a War Department vehicle.

LC 5373: Its origins are unknown, but it was new as a car.

TX 1965: Its origins are unknown.

VF 1381: New to United Automobile Services Ltd, Darlington (DM) H11; H Lane & Co Ltd (dealer), London SW10 1/29; ET Rolfe, Lane End (BK) 3/29, from whom it was acquired.

VX 6462: A vehicle with this chassis number was new to Irish Express, Dublin (EI) registered ZI 1810 passing to J Dwyer {Rocksavage Bus Co}, Cork (EI) at an unknown date and to Irish Omnibus Co / Great Southern Railway (EI) in 1932. It is not clear whether VX 6462 is the same vehicle (as the dates conflict); this was first registered to G Barney, Grays (EX) in 6/30, from whom it was acquired.

Notes:

? (Garford): Displayed the legend 'Don't Worry'.

LC 5373: Was named 'Victory'.

Disposals:

? (Bean):	No known disposal.
? (Garford):	No known disposal.
LC 5373:	No known disposal.
TX 1965:	No known disposal.
VF 1381:	Converted to a lorry at an unknown date; last licensed 3/32.
VX 6462 (ex ZI 1810):	No known disposal.
XV 5867:	H Lane & Co Ltd (dealer), London SW10 6/31; scrapped by 6/32.
YV 5053:	FJ Lintott {Direct Bus Service}, Basingstoke (HA) 11/31; Smith, location unknown at an unknown date; Burnell & Pugsley, Wootton Courtney (SO) 9/35; scrapped 11/36.

A JESTY & ? TUDOR {Wycombe & District Bus Co}

KX 1795	Bean model 11	1601/11W	?	B14-	1/29	1/29	by6/30
PK 1822	?	?	?	B14-	-/--	9/29	-/--
TD 5974	Chevrolet X	8479	?	B14-	5/26	10/29	10/30
PP 8497	Chevrolet LM	16643	?	B14F	6/27	3/30	-/--
KX 3159	Chevrolet LQ	55120	?	B14F	7/29	3/30	9/31
KX 3279	Chevrolet LQ	53994	?	B14F	8/29	3/30	-/--
PY 7380	?	?	?	B14F	-/--	6/30	-/--
KX 4530	Chevrolet LQ	56734	?	B14F	3/30	3/30	2/33
KX 5010	Commer Invader	6TK28027	?	B20D	5/30	5/30	-/--
YV 3567	TSM B10A	5546	?	C28-	4/28	12/30	12/31

Previous histories:

KX 3159:	New to F & T Brown {Brown Bros / Lane End & District Motor Services}, Lane End (BK), from whom it was acquired.
KX 3279:	New to F & T Brown {Brown Bros / Lane End & District Motor Services}, Lane End (BK), from whom it was acquired.
PK 1822:	New to G Weller {Gastonia}, Cranleigh (SR), from whom it was acquired.
PP 8497:	New to C Wilkinson {Wilkinson's Service}, Lane End (BK); F & T Brown {Brown Bros / Lane End & District Motor Services}, Lane End (BK) 5/29, from whom it was acquired.
PY 7380:	Its origins are unknown; it was previously with RS Harrison, Lane End (BK), from whom it was acquired.
TD 5974:	Its origins are unknown; it was previously with Ideal Coachways, Ruddington (NG), from whom it was acquired.
YV 3567:	New to AR & Mrs EF Thorne {Thorne Bros}, SW2 (LN), from whom it was acquired.

Disposals:

KX 1795:	Stacys Garage, High Wycombe (BK) 1930; unidentified dealer 1931.
KX 3159:	AE Roberts, Llanllechid (CN) 9/31; unidentified owner as a lorry 1934.
KX 3279:	Scammell (dealer?), location unknown 1934
KX 4530:	W Thomson {TT Bus}, Slough (BK) 2/33; London Passenger Transport Board, London SW1 (LN) 2/34; withdrawn 1934; C&P Sales (dealer), London SE15 5/35.
KX 5010:	No known disposal.
PK 1822:	No known disposal.
PP 8497:	No known disposal.
PY 7380:	No known disposal.
TD 5974:	Last licensed 10/30.
YV 3567:	Summerson Bros {The Eden}, West Auckland (DM) 12/31; unidentified operator / dealer 9/36; scrapped 11/38.

F & T BROWN {Brown Bros / Lane End & District Motor Services}

See entries under Jesty & Tudor (above) and Wilkinson (below) for all of Brown's known vehicles.

C WILKINSON {Wilkinson's Service}

PP 2700	Ford TT	10627177	?	B14-	10/24	10/24	6/26
PP 3133	Reo	111492	?	B14-	1/25	1/25	6/27
PP 4281	Ford TT	11274764	?	B14-	6/25	6/25	6/28
PP 6432	Chevrolet X	10052	?	B14F	6/26	6/26	5/29
PP 8497	Chevrolet LM	16643	?	B14F	6/27	6/27	5/29
KX 760	Dennis G	70286	?	B20F	6/28	6/28	5/29

Disposals:

PP 2700:	No known disposal.
PP 3133:	No known disposal.
PP 4281:	No known disposal.
PP 6432:	F & T Brown {Brown Bros / Lane End & District Motor Services}, Lane End (BK) 5/29.
PP 8497:	F & T Brown {Brown Bros / Lane End & District Motor Services}, Lane End (BK) 5/29; Jesty & Tudor {Wycombe & District Bus Co}, 3/30; withdrawn 9/31.
KX 760:	F & T Brown {Brown Bros / Lane End & District Motor Services}, Lane End (BK) 5/29; JRG Dell {Rover Bus Service}, Lye Green (BK) at an unknown date; unidentified owner as a lorry 1933.

ADDITIONAL VEHICLES OF PREDECESSORS TO PIONEER BUS SERVICE Ltd

C HOLLAND {Pioneer}

?	Mercedes	?	Clinkard	B10R	-/--	-/18	-/--
X 8161	Buick	?	?	B14R	-/--	4/19	-/--
?	Ford 1-ton	?	?	?	4/21	4/21	-/--
FX 4922	Buick	?	?	B14R	-/--	-/22	-/--
BL 9861	Delaunay-Belleville	432	(Andrews?)	Ch14	4/22	7/23	8/24
NB 1215	?	?	?	?	-/20	-/--	-/29
?	?	?	?	C---	-/--	by-/28	-/--
NW 8018	Leyland A13	35143	?	B26-	11/24	12/28	10/29
PP 6279	Graham Dodge	A546421	?	B20-	6/26	6/26	-/--
PP 9943	Graham Bros	GB5080	Petty	B20-	3/28	3/28	-/--

Previous histories:

? (Mercedes):	Its origins are unknown, but it was new as a car.
? (Ford):	Its origins are unknown.
? (?):	Its origins are unknown.
X 8161:	Was originally a War Department vehicle.
BL 9861:	Was originally a large private car in 1918; TA Denham, Newbury (BE) c4/22, from whom it was acquired.
FX 4922:	Was originally a War Department vehicle.
NB 1215:	Its origins are unknown.
NW 8018:	New to J Cole & Sons (Leeds) Ltd, Leeds (WR), from whom it was acquired.

Notes:

X 8161:	Was a left-hand drive vehicle.
FX 4922:	Was a left-hand drive vehicle.

Disposals:

? (Mercedes):	No known disposal.
? (Ford):	No known disposal.
? (?):	No known disposal.
X 8161:	No known disposal.
BL 9861:	No known disposal.
FX 4922:	No known disposal.
NB 1215:	No known disposal.
NW 8018:	EG Smith, Liverpool (GLA) at an unknown date; last licensed 12/37.
PP 6279:	No known disposal.
PP 9943:	No known disposal.

Albert E COWLEY {Lower Road Bus Service}   8 South View, COOKHAM RISE (BE)

Cowley commenced a Maidenhead to Cookham Rise (via Boulter's Lock) service in October 1928. This together with Cowley's solitary vehicle was purchased by Thames Valley on 29 October 1931.

RX 3131	Dennis 1½ ton	53685	Willmott	B14F	10/28	10/28	10/31

Notes:

RX 3131:	Fitted with pneumatic tyres 1/30.

The following vehicle marked with an asterisk above, transferred to Thames Valley 10/31 (qv):
RX 3131 (243).

Henry David FARMER {Gem Bus Service}

Harrow Lane, HUGHENDEN VALLEY (BK)
Kiln (or Lily?) Lane, LACEY GREEN (BK) (3/32)
Warrens Row, LACEY GREEN (BK) (1/35)
Aylesbury Road, MONKS RISBOROUGH (BK) (1937)

Farmer had commenced operations in 1923 and had run continuously for 26 years until selling out to Thames Valley on 26 March 1949 for £1,200. The deal included Farmer's service High Wycombe to Princes Risborough via Lacey Green and Hampden. No vehicles were taken into Thames Valley stock.

PP 9413	Willys Overland	BMT6481	?	B14-	12/27	12/27	-/--
SK 1505	Reo Sprinter	FA2809	?	B14-	11/28	by6/30	-/38
CH 9864	Reo FB (Gold Crown)	FB?	?	C---	4/31	-/--	-/--
TM 8402	Reo Pullman	GE186	?	B20F	4/31	c-/35	-/40
ADF 797	Dodge PLB	1052	REAL	B20F	8/35	by8/39	9/49
FV 3795	Leyland KP3	1459	EEC	C20R	7/33	2/45	-/52
DW 7353	Reo	?	?	-24F	2/31	by6/47	by9/49
CRR 820	Leyland KPZ2	7002	Brush	C20F	1/37	8/49	-/--

Previous histories:

CH 9864: New to Monk, Derby (DE), from whom it was acquired.

DW 7353: New to WA Pugh, Newport (MH) (as -20F); DJ Davies {Wheatsheaf Motors}, Merthyr Tydfil (GG) at an unknown date; TJ Headington, Weston-Super-Mare (SO) by 1938, from whom it was acquired.

FV 3795: New to W Marshall & Sons (Blackpool) Ltd, Blackpool (LA); Walton & Helliwell Ltd, Mytholmroyd (WR) 6/42, from whom it was acquired.

SK 1505: New to W Black, Watten (CS), from whom it was acquired.

TM 8402: New to an unidentified owner (as B26F); unidentified dealer, Norwich at an unknown date; AM Bonham {The Milton Bus Service}, Milton Ernest (BD) 1932; Eastern National Omnibus Co Ltd, Chelmsford (EX) 3472 9/33 [withdrawn 5/35], from whom it was acquired.

ADF 797: New to ATW Ayland, Westbury-on-Severn (GL), from whom it was acquired.

CRR 820: New to Barton Transport Ltd, Chilwell (NG) 285; withdrawn 3/48; Nudd Bros & Lockyer (dealer), Kegworth 9/48; NJ & KB Kilby, London N18 (LN) 9/48, from whom it was acquired.

Disposals:

CH 9864: No known disposal.

DW 7353: No known disposal.

FV 3795: Last licensed 1952 – no further operator.

PP 9413: No known disposal.

SK 1505: Horne Products Ltd (dealer), London NW10 1938; scrapped 7/38.

TM 8402: Greenslade's Tours Ltd, Exeter (DN) 1940; withdrawn 1940 and scrapped.

ADF 797: Last licensed 9/49 – no further operator.

CRR 820: HE Edwards, West Drayton at an unknown date; last licensed 6/59.

James H HARRIS {Pixey Bus / Pixey Omnibus Service}

Long Lane, FIFIELD (BE)

The Pixey Bus operation was a serious competitor to Thames Valley on routes between Maidenhead and Windsor. In addition, Windsor local services were run and a licence was held for express workings between Maidenhead and Ascot Races. The business (including seven vehicles) was purchased on 7 April 1933.

?	Renault	?	?	B14F	by7/22	by7/22	-/--
RX 1162	Chevrolet LM	17081	?	B14F	11/27	11/27	*
NK 8073	Chevrolet B	?	?	B14-	6/24	-/--	-/--
RM 3889	Chevrolet	15372	?	B14-	5/27	-/--	*
TM 1258	Chevrolet	?	?	B14F	7/27	-/--	*
TW 8979	Chevrolet LM	15202	?	B14-	5/27	-/--	*
VF 3004	Chevrolet LO	40895	Waveney	B14F	9/27	-/--	*
EF 3469	Chevrolet LM	16050	Strachan & Brown	B14-	4/27	-/30	*
RT 4952	Chevrolet LP	46367	?	B14F	10/28	-/30	*

Previous histories:

Unidentified Renault: Was of unknown origin.

EF 3469: New to Eastern Express Motors Ltd, West Hartlepool (DM) 25; United Automobile Services Ltd, York (YK) H39 1/30; H Lane & Co Ltd (dealer), London SW10 8/30, from whom it was acquired.

NK 8073: Was of unknown origin.

RM 3889:	New to J Wood, Heads Nook (CU), from whom it was acquired.								

RM 3889:   New to J Wood, Heads Nook (CU), from whom it was acquired.
RT 4952:   New to D Kerridge, Needham Market (EK); Eastern Counties Road Car Co Ltd, Ipswich (EK) 41 6/30; Child & Pullen (dealer), Ipswich 9/30; J Ross (dealer), London E15 10/30; H Lane & Co Ltd (dealer), London SW10 10/30, from whom it was acquired.
TM 1258:   New to EJ Cooper, Elstow (BD), from whom it was acquired.
TW 8979:   New to EJ Gray, London E11 (GLN), from whom it was acquired.
VF 3004:   New to United Automobile Services Ltd, York (YK) H19, from whom it was acquired.

Notes:
TW 8979:   Was fitted with a bus body, but it is not known whether by Harris or its previous owner.
VF 3004:   Was reduced to chassis only form by 4/33.

Disposals:
? (Renault): No known disposal.
NK 8073:   No known disposal.
RM 3889:   Thames Valley Traction Co Ltd 4/33 (qv).

The following vehicles marked with an asterisk above, transferred to Thames Valley 5/36 (qv):
EF 3469, RM 3889, RT 4952, RX 1162, TM 1258, TW 8978, VF 3004 (chassis only).

LEDBURY TRANSPORT Co Ltd {Thackray's Way}   Westbourne Grove, LONDON W11 (LN)

Robert Thackray operated buses in London W11 from January 1925 until he sold out to London Public Omnibus Co Ltd in October 1927.

He recommenced in 1929 forming Ledbury Transport Co Ltd and started a Reading to London (via Maidenhead and Slough) service in direct competition to Thames Valley in September 1929. The following month saw Newbury to Reading link introduced. The livery was dark red and cream, very similar to that of Thames Valley. The Pride of the Valley business of H Cordery was taken over in December 1929 which provided Ledbury Transport with a network of services to the south of Reading together with a garage in Spencers Wood. This was followed by the acquisition of the EM Hope business which gave Ledbury some coaching and excursions. A fire however at the Spencers Wood garage in April 1930 proved to be a major setback with the building and four vehicles being destroyed.

In order to obtain more licences in Reading, the company offered to build a coach station which duly materialised at Crown Colonnade, Cemetery Junction, east of the town centre. The former Pride of the Valley licences were surrendered and a new service to London (via Wokingham, Bracknell, Ascot and Staines) was commenced. This however was curtailed in 1931 when the Traffic Commissioners took the decision not to licence this service.

Fleet numbers (even numbers only) were not applied until 8/32, following the arrival of GP 5139-45.

Ledbury Transport had been seeking a buyer for several years but Thames Valley had shown little interest until Birch Bros Ltd prepared an offer. As a result of this, Tilling Transport Ltd stepped in and purchased the business (together with the Crown Colonnade station) for £68,000 in December 1935, placing it under Thames Valley control in the following month.

Thames Valley based the business at Crown Colonnade and maintained it as a separate operation largely in order to protect the lucrative Reading to London express service licences.

Ledbury Transport Co Ltd was wound up on 26 July 1950 with the vehicles in the fleet at that time transferring back to the main Thames Valley fleet.

16	UV 7962	Gilford 166SD	10930	Duple	1736	C26D	9/29	9/29	4/37
18	UV 7963	Gilford 166SD	11030	Duple	1732	C26D	9/29	9/29	4/37
20	UV 7964	Gilford 166SD	11034	Duple	1733	C26D	9/29	9/29	4/37
22	UV 7965	Gilford 166SD	11032	Duple	1731	C26D	9/29	9/29	4/37
24	UV 7966	Gilford 166SD	11031	Duple	1734	C26D	9/29	9/29	4/37
26	UV 7967	Gilford 166SD	10978	Duple	1735	C26D	9/29	9/29	4/37
38	UW 2615	Gilford 166SD	11046	Duple	1754	C26D	10/29	10/29	9/36
40	UW 2616	Gilford 166SD	10931	Duple	1610	C26D	10/29	10/29	4/37
48	UW 6646	Gilford 166SD	11075	Duple	1782	C26D	11/29	11/29	4/37
	HO 6335	Thornycroft BOA	10920	Vickers		B26D	9/24	12/29	9/30
	MO 7526	Chevrolet 1 ton	?	?		B14F	4/26	12/29	----
	MO 7924	Talbot 25/50 hp	10036	Andrews		Ch14	5/26	12/29	----
	MO 9039	Thornycroft A1 Long	12840	Vickers		B20F	1/27	12/29	4/30

	Reg	Chassis	No	Body		Code			
	OT 1339	Thornycroft LB	12927	NCME		B28D	1/27	12/29	4/30
	RX 1456	Chevrolet LM 6-wheel	18393	?		B20F	3/28	12/29	9/30
	RX 1590	Chevrolet LM 4-wheel	17490	?		B14F	2/28	12/29	9/30
28	UW 7597	Gilford 166SD	11118	Duple	1785	C26D	12/29	12/29	4/37
30	UW 7598	Gilford 166SD	11122	Duple	1783	C26D	12/29	12/29	4/37
32	UW 7599	Gilford 166SD	11067	Duple	1784	C26D	12/29	12/29	4/37
34	UW 7600	Gilford 166SD	11068	Duple	1786	C26D	12/29	12/29	4/37
36	UW 7601	Gilford 166SD	11074	Duple	1787	C26D	12/29	12/29	4/37
	GC 1866	Gilford 168SD	11160	Duple	1781	C26D	1/30	1/30	4/30
42	GC 1867	Gilford 168SD	11161	Duple	1780	C26D	1/30	1/30	10/36
	GC 1868	Gilford 168SD	11162	Duple	1845	C26D	2/30	2/30	4/30
	GC 1869	Gilford 168SD	11163	Duple	1797	C26D	2/30	2/30	4/30
44	GC 1870	Gilford 168SD	11164	Duple	1792	C26D	2/30	2/30	11/37
46	GC 1871	Gilford 168SD	11165	Duple	1793	C26D	2/30	2/30	1/38
	?	GMC	?	?		Ch20	c-/24	4/30	10/31
50	GF 6676	Gilford 168SD	11222	Duple	1860	C26D	4/30	4/30	1/38
52	GF 6677	Gilford 168SD	11223	Duple	1861	C26D	4/30	4/30	6/37
54	GF 6678	Gilford 168SD	11224	Duple	1862	C26D	4/30	4/30	1/38
56	GF 6679	Gilford 168SD	11225	Duple	1863	C26D	4/30	4/30	10/37
60	GJ 1331	Gilford 168SD	11176	Duple	1788	C26D	5/30	5/30	1/38
62	GJ 1332	Gilford 168SD	11177	Duple	1790	C26D	5/30	5/30	by10/39
58	GJ 8024	Gilford 168SD	11226	Duple	1846	C26D	6/30	5/30	1/38
	DP 3590	Dennis 1½ ton	?	Vincent		Ch20	3/21	6/30	9/30
	DP ?	Lancia Tetraiota	?	Vincent		C20D	-/25	6/30	----
	DP 7669	Delahaye 83/59	24630	Vincent		Ch20	6/26	6/30	9/31
	RD 1886	Gilford 168OT	11464	Vincent		C30D	6/30	6/30	----
	VM 8638	Gilford 166SD	?	Lewis & Crabtree		C26-	4/29	6/30	5/31
2	GP 5139	Gilford 168OT	11957	Wycombe		C26F	7/31	8/32	3/40
4	GP 5140	Gilford 168OT	11958	Wycombe		C26F	7/31	8/32	3/40
6	GP 5141	Gilford 168OT	11959	Wycombe		C26F	7/31	8/32	3/40
8	GP 5142	Gilford 168OT	11960	Wycombe		C26F	7/31	8/32	3/40
10	GP 5143	Gilford 168OT	11961	Wycombe		C26F	7/31	8/32	3/40
12	GP 5144	Gilford 168OT	11962	Wycombe		C26F	7/31	8/32	3/40
14	GP 5145	Gilford 168OT	11963	Wycombe		C26F	7/31	8/32	3/40

Previous histories:

Unidentified GMC: First recorded with AE Ireland {Alexander Coaches}, Reading (BE), from whom it was acquired.

DP ?: New to EM Hope, Reading (BE), from whom it was acquired.

DP 3590: New to EM Hope, Reading (BE), from whom it was acquired.

DP 7669: New to EM Hope, Reading (BE), from whom it was acquired.

GP 5139 (2): New to Main Lines Ltd, London SW1 (LN) 16, from whom it was acquired.

GP 5140 (4): New to Main Lines Ltd, London SW1 (LN) 17, from whom it was acquired.

GP 5141 (6): New to Main Lines Ltd, London SW1 (LN) 18, from whom it was acquired.

GP 5142 (8): New to Main Lines Ltd, London SW1 (LN) 19, from whom it was acquired.

GP 5143 (10): New to Main Lines Ltd, London SW1 (LN) 20, from whom it was acquired.

GP 5144 (12): New to Main Lines Ltd, London SW1 (LN) 21, from whom it was acquired.

GP 5145 (14): New to Main Lines Ltd, London SW1 (LN) 22, from whom it was acquired.

HO 6335: New as a demonstrator with John I Thornycroft Ltd (dealer), Basingstoke; H Cordery {Pride of the Valley}, Spencers Wood (BE) 5/27, from whom it was acquired.

MO 7526: New to H Cordery {Pride of the Valley}, Spencers Wood (BE), from whom it was acquired.

MO 7924: New to JC Durnford {C Durnford & Sons}, Newbury (BE); H Cordery {Pride of the Valley}, Spencers Wood (BE) c4/29 [last licensed 9/29], from whom it was acquired.

MO 9039: New to H Cordery {Pride of the Valley}, Spencers Wood (BE), from whom it was acquired.

OT 1339: New as a demonstrator with John I Thornycroft Ltd (dealer), Basingstoke (with a Hall Lewis B30R body); rebodied NCME B28D by 11/27; H Cordery {Pride of the Valley}, Spencers Wood (BE) 11/27, from whom it was acquired.

RX 1456: New to H Cordery {Pride of the Valley}, Spencers Wood (BE), from whom it was acquired.

RX 1590: New to H Cordery {Pride of the Valley}, Spencers Wood (BE), from whom it was acquired.

RD 1886: New to CR Tanton {Tanton's Coaches}, Reading (BE), from whom it was acquired.

VM 8638: New to an unidentified Manchester area operator; CR Tanton {Tanton's Coaches}, Reading (BE) at an unknown date, from whom it was acquired.

Notes:

GMC: Converted to a breakdown tender and transferred to the service fleet from 10/31.

DP ?: Not operated by Ledbury Transport Co Ltd.

DP 7669: Converted to a breakdown tender and transferred to the service fleet 10/31 (presumably operated on trade plates as it was last licensed 9/31).

GC 1866: Destroyed by fire at Cordery's Garage, Spencers Wood 4/30.

GC 1868-1869: Destroyed by fire at Cordery's Garage, Spencers Wood 4/30.

GJ 1332 (62): Cannibalised for spares by 10/39.

HO 6335: Used as a painter's store at the Crown Colonnade Garage, Reading from 9/30 until 5/33.

MO 7526: Not operated by Ledbury Transport Co Ltd.

MO 7924: Not operated by Ledbury Transport Co Ltd.

MO 9039: Destroyed by fire at Cordery's Garage, Spencers Wood 4/30.

OT 1339: Damaged by fire at Cordery's Garage, Spencers Wood 4/30, but subsequently repaired.

RX 1456: Converted to a lorry and transferred to the service fleet from 9/30; its body used as a changing room at Ford's Farm, Calcot.

RD 1886: Not operated by Ledbury Transport Co Ltd.

Disposals:

GMC: Unidentified dealer for scrap 4/33.

DP ?: A & PA Andrews & Son {A Andrews & Son / Favourite Coaches}, Newbury (BE) 5/31 (qv).

DP 3590: Unidentified owner, Berkshire 12/30.

DP 7669: H Goodey (dealer), Twyford for scrap 6/35.

GC 1866: Chassis salvaged for use as a farm trailer at Thackray's Farm, Calcot; registration voided 3/34.

GC 1867 (42): W & G Chandler, Wantage (BE) 10/36; last licensed 9/39.

GC 1868: Chassis salvaged for use as a farm trailer at Thackray's Farm, Calcot; registration voided 3/34.

GC 1869: Chassis salvaged for use as a farm trailer at Thackray's Farm, Calcot; registration voided 3/34.

GC 1870 (44): GJ Neville, Kempsford (GL) by 10/38; withdrawn 1939; possibly to War Department (GOV) at an unknown date; PR Hooper, Castle Eaton (WI) at an unknown date; AW Giles {Cricklade Motor Services}, Cricklade (WI) 11/44; last licensed 3/45.

GC 1871 (46): Horne Products (dealer), London NW10 for scrap 1/38.

GF 6676 (50): Horne Products (dealer), London NW10 for scrap 1/38.

GF 6677 (52): RA Ford {A Ford & Son}, Silchester (HA) 6/37; Newbury & District Motor Services Ltd for spares 7/40 (qv).

GF 6678 (54): FC Killick, Dallington (ES) 1/38.

GF 6679 (56): Showman 7/39.

GJ 1331 (60): Horne Products (dealer), London NW10 1/38; Stephens, Tredegar (MH); Hereford Motor Co Ltd, Hereford (HR) 14 by 6/42 (rebuilt as a Gilford 168OT); showman by 1953.

GJ 1332 (62): Unidentified operator / dealer 3/40; Air Raid Precautions (ARP) 1940; unidentified dealer for scrap, probably in a damaged condition 4/40.

GJ 8024 (58): Horne Products (dealer), London NW10 for scrap 1/38.

GP 5139 (2): H Lane & Co Ltd (dealer), London SW10 3/40; National Fire Service (GOV) by 2/46.

GP 5140 (4): H Lane & Co Ltd (dealer), London SW10 3/40; Trower Bros, London SW8 (LN) 9/40; P Crouch & Son Ltd {Blue Bus}, Guildford (SR) c7/43; withdrawn by 4/45.

GP 5141 (6): H Lane & Co Ltd (dealer), London SW10 3/40; EA Seager {Enterprise Tours}, Sherborne (DT) 7/40; fitted with an Alexander DP27F body by 10/53; AW Latham {Enterprise Coaches}, Kenton (MX) 7/54; withdrawn 11/54; showman at an unknown date.

GP 5142 (8): H Lane & Co Ltd (dealer), London SW10 3/40; Trower Bros, London SW8 (LN) 9/40; P Crouch & Son Ltd {Blue Bus}, Guildford (SR) c7/43 (used 1943-5 for transporting Prisoners of War); withdrawn by 4/45; Keen Brickworks, Worplesden as a caravan 7/63; later used as a shed.

GP 5143 (10): H Lane & Co Ltd (dealer), London SW10 3/40; CAJ Scarrott {Luxury Coaches}, Stow-on-the-Wold (GL) by 1/43; withdrawn at an unknown date and scrapped.

GP 5144 (12): H Lane & Co Ltd (dealer), London SW10 3/40; JA Watson {Watson's Coaches}, Gunnislake (CO) c1940; SK Hill {Hill's Services}, Stibb Cross (DN) 1942 (as C32F); withdrawn 1/51 and scrapped.

GP 5145 (14): H Lane & Co Ltd (dealer), London SW10 3/40; EA Seager {Enterprise Tours}, Sherborne (DT) 7/40; withdrawn 4/50 and scrapped.

HO 6335: Unidentified operator / dealer, Middlesex 5/33.

MO 7526: No known disposal.

MO 7924: No known disposal.

MO 9039: No known disposal.

OT 1339: Unidentified owners, Gloucestershire at an unknown date and Glamorgan 4/34; scrapped 12/37.

RX 1456: WG Cook, Tilehurst (GBE) at an unknown date; last licensed 12/32.

RX 1590: B Smith, Wantage (GBE) at an unknown date; last licensed 9/33.

RD 1886: A & PA Andrews & Son {A Andrews & Son / Favourite Coaches}, Newbury (BE) 5/31 (qv).

UV 7962 (16): FW Buckmaster, Leighton Buzzard (BD) 4/37; withdrawn 4/39 and scrapped.

UV 7963 (18): Horne Products Ltd (dealer), London NW10 4/37.

UV 7964 (20): Horne Products Ltd (dealer), London NW10 4/37.

UV 7965 (22): PA Skinner {Percival's Motors}, Cambridge (CM) 6/37; moved to Oxford (OX) 7/38; last licensed 12/41.

UV 7966 (24): OA Slatter, Long Hanborough (OX) 1/39; Allday (dealer), Northampton 4/41; showman by 1944.

UV 7967 (26): Horne Products Ltd (dealer), London NW10 4/37.

UW 2615 (38): BC & CV Lovick {Lovick Motors}, Crowthorne (BE) 12/36; Hards & Taylor {Lovick Motors}, Crowthorne (BE) 4/49; Lovick Motors Ltd, Crowthorne (BE) 7/50; withdrawn 4/52.

UW 2616 (40): H Crapper, Oxford (OX) 6/37.

UW 6646 (48): Horne Products Ltd (dealer), London NW10 4/37; HJ Sargeant {East Grinstead Motor Coaches}, East Grinstead (ES) 7/37; withdrawn 7/39; Hall, London NW8 9/51; scrapped 10/60.

UW 7597 (28): Horne Products Ltd (dealer), London NW10 for scrap 4/37.

UW 7598 (30): Horne Products Ltd (dealer), London NW10 for scrap 4/37.

UW 7599 (32): Horne Products Ltd (dealer), London NW10 4/37; GC Cook (dealer), Lambeth for scrap 6/37.

UW 7600 (34): Horne Products Ltd (dealer), London NW10 for scrap 4/37.

UW 7601 (36): Horne Products Ltd (dealer), London NW10 for scrap 4/37.

VM 8638: A & PA Andrews & Son {A Andrews & Son / Favourite Coaches}, Newbury (BE) 5/31 (qv).

No vehicles were purchased for the Ledbury fleet after 1932. Instead, vehicles were transferred from the main Thames Valley fleet for varying periods. Although nominally Ledbury vehicles, these were fully integrated with the rest of the Thames Valley fleet and operated on Thames Valley services. Although these vehicles displayed Ledbury legal lettering (and carried Ledbury fleet numbers), the Ledbury operation was separate on paper only. Full details of these vehicles can be found in the Thames Valley section.

22	JB 8346	Leyland TS7	9399	Brush			DP32R	3/36	12/37	5/38
24	JB 8348	Leyland TS7	9401	Brush			B32R	3/36	12/37	7/50
26	JB 8349	Leyland TS7	9402	Brush			B32R	3/36	12/37	7/50
28	JB 8350	Leyland TS7	9403	Brush			B32R	3/36	12/37	7/50
16	KX 8481	Karrier Coaster	35189	Weymann	W905		B24F	4/32	12/37	----
20	RD 6270	Thornycroft Ardent FE	24776	?			B26F	12/34	12/37	10/38
18	RX 188	Thornycroft A2 Long	14060A	Challands Ross			B20F	5/27	12/37	c1/38
52	VX 6549	Reo Pullman	GE193	?			B20F	7/30	12/37	5/38
30	ABL 751	Leyland TS7	12599	ECW		4870	B32R	3/37	12/37	7/50
32	ABL 752	Leyland TS7	12600	ECW		4871	B32R	3/37	12/37	7/50
34	ABL 753	Leyland TS7	12601	ECW		4872	B32R	3/37	12/37	7/50
36	ABL 754	Leyland TS7	12602	ECW		4873	B32R	3/37	12/37	7/50
40	ABL 755	Leyland TS7	12603	ECW		4874	B32R	3/37	12/37	7/50
44	ABL 756	Leyland TS7	12604	ECW		4875	B32R	3/37	12/37	7/50
48	ABL 761	Leyland TS7	12609	ECW		4880	B32R	3/37	12/37	7/50
50	KX 6094	AEC Regal	662599	Petty			C32F	12/30	3/38	10/38
46	KX 7157	AEC Regal	662644	Petty			C32F	6/31	3/38	8/38
58	MT 1330	AEC Reliance	660002	Hall Lewis			B31D	12/28	3/38	10/38
54	MY 639	AEC Reliance	660311	Short			B32F	7/29	3/38	10/38
60	UR 3767	AEC Reliance	660239	Craven			C31R	7/29	3/38	10/38
56	UV 4080	Thornycroft BC	18816	Vickers			B26R	7/29	3/38	10/38
18	JB 7494	Leyland TS7	8543	Brush			B32R	12/35	5/38	7/50
20	RX 5577	Leyland LT1	50776	Brush			B32R	2/30	11/38	3/50
22	RX 5578	Leyland LT1	50777	Brush			B32R	2/30	11/38	2/50
38	RX 5579	Leyland LT1	50778	Brush			B32R	2/30	11/38	3/50
42	RX 5580	Leyland LT1	50779	Brush			B32R	2/30	11/38	2/50
46	RX 6245	Leyland LT2	51208	Brush			DP32R	7/30	11/38	7/50
50	RX 6246	Leyland LT2	51209	Brush			DP32R	7/30	11/38	4/50
52	RX 6247	Leyland LT2	51210	Brush			DP32R	7/30	11/38	7/50
54	RX 6248	Leyland LT2	51211	Brush			DP32R	7/30	11/38	7/50
2	RX 5571	Leyland LT1	50770	Brush			B32R	2/30	4/40	2/50
4	RX 5572	Leyland LT1	50771	Brush			B32R	2/30	4/40	2/50
6	RX 5573	Leyland LT1	50772	Brush			B32R	2/30	4/40	2/50
8	RX 5574	Leyland LT1	50773	Brush			B32R	2/30	4/40	2/50
10	RX 5575	Leyland LT1	50774	Brush			B32R	2/30	4/40	7/50

12	RX 5576	Leyland LT1	50775	Brush		B32R	2/30	4/40	2/50
14	RX 6249	Leyland LT2	51212	Brush		DP32R	7/30	4/40	7/50
62	RX 6250	Leyland TS3	61065	Brush		C28D	8/30	4/40	7/40

Reginald CLAYTON {Marlow & District Motor Services}   **Heights Lodge, Henley Road, MARLOW (BK)**
MARLOW & DISTRICT MOTOR SERVICES Ltd (10/25)   **8 Glade Road, MARLOW (BK)** (10/25)
83 Lower Thorn Street, READING (BE) (4/32)

Marlow & District Motor Services Ltd was formed on 28 March 1925 by Reginald Clayton, a director of Karrier Motors of Huddersfield. Clayton who lived near Marlow, identified an opportunity to run bus services in the area and also provide a test bed for Karrier vehicles and engines. Routes from Marlow to High Wycombe, Maidenhead and Henley were started, and within a year, the fleet had expanded to ten vehicles. Vehicles were initially painted brown and later chocolate and cream in a style very similar to the GWR livery. Ernest Jeffries, a driver, was promoted to manage the business and a garage was constructed in Victoria Road, Marlow. Discussions with Thames Valley on a possible merger of operations commenced in June 1928 and an agreement was struck for the sale of Marlow & District's shares with effect from 1 January 1929. Reginald Clayton received Thames Valley shares to the value of £7,800 and was made a director. Ernest Jeffries continued to manage Marlow & District as a separate entity with its own distinct identity. The Marlow to High Wycombe service operated by FH Crook, was acquired in October 1932 for £400. It was decided to wind up the Marlow & District company with the operations being absorbed into the main Thames Valley fleet from 13 May 1933.

	PP 3343	Karrier Z	?	?		B14F	2/25	2/25	by6/29
	PP 3344	Karrier Z	30144	?		B14F	2/25	2/25	12/29
	PP 3649	Karrier CY	20749	?		B20F	4/25	4/25	12/29
	PP 3940	Karrier Z	30100	?		Ch14	5/25	5/25	by6/31
6	PP 4107	Karrier CY	20847	?		B20F	5/25	5/25	*
	PP 4308	Karrier CY	20864	?		B20F	6/25	6/25	12/29
3	PP 4388	Karrier WJ	?	?		Ch18	6/25	6/25	*
	PP 4837	Karrier CY	20912	?		B20F	9/25	9/25	12/29
	PP 4884	Karrier CY	20910	?		B20F	9/25	9/25	12/29
	PP 4885	Karrier CY	20738	?		B20F	9/25	9/25	12/29
4	PP 5930	Morris T	9258T	Morris		B14F	4/26	4/26	*
	PP 6302	Karrier CL4	?	?		B26F	5/26	5/26	*
2	PP 8371	Karrier CL4	35011	?		B20F	5/27	5/27	*
5	RF 1625	Karrier CL4	?	Lawton		B28F	3/26	4/28	*
	RF 1708	Karrier CL4	?	Lawton		B28F	3/26	4/28	*
9	KX 3638	Karrier CL4	35073	Ramsden		B24F	10/29	10/29	*
7	KX 3869	Karrier CL4	35072	Ramsden		B24F	12/29	12/29	*
8	KX 3870	Karrier CL4	35070	Ramsden		B24F	12/29	12/29	*
11	KX 3898	Karrier CL4	35076	Ramsden		B24F	12/29	12/29	*
12	KX 3899	Karrier CL4	35075	Ramsden		B24F	12/29	12/29	*
6	KX 3900	Karrier CL4	35069	Ramsden		B24F	12/29	12/29	*
10	KX 3901	Karrier CL4	35077	Ramsden		B24F	12/29	12/29	*
3	YW 1721	Maudslay ML3B	4177	Buckingham		C26D	5/28	3/31	*
15	KX 8481	Karrier Coaster	35189	Weymann	W905	B24F	4/32	4/32	*
14	KX 8482	Karrier Coaster	35190	Weymann	W904	B24F	4/32	4/32	*

Previous histories:

RF 1625 (5): New to R Mallinson {Stafford Transport Co}, Stafford (ST); Karrier Motors Ltd (dealer), Huddersfield 3/28, from whom it was acquired.

RF 1708: New to R Mallinson {Stafford Transport Co}, Stafford (ST); Karrier Motors Ltd (dealer), Huddersfield 3/28, from whom it was acquired.

YW 1721: New to Great Western Railway, London W2 (LN) 1229; Thames Valley Traction Co Ltd 1/31, from whom it was acquired.

Notes:

Thames Valley MO 6843 (99) was hired to Marlow & District c4/32 whilst vehicles were being overhauled.

PP 4388 (3): Fitted with an experimental Tylor engine; its chassis number has been recorded as 50/000WJ, but this is possibly the engine number; renumbered 1 c4/32.

PP 5930 (4): Renumbered 2 c4/32.

RF 1625: Had been reduced to a chassis only by 5/33.

Disposals:

> PP 3343-3344: No known disposals.
> PP 3649:   No known disposal.
> PP 3940:   No known disposal.
> PP 4308:   No known disposal.
> PP 4837:   No known disposal.
> PP 4884-4885: No known disposals.

The following vehicles marked with an asterisk above, transferred to Thames Valley 5/33 (qv):

> KX 3638 (9), KX 3869 (7), KX 3870 (8), KX 3898 (11), KX 3899 (12), KX 3900 (6), KX 3901 (10), KX 8481
> (15), KX 8482 (14), PP 4107 (withdrawn), PP 4388 (1), PP 5930 (2), PP 6302 (withdrawn); PP
> 8371 (withdrawn), RF 1625 (as a chassis only), RF 1708 (withdrawn), YW 1721 (3).

Two additional vehicles were transferred from the main Thames Valley fleet for a period prior to 5/33. Full details of
these vehicles can be found in the Thames Valley section.

4	MO 9316	TSM B9A	5272	Brush	225	B35R	6/27	4/32	5/33
5	MO 9327	TSM B9A	5283	Brush	231	B35R	6/27	4/32	5/33

FJ SUGG {Penn Bus Co}   St John's Wood Road, TYLERS GREEN (BK)

to PENN BUS Co Ltd (4/31)

Negotiations between Fred Sugg, the London Passenger Transport Board and Thames Valley came to fruition in
June 1935, pre-empting the prospect of a compulsory takeover by LPTB as some of the routes fell within their
designated area. The price paid by Thanes Valley was £29,000 but this was offset by LPTB subsequently paying
£13,750 for the routes in their area plus seven vehicles and the Tylers Green garage. The takeover date was 1
August 1935 and all 85 employees were retained by the purchasers.

	BH 0311	Austin 2 ton	?	Coles		B20R	1/20	1/20	c9/26
	BH 5951	Ford T	?	Coles		B14R	7/20	7/20	c8/26
	BH 9409	Ford T	5412167	Coles		B14R	8/22	8/22	c2/27
	BH 9991	Ford T	6488954	Coles		B14R	3/23	3/23	c2/27
	PP 820	Ford T	7900142	?		B14-	9/23	9/23	-/--
	PP 1119	Ford T	7943334	?		B14-	12/23	12/23	-/--
1	PP 1194	Dennis 2½ ton	?	Strachan & Brown		B26R	1/24	1/24	by8/35
2	PP 2245	Dennis 2½ ton	30773	Strachan & Brown		B26R	7/24	7/24	*
4	PP 3005	Dennis 2½ ton	30924	Strachan & Brown		B26R	12/24	12/24	by8/35
3	PP 3006	Dennis 2½ ton	30922	Strachan & Brown		B26R	12/24	12/24	by8/35
5	PP 3811	Dennis 2½ ton	31023	Strachan & Brown		B26R	4/25	4/25	by8/35
6	PP 4616	Dennis 1½ ton	50033	Strachan & Brown		B14R	7/25	7/25	3/29
7	PP 4875	Dennis 2½ ton	31245	Strachan & Brown		B26R	9/25	9/25	*
8	PP 5166	Dennis 2½ ton	31296	Strachan & Brown		B26R	12/25	12/25	*
9	PP 6811	Dennis 2½ ton	31572	Strachan & Brown		B26R	8/26	8/26	by8/35
10	PP 6918	Chevrolet X	10698	?Coles?		B14F	9/26	9/26	by8/35
11	PP 7563	Chevrolet LM	15131	Coles		B14R	2/27	2/27	c1/30
12	PP 7564	Chevrolet LM	15170	Coles		B14R	2/27	2/27	by8/35
15	PP 8721	Dennis 2½ ton	45522	Strachan & Brown		B26F	7/27	7/27	by8/35
14	PP 9263	Dennis 2½ ton	31886	Strachan & Brown		B26F	10/27	10/27	10/29
16	PP 9657	Leyland LSC1	46414	Strachan & Brown		B32F	1/28	1/28	*
17	KX 498	Dennis 2½ ton	45542	Strachan & Brown		B26F	5/28	5/28	*
18	KX 1312	Dennis 2½ ton	45551	Strachan & Brown		B26F	10/28	10/28	*
19	KX 1541	Dennis E	17614	Strachan		B32R	12/28	12/28	*
20	KX 1734	Dennis 2½ ton	45558	Strachan		B26F	1/29	1/29	*
21	KX 3484	Gilford 166OT	11070	Wycombe		B32F	9/29	9/29	*
22	UV 7778	Gilford 166OT	11015	Wycombe		B32F	8/29	1/30	*
23	KX 5733	Gilford 168OT	11312	Wycombe		B32F	9/30	9/30	*
24	KX 7382	Gilford 168OT	11967	Wycombe		B32F	7/31	7/31	*
25	KX 7843	Gilford 168OT	12008	Wycombe		C32F	12/31	12/31	*
26	KX 8092	Dennis Lancet	170008	Wycombe		B32F	1/32	1/32	*
27	KX 8744	Dennis Lancet	170116	Dennis		B32R	6/32	6/32	*
28	ABH 350	Dennis Lancet	170390	Dennis		B32F	5/33	5/33	*
29	APP 271	Dennis Lancet	170657	Dennis		C32F	4/34	4/34	*
30	APP 272	Dennis Lancet	170652	Dennis		B32F	4/34	4/34	*
31	APP 273	Dennis Ace	200003	Dennis		B20F	4/34	4/34	*

32	BBH 755	Dennis Mace	240028	Dennis	B26C	1/35	12/34	*
33	BKX 431	Dennis Lancet	170827	Dennis	C32C	3/35	3/35	*
34	BKX 696	Dennis Lancet	170905	Dennis	C32C	5/35	4/35	*
35	BKX 898	Dennis Lancet	170904	Dennis	C32C	5/35	5/35	*

Previous history:

UV 7778 (22): New as a demonstrator with Gilford Motor Co Ltd, Upper Holloway, from whom it was acquired.

Notes:

KX 498 (17): Reseated to B25F 1/34.

KX 1312 (18): Reseated to B25F at an unknown date.

PP 1194 (1): Rebodied Wycombe B26F 1927.

PP 2245 (2): Rebodied Wycombe B26F 1928/9.

PP 3005 (4): Body also recorded as Dennis B25R.

PP 3006 (3): Body also recorded as Dennis B25R.

PP 3811 (5): Rebodied Wycombe B26F at an unknown date.

PP 4875 (7): Rebodied Wycombe B26F 8/27.

PP 5166 (8): Rebodied Wycombe B26F 9/30.

PP 6811 (9): Probably rebodied Wycombe B26R at an unknown date.

PP 8721 (15): Rebodied Strachan & Brown B26F after being crushed by a tree 1/28.

PP 7563-7564 (11-12): Fitted with the bodies from BH 9409 and BH 9991 (order unknown).

Disposals:

BH 0311: No known disposal.

BH 5951: No known disposal.

BH 9409: No known disposal (body to PP 7563 or PP 7564).

BH 9991: No known disposal (body to PP 7563 or PP 7564).

PP 820: No known disposal.

PP 1119: No known disposal.

PP 1194 (1): No known disposal.

PP 3005 (4): No known disposal.

PP 3006 (3): No known disposal.

PP 3811 (5): No known disposal.

PP 4616 (6): P Crouch & Son {Blue Bus Service}, Guildford (SR) 3/29.

PP 6811 (9): No known disposal.

PP 6918 (10): No known disposal.

PP 7563-7564 (11-12): No known disposals.

PP 8721 (15): No known disposal.

PP 9263 (14): Unidentified owner (G??) 10/29.

The following vehicles marked with an asterisk above, transferred to Thames Valley 8/35 (including those subsequently transferred to London Passenger Transport Board - (qv)):

KX 498 (281), KX 1312 (282), KX 1541, KX 1734 (283), KX 3484 (284), KX 5733 (285), KX 7382 (286), KX 7843, KX 8092 (287), KX 8744 (288), PP 2245, PP 4875 (278), PP 5166 (279), PP 9657 (280), UV 7778, ABH 350, APP 271 (289), APP 272 (290), APP 273 (291), BBH 755, BKX 431 (292), BKX 696, BKX 898 (293).

Cyril Apsley RANGER   **17 York Road, MAIDENHEAD (BE)**

Alfred William SIMMONDS   **The Pines, Upper Road, SLOUGH (BK)**

Cyril Apsley RANGER & Alfred William SIMMONDS {Reliance Omnibus Co} (-/24)

Hebron, Forlease Road, MAIDENHEAD (BE)

Cyril Ranger and Alfred Simmonds had each started operations separately; Ranger from Maidenhead with a service to Reading and Simmonds from Slough with a service to Maidenhead. Both operated in direct competition to Thames Valley. They formed a partnership in 1924 as Reliance Omnibus Co and concentrated on the busy Maidenhead to Slough corridor. Thames Valley eventually purchased the business (including four vehicles) for £4,700 on 27 May 1933.

BH 9063	Ford T	2594056	?	B6-	5/22	5/22	1/24
BH 9638	Ford T	6485972	?	B14-	11/22	11/22	3/24
MO 2850	Berliet	?	?	B20-	3/24	3/24	10/26
MO 2851	Berliet	14520	?	B20-	3/24	3/24	10/26
MO 3558	Berliet 20 hp	?	?	B20-	7/24	7/24	6/27

MO 4695	Thornycroft J	?	?	B26-	3/25	3/25	10/26
KO 4530	Dennis G	?	Strachan & Brown	C14F	8/27	-/--	6/29
RX 4101	Chevrolet	50030	?	?	3/29	3/29	-/--
RX 8373	Dodge	8341677	Willmott	B14F	4/31	4/31	*
RX 8374	Dodge	8341607	Willmott	B14F	4/31	4/31	*
RX 8375	Dodge	8341784	Willmott	B14F	4/31	4/31	*
GW 540	Dennis 1½ ton	55654	Willmott	B14F	12/31	12/31	*

Previous histories:

KO 4530: New to Goddard & Kelcey {Orange Coaches}, Chatham (KT) 10, from whom it was acquired.

Notes:

Vehicles were licensed separately to the partners. Those known were:
> Ranger – BH 9063, BH 9638, GW 540, MO 2850, RX 8373, RX 8374.
> Simmonds – MO 2851, MO 3558, MO 4695, RX 8375.

BH 9063: Reseated to B14- 1/24.

Disposals:

BH 9063: G Thomas, Slough (BK) 1/24.
BH 9638: No known disposal.
KO 4530: No known disposal.
MO 2850: F Martin, Cheltenham (GL) 10/26; last licensed 6/27.
MO 2851: Mrs EAM Harrington {Scarlet Runner}, Chatham (KT) 10/26; last licensed 3/27.
MO 3558: Last licensed 6/27 – no further operator.
MO 4695: R Turton, Reading (GBE) 6/29; last licensed 9/29.
RX 4101: No known disposal; last licensed 9/37.

The following vehicles marked with an asterisk above, transferred to Thames Valley 5/33 (qv):
GW 540, RX 8373, RX 8374, RX 8375.

Reginald J ROBSON {Premier Motor Omnibus Co}   COOKHAM GREEN (BE)

Robson had started a service between Cookham Dean and Maidenhead (via Boulter's Lock) in August 1925 which was expanded to include excursions. The business of W Jordan, Cookham (who ran a charabanc and a car hire operation) was acquired in 1926. Thames Valley acquired the Cookham Dean service together with one vehicle for £850 on 8 June 1931.

MO 6078	Morris (T?)	?	?	B14-	8/25	-/--	by6/31
RX 215	Morris (Z?) 1½ ton	3693	?	B20-	6/27	-/--	by6/31
GU 7544	Dennis 1½ ton	54233	?	B14F	4/29	-/--	*

Notes:

GU 7544: May have been fitted with the body from MO 6078.

Disposals:

MO 6078: No known disposal.
RX 215: Unidentified owner as a goods vehicle by 7/31; last licensed 9/31.

The following vehicle marked with an asterisk above, transferred to Thames Valley 6/31 (qv):
GU 7544 (239).

Fred SIMMONDS   READING (BE)

Simmonds commenced operations in April 1922 with a service between Reading and Stoke Row. This was acquired by Thames Valley (their first acquisition) in March 1923 together with Simmonds' solitary vehicle.

| DP 4400 | Ford T | ? | Russell & Paddick | B14F | 8/22 | 8/22 | * |

Notes:

DP 4400: Russell & Paddick were a firm of local builders and the body for DP 4400 was taken on as a carpentry job.

The following vehicle marked with an asterisk above, transferred to Thames Valley 3/23 (qv):
DP 4400 (56).

T SPRAGG & J WOOFF {Progressive Bus Service}   London Road, BRACKNELL (BE)

T SPRAGG Ltd {Progressive Bus Service} (by 7/24)

Operations commenced March 1923 with a service between Ascot and Reading in direct competition with Thames Valley. Spragg saw an opportunity to sell his business to Thames Valley and the deal was completed on 31 October 1925 for £5,500. This included the entire fleet of five vehicles and Spragg's garage in Bracknell. Thames Valley almost immediately recovered £1,100 by selling the Dennis to Aldershot & District. Spragg then bought the garage back for £1,000 as a base for his newly formed sand and gravel haulage business.

MO 1196	Ford T	6499451	Rice & Harper	B14F	3/23	3/23	-/25
MO 1197	Ford T	6499023	Rice & Harper	B14F	3/23	3/23	-/25
MO 1647	Ford T	6498030	?	B14-	7/23	7/23	-/--
MO 2213	Lancia Tetraiota	224E	Bartle	B20F	10/23	10/23	*
MO 3530	Lancia Z	3394	Vincent / Manners	B20F	7/24	7/24	*
MO 4648	Lancia Pentaiota	702	Strachan & Brown	B25F	2/25	2/25	*
MO 5443	Lancia Pentaiota	846	Strachan & Brown	B25F	5/25	5/25	*
MO 6184	Dennis 2½ ton	45158	Strachan & Brown	B30R	9/25	9/25	*

Notes:

MO 2213:   Bartle was a London W11 coachbuilder.

MO 3530:   Had a reconditioned chassis; The bodywork was started by Vincent of Reading, but finished by T Manners, a Bracknell coachbuilder.

Disposals:

MO 1196:   Unidentified owner as a goods vehicle at an unknown date; last licensed 6/30.

MO 1197:   CE Butterfield, Sandy 7/25; Viscount Lee of Fareham, London SW7 4/27; moved to Richmond Park 3/28; last licensed 9/29.

MO 1647:   J Lynch, Ide Hill, Sevenoaks (KT) at an unknown date; last licensed 9/29.

The following vehicles marked with an asterisk above, transferred to Thames Valley 10/25 (qv):

MO 2213 (95), MO 3530 (94), MO 4648 (96), MO 5443 (97), MO 6184.

NEWBURY & DISTRICT MOTOR SERVICES LTD, NEWBURY (BE)

The origins of Newbury & District Motor Services Ltd came about in March 1932 as a result of Theo Denham, local bus operator and Chairman of the South Berkshire Bus Proprietors & Carriers Association, convening a meeting to discuss the concept of co-operative bus operations in the area. This was in response to the demands of the 1930 Transport Act which had increased administrative burdens on individual operators and left them vulnerable to large and financially powerful concerns.

Initially, the main players in the town – Arthur Andrews, Charlie Durnford and Theo Denham – formed the new company on 26 April 1932, each being allocated 2,000 £1 shares. Durnford was Chairman and Denham was Company Secretary. The registered address was 16 Market Street, Newbury, which were Durnford's offices. The company successfully applied for the licences held by the individual operators although a restriction was placed initially on vehicle numbers to just five. The associated taxi businesses (Andrews & Denham), haulage operations (all three) and removals businesses (Durnford) were also absorbed and maintained.

After all the activity of 1932, the following year was one of consolidation. Efforts to gain footholds in key locations such as Hungerford and Kintbury failed due to the complexity of the applications and objections from other local operators. Efforts were made to launch an express service to Southsea, probably the most popular destination on the south coast, also failed.

A major blow was the withdrawal of Charlie Durnford from active participation in the company from July 1933. As a result, the registered office of the company was changed to 7 The Wharf, Newbury. Durnford immediately went back to operating as an independent, setting his sons up as Durnford Bros. He wasn't away for long however and in an extraordinary meeting he (along with Freddie Spanswick) were elected to the board on the condition that he curtailed his outside interests. The breakaway Durnford Bros business (including the removals and haulage interests) duly returned to Newbury & District fold in January 1934.

John Prothero left the business in April 1934 and his shares were purchased by James Davies (recently appointed as Inspector and Traffic Assistant), Charlie Durnford and a number of employees. At the AGM in September, George Hedges was replaced on the board by Davies; Hedges immediately decided to break away from Newbury & District and an agreement was struck for him to buy back his Reliance Motor Services business for the price he sold it for. He departed with four vehicles in December 1934.

After the departures of Prothero and Hedges, attempts were made to stabilise the board which comprised of Charlie Durnford (Engineer, Coach & Haulage Manager), Theo Denham (Company Secretary), Arthur Andrews (Chairman and Coachbuilder), Freddie Spanswick (Rolling Stock Manager) and James Davies (Traffic Manager).

In late 1935, Thames Valley took over managing the operations of Ledbury Transport Co Ltd, both companies having established services between Reading and Newbury. This encouraged Thames Valley to look towards expanding its operations west of Reading and an approach to Newbury & District was made for the Thatcham area routes or alternatively, the entire company. The prices quoted (£15,000 and £50,000 respectively) were considered too high by Thames Valley and discussions ended there. In addition, both Wilts & Dorset Motor Services Ltd (based in Salisbury) and Venture Transport Ltd (of Basingstoke) considered making offers for the business but again nothing transpired.

Charlie Durnford resigned for the second time in August 1937, his place on the board passed to Angus Marshall, a local solicitor. Durnford purchased Kennet Motor Works (a motor garage) and left Newbury & District. Arthur Andrews, another of the original founders, resigned in October 1937 (although he continued as coachbuilder), with his place being filled by Frank Frampton, a new investor.

From 1938 onwards, for the first time a policy on future vehicle acquisitions was implemented which broadly consisted of small buses to be of Dennis manufacture, with larger buses and coaches to be Leylands. At the outbreak of World War 2, the operational fleet had grown to 51 vehicles. The building of airfields in the region together with the aircraft manufacturing establishment at Eddington near Hungerford intensified demand. Evacuation of children from Southampton and London to the relatively safe Newbury area also required meant that regular services had to be curtailed. Records are sketchy, but it appears that in addition, at least a dozen vehicles were impressed by the War Department in the 1940/41 period. Despite the difficulties in obtaining vehicles, there was a steady stream of second-hand buses coming into the fleet replacing older vehicles that had come to the end of the line. This had slowed up by 1942 but the fleet was maintained well and vehicles refurbished in order to extend their lives. The company was also allocated four new Bedford OWBs which arrived over 1942/43.

By 1943 however, wartime restrictions had placed a severe strain on maintenance standards and finances and it was agreed to seek a purchaser for the company. Towards the end of the year, a prospectus was drawn up including 63 buses and coaches (7 Bedford, 24 Dennis, 23 Leyland and 9 Thornycroft) plus four Bedford lorries.

The sale to Red & White United Transport Ltd of Chepstow for £62,000 was approved by the Board on 23 December 1943 with the take-over date set for 1 January 1944. The haulage business however was not continued under Red & White.

Almost immediately, efforts to standardise the fleet were implemented. An outstanding order for two Bedford OWBs was successfully switched to Guy Arab double-deckers, with seven of this type being received over 1944/5. Single-deck requirements were met by the acquisition of a number of AEC Regals, ten of which received ten-year old second-hand bodies. Newbury & District's Dennis and Thornycroft types were not required by the new regime and ten Bedford OWBs from the Red & White and United Welsh fleets were drafted in, initially on hire and later permanently.

1947 saw an influx of 15 new vehicles (ten buses and five coaches) and this together with a reduction in contract commitments, enabled a number of older vehicles to be disposed of. In all, 28 new vehicles were received up to 1951.

As Governmental pressure grew on large bus operators to sell out to the nationalised British Transport Commission (BTC), Red & White decided to voluntarily sell their bus and coaching interests to BTC with effect from 10 February 1950. Newbury & District (as well as South Midland) was placed under the control of Thames Valley. For the first two years, the fleets were kept separate, with Newbury & District taking in Guy Arab double-deck vehicles into 1951. Vehicles from Thames Valley's own fleet were soon drafted in and within a couple of years, most traces of the Newbury & District identity were erased. The last vestiges of the Newbury & District operation, the Guy Arabs, lasted however until 1968.

PREMISES
The initial premises acquired were (all in Newbury):

Market Street (offices), Mayors Lane and Mill Lane (garages)	ex Durnford
Wharf Road (garage and workshop) and Mill Lane (garage)	ex Denham
Northcroft Lane (coach building shop, maintenance facilities and garage)	ex Andrews

Various garages, outstations and dormy shed were added with the amalgamated and acquired businesses over the next six years including those at Brightwalton, Bucklebury, Chieveley, Cold Ash, East Ilsley, Hermitage, Kingsclere, Kintbury, Lambourn Woodlands and Thatcham.

From 1932 to 1937, Newbury & District rented Thames Valley's dormy shed with the latter garaging two vehicles there as part of the agreement.

At the end of 1936, land in Mill Lane, Newbury was purchased for the construction of a new main depot which commenced in February 1937. This was replaced by a new structure nearby built over 1945/46. After this came into use, servicing of South Midland vehicles took place there.

LIVERIES
Vehicles were painted in a variety of liveries initially with a few repainted into maroon and cream in the 1932-34 period. From the start of 1934, a fleet livery was decided on – green with cream relief for buses and the reverse for coaches. Following the Red & White United Transport Ltd takeover in 1944, that operator's crimson and broken white livery was introduced. From 1950, vehicles were repainted into Thames Valley livery, although Newbury & District fleet names continued to be applied until 1952/53.

FLEET NUMBERS
The original scheme in 1932 was for service buses to be numbered between 1 and 20, with the coach series starting at 21. Thereafter however, vehicles were largely numbered randomly, a mixture of sequential numbering and gap filling. By 1942, number 94 had been reached and thereafter (with only a few exceptions), vehicles were numbered sequentially, finishing at 178 in 1951.

1932

Vehicles acquired from A & PA Andrews {A Andrews & Son / Favourite Coaches}, Newbury (BE) 6/32:

	?	Guy J	?	Andrews	C20D	c-/25	6/33
21	BL 6490	Talbot 25/50 hp	4SW10379	Andrews	C14D	4/20	9/35
	DP ?	Lancia Tetraiota	?	Vincent	C20D	-/25	by4/33
22	RD 1886	Gilford 168OT	11464	Vincent	C30D	6/30	c7/43
6	RX 8261	Ford AA	4453106	Andrews	B20F	3/31	12/34
	VA 3156	Lancia Tetraiota	650	?	B20-	12/24	-/32
25	VM 8638	Gilford 166SD	?	Lewis & Crabtree	C26-	4/29	8/38

Previous histories:

These vehicles were acquired with the Andrews business; their previous histories are detailed in the Vehicles of Acquired Operators section.

Notes:

RD 1886: Fitted with the Wilton C32D body (rebuilt to C32R) from MT 1842 c12/36 (qv).

VA 3156: Probably not operated by Newbury & District Motor Services Ltd.

Disposals:

Guy J: No known disposal.

BL 6490 (21): Penn, Whitchurch 9/35; last licensed 12/35.

DP   ?: No known disposal.

RD 1886 (22): D Penfold (dealer), Thatcham c7/43; War Department (GOV) 7/43.

RX 8261 (6):   GE Hedges {Reliance Motor Services}, Brightwalton (BE) 1 12/34 (qv).

VA 3156: Richards, Towyn by 12/32.

VM 8638 (25): T Goodman (Transport) Ltd {Coliseum Coaches}, Gosport (HA) by 3/44; withdrawn 10/51.

Vehicles acquired from AH & TA Denham {Denham Bros}, Newbury (BE) 6/32:

	?	Gilford	?	?	B28-	-/--	6/33
5	BU 5690	TSM B10A2	5869	NCME	C32F	11/28	9/36
27	HX 1059	Star Flyer VB4	D639	Strachan	C26D	7/30	8/39
	KE 3196	Talbot 25/50 hp	?	Andrews	B14F	2/21	-/33
9	MW 825	Thornycroft A2	?	Challands Ross	B20F	11/27	6/40
23	TO 9554	Gilford 166OT	10614	Strachan	B32F	3/29	c7/39
	TR 1231	Leyland A13	35879	Southampton Corporation	B26F	11/25	-/33
12	TR 8198	Thornycroft A2	?	Wadham	B20F	2/30	6/40
7	VT 184	TSM B10A	?	Strachan & Brown	B32F	7/27	7/40
	WU 9870	Minerva	?	Metcalfe	B20-	2/27	10/32

Previous histories:

These vehicles were acquired with the Denham business; their previous histories are detailed in the Vehicles of Acquired Operators section.

Disposals:

Unidentified (Gilford): Unidentified operator / dealer 6/33.

BU 5690 (5): AE Warwick {Wem Service}, Farnham Common (BK) 9/36.

HX 1059 (27): Last licensed 8/39.

KE 3196: Unidentified operator / dealer 1933.

MW 825 (9): War Department (GOV) 6/40; Air Raids Precautions, West Ham as a mobile unit (GOV) 8/42.

TO 9554 (23): Unidentified operator / dealer 1939.

TR 1231: Unidentified operator / dealer 1933, possibly Read, London E11 (LN); last licensed 12/38.

TR 8198 (12): War Department (GOV) 12/40; Air Raids Precautions, location unknown (GOV) as a mobile unit 12/40.

VT 184 (7): War Department (GOV) 7/40.

WU 9870: Unidentified operator, Birmingham 10/32.

Vehicles acquired from JC Durnford {C Durnford & Sons}, Newbury (BE) 6/32:

	?	Reo Major	?	?	C20F	c-/27	-/35
	?	Lancia Pentaiota	?	London Lorries	C25F	-/--	-/--
26	RX 6264	Reo Pullman	?	Wray	C25D	3/30	9/38
30	UU 7594	GMC T42	D2287	Wilton	C26-	6/29	12/37
	UV 9116	Gilford CP6	11005	Wycombe	C20F	7/29	----
	VX 43	Gilford CP6	10743	Thurgood	C20D	5/29	6/33

	YB 7442	Lancia Pentaiota	583	Wray	C20F	9/26	6/34
28	YE 8768	Maudslay ML4	4028	London Lorries	C28D	3/27	6/34
29	YT 9565	Garner 55 hp	74182	Buckingham	C26D	9/27	8/36

Previous histories:
>These vehicles were acquired with the Durnford business; their previous histories are detailed in the Vehicles of Acquired Operators section.

Notes:
>UV 9116: Not operated by Newbury & District Motor Services Ltd.

Disposals:
>Unidentified (Lancia): No known disposal.
>Unidentified (Reo): Fitted with a flat-bed lorry body 1935 and transferred to the service fleet (qv); coach body probably fitted to RX 9463 (18) 7/35 (qv).
>RX 6264 (26): Last licensed 9/38.
>UU 7594 (30): Last licensed 12/37.
>UV 9116: W Kemp & F Wright {Wright's Bus Service}, Louth (LI) 7/32; Dawson & Goult {Pioneer}, Felixstowe (EK) 1940s; VT Faiers {WG Clarke}, Felixstowe (EK) 3/47.
>VX   43: JR Killip {The Wayfarer}, Douglas (IM) re-registered MN 8844 6/33; JW Kneen {Cornflower Motors}, Douglas (IM) 6/38; GC Gale {Gales Western Motors}, Peel (IM) 6/39; withdrawn 12/39.
>YB 7442: Last licensed 6/34; unidentified dealer (probably for scrap) 12/34.
>YE 8768 (28): E Snow, Merthyr Tydfil (GG) 6/34; scrapped 1/37.
>YT 9565 (29): Last licensed 8/36.

Vehicle acquired from Aldershot & District Traction Co Ltd, Aldershot (HA) 6/32:

PE 2077	Dennis 2½ ton	51020	Strachan & Brown	B20F	4/25	6/33

Previous history:
>PE 2077:   New to S Tanner {Chobham Bus Service}, Chobham (SR); Aldershot & District Traction Co Ltd D240.

Disposal:
>PE 2077:   Unidentified operator / dealer, Hampshire c1933; showman, West Suffolk 11/43; CW English (showman), Bishops Stortford by 3/48.

Vehicles acquired from GE Hedges {Reliance Motor Services}, Brightwalton (BE) 9/32:

?	Talbot 25/50 hp		Andrews	C14-	-/25	-/--
RX 4556	Ford AA	1045538	?	C14D	5/29	12/34
RX 6888	Ford AA	3015658	Duple	C14D	6/30	12/34

Previous histories:
>These vehicles were acquired with the Hedges business; their previous histories are detailed in the Vehicles of Acquired Operators section.

Disposals:
>Talbot: No known disposal.
>RX 4556: GE Hedges {Reliance Motor Services}, Brightwalton (BE) 12/34.
>RX 6888: GE Hedges {Reliance Motor Services}, Brightwalton (BE) 12/34.

Vehicles acquired from J Prothero {XLCR Motor Service}, Beedon (BE) 9/32:

?	Gilford f/c		?	C32-	-/--	-/--
RX 4272	Ford AA	763071	Andrews	B14F	4/29	1/34
RX 7256	Ford AA	3458473	Andrews	B14F	7/30	c1/34
RX 7772	Ford AA	3950354	(Andrews?)	B20F	12/30	11/35
RX 9005	Ford AA	4486474	(Andrews?)	B20F	7/31	9/36

Previous histories:
>These vehicles were acquired with the Prothero business; their previous histories are detailed in the Vehicles of Acquired Operators section.

Disposals:

Unidentified (Gilford): No known disposal.
RX 4272: JF Burt, Inkpen (GBE) 1/34; last licensed 12/36.
RX 7256: J Cook, London NW1 c1/34; last licensed 9/37.
RX 7772: Last licensed 11/35.
RX 9005: Last licensed 9/36.

Vehicles acquired from WC, PB & NW Pocock {Pocock Bros}, Cold Ash (BE) 10/32:

	?	Chevrolet	?	?	C14-	-/--	6/33
	MO 8231	Chevrolet X	10150	?	B14F	7/26	----
19	RX 9971	Bedford WLB	108401	?	B20F	3/32	8/40

Previous histories:

These vehicles were acquired with the Pocock business; their previous histories are detailed in the Vehicles of Acquired Operators section.

Notes:

MO 8231: Not operated by Newbury & District Motor Services Ltd.

Disposals:

Chevrolet: No known disposal.
MO 8231: Pocock Bros, Cold Ash (GBE) c1933; last licensed 6/35.
RX 9971 (19): T & J Wood {T Wood & Sons / Empress Motor Service}, Worting (HA) 8/40; last licensed 12/43.

1933

Vehicles acquired from FG Spanswick {Spanswicks's Bus Service}, Thatcham (BE) 1/33:

MO 6744	Ford TT	11279654	Andrews	B14F	1/26	6/33
RX 6662	Ford AA	1843020	Andrews	B20F	4/30	c7/35

Previous histories:

These vehicles were acquired with the Spanswick business; their previous histories are detailed in the Vehicles of Acquired Operators section.

Disposals:

MO 6744: No known disposal.
RX 6662: GT Perry, Whitchurch (HA) c7/35; last licensed 3/39.

Vehicle acquired from CA Usher {Victory Safety Coaches}, London E3 (LN) 7/33:

53	UV 6002	Dennis GL	70550	Wray	C20-	7/29	3/36

Previous history:

UV 6002 (53): New to CA Usher {Victory Safety Coaches}.

Disposal:

UV 6002 (53): Unidentified owner (G??) 3/36.

Vehicle acquired from J Spratley & Son {Blue Star Coaches}, Mortimer (BE) 7/33:

10	OU 3317	Thornycroft A2	?	Wadham	B20F	8/29	4/44

Previous history:

OU 3317 (10): New to John I Thornycroft Ltd, Basingstoke as a demonstrator; Lovegrove Bros (dealer), Silchester 1929; J Spratley & Son {Blue Star Coaches} 8/29.

Disposal:

OU 3317 (10): D Penfold (dealer), Thatcham 4/44; J Brown (showman), West Drayton 4/44.

Vehicle acquired from United Automobile Services Ltd, Darlington (DM) c7/33:

3	TY 6174	Star Flyer VB4	1004/D022	Robson	B20-	6/29	12/35

Previous history:
TY 6174 (3): New to W Rutherford, Craster (ND) 4; United Automobile Services Ltd B136 10/32.

Notes:
TY 6174 (3): Its body builder is also quoted as Blagg.

Disposal:
TY 6174 (3): Unidentified operator / dealer 12/35.

Vehicle acquired from Midland General Omnibus Co Ltd, Langley Mill (DE) 9/33:

RA 1794	Thornycroft A2 Long	14076	Challands Ross	B20R	2/27	by8/38

Previous history:
RA 1794: New to AWN Henshaw, Ilkeston (DE); Williamson's Garage Ltd, Heanor (DE) 1929; Midland General Omnibus Co Ltd (not operated) 1931.

Disposal:
RA 1794: No known disposal.

Vehicles acquired from Central SMT Co Ltd, Motherwell (LK) c9/33:

39	VA 7942	Leyland LSC1	47336	Leyland	B31F	7/28	c4/37
40	VA 7943	Leyland LSC1	47337	Leyland	B31F	8/28	8/38

Previous histories:
VA 7942-7943 (39-40): New to W Baxter & Sons {Baxter's Bus Services}, Blantyre (LK) 9-10; JW & R Torrance Ltd, Hamilton (LK) 52-53 4/29; Central SMT Co Ltd E10-11 6/32.

Notes:
VA 7943 (40): Probably cannibalised for spares after 8/38.

Disposals:
VA 7942 (39): Last licensed c4/37 – no further owner.
VA 7943 (40): Last licensed 9/38 – no further owner.

Vehicle acquired from Southern National Omnibus Co Ltd, Exeter (DN) 11/33:

41	PR 9053	Dennis E	17166	Strachan & Brown	B32D	4/27	9/37

Previous history:
PR 9053 (41): New to National Omnibus & Transport Co Ltd, Exeter (DN); Southern National Omnibus Co Ltd 1/29.

Notes:
PR 9053 (41): Cannibalised for spares from 9/37 to 7/38 at least.

Disposal:
PR 9053 (41): Scrapped at an unknown date.

1934

Vehicle acquired from Mrs C Geary {Joy Coaches}, Great Shefford (BE) 1/34:

RX 5432	Ford AA	1158124	(Pass & Co?)	C14-	10/29	----

Previous history:
This vehicle was acquired with the Geary business; its previous history is detailed in the Vehicles of Acquired Operators section.

Notes:
RX 5432: Not operated by Newbury & District Motor Services Ltd.

Disposal:
RX 5432: A Low {Pass & Co}, Newbury (probably as dealer) 1/34.

Bristol LS6B HMO 835 had been a coach in the South Midland fleet, but in 1964 it re-emerged after being rebuilt as a service bus and re-numbered S309. It was one of a trio prepared for the commencement of the new joint service 19 to Long Lane with Reading Corporation Transport. (Geoffrey Morant, courtesy Richard Morant)

In 1957, a summer service along the River Thames between Maidenhead and Reading was introduced. Four Bristol K5G dating from 1940 were obtained from Brighton Hove & District, painted in a special livery and converted to open-top. CAP 132 (771) is seen here at Reading Stations with some hopeful passengers on the top deck. (Roy Marshall collection, Omnibus Society)

From 1957, the Marlow Bridge service was taken over by five Bristol SC4LK with ECW 35-seat bodies, one of which was NBL 732 (775), seen here at Maidenhead Coach Station which was used by buses whilst the Bus Station underwent repairs. Four of these vehicles survived in service until 1969 and all saw further use elsewhere. (John May, courtesy Mike Eyre)

The second batch of Bristol LDs delivered in 1957 included NBL 736 (779) which was an uncommon LDL model seating 70. Nicknamed 'Big Bertha', its extra length made it prone to accidents although ironically its days were finally ended when it came to grief in a low bridge accident in 1973. (Derek Giles collection, Omnibus Society)

Three Bristol K5G / ECW dating from 1938 were obtained from Hants & Dorset in 1960. These had been bodied by Brush when new but received ECW bodies in 1949. They survived until 1964 and despite their age, all saw further service elsewhere. JT 9355 (473) is seen here at Reading Stations. (Norris Collection, Omnibus Society)

The successor to the Bristol LS was the Bristol MW saloon of which VJB 945 (181), seen at Newbury Wharf, arrived in 1960. Six were delivered in that year, two of which had dual-purpose seating for the Reading to London services whilst the remainder were sent to Newbury to replace the last of the AEC Regals there. (Derek Giles collection, Omnibus Society)

Surprising acquisitions were five 15-year old Bristol L6A / ECW half-cabs which arrived from Crosville in 1963, long after native examples had disappeared. Their stay at Thames Valley was brief but all saw further service elsewhere. GFM 882 (S302) survived into preservation and is a familiar sight at rallies today. (Norris Collection, Omnibus Society)

The Bristol FLF replaced the LD in 1960 and numerous examples were obtained. GRX 140D (D40) was received in 1966 and is seen here at Maidenhead's modified Bus Station. This particular vehicle has been preserved locally since 1986 and will celebrate its 50th birthday in 2016. (John May, courtesy Mike Eyre)

There were quite a few more conversions of former coaches to service saloons. Here ex-South Midland Bristol LS6B TWL 55 (now as S315) is seen alongside LWN 52, one of the many LD-types acquired from United Welsh, which was the second Thames Valley bus to carry fleet number 770. (John May, courtesy Mike Eyre)

The intake for 1967 comprised eight Bristol RESL6Gs fitted with 'standee' ECW bodies, but the Union objected to their proposed use on the busy Slough cross-town services. After a winter in store they were reseated and distributed amongst various garages with LJB 332F (S332) being caught on Station Hill in Reading. (Peter Henson, Omnibus Society)

The last double-deck development was the Bristol VR, of which 21 were delivered by the end of operations in 1971. UBL 247G (506) was a VRT/SL6G variant, seating 70. Despite its bus seats, it is operating express service B (Reading - London) and is seen at Victoria Coach Station. (Geoffrey Morant, courtesy Richard Morant)

The final vehicles for the Marlow Bridge service were five Bristol SUS4A with ECW 30-seat bodies. They were acquired in 1969/70 as replacements for the SC4LKs with two sourced from Western National and three, including 846 THY (199), coming from Bristol Omnibus Co. (John May, courtesy Mike Eyre)

Newbury & District ordered few new vehicles in the 1930s but one such example was JB 6834 (63), a Dennis Ace with King & Taylor 20 seat bodywork, which arrived in 1935. It saw 11 years' service but ended its days in Czechoslovakia transporting displaced persons from camps after the War. (JF Parke, Omnibus Society)

Newbury & District JY 4752 (65) was one of the numerous Dennis Aces that were acquired in the late 1930s and early 1940s with their snout-like bonnets gave them the nickname 'Flying Pigs'. This was a fine coach seated example, seating 20 and was bodied by Mumford. (Paul Lacey)

HD 4371 (56) was one of four 1931 Leyland LT2 which were acquired by Newbury & District from Yorkshire Woollen in 1939. It is seen here at Bucklebury Common in wartime as signified by its masked headlights and white painted mudguards. It lasted here until 1947 but survived elsewhere until the late 1950s. (John C Gilham, Omnibus Society)

EKP 140 (74) was a Thornycroft 'Dainty' with Thurgood bodywork and was acquired from London Transport when only just over two years old. It seated 20 and typified the small capacity vehicles operated by Newbury & District at the time. It is seen here at Newbury Wharf. (JF Parke, Omnibus Society)

After its acquisition by Red & White in 1944, Newbury & District standardised on the Guy Arab for its double-deck requirements. CRX 280 (100) was one of five such vehicles obtained new in 1944 and fitted with Park Royal 56-seat bodywork. It was renumbered H2 in 1954 to signify it was of highbridge design after one of its sisters was decapitated under a low bridge. (John Clarke collection, Omnibus

To replace its ageing fleet, Newbury & District obtained a number of Bedford OWBs in 1944 through Red & White's Welsh subsidiaries. DWN 295 (661) and EWO 454 (454) were fitted Duple 32-seat bodies and are seen here at Newbury Wharf in the new fleet livery of red and white. (John Clarke collection, Omnibus Society)

TX 9498 (108) was one of a trio of AEC Regals obtained from Red & White in 1944 as the fleet was continued to be standardised. This was originally fitted with a Short body in 1930, but was rebodied in 1942 with a Duple 35-seat body. It is seen here at Newbury Wharf. (John Clarke collection, Omnibus Society)

Ten ex-SMT AEC Regal 4s with dilapidated Burlingham bodies were acquired in 1945 by Red & White for the Newbury & District fleet. These were thoroughly rebuilt and fitted with refurbished nine-year old ECOC / ECW bodies. FS 8560 (122) is seen at Newbury Wharf and saw five further years' service in this form. (John Clarke collection, Omnibus Society)

FAX 349 (157) was new as a Burlingham bodied coach in 1931 registered FV 1665. It was impressed by the War Department in 1940 before being later acquired by Red & White who were earning a reputation for rebuilding vehicles. They fitted it with a Burlingham 34-seat bus body before passing it to Newbury & District in 1948. (Roy Marshall collection, The Omnibus Society)

FMO 517 (172, later H10) was another highbridge Guy Arab, with Duple 57-seat bodywork and was amongst the last vehicles acquired by Newbury & District in 1950. Like its sisters, it lasted until 1968, by which time, they were the only non Bristol / ECW double-deckers in the fleet. (John Clarke collection, Omnibus Society)

Body builders were finding it difficult to keep up with demand in the immediate post-war period, so South Midland overcame this by fitting a refurbished 1936 ECOC 31-seat body on LWL 995 (38), a new Leyland PS1/1 chassis delivered in 1947. It was transferred to Newbury & District in 1950 where it became fleet number 169. (SNJ White, Roy Marshall collection)

The Thames Valley Chief Engineer saw a potential for the PS1/1 as a much-needed coach, so its chassis was lengthened to 30ft and fitted with this ECW 8ft-wide body. In this form it returned as Newbury & District 169 and it seen at the Thames-side Promenade at Reading with Festival of Britain adornments. (Paul Lacey & Mike Sutcliffe collections)

Typifying the Leyland Tiger TS8 in its final bus form is BBL 565 (379), an ECW 32-seat example. It is seen here at Newbury Wharf, having been transferred late in life, to the Newbury & District fleet from Thames Valley during the period the fleets were being integrated. (Derek Giles collection, Omnibus Society)

South Midland managed to achieve the look of a much larger outfit, purchasing quality coaches such as this Gilford WL 9058 (19) with Arnold & Comben of Farnham bodywork. It is seen ready to leave Gloucester Green in Oxford for Worcester. During WW2, it was made available for conversion to an ambulance. (AB Cross, Omnibus Society)

South Midland moved on to Leylands in due course with small batches of various models. On the left is Leyland Tiger TS3 JO 1593 (30), by now rebodied by Harrington, alongside which is Burlingham-bodied Cheetah LZ2A HFC 550 (27), both seen outside the cafe also owned by the Company. (The Omnibus Society)

Post-war, Red & White ordered various batches of Duple-bodied AEC Regal coaches in order to replace the ageing South Midland fleet. One of these was NWL 879 (62) which is seen parked in a London street awaiting a journey from Victoria. (Roy Marshall collection, Omnibus Society)

From 1950, the Thames Valley influence in the South Midland fleet became apparent with a batch of Bristol LS6G / ECW 37-seat coaches arriving in 1952. The livery had changed to maroon and cream in the mid-1950s, as worn by SFC 565 (79). (Derek Giles collection, Omnibus Society)

Inherited through outstanding Red & White orders was a batch of Guy underfloor-engine coaches, with bodies started by the ill-fated Lydney Coachworks and completed in 1953 by BBW under ECW guidance. SFC 501 (86) is shown at Newbury Wharf (despite the indicator settings), probably just in from Oxford for servicing. (Chris Carter, Omnibus Society)

Lightweight Bedfords were a regular purchase for South Midland, primarily for use on touring work and 1962 SB8-type with Duple Super Vega bodywork 517 ABL (863) is shown at work on the Irish Tour. Fleet numbers were by now integrated in the main Thames Valley scheme. (Mike Sutcliffe)

The South Midland fleet was chosen as the working ground for the prototype high-floor Bristol RE-type. 521 ABL (867) arrived in 1963 fitted with the first 36ft long ECW coach body. It was also fitted with forced-air ventilation and is seen here at Gloucester Green. (Derek Giles collection, Omnibus Society)

Vehicle acquired from JF Burt & AV Greenwood, Inkpen (BE) 1/34:

	GJ 7973	Federal AB6	?	?		C28-	c7/30	by8/38

Previous history:

This vehicle was acquired with the Burt & Greenwood business; its previous history is detailed in the Vehicles of Acquired Operators section.

Notes:

GJ 7973: Its registration is uncertain, being also recorded as GJ 9733.

Disposal:

GJ 7973: No known disposal.

Vehicle acquired from G Brown {Wash Common Bus Service}, Wash Common (BE) 1/34:

	RX 3553:	Morris R	128R	Morris		B14F	1/29	9/35

Previous history:

This vehicle was acquired with the Brown business; its previous history is detailed in the Vehicles of Acquired Operators section.

Disposal:

RX 3553: Last licensed 9/35.

Vehicles acquired from LC, EA & HA Durnford {Durnford Bros}, Newbury (BE) 1/34:

28	GU 7545	Star Flyer VB4	C884/1055	Thurgood		C26-	4/29	by7/38
51	HJ 8718	Gilford 166SD	10499	?		C26-	3/29	c7/39

Previous histories:

These vehicles were acquired with the Durnford Bros business; their previous histories are detailed in the Vehicles of Acquired Operators section.

Disposals:

GU 7545 (28): Scrapped 7/39.

HJ 8718 (51): Last licensed 9/39.

Vehicle acquired from Maidstone & District Motor Services Ltd, Maidstone (KT) c2/34:

11	KM 3028	Thornycroft A2	20918	Strachan & Brown		B20F	3/26	c8/39

Previous history:

KM 3028 (11): New to Weald of Kent Transport Co Ltd, Tenterden (KT) 7; Maidstone & District Motor Services Ltd at an unknown date; unidentified dealer, London c1934, from whom it was acquired.

Disposal:

KM 3028 (11): Unidentified operator / dealer c8/39.

Vehicle acquired from HE Hill {Strawhatter Motor Coaches}, Luton (BD) c2/34: ·

	TM 5639	Gilford 166OT	11047	Strachan		C32F	9/29	by8/38

Previous history:

TM 5639: New to HE Hill {Strawhatter Motor Coaches} 7.

Notes:

TM 5639: A Gilford was acquired in early 1934; whilst its identity has not been absolutely confirmed, it is believed to have been TM 5639.

Disposal:

TM 5639: No known disposal.

Vehicles acquired from GP Howlett {Kennet Bus Service}, Bucklebury (BE) 2/34:

	MY 3052	Star Flyer VB4	1007/D403	Star		C26D	3/30	1/37
4	MY 4213	Star Flyer VB4	1172/D436	Star		C26D	4/30	3/38
	SH 3380	GMC T30C	302813	Alexander Motors		B20F	5/29	12/34

Previous histories:

These vehicles were acquired with the Howlett business; their previous histories are detailed in the Vehicles of Acquired Operators section.

Disposals:

MY 3052: H Lane & Co Ltd (dealer), London SW10 1/37; Eva's Motor Coaches Ltd, London EC2 5 (LN) at an unknown date; George Ewer & Co Ltd {Grey-Green}, London N16 (LN) 75 at an unknown date; RW Toop & WJ Ironside {Pioneer}, Bere Regis (DT) at an unknown date.

MY 4213 (4): Last licensed 3/38.

SH 3380: GE Hedges {Reliance Motor Services}, Brightwalton (BE) 3 12/34.

Vehicles acquired from EG White {WJ White & Son / Tony Coaches}, Hermitage (BE) 3/34:

44	MW 6161	AJS Pilot	?	Eaton	B26F	12/29	c6/37
42	RX 5493	Dennis 1½ ton	55318	?	C14D	11/29	9/34
43	RX 6401	Dennis 1½ ton	55716	?	C17-	5/30by10/35	
	TP 7118	Dennis 1½ ton	53913	Dennis	B14F	12/28	3/35

Previous histories:

These vehicles were acquired with the White business; their previous histories are detailed in the Vehicles of Acquired Operators section.

Notes:

RX 5493 (42): Refurbished and rebuilt to C16F c9/34; extensively damaged by fire shortly after its return to service 9/34.

Disposals:

MW 6161 (44): Unidentified operator / dealer c6/37.

RX 5493 (42): Unidentified dealer for scrap 1934.

RX 6401 (43): Unidentified owner (G??) by 10/35; last licensed 1/48.

TP 7118: Unidentified owner (G??) 3/35.

Vehicles acquired from Crosville Motor Services Ltd, Chester (CH) 12/34:

31	CC 9415	GMC T60	921D	Strachan	B26D	3/30	1/37
36	FM 6486	GMC T30C	308362	Hughes	B20F	12/30	c2/41
37	FM 6487	GMC T30C	308433	Hughes	B20F	12/30	8/39
35	FM 6488	GMC T30C	308435	Hughes	B20F	12/30	c2/41

Previous histories:

CC 9415 (31): New to Tocia Motor Omnibus Co Ltd, Aberdaron (CN); Crosville Motor Services Ltd 92 2/34; H Lane & Co Ltd (dealer), London SW10 by 12/34, from whom it was acquired.

FM 6486-6487 (36-37): New to Crosville Motor Services Ltd 629-630 (having been ordered by W Edwards {Red Dragon Motor Services}, Denbigh (DH)); H Lane & Co Ltd (dealer), London SW10 by 12/34, from whom it was acquired.

FM 6488 (35): New to Crosville Motor Services Ltd 631 (having been ordered by W Edwards {Red Dragon Motor Services}, Denbigh (DH)); H Lane & Co Ltd (dealer), London SW10 by 12/34, from whom it was acquired.

Disposals:

CC 9415 (31): H Lane & Co Ltd (dealer), London SW10 1/37.

FM 6486-6487 (36-37): No known disposal.

FM 6488 (35): No known disposal.

1935

New vehicle:

63	JB 6834	Dennis Ace	200399	King & Taylor	C20F	7/35	12/46

Notes:

JB 6834 (63): Received a major rebuild during World War 2.

Disposal:

JB 6834 (63): Last licensed 12/46; Wootten (dealer), Birmingham 1/47; United Nations Refugee Rehabilitation Agency (UNRRA) (for transporting displaced persons from camps in Czechoslovakia) 6/47; probably ultimately burnt as a health precaution.

Vehicle acquired from Southdown Motor Services Ltd, Brighton (ES) 4/35:

50	JK 1911	Gilford 168OT	11526	Duple	1956 C31F	7/31	7/40

Previous history:

JK 1911 (50): Ordered by Miller {Starline}, Ilford (EX) 5, but new to Southern Glideway Coaches Ltd, Eastbourne (ES); Southdown Motor Services Ltd 37 3/32; H Lane & Co Ltd (dealer), London SW10 1/35, from whom it was acquired.

Notes:

JK 1911 (50): It was recorded as C28- when new, then C31F, but at some point had been rebuilt to C28D with a rear door; it was converted back to C31F by Newbury & District before entry into service.

Disposal:

JK 1911 (50): War Department (GOV) 7/40.

Vehicle acquired from General Motor Carrying Co Ltd, Kirkcaldy (FE) 4/35:

6	FG 4427	Maudslay ML4B	4444	Buckingham	B29F	10/28	6/37

Previous history:

FG 4427 (6): New to Cormie Bros Ltd {Cormie Comfort Coaches}, Kirkcaldy (FE); General Motor Carrying Co Ltd 10/31 (as B26-); numbered 0185 1932; Leyland Motors Ltd (dealer), Leyland 7/32; GJ Dawson (Clapham) Ltd (dealer), London SW9 by 4/35, from whom it was acquired.

Disposal:

FG 4427 (6): Last licensed 6/37.

Vehicle acquired from -?-, Manchester (LA) 6/35:

VM 3669	Gilford 166OT	?	Lewis & Crabtree	C32R	8/28	by8/38

Previous history:

VM 3669: Its origins are unknown other than it is believed to have been new to a Manchester area operator.

Disposal:

VM 3669: No known disposal.

Vehicle acquired from East Yorkshire Motor Services Ltd, Kingston upon Hull (ER) 6/35:

24	RH 2257	Gilford 168OT	11640	HC Motor Works	B32R	6/30	4/41

Previous history:

RH 2257 (24): New to HC Motor Works Ltd {Kingston Motor Services}, Kingston upon Hull (ER) 46; East Yorkshire Motor Services Ltd 206 6/32 (as B31R); withdrawn 10/34; Allday's Commercial Motors (dealer), London SW1 5/35, from whom it was acquired.

Disposal:

RH 2257 (24): A & AE Blackbourn {Granville Tours}, Grimsby (LI) 4/41; last licensed 12/43.

Vehicles acquired from Hants & Dorset Motor Services Ltd, Bournemouth (DT) c6/35:

RU 5796	Leyland Leveret LA2	40067	Leyland	B20F	7/27	-/36
RU 5843	Leyland Leveret LA2	40006	Leyland	B20F	8/27	-/35

Previous histories:

RU 5796: New to Hants & Dorset Motor Services Ltd 2 [renumbered D2 c1930; withdrawn 3/35].
RU 5843: New to Hants & Dorset Motor Services Ltd 216 [renumbered D216 c1930; withdrawn 6/35].

Disposals:

RU 5796: Unidentified operator / dealer 1936.
RU 5843: Unidentified operator / dealer by 12/35.

Vehicle acquired from C King, Little Coxwell (GBE) 7/35:

18	RX 9463	Bedford WLG	114997	cattle truck		11/31	9/37

Previous history:
> RX 9463 (18): New to C King [as a cattle truck].

Notes:
> RX 9463 (18): Rebuilt as a coach (as C20F) before entry into service; the body probably came from the 1927 Reo Major (identity unknown, ex JC Durnford 6/32, qv) which was rebuilt as a lorry 1935.

Disposal:
> RX 9463 (18): Last licensed 9/37.

Vehicle acquired from Wilts & Dorset Motor Services Ltd, Salisbury (WI) 9/35:

49	MW 4028	Gilford 166OT	10493	Wycombe	C31F	3/29	by6/40

Previous history:
> MW 4028 (49): New to Sparrow & Vincent {Victory Motor Services}, Salisbury (quoted variously as C32R and C31D; rebuilt to C31F and fitted with a sunshine roof by Heaver c1931); Wilts & Dorset Motor Services Ltd 134 12/33.

Disposal:
> MW 4028 (49): Sir Alexander Gibb & Partners (contractor) (X) by 6/40.

Vehicle acquired from CH Ballard {Southend Garage}, Bradfield (BE) 10/35:

43	UL 7692	Dennis F	80095	Dodson	C20D	3/29	1/37

Previous history:
> This vehicle was acquired with the Ballard business; its previous history is detailed in the Vehicles of Acquired Operators section.

Disposal:
> UL 7692 (43): H Lane & Co Ltd (dealer), London SW10 1/37; D Penfold, Thatcham (GBE or dealer) 1/37.

Vehicle acquired from ER & EM Whitren {Billie's Coaches}, Pennington (HA) 10/35:

58	OU 2885	GMC T30C	4523C	London Lorries	C20D	7/29	12/40

Previous history:
> OU 2885 (58): New to ER & EM Whitren {Billie's Coaches}.

Notes:
> OU 2885 (58): Probably cannibalised for spares after 12/40.

Disposal:
> OU 2885 (58): No known disposal.

Vehicles acquired from Crosville Motor Services Ltd, Chester (CH) 12/35:

UN 5227	Bedford WLB	108014	Willmott	C20F	10/31	12/38
UN 5381	Bedford WLB	108111	Willmott	C20F	1/32	12/36
UX 9410	Bedford WLB	108151	Dobson	B20F	11/31	7/36

Previous histories:
> UN 5227: New to J Price, New Broughton (DH); Crosville Motor Services Ltd U32 4/35; H Lane & Co Ltd (dealer), London SW10 1935, from whom it was acquired.
> UN 5381: New to J Price, New Broughton (DH); Crosville Motor Services Ltd U33 4/35; H Lane & Co Ltd (dealer), London SW10 1935, from whom it was acquired.
> UX 9410: New to WB Jones, Ifton Heath (SH); Crosville Motor Services Ltd U30 3/35; H Lane & Co Ltd (dealer), London SW10 1935, from whom it was acquired.

Disposals:
> UN 5227: MJ Eagle, Castle Acre (NK) 12/38; withdrawn 6/39.
> UN 5381: Unidentified operator / dealer 12/36.
> UX 9410: Surfleet PSV School, Thornton Heath (XSR) 7/36.

Vehicle acquired from W Alexander & Sons Ltd, Falkirk (SN) 12/35:

RG 881	GMC T30C		303764	?		-20-	12/29	-/38

Previous history:
RG 881: R Raffan {Radio Bus Service}, Aberdeen (AD); W Alexander & Sons Ltd (not operated) 7/35; E & N Sanderson {Millburn Garage} (dealer), Glasgow 9/35, from whom it was acquired.

Disposal:
RG 881: No known disposal.

Vehicle acquired from Eastern National Omnibus Co Ltd, Chelmsford (EX) 12/35:

48	MS 9336	Gilford 166OT		10955	Wycombe		B32F	11/29 by3/39

Previous history:
MS 9336: New to James Penman & Co Ltd, Bannockburn (SN); numbered 21 by 1930; W Alexander & Sons Ltd, Falkirk (SN) 16 11/31; renumbered Y1 1932; Gilford Motor Co Ltd (dealer), London NW10 8/32; Stanford Motors Ltd, Stanford-le-Hope (EX) 3/33; Eastern National Omnibus Co Ltd 7/35; withdrawn 9/35; unidentified dealer 11/35, from whom it was acquired.

Disposal:
MS 9336: Unidentified operator / dealer by 3/39; at Felsted as a caravan by 1956.

Vehicle acquired from Midland General Omnibus Co Ltd, Langley Mill (DE) 12/35:

32	RA 9830	GMC T42		423043D	Duple	1742	B24F	10/29	1/41

Previous history:
RA 9830 (32): New to GF Eaton, Heage (DE) (as B26F); JH Booth, Westhouses (DE) c1930; Midland General Omnibus Co Ltd (not operated) 7/34.

Disposal:
RA 9830 (32): No known disposal.

Vehicle acquired from London Passenger Transport Board, London SW1 (LN) 12/35:

53	HX 1855	Gilford AS6		11579	Petty		C20D	11/30	4/39

Previous history:
HX 1855 (53): New to Western Star Motorways Ltd, Hayes (MX); Chesham & District Bus Co Ltd, Chesham (BK) 9 1932; Amersham & District Motor Bus & Haulage Co Ltd, Amersham (BK) 11/32; London Passenger Transport Board, London SW1 (LN) 11/33; H Lane & Co Ltd (dealer), London SW10 9/35, from whom it was acquired.

Disposal:
HX 1855 (53): Unidentified operator / dealer 4/39; A Ott (showman), Feltham by 3/48; last licensed 9/53.

Vehicle acquired from EA Dyer {Regal Coaches}, Croydon (SR) 12/35:

61	OY 2093	Bedford WLB		?	REAL		C20F	12/31	c3/38

Previous history:
OY 2093 (61): New to EA Dyer {Regal Coaches}.

Disposal:
OY 2093 (61): WT Blewett {Crimson Tours}, St Ives (CO) 1938; Blewetts Ltd {Crimson Tours}, St Ives (CO) 1948; last licensed 4/49.

Vehicle acquired from L Park {Fram Coaches}, Addiscombe (SR) 12/35:

62	OY 5807	Bedford WLB		109129	Duple	3659	C20F	5/33	c3/38

Previous history:
OY 5807 (62): New to L Park {Fram Coaches}; Arlington Motor Co Ltd (dealer), London SW1 by 5/33, from whom it was acquired.

Disposal:
OY 5807 (62): No known disposal.

Vehicle acquired from Mrs EG Kent {Kingsclere Coaches}, Baughurst (HA) 12/35:

(OT 816?)	Thornycroft A1	?	Hall Lewis		Ch20	-/25	----

Previous history:
(OT 816?): New as a demonstrator with John I Thornycroft Ltd (dealer), Basingstoke; Mrs EG Kent {Kingsclere Coaches} 3/26 [withdrawn 1932].

Notes:
(OT 816?): Its registration is not confirmed; acquired for spares only.

Disposal:
(OT 816?): Scrapped c1938.

1936

Vehicles acquired from London Passenger Transport Board, London SW1 (LN) 5/36:

21	JH 492	Thornycroft A12	20914	Thurgood	427	B20F	9/31	8/45
	MY 346	Gilford 166SD	10830	Duple	1605	C26D	7/29	c3/38
20	UR 7968	Thornycroft A2 Long	18742	Thurgood	376	B20F	11/30	6/40

Previous histories:
JH 492 (21): New to People's Motor Services Ltd, Ware (HT) 27; London Passenger Transport Board NY1 11/33; GJ Dawson (Clapham) Ltd (dealer), London SW9 5/36, from whom it was acquired.
MY 346: New to Skylark Motor Coach Co Ltd, London W3 (LN) 7; Green Line Coaches Ltd, London SW1 (LN) GF7 2/32; London Passenger Transport Board (Country Bus Department) GF130 10/33 (as C20D); GJ Dawson (Clapham) Ltd (dealer), London SW9 2/36, from whom it was acquired.
UR 7968 (20): New to People's Motor Services Ltd, Ware (HT) 25; London Passenger Transport Board NY8 11/33; GJ Dawson (Clapham) Ltd (dealer), London SW9 4/36, from whom it was acquired.

Disposals:
JH 492 (21): Showman 8/45.
MY 346: TR Davies (showman), Reigate 1938; still with a showman 4/49.
UR 7968 (20): War Department (GOV) 12/40; Tottenham Corporation (GOV) as a mobile ARP unit 12/40.

Vehicle acquired from J Carruthers junior {Carruthers Bus Service}, New Abbey (KK) 12/36:

52	TY 8886	Gilford 168MOT	11996	Strachan		C26R	12/31	2/41

Previous history:
TY 8886 (52): New to Orange Bros Ltd, Bedlington (ND) 34 (having been exhibited at the 1931 Commercial Vehicle Show); United Automobile Services Ltd, Darlington (DM) (not operated) 5/33; J Carruthers junior by 1934; fitted with a Lycoming engine (to 168OT specification) at an unknown date; Albion Motors Ltd (dealer), Scotstoun 5/36; E & N Sanderson {Millburn Garage} (dealer), Glasgow 1936; Horne Products Ltd (dealer), London NW10 1936, from whom it was acquired.

Notes:
TY 8886 (52): Reseated to C31R c12/36.

Disposal:
TY 8886 (52): H Lane & Co Ltd (dealer), London SW10 2/41; CJ Towler & Sons, Emneth (NK) 4/41; T Wood (showman), Norwich 3/46.

Vehicle acquired from The Borough Services Ltd, Southend-on-Sea (EX) 12/36:

	MT 1842	Gilford 166OT	10587	Wilton		C32D	1/29	----

Previous history:
MT 1842: New to WD Beaumont & A Priest {Beaumont-Safeway Saloon Coaches}, Enfield (MX); The Borough Services Ltd 8/30; Horne Products Ltd (dealer), London NW10 by 12/36, from whom it was acquired.

Notes:
>MT 1842: Acquired for spares only; body transferred to RD 1886 (rebuilt to C32R) c12/36 (qv); its chassis
>was cannibalised for spares.

Disposal:
>MT 1842: Scrapped at an unknown date.

1937

Vehicles acquired from London Passenger Transport Board, London SW1 (LN) 1/37:

46	PG 1099	Thornycroft A2 Long	15924	Challands Ross	B20F	6/29	12/40
14	PG 2018	Thornycroft A2 Long	15945	Challands Ross	B20F	7/29	4/44
16	PG 3236	Thornycroft A2 Long	18665	Challands Ross	B20F	9/29	2/41
17	PG 4226	Thornycroft A2 Long	18664	Challands Ross	B20F	11/29	11/40

Previous histories:
>PG 1099 (46): New to JR Fox & Sons {Woking & District}, Woking (SR); London General Omnibus Co Ltd,
>London SW1 (LN) 1/31; loaned to East Surrey Traction Co Ltd, Reigate (SR); London
>Passenger Transport Board 7/33; GJ Dawson (Clapham) Ltd (dealer), London SW9 4/36, from
>whom it was acquired.
>PG 2018 (14): New to JR Fox & Sons {Woking & District}, Woking (SR) 3; London General Omnibus Co Ltd,
>London SW1 (LN) 1/31; loaned to East Surrey Traction Co Ltd, Reigate (SR); London
>Passenger Transport Board 7/33; GJ Dawson (Clapham) Ltd (dealer), London SW9 4/36, from
>whom it was acquired.
>PG 3236 (16): New to JR Fox & Sons {Woking & District}, Woking (SR) 4; London General Omnibus Co Ltd,
>London SW1 (LN) 1/31; loaned to East Surrey Traction Co Ltd, Reigate (SR); London
>Passenger Transport Board 7/33; GJ Dawson (Clapham) Ltd (dealer), London SW9 4/36, from
>whom it was acquired.
>PG 4226 (17): New to JR Fox & Sons {Woking & District}, Woking (SR) 5; London General Omnibus Co Ltd,
>London SW1 (LN) 1/31; loaned to East Surrey Traction Co Ltd, Reigate (SR); London
>Passenger Transport Board 7/33; GJ Dawson (Clapham) Ltd (dealer), London SW9 4/36, from
>whom it was acquired.

Disposals:
>PG 1099 (46): War Department (GOV) 12/40; Cheshunt Urban District Council (GOV) as a mobile ARP unit
>12/40; Middlesex County Council, London NW2 (GOV) as a mobile ARP unit 9/42.
>PG 2018 (14): D Penfold (dealer), Thatcham for scrap 4/44.
>PG 3236 (16): Eagle Star Insurance Co Ltd, London EC2 (XLN) 2/41.
>PG 4226 (17): War Department (GOV) 12/40; Erith Borough Council (GOV) as a mobile ARP unit 12/40.

Vehicles acquired from Southdown Motor Services Ltd, Brighton (ES) 1/37:

31	TP 7951	Thornycroft A2	15927	Wadham	B20F	6/29	4/44
43	TP 8693	Thornycroft A2	18705	Wadham	B20F	2/30	4/44
57	TP 9164	Thornycroft A2	18732	Wadham	B20F	5/30	4/44

Previous histories:
>TP 7951 (31): New to FG Tanner {Denmead Queen}, Denmead (HA) 6; Southdown Motor Services Ltd 41
>3/35; renumbered 541 1936; withdrawn 1936; H Lane & Co Ltd (dealer), London SW10 1/37,
>from whom it was acquired.
>TP 8683 (43): New to FG Tanner {Denmead Queen}, Denmead (HA) 7; Southdown Motor Services Ltd 42
>3/35; renumbered 542 1936; withdrawn 1936; H Lane & Co Ltd (dealer), London SW10 1/37,
>from whom it was acquired.
>TP 9164 (57): New to FG Tanner {Denmead Queen}, Denmead (HA) 8; Southdown Motor Services Ltd 43
>3/35; renumbered 543 1936; withdrawn 1936; H Lane & Co Ltd (dealer), London SW10 1/37,
>from whom it was acquired.

Disposals:
>TP 7951 (31): D Penfold (dealer), Thatcham for scrap 4/44.
>TP 8693 (43): D Penfold (dealer), Thatcham for scrap 4/44.
>TP 9164 (57): D Penfold (dealer), Thatcham 4/44; Ruggles (showman?), Stambourne, Essex 8/48.

Vehicles acquired from CW Banfield, London SE17 (LN) 2/37:

54	HX 7560	Gilford 168OT	11750	Duple	C32F	3/31	c6/40
55	JJ 8873	Gilford 168OT	12137	Duple	C32F	3/33	6/40

Previous histories:
> HX 7560 (54): New to CW Banfield (as C31F); Arlington Motor Co Ltd (dealer), London SW1 by 2/37, from whom it was acquired.
> JJ 8873 (55): New to CW Banfield; Arlington Motor Co Ltd (dealer), London SW1 by 2/37, from whom it was acquired.

Disposals:
> HX 7560 (54): EA Seager {Enterprise}, Sherborne (DT) c6/40; withdrawn 2/49.
> JJ 8873 (55): War Department (GOV) 6/40.

Vehicle acquired from Milton's Services (Crediton) Ltd, Crediton (DN) 3/37:

64	FJ 9581	Dennis Ace	200026	Duple		B20F	3/34	12/44

Previous history:
> FJ 9581 (64): New to Milton's Services (Crediton) Ltd.

Notes:
> FJ 9581 (64): Wrecked in an accident at Worthy Down 7/37; rebuilt by Duple and renumbered 66 c3/38.

Disposal:
> FJ 9581 (66): Unidentified operator / dealer 12/44; Mann, Wootten Green 4/46; Brook, Aylesbury 3/47; last licensed 7/51.

Vehicle acquired from CA Gayton, Ashburton (DN) 3/37:

65	JY 4752	Dennis Ace	200317	Mumford		C20F	12/34	12/44

Previous history:
> JY 4752 (65): New to CA Gayton.

Disposal:
> JY 4752 (65): AW Braybrooke {AF Braybrooke & Son}, Mendlesham (EK) c12/44; RH Tye, Mendlesham (EK) 4/47; last licensed 10/50.

Vehicles acquired from Mrs EG Kent {Kingsclere Coaches}, Baughurst (HA) 4/37:

38	CG 1724	Commer B40	46056	Petty	C20F	8/32	2/38
15	OT 4452	Thornycroft A2 Long	14119	Wadham	B20F	4/27	c7/39
42	OU 6047	AJS Pilot	1004	Petty	B28F	6/30	c7/39
8	TK 2740	Guy OND	OND9218	Guy	B20F	5/29	5/37
5	UN 3196	Chevrolet LR	57315	?	B16F	12/29	12/39
39	ACG 644	Commer B3	?	Petty	C20F	4/35	6/40

Previous histories:
> These vehicles were acquired with the Kent business; their previous histories are detailed in the Vehicles of Acquired Operators section.

Disposals:
> CG 1724 (38): Last licensed 2/38.
> OT 4452 (15): No known disposal.
> OU 6047 (42): No known disposal.
> TK 2740 (8): No known disposal.
> UN 3196 (5): Last licensed 12/39.
> ACG 644 (39): Baddeley Bros Ltd {Green & White Services}, Holmfirth (WR) 29 6/40.

Vehicles acquired from AJ Low {Pass & Co}, Newbury (BE) 5/37:

	JB 437	Ford AA	4839808	?	C20-	6/32	12/37
60	JB 5701	Ford BB	1056354	?	C20-	2/35	3/41
	RX 7150	Ford AA	3452798	?	C14F	7/30	c9/37

Previous histories:
> These vehicles were acquired with the Low business; their previous histories are detailed in the Vehicles of Acquired Operators section.

Notes:

RX 7150:   May not have operated for Newbury & District Motor Services Ltd.

Disposals:

JB 437:   WH Martin, Howden (ER) 12/37; Bailey's Bus Service Ltd, Fangfoss (ER) 6/45; converted to a goods vehicle 9/50; last licensed 5/53 and scrapped.

JB 5701 (60): Last licensed 3/41.

RX 7150:   BC Leather {Maiden Bradley Service}, Maiden Bradley (WI) c9/37; last licensed 12/43.

Vehicle acquired from Tillingbourne Valley Bus Services Ltd, Chilworth (SR) 5/37:

8	UO 9841	Thornycroft A2 Long	15871	Wadham		B20F	3/29	12/40

Previous history:

UO 9841 (8): New to J Geddes {Burton Cars}, Brixham (DN); Tillingbourne Valley Bus Services Ltd 2/33.

Disposal:

UO 9841 (8): War Department (GOV) 12/40; Air Raids Precautions, Tottenham (GOV) 12/40.

Vehicles acquired from Trent Motor Traction Co Ltd, Derby (DE) 6/37:

44	TV 5363	TSM B10A	8551	Beadle	194	B32F	12/31	6/42
45	TV 6036	TSM B49A7	8682	Willowbrook		B32F	4/32	9/40

Previous histories:

TV 5363 (44): New to W, AW, L, E, F & S Dutton {Unity Bus Service}, Nottingham (NG); Dutton's Unity Services Ltd {Unity Bus Service}, Nottingham (NG) 6/32; Trent Motor Traction Co Ltd 1220 8/35; W North Ltd (dealer), Leeds 9/36; H Lane & Co Ltd (dealer), London SW10 by 6/37, from whom it was acquired.

TV 6036 (45): New to W, AW, L, E, F & S Dutton {Unity Bus Service}, Nottingham (NG); Dutton's Unity Services Ltd {Unity Bus Service}, Nottingham (NG) 6/32; Trent Motor Traction Co Ltd 1219 8/35; W North Ltd (dealer), Leeds 9/36; H Lane & Co Ltd (dealer), London SW10 by 6/37, from whom it was acquired.

Disposals:

TV 5363 (44): Salopia Coaches Ltd, Whitchurch (SH) 32 6/42 (as B30F); WJ Hanmer & Sons, Southsea (DH) 10/48 (as B32F); withdrawn 12/50.

TV 6036 (45): A Jones {Bryn Melyn Motor Services}, Llangollen (DH) 9/40; last licensed 12/44.

Vehicle acquired from AJ Low {Pass & Co}, Newbury (BE) 7/37:

64	RX 2907	Ford AA	?	Vincent		C14D	8/28	11/39

Previous history:

RX 2907 (64): New to G Salkeld {Pass & Co}, Newbury (BE); AJ Low 7/31; Pass & Co (dealer), Newbury 5/37, from whom it was acquired.

Disposal:

RX 2907 (64): Last licensed 11/39.

1938

Vehicle acquired from J & W Hawkins {Hawkins Bros / Scarlet Pimpernel Coaches}, Minehead (SO) 3/38:

67	AYA 102	Dennis Ace	200170	Harrington		C20R	6/34	5/46

Previous history:

AYA 102 (67): New to J & W Hawkins {Hawkins Bros / Scarlet Pimpernel Coaches}.

Disposal:

AYA 102 (67): P & M, Ipswich (EK) 29 5/46; scrapped 11/52.

Vehicle acquired from FC Cottrell, Mitcheldean (GL) 3/38:

68	DG 9516	Dennis Ace	200194	Duple	4307	C20F	6/34	12/44

Previous history:

DG 9516 (68): New to FC Cottrell.

Disposal:

DG 9516 (68): Unidentified operator / dealer 12/44; J Hacking {Yellow Rose Coaches}, Morecambe (LA) 3/48; withdrawn 11/48; JJ McGahon (showman), Inverness by 9/50; last licensed 9/50.

Vehicle acquired from Glenton Tours Ltd, London SE14 (LN) 3/38:

69	DYF 184	Dennis Ace	200522	Strachan	C20F	5/37	12/44

Previous history:

DYF 184 (69): New to Glenton Tours Ltd.

Disposal:

DYF 184 (69): F Wightman {F Wightman & Son}, Saxmundham (EK) c12/44; WJ Cooper {Combs Coaches}, Combs (EK) 3/47; AC Bickers, Coddenham (EK) 2/50.

Vehicles acquired from A Young {Red Warrior}, Birmingham (WK) 3/38:

70	BON 886	Bedford WTB	110402	Duple	6905	C25F	4/36	6/46
71	BON 887	Bedford WTB	110430	Duple	6906	C25F	4/36	5/47

Previous histories:

BON 886-887 (70-71): New to A Young {Red Warrior} 9-10.

Disposals:

BON 886-887 (70-71): No known disposals.

Vehicle acquired from London Passenger Transport Board, London SW1 (LN) 7/38:

30	JD 1220	Gilford 168OT	11803	Wycombe	C26F	4/31	----

Previous history:

JD 1220 (30): New to EH Hillman {Hillman Saloon Coaches}, London E15 (LN) 73; moved to Romford (EX) 8/32; London Passenger Transport Board GF67 1/34; GJ Dawson (Clapham) Ltd (dealer), London SW9 12/37, from whom it was acquired.

Notes:

JD 1220 (30): Not operated by Newbury & District Motor Services Ltd.

Disposal:

JD 1220 (30): Unidentified operator / dealer by 3/39; War Department (GOV) 1940; Ministry of Supply (GOV) for disposal by 4/42; JR Munday & Sons Ltd, London SW11 (LN) re-registered GLB 887 4/42.

Vehicle acquired from EE Nobes, Lambourn Woodlands (BE) 7/38:

	TM 5726	Chevrolet LQ	?	Economy	B16F	9/29	----

Previous history:

TM 5726: This vehicle was acquired with the Nobes business; its previous history is detailed in the Vehicles of Acquired Operators section.

Notes:

TM 5726: Not operated by Newbury & District Motor Services Ltd.

Disposal:

TM 5726: No known disposal.

Vehicles acquired from Hants & Dorset Motor Services Ltd, Bournemouth (HA) 7-9/38:

40	RU 5072	Leyland LSC3	45703	Leyland	B35F	4/27	c6/46
	RU 5394	Leyland LSC3	45808	Brush	B32F	5/27	----
29	RU 7559	Leyland LSC3	47239	Leyland	B35F	6/28	6/46
41	RU 7560	Leyland LSC3	47242	Leyland	B35F	7/28	6/46
28	RU 8058	Leyland LSC3	47607	Leyland	B35F	10/28	8/45

Previous histories:

RU 5072 (40): New to Hants & Dorset Motor Services Ltd 106 [renumbered B106 c1930]; T Jefferis (dealer), Hedge End 1938, from whom it was acquired in 9/38.

RU 5394: New to Hants & Dorset Motor Services Ltd 38 (fitted with a Tilling C33D body); renumbered B38 c1930; rebodied Beadle (216) B32- 1932; fitted with the Brush B32F body from Leyland LT1 TK 4687 c1938; T Jefferis (dealer), Hedge End 9/38, from whom it was acquired in 9/38.
RU 7559 (29): New to Hants & Dorset Motor Services Ltd 250; renumbered B250 c1930; T Jefferis (dealer), Hedge End 6/38, from whom it was acquired in 7/38.
RU 7560 (41): New to Hants & Dorset Motor Services Ltd 254; renumbered B254 c1930; T Jefferis (dealer), Hedge End 9/38, from whom it was acquired in 9/38.
RU 8058 (28): New to Hants & Dorset Motor Services Ltd 144; renumbered B144 c1930; T Jefferis (dealer), Hedge End 6/38, from whom it was acquired in 7/38.

Notes:
RU 5394: Acquired for spares only and not operated by Newbury & District Motor Services Ltd.

Disposals:
RU 5072 (40): D Alderton (showman), Chalfont c6/46; withdrawn 1949.
RU 5394: No known disposal.
RU 7559 (29): Classique Coaches Ltd, London E10 (LN) 6/46; withdrawn 10/46.
RU 7560 (41): Classique Coaches Ltd, London E10 (LN) 6/46; withdrawn 10/46; T Tamblyn (showman), Newquay c1947; withdrawn 1947.
RU 8058 (28): No further operator.

Vehicle acquired from S Lovegrove {Lovegrove Bros}, Silchester (HA) c8/38:

	VR 9822	Gilford 168OT	?	?		B32-	7/30 by8/41

Previous history:
VR 9822: New to T McLaw {Curtis Motor Tours}, Manchester (LA); S Lovegrove {Lovegrove Bros}, Silchester (HA) (probably not used) c8/38.

Disposal:
VR 9822: AJ Bayliss, Dymock (GL) by 8/41; withdrawn 6/48.

Vehicle acquired from RA Ford {A Ford & Son}, Silchester (HA) 10/38:

26	RD 6270	Thornycroft Ardent FE	24776	?		B26F	12/34 c8/45

Previous history:
RD 6270 (26): New to G Jarvis & Son {Reading & District Motor Services}, Reading (BE); Thames Valley Transport Co Ltd 300 1/36 (licensed to Ledbury Transport Co Ltd 20 12/37-10/38); RA Ford {A Ford & Son} 10/38.

Disposal:
RD 6270 (26): BG Howse, Aldsworth (GL) 1945; EH & A Jones {Jones Motors}, Ynysybwl (GG) by 4/48.

1939
Vehicle acquired from WP Julius {Julius & Lockwood}, London SE15 (LN) 2/39:

72	MS 8438	Leyland TS1	60259	Alexander	1414	C32F	4/29 7/40

Previous history:
MS 8438 (72): New to W Alexander & Sons Ltd, Falkirk (SN) 142 (with an Alexander (509) B32F body); renumbered 442 6/30; renumbered P15 1932; rebodied 12/35; GJ Dawson (Clapham) Ltd (dealer), London SW9 10/37; WP Julius 4/38.

Disposal:
MS 8438 (72): War Department (GOV) 7/40; Ministry of Works & Buildings (GOV) 10/44.

Vehicle acquired from G Burnham {Grey Luxury Coaches}, Clifton-on-Teme (WO) 5/39:

73	WP 6206	Leyland LT5A	4484	Burlingham		C32R	5/34 11/47

Previous history:
WP 6206 (73): New to G Burnham {Grey Luxury Coaches} 22.

Disposal:
WP 6206 (73): Supremacy, Riseley 11/47

Vehicles acquired from Yorkshire (Woollen District) Transport Co Ltd, Dewsbury (WR) 7/39:

48	HD 4368	Leyland LT2	51530	Leyland	B30F	5/31	6/47
47	HD 4369	Leyland LT2	51531	Leyland	B30F	5/31	6/47
51	HD 4370	Leyland LT2	51532	Leyland	B30F	5/31	5/45
56	HD 4371	Leyland LT2	51533	Leyland	B30F	5/31	7/47

Previous histories:
> HD 4368 (48): New to Yorkshire (Woollen District) Transport Co Ltd 183.
> HD 4369 (47): New to Yorkshire (Woollen District) Transport Co Ltd 184.
> HD 4370 (51): New to Yorkshire (Woollen District) Transport Co Ltd 185.
> HD 4371 (56): New to Yorkshire (Woollen District) Transport Co Ltd 186.

Disposals:
> HD 4368 (48): JA Cassels {Lancaster Coaches}, Woburn Sands (BK) 7/47; withdrawn 5/49.
> HD 4369 (47): J Nicholson & Sons (New Washington) Ltd, New Washington (DM) LL16 6/47; Crown Coaches Group, Newcastle upon Tyne (ND) 9/46; Bedlington & District Luxury Coaches Ltd, Ashington (ND) at an unknown date; TA Wright {Grey Saloon Coaches}, Southend-on-Sea (EX) 3/48; withdrawn 9/49.
> HD 4370 (51): Beeline Roadways (Teesside) Ltd, West Hartlepool (DM) 5/45; J Nicholson & Sons (New Washington) Ltd, New Washington (DM) L036 1/46; Crown Coaches Group, Newcastle upon Tyne (ND) 9/46; Bedlington & District Luxury Coaches Ltd, Ashington (ND) 12/47; withdrawn 11/50.
> HD 4371 (56): CS Flint, Carr Vale (DE) 1/48; Comberhill Motors Ltd (dealer), Wakefield 5/50; Rawson (dealer), Lupsett 5/50; R Forrest (dealer), Bradford 1950; SE Crowe, Ilkley for conversion to a caravan at an unknown date; unidentified dealer for scrap 10/58.

Vehicle acquired from WH Johnson & Sons Ltd, Kings Lynn (NK) 8/39:

18	VF 9339	Thornycroft A2 Long	18731	Challands Ross	B20F	7/30	4/44

Previous history:
> VF 9339 (18): New to B Mace, Shouldham (NK); WH Johnson & Sons Ltd at an unknown date.

Disposal:
> VF 9339 (18): D Penfold (dealer), Thatcham for scrap 6/44.

Vehicle acquired from HJ Eagles {Eagles Coaches}, Kenny Hill (EK) 11/39:

UR 2932	GMC T30	301890	Strachan	B20F	4/29	----

Previous history:
> UR 2932: New to FJ Cobb {Albanian Bus Co}, St Albans (HT) 5; London Passenger Transport Board, London SW1 (LN) 2/34; C & P Sales (dealer), London SW9 10/34; HJ Eagles {Eagles Coaches} 1/35.

Notes:
> UR 2932: Acquired for spares only.

Disposal:
> UR 2932: Scrapped 1940.

1940

Vehicles acquired from Maidstone Corporation (KT) 6/40:

49	KP 8371	Leyland LT1	50352	RSJ	B31R	7/29	6/46
42	KP 8372	Leyland LT1	50353	RSJ	B31R	7/29	6/46

Previous histories:
> KP 8371 (49): New to Maidstone Corporation 19.
> KP 8372 (42): New to Maidstone Corporation 20.

Disposals:
> KP 8371 (49): Black & White, London E17 as a breakdown tender c6/46.
> KP 8372 (42): D Gordon {Radio Coaches}, Luton (BD) c6/46.

Vehicle acquired from CJ Payne, Buckingham (BK) 6/40:

59	YD 9912	Dennis Ace	200207	Dennis		B20F	6/34	4/45

Previous history:
> YD 9912 (59): New to WLG Waterman, Bridgwater (SO); CJ Payne 6/39.

Notes:
> YD 9912 (59): Was rebuilt or refurbished 1943.

Disposal:
> YD 9912 (59): Pearce, location unknown 4/45; last licensed 1950.

Vehicles acquired from London Passenger Transport Board, London SW1 (LN) 6-7/40:

23	EV 5909	Dennis Dart	75783	Metcalfe		B20F	4/32	12/43
	GX 5327	Dennis Dart	75791	LGOC		B18F	12/32	----
61	CKL 719	Dennis Ace	200453	Dennis		B20F	1/36	3/46
74	EKP 140	Thornycroft CF/FB4/1 Dainty	26572	Thurgood	667	B20F	4/38	-/44

Previous histories:
> EV 5909 (23): New to C & A Roberts & E Hammer {Romford & District Motor Services}, Romford (EX); London Passenger Transport Board DA44 7/34; Steel Breaking & Dismantling Co (dealer), Edgware 3/40, from whom it was acquired in 6/40.
> GX 5327: New to London General Omnibus Co Ltd, London SW1 (LN) DA36; London Passenger Transport Board DA36 4/33; Steel Breaking & Dismantling Co (dealer), Edgware 3/40, from whom it was acquired in 7/40.
> CKL 719 (61): New to West Kent Motor Services Ltd, Sundridge (KT) 9 (fitted with a Perkins Wolf diesel engine); London Passenger Transport Board 10/39; H Lane & Co Ltd (dealer), London SW10 by 6/40, from whom it was acquired in 6/40.
> EKP 140 (74): New to West Kent Motor Services Ltd, Sundridge (KT) 4; London Passenger Transport Board 10/39; H Lane & Co Ltd (dealer), London SW10 by 6/40, from whom it was acquired in 6/40.

Notes:
> GX 5327: Acquired for spares only and not operated by Newbury & District Motor Services Ltd.
> CKL 719 (61): Had a Dennis petrol engine whilst with Newbury & District, but it is not known when this was fitted; was rebuilt or refurbished 1943.

Disposals:
> EV 5909 (23): Last licensed 12/43; D Penfold (dealer), Thatcham 4/44; A Uzzell, Thatcham by 9/46.
> GX 5327: War Department (GOV) 10/40; Air Raids Precautions (ARP) (GOV) 10/40; Crystal Palace Vehicle Reserve, Ministry of Supply Dump (GOV) by 10/43; National Fire Service (GOV) by 7/46.
> CKL 719 (61): F Wightman {F Wightman & Son}, Saxmundham (EK) 3/46; PE King, Lavenham (EK) 12/47; withdrawn 12/50.
> EKP 140 (74): AA Austin, Cold Ash (BE) 1944; withdrawn 5/52.

Vehicle acquired from RA Ford {A Ford & Son}, Silchester (HA) 7/40:

	GF 6677	Gilford 168SD	11223	Duple	1861	C26D	4/30	----

Previous history:
> GF 6677: New to Ledbury Transport Co Ltd 52; RA Ford {A Ford & Son} 6/37.

Notes:
> GF 6677: Acquired for spares only and not operated by Newbury & District Motor Services Ltd; it was put back into roadworthy condition by its subsequent operator.

Disposal:
> GF 6677: L Coleman, Tydd St Giles (EY) 4/41; last licensed 12/45.

Vehicle acquired from S Hayter {Yellow Bus Service}, Guildford (SR) 10/40:

75	BPG 531	Dennis Ace	200182	Dennis		B20F	6/34	1/47

Previous history:
> BPG 531 (75): New to S Hayter {Yellow Bus Service} 6.

Notes:
    BPG 531 (75): Rebuilt or refurbished 1943.

Disposal:
    BPG 531 (75): Wootten (dealer), Birmingham 1/47; United Nations Refugee Rehabilitation Agency (UNRRA) (for transporting displaced persons from camps in Czechoslovakia) 6/47; probably ultimately burnt as a health precaution.

Vehicle acquired from A, A, J, W & H Rowe {A Rowe & Sons}, Cudworth (WR) 10/40:

80	HL 5228	Leyland LT5	468	Roe		GO2061	B32F	4/32	3/48

Previous history:
    HL 5228 (80): New to West Riding Automobile Co Ltd, Wakefield (WR) 342; A, A, J, W & H Rowe {A Rowe & Sons} 5/39.

Disposal:
    HL 5228 (80): AJ Roberts & J Dickinson {Ashford Belle Coaches / Martindale Coaches}, Ashford (MX) 8/48; AE Banwell {Regent Coaches}, Biddisham (SO) 10/48; TR Banwell, Newport (MH) 4/49; last licensed 3/50; scrapped by 11/52.

Vehicle acquired from WR Taylor {Taylor's Garage}, Ryde (IW) 11/40:

45	YV 5499	Leyland LSC3	46384	Birch		C32F	6/28	by6/42

Previous history:
    YV 5499 (45): New to Birch Bros Ltd, London NW5 (LN) K11; WR Taylor {Taylor's Garage} 10/34.

Disposal:
    YV 5499 (45): War Department (GOV) by 6/42; scrapped 11/43.

Vehicle acquired from S Hayter {Yellow Bus Service}, Guildford (SR) 12/40:

72	CPA 828	Dennis Ace	200359	Dennis		B20F	12/34	1/46

Previous history:
    CPA 828 (72): New to S Hayter {Yellow Bus Service}.

Notes:
    CPA 828 (72): Rebuilt or refurbished 1943.

Disposals:
    CPA 828 (72): JB Morgan, Brynhyfryd (GG) 1/46; showman, Birmingham 6/52; registration voided 12/57.

Vehicle acquired from F Homer, Cannock (ST) 12/40:

50	UR 9658	Leyland LT2	51626	Birch		B32F	5/31	10/47

Previous history:
    UR 9658 (50): New to AE & CF Russett {Charles Russett & Son / St Albans & District}, St Albans (HT); London Passenger Transport Board, London SW1 (LN) 11/33; William R Wintour & Co (dealer), London W1 4/36; F Homer 1936.

Disposal:
    UR 9658 (50): T Baker & Sons, Compton (XBE) 10/47; scrapped 1952.

Vehicles acquired from W Emmerson {OK Motor Services}, Evenwood (DM) 12/40:

82	KV 9903	Dennis Ace	200251	Willowbrook	2708	C20F	6/34	7/46
77	ARA 370	Dennis Ace	200221	Willowbrook		B20F	6/34	6/46
81	AVO 977	Dennis Ace	200254	Willowbrook		DP20F	12/34	6/46

Previous histories:
    KV 9903 (82): New to RGW Coombs {Park & Bunty Motorways}, Coventry (WK); Saunt, Ellistown (LE) at an unknown date; W Emmerson {OK Motor Services} c1939.
    ARA 370 (77): New to A Turner, Brampton (DE); W Emmerson {OK Motor Services} 1939.

AVO 977 (81): New to CH Wright, Newark (NG); CH, LC & FD Wright {CH Wright & Sons}, Newark (NG) at an unknown date; W Emmerson {OK Motor Services} 1939.

Disposals:

KV 9903 (82): No known disposal.

ARA 370 (77): G Woolston {Keysonian}, Keysoe (BD) 9/46; last licensed 10/51.

AVO 977 (81): AE Marshall {Eagle Coaches}, Bedford (BD) 6/46; Phillimore & Holloway, Bedford (BD) 11/47; withdrawn 8/49.

Vehicle acquired from WF Alexander {Comfy Bus Service}, Horsham (WS) 12/40:

79	RV 6259	Dennis Ace	200349	Dennis		B20F	1/35	1/47

Previous history:

RV 6259 (79): New to WR Parsons {Blue Bird Service}, Winterslow (WI); WF Alexander {Comfy Bus Service} 7/39.

Notes:

RV 6259 (79): Rebuilt or refurbished 1943.

Disposal:

RV 6259 (79): Wootten (dealer), Birmingham 1/47; United Nations Refugee Rehabilitation Agency (UNRRA) (for transporting displaced persons from camps in Czechoslovakia) 10/47; probably ultimately burnt as a health precaution.

Vehicle acquired from JWH & P Marson {J Marson & Sons}, Bentley (WR) 12/40:

83	AUB 354	Dennis Ace	200345	?		B20F	12/34	6/47

Previous history:

AUB 354 (83): New to JWH & P Marson {J Marson & Sons}.

Disposal:

AUB 354 (83): Ashline Ltd {Ashline Coaches}, Tonbridge (KT) 6/47; F Fuggle {Fuggle's Garage}, Benenden (KT) 5/49; withdrawn 9/60; PF Wilks et al, High Wycombe for preservation (but not restored) 4/61; unidentified dealer for scrap by 12/73 (probably much earlier).

1941

Vehicle acquired from Gregory & Richards, Oldham (LA) 1/41:

84	CK 4573	Leyland TS2	61661	Weymann	W850	B32F	4/31	7/48

Previous history:

CK 4573 (84): New to J Watkinson {Scout Motor Services}, Preston (LA) 29 (with a Weymann (W850) C30D body); Scout Motor Services Ltd, Preston (LA) 29 12/32; Elgin & District Bus Co Ltd, Elgin (MR) 20 4/34 (as C32D); W Alexander & Sons Ltd, Falkirk (SN) P294 11/35; Coaches & Components (dealer), London N7 2/37; J Riley {Riley's Motor Tours}, Belper (DE) 6/38; Gregory & Richards, Oldham (LA) (not operated) c1939; H Lane & Co Ltd (dealer), London SW10 1940, from whom it was acquired having been fitted with a second-hand Leyland B32F body at an unknown date.

Disposal:

CK 4573 (84): AJ Roberts & J Dickinson {Ashford Belle Coaches / Martindale Coaches}, Ashford (MX) (not operated) 8/48; fitted with a post-war Strachan C33F body by 3/49; TR Banwell, Newport (MH) 3/49; TR Banwell Ltd, Newport (MH) by 12/50; last licensed 12/52 (or possibly 11/53); scrapped by 11/55.

Vehicle acquired from KW Services Ltd, Daventry (NO) 2/41:

58	MJ 4550	Dennis Ace	200192	Grose		DP20F	6/34	1/47

Previous history:

MJ 4550 (58): New to RLH & A Seamarks {Seamarks Bros}, Higham Ferrers (NO); KW Services Ltd, Daventry at an unknown date.

Notes:

MJ 4550 (58): Rebuilt or refurbished 1942.

Disposal:
> MJ 4550 (58): Wootten (dealer), Birmingham 1/47; United Nations Refugee Rehabilitation Agency (UNRRA) (for transporting displaced persons from camps in Czechoslovakia) 6/47; probably ultimately burnt as a health precaution.

Vehicle acquired from WF Alexander {Comfy Bus Service}, Horsham (WS) 2/41:

76	BBP 339	Dennis Ace	200412	Dennis		B20F	9/35	12/44

Previous history:
> BBP 339 (76): New to WF Alexander {Comfy Bus Service}.

Notes:
> BBP 339 (76): Rebuilt or refurbished 1943.

Disposal:
> BBP 339 (76): Unidentified operator / dealer 12/44; unidentified operator 4/48; withdrawn 7/50.

Vehicle acquired from C Bourne, Tenterden (KT) 2/41:

78	BKE 720	Dennis Ace	200135	Duple	4177	C20F	4/34	7/45

Previous history:
> BKE 720 (78): New to C Bourne.

Disposal:
> BKE 720 (78): CLW Rayner {Rayner's Coachways}, Feltham (MX) 7/45; Rayner's Coachways Ltd, Feltham (MX) 1/46.

Vehicle acquired from H Lee {Whippet Coaches}, Hilton (HN) 2/41:

85	JB 3354	Dennis Ace	200196	Dennis		C20F	5/34	8/45

Previous history:
> JB 3354 (85): New to Windsorian Motor Coach Service Ltd, Windsor (BE); H Lee {Whippet Coaches} 6/39.

Disposal:
> JB 3354 (85): No known disposal.

Vehicle acquired from Davis Bros, London SW18 (LN) 2/41:

86	CK 3951	Leyland TS2	60059	Leyland		DP29R	9/28	9/48

Previous history:
> CK 3951 (86): New to Ribble Motor Services Ltd, Preston (LA) 493; E & N Sanderson {Millburn Garage} (dealer), Preston 2/37; W Alexander & Sons Ltd, Falkirk (SN) P297 2/37; licensed 6/37; E & N Sanderson {Millburn Garage} (dealer), Glasgow 10/37; Davis Bros 5/38 [reseated to B32R at an unknown date].

Notes:
> CK 3951 (86): Extended to 27ft 6in with longer side panels and square windows during World War 2.

Disposal:
> CK 3951 (86): AE Banwell {Regent Coaches}, Biddisham (SO) 3/49; LC Munden {Airborne Coaches}, Bridgwater (SO) 1/53; last licensed 9/53; AE Banwell {Regent Coaches}, Biddisham (SO) (not operated) by 8/56 (probably by 11/53); scrapped at an unknown date.

Vehicle acquired from AW Latham {Enterprise Coaches}, Kenton (MX) 2/41:

87	DF 7841	Leyland TS2	60191	Alexander		C32F	5/29	9/47

Previous history:
> DF 7841 (87): New to Black & White Motorways Ltd, Cheltenham (GL) L28 (with a Leyland / Abbot C26DT body); Horne Products (dealer), London NW10 12/37; AW Latham {Enterprise Coaches} 2/38, having been fitted with a 1934/5 Alexander body at an unknown date.

Notes:
> DF 7841 (87): Rebuilt or refurbished 1943.

Disposal:
> DF 7841 (87): Feltham Transport Ltd, Bedfont (MX) 2/48; last licensed 12/50.

Vehicle acquired from A Brain {St Leger}, Armthorpe (WR) 3/41:

46	WX 7898	Leyland TS2		Roberts	B32F	7/31	1/47

Previous history:
> WX 7898 (46): New to A Brain {St Leger}.

Disposal:
> WX 7898 (46): Unidentified operator / dealer 1/47.

Vehicle acquired from H Wray & Sons {Ideal Service}, Hoyle Mill (WR) 3/41:

52	TF 4155	Leyland LT2	51470	Leyland	B30F	2/31	9/47

Previous history:
> TF 4155 (52): New to Dallas Services Ltd, Earnshaw Bridge (LA) (as B35F), Arlington Motor Co Ltd (dealer), Ponders End 7/35; H Wray & Sons {Ideal Service} c8/35 (as B32F).

Notes:
> TF 4155 (52): Reseated to B30F at an unknown date.

Disposal:
> TF 4155 (52): TW Earth {Earth's Tours}, Boston (HD) 10/47; C Pell, Cumberworth at an unknown date; last licensed 1/49.

Vehicle acquired from Yorkshire Traction Co Ltd, Barnsley (WR) 3/41:

53	HE 5229	Leyland LT2	51544	Leyland	B30F	5/31	1/47

Previous history:
> HE 5229 (53): New to Yorkshire Traction Co Ltd 345.

Disposal:
> HE 5229 (53): No further operator.

Vehicle acquired from GR Ayres {Ayres Luxury Coaches}, Dover (KT) 3/41:

88	MS 8834	Leyland TS1	60274	Alexander	1435	C32F	3/29	10/47

Previous history:
> MS 8834 (88): New to W Alexander & Sons Ltd, Falkirk (SN) 151 (with an Alexander (520) B32F body and a petrol engine); renumbered 451 6/30; renumbered P30 1932; fitted with a Leyland 8.6 litre diesel engine at an unknown date; rebodied 12/35; GJ Dawson (Clapham) Ltd (dealer), London SW9 10/37; GR Ayres {Ayres Luxury Coaches} at an unknown date.

Disposal:
> MS 8834 (88): Unidentified dealer 10/47; Feltham Transport Ltd, Bedfont (MX) 6/48; withdrawn 5/52.

Vehicle acquired from JWH & P Marson {J Marson & Sons}, Bentley (WR) 3/41:

89	DNW 359	Dennis Ace	200483	Fielding & Bottomley	B20F	6/36	10/43

Previous history:
> DNW 359 (89): New to JWH & P Marson {J Marson & Sons}.

Notes:
> DNW 359 (89): Wrecked in a collision with a train at Didcot Ordnance Factory 1/10/43.

Disposal:
> DNW 359 (89): Scrapped 1943/4.

Vehicle acquired from Ribble Motor Services Ltd, Preston (LA) 3/41:

91	CK 4312	Leyland TS2	61106	Leyland	B26F	5/30	6/47

Previous history:

CK 4312 (91): New to Ribble Motor Services Ltd, Preston (LA) 852; E & N Sanderson {Millburn Garage} (dealer), Preston 9/38, from whom it was acquired.

Disposal:

CK 4312 (91): AE Butler {Sunshine Coaches}, Bagshot (SR) 6/47; fitted with an unidentified C33F body 6/49; Price, Frimley Green (SR) at an unknown date; WGT Worrell {W & O Worrell}, New Addington (SR) 3/53; last licensed 9/54.

Vehicle acquired from JW, E, WC & HW Kitchin {JW Kitchin & Sons}, Pudsey (WR) 5/41:

90	JU 4374	Dennis Ace	200159	Willowbrook	2655	B20F	6/34	8/46

Previous history:

JU 4374 (90): New to R, SL & AH Wheildon {R Wheildon & Sons}; Castle Donington (LE); JW, E, WC & HW Kitchin {JW Kitchin & Sons} 1938/9.

Disposal:

JU 4374 (90): J Hannington, Kettering (NO) 8/46; TG Dilkes, Desborough (NO) by 9/49; SB Lord, Rushden (NO) by 1954; withdrawn by 1955.

Vehicle acquired from Oakland's Hotel, Weybridge (XSR) c5/41:

55	BPH 293	Dennis Ace	200174	Weymann	W993	C20F	6/34	12/44

Previous history:

BPH 293 (55): New to Oakland's Hotel [as C23F].

Disposal:

BPH 293 (55): AJ Hiscock {Silver Queen}, Vernham Dean (HA) 12/44; AH Razey {Amport & District}, Thruxton (HA) 2/49; registration voided 5/51.

Vehicle acquired from H & G Hartshorn {Hartshorn Bros}, Doncaster (WR) c5/41:

92	BUA 795	Dennis Mace	240046	Brush		DP24C	10/35	12/44

Previous history:

BUA 795 (92): New to H & G Hartshorn {Hartshorn Bros}.

Disposal:

BUA 795 (92): Unidentified operator / dealer 12/44; A, A & KM Soames {Forget Me Not}, Clopton (EK) 6/46; AC Bickers, Coddenham (EK) 10/47, HG Reynolds {Forge Coaches}, Whitfield (KT) 12/50 to 6/52.

Vehicle acquired from Scottish Motor Traction Co Ltd, Edinburgh (MN) 12/41:

93	SY 4441	Leyland LT2	51352	Roberts		C28D	6/31	12/45

Previous history:

SY 4441 (93): New to J Bowen & Co {Bowen's Tours}, Musselburgh (MN); Scottish Motor Traction Co Ltd G61 5/35.

Disposal:

SY 4441 (93): Last licensed 12/45.

1942

New vehicle:

94	CMO 523	Bedford OWB	10227	Duple	31781	B32F	11/42	10/51

Notes:

CMO 523 (94): Fitted with utility bodywork; reseated to B30F by 5/50.

Disposal:

CMO 523 (94): Royal Army Education Corps, Beaconsfield (XBK) as a Sergeants' mess 10/51.

Vehicle acquired from Ribble Motor Services Ltd, Preston (LA) 6/42:

| 45 | CK 4518 | Leyland LT2 | 51383 | Leyland | B30F | 3/31 | 6/47 |

Previous history:

CK 4518 (45): New to Ribble Motor Services Ltd 1161; William R Wintour & Co (dealer), London SE17 7/40, from whom it was acquired.

Notes:

CK 4518 (45): There is evidence to suggest that this vehicle was impressed by the War Department (GOV) between 7/40 and 6/42 as Newbury & District wrote to the Ministry of War Transport in 5/42 'seeking its return'.

Disposal:

CK 4518 (45): HC Luff & Son, Leatherhead (SR) 6/47; last licensed 12/49; static caravan, Chavey Down c1950; MA Sutcliffe, Studham (later moved to Tottenhoe) & B Weatherhead, Woburn Sands for preservation 1/81; W Ashcroft, Lostock Hall for preservation c2002; restoration complete c2012; Ribble Vehicle Preservation Group, Freckleton for preservation c2014.

Vehicle acquired from Tom Tappin Ltd {Rambler Coaches}, Wallingford (BK) c11/42:

| 93 | EX 2861 | Thornycroft A12 | 20906 | Economy | C20F | 6/31 | 4/44 |

Previous history:

EX 2861 (93): New to S Page {Beeline}, Gorleston (NK); George Ewer & Co Ltd {Grey-Green}, London N16 (LN) 1934; Tom Tappin Ltd {Rambler Coaches} by 1939.

Notes:

EX 2861 (93): Possibly impressed by the Air Ministry (Royal Air Force) (GOV) 1939-1942.

Disposal:

EX 2861 (93): D Penfold (dealer), Thatcham for scrap 4/44.

1943

New vehicles:

95	CMO 624	Bedford OWB	11719	Duple	31922	B32F	1/43	10/51
96	CMO 657	Bedford OWB	12598	Duple	32014	B32F	2/43	10/51
97	CMO 658	Bedford OWB	12610	Duple	32007	B32F	2/43	2/50
98	CMO 659	Bedford OWB	12604	Duple	32009	B32F	2/43	2/50

Notes:

CMO 624 (95): Fitted with utility bodywork; reseated to B30F by 5/50
CMO 657 (96): Fitted with utility bodywork; reseated to B30F by 5/50
CMO 658 (97): Fitted with utility bodywork; motor tax records quote its chassis number as 12604.
CMO 659 (98): Fitted with utility bodywork; motor tax records quote its chassis number as 12610.

Disposals:

CMO 624 (95): F Cowley (dealer), Salford 10/51.
CMO 657 (96): F Cowley (dealer), Salford 10/51.
CMO 658 (97): A & C McLennan, Spittalfield (PH) 15 c1950; Markinch & District Co-operative Society Ltd, Markinch as a mobile shop (XFE) at an unknown date; last licensed 1/66.
CMO 659 (98): A & C McLennan, Spittalfield (PH) 16 c1950; Auchterader Motors Ltd, Auchterader (PH) by 5/54; A & C McLennan, Spittalfield (PH) 16 c1956; JL Skinner, Clydebank as a goods vehicle (XDB) at an unknown date; last licensed 12/64.

Vehicle acquired from War Department (GOV) 10/43:

| 60 | DL 9011 | Dennis Ace | 200195 | Harrington | B20F | 6/34 | 2/45 |

Previous history:

DL 9011 (60): New to Southern Vectis Omnibus Co Ltd, Newport (IW) 401; War Department (GOV) 7/41.

Disposal:

DL 9011 (60): Unidentified operator / dealer 2/45; FC Hill {London Road Coaches}, Slough (BK) 6 4/46; Bews Booking Office Coaches Ltd, Hillingdon (MX) 8/46; Car Contracts Ltd, London SE5 (LN) 4/49; Olsen Bros Ltd {Pickwick Coaches}, Strood (KT) 6/51; withdrawn 11/51.

1944

New vehicles:

99	CRX 279	Guy Arab II	FD27063	Park Royal	B28565	H30/26R	11/44	7/56
100	CRX 280	Guy Arab II	FD27066	Park Royal	B28567	H30/26R	11/44	6/56
101	CRX 281	Guy Arab II	FD27067	Park Royal	B28566	H30/26R	10/44	12/54
102	CRX 282	Guy Arab II	FD27107	Park Royal	B28568	H30/26R	11/44	5/56
103	CRX 283	Guy Arab II	FD27176	Park Royal	B28590	H30/26R	11/44	5/56

Notes:

CRX 279-283 (99-103): Fitted with Gardner 5LW engines and utility bodywork including wooden slatted seats; fitted with upholstered seats by 5/50.

CRX 279-280 (99-100): Renumbered H1-H2 c12/54.
CRX 281 (101): Decapitated under a low bridge at Boxford 12/54; following this, all high bridge double-deckers were renumbered in a new series prefixed 'H'; allocated H3 in this scheme, but not carried as the vehicle was already withdrawn.
CRX 282-283 (102-103): Renumbered H4-H5 c12/54.

Disposals:

CRX 279 (H1): F Pelham (showman), Hurst 7/56.
CRX 280 (H2): Remblance (dealer), Southampton (minus engine) for scrap 6/56.
CRX 281 (H3): J Mattia (dealer), Nether Wallop for scrap 6/55; chassis returned for spares.
CRX 282-283 (H4-H5): J Mattia (dealer), Nether Wallop for scrap 5/56.

Vehicles hired (and later transferred) from Red & White Services Ltd, Chepstow (MH) c4/44:

447	EAX 647	Bedford OWB	8708	Duple	31681	B32F	8/42	10/49
454	EWO 454	Bedford OWB	9940	Duple	31759	B32F	10/42	10/49
476	EWO 476	Bedford OWB	11825	Mulliner		B32F	1/43	12/48
479	EWO 479	Bedford OWB	13263	Duple	32086	B32F	4/43	12/48
480	EWO 480	Bedford OWB	13276	Duple	32067	B32F	4/43	12/48
481	EWO 481	Bedford OWB	13273	Duple	32069	B32F	4/43	10/49

Previous histories:

EAX 647 (447): New to Red & White Services Ltd 447.
EWO 454 (454): New to Red & White Services Ltd 454.
EWO 476 (476): New to Red & White Services Ltd 476.
EWO 479-481 (479-481): New to Red & White Services Ltd 479-481.

Notes:

These vehicles were fitted with utility bodywork and were permanently transferred to Newbury & District Motor Services Ltd 1/46.

EAX 647 (447): Renumbered 120 1/46.
EWO 454 (454): Renumbered 112 1/46.
EWO 476 (476): Renumbered 118 c6/46.
EWO 479 (479): Renumbered 111 1/46.
EWO 480 (480): Renumbered 110 1/46.
EWO 481 (481): Renumbered 119 c6/46.

Disposals:

EAX 647 (120): Taylor, Marlow (BK) at an unknown date; showman, London E10 by 9/56; noted Barking 9/57.
EWO 454 (112): Cowley Metals Ltd (dealer), Salford at an unknown date; Dowsett (contractor), London at an unknown date; Cowley Metals Ltd (dealer), Salford by 5/53.
EWO 476 (118): Horseshoe Coaches Ltd, Kempston (BD) 6/49; Horseshoe Coaches Ltd, London N15 (LN) 3/51; rebodied Duple (44626) C29F 1951; Horseshoe Coaches Ltd, Kempston (BD) 2/59.
EWO 479 (111): Doolan Bros, Neath (GG) (1/49?); TB Gravell, Kidwelly (CR) 11/50; withdrawn 10/55.
EWO 480 (110): CG & KTJ Williams, Gloucester (GL) 2/49; withdrawn 7/52; T Pearmain & Sons, Southend-on-Sea (EX) 10/52; withdrawn 7/54; Grisby & Son, Kingston-upon-Thames (GSR) by 11/57.
EWO 481 (119): Eddiways, Manchester (GLA) 2/57.

Vehicles hired (and later transferred) from United Welsh Services Ltd, Swansea (GG) c4/44:

659	DWN 258	Bedford OWB	10713	Mulliner		B32F	11/42	9/49
661	DWN 295	Bedford OWB	10588	Duple	31825	B32F	11/42	12/48
664	DWN 298	Bedford OWB	10784	Duple	31846	B32F	11/42	10/49
665	DWN 299	Bedford OWB	11160	Mulliner		B32F	11/42	10/49

Previous histories:
DWN 258 (659): New to United Welsh Services Ltd 659.
DWN 295 (661): New to United Welsh Services Ltd 661.
DWN 298-299 (664-665): New to United Welsh Services Ltd 664-665.

Notes:
These vehicles were fitted with utility bodywork and were permanently transferred to Newbury & District Motor Services Ltd 1/46.

DWN 258 (659): Renumbered 114 1/46.
DWN 295 (661): Renumbered 113 1/46.
DWN 298-299 (664-665): Renumbered 115-116 1/46.

Disposals:
DWN 258 (114): Morley's Grey Coaches Ltd, West Row (WF) (not operated) at an unknown date; scrapped at an unknown date.
DWN 295 (113): H Holmes {Horseshoe Coaches}, Kempston (BD) 1/49; Horseshoe Coaches Ltd, London N15 (LN) 1949; rebodied Duple (44627) C29F 3/51; Horseshoe Coaches Ltd, Kempston (BD) 2/59.
DWN 298 (115): Morley's Grey Coaches Ltd, West Row (WF) (not operated) at an unknown date; scrapped at an unknown date.
DWN 299 (116): Unidentified owner, Hinckley (XLE) as a mobile shop at an unknown date; unidentified dealer for scrap by 1/70.

Vehicle hired (and later transferred) from Red & White Services Ltd, Chepstow (MH) 11/44:

89	PJ 3827	AEC Regal	6621169	Duple	3900	B35C	3/32	12/48

Previous history:
PJ 3827 (89): Exhibited at the 1931 Commercial Motor Show; new to South Wales Express Co Ltd, London W2 (LN) (with a Meltz C30R body); Red & White Services Ltd 89 6/33 [rebodied 1940; fitted with a Gardner diesel engine at an unknown date].

Notes:
PJ 3827 (89): Permanently transferred to Newbury & District Motor Services Ltd and renumbered 109 1/46.

Disposal:
PJ 3827 (109): AJ Roberts & J Dickinson {Ashford Belle Coaches / Martindale Coaches}, Ashford (MX) 1/49; AJ Roberts {Martindale Coaches}, Ashford (MX) 6/49; withdrawn 12/49; HC Martin, Hillingdon (MX) 5/50; fitted with coach seats 1950; withdrawn 9/50.

Vehicles transferred from Red & White Services Ltd, Chepstow (MH) 11/44:

107	TG 1568	AEC Regal	662967	Short		B32R	5/31	7/48
108	TX 9498	AEC Regal	662204	Duple	32210	B35C	5/30	12/48

Previous histories:
TG 1568 (107): New to D Bassett & Sons (Gorseinon) Ltd, Gorseinon (GG) (10) (as B31R); United Welsh Services Ltd, Swansea (GG) 570 1/39; Red & White Services Ltd 570 11/40 [fitted with a Gardner diesel engine at an unknown date].
TX 9498 (108): New to D Bassett & Sons (Gorseinon) Ltd, Gorseinon (GG) 6 (with a Short B31R body); United Welsh Services Ltd, Swansea (GG) 568 1/39 [rebodied 1942]; Red & White Services Ltd 568 7/43 [fitted with a Gardner diesel engine at an unknown date].

Disposals:
TG 1568 (107): EHV Sharpe {Hertfordian Coaches}, South Harrow (MX) at an unknown date.
TX 9498 (108): AJ Roberts & J Dickinson {Ashford Belle Coaches / Martindale Coaches}, Ashford (MX) 1/49; AJ Roberts {Martindale Coaches}, Ashford (MX) 6/49; withdrawn 5/51; showman by 4/54; noted Hampstead Heath 4/55.

1945

New vehicles:

105	CRX 595	Guy Arab II		FD27826	Massey	1680	H30/26R	9/45	6/56
106	CRX 596	Guy Arab II		FD27850	Massey	1681	H30/26R	9/45	6/57

Notes:

CRX 595-596 (105-106): Fitted with Gardner 5LW engines and utility bodywork including wooden slatted seats; fitted with upholstered seats by 5/50; renumbered H7-H8 c12/54.

Disposals:

CRX 595 (H7): Remblance (dealer), Southampton (minus engine) for scrap 6/56.
CRX 596 (H8): J Mattia (dealer), Nether Wallop (minus engine) for scrap 6/57; chassis returned for spares.

Vehicles acquired from Scottish Motor Traction Co Ltd, Edinburgh (MN) 2/45:

122	FS 8560	AEC Regal 4	O642089	Burlingham	B34R	6/34	3/51
123	FS 8562	AEC Regal 4	O642092	Burlingham	B34R	7/34	2/51
130	FS 8565	AEC Regal 4	O642095	Burlingham	B34R	7/34	3/51
127	FS 8566	AEC Regal 4	O642096	Burlingham	B34R	6/34	3/51
124	FS 8567	AEC Regal 4	O642097	Burlingham	B34R	7/34	3/51
126	FS 8572	AEC Regal 4	O642103	Burlingham	B34R	7/34	3/51
128	FS 8574	AEC Regal 4	O642105	Burlingham	B34R	7/34	3/51
129	FS 8575	AEC Regal 4	O642106	Burlingham	B34R	7/34	3/51
125	FS 8576	AEC Regal 4	O642107	Burlingham	B34R	7/34	3/51
121	FS 8582	AEC Regal 4	O642113	Burlingham	B34R	6/34	10/51

Previous histories:

FS 8560 (122): New to Scottish Motor Traction Co Ltd B100 (impressed by the War Department (GOV) 7/40 to 1/43); Broadhead (dealer), Bollington by 1944, from whom it was acquired.
FS 8562 (123): New to Scottish Motor Traction Co Ltd B102 (impressed by the War Department (GOV) 7/40 to 12/44); Broadhead (dealer), Bollington by 1944, from whom it was acquired.
FS 8565 (130): New to Scottish Motor Traction Co Ltd B105 (impressed by the War Department (GOV) 7/40 to 12/42); Broadhead (dealer), Bollington by 1944, from whom it was acquired.
FS 8566 (127): New to Scottish Motor Traction Co Ltd B106 (impressed by the War Department (GOV) 7/40 to 4/43); Broadhead (dealer), Bollington by 1944, from whom it was acquired.
FS 8567 (124): New to Scottish Motor Traction Co Ltd B107 (impressed by the War Department (GOV) 7/40 to 9/42); Broadhead (dealer), Bollington by 1944, from whom it was acquired.
FS 8572 (126): New to Scottish Motor Traction Co Ltd B112 (impressed by the War Department (GOV) 7/40 to 3/43); Broadhead (dealer), Bollington by 1944, from whom it was acquired.
FS 8574 (128): New to Scottish Motor Traction Co Ltd B114 (impressed by the War Department (GOV) 7/40 to 10/42); Broadhead (dealer), Bollington by 1944, from whom it was acquired.
FS 8575 (129): New to Scottish Motor Traction Co Ltd B115 (impressed by the War Department (GOV) 7/40 to 12/42); Broadhead (dealer), Bollington by 1944, from whom it was acquired.
FS 8576 (125): New to Scottish Motor Traction Co Ltd B116 (impressed by the War Department (GOV) 7/40 to 1/43); Broadhead (dealer), Bollington by 1944, from whom it was acquired.
FS 8582 (121): New to Scottish Motor Traction Co Ltd B122 (impressed by the War Department (GOV) 7/40 to 12/43); Broadhead (dealer), Bollington by 1944, from whom it was acquired.

Notes:

These vehicles were acquired in a dilapidated condition and were thoroughly repaired and refurbished over 1945/6; fitted with rebuilt 1936 ECOC B35R bodies (originally DP31R, from nos. 4217-4240) or 1936 ECW B35R bodies (originally B31R, from nos. 4404-4453) from North Western Road Car Co Ltd Bristol JO5Gs (22 of these bodies were purchased by Red & White United Transport Ltd from Broadhead (dealer), Bollington in 5/46; fitted with Gardner 5LW diesel engines, before entering service.

FS 8560 (122): Entered service 7/46.
FS 8562 (123): Entered service 8/46.
FS 8565 (130): Entered service 5/47.
FS 8566 (127): Entered service 2/47.
FS 8567 (124): Entered service 9/46.
FS 8572 (126): Entered service 11/46.
FS 8574 (128): Entered service 3/47.
FS 8575 (129): Entered service 4/47.

FS 8576 (125): Entered service 10/46.
FS 8582 (121): Entered service 6/46.

Disposals:
FS 8560 (122): F Cowley (dealer), Salford 3/51; LW Vass (dealer), Ampthill 1951; last licensed 12/51.
FS 8562 (123): Hanslip (showman), Southampton 2/51; last licensed 9/56.
FS 8565 (130): Wright (dealer?), Salford 3/51; WC French (contractor), Buckhurst Hill 708 8/51; last licensed 12/51.
FS 8566 (127): Unidentified operator / dealer 3/51; Taylor {Riviera Services}, Falmouth 8/51; withdrawn 8/57 and scrapped.
FS 8567 (124): F Cowley (dealer), Salford 3/51; LW Vass (dealer), Ampthill 1951; last licensed 12/51.
FS 8572 (126): Parks (dealer?), Northwich 3/51; WC French (contractor), Buckhurst Hill 709 by 2/52.
FS 8574 (128): W Phillips, Grafton Flyford (WO) 3/51; last licensed 3/52.
FS 8575 (129): AAP (dealer) Dukinfield 3/51; Last licensed 12/53; F Cowley (dealer), Salford 10/55.
FS 8576 (125): F Cowley (dealer), Salford 3/51; LW Vass (dealer), Ampthill 1951; showman, Wormwood Scrubs 4/52; last licensed 9/57.
FS 8582 (121): Desnos (showman), Croydon 10/51; noted Blackheath 5/53; noted London 4/56; last licensed 6/61.

Vehicle transferred from Cheltenham District Traction Co Ltd, Cheltenham (GL) c8/45:

104	FAD 253	Guy Arab II	FD26616	Park Royal	B27164	H30/26R	3/44	6/56

Previous history:
FAD 253 (104): New to Cheltenham District Traction Co Ltd 52.

Notes:
FAD 253 (104): Fitted with a Gardner 5LW engine and utility bodywork including wooden slatted seats; did not enter service until 11/44; reseated with upholstered seats by 5/50; renumbered H6 c12/54.

Disposal:
FAD 253 (H6): Remblance (dealer), Southampton (minus engine) for scrap 6/56.

1946

Vehicle transferred from Cheltenham District Traction Co Ltd, Cheltenham (GL) 4/46:

117	HG 1221	AEC Regent	6611659	Brush		H28/23C	3/32	9/48

Previous history:
HG 1221 (117): New to Burnley Corporation (LA); Burnley, Colne & Nelson Joint Transport Committee (LA) 4/33; Cheltenham District Traction Co Ltd 61 7/45 (as H28/22C).

Disposal:
HG 1221 (117): Unknown owner as a static caravan 9/48.

1947

New vehicles:

131	DMO 320	AEC Regal	O6624583	Duple	45107	B35F	4/47	12/60
132	DMO 321	AEC Regal	O6624584	Duple	45108	B35F	4/47	12/60
133	DMO 322	AEC Regal	O6624667	Duple	45109	B35F	4/47	9/60
134	DMO 323	AEC Regal	O6624668	Duple	45110	B35F	4/47	12/60
135	DMO 324	AEC Regal	O6624585	Duple	45111	B35F	4/47	7/58
136	DMO 325	AEC Regal	O6624586	Duple	45112	B35F	4/47	7/58
137	DMO 326	AEC Regal	O6624588	Duple	45113	B35F	4/47	12/60
138	DMO 327	AEC Regal	O6624589	Duple	45114	B35F	4/47	7/58
139	DMO 328	AEC Regal	O6624587	Duple	45115	B35F	4/47	8/60
140	DMO 329	AEC Regal	O6624669	Duple	45116	B35F	4/47	7/58
141	DMO 330	AEC Regal	O6624957	Duple	45136	C35F	8/47	12/58
142	DMO 331	AEC Regal	O6624960	Duple	45138	C35F	10/47	10/57
143	DMO 332	AEC Regal	O6624958	Duple	45139	C35F	10/47	1/59
144	DMO 333	AEC Regal	O6624963	Duple	45141	C35F	10/47	12/58
145	EBL 736	AEC Regal	O6624965	Duple	45143	C35F	11/47	1/59

Notes:
DMO 320 (131): Equipped for one-man-operation and reseated to B34F 2-7/58.
DMO 321 (132): Equipped for one-man-operation and reseated to B34F c9/57-1/58.

DMO 322-323 (133-134): Equipped for one-man-operation and reseated to B34F 2-7/58.
DMO 326 (137): Equipped for one-man-operation and reseated to B34F 2-7/58.
DMO 328 (139): Equipped for one-man-operation and reseated to B34F 2-7/58.
DMO 331-333 (142-144): Did not enter service until 3/55.
EBL 736 (145): Did not enter service until 3/55.

Disposals:
DMO 320 (131): Unidentified dealer 12/60; Deiniolen Motors (CN) 12/60; Purple, Bethesda (CN) 3/64; Jones {Express}, Rhostryfan (CN) 1/66.
DMO 321 (132): Unidentified dealer 12/60; Creamline Motor Services Ltd, Bordon (HA) 3/61; scrapped 2/63.
DMO 322 (133): Passenger Vehicle Disposals Ltd (dealer), Dunchurch 9/60; Henley, Abertillery (MH) by 2/61; withdrawn 8/64.
DMO 323 (134): Unidentified dealer 12/60; Creamline Motor Services Ltd, Bordon (HA) 2/61; withdrawn 4/63.
DMO 324 (135): Passenger Vehicle Disposals Ltd (dealer), Dunchurch 7/58; Woodhall-Duckham (contractor).
DMO 325 (136): Passenger Vehicle Disposals Ltd (dealer), Dunchurch 7/58; Lloyd, Nuneaton 9/58; W Clayton (contractor), (Ulting?) 1962.
DMO 326 (137): Purple, Bethesda (CN) 12/60; withdrawn 1/65.
DMO 327 (138): Passenger Vehicle Disposals Ltd (dealer), Dunchurch 7/58; Lloyd, Nuneaton 9/58; Arlington Motor Co Ltd (dealer), Potters Bar 6/62.
DMO 328 (139): Passenger Vehicle Disposals Ltd (dealer), Dunchurch 8/60; Hall & Co (contractor), Aberdeen (XAD) 1962; Mills {Wallington Commercials} (dealer), Fareham for scrap c1965.
DMO 329 (140): Passenger Vehicle Disposals Ltd (dealer), Dunchurch 7/58; Millburn Motors (Preston) Ltd (dealer), Preston 3/59; Millburn Motors Ltd (dealer), Glasgow 6/62.
DMO 330 (141): Passenger Vehicle Disposals Ltd (dealer), Dunchurch 12/58; Ellis Bros, Buckley (FT) by 4/59; unidentified operator / dealer 8/61.
DMO 331 (142): AE Connorton Motors (dealer), London SW9 10/57; WL Thurgood (Coachbuilders) Ltd (dealer), Ware 10/57; RS Marchant, Cheltenham (GL) 11/57; Jelf (dealer), Gloucester for scrap 2/60.
DMO 332 (143): Fleet Car (Sales) Ltd (dealer), Dunchurch 1/59; Contract Bus Services Ltd, Caerwent (MH) 7/60; County & Mullins (dealer), Fleur-de-Lys for scrap 1/62.
DMO 333 (144): Passenger Vehicle Disposals Ltd (dealer), Dunchurch 12/58; Thomas, Barry (GG) 12/58; Red Dragon Coaches, Pontllanfraith (MH) 1/59; Bryn Motor Co Ltd, Pontllanfraith (MH) 1960 to 2/61 at least.
EBL 736 (145): Fleet Car (Sales) Ltd (dealer), Dunchurch 1/59; George Wimpey & Co Ltd (contractor), London W6 (XLN) 119 (noted Portsmouth) 3/59; General Auctions 11/61.

Vehicles on hire from Red & White Services Ltd, Chepstow (MH):

240	EM 2730	Albion PW65 (5LW)	16016J	Burlingham (1944)	B34F	8/32	5/47	by1/50
243	EM 2735	Albion PW65 (5LW)	16018B	Burlingham (1944)	B34F	8/32	5/47	by1/50
244	EM 2736	Albion PW65 (5LW)	16018F	Burlingham (1944)	B34F	8/32	5/47	by1/50
249	EM 2741	Albion PW65 (5LW)	16017H	Burlingham (1944)	B34F	8/32	5/47	by1/50

Notes:
These vehicles were on extended hire from Red & White Services Ltd. The dates of their return are unknown but all were back with Red & White by 1/50 (EM 2741 (249) was not licensed after 12/49).

1948

New vehicles:

146	EJB 146	AEC Regal III	O682386	Duple	45367	C35F	3/48	1/59
147	EJB 147	AEC Regal III	O682387	Duple		45368	C35F	3/48	1/59
148	EJB 148	AEC Regal III	O682391	Duple		45369	C35F	3/48	1/59
151	EJB 521	AEC Regent III	O9611887	Weymann / Lydney	M3302	H30/26R	3/48	1/51
149	EJB 649	AEC Regal III	6821A419	Duple	45371	C35F	9/48	1/50
150	EJB 650	AEC Regal III	6821A420	Duple	45370	C35F	9/48	1/50

Notes:
EJB 521 (151): Body finished by Lydney (Mumford prior to 2/48) on a Weymann frame; it was originally built for Venture Transport Ltd, but diverted to Newbury & District.

Disposals:

EJB 146 (146): Fleet Car (Sales) Ltd (dealer), Dunchurch 1/59; Contract Bus Services Ltd, Caerwent (MH) 1959; noted Dungeness 10/60; Wade (dealer), Cardiff for scrap 5/63.

EJB 147 (147): Fleet Car (Sales) Ltd (dealer), Dunchurch 1/59; Contract Bus Services Ltd, Caerwent (MH) 10/59; noted Dover 8/62.

EJB 148 (148): Fleet Car (Sales) Ltd (dealer), Dunchurch 1/59; Contract Bus Services Ltd, Caerwent (MH) by 8/60; noted Llanwern 8/60; noted Dover 6/62; noted Dungeness 8/62.

EJB 521 (151): Venture Transport Ltd, Basingstoke (HA) 102 1/50; Wilts & Dorset Motor Services Ltd, Salisbury (WI) 500 1/51; AW Stephens (dealer), Gloucester for scrap 10/62.

EJB 649-650 (149-150): South Midland Motor Services Ltd 68-69 1/50 (qv).

Vehicles transferred from Red & White Services Ltd, Chepstow (MH) 10-12/48:

154	TG 1819	AEC Regal	662835	Burlingham		B34F	7/31	10/51
152	AGJ 929	AEC Regal	6621433	ECOC		B32R	4/33	1/52
155	AGP 841	AEC Regal	6621427	Burlingham		B34F	4/33	10/51
153	AGX 455	AEC Regal	6621431	Burlingham		B34F	4/33	10/51
156	AMD 47	AEC Regal 4	642010	Duple	4929	B35C	3/33	by5/50
157	FAX 349	AEC Regal	662664	Burlingham		B34F	3/31	10/53

Previous histories:

TG 1819 (154): New to Gough's Welsh Motorways, Mountain Ash (GG) (with a Metcalfe C31- body); Red & White Services Ltd 284 4/36 [rebodied and fitted with a Gardner 5LW diesel engine 7/44]; acquired 11/48.

AGJ 929 (152): New to Blue Belle Motors Ltd, London SW2 (LN) 34 (with a London Lorries / Beadle (321) RC35C body); fitted with a Gardner 6LW diesel engine 7/38; Red & White Services Ltd B34 1/39 [renumbered 734 at an unknown date; fitted with a rebuilt 1936 ECOC B35R (ex-North Western Road Car Co Ltd Bristol JO5G) 1947; fitted with a Gardner 5LW diesel engine at an unknown date]; acquired 10/48.

AGP 841 (155): New to Blue Belle Motors Ltd, London SW2 (LN) 30 (with a London Lorries / Beadle (327) RC35C body); fitted with a Gardner 6LW diesel engine 4/38; Red & White Services Ltd B30 1/39 [renumbered 730 at an unknown date; rebodied 1944; fitted with a Gardner 5LW diesel engine at an unknown date]; acquired 11/48.

AGX 455 (153): New to Blue Belle Motors Ltd, London SW2 (LN) 28 (with a London Lorries / Beadle (325) RC35C body); Red & White Services Ltd B28 1/39 [renumbered 728 at an unknown date; rebodied 1/45; fitted with a Gardner 5LW diesel engine by 2/48]; acquired 11/48.

AMD 47 (156): New as a demonstrator with AEC Ltd, Southall (with a Park Royal (B3227?) B33- body and a petrol engine); fitted with a diesel engine by 2/35; Gough's Welsh Motorways, Mountain Ash (GG) 2/35; Red & White Services Ltd 290 1936 [rebodied 1942; fitted with a Gardner 5LW diesel engine by 2/48]; acquired 11/48.

FAX 349 (157): New to W Salisbury & Sons Ltd, Blackpool (LA) with a Burlingham C26R body and registered FV 1665; WC Standerwick Ltd, Blackpool (LA) 32 7/36; War Department (GOV) 1940; Ministry of Supply (GOV) at an unknown date; Red & White Services Ltd, Chepstow (MH) 795 c1945 [rebodied Burlingham B34F and fitted with a Gardner 5LW diesel engine 1-3/46, entering service 3/46]; acquired 12/48.

Disposals:

TG 1819 (154): E Tucker {Joyride Coaches}, Taunton 10/51; W North Ltd (dealer), Leeds c5/53; showman by 5/55.

AGJ 929 (152): Plant & Son, Reading (minus engine and gearbox) 1/52; caravan 7/52.

AGP 841 (155): E Tucker {Joyride Coaches}, Taunton 10/51; derelict at Dundee 1953.

AGX 455 (153): E Tucker {Joyride Coaches}, Taunton 10/51; showman, Hampton Court 4/52.

AMD 47 (156): Unidentified dealer, probably for scrap by 3/51.

FAX 349 (157): J Mattia (dealer), Nether Wallop 10/53; agricultural engineer, Basingstoke (GHA) 1953.

1949

New vehicle:

158	ERX 937	AEC Regal III	6821A168	Duple	45372	C35F	7/49	1/50

Disposal:

ERX 937 (158): South Midland Motor Services Ltd 70 1/50 (qv).

Vehicle transferred from Cheltenham District Traction Co Ltd, Cheltenham (GL) 3/49:

159	HAD 745	AEC Regent	O961881	Weymann/Mumford M3076	H30/26R	1/48	1/50

Previous history:
> HAD 745 (159): New to Cheltenham District Traction Co Ltd 65.

Notes:
> HAD 745 (159): Body finished by Mumford on a Weymann frame; it was originally built for Venture Transport Ltd, but diverted to Cheltenham District Traction Co Ltd.

Disposal:
> HAD 745 (159): Venture Transport Ltd, Basingstoke (HA) 99 1/50; Wilts & Dorset Motor Services Ltd, Salisbury (WI) 499 1/51; last licensed 10/62; AW Stephens (dealer), Gloucester for scrap 10/62.

Vehicle transferred from Red & White Services Ltd, Chepstow (MH) 9/49:

160	EWO 484	Guy Arab I	FD25937	Lydney			H30/26R	6/43	6/57

Previous history:
> EWO 484 (160): New to Red & White Services Ltd 484 (with a Strachan L27/28R body) [rebodied 1949].

Notes:
> EWO 484 (160): Fitted with a Gardner 5LW engine; renumbered H9 c12/54.

Disposal:
> EWO 484 (H9): J Mattia (dealer), Nether Wallop (minus engine) for scrap 6/57; chassis returned for spares.

1950

New vehicles:

161	FBL 919	AEC Regal III	6821A425	Lydney		B35F	2/50	9/59
162	FBL 920	AEC Regal III	6821A427	Lydney		B35F	2/50	9/59
163	FBL 921	AEC Regal III	6821A426	Lydney		B35F	3/50	9/59
170	FMO 515	Guy Arab III	FD70107	Duple	46098	L27/26RD	2/50	4/68
171	FMO 516	Guy Arab III	FD70177	Duple	46097	L27/26RD	2/50	4/68
172	FMO 517	Guy Arab III	FD70459	Duple	53146	H31/26R	5/50	4/68

Notes:
> FMO 515-516 (170-171): Fitted with Gardner 6LW engines.
> FMO 517 (172): Fitted with a Gardner 6LW engine; renumbered H10 c12/54.

Disposals:
> FBL 919 (161): Fleet Car (Sales) Ltd (dealer), Dunchurch 11/59.
> FBL 920 (162): Fleet Car (Sales) Ltd (dealer), Dunchurch 11/59; Wilson Lovatt & Sons Ltd (contractor), London SW1 (XLN) 11/61.
> FBL 921 (163): Fleet Car (Sales) Ltd (dealer), Dunchurch 11/59; Wilson Lovatt & Sons Ltd (contractor), London SW1 (XLN) 4/60.
> FMO 515-516 (170-171): C Morgan (dealer), Waltham Chase 5/68; Mills {Wallington Commercials} (dealer), Fareham for scrap 5/68.
> FMO 517 (H10): C Morgan (dealer), Waltham Chase 4/68; Mills {Wallington Commercials} (dealer), Fareham for scrap 4/68.

Vehicles transferred from South Midland Motor Services Ltd 1/50:

167	BWL 349	Leyland TS7	6061	Harrington		C32R	5/35	c3/51
168	CWL 951	Leyland TS7	9137	Harrington		C32F	4/36	c3/51
166	CWL 953	Leyland TS7	9138	Harrington		C32F	4/36	c3/51
164	LJO 756	Bedford OB	54661	Duple	46745	C29F	7/47	4/50
165	LJO 757	Bedford OB	61338	Duple	46751	C29F	3/48	4/50
169	LWL 995	Leyland PS1/1	462028	ECOC		DP31R	2/47	6/58

Previous histories:
> BWL 349 (167): New to South Midland Motor Services Ltd 35.
> CWL 951 (168): New to South Midland Motor Services Ltd 36.
> CWL 953 (166): New to South Midland Motor Services Ltd 37.
> LJO 756 (164): New to South Midland Motor Services Ltd 43.
> LJO 757 (165): New to South Midland Motor Services Ltd 44.
> LWL 995 (169): New to South Midland Motor Services Ltd 38.

Notes:

BWL 349 (167): Reseated to B31F at an unknown date.
CWL 951 (168): Reseated to B35F at an unknown date.
CWL 953 (166): Reseated to B35F at an unknown date.
LWL 995 (169): Rebuilt to 30ft long by Thames Valley 11-12/50; rebodied ECW (5464) FC37F (8ft wide) 2/51, returning to service 6/51; reseated to FC34F c2/58; it became the last Leyland vehicle in the Thames Valley fleets.

Disposals:

BWL 349 (167): F Cowley (dealer), Salford c3/51; Wootten, Deeping St James 1955.
CWL 951 (168): F Cowley (dealer), Salford c3/51; E Tucker {Joyride Coaches}, Taunton (SO) 3/51; WEMS, Clevedon (SO) 72 7/53; A Walker {Wivey Coaches}, Wiveliscombe (SO) 10/53; withdrawn 7/56 and scrapped.
CWL 953 (166): F Cowley (dealer), Salford c3/51; E Tucker {Joyride Coaches}, Taunton (SO) 2/52; Champion, Woking c5/52; Lansdowne Luxury Coaches, London E11 (LN) by 6/54; Arscott, Chagford 6/54 to 3/59.
LJO 756-757 (164-165): Thames Valley Traction Co Ltd 164-165 4/50 (qv).
LWL 995 (169): South Midland Motor Services Ltd 169 6/58 (qv); its 1936 ECOC body was sold to Shirley (dealer), Darby Green 11/50.

Vehicles transferred from Thames Valley Traction Co Ltd 4/50:

262	JB 5841	Leyland TS7	7126	Duple	5015	C33F	4/35	4/50	10/53
264	JB 5843	Leyland TS7	7128	Duple	5013	C32F	4/35	4/50	4/54
179	RX 4341	Leyland TD1	70669	Leyland		L27/24R	6/29	4/50	9/52
181	RX 4343	Leyland TD1	70671	Leyland		L27/24R	6/29	4/50	8/52
50	RX 6246	Leyland LT2	51209	Brush		DP32R	7/30	4/50	9/51
246	RX 9700	Leyland TS4	586	Brush		B32R	3/32	4/50	c3/51
255	RX 9709	Leyland TS4	595	Brush		B29R	5/32	4/50	7/51

Previous histories:

JB 5841 (262): New to Thames Valley Traction Co Ltd 262; War Department (GOV) 7/40; re-acquired by Thames Valley Traction Co Ltd 262 3/43.
JB 5843 (264): New to Thames Valley Traction Co Ltd 264; War Department (GOV) 7/40; re-acquired by Thames Valley Traction Co Ltd 264 8/48.
RX 4341 (179): New to Thames Valley Traction Co Ltd 179.
RX 4343 (181): New to Thames Valley Traction Co Ltd 181.
RX 6246 (50): New to Thames Valley Traction Co Ltd 226; Ledbury Transport Co Ltd 50 11/38.
RX 9700 (246): New to Thames Valley Traction Co Ltd.
RX 9709 (255): New to Thames Valley Traction Co Ltd 255; War Department (GOV) 7/40; re-acquired by Thames Valley Traction Co Ltd 255 c4/43.

Disposals:

JB 5841 (262): FG Hobbs {Watling Street Motors} (dealer), Redbourn 4/54.
JB 5843 (264): Schwartz {Baker Street Trading Co} (dealer), London SW7 10/54; exported to Yugoslavia (probably operated for Belgrade City Transport, Belgrade (O-YU)).
RX 4341 (179): Davies (showman), London SW6 10/52; noted Tooting Bec 4/53 and Epsom 6/58.
RX 4343 (181): EW Ross (showman), Lambourn (minus engine and not licensed) 1/53; noted Reading 4/53.
RX 6246 (50): Searle, Harlington (MX) 9/51.
RX 9700 (246): OP Glanville (showman), London SW19 4/51; noted Windsor 5/51 and Stevenage 9/59.
RX 9709 (255): FG Hobbs {Watling Street Motors} (dealer), Redbourn 7/51; rebuilt to FC33F and re-registered MUR 500 1951; Hillside Coaches Ltd, Luton (BD) 2 1951.

1951

Vehicles transferred from Venture Transport Ltd, Basingstoke (HA) 1/51:

173	EWO 490	Guy Arab II	FD26085	Park Royal / Guy	B34341	H30/26R	7/43	10/55
174	EWO 492	Guy Arab II	FD26121	Park Royal / Guy	B34338	H30/26R	7/43	10/55
175	HOT 391	Guy Arab III	FD70240	Duple	53140	H31/26R	6/50	2/68
176	HOT 392	Guy Arab III	FD70349	Duple	53142	H31/26R	5/50	4/68
177	HOT 393	Guy Arab III	FD70379	Duple	53144	H31/26R	6/50	4/68
178	HOT 394	Guy Arab III	FD70436	Duple	53145	H31/26R	6/50	4/68

Previous histories:

EWO 490 (173): New to Red & White Services Ltd, Chepstow (MH) 490 (with a Strachan L27/28R body); rebodied with frames supplied by Park Royal, completed by Guy early 1950 (the Guy body number is unconfirmed, but was probably 164); Venture Transport Ltd, Basingstoke (HA) 100 4/50.

EWO 492 (174): New to Red & White Services Ltd, Chepstow (MH) 492 (with a Strachan L27/28R body); rebodied with frames supplied by Park Royal, completed by Guy early 1950 (the Guy body number is unconfirmed, but was probably 161); Venture Transport Ltd, Basingstoke (HA) 101 4/50.

HOT 391-394 (175-178): New to Venture Transport Ltd 103-106.

Notes:

EWO 490 (173): Fitted with a Gardner 5LW engine; renumbered H11 c12/54.
EWO 492 (174): Fitted with a Gardner 5LW engine; renumbered H12 c12/54.
HOT 391-394 (175-178): Fitted with Gardner 6LW engines; renumbered H13-16 c12/54.

Disposals:

EWO 490 (H11): Remblance (dealer), Stepney (minus engine) 10/55.
EWO 492 (H12): Remblance (dealer), Stepney (minus engine) 10/55.
HOT 391 (H13): J Mattia (dealer), Nether Wallop 2/68.
HOT 392-394 (H14-H16): C Morgan (dealer), Waltham Chase 4/68; Mills {Wallington Commercials} (dealer), Fareham for scrap 4/68.

Vehicles transferred from Thames Valley Traction Co Ltd 5/51:

184	ABL 763	Leyland TS7	12611	ECW		4882	B35R	3/37	10/52
179	AJB 814	Leyland TS8	14374	Brush			B35R	5/37	4/53
185	AJB 815	Leyland TS8	14375	Brush			B35R	5/37	c5/53
180	AJB 816	Leyland TS8	14376	Brush			B35R	5/37	10/53
182	AJB 818	Leyland TS8	14378	Brush			B35R	5/37	4/53
186	ARX 990	Leyland TS8	16995	ECW		5517	B35R	3/38	10/53
181	BBL 558	Leyland TS8	300219	ECW		5663	B35R	6/38	10/53
183	BBL 565	Leyland TS8	300226	ECW		5670	B35R	6/38	10/53
187	CJB 139	Guy Arab 1	FD25546	Strachan			L27/26R	1/43	8/55

Previous histories:

ABL 763 (184): New to Thames Valley Traction Co Ltd 184.
AJB 814-816 (342-344): New to Thames Valley Traction Co Ltd 342-344.
AJB 818 (346): New to Thames Valley Traction Co Ltd 346.
ARX 990 (368): New to Thames Valley Traction Co Ltd 368.
BBL 558 (372): New to Thames Valley Traction Co Ltd 372.
BBL 565 (379): New to Thames Valley Traction Co Ltd 379.
CJB 139 (420): New to Thames Valley Traction Co Ltd 420.

Disposals:

ABL 763 (184): Disposed of through an auction, London c10/52; D Davis (dealer), South Mimms 8/53; showman, Bromley (7/53?); noted Sittingbourne 8/58.
AJB 814 (342): Rodgers Bros, Felixstowe 4/53.
AJB 815 (343): TJ Richardson & Sons (dealer), Oldbury 7/53; unidentified showman, Hastings 7/54; noted Crawley 9/59.
AJB 816 (344): Shufflebottom, Billericay 11/53; showman, Lewes 4/58; noted Shoreham 6/60 and 5/61.
AJB 818 (346): Crowe (showman), March 4/53.
ARX 990 (368): Token Construction Co Ltd (contractor), London (XLN) 12/53.
BBL 558 (372): RA Ford {A Ford & Son}, Silchester (HA) (not operated) 3/54.
BBL 565 (379): Token Construction Co Ltd (contractor), London (XLN) 12/53.
CJB 139 (420): Guy Motors Ltd (dealer), Wolverhampton 8/55; REICOM (O-IC) 1/56.

ANCILLARY VEHICLES

New & acquired vehicles:

	Reg	Make	No	Type			
	?	Thornycroft J		lorry	-/--	6/32	by4/33
	?	Guy		lorry or van	-/--	6/32	by4/33
	?	GMC K41		lorry	c-/25	6/32	by4/33
	?	Star 2½ ton		lorry	c-/23	6/32	by4/33
	TB 2522	Daimler CK		lorry	-/20	6/32	----
L4	CW 6802	Maudslay ML2	3955	van	6/26	6/32	6/37
	?	?		lorry	-/--	9/32	-/--
	OT 6861	Dennis G		lorry	12/27	9/32	3/35
	OT 6862	Dennis G		lorry	12/27	9/32	3/35
	OT 7923	Dennis G		lorry	3/28	9/32	7/35
	RX 4356	Ford AA		lorry	4/29	1/34	12/37
	RD 5922	Bedford 2½ ton		lorry	9/34	9/34	7/45
	JB 1930	Bedford 2½ ton		lorry	5/33	1/35	2/42
	JB 1984	Bedford 2½ ton		lorry	5/33	1/35	2/42
	?	Reo Major		lorry	c-/27	-/35	by4/36
	JB 6909	Bedford 3 ton		(chassis only)	7/35	7/35	4/41
	?	Bedford 2½ ton		lorry	-/34	c2/36	-/--
	HO 6306	Dennis 4 ton		lorry	5/24	3/36	by2/42
	AMO 455	Bedford 2½ ton		van	5/37	5/37	7/44
	JB 5917	Bedford 2½ ton		lorry	3/35	2/39	4/47
	ABL 459	Bedford 2½ ton		lorry	10/36	2/39	7/45
	CMO 963	Bedford OW 5 ton		lorry	-/43	9/47	-/--

Previous histories:

Unidentified (lorry): Acquired from GE Hedges {Reliance Motor Services}, Brightwalton (GBE).

Unidentified (Bedford): Acquired from Great Western Motors (dealer), Reading.

Unidentified (Thornycroft): New as a War Department (GOV) lorry; A & PA Andrews {A Andrews & Son / Favourite Coaches}, Newbury (GBE) at an unknown date, from whom it was acquired.

Unidentified (Guy): Acquired from JC Durnford {C Durnford & Sons}, Newbury (GBE).

Unidentified (Star): Its origins are not known; JC Durnford {C Durnford & Sons}, Newbury (BE) by 7/24 (as Ch18 - converted to a lorry at an unknown date), from whom it was acquired.

Unidentified (GMC): Its origins are not known; JC Durnford {C Durnford & Sons}, Newbury (BE) by 5/28 (as C20- - converted to a lorry at an unknown date), from whom it was acquired.

Unidentified (Reo): Previously in the PSV fleet (qv); its body was removed and rebuilt as a flatbed lorry for the haulage of bricks for the redevelopment of the Jack Hotel site, Newbury 1935.

CW 6802: New to J Bracewell, Blackpool (LA); RJA Allison {Prudence Motor Coaches}, London W6 (LN) 4/28; JC Durnford {C Durnford & Sons}, Newbury (BE) 1/30 [rebodied as a pantechnicon 1/32], from whom it was acquired.

HO 6306: New to Aldershot & District Traction Co Ltd, Aldershot (HA) D100 (fitted with Dennis B36R body); withdrawn 1930; King & Taylor (dealer), Godalming (as a chassis only) 10/30; CG Colliver, Wickham (GBE) 11/30, from whom it was acquired (with his business) (qv).

JB 1930: New to WGR Cleeveley, Newbury (GBE), from whom it was acquired.

JB 1984: New to WGR Cleeveley, Newbury (GBE), from whom it was acquired.

JB 5917: New to James & Co, Hungerford (GBE), from whom it was acquired.

JB 6909 (chassis): Acquired from Great Western Motors (dealer), Reading as a chassis only; fitted with a lorry body by Newbury & District Motor Services Ltd.

OT 6861-6832: New to Aldershot & District Traction Co Ltd, Aldershot (HA) D181-182 [fitted with Hoyal B20F bodies, withdrawn 8/32], from whom they were acquired, probably as chassis only.

OT 7923: New to Aldershot & District Traction Co Ltd, Aldershot (HA) D205 [fitted with a Strachan & Brown C18R body], from whom it was acquired, probably as a chassis only.

RX 4356: New to A Bason, Woolhampton (GBE); JC & WG Durnford, Newbury (GBE) 6/33, from whom it was acquired.

TB 2522: Its origins are not known; AH & TA Denham {Denham Bros}, Newbury (BE) 1925 (as Ch28 – converted to a lorry at an unknown date) [last licensed 4/32], from whom it was acquired.

ABL 459: Its origin is unknown.

AMO 960: Its origin is unknown.

CMO 963: Its origin is unknown.

Notes:

CW 6802: Operated for JC & WG Durnford, Newbury (GBE) as a pantechnicon 7/33 to 1/34 before returning to Newbury & District Motor Services Ltd.

RD 5922: Loaned to Newbury Volunteer Fire Brigade from late 1939 to 7/45.

ABL 759: Loaned to Newbury Volunteer Fire Brigade from late 1939 to 7/45.

Disposals:

Only those vehicles listed below have a known disposal:

CW 6802: Last licensed 6/37; GJ Dawson (Clapham) Ltd (dealer), London SW9 9/37.

OT 6861: Unidentified owner, Hampshire (GHA) 3/35.

OT 6862: Unidentified owner, Middlesex (GMX) 3/35; Inaflash, location unknown (G??) by 2/43.

OT 7923: JC McDermott, London N1 (GLN) 7/35; registration voided 3/39 (as scrapped).

OPERATORS ACQUIRED BY NEWBURY & DISTRICT

Newbury & District was formed by the amalgamation of three established operators in the town:

6/32	A & PA Andrews {A Andrews & Son / Favourite Coaches}, Newbury
6/32	AH & TA Denham {Denham Bros}, Newbury
6/32	JC Durnford {C Durnford & Sons}, Newbury

Over the next six years, a further 17 concerns were absorbed. A number of these were by amalgamation (where their business was merged into the main operation and the former owners became shareholders (and in some cases, employees) of Newbury & District):

9/32	GE Hedges {Reliance Motor Services}, Brightwalton
9/32	J Prothero {XLCR Motor Service}, Beedon
10/32	WC, PB & NW Pocock {Pocock Bros}, Cold Ash
1/33	FG Spanswick {Spanswicks's Bus Service}, Thatcham
1/34	JF Burt & AV Greenwood, Inkpen
1/34	LC, EA & HA Durnford {Durnford Bros}, Newbury
2/34	GP Howlett {Kennet Bus Service}, Bucklebury
3/34	EG White {WJ White & Son / Tony Coaches}, Hermitage
7/38	EE Nobes, Lambourn Woodlands

The remainder were by acquisition (where the business was purchased outright and the seller had no further involvement). In some of these cases, no vehicles were taken into stock by Newbury & District; these operators are marked *):

10/32	*T Holman, Ecchinswell
1/34	Mrs C Geary {Joy Coaches}, Great Shefford
1/34	G Brown {Wash Common Bus Service}, Wash Common
1/35	*WGR Cleeveley, Newbury
10/35	CH Ballard {Southend Garage}, Bradfield
3/36	*CG Colliver, Wickham
4/37	Mrs EG Kent {Kingsclere Coaches}, Baughurst
5/37	AJ Low {Pass & Co}, Newbury

VEHICLES OF ACQUIRED OPERATORS (NEWBURY & DISTRICT)

Arthur & Percy Arthur ANDREWS {A Andrews & Son / Favourite Coaches} Northcroft Lane, NEWBURY (BE)

Arthur Andrews trained as a coachbuilder and wheelwright, setting up his own business in the 1890s to build carts and vans for local tradesmen. His son Percy trained as a motor mechanic and after the World War 1 began refurbishing chassis for his father to body. They jointly embarked on a charabanc operation in 1922, running excursions to the south coast; whilst out of season, a haulage operation was also developed. Further ventures included a car and van hire and a motor repair business. Bus operations commenced in 1931 with a workers' transport contract to Colthrop Mill. The Andrews operation contributed seven vehicles (plus a lorry and a taxi) as well as the coach building shop, maintenance facilities and garage in Northcroft Lane to the initial Newbury & District fleet in June 1932.

Reg	Make	Chassis	Source	Body			
MO 218	Ford T	5824128	Andrews	B14-G	7/22	7/22	1/25
MO 1714	FIAT 15TER	SM33807	Andrews	Ch14	6/23	6/23	c-/27
BL 6490	Talbot 25/50 hp	4SW10379	Andrews	Ch14	4/20	10/25	*
XK 7225	Dennis 3 ton	8397	Andrews?	Ch28	4/22	5/25	8/26
?	Lancia Z	?	Andrews	Ch14	-/--	c-/26	by-/30
?	Lancia Tetraiota	?	Andrews	Ch18	-/--	c-/27	by6/32
?	Guy J	?	Andrews	C20D	c-/25	c-/27	*
?	Reo	?	?	C26-	-/--	c-/29	by6/32
?	Lancia Pentaiota	?	?	B26F	-/28	by-/31	c1/32
VA 3156	Lancia Tetraiota	650	?	B20-	12/24	c3/31	*
DP ????	Lancia Tetraiota	?	Vincent	C20D	-/25	5/31	*
RD 1886	Gilford 168OT	11464	Vincent	C30D	6/30	5/31	*
RX 8261	Ford AA	4453106	Andrews	B20F	3/31	3/31	*
VM 8638	Gilford 166SD	?	Lewis & Crabtree	C26-	4/29	5/31	*

Previous histories:

DP ????: New to EM Hope, Reading (BE); Ledbury Transport Co Ltd {Thackray's Way}, Reading (BE) (not operated) 6/30 (qv), from whom it was acquired.

BL 6490: Originally registered as a private car; rebuilt 1925 as a charabanc.

RD 1886: New to CR Tanton {Tanton's Coaches}, Reading (BE); Ledbury Transport Co Ltd {Thackray's Way}, Reading (BE) (not operated) 6/30 (qv), from whom it was acquired.

VA 3156: New to Rankin Brothers, Glasgow (LK); United Automobile Services Ltd, York (YK) B303 11/28, from whom it was acquired.

VM 8638: New to an unidentified Manchester area operator; CR Tanton {Tanton's Coaches}, Reading (BE) at an unknown date; Ledbury Transport Co Ltd {Thackray's Way}, Reading (BE) 6/30 (qv), from whom it was acquired.

XK 7225: Was an ex-War Department (GOV) lorry, rebuilt 1925 as a charabanc.

Notes:

The unidentified Lancia Pentaiota was offered for sale in 1/32 and was advertised to having been in use up to the end of 1931.

A Thornycroft lorry and a Daimler taxi also passed to Newbury & District Motor Services Ltd (qv).

BL 6490: Rebodied C14D (probably by Andrews) c1930/1.
MO 1714: Its chassis was probably ex-War Department (GOV).

Disposals:

Unidentified (Lancia Pentaiota): Unidentified operator / dealer c1/32.
Unidentified (1927 Lancia Tetraiota): No known disposal.
Unidentified (Lancia Z): No known disposal.
Unidentified (Reo): No known disposal.
MO 218: Newbury Sanitary Steam Laundry, Newbury (GBE) 1/25; unidentified owner (G??) 4/28.
MO 1714: AH & TA Denham {Denham Bros}, Newbury (BE) c1927 (qv).
XK 7225: Unidentified owner (G??) 8/26.

The following vehicles marked with an asterisk above, transferred to Newbury & District 6/32 (qv):

Unidentified Guy, DP ????, BL 6490 (21), RD 1886 (22), RX 8261 (6), VA 3156, VM 8638 (25).

Charles Henry BALLARD {South End Garage}   South End Garage, BRADFIELD (BE)

Charlie Ballard had established South End Garage by 1924. By 1929 he set about developing a coaching business concentrating on excursions and private hire. He sold this business to Newbury & District in October 1935 and concentrated thereafter on his garage business.

RX 4706	Chevrolet LQ	54449	?	C14-	6/29	6/29	6/34
UL 7692	Dennis F	80095	Dodson	C20D	3/29	7/34	*

Previous history:

UL 7692: New to FJ Pike {Claremont Coaching Services}, London SW3 (LN); Westminster Coaching Services Ltd, London N7 (LN) 6/29; Eastern National Omnibus Co Ltd, Chelmsford (EX) 3496 (not operated) 7/33, from whom it was acquired.

Notes:

RX 4706: Had an interchangeable van body.

Disposal:

RX 4706: Last licensed 6/34.

The following vehicle marked with an asterisk above, transferred to Newbury & District 10/35 (qv):
UL 7692 (43).

Richard Augustine PESTELL {Wash Common Bus Service} The Stores, Essex Street, WASH COMMON (BE)
George BROWN {Wash Common Bus Service}   Bourne Terrace, WASH COMMON (BE) (10/33)

Richard Pestell started the Wash Common Bus Service in March 1925 with a service to Newbury. He sold the business to George Brown in October 1933 who promptly sold out to Newbury & District in January 1934 for £350.

MO 4614	Ford TT	10630775	{Pass & Co?}	B14-	2/25	2/25	1/29
RX 3553	Morris R	128R	Morris	B14F	1/29	1/29	*

Notes:

MO 4614: Also carried the fleet name 'The Doris'.

Disposal:

MO 4614: EE Nobes, Lambourn Woodlands (BE) -/29 (qv).

The following vehicle marked with an asterisk above, transferred to Newbury & District 1/34 (qv):
RX 3553.

John Francis BURT
John Francis BURT & Albert Victor GREENWOOD (1930)   INKPEN (BE)

Jack Burt took over a carrier service between Inkpen and Newbury in 1930 utilising a vehicle that could serve as both passenger and goods carrying purposes. Bert Greenwood joined him in partnership shortly after commencement. Newbury & District acquired the bus service and one vehicle in January 1934 for £220 and 640 £1 shares. Burt retained the carrier and coal delivery business but Greenwood went to work for Newbury & District.

MO 2059	Ford T	7403125	(Pass & Co?)	Ch--	8/23	-/29	-/30
MO 7517	Ford TT	12976420	(Pass & Co?)	B14-G	4/26	-/30	12/33
GJ 7973	Federal AB6	?	?	C28-	c7/30	c-/33	*

Previous histories:

GJ 7973: Its origins are unknown (Beattie Coaches Ltd, London W12 (LN) had an unidentified Federal, which may have been this one).

MO 2059: New to H Pass {Pass & Co}, Newbury (BE), from whom it was (probably) acquired.

MO 7517: New to AFW Davis, Inkpen (BE), from whom it was acquired.

Notes:

GJ 7973: Its registration is uncertain, being also recorded as GJ 9733.

MO 2059: Saw some use as a charabanc, but was mostly used as a lorry for coal deliveries.

Disposals:

MO 2059:	No known disposal.
MO 7517:	Last licensed 12/33.

The following vehicle marked with an asterisk above, transferred to Newbury & District 1/34 (qv):
GJ 7973.

Charles George COLLIVER   WICKHAM (BE)

Charles Colliver was a brick haulier who had been established from at least 1931. Newbury & District purchased the business (which included one lorry) in March 1936.

Walter George R CLEEVELEY   Robin Hood Public House, London Road, NEWBURY (BE)

Walter Cleeveley was a publican. In May 1933, he purchased two Bedford 2½ ton trucks and started a sand and gravel supply business as well as undertaking general haulage work. In January 1935, he was approached by Newbury & District and agreed to sell his business (including the two lorries) for £200.

Theophilus Albert DENHAM {Denham's}
Ambrose Henry & Theophilus Albert DENHAM {Denham Bros} (1925)   Wharf Road, NEWBURY (BE)

Theo Denham set up a motor repairs garage in December 1921, shortly thereafter acquiring a trio of second-hand vehicles for overhaul which were to become the basis of his passenger carrying fleet. The initial route was from Newbury to Woolton Hill and this was quickly augmented with Newbury-Thatcham-Cold Ash and Newbury-Chieveley-Beedon-East Ilsley services. Excursions were scheduled to the south and south-west coastal resorts as well as other tourist attractions such as Glastonbury and Stratford-upon-Avon. Further extensions to bus services occurred in 1926/7 with West Woodhay, Hungerford, Inkpen and Highclere being additional destinations reached. By the time the Road Traffic Act took force in April 1931, Denhams had nine registered services operating out of Newbury. The Denham Bros operation contributed 10 vehicles (plus a lorry and a taxi), the garage in Wharf Road and a second garage in Mill Lane - to the initial Newbury & District fleet in June 1932.

AF 1344	Star 20-25 hp	?	?	B12F	6/14	c4/22	-/--
?	Buick 25 cwt	?	?	B10R	c-/16	c4/22	1/27
BL 9861	Delaunay-Belleville	432	(Andrews?)	Ch14	-/18	c4/22	7/23
?	GMC K16	?	?	Ch14	-/--	8/22	by6/27
MD 8213	Talbot 25/50 hp	10288	Andrews	-12-	7/21	by7/23	3/32
MO 1797	Ford T	7897211	(Pass & Co?)	B14-	7/23	7/23	1/27
MO 2406	FIAT 15TER	?	?	B20R	12/23	12/23	by-/30
OR 4295	Chevrolet B	?	?	B14F	7/24	7/24	6/30
AE 3792	Bristol C50	1158	Bristol	B26R	7/14	-/24	----
LF 9044	TSM TTA1	?	Tilling	O18/16RO	5/13	9/24	12/26
?	TSM TTA1	?	Tilling	O18/16RO	-/13	3/25	5/27
BL 7936	Daimler CC	796	?	B---	12/20	-/25	12/28
TB 2522	Daimler CK	3799	?	Ch28	-/20	-/25	*
PM 581	Talbot 25/50 hp	?	Andrews	B10F	-/22	by5/26	by6/32
KE 3196	Talbot 25/50 hp	?	Andrews	B14F	2/21	-/27	*
MO 1714	FIAT 15TER	SM33807	Andrews	Ch14	6/23	-/27	6/30
BL 8006	Ford T	4026000	?	Ch14	10/20	8/29	----
HX 1059	Star Flyer VB4	D639	Strachan	C26D	7/30	-/30	*
TR 8198	Thornycroft A2	?	Wadham	B20F	2/30	-/30	*
MW 825	Thornycroft A2	?	Challands Ross	B20F	11/27	4/31	*
TR 1231	Leyland A13	35879	Southampton Corporation	B26F	11/25	-/31	*
VT 184	TSM B10A	?	Strachan & Brown	B32F	7/27	5/31	*
BU 5690	TSM B10A2	5869	NCME	C32F	11/28	c5/31	*
TO 9554	Gilford 166OT	10614	Strachan	B32F	3/29	9/31	*
?	Gilford	?	?	B28-	-/--	by-/31	*
WU 9870	Minerva	?	Metcalfe	B20-	2/27	1/32	*

Previous histories:

Unidentified (Buick): Was acquired from Military Disposal Sales (GOV).

Unidentified (TSM): Was new to Thomas Tilling Ltd, London SE6 (LN), but otherwise its identity is not known (it may have been one of the others of the batch that was hired to Ortona Motor Co Ltd, Cambridge (CM) 7-8/22 with LF 9044 (below) – LF 9026/8/43/5/6, LF 9917/21, LH 8619/20).

AE 3792: New to Bristol Tramways & Carriage Co Ltd, Bristol (GL) 1158 (with a Ch28 body); Shoplaw, Clevedon (SO) 11/23, from whom it was acquired.

AF 1344:	New to W Randall, Penryn (CO) (with a Ch—body) [rebodied B12F at an unknown date]; from whom it was acquired via several unidentified operators.
BL 7936:	·New to JC Durnford, Newbury (BE) (with a Ch25 / goods body) (qv) [its chassis originated as a War Department lorry, new 12/12]; unidentified operator, Woolhampton (BE) 4/22 [rebodied to B-- at an unknown date], from whom it was acquired (qv).
BL 8006:	New to HG Williams, Kintbury (BE); J Baldwin, Peasemore (BE) at an unknown date, from whom it was acquired.
BL 9861:	Was originally a large private car new in 1918.
BU 5690:	New to TH Lockett, Ashton-under-Lyne (LA); JH Robinson, Oldham (LA) 1929; S Whittle, Hyde (CH) 1929; withdrawn 1929; unidentified operator, Co Durham at an unknown date, from whom it was acquired.
HX 1059:	New to W Gotobed & D Kinch {Spartan Coaches}, London SW3 (LN), from whom it was acquired.
KE 3196:	Its origins are not known; it was probably originally a large private car, rebodied as a bus 1927.
LF 9044:	New to Thomas Tilling Ltd, London SE6 (LN) 219 [hired to Ortona Motor Co Ltd, Cambridge (CM) 7-8/22], from whom it was acquired.
MD 8213:	Its origins are not known.
MO 1714:	New to A & PA Andrews {A Andrews & Son / Favourite Coaches}, Newbury (BE) (qv), from whom it was acquired.
MW 825:	New to C Haines {Charlie's Cars}, Durrington (WI), from whom it was acquired.
PM 581:	Its origins are not known; it was probably originally a large private car, rebodied as a bus 1926.
TB 2522:	Its origins are not known.
TO 9554:	New to R Reynolds {Bulwell Bus Service}, Bulwell (NG) (as B36F); RT & W Reynolds {Reynolds Bros / Bulwell Bus Service}, Bulwell (NG) 1930; Nottingham Corporation Transport (NG) 108 3/31 [reseated to B32F 8/31], from whom it was acquired.
TR 1231:	New to Southampton Corporation Transport (HA) 7, from whom it was acquired.
TR 8198:	New to Mrs EL Easson & RJ Essex {EL Easson}, Southampton (HA), from whom it was acquired.
VT 184:	New to A Lowe {Norton Bus Co}, Norton-in-the-Moors (ST), from whom it was acquired.
WU 9870:	New to C Booth {Booth's Bus Service}, Otley (WR); B & B Tours Ltd, Sheffield (WR) 10/30, from whom it was acquired.

Notes:

A 1920 Palladium YE 3-4 ton lorry registered BL 8474 (originally BL 0301) was operated for a period after 4/27.

A taxi (no details known) also passed to Newbury & District in 6/32.

Unidentified (Buick): Was a left hand drive ex-War Department field ambulance fitted with a bus body with face-to-face seating and an entrance at the back; it was being used as a van by the time of its disposal in 1/27.

Unidentified (GMC): Named 'The Newbury Rover'.

Unidentified (TSM): Its Tilling O18/16RO body was cut down to single-deck (as B20R) and the vehicle re-registered MO 4984 before entry into service 3/25.

AE 3792:	Was acquired for use as a goods vehicle and was not operated as a bus; its Bristol body was removed and fitted to MO 3875 5/25; it was then rebuilt as a lorry.
BL 8006:	Not operated by Denham.
BL 9861:	Named 'Pride of Newbury'.
LF 9044:	Re-registered MO 3875 before entry into service 9/24; its Tilling O18/16RO body was cut down to single-deck (as B20R) 1/25; fitted with the Bristol B26R body from AE 3792 5/25.
MD 8213:	Was probably rebodied 1923, before entry into service.
MO 1797:	Was also used as a lorry.
PM 581:	Rebodied Andrews B14F at an unknown date (probably 1929-31 period).
TB 2522:	Was also used as a lorry.

Disposals:

Unidentified (Buick):	Unidentified operator / dealer 1/27.
Unidentified (GMC):	Unidentified operator / dealer by 6/27.
AE 3792:	No known disposal.
AF 1344:	No known disposal.
BL 7936:	Last licensed 12/28.
BL 8006:	Last licensed 9/29.
BL 9861:	C Holland {Pioneer Bus Service}, Lane End (BK) 7/23 (qv).

MD 8213: Last licensed 3/32.
MO 1714: Last licensed 6/30.
MO 1797: Unidentified owner as a goods vehicle 1/27; last licensed 6/27.
MO 2406: Lavington & Devizes Motor Services Ltd, Devizes (GWI) by 1930; Bath Electric Tramways Co, Bath (GSO) 5/33; last licensed 10/33.
MO 3875: Unidentified operator / dealer 12/26.
MO 4984: Unidentified operator / dealer 5/27.
OR 4295: No known disposal.
PM 581:   No known disposal.

The following vehicles marked with an asterisk above, transferred to Newbury & District 6/32 (qv):
Unidentified Gilford, BU 5690 (5), HX 1059 (27), KE 3196, MW 825 (9), TB 2522 (as a lorry), TO 9554 (23), TR 1231, TR 8198 (12), VT 184 (7), WU 9870.

John Charles DURNFORD {C Durnford & Sons}   MIDGHAM GREEN (BE)
16/7 Market Street, NEWBURY (BE) (1922)

Charlie Durnford's early training was with Vincent, the Reading coachbuilders and motor engineers. By World War 1, he was dealing in motorcycles and by 1920, was establishing a sand and gravel haulage operation and also a house removals business. During the summer of 1920, he converted his lorry for use as a charabanc on excursions to Southsea, Bournemouth and Brighton as well as a bus service to Woolhampton. Throughout the 1920s, the excursions were developed into an extensive network whilst the haulage and removals businesses ensured that vehicles could be utilised out of season. The Durnford operation contributed nine vehicles (plus four goods vehicles), office premises at Market Street, an adjoining garage in Mayors Lane and an additional garage in Mill Lane to the initial Newbury & District fleet in June 1932.

Reg	Chassis	Chassis No	Body	Seating	New	Acq	Disp
BL 0336	Commer WP3	?	?	Ch25	1/20	1/20	-/--
BL 7936	Daimler CC	796	?	Ch28	12/20	12/20	4/22
BL 8804	Daimler B	B2949	?	Ch25	7/21	7/21	-/--
CR 4021	Hallford EA	402	?	Ch30	-/19	5/22	-/--
MO 53	Dennis 3 ton	3460	?	Ch20	5/22	5/22	12/26
MC 3937	Dennis 1½ ton	3031	?	Ch14	8/22	8/22	9/25
?	Maudslay A	?	?	Ch30	-/--	10/22	-/--
MO 1763	Dennis 3 ton	3696	?	Ch25	6/23	6/23	9/26
EL 3769	Dennis 3 ton	?	?	Ch30	6/19	-/23	9/29
?	Leyland	?	?	Ch28	-/--	5/24	-/--
MO 3343	Dennis 3 ton	?	?	Ch25	6/24	6/24	3/31
?	Star 50 cwt	?	?	Ch14	c-/23	by7/24	*
?	Thornycroft J	?	?	Ch28	-/--	by6/25	-/--
MO 7924	Talbot 25/50 hp	10036	Andrews	Ch14	5/26	5/26	c4/29
CC 5083	Lancia Z	5499	Spicer	C20F	12/24	6/26	6/29
RX 1992	Dennis G	30938?	?	C18-	3/28	3/28	2/31
DL 2122	Dennis 2 ton	?	Margham	C20-	-/21	by5/28	-/--
?	GMC K41	?	?	C20-	c-/25	by5/28	*
YB 7442	Lancia Pentaiota	583	Wray	C20F	9/26	2/29	*
YE 8768	Maudslay ML4	4028	London Lorries	C28D	3/27	11/29	*
?	Lancia Pentaiota	?	London Lorries	C25F	-/--	by-/30	*
?	Reo Major	?	?	C20F	c-/27	by-/30	*
?	Guy	?	?	?	-/--	by-/30	*
CW 6802	Maudslay ML2	3956	?	C28-	6/26	1/30	*
YT 9565	Garner 55 hp	74182	Buckingham	C26D	9/27	2/30	*
RX 6264	Reo Pullman	GE---	Wray	C25D	3/30	3/30	*
VX 43	Gilford CP6	10743	Thurgood	C20D	5/29	-/30	*
UV 9116	Gilford CP6	11005	Wycombe	C20F	7/29	12/30	*
RX 8210	Diamond T	43505	Newns	C20-	3/31	3/31	4/32
UU 7594	GMC T42	D2287	Wilton	C26-	6/29	1/32	*

Previous histories:
CC 5083: New to Caernarvon Motors, Caernarvon (CN); Northwood (dealer?), London SE1 4/26, from whom it was acquired.
CR 4021: New to R Leach, Southampton (HA), from whom it was acquired.
CW 6802: New to J Bracewell, Blackpool (LA); RJA Allison {Prudence Motor Coaches}, London W6 (LN) 4/28, from whom it was acquired.
DL 2122: New to F Plater {Isle of Wight Tourist}, Ryde (IW), from whom it was acquired.

EL 3769: New to TR Brooke, Bournemouth (HA); JG Pounds {Charlie's Cars}, Bournemouth (HA) 3 2/20, from whom it was acquired.

UU 7594: New to HT Ross {Kings Service Coaches}, London SW12 (LN), from whom it was acquired.

UV 9116: New to Blue Belle Motors Ltd, London SW2 (LN), from whom it was acquired.

VX 43: New to GFC Croxon {Essex County Coaches}, London E10 (LN), from whom it was acquired.

YB 7442: New to FJ Webb {Tor Coaches}, Street (SO), from whom it was acquired.

YE 8768: New to G Ewer & Co {Grey-Green}, London N16 (LN), from whom it was acquired.

YT 9565: New to F Sands, Hoo St Werburgh (KT); Wrays Motors (dealer), London SW6 c1929; Banks, Southampton (HA) 10/29, from whom it was acquired.

Notes:

Unidentified (Guy): Was also used as a lorry.

Unidentified (Leyland): Was also used as a lorry.

Unidentified (Maudslay): Its chassis was from an ex-War Department (GOV) lorry, new 1915, rebodied as a charabanc; was also used as a van.

Unidentified (Reo): Was also used as a lorry.

Unidentified (Star): Was also used as a lorry.

Unidentified (Thornycroft): Its chassis was from an ex-War Department (GOV) lorry, rebodied as a charabanc; was also used as a lorry.

BL 0336: Was new as a lorry, but was fitted with detachable seats and a canvas top for use as a charabanc from c6/20.

BL 7936: Its chassis was from an ex-War Department (GOV) lorry, new 12/12, rebodied as a charabanc; was also used as a van.

BL 8804: Its chassis was from an ex-War Department (GOV) lorry, new 1914, rebodied as a charabanc; was also used as a lorry; it was used as a lorry only from 1922.

CR 4021: Its chassis was from an ex-War Department (GOV) lorry, new 1912, rebodied as a charabanc.

CW 6802: Rebodied as a pantechnicon (by Andrews) for removals work 1/32.

EL 3769: It was solely being used as a removals van by the time of its disposal 9/29.

MC 3937: Its chassis was new to Maple & Co (Furnishers), London in 1911; later impressed by the War Department (GOV) as a lorry; rebodied as a charabanc at an unknown date and was also used as a lorry.

MO 53: Its chassis was from an ex-War Department (GOV) lorry, new 1912 (purchased through Slough Trading Co Ltd (dealer), Slough), rebodied as a charabanc; was also used as a lorry; named 'Pride of Newbury' by 6/23; it was solely being used as a lorry by the time of its disposal 12/26.

MO 1763: Its chassis was from an ex-War Department (GOV) lorry, new 1915 (purchased through Slough Trading Co Ltd (dealer), Slough), rebodied as a charabanc; was also used as a lorry; it was solely being used as a lorry by the time of its disposal 9/26.

MO 3343: Its chassis was from an ex-War Department (GOV) lorry, new 1915 (purchased through Slough Trading Co Ltd (dealer), Slough), rebodied as a charabanc; fitted with a van body for removals work at an unknown date.

MO 7924: Its chassis was from an ex-War Department (GOV) ambulance, new 1918, rebodied as a charabanc.

RX 1992: Fitted with a van body for removals work at an unknown date.

Disposals:

Unidentified (Leyland): No known disposal.

Unidentified (Maudslay): No known disposal.

Unidentified (Thornycroft): No known disposal.

BL 0336: No known disposal.

BL 7936: Unidentified operator, Woolhampton (BE) 4/22; rebodied to B--- at an unknown date; AH & TA Denham {Denham Bros}, Newbury (BE) 1925 (qv).

BL 8804: No known disposal.

CC 5083: Wrays Motors (dealer), London SW6 6/29; JHN Horner, Portsmouth (HA) 6/29; last licensed 1931.

CR 4021: No known disposal.

DL 2122: No known disposal.

EL 3769: Last licensed 9/29.

MC 3937: Last licensed 9/25.

MO 53: Last licensed 12/26.

MO 1763: Last licensed 9/26.

MO 3343: Last licensed 3/31.

MO 7924: H Cordery {Pride of the Valley}, Spencers Wood (BE) c4/29; last licensed 9/29; Ledbury Transport Co Ltd {Thackray's Way}, Reading (BE) (not operated) 12/29 (qv).

RX 1992:   Unidentified owner (G??) 2/31; last licensed 12/37.
RX 8210:   Last licensed 4/32.

The following vehicles marked with an asterisk above, transferred to Newbury & District 6/32 (qv):
Unidentified GMC (as a goods vehicle), unidentified Guy (as a goods vehicle), unidentified Lancia, unidentified Reo, unidentified Star (as a goods vehicle), CW 6802 (L4) (pantechnicon), RX 6264 (26), UU 7594 (30), UV 9116, VX 43, YB 7442, YE 8768 (28), YT 9565 (29).

Leonard Charles, Ernest A & Henry Albert DURNFORD {Durnford Bros} 16/7 Market Street, NEWBURY (BE)

Having broken away from Newbury & District, Charlie Durnford and his sons set up on their own from their old Market Street premises in June 1933. Charlie and his son William George (Bill) ran the removals and haulage business, whilst the other three sons, trading as Durnford Bros, started up a new motor coach business. The excursions and tours licenses of A Bason, Woolhampton were acquired in August 1933 and his 'Scarlet Runners' fleet name was also adopted by the Durnfords. Before the end of 1933 however, Charlie Durnford returned to the Newbury & District fold and following his appointment to the board, the Durnford Bros business (including two coaches, a lorry and the pantechnicon) was amalgamated back into Newbury & District.

HJ 8718	Gilford 166SD	10499	?	C26-	3/29	6/33	*
GU 7545	Star Flyer VB4	C884/1055	Thurgood	C26-	4/29	6/33	*

Previous histories:
GU 7545:   New to HE Lang {Lang's Luxury Coaches}, London SW8 (LN), from whom it was acquired.
HJ 8718:   New to E Brazier, Southend-on-Sea (EX); Mrs LE Brazier, Southend-on-Sea (EX) c1931, from whom it was acquired.

Notes:
In order to augment the above two vehicles, vehicles were hired in from a number of sources including GP Howlett of Bucklebury and A Bason of Woolhampton.
The pantechnicon (CW 6802) which had passed to Newbury & District in 6/32 with the JC Durnford business, returned with the removals business. This together with another lorry (RX 4356) which had been acquired from Bason, returned to Newbury & District Motor Services Ltd in 1/34.

The following vehicles marked with an asterisk above, transferred to Newbury & District 1/34 (qv):
GU 7545 (28), HJ 8718 (51).

Mrs Catherine GEARY {Joy Coaches & Cars}   Church Road, GREAT SHEFFORD (BE)

Mrs Geary began operating a haulage and removals business in March 1929. In that year, she also established passenger carrying services from Fawley to Newbury. She sold this to Newbury & District in January 1934 for £240, continuing thereafter her haulage activities.

RX 3981	Ford AA	845179	(Pass & Co?)	B14-	3/29	3/29	1/34
RX 5432	Ford AA	1158124	(Pass & Co?)	C14-	10/29	10/29	*

Notes:
RX 3981:   Was also solely used as a good vehicle after 1/34.

Disposals:
RX 3981:   Mrs C Geary, Great Shefford (GBE) 1/34; last licensed 1/37.

The following vehicles marked with an asterisk above, transferred to Newbury & District 1/34 (qv):
RX 5432.

George Edmund HEDGES {Reliance Motor Services}   BRIGHTWALTON (BE)

After a spell as the local carrier in Brightwalton, George Hedges purchased a van with bench seating which allowed him to add passenger carrying to his services. He also won a coal delivery contract with supplies being collected from Great Shefford station. The name Reliance Motor Services was introduced in October 1931 and by the time Newbury & District was being formed, Hedges was running services between Brightwalton and Newbury as well a flourishing excursions business to a variety of towns in the south of England as well as the usual seaside resorts. Newbury & District was keen to build on the excursions business in particular, so an agreement was struck to amalgamate the Reliance Motor Services operation (three vehicles plus a lorry and a garage at Brightwalton) in September 1932. In return, George Hedges received 2,000 £1 shares in Newbury & District.

BL 9886	Ford T	5406956	Andrews?	B14-G	4/22	4/22	-/--
MO 3514	Ford TT	9137153	Andrews?	B14-	8/24	8/24	10/30
?	Talbot 25/50 hp		Andrews	Ch14	-/25	-/25	*
RX 4556	Ford AA	1045538	?	C14D	5/29	5/29	*
RX 6888	Ford AA	3015658	Duple	C14D	6/30	6/30	*

Notes:

An unidentified lorry was also transferred to Newbury & District Motor Services Ltd.

Unidentified (Talbot): Had an interchangeable van body.
BL 9886: Was a van with detachable seats; it was used for coal deliveries only after 8/24.
MO 3514: Reseated to B8- 1/29; by the time of its withdrawal in 10/30, it was being solely used for goods.

Disposals:

BL 9886: Unidentified owner (G??) at an unknown date; last licensed 12/29.
MO 3514: Unidentified owner (G??) 10/30.

The following vehicles marked with an asterisk above, transferred to Newbury & District 9/32 (qv):
Unidentified Talbot, RX 4556, RX 6888.

Thomas HOLMAN   ECCHINSWELL (HA)

Tom Holman became a carrier between Ecchinswell, Sydmonton and Newbury during the World War 1. By 1923, he purchased a carrier's van with removable seats which enabled passengers to be carried. He also became a coal merchant, collecting supplies from Highclere Station. He sold the goodwill and his Ecchinswell-Newbury service to Newbury & District in October 1932 for £30 and 50 £1 shares but retained his vehicle to carry on his coal business and a goods carrier until 1941 at least.

OR 2576	Ford T	?	?	B14-G	9/23	9/23	6/29

Notes:

Two further unidentified vehicles were operated between 1929 and 1932.

OR 2576: Was a van with detachable seats.

Disposals:

OR 2576: No known disposal.

George Perry HOWLETT {Kennet Bus Service}   The Oak Tree Garage, BUCKLEBURY COMMON (BE)

George Howlett was operating a horse-drawn carrier's service between Cold Ash and Newbury as far back as 1908. He became motorised in 1914 and set about developing haulage and removals businesses as well as passenger carrying services. In 1917, he established a second service to Reading as well as building private hire and excursion work. In 1919, he divested the carrier business to A Austin, although later resuming a passenger service between Cold Ash and Newbury. After 1930, services run were Bucklebury-Newbury and Cold Ash-Reading. Howlett amalgamated the business (including three vehicles) into Newbury & District in February 1934 for £270 and 1,000 £1 shares. Howlett retained The Oak Tree Garage and subsequently rented it to Newbury & District as an outstation.

1	BL 3415	Wolseley-Siddeley 18/24 hp ?	?		B---G	1/14	1/14	3/14
2	BL 027	CPT 18-20 hp	H8153	?	B---G	3/14	3/14	9/27
3	BL 8684	Garner 15 Busvan	8070	Garner	B20-G	6/21	6/21	3/30
	MO 3959	FIAT 15TER	2300	City Carriage	B20F	9/24	9/24	3/30
	MY 3052	Star Flyer VB4	1007/D403	Star	C26D	2/30	2/30	*
	MY 4213	Star Flyer VB4	1172/D436	Star	C26D	4/30	4/30	*
	SH 3380	GMC T30C	302813	Alexander Motors	B20F	5/29	-/33	*

Previous history:

SH 3380: New to W Gardiner, Leitholm (BW); Scottish Motor Traction Co Ltd, Edinburgh (MN) C9 7/32; Leyland Motors Ltd (dealer), Leyland 1933; unidentified dealer 1933, from whom it was acquired.

Notes:

BL 027 (1): Re-registered BL 3850 7/14; it was a carrier's van with bench seats; used mainly for goods haulage after 1921.

BL 3415: Was a carrier's van with seats; displayed 'The Kennet' branding.

BL 8684 (2): Was a carrier's van with seats.

MO 3959 (3): Its chassis was new in 1918 (use unknown), being rebodied as a bus and re-registered in 1924; displayed 'The Kennet' branding.

MY 3052: Displayed 'The Spartan by Howlett' branding (was also recorded as new to W Gotobed & D Kinch {Spartan Coaches}, London W3 (LN), but this may have arisen as a result of the branding carried by the vehicle).

MY 4213: Displayed 'The Spartan by Howlett' branding (was also recorded as new to W Gotobed & D Kinch {Spartan Coaches}, London W3 (LN), but this may have arisen as a result of the branding carried by the vehicle).

Disposals:

BL 3415: No known disposal.

BL 3850 (1): Last licensed 9/27.

BL 8684 (2): Last licensed 3/30.

MO 3959 (3): Last licensed 3/30.

The following vehicles marked with an asterisk above, transferred to Newbury & District 2/34 (qv):

MY 3052, MY 4213 (4), SH 3380.

Mrs Edith Gertrude KENT {Kingsclere Coaches}   **BAUGHURST (HA)**

Following the death of her husband in 1914, Edith Kent set up a milk carrying round, collecting milk from farms to Basingstoke railway station for onward transportation to the London dairies. By the early 1920s, she was using a Ford T van for this purpose and seems to have been persuaded that there was a demand to take passengers from Kingsclere to Basingstoke and Newbury. This got underway in 1926 with the acquisition of a charabanc and a small bus. The business expanded rapidly and by the end of 1928, six vehicles were operated from a garage in Baughurst and an outstation in Kingsclere. In April 1936, she took over the business of Vincent, Headley which included one vehicle and a Kingsclere to Newbury service. At this point, she was running four services: two between Kingsclere and Newbury (her own and Vincent's), Basingstoke to Newbury and Basingstoke to Kingsclere. By 1937, Edith Kent was looking to retire, so first approached Venture Ltd of Basingstoke. That option was blocked by the Traffic Commissioners, so she approached Newbury & District who concluded a deal in April 1937. Her four sons all had interests in passenger carrying businesses and Kent's Coaches Ltd, originally started by her son Bill, survived until 1978.

(OT 816?)	Thornycroft A1	?	Hall Lewis	Ch20	-/25	3/26	-/32
OT 1333	Morris (Z?) 25 cwt	?	?	B14F	6/26	6/26	by4/37
OT 3284	Reo Sprinter	5352	Wray	C20D	12/26	12/26	-/35
OT 4452	Thornycroft A2 Long	14119	Wadham	B20F	4/27	4/27	
OT 7672	Reo	?	?	B20F	3/28	3/28	by4/37
OT 9741	Chevrolet	?	?	B14F	9/28	9/28	by4/37
OU 6047	AJS Pilot	1004	Petty	B28F	6/30	6/30	*
TK 2740	Guy OND	OND9218	Guy	B20F	5/29	c10/30	*
CG 1724	Commer B40	46056	Petty	C20F	8/32	8/32	*
ACG 644	Commer B3	?	Petty	C20F	4/35	4/35	*
UN 3196	Chevrolet LR	57315	?	B16F	12/29	4/36	*

Previous histories:

(OT 816?): New as a demonstrator with John I Thornycroft Ltd (dealer), Basingstoke, from whom it was acquired.

TK 2740: New to Poole & District & District Motor Services Ltd, Parkston (DT); Hants & Dorset Motor Services Ltd, Bournemouth (DT) 9/30, from whom it was acquired.

UN 3196: Its first operator not known; R Vincent, Headley (HA) at an unknown date, from whom it was acquired (it is thought to have been with Barrett & Cant {Colne Valley Coaches}, Watford (HT) at some point, but this is unconfirmed).

Notes:

(OT 816?): Its registration is not confirmed; it was not used after 1932.

OT 1333: Was also run as a lorry.

Disposals:

(OT 816?):	Newbury & District Motor Services Ltd for spares 12/35 (qv).
OT 1333:	No known disposal.
OT 3284:	No known disposal.
OT 7672:	No known disposal.
OT 9741:	No known disposal.

The following vehicles marked with an asterisk above, transferred to Newbury & District 4/37 (qv):
    CG 1724 (38), OT 4452 (15), OU 6047 (42), TK 2740 (8), UN 3196 (5), ACG 644 (39).

Henry PASS {Pass & Co}

George SALKELD {Pass & Co} (1925)

Arthur J LOW {Pass & Co} (7/31)   NEWBURY (BE)

The Pass & Co business was started by Henry Pass in the 1890s when he acquired a coachworks business. The business later added motor workshops, became Ford agents in 1915 and also hired out cars, vans and lorries. In the same way as Arthur Andrews, many early local operators' bus bodies were manufactured by Pass & Co. A move into passenger carrying services was underway in 1922 with a service between Newbury and Wash Common, but it was mainly excursions and tours that were developed. Henry Pass died in 1925 and it seems that the business passed to George Salkeld who worked there since 1901. In any event, it was he who sold the business on to Arthur Low in 1931. Newbury & District were keen to eliminate competing businesses engaged in excursions and tours and an offer of £1,500 was accepted in May 1937.

BL 9316	Ford T	4677457	(Pass & Co?)	B14-G	11/21	11/21	12/21
BL 9713	Ford T	4693653	(Pass & Co?)	B14-G	3/22	3/22	12/22
MO 659	Ford T	5825166	(Pass & Co?)	Ch14	11/22	11/22	-/--
MO 2059	Ford T	7403125	(Pass & Co?)	Ch14	8/23	8/23	4/25
BL 5420	CPT	H8684	(Pass & Co?)	Ch14	6/17	1/25	9/28
MO 5313	Ford T	10637049	?	Ch14	5/25	5/25	-/--
MO 5899	Ford T	11273815	?	Ch14	7/25	7/25	9/28
MO 7520	Ford 1-ton	12973827	?	Ch14	5/26	5/26	-/--
RX 2907	Ford AA	?	Vincent	C14D	8/28	8/28	5/37
RX 4109	Ford T rebuild	15097146	?	Ch14	3/29	3/29	-/--
RX 6887	Ford AA	1478349	?	C14-	6/30	6/30	-/--
RX 7150	Ford AA	3452798	?	C14F	7/30	7/30	*
JB 437	Ford AA	4839808	?	C20-	6/32	6/32	*
RX 5432	Ford AA	1158124	(Pass & Co?)	C14-	10/29	1/34	----
JB 5701	Ford BB	1056354	?	C20-	2/35	2/35	*

Previous histories:

BL 5420:	Was owned by Pass & Co from new, being rebodied as a charabanc 1/25.
RX 5432:	New to Mrs C Geary, Great Shefford (BE); Newbury & District Motor Services Ltd (not operated) 1/34, from whom it was acquired.

Notes:

A vehicle registered P 942 was operated from 4/23. It was probably a private car rebodied as a charabanc.

BL 9316:	Was a carrier's van with detachable seats.
BL 9713:	Was a carrier's van with detachable seats.
RX 5432:	Was probably acquired in a dealing capacity only.

Disposals:

BL 5420:	Last licensed 9/28.
BL 9316:	J Prothero, Beedon (BE) 12/21.
BL 9713:	A Cooke, Kingsclere (GHA) 12/22; last licensed 9/28.
MO 659:	FJ Feltham, Burghfield Common (GBE) at an unknown date; last licensed 9/29.
MO 2059:	JF Burt, Inkpen (BE) 1929.
MO 5313:	Unidentified owner (G??) at an unknown date; last licensed 7/32.
MO 5899:	Scrapped 9/28.
MO 7520:	H Galpin, Yattenden at an unknown date; last licensed 7/32.
RX 2907:	Pass & Co (dealer), Newbury 5/37; Newbury & District Motor Services Ltd 64 7/37 (qv).
RX 4109:	Unidentified owner (G??) at an unknown date; last licensed 11/37.
RX 5432:	Unidentified owner (G??) c1934; last licensed 6/47; scrapped 3/48.
RX 6887:	Unidentified owner at an unknown date; converted to a hearse 3/40; last licensed 8/44.

The following vehicles marked with an asterisk above, transferred to Newbury & District 5/37 (qv):
JB 437, JB 5701 (60), RX 7150.

Ernest Edward NOBES   Hurst Farm, LAMBOURN WOODLANDS (BE)

Ernie Nobes started a service between Lambourn Woodlands and Newbury in 1923, quickly augmenting this to serve Baydon, Swindon and Hungerford and by the 1930s, occasional excursions. In July 1938, Nobes sold his vehicle and services to Newbury & District for £50 but continued to drive for the company. He was tragically killed in the collision with a train at Didcot Ordnance Factory on 1/10/43 whilst driving DNW 359.

MO 1846	Ford T	7898903	(Pass & Co?)	-14-	7/23	7/23	4/30
MO 4614	Ford TT	10630775	(Pass & Co?)	B14F	2/25	-/29	8/36
TM 5726	Chevrolet LQ	?	Economy	B16F	9/29	by8/36	*

Previous histories:
MO 4614:   New to RA Pestell {Wash Common Bus Service}, Wash Common (BE), from whom it was acquired.
TM 5726:   New to FA Jenkins {Perseverance}, Shillington (BD); unidentified dealer, London W12, from whom it was acquired.

Notes:
MO 1846:   Was a carrier's van with detachable seats.

Disposals:
MO 1846:   Last licensed 4/30.
MO 4614:   Last licensed 8/36.

The following vehicle marked with an asterisk above, transferred to Newbury & District 7/38 (qv):
TM 5726.

William Charles POCOCK   Cold Ash Hill, COLD ASH (BE)
William Charles, Percival Brice & Norman William POCOCK {WC Pocock & Sons, later Pocock Bros}

Like many of his contempories, William Pocock started off in the early 1920s with a van fitted with detachable seats. His son Norman was responsible for growing an associated garage and taxi business which became very successful. The Pococks also had a market garden business and for this, three former LGOC bus bodies were purchased from Thames Valley in October 1926 for use as greenhouses. The main bus operation was a service between Cold Ash and Newbury augmented in the summer by excursions and tours to the usual south coast seaside resorts plus other events in the south of England. The business (comprising three vehicles) was amalgamated for £300 plus 500 £1 shares in Newbury & District. The Pococks continued their market garden business (which continued until 1947 at least) and the Cold Ash Garage business which did not close until 1976.

MO 1573	Ford T	7897170	(Pass & Co?)	B14-G	6/23	6/23	9/32
?	FIAT	?	?	Ch14	by7/26	by7/26	-/--
MO 8231	Chevrolet X	10150	?	B14F	7/26	7/26	*
MO 6416	Chevrolet T	R6089T	?	B14F	10/25	7/29	12/30
RX 9971	Bedford WLB	108401	?	B20F	3/32	3/32	*
?	Chevrolet	?	?	C14-	-/--	-/--	*

Previous histories:
MO 6416:   New to WJ White & Son {Tony Coaches}, Hermitage (BE), from whom it was acquired (qv).

Notes:
During the summer of 1927, charabancs were being advertised, but only the FIAT is known to have been operated.

Unidentified (FIAT): Was named 'The Scout'.
MO 1573:   Was a carrier's van with detachable seats; after 7/26, it was used for goods only.

Disposals:
Unidentified (FIAT):   No known disposal.
MO 1573:   Unidentified owner (G??) 9/32; last licensed 9/36.
MO 6416:   Last licensed 12/30.

The following vehicles marked with an asterisk above, transferred to Newbury & District 10/32 (qv):
Unidentified Chevrolet, MO 8231, RX 9971 (19).

John PROTHERO & Robert Valentine REVELL {Beedon & Chieveley Motor Service}   BEEDON (BE)
John PROTHERO {Prothero's Bus Service / Beedon & Chieveley Bus Service / XLCR Motor Service} (12/21)
John PROTHERO & ? WILD {XLCR Motor Service} (1/25)
John PROTHERO {XLCR Motor Service} (1930)

In January 1921, John Prothero and his brother-in-law Robert Revell started up a carrier service between West Ilsley and Newbury (via Beedon and Chieveley). The partnership was however dissolved at the end of the year with Revell retaining the service and the vehicle. Prothero purchased another vehicle in November 1921 and set about establishing a passenger service between Beedon and Newbury. The acquisition of a charabanc in 1926 coincided with the adoption of the XLCR ('Excelsior') fleet name. Following the partnership with a Mr Wild, a garage was opened in Beedon from where Wild developed a haulage business (when the partnership ended in 1930, Wild took the haulage business with him). Meanwhile, the Beedon service was extended to East Ilsley and from December 1930, this ran all the way to Reading. By 1932, three routes were served: East Ilsley-Newbury, East Ilsley-Reading and Peasemore-Newbury. Following an approach by Newbury & District, an agreement was struck to amalgamate the XLCR operation (five vehicles) in September 1932. In return, John Prothero received 2,000 £1 shares in Newbury & District. As Prothero had retained his Beedon premises (from where he ran a separate garage business), the vehicles were out stationed at the Swan Inn, East Ilsley.

Reg	Make	Chassis	Body	Type			
BL 8278	Ford TT	4029187	(Pass & Co?)	B12-G	1/21	1/21	12/21
BL 9316	Ford T	4677457	(Pass & Co?)	B14-G	11/21	11/21	9/25
?	Austin 20 hp	?	Prothero/Andrews	B14F	-/--	c-/23	-/--
XH 8592	Ford TT	?	Prothero/Andrews	B14F	12/21	5/25	c-/29
?	Talbot 25/50 hp	?	Andrews	Ch14	-/--	4/26	by9/32
?	Chevrolet	?	?	B14F	-/--	by-/29	by9/32
RX 4272	Ford AA	763071	Andrews	B14F	4/29	4/29	*
RX 7256	Ford AA	3458473	Andrews	B14F	7/30	7/30	*
RX 7772	Ford AA	3950354	(Andrews?)	B20F	12/30	12/30	*
RX 9005	Ford AA	4486474	(Andrews?)	B20F	7/31	7/31	*
?	Gilford f/c	?	?	C32-	-/--	c-/31	*

Previous histories:
Unidentified (Austin):Was probably originally a large private car; fitted with a bus body c1923.
XH 8592:   Was new as a van in McNamara's contract hire fleet; it was fitted with a bus body in 5/25.

Notes:
BL 8278:   Was a carrier's van with detachable seats.
BL 9316:   Was a carrier's van with detachable seats.

Disposals:
Unidentified (Austin):   No known disposal.
Unidentified (Chevrolet): No known disposal.
Unidentified (Talbot):   No known disposal.
BL 8278:   RV Revell, Beedon (BE) 12/21; unidentified owner (G??) 6/28; last licensed 9/37.
BL 9316:   Last licensed 9/25.
XH 8592:   EJ Claridge {Ramsbury Motor Services}, Ramsbury (WI) c1929; withdrawn c4/32.

The following vehicles marked with an asterisk above, transferred to Newbury & District 9/32 (qv):
Unidentified Gilford, RX 4272, RX 7256, RX 7772, RX 9005.

Frederick George SPANSWICK {Spanswicks's Bus Service}   21 The Broadway, THATCHAM (BE)
Freddie Spanswick was a cycle agent and petroleum spirit dealer who took over the Thatcham-Newbury carrier business in 1915 from Fred Maslin whom he was related to by marriage. Despite competition, Spanswick persevered with his Thatcham-Newbury service which was augmented with private hire work and local excursions. From 1930, a second service between Newbury and Lambourn was started. An approach from Newbury & District persuaded Spanswick to amalgamate his two-vehicle business in January 1933 for £300 and 1,500 £1 shares.

Reg	Make	Chassis	Body	Type			
BL 946	Argyll 45LS	?	?	B---G	8/06	-/15	4/22
BL 884	Ford T	?	?	B14-G	-/19	1/21	4/30
MO 6744	Ford TT	11279654	Andrews	B14F	1/26	1/26	*
MO 7043	Morris 25 cwt	8912T	Andrews	B14F	1/26	1/26	8/32
RX 6662	Ford AA	1843020	Andrews	B20F	4/30	4/30	*

Previous histories:

BL 946:   New as a private car, acquired in 7/12 and initially used by Spanswick as a hackney cab and goods carrying vehicle from 7/13.

Notes:

Another carrier's van with seats acquired from F Maslin, Thatcham (BE), was operated from 1915 to 1/21.

BL 884:   The originally bearer of this registration was a Covre car new in 5/06 and owned by Spanswick from 9/11. The registration was later re-used on a Ford T carrier's van fitted with detachable seats, purchased new in 1919. It was used for goods only from 1926.

BL 946:   Appears to have first been used as a passenger carrying vehicle in 1915; it was essentially as carriers van fitted with detachable seats.

Disposals:

BL 884:   W Pinnock, Thatcham (GBE) 4/30; withdrawn 12/30.

BL 946:   W Bone, Reading (GBE) 4/22; A Wells, Reading (GBE) at an unknown date; last licensed 3/23.

MO 7043:   A Austin {Cold Ash & District Service}, Cold Ash (BE) 8/32; last licensed 12/36.

The following vehicles marked with an asterisk above, transferred to Newbury & District 1/33 (qv):
MO 6744, RX 6662.

William James WHITE {Tony Coaches}   **Fernbank Garage, HERMITAGE (BE)**
William James & Edwin George WHITE {WJ White & Son / Tony Coaches} (by12/28)
Edwin George WHITE {WJ White & Son / Tony Coaches} (by3/31)

William White had started a motorised carrier service between Hermitage and Newbury by 1922 and in the following year, added a service to Reading. By 1924, he was also a coal merchant, collecting supplies from Hermitage railway yard, operating a taxi service and running excursions to the south coast resorts. William White died early in 1931 and the business was continued by his son Edwin who had joined his father a few years earlier. The business (including four vehicles) was amalgamated into Newbury & District in March 1934 for £500 plus 1,000 £1 shares.

MO 5620	Mason	A2604	?	Ch14/B14F 6/25	6/25	9/31	
MO 6416	Chevrolet T	R6089T	(Vincent?)	B14F	10/25	10/25	7/29
MO 7182	Chevrolet T	R6500T	(Vincent?)	B14F	3/26	3/26	12/33
RX 3330	Chevrolet LP	47318	?	B14F	12/28	12/28	10/33
RX 5493	Dennis 1½ ton	55318	?	C14D	11/29	11/29	*
RX 6401	Dennis 1½ ton	55716	?	C17-	5/30	5/30	*
MW 6161	AJS Pilot	?	Eaton	B26F	12/29	-/31	*
TP 7118	Dennis 1½ ton	53913	Dennis	B14F	12/28	10/33	*

Previous histories:

MW 6161:   New to WC King & Son {Kingson Motor Services}, Nomansland (WI); Wilts & Dorset Motor Services Ltd, Salisbury (WI) 1/31, from whom it was acquired.

TP 7118:   New to PW Lambert {The Little Wonder Bus Service}, East Meon (HA) [as B18F, reseated to B14F 10/33], from whom it was acquired.

Notes:

An unidentified van with seats was operated to c11/29.

MO 5620:   Was named 'The Tony'; its charabanc body was interchangeable with a B14F bus body; it was used solely on haulage work after 11/29.

Disposals:

MO 5620:   Last licensed 9/31.

MO 6416:   WC, PB & NW Pocock {Pocock Bros}, Cold Ash (BE) 7/29 (qv).

MO 7182:   Last licensed 12/33.

RX 3330:   Last licensed 10/33.

The following vehicles marked with an asterisk above, transferred to Newbury & District 3/34 (qv):
MW 6161 (44), RX 5493 (42), RX 6401 (43), TP 3118.

WF BEESLEY {SOUTH MIDLAND TOURING & TRANSPORT CO} (4/21-4/22)
SOUTH MIDLAND TOURING & TRANSPORT CO LTD (4/22-11/30)
SOUTH MIDLAND MOTOR SERVICES LTD (11/30-12/70)

The South Midland operation began on 1 April 1921 when William Frank Beesley, a 22 year old former Army and Forestry Commission mechanic, launched a charabanc service in Oxford using a top-of-the-range Dennis. This was quickly joined by a second similar vehicle and the operation was marketed as 'Grey Torpedo Coaches'. As well as excursions and tours, an early express service from Oxford to London (via Henley-on-Thames and Hounslow) was started, with the sixty mile route being covered in a remarkable journey time of 3¼ hours. In a short time, City of Oxford Motor Services Ltd (COMS), the dominant operator in the region commenced their own London service and fierce competition broke out.

On 4 April 1922, the operation was incorporated as South Midland Touring & Transport Co Ltd with WF Beesley as Managing Director. An elaborate network of tours and excursions (48 in total) was advertised as well as the London service and a third Dennis charabanc was obtained. The British Empire Exhibition in 1924 provided such demand that the London service was suspended in favour of one to Wembley for the season. Despite competition again from COMS, the exhibition generated significant profits for South Midland which stabilised the company after a financially precarious start. Business was augmented with sales of wirelesses, petrol and cigarettes together with car hire and battery-charging services. Excursions to Wembley continued through 1925 and although the London service resumed, both South Midland and COMS suspended these services from May 1926 as a result of the General Strike.

With private hires, tours and excursions more than adequately sustaining the company, it was something of a surprise when the London service was resumed in 1928 using three high-specification Lancia coaches. Additional garaging in Iffley Road was secured with the acquisition of a haulage and garage business called Oxford Motor Carriers & Repairers Ltd. The main competition was now from London based operators such as Samuelson Saloon Coaches, Varsity Express Motors and Grays {Red & Black}. In order to combat these, additional investment was generated in order to purchase four new vehicles for the 1929 season, specifically to increase frequencies on the London service and also to commence a service to Bournemouth. By the end of the decade, the fleet strength was 12 comprising of the three original Dennis charabancs and nine coaches of Dennis, Lancia and Gilford manufacture. By the following year, there were 18 operators running 58 services per day between Oxford and London.

Further investment was obtained in 1930 with the share capital of the company increased to £10,000 together with the sale of the garage business at Iffley Road. This facilitated the purchase of a further nine new Gilfords which enabled frequencies to be increased still further and also allowed the introduction of a new service to Worcester. Attempts to register a stage carriage service to Reading however failed. On 25 November 1930, the company's name was changed to South Midland Motor Services Ltd.

1931 saw the introduction of the Leyland marque with the arrival of four TS3s – Leyland was to supply most of the new arrivals over the next decade. The 1930 Road Traffic Act required services to be registered and South Midland had four express services granted – these were to remain as the company's core routes for the next 40 years:

J73	Worcester – Oxford – Henley – Maidenhead - London
J74	Oxford – Newbury – Winchester - Southsea
J75	Oxford – Henley – Maidenhead - London
J76	Worcester – Oxford – Newbury – Winchester - Southsea

Two additional routes terminating at Coventry were applied for, but in the event, were not taken up despite publicity being produced. Six half-day, 14 full-day and two evening excursions were also approved.

During 1933, a booking office and café were opened at the Gloucester Green bus station in Oxford in order to capture uncommitted passengers. One of the aims of the 1930 Road Traffic Act was to encourage integration and avoid wasteful competition and as a result, through-ticketing agreements were reached with Red & White (who had extensive services to the North West and Wales) and Royal Blue (Midlands to the South and West).

Another innovation was to trial one of the Gilford coaches to run on creosote as an alternative fuel. There were some drawbacks (petrol was still needed to operate the engine at slow speeds), but on the whole, the trial was successful. The rapid development of diesel engine technology however meant that it wasn't taken further.

The other major development was that a buyer was being sought for the business. It is not clear why this decision was taken but in any event, rather surprisingly no interested party emerged. Elsewhere in the industry, the Associated Motorways consortium was formed on 1 July 1934, its member companies comprising of Midland Red,

Black & White Motorways, Royal Blue, Greyhound Motors, Red & White and United Counties. The latter had previously taken over the Varsity Express business which included a significate share in the Oxford to London service and there was some evidence that it had some interest in acquiring South Midland although nothing further transpired.

Away from Oxford, a new venture in Brighton was started in March 1936 – a hire car business called 'Britax'. 26 Austin Ascot saloons were ordered in the first year and although business flourished, the fact that bookings could only be made by telephone restricted the clientele of the era to certain demographics only. Nevertheless, the business ran until August 1942 until brought to an end by the unavailability of replacement vehicles and fuel rationing.

Since 1932, Thomas Harrington Ltd of Hove had been the coachbuilder of choice for South Midland vehicles and in 1936, the Scammell & Nephew bodies on the 1931 Leylands which had badly deteriorated, were replaced with Harrington bodies which extended their lives until well into the 1950s. This was timely as passenger numbers on express services nationally increased quite significantly in the years leading up to World War 2.

The 1939 intake showed a change in policy with the acquisition of lightweight chassis – a pair of Leyland 'Cheetahs' and a pair of Austin K3s. A third Austin was acquired in 1940; the only vehicle obtained during the war years and although two coaches were impressed by the War Department for military use and further three were made available for conversion to ambulances, the South Midland fleet survived the period relatively unscathed. By 1942, the company was heavily involved in transporting military personnel (there were 25 RAF airfields in Oxfordshire alone) which together with a growing shortage of fuel, inevitably curtailed the number of express services that could be run. During 1943 and 1944, much mileage was also accounted for with the movement of Prisoners of War and indeed, the company made record profits during this period.

By early 1944, wartime privations were taking their toll on the ageing fleet. Consideration was given to selling the company, probably in the knowledge that serious reinvestment would become a necessity once new vehicles were available again. A number of informal discussions were held with Red & White United Transport Ltd of Chepstow which came to fruition on 8 October 1945 when that company paid £46,695 for the business. The deal included the High Street head office and the Gloucester Green café. William Beesley left the business and a Red & White man, Gerald Nowell, was appointed Director & General Manager in his place. The agreement with Red & White included 16 vehicles with an average age of over 9 years.

During 1946, express coach services returned to pre-war levels producing an even more acute need for new vehicles. In the event, replacements came quickly and 30 AEC Regals with Duple bodywork arrived over the four year period from 1947 to 1950 with the business expanding into 8-day and other innovative tours as well as excursions and contract work.

As Governmental pressure grew on large bus operators to sell out to the nationalised British Transport Commission (BTC), Gerald Nowell moved on to Hants & Sussex Motor Services Ltd at the end of 1949 and was replaced by another Red & White man, LH Grimmett who had latterly served with Newbury & District. In the event, Red & White decided to voluntarily sell their bus and coaching interests to BTC with effect from 1 January 1950. Of the Red & White subsidiaries in the region, South Midland together with Newbury & District was placed under the control of Thames Valley, whilst the third company, Venture Transport of Basingstoke, was aligned with Wilts & Dorset. The agreement with BTC included 34 vehicles with an average age now reduced to 5 years.

All the non-AEC vehicles were quickly disposed of, three being exchanged for AEC Regals that had recently entered service with Newbury & District. Although the Newbury & District name was to vanish within a few years, Thames Valley decided to retain South Midland as a separate operation. With Thames Valley's own works in Reading fully utilised, it was decided that vehicle overhauls would be carried out by Newbury & District.

By the early 1950s, the express routes in addition to the four original services above were:

> Oxford – London – Margate (joint with East Kent)
> Worcester – London – Brighton (joint with Southdown)
> Oxford – London – Brighton (joint with Southdown)

With effect from 1 May 1952, BTC transferred United Counties' Oxford-High Wycombe-London service to South Midland, which had originally been operated by Varsity Express from 1929. With the service came six Bristol coaches and two dual-purpose buses as well as United Counties' garage in Botley Road, Oxford. The capacity of the garage was quickly extended to accommodate 41 vehicles.

Apart from a quartet of heavyweight Guy Arab single-deckers that had been on order for some time, Bristol / ECW products became the standard for the rest of the decade.

Demand remained high through the early 1950s and vehicles from the Thames Valley fleet were drafted in for both short and long term hires. The ready availability now of vehicles at short notice plus a refurbishment programme for some of the older AEC Regals meant that no more new vehicles were obtained until 1958.

Integration with Thames Valley took a step closer when the South Midland Road Services licenses were transferred to the parent company during 1954. The appointment of Tom Pruett as General Manager of Thames Valley from January 1955, saw a steadily decline in coaching activities within that company, but South Midland was left untouched.

In 1957, a unique occurrence was the transfer of one of Thames Valley's Bristol K5G open top double-deckers to South Midland. It was used (with limited success) on a tour of the Oxford Colleges and Blenheim Palace but saw little service after 1959. It remained the only double-deck ever operated by South Midland.

A tour of the Irish Republic was introduced in from June 1958 and for this purpose, a former South Midland rebodied Leyland coach was re-acquired from Newbury & District. The other major event of the year was the entry of a new Bristol MW coach at the British Coach Rally where it won the Concours d'Elegance.

1961 saw the first of a number of lightweight Bedford coaches and deliveries of these interspersed with Bristols which were the standard chassis type for the remainder of the decade. The year also saw the introduction of coach-air travel, with the tour of Ireland, extended into Northern Ireland for the first time, being broken with a flight from Bristol Airport.

For 1963, the express services were given route letters following on from Thames Valley's A & B Reading-London routes and G, H and J from High Wycombe:

C	Oxford – Henley – Maidenhead - London
D	Oxford – High Wycombe – Uxbridge - London
E	Worcester – Oxford –Maidenhead - London
F	Worcester – Oxford – Newbury – Winchester – Southsea

Operation of the Gloucester Green café passed to Coach Caterers (Southern) Ltd in February 1964, having been in South Midland's ownership since 1933.

An important milestone occurred in February 1965 when ownership of all South Midland vehicles (plus plant, machinery, fixtures and fittings) passed to Thames Valley Traction Co Ltd. Separate operations however continued as before (including vehicles being transferred between the two companies). Discussions with Bristol Omnibus Co Ltd in early 1966 led to a close working arrangement with their Greyhound network with South Midland taking over a significant share of their express routes.

In 1968, the Transport Holding Company (the successors to BTC) acquired the bus interests of the BET Group which brought South Midland and City of Oxford Motor Services under common ownership. As a direct result of this, the National Bus Company was set up with effect from 1 January 1969. Perhaps inevitably, plans were drawn up to rationalise the operating companies and South Midland was merged with City of Oxford with effect from 1 January 1971. 33 coaches passed into COMS ownership which adopted the fleet name 'Oxford-South Midland'.

Premises
5/6 Brewers Street, Oxford	1921-1927	
Sandford Farm, Sandford on Thames	1927-1928	
Iffley Road, Oxford	1928-1961	(former Oxford Motor Carriers & Repairers Ltd)
Botley Road, Oxford	1952-1970	(former United Counties)

Liveries
The early charabancs were grey (hence the fleet name 'Grey Torpedo Coaches'). 1927-28 arrivals were painted in maroon or silver & maroon liveries, but in the following year, a new livery of cream & dark red was introduced. HFC 42 (22) was painted in (a possibly experimental) red & yellow livery, but this was not repeated.

Red & White's livery was adopted for the immediate post-war deliveries, this being predominantly red, with white flash and black mudguards. Some of the pre-war vehicles were repainted with white window surrounds. The new underfloor engined Bristol and Guy coaches arrived in the standard Tilling coach livery of cream with black window surrounds and black mudguards, though the black gave way to maroon around 1954. The AEC Regals then became predominantly cream with maroon mudguards.

From 1958, the maroon was applied to the lower panels with cream window surrounds and roof. This livery was also applied to Thames Valley vehicles on long term hire and remained the South Midland livery to the end.

Fleet numbering
The first known fleet number was 14 which was used on a Lancia new in 1928 (it is known that the series was not started at 1 in order to give the impression that the fleet was larger than it was). Thereafter, vehicles were numbered more or less sequentially (apart from some gap filling in 1938-40) until 95 had been reached in 1954. After this date, vehicles were included in the main Thames Valley scheme. The first South Midland vehicle was numbered 800 in 1958 and the last in this series was 867 in 1963. A new Thames Valley coach series was started in that year at C401, reaching 439 by 1970 (the C prefix having been discontinued in early 1969).

1921

New Vehicles:

FC 3902	Dennis 2½ ton	20049	Dennis		Ch30	4/21	by-/31
FC 4010	Dennis 2½ ton	20047	Dennis		Ch30	5/21	by-/31

Disposals:
FC 3902: No known disposal.
FC 4010: No known disposal.

1922

New Vehicle:

FC 4501	Dennis 2½ ton	20086	Dennis	Ch30	5/22	by-/31

Disposal:
FC 4501: No known disposal.

1923

Vehicle acquired from an unknown source 1923:

LK 8069	Crossley	?	?	C16-	-/--	by-/31

Previous history:
LK 8069: Its origins are not known.

Notes:
LK 8069: Was an 'all-weather' coach fitted with pneumatic tyres.

Disposal:
LK 8069: No known disposal.

1925

New Vehicle:

FC 8130	Dennis 2½ ton	45030	Dennis	C29D	4/25	by-/32

Notes:
FC 8130: Was an 'all-weather' coach fitted with pneumatic tyres.

Disposal:
FC 8130: No known disposal (its last owner was ?F Bunke 12/37?).

1927

New Vehicle:

WL 2696	Lancia Pentaiota	?	?	C24D	6/27	c5/34

Disposal:
WL 2696: No known disposal.

1928

New Vehicles:

	WL 4131	Lancia Pentaiota	2074	Weymann	C26D	2/28	5/35
14	WL 5055	Lancia Pentaiota	?	?	C28D	5/28	6/35

Disposal:
WL 4131: No known disposal.
WL 5055 (14): No known disposal.

Vehicle acquired from House Bros, Watlington (OX) 7/28:

BL 1351	Hotchkiss 30/40 hp	979	?	Ch14	5/14	9/28

Previous history:
BL 1351: New as a private 4-seat car; House Bros 3/26 [rebodied Ch14 at an unknown date].

'

Disposal:
      BL 1351: Last licensed 9/28.

1929

New Vehicles:

15	WL 7221	Dennis GL	70504	Arnold & Comben	C20D	5/29	4/32
18	WL 7233	Gilford 166SD	10737	Arnold & Comben	C26D	5/29	5/39
16	WL 7240	Dennis F	80102	Arnold & Comben	C28D	6/29	5/37
17	WL 7456	Dennis F	80104	Arnold & Comben	C28D	6/29	5/37

Disposals:
      WL 7221 (15): No known disposal.
      WL 7233 (18): S Henderson, Penygraig (GG) 5/39; scrapped at an unknown date.
      WL 7240 (16): Morgan, Tonypandy (GG) at an unknown date; Sir Alexander Gibb & Partners (contractor) (X)
            T91 at an unknown date.
      WL 7456 (17): Scrapped 3/38.

1930

New Vehicles:

27	JO 200	Gilford 168OT	11460	Arnold & Comben	C32F	8/30	2/35
19	WL 9058	Gilford 168OT	11197	Arnold & Comben	C30F	2/30	6/45
20	WL 9076	Gilford 168OT	11239	Arnold & Comben	C30F	3/30	2/40
21	WL 9079	Gilford 168OT	11284	Arnold & Comben	C28F	3/30	6/36
22	WL 9081	Gilford 168OT	11331	Arnold & Comben	C30F	4/30	6/39
23	WL 9415	Gilford 168OT	11344	Arnold & Comben	C30F	4/30	3/35
24	WL 9810	Gilford 168OT	11355	Arnold & Comben	C30F	5/30	1/35
25	WL 9862	Gilford 168OT	11406	Arnold & Comben	C30F	5/30	10/35
26	WL 9942	Gilford 168OT	11407	Arnold & Comben	C28F	6/30	5/39

Notes:
      WL 9058 (19): Converted for use as an ambulance from 1940 (one of three vehicles so treated – the
            identities of the other two are unknown).

Disposals:
      JO 200 (27): AH Kearsey, Staverton (GL) 2/35; last licensed 9/42 [it is also quoted with the War Department
            in 1941].
      WL 9058 (19): No known disposal.
      WL 9076 (20): War Department (GOV) 2/40; Tolley, Grafton Flyford (WO) 1940 to 2/45; CJ Marks {BlueBus},
            Worcester (WO) at an unknown date.
      WL 9079 (21): S Henderson, Penygraig (GG) 6/39; scrapped at an unknown date.
      WL 9081 (22): S Henderson, Penygraig (GG) 6/39; scrapped at an unknown date.
      WL 9415 (23): F & E Beedon, Northampton (NO) 50 3/35; United Counties Omnibus Co Ltd, Northampton
            (NO) 523 6/38; A Robertson {Excelsior}, Leith (MN) at an unknown date.
      WL 9810 (24): A Cox {Godiva}, Coventry (WK) 1/35; A Cox & FW Sephton {Godiva}, Coventry (WK) 6/37.
      WL 9862 (25): No known disposal.
      WL 9942 (26): S Henderson, Penygraig (GG) 5/39; scrapped at an unknown date.

1931

New Vehicles:

30	JO 1593	Leyland TS3	61519	Scammell & Nephew	C28C	4/31by12/50
31	JO 1595	Leyland TS3	61520	Scammell & Nephew	C28C	4/31 by9/49
28	JO 1597	Leyland TS3	61703	Scammell & Nephew	C28C	3/31by12/50
29	JO 1599	Leyland TS3	61704	Scammell & Nephew	C28C	3/31 by9/50

Notes:
      JO 1593 (30): Rebodied Harrington C31F 1936.
      JO 1595 (31): Rebodied Harrington C31F 1936.
      JO 1597 (28): Rebodied Harrington C31F 1936.
      JO 1599 (29): Rebodied Harrington C31F 1936.

Disposals:
      JO 1593 (30): FG Hobbs {Watling Street Motors} (dealer), Redbourn at an unknown date; last licensed
            12/56.

JO 1595 (31): H Crapper & Son Ltd, Oxford (OX) 29 by 9/49; withdrawn 1/52; Middleton & Davies, (contractor), Cardiff (XGG) at an unknown date.

JO 1597 (28): H Crapper & Son Ltd, Oxford (OX) 28 1/51; withdrawn 10/52; Hambridge, Kidlington (OX) at an unknown date; last licensed 12/54.

JO 1599 (29): H Crapper & Son Ltd, Oxford (OX) 31 1/51; withdrawn by 11/55.

1932

New Vehicles:

32	JO 4789	Leyland TS4	1551	Harrington	C32R	6/32	by8/46

Disposals:

JO 4789 (32): H Crapper & Son Ltd, Oxford (OX) 32 by 8/46; withdrawn and scrapped at an unknown date.

1934

New Vehicles:

33	AFC 531	Leyland TS6	4670	Harrington	C32F	5/34	c3/40

Disposals:

AFC 531 (33): War Department (GOV) c3/40; JW Hurst & Sons Ltd, Winlaton (DM) 7/44; rebodied ACB B35F date unknown (but whilst with Hurst); Northern General Transport Co Ltd, Gateshead (DM) 1446 8/51; Lancashire Motor Traders (dealer), Salford 1/56.

1935

New Vehicles:

34	BFC 675	Leyland TS7	6060	Harrington	C32F	4/35	9/50
35	BWL 349	Leyland TS7	6061	Harrington	C32R	5/35	1/50

Disposals:

BFC 675 (34): SG Taylor & E Whittington {Enterprise Coaches}, Newbury (BE) 1/51.

BWL 349 (35): Newbury & District Motor Services Ltd 167 1/50 (qv).

Vehicle acquired from Morris Commercial Cars Ltd, Birmingham by 7/35:

?23?	HA 7493	Morris Viceroy	163Y	?	C20F	7/31	c1940

Previous history:

HA 7493: New as a Morris demonstrator with Morris Commercial Cars Ltd; its acquisition date is uncertain and it may have had intermediate operators).

Disposal:

HA 7493: House Bros, Watlington (OX) c1940.

1936

New Vehicles:

36	CWL 951	Leyland TS7	9137	Harrington	C32F	4/36	1/50
37	CWL 953	Leyland TS7	9138	Harrington	C32F	4/36	1/50

Disposals:

CWL 951 (36): Newbury & District Motor Services Ltd 168 1/50 (qv).

CWL 953 (37): Newbury & District Motor Services Ltd 166 1/50 (qv).

1938

New Vehicles:

24	FWL 795	Leyland SKPZ2	8434	Harrington	C26F	3/38	10/47
25	FWL 797	Leyland SKPZ2	8435	Harrington	C26F	2/38	10/47

Disposals:

FWL 795 (24): Unidentified dealer 10/47; AE Banwell {Regent Coaches}, Biddisham (SO) 4/48; F Dare {Avalon Coaches, Weston-Super-Mare (SO) 5/48; Western Engineering & Motor Services Ltd {WEMS}, Clevedon (SO) 17 (not operated) 10/49; Harry Lester & His Hayseeds (band), location and date unknown.

FWL 797 (25): Unidentified dealer 10/47; AE Banwell {Regent Coaches}, Biddisham (SO) 2/48; B Banwell {Regent Coaches}, Biddisham (SO) 9/53; RW Chandler {Cathedral Coaches}, Gloucester (GL) 9/54; withdrawn 1/56.

1939

New Vehicles:

26	HFC 548	Leyland LZ2A	?	Burlingham		C32F	3/39	12/47
27	HFC 550	Leyland LZ2A	201314	Burlingham		C32F	3/39	10/47
23	JFC 12	Austin K3/CL	1552	Burlingham		C26F	8/39	5/48
22	JFC 42	Austin K3/CL	1893	Harrington		C26F	8/39	5/48

Disposals:

HFC 548 (26): Unidentified dealer 12/47; AE Banwell {Regent Coaches}, Biddisham (SO) 2/48; G Alford & Sons, Coleford (SO) 5/48; withdrawn 8/50.

HFC 550 (27): Unidentified dealer 10/47; AE Banwell {Regent Coaches}, Biddisham (SO) 3/48; withdrawn 9/51; LC Munden {Airborne Coaches}, Bridgwater (SO) 3/52; LC Munden {Crown Coaches}, Bristol (GL) 9/53; withdrawn 5/60.

JFC 12 (23): BC Leather, Maiden Bradley (WI) 6/48; withdrawn 7/55; possibly to DGH Bissell {Trans-Orient Tours), London NW3 (LN) at an unknown date.

JFC 42 (22): Babbage & Son (Cromer) Ltd, Cromer (NK) 7/48; AG Rix, Foulsham (NK) 9/50; withdrawn 9/57; unidentified dealer, East Dereham for scrap at an unknown date.

1940

New Vehicles:

21	JFC 707	Austin K3/CL	2149	Harrington		C26F	3/40	5/48

Disposals:

JFC 707 (21): H Semmance & Co Ltd, Wymondham (NK) 9/48; WC Cunningham & Son, Hempnall (NK) 5/60; withdrawn 1/62.

1947

New Vehicles:

43	LJO 756	Bedford OB	54661	Duple	46745	C29F	7/47	1/50
45	LJO 758	AEC Regal	O6624671	Duple	45151	C33F	8/47	10/57
46	LJO 759	AEC Regal	O6624949	Duple	45150	C33F	8/47	10/58
47	LJO 760	AEC Regal	O6624961	Duple	45152	C33F	8/47	10/58
38	LWL 995	Leyland PS1/1	462028	ECOC		DP31R	2/47	1/50
39	LWL 996	AEC Regal	O6624593	Duple	45146	C33F	5/47	7/58
40	LWL 997	AEC Regal	O6624591	Duple	45147	C33F	5/47	7/58
41	LWL 998	AEC Regal	O6624594	Duple	45148	C33F	5/47	10/58
42	LWL 999	AEC Regal	O6624670	Duple	45149	C33F	5/47	7/58

Notes:

LJO 758 (45): Refurbished by ECW and reseated to C35F (rebuild no R634) 5-7/55.

LJO 759 (46): Refurbished by ECW and reseated to C35F (rebuild no R635) 11/54-2/55.

LJO 760 (47): Refurbished by ECW and reseated to C35F (rebuild no R630) 1-4/55.

LWL 995 (38): Fitted a with rebuilt 1936 ECOC B35R body (originally DP31R, one of nos. 4217-4240) from a North Western Road Car Co Ltd Bristol JO5G (22 of these bodies were purchased by Red & White United Transport Ltd from Broadhead (dealer), Bollington in 5/46).

LWL 997 (40): Refurbished by ECW and reseated to C35F (rebuild no R631) 4-7/55.

LWL 998 (41): Refurbished by ECW and reseated to C35F (rebuild no R629) 10/54-1/55.

LWL 999 (42): Refurbished by ECW and reseated to C35F (rebuild no R633) 2-4/55.

Disposals:

LJO 756 (43): Newbury & District Motor Services Ltd 164 1/50 (qv).

LJO 758 (45): AE Connorton Motors (dealer), London SW9 10/57; R Taylor, London SE1 (LN) 3/58; Freedman Upholstery, Basildon as a mobile showroom (XEX) 5/59.

LJO 759 (46): Passenger Vehicle Disposals Ltd (dealer), Dunchurch 10/58; Contract Bus Services Ltd, Caerwent (MH) 3/60.

LJO 760 (47): Passenger Vehicle Disposals Ltd (dealer), Dunchurch 10/58; Contract Bus Services Ltd, Caerwent (MH) 10/58; awaiting scrapping at Tredegar depot 4/62.

LWL 995 (38): Newbury & District Motor Services Ltd 169 1/50 (qv).

LWL 996 (39): Passenger Vehicle Disposals Ltd (dealer), Dunchurch 7/58; Lloyd, Nuneaton 7/58; HE Clarke, Newcastle Emlyn (CR) 7/58; withdrawn by 7/64.

LWL 997 (40): Passenger Vehicle Disposals Ltd (dealer), Dunchurch 7/58; George Wimpey & Co Ltd (contractor), London W6 (XLN) 8/60; St George's Ambulance Station, Cheam (XSR) 11/65.

LWL 998 (41): Passenger Vehicle Disposals Ltd (dealer), Dunchurch 10/58; Contract Bus Services Ltd, Caerwent (MH) 1959; Wade (dealer), Cardiff for scrap 8/62.

LWL 999 (42): Passenger Vehicle Disposals Ltd (dealer), Dunchurch 7/58; George Wimpey & Co Ltd (contractor), London W6 (XLN) 112 at an unknown date; noted Stockton 10/58.

Vehicles on hire from Red & White Services Ltd, Chepstow (MH):

233	EM 2723	Albion PW65 (5LW)	16016E	Burlingham (1944)	B34F	7/32	5/47	1/48
251	EM 2743	Albion PW65 (5LW)	16018C	Burlingham (1944)	B34F	12/32	5/47	1/48

1948

New Vehicles:

44	LJO 757	Bedford OB	61338	Duple	46751	C29F	3/48	1/50
48	LJO 761	AEC Regal	O6625639	Duple	45153	C33F	1/48	10/57
53	MJO 278	AEC Regal	O6625645	Duple	45158	C33F	1/48	12/58
54	MJO 664	AEC Regal III	O682385	Duple	45382	C33F	3/48	12/58
55	MJO 665	AEC Regal III	O682389	Duple	45383	C33F	4/48	12/58
56	MJO 667	AEC Regal III	O682390	Duple	45384	C33F	4/48	11/59
49	MWL 741	AEC Regal	O6625643	Duple	45154	C33F	1/48	10/58
50	MWL 742	AEC Regal	O6625641	Duple	45155	C33F	1/48	10/58
51	MWL 743	AEC Regal	O6625642	Duple	45156	C33F	1/48	8/58
52	MWL 744	AEC Regal	O6625644	Duple	45157	C33F	1/48	10/57
57	NFC 128	AEC Regal III	6821A415	Duple	45387	C33F	9/48	11/59

Notes:

LJO 761 (48): Refurbished by ECW and reseated to C35F (rebuild no R636) 2-5/55.

MJO 278 (53): Refurbished by ECW and reseated to C35F (rebuild no R640) 7-9/55.

MWL 741 (49): Refurbished by ECW and reseated to C35F (rebuild no R637) 6-9/55.

MWL 742 (50): Refurbished by ECW and reseated to C35F (rebuild no R638) 11/54-3/55.

MWL 743 (51): Refurbished by ECW and reseated to C35F (rebuild no R632) 11/54-2/55.

MWL 744 (52): Refurbished by ECW and reseated to C35F (rebuild no R639) 3-5/55.

NFC 128 (57): Did not enter service until 12/48.

Disposals:

LJO 757 (44): Newbury & District Motor Services Ltd 165 1/50 (qv).

LJO 761 (48): AE Connorton Motors (dealer), London SW9 10/57; WL Thurgood (Coachbuilders) Ltd (dealer), Ware 10/57.

MJO 278 (53): Passenger Vehicle Disposals Ltd (dealer), Dunchurch 12/58; Bryn Motor Co Ltd, Pontllanfraith (MH) 1/59; derelict by 9/63.

MJO 664 (54): Passenger Vehicle Disposals Ltd (dealer), Dunchurch 12/58; G Williams, Blaina (MH) 7/59.

MJO 665 (55): Passenger Vehicle Disposals Ltd (dealer), Dunchurch 12/58; W & EF Kershaw {County}, Batford (HT) 2/59; unidentified dealer 11/61; chassis to Strowger's, Manchester 9/62.

MJO 667 (56): Fleet Car (Sales) Ltd (dealer), Dunchurch 11/59; C Davies, Pontlottyn (GG).

MWL 741-742 (49-50): Passenger Vehicle Disposals Ltd (dealer), Dunchurch 10/58; Contract Bus Services Ltd, Caerwent (MH) 1959.

MWL 743 (51): Passenger Vehicle Disposals Ltd (dealer), Dunchurch 8/58; Superb, Birmingham (WK) 9 1959; Goddard, Birmingham (WK) 33 9/59; Bailey, Birmingham (WK) 10/60.

MWL 744 (52): AE Connorton Motors (dealer), London SW9 10/57; WL Thurgood (Coachbuilders) Ltd (dealer), Ware 10/57.

NFC 128 (57): Fleet Car (Sales) Ltd (dealer), Dunchurch 11/59; C Davies, Pontlottyn (GG).

1949

New Vehicles:

58	NFC 129	AEC Regal III	6821A416	Duple	45386	C33F	5/49	11/59
59	NFC 130	AEC Regal III	6821A418	Duple	45385	C33F	5/49	11/59
63	NJO 217	AEC Regal III	6821A169	Duple	45375	C30F	7/49	1/59
64	NJO 218	AEC Regal III	6821A170	Duple	45381	C30F	7/49	1/59
60	NWL 877	AEC Regal III	6821A163	Duple	45373	C30F	6/49	12/58
61	NWL 878	AEC Regal III	6821A164	Duple	45380	C30F	6/49	1/59
62	NWL 879	AEC Regal III	6821A165	Duple	45388	C30F	6/49	10/57

Disposals:

NFC 129-130 (58-59): Fleet Car (Sales) Ltd (dealer), Dunchurch 11/59; C Davies, Pontlottyn (GG) at an unknown date.

NJO 217 (63): J Deacon (dealer), Dorchester-on-Thames 1/59; Frostways (Oxford) Ltd, Kennington (BE) 5/59; PG & JD Bryan {Reliable Cars}, Didcot (BE) 4/62; yard near Ampthill, Bedfordshire 7/66.

NJO 218 (64): Fleet Car (Sales) Ltd (dealer), Dunchurch 1/59; Bryn Motor Co Ltd, Pontllanfraith (MH) 2/59; derelict by 9/63.

NWL 877 (60): Passenger Vehicle Disposals Ltd (dealer), Dunchurch 12/58; Bryn Motor Co Ltd, Pontllanfraith (MH) 1/59; derelict by 9/63.

NWL 878 (61): Fleet Car (Sales) Ltd (dealer), Dunchurch 1/59; Contract Bus Services Ltd, Caerwent (MH) 1/59; derelict by 9/63.

NWL 879 (62): AE Connorton Motors (dealer), London SW9 10/57; WL Thurgood (Coachbuilders) Ltd (dealer), Ware 10/57; Williams, Llantwit Major (GG) 11/65; withdrawn 5/66.

Vehicles on hire from Liberty Motors Ltd, Cardiff (GG):

7	HAX 657	Bedford OB	96712	Duple	52382	C29F	1/49	6/49	9/49
8	HAX 828	Bedford OB	100318	Duple	54085	C29F	2/49	6/49	9/49

1950

New Vehicles:

65	OFC 204	AEC Regal III	6821A422	Duple	51608	C30F	3/50	1/59
66	OFC 205	AEC Regal III	6821A423	Duple	51609	C30F	3/50	1/59
67	OFC 206	AEC Regal III	6821A424	Duple	51610	C30F	3/50	1/59

Disposals:

OFC 204 (65): Fleet Car (Sales) Ltd (dealer), Dunchurch 1/59; Contract Bus Services Ltd, Caerwent (MH) 1959; Edwards Coaches Ltd, Joys Green (GL) c1964; broken up by Edwards 3/64.

OFC 205 (66): J Deacon (dealer), Dorchester-on-Thames 1/59; Frostways (Oxford) Ltd, Kennington (BE) 5/59; Passenger Vehicle Disposals Ltd (dealer), Dunchurch 4/62; James, Blaenporth (CG) at an unknown date; TS Lewis, Rhydlewis (CG) 11/63 (as C32F); withdrawn by 7/75; MD Shaw, Oxford for preservation 1/80; moved to Farmoor 1/81; Oxford Bus Museum Trust, Oxford for preservation by 4/09.

OFC 206 (67): Fleet Car (Sales) Ltd (dealer), Dunchurch 1/59; AS Shurrock {Ann Marie Coaches}, Brill (BK) 7/59.

Vehicles transferred from Newbury & District Motor Services Ltd 1/50:

68	EJB 649	AEC Regal III	6821A419	Duple	45371	C33F	9/48	10/59
69	EJB 650	AEC Regal III	6821A420	Duple	45370	C33F	9/48	7/58
70	ERX 937	AEC Regal III	6821A168	Duple	45372	C33F	7/49	2/60

Previous histories:

EJB 649-650 (68-69): New to Newbury & District Motor Services Ltd 149-150 (as C35F).

ERX 937 (70): New to Newbury & District Motor Services Ltd 158 (as C35F).

Disposals:

EJB 649 (68): Fleet Car (Sales) Ltd (dealer), Dunchurch 10/59; Contract Bus Services Ltd, Caerwent (MH) 8/60 to 1965 at least.

EJB 650 (69): Passenger Vehicle Disposals Ltd (dealer), Dunchurch 7/58; Dickson, Stoke Mandeville (BK) 6 10/58; Passenger Vehicle Disposals Ltd (dealer), Dunchurch 4/62; T Edmunds, Rassau (BC) 5/62.

ERX 937 (70): Frostways (Oxford) Ltd, Kennington (BE) 2/60; withdrawn 7/64.

1952

New Vehicles:

79	SFC 565	Bristol LS6G	89.010	ECW	6204	C37F	6/52	9/65
80	SFC 566	Bristol LS6G	89.011	ECW	6205	C37F	6/52	9/65
81	SFC 567	Bristol LS6G	89.012	ECW	6206	C37F	6/52	9/65
82	SFC 568	Bristol LS6G	89.116	ECW	6207	C37F	10/52	9/65
83	SFC 569	Bristol LS6G	89.117	ECW	6208	C37F	10/52	9/65
84	SFC 570	Bristol LS6G	89.118	ECW	6209	C37F	10/52	10/61
85	SFC 571	AEC Regal IV	9821E182	ECW	5772	C37F	8/52	10/67

Notes:

SFC 565 (79): Reseated to C39F in early 1961; hired to City of Oxford Motor Services Ltd, Oxford (OX) at various times between 1-2/63.

SFC 566 (80): Reseated to C39F in early 1961; hired to City of Oxford Motor Services Ltd, Oxford (OX) at various times between 1-3/63.

SFC 567 (81): Reseated to C39F in early 1961; hired to City of Oxford Motor Services Ltd, Oxford (OX) at various times in 1/63; hired (seat-less) to Post Office, Oxford 12/64.

SFC 568 (82): Reseated to C39F in early 1961; hired to City of Oxford Motor Services Ltd, Oxford (OX) at various times between 2-3/63; hired (seat-less) to Post Office, Oxford 12/64.

SFC 569 (83): Reseated to C39F in early 1961; hired to City of Oxford Motor Services Ltd, Oxford (OX) at various times in 1/63; renumbered C83 (in error) c1/64.

SFC 570 (84): Reseated to C39F in early 1961; wrecked in an accident at Ashridge Hill, near East Ilsley 6/10/61; cannibalised for spares from 10/61 to 5/62.

SFC 571 (85): Originally intended to be fitted with a Duple (Ambassador) body, but due to delays, the order was reassigned to ECW; reseated to C39F 2/62; hired to City of Oxford Motor Services Ltd, Oxford (OX) at various times in 1/63.

Disposals:

SFC 565 (79): TD Alexander {Greyhound Luxury Coaches}, Arbroath (AS) 12/65; TD Alexander {Greyhound Luxury Coaches}, Sheffield (WR) 6/66; withdrawn and cannibalised for spares 5/68.

SFC 566 (80): TD Alexander {Greyhound Luxury Coaches}, Arbroath (AS) 12/65; TD Alexander {Greyhound Luxury Coaches}, Sheffield (WR) by 3/66.

SFC 567 (81): TD Alexander {Greyhound Luxury Coaches}, Sheffield (WR) 1/66; TD Alexander {Greyhound Luxury Coaches}, Arbroath (AS) 4/67; withdrawn by 1969.

SFC 568 (82): TD Alexander {Greyhound Luxury Coaches}, Sheffield (WR) 12/65; TD Alexander {Greyhound Luxury Coaches}, Arbroath (AS) by 10/68; Hartwood Finance Ltd (dealer), Birdwell 10/70.

SFC 569 (83): Westbrick Products, Dorset as a mobile showroom 12/65; Quickover, noted Colchester as a mobile demonstration unit 7/67.

SFC 570 (84): Dismantled for spares / scrap by Thames Valley 5/62.

SFC 571 (85): Winlon Autos Ltd, Harrow (LN) 10/67; 6th Newtownards Scout Group, Newtownards (XDO) 2/70.

Vehicles acquired from United Counties Omnibus Co Ltd, Northampton (NO) 5/52:

71	EBD 234	Bristol L6B	71.023	ECW	2963	DP31R	9/48	1/53
72	EBD 235	Bristol L6B	71.024	ECW	2964	DP31R	9/48	1/53
73	EBD 236	Bristol L6B	73.039	ECW	4195	FC31F	2/50	10/61
74	EBD 237	Bristol L6B	73.042	ECW	4196	FC31F	2/50	11/60
75	FRP 832	Bristol LL6B	83.012	ECW	4930	FC37F	2/51	12/62
76	FRP 833	Bristol LL6B	83.013	ECW	4931	FC37F	2/51	5/63
77	FRP 834	Bristol LL6B	83.068	ECW	4932	FC37F	2/51	8/63
78	FRP 836	Bristol LL6B	83.070	ECW	4934	FC37F	2/51	3/63

Previous histories:

EBD 234-237 (71-74): New to United Counties Omnibus Co Ltd 107-110 [renumbered 807-810 2/50 and 71-74 3/52].

FRP 832-834 (75-77): New to United Counties Omnibus Co Ltd 832-834 [renumbered 75-77 3/52].

FRP 836 (78): New to United Counties Omnibus Co Ltd 836 [renumbered 78 3/52].

Notes:

FRP 833 (76): Hired to City of Oxford Motor Services Ltd, Oxford (OX) during 2/63.

Disposals:

EBD 234-235 (71-72): Thames Valley Traction Co Ltd 71-72 1/53 (qv).

EBD 236 (73): Creamline Motor Services Ltd, Bordon (HA) 10/61; P Jeffreys {Liss & District}, Grayshott (HA) 4/64; James (dealer), Hedge End 11/66.

EBD 237 (74): Passenger Vehicle Disposals Ltd (dealer), Dunchurch 11/60; Worth, Enstone (OX) 12/60 to 8/62; F Cowley (dealer), Dunchurch 5/66.

FRP 832 (75): S Leavy & C Conlon, Botley (BE) 12/62; Hargreaves, Childrey (BE) 12/66; Aston, Marton (WK) 5/67.

FRP 833 (76): Clack {B & C Coaches}, Cumnor (BE) 5/63; withdrawn 8/67; Main Motors (dealer), Ewelme 6/71.

FRP 834 (77): TD Alexander {Greyhound Luxury Coaches}, Arbroath (AS) 12/63; TD Alexander {Greyhound Luxury Coaches}, Sheffield (WR) 12/64; withdrawn 2/65.

FRP 836 (78): Creamline Motor Services (Bordon) Ltd, Bordon (HA) 3/63; withdrawn 11/64.

Vehicles on hire from Red & White Services Ltd, Chepstow (MH):

JWO 213	Leyland PSU1/13	505913	Lydney		C41F	4/52	5/52	11/52
JWO 546	Leyland PSU1/13	510614	Lydney		C41F	4/52	5/52	11/52

Notes:

JWO 213: Was numbered UC951 in the Red & White fleet.
JWO 546: Was numbered UC2051 in the Red & White fleet.

1953

New Vehicles:

86	SFC 501	Guy Arab UF	UF71338	Lydney / BBW		C41C		4/53	7/60
87	SFC 502	Guy Arab UF	UF71339	Lydney / BBW		C41C		5/53	7/60
88	SFC 503	Guy Arab UF	UF71340	Lydney / BBW		C41C		3/53	7/60
89	SFC 504	Guy Arab UF	UF71341	Lydney / BBW		C41C		4/53	7/60
90	TWL 55	Bristol LS6B	97.017	ECW	6975	C37F		6/53	2/66
91	TWL 56	Bristol LS6B	97.018	ECW	6976	C37F		6/53	5/66
92	TWL 57	Bristol LS6B	97.019	ECW	6977	C37F		6/53	7/66
93	TWL 58	Bristol LS6B	97.020	ECW	6978	C37F		7/53	7/66
94	TWL 59	Bristol LS6B	97.041	ECW	6979	C37F		8/53	6/67
95	TWL 60	Bristol LS6B	97.042	ECW	6980	C37F		10/53	1/67

Notes:

SFC 501-504 (86-89): Fitted with Gardner 6HLW engines.

SFC 502 (87): Swerved to avoid a cyclist and collided with a building 26/6/58 en-route to Newbury; subsequently had its front end completely rebuilt by Thames Valley.

TWL 55 (90): Reseated to C39F 2/62; delicensed 10/65; probably hired (seat-less) to the Post Office 12/65; reseated to DP41F, equipped for one-man-operation and renumbered S315 2/66; it did not re-enter service with South Midland in this form.

TWL 56 (91): Reseated to C39F 7/62; delicensed 11/65; probably hired (seat-less) to the Post Office 12/65; reseated to DP39F, equipped for one-man-operation and renumbered S316 5/66; it did not re-enter service with South Midland in this form.

TWL 57 (92): Reseated to C39F 2/62; delicensed 2/66; reseated to DP39F, equipped for one-man-operation and renumbered S317 7/66; it did not re-enter service with South Midland in this form.

TWL 58 (93): Reseated to C39F 5/62; hired to City of Oxford Motor Services Ltd, Oxford (OX) at various times during 1/63; hired (seat-less) to the Post Office 12/63; delicensed 2/66; reseated to DP39F, equipped for one-man-operation and renumbered S318 7/66; it did not re-enter service with South Midland in this form.

TWL 59 (94): Reseated to C39F 1/64; delicensed 12/66; reseated to DP39F, equipped for one-man-operation and renumbered S319 6/67; it did not re-enter service with South Midland in this form.

TWL 60 (95): Did not enter service until 3/54; reseated to C39F 1/64; delicensed 4/66; hired (seat-less) to the Post Office 12/66; reseated to DP39F, equipped for one-man-operation and renumbered S320 1/67; it did not re-enter service with South Midland in this form.

Disposals:

SFC 501 (86): Red & White Services Ltd, Chepstow (MH) UC1552 7/60; renumbered DS1552 5/62; Woodland (dealer), Chepstow 7/66; E, T & W Williams {Tudor Williams Brothers / Pioneer}, Laugharne (CR) 7/66; Smith (dealer), Sutton St Nicholas 5/70 to 5/72 at least.

SFC 502 (87): Red & White Services Ltd, Chepstow (MH) UC1652 7/60; renumbered DS1652 5/62; F Cowley (dealer), Salford 8/65; AC Brew (contractor), Irlam (XLA) 1/66; unidentified operator / dealer by 1968.

SFC 503 (88): Red & White Services Ltd, Chepstow (MH) UC1752 7/60; renumbered DS1752 5/62; F Cowley (dealer), Salford 8/65; AC Brew (contractor), Irlam (XLA) 1/66; unidentified owner, London E17 as a furniture display vehicle 7/66.

SFC 504 (89): Red & White Services Ltd, Chepstow (MH) UC1852 7/60; renumbered DS1852 5/62; F Cowley (dealer), Salford 8/65; AC Brew (contractor), Irlam (XLA) 1/66; unidentified operator / dealer by 1968.

TWL 55 (S315): Thames Valley Traction Co Ltd S315 2/66 (qv).

TWL 56 (S316): Thames Valley Traction Co Ltd S316 5/66 (qv).

TWL 57-58 (S317-318): Thames Valley Traction Co Ltd S317-318 7/66 (qv).

TWL 59 (S319): Thames Valley Traction Co Ltd S319 6/67 (qv).

TWL 60 (S320): Thames Valley Traction Co Ltd S320 1/67 (qv).

1955

Vehicles transferred from Thames Valley Traction Co Ltd 1/55:

548	FMO 23	Bristol L6B	79.116	Windover	6857	C33F	3/50	10/58
553	FMO 935	Bristol L6B	81.071	Windover	6909	C33F	7/50	10/60

Previous histories:
FMO 23 (548): New to Thames Valley Traction Co Ltd 548.
FMO 935 (553): New to Thames Valley Traction Co Ltd 553.

Disposals:
FMO 23 (548): Thames Valley Traction Co Ltd 548 10/58 (qv).
FMO 935 (553): Passenger Vehicle Disposals Ltd (dealer), Dunchurch 11/60; S Davies Ltd, Cardiff (GG) 5/61; C Davies, Pontlottyn (GG) by 11/61; Kenfig Motor Services, Kenfig Hill (GG) at an unknown date; last licensed 11/63; derelict by 5/65; WA Way & Sons (dealer), Cardiff 12/65; unidentified owner, St Clears 5/66.

1957

Vehicle transferred from Thames Valley Traction Co Ltd 8/57:

770	CAP 206	Bristol K5G	55.070	ECW	6932	O30/26R	9/40	7/60

Previous history:
CAP 206 (770): New to Brighton, Hove & District Omnibus Co Ltd, Brighton (ES) 6353 (as H30/26R); renumbered 353 1955; rebuilt to O30/26R 1956; Thames Valley Traction Co Ltd 770 11/56.

Notes:
CAP 206 (770): Used on tours of the Oxford colleges and Blenheim Palace.

Disposal:
CAP 206 (770): Passenger Vehicle Disposals Ltd (dealer), Dunchurch 7/60; Colbro Ltd (dealer), Rothwell 8/60.

1958

New Vehicles:

800	ORX 631	Bristol MW6G	135.069	ECW	10652	C34F	3/58	12/68
801	ORX 632	Bristol MW6G	135.074	ECW	10653	C34F	3/58	3/69
802	ORX 633	Bristol MW6G	135.075	ECW	10654	C34F	4/58	3/69
803	ORX 634	Bristol MW6G	135.089	ECW	10655	C32F	4/58	12/68

Notes:
ORX 631 (800): Reseated to C38F 1/63; delicensed 12/68; reseated to DP41F with folding doors, altered front dome, fitted for one-man-operation and renumbered 159 3/69; it did not re-enter service with South Midland in this form.
ORX 632 (801): Reseated to C38F 1/63; delicensed 3/69; reseated to DP41F with folding doors, altered front dome, fitted for one-man-operation and renumbered 160 7/69; it did not re-enter service with South Midland in this form.
ORX 633 (802): Hired to the Post Office 12/63; reseated to C38F 1/64; delicensed 3/69; reseated to DP41F with folding doors, altered front dome, fitted for one-man-operation and renumbered 161 6/69; it did not re-enter service with South Midland in this form.
ORX 634 (803): Exhibited at the British Coach Rally, Brighton winning the Concours d'Elegance 4/58; reseated to C34F 10/58; reseated to C38F 11/62; delicensed 12/68; reseated to DP41F with folding doors, altered front dome, fitted for one-man-operation and renumbered 162 4/69; it did not re-enter service with South Midland in this form.

Disposals:
ORX 631 (159): Thames Valley Traction Co Ltd 159 3/69.
ORX 632 (160): Thames Valley Traction Co Ltd 160 7/69.
ORX 633 (161): Thames Valley Traction Co Ltd 161 6/69.
ORX 634 (162): Thames Valley Traction Co Ltd 162 4/69.

Vehicles transferred from Thames Valley Traction Co Ltd 6/58:

689	HMO 835	Bristol LS6B	97.068	ECW	6982	C39F	10/53	11/63
690	HMO 836	Bristol LS6B	97.069	ECW	6983	C39F	10/53	11/63
692	HMO 838	Bristol LS6B	101.062	ECW	6985	C39F	3/54	12/64
693	HMO 839	Bristol LS6B	101.063	ECW	6986	C39F	3/54	11/64

Previous histories:
HMO 835-836 (689-690): New to Thames Valley Traction Co Ltd 689-690.
HMO 838-839 (692-693): New to Thames Valley Traction Co Ltd 692-693.

Notes:
HMO 835 (689): Reseated to C37F from c5/59 to 11/59; reverted to C39F by 4/60; delicensed 11/63, equipped for one-man-operation, reseated to DP41F and renumbered S309 4/64 (it was hired (seat-less) to the Post Office, Oxford in 12/63, during the course of this rebuild); it did not re-enter service with South Midland in this form.

HMO 836 (690): Reseated to C37F from c3/59 to 8/59; delicensed 11/63, equipped for one-man-operation, reseated to DP41F and renumbered S310 4/64; it did not re-enter service with South Midland in this form.

HMO 838 (692): Reseated to C37F from c1/59 to c8/60; delicensed 12/64, equipped for one-man-operation, reseated to DP39F and renumbered S312 3/65 (it was hired (seat-less) to the Post Office, Oxford in 12/64, during the course of this rebuild); it did not re-enter service with South Midland in this form.

HMO 839 (693): Reseated to C34F and fitted with a luggage rack in place of the rear five seats (for American tourist work) 5/58 to late 1958; delicensed 11/64, equipped for one-man-operation, reseated to DP39F and renumbered S313 2/65 (it was hired (seat-less) to the Post Office, Oxford in 12/64, during the course of this rebuild); it did not re-enter service with South Midland in this form.

Disposals:
HMO 835-836 (S309-310): Thames Valley Traction Co Ltd S309-310 4/64 (qv).
HMO 838 (S312): Thames Valley Traction Co Ltd S312 3/65 (qv).
HMO 839 (S313): Thames Valley Traction Co Ltd S313 2/65 (qv).

Vehicle transferred from Newbury & District Motor Services Ltd 6/58:

169	LWL 995	Leyland PS1/1	462028	ECW	5464	FC34F	2/47	7/60

Previous history:
LWL 995 (169): New to South Midland Motor Services Ltd 38 (with a 1936 ECOC DP31R body); Newbury & District Motor Services Ltd 169 1/50 [rebuilt to 30ft long 11-12/50 and rebodied ECW (5464) FC37F (8ft wide) 2/51; reseated to FC34F c2/58].

Disposal:
LWL 995 (169): Frostways (Oxford) Ltd, Kennington (BE) 7/60; Sealandair, West Bromwich (ST) 5/63; unidentified operator / dealer 11/63; contractor, Bewdley by 5/64.

1959

New Vehicles:

804	PRX 930	Bristol MW6G	139.256	ECW	11316	C34F	3/59	10/69
805	PRX 931	Bristol MW6G	139.257	ECW	11317	C34F	4/59	10/69
806	PRX 932	Bristol MW6G	139.258	ECW	11318	C34F	4/59	8/69
807	PRX 933	Bristol MW6G	139.259	ECW	11319	C34F	3/59	12/69

Notes:
PRX 930 (804): Reseated to C38F 11/62; delicensed 10/69, reseated to DP41F with folding doors, altered front dome, fitted for one-man-operation and renumbered 163 11/69; it did not re-enter service with South Midland in this form.

PRX 931 (805): Renumbered C805 (in error) 1/64, reverted to 805 1965; reseated to C38F c3/66; delicensed 10/69, reseated to DP41F with folding doors, altered front dome, fitted for one-man-operation and renumbered 164 12/69; it did not re-enter service with South Midland in this form.

PRX 932 (806): Reseated to C38F 4/63; delicensed 8/69, reseated to DP41F with folding doors, altered front dome, fitted for one-man-operation and renumbered 165 10/69; it did not re-enter service with South Midland in this form.

PRX 933 (807): Renumbered C807 (in error) 1/64, reverted to 807 1965; reseated to C38F c3/66; delicensed 12/69, reseated to DP41F with folding doors, altered front dome, fitted for one-man-operation and renumbered 166 2/70; it did not re-enter service with South Midland in this form.

Disposals:
PRX 930 (163): Thames Valley Traction Co Ltd 163 11/69 (qv).
PRX 931 (164): Thames Valley Traction Co Ltd 164 12/69 (qv)
PRX 932 (165): Thames Valley Traction Co Ltd 165 10/69 (qv)
PRX 933 (166): Thames Valley Traction Co Ltd 166 2/70 (qv)

Vehicles acquired from United Counties Omnibus Co Ltd, Northampton (NO) 1/59:

821	FRP 835	Bristol LL6B	83.069	ECW	4933	FC37F	3/51	10/61
822	FRP 837	Bristol LL6B	83.071	ECW	4935	FC37F	3/51	3/62
823	FRP 838	Bristol LL6B	83.072	ECW	4936	FC37F	5/51	7/63
824	FRP 839	Bristol LL6B	83.084	ECW	4946	FC37F	6/51	3/62
825	FRP 840	Bristol LL6B	83.085	ECW	4947	FC37F	6/51	1/62
826	FRP 841	Bristol LL6B	83.087	ECW	4948	FC37F	6/51	10/61
827	FRP 842	Bristol LL6B	83.113	ECW	4949	FC37F	5/51	3/62

Previous histories:
FRP 835 (821): New to United Counties Omnibus Co Ltd 835 [built with an 8ft wide body on a 7ft 6in chassis; fitted with wider axles 1952; renumbered 371 3/52]; entering service 2/59.
FRP 837 (822): New to United Counties Omnibus Co Ltd 837 [built with an 8ft wide body on a 7ft 6in chassis; fitted with wider axles 1952; renumbered 372 3/52]; entering service 3/59.
FRP 838 (823): New to United Counties Omnibus Co Ltd 838 [built with an 8ft wide body on a 7ft 6in chassis; fitted with wider axles 1952; renumbered 373 3/52]; entering service 2/59.
FRP 839 (824): New to United Counties Omnibus Co Ltd 839 [built with an 8ft wide body on a 7ft 6in chassis; rebuilt by ECW (rebuild R623) following a fire 6/51; renumbered 374 3/52]; entering service 2/59.
FRP 840-842 (825-827): New to United Counties Omnibus Co Ltd 840-842 [built with 8ft wide bodies on 7ft 6in chassis; fitted with wider axles 1952; renumbered 375-377 3/52]; entering service 3/59.

Disposals:
FRP 835 (821): Frostways Ltd, Kennington (BE) 11/61; Frostways Ltd, Kingston upon Hull (ER) 10/63; W Norths (PV) Ltd (dealer), Sherburn in Elmet 1/66.
FRP 837 (822): Alexander & Walker (dealer), Bretforton 3/62; El Peake, Pontnewynydd (MH) 2/62; WG & CS Peake, Pontnewynydd (MH) 7/62; withdrawn 7/65.
FRP 838 (823): W Welch, Llangeinor (GG) 7/63; F Stanton, Ogmore Vale (GG) 7/63; withdrawn 4/66; R & D Burrows, Ogmore Vale (GG) 12/66.
FRP 839 (824): Alexander & Walker (dealer), Bretforton 3/62; El Peake, Pontnewynydd (MH) 2/62; WG & CS Peake, Pontnewynydd (MH) 7/62; reseated to FDP39F by 8/64; withdrawn 10/65.
FRP 840 (825): Frostways Ltd, Kennington (BE) 1/62; Frostways Ltd, Kingston upon Hull (ER) 1/62; W Norths (PV) Ltd (dealer), Sherburn in Elmet (minus engine) 7/66.
FRP 841 (826): Frostways Ltd, Kennington (BE) 11/61; Frostways Ltd, Kingston upon Hull (ER) 10/63; scrapped 1/64.
FRP 842 (827): Frostways Ltd, Kennington (BE) (but based at Frostways Ltd, Kingston upon Hull (ER)) 3/62; unidentified operator / dealer 9/65.

1960

New Vehicles:

830	UJB 196	Bristol MW6G	164.001	ECW	11949	C34F	3/60	9/70
831	UJB 197	Bristol MW6G	164.002	ECW	11950	C34F	3/60	12/70
832	UJB 198	Bristol MW6G	164.003	ECW	11951	C34F	3/60	12/70
833	UJB 199	Bristol MW6G	164.004	ECW	11952	C34F	4/60	12/70

Notes:
UJB 196 (830): Did not enter service until 5/60; renumbered C830 (in error) c1/64, reverted to 830 1965; reseated to C38F c3/66; delicensed 9/70, reseated to DP41F with folding doors, altered front dome, fitted for one-man-operation and renumbered 167 11/70; it did not re-enter service with South Midland in this form.
UJB 197-198 (831-832): Did not enter service until 5/60; reseated to C38F c3/66; hired to City of Oxford Motor Services Ltd, Oxford (OX) at various times in 11/68.

UJB 199 (833): Did not enter service until 5/60; reseated to C38F c3/66; hired to City of Oxford Motor Services Ltd, Oxford (OX) at various times in 11/68 and 1/70.

Disposals:

UJB 196 (167): Thames Valley Traction Co Ltd 167 11/70 (qv).

UJB 197 (831): City of Oxford Motor Services Ltd, Oxford (OX) 831 1/71; renumbered 43 2/71; withdrawn 9/71; South Wales Transport Co Ltd, Swansea (GG) 283 11/71; reseated to DP45F and equipped for one-man-operation during 1972; withdrawn 6/75.

UJB 198 (832): City of Oxford Motor Services Ltd, Oxford (OX) 832 1/71; renumbered 44 2/71; withdrawn 9/71; South Wales Transport Co Ltd, Swansea (GG) 284 11/71; reseated to DP45F and equipped for one-man-operation during 1972; withdrawn 6/75; unidentified dealer 4/76.

UJB 199 (833): City of Oxford Motor Services Ltd, Oxford (OX) 833 1/71; renumbered 45 2/71; withdrawn 9/71; South Wales Transport Co Ltd, Swansea (GG) 285 11/71; reseated to DP45F and equipped for one-man-operation during 1972; withdrawn 2/76.

Vehicles transferred from Thames Valley Traction Co Ltd 3-7/60:

545	FMO 20	Bristol L6B	79.058	Windover	6844	C33F	3/50	5/60	10/60
550	FMO 25	Bristol L6B	81.068	Windover	6906	C33F	7/50	7/60	10/60
551	FMO 26	Bristol L6B	81.069	Windover	6907	C33F	7/50	5/60	11/60
552	FMO 934	Bristol L6B	81.070	Windover	6908	C33F	7/50	3/60	10/60
554	FMO 936	Bristol L6B	81.072	Windover	6910	C33F	7/50	5/60	10/60
555	FMO 937	Bristol L6B	81.120	Windover	6911	C33F	7/50	5/60	10/61
608	GBL 872	Bristol LWL6B	85.109	ECW	5435	FC37F	7/51	7/60	4/64
609	GBL 873	Bristol LWL6B	85.110	ECW	5436	FC37F	8/51	7/60	5/64

Previous histories:

FMO 20 (545): New to Thames Valley Traction Co Ltd 545; transferred 6/60.

FMO 25 (550): New to Thames Valley Traction Co Ltd 550; transferred 7/60.

FMO 26 (551): New to Thames Valley Traction Co Ltd 551; transferred 6/60.

FMO 934 (552): New to Thames Valley Traction Co Ltd 552; transferred 3/60.

FMO 936-937 (554-555): New to Thames Valley Traction Co Ltd 554-555; transferred 6/60.

GBL 872-873 (608-609): New to Thames Valley Traction Co Ltd 608-609; transferred 7/60.

Notes:

GBL 872 (608): Hired to City of Oxford Motor Services Ltd, Oxford (OX) at various times during 2/63.

Disposals:

FMO 20 (545): Passenger Vehicle Disposals Ltd (dealer), Dunchurch 11/60; RJ Jordan, Wantage (BE) 3/61; PG & JD Bryan {Reliable Cars}, Didcot (BE) 4/64; showman by 8/66.

FMO 25 (550): Passenger Vehicle Disposals Ltd (dealer), Dunchurch 11/60; Cosy Coaches, Meadowfield (DM) 12/60; Cummins, Sunderland (XDM) 2/68; withdrawn 1969.

FMO 26 (551): Passenger Vehicle Disposals Ltd (dealer), Dunchurch 11/60; Cosy Coaches, Meadowfield (DM) 12/60; Transport (Passenger Equipment) Ltd (dealer), Macclesfield by 10/64; S & JR Cubbins (dealer), Farnworth 12/64.

FMO 934 (552): Passenger Vehicle Disposals Ltd (dealer), Dunchurch 11/60; Worth's Motor Services Ltd, Enstone (OX) 12/60; withdrawn 10/64; scrapped 1/67.

FMO 936 (554): Passenger Vehicle Disposals Ltd (dealer), Dunchurch 11/60; AGH Jordan, Blaenavon (MH) 12/60; W Norths (PV) Ltd (dealer), Sherburn in Elmet 7/65.

FMO 937 (555): Creamline Motor Services Ltd, Bordon (HA) 11/61; withdrawn 11/63; engine, radiator and registration plate noted on a showman's generator vehicle at London E10 4/65; remainder of vehicle to Transport (Passenger Equipment) Ltd (dealer), Macclesfield for scrap.

GBL 872 (608): HJ Clack {B & C Coaches}, Cumnor (BE) 5/64; withdrawn 9/67; Main Motors (dealer), Ewelme 6/71.

GBL 873 (609): GP Holder {Charlton Services}, Charlton-on-Otmoor (OX) 6/64; withdrawn 2/70; unidentified operator, Maidenhead (XBE) 6/71; The Princess Margaret Royal Free School, Windsor (XBE) 8/78.

1961

New Vehicles:

858	WRX 773	Bristol MW6G	184.022	ECW		12215	C34F	5/61	12/70
859	WRX 774	Bristol MW6G	184.023	ECW		12216	C34F	5/61	12/70
860	WRX 775	Bristol MW6G	184.049	ECW		12217	C34F	6/61	12/70
861	WRX 776	Bedford SB8	88067	Duple		1133/417	C37F	5/61	2/68

Notes:

WRX 773 (858): Reseated to C38F c3/66; hired to City of Oxford Motor Services Ltd, Oxford (OX) at various
times in 11/68 and 1/70.
WRX 774-775 (859-860): Reseated to C38F c3/66.
WRX 776 (861): Was 7ft 6in wide.

Disposals:

WRX 773 (858): City of Oxford Motor Services Ltd, Oxford (OX) 858 1/71; renumbered 46 2/71; withdrawn
3/73; Transport (Passenger Equipment) Ltd (dealer), Macclesfield 6/73; Rennies Lion &
Comfort Coaches Ltd, Dunfermline (FE) 7/73; Paul Sykes Organisation Ltd (dealer), Carlton
6/74; WG & CS Peake, Pontypool (GT) 1/75.
WRX 774 (859): City of Oxford Motor Services Ltd, Oxford (OX) 859 1/71; renumbered 47 2/71; withdrawn
3/73; Transport (Passenger Equipment) Ltd (dealer), Macclesfield 7/73; Rennies Lion &
Comfort Coaches Ltd, Dunfermline (FE) 7/73; Jack, Oakley (FE) by 2/74; WG & CS Peake,
Pontypool (GT) 7/74; withdrawn 1/77.
WRX 775 (860): City of Oxford Motor Services Ltd, Oxford (OX) 860 1/71; renumbered 48 2/71; withdrawn,
following an accident 8/71; South Wales Transport Co Ltd, Swansea (GG) for spares 11/71.
WRX 776 (861): FJ Miller (Bristol) Ltd (dealer), Bristol 2/68; FJ Miller (Bristol) Ltd {Rambling Rose},
Whitchurch (SO) 5/68; DC Venner, Witheridge (DN) 6/69; Terraneau, South Molton (DN) 2/71;
destroyed by fire by 11/71.

Vehicles transferred from Thames Valley Traction Co Ltd 12/61:

673	HBL 75	Bristol LS6G	89.087	ECW		6212	C39F	7/52	10/65
688	HMO 834	Bristol LS6B	97.067	ECW		6981	C39F	10/53	10/64

Previous histories:

HBL 75 (673): New to Thames Valley Traction Co Ltd 673.
HMO 834 (688): New to Thames Valley Traction Co Ltd 688.

Notes:

HBL 75 (673): Hired to City of Oxford Motor Services Ltd, Oxford (OX) at various times between 2-3/63.
HMO 834 (688): Hired to City of Oxford Motor Services Ltd, Oxford (OX) at various times between 2-3/63;
delicensed 10/64, equipped for one-man-operation, reseated to DP41F and renumbered S314
6/65; it did not re-enter service with South Midland in this form.

Disposals:

HBL 75 (673): TD Alexander {Greyhound Luxury Coaches}, Arbroath (AS) 11/65.
HMO 834 (S314): Thames Valley Traction Co Ltd S314 7/65 (qv).

1962

New Vehicles:

862	516 ABL	Bedford SB8	88965	Duple	1145/233	C37F	4/62	4/65
863	517 ABL	Bedford SB8	89057	Duple	1145/234	C37F	5/62	4/65
864	518 ABL	Bedford SB8	89058	Duple	1145/235	C37F	5/62	5/68
865	519 ABL	Bedford SB8	89060	Duple	1145/236	C37F	5/62	6/68

Notes:

516 ABL (862): Was 7ft 6in wide; did not enter service until 4/62.
517 ABL (863): Was 8ft wide; did not enter service until 5/62.
518 ABL (864): Was 8ft wide; did not enter service until 5/62; carried Ulster Transport Authority fleet number
3158 for the 1962 and 1963 seasons.
519 ABL (865): Was 8ft wide; did not enter service until 5/62.

Disposals:

516-517 ABL (862-863): Thames Valley Traction Co Ltd 862-863 4/65.
518 ABL (864): Shamrock & Rambler (THC) Ltd, Bournemouth (HA) 5/68 (as C41F); Southern Vectis
Omnibus Co Ltd, Newport (IW) 111 5/69; withdrawn 8/76.
519 ABL (865): Shamrock & Rambler Motor Coaches Ltd, Bournemouth (HA) named 'Theseus' 5/68;
Swanmore County Secondary School, Swanmore (XHA) 1/73; withdrawn 11/77.

Vehicles transferred from Thames Valley Traction Co Ltd 1-2/62:

610	GBL 874	Bristol LWL6B	85.111	ECW		5437	FC37F	8/51	4/64
671	HBL 73	Bristol LS6G	89.036	ECW		6210	C39F	6/52	10/67
691	HMO 837	Bristol LS6B	101.061	ECW		6984	C39F	3/54	11/63

Previous histories:

GBL 874 (610): New to Thames Valley Traction Co Ltd 610; transferred 2/62.
HBL 73 (671): New to Thames Valley Traction Co Ltd 671; transferred 2/62.
HMO 837 (691): New to Thames Valley Traction Co Ltd 691; transferred 1/62.

Notes:

GBL 874 (610): Hired to City of Oxford Motor Services Ltd, Oxford (OX) at various times during 1/63.
HBL 73 (671): Hired to City of Oxford Motor Services Ltd, Oxford (OX) at various times between 2-3/63;
carried fleet number C671 (in error) 1/64, reverting to 671 in 1965.
HMO 837 (691): Delicensed 11/63, equipped for one-man-operation, reseated to DP41F and renumbered
S311 4/64 (it was hired (seat-less) to the Post Office, Oxford in 12/63, during the course of this
rebuild); it did not re-enter service with South Midland in this form.

Disposals:

GBL 874 (610): Creamline Motor Services Ltd, Bordon (HA) 4/64; last licensed 7/65; Mitchell, Camberley at
an unknown date; scrapped 2/66.
HBL 73 (671): Elm Park Coaches Ltd, Romford (EX) 4/68; withdrawn 1/70.
HMO 837 (S311): Thames Valley Traction Co Ltd S311 4/64 (qv).

1963

New Vehicles:

867	521 ABL	Bristol RELH6G	REX.002	ECW		EX7	C47F	4/63	12/70
C401	831 CRX	Bedford SB8	92010	Duple		1159/159	C37F	2/63	10/68
C402	832 CRX	Bedford SB8	91997	Duple		1159/160	C37F	4/63	10/68
C403	833 CRX	Bedford SB8	92032	Duple		1159/161	C37F	4/63	10/68

Notes:

521 ABL (867): Fitted with a Gardner 6HLX diesel engine; renumbered 403 4/69.
831 CRX (C401): Fitted with a Leyland O.350 diesel engine; was delivered in 2/63 for a publicity tour, but did
not enter service until 5/63; carried Ulster Transport Authority fleet number 3158 for the 1965
season.

Disposals:

521 ABL (403): City of Oxford Motor Services Ltd, Oxford (OX) 403 1/71; renumbered 3 2/71; withdrawn
12/73; P Sykes (dealer), Barnsley 3/74; R Askin (dealer), Barnsley for scrap 10/74.
831 CRX (C401): FJ Miller (Bristol) Ltd (dealer), Bristol 12/68; FJ Miller (Bristol) Ltd {Rambling Rose},
Whitchurch (SO) 2/69; withdrawn 4/71; unidentified owner, Bristol 11/70; HML Motors Ltd,
Oakdale (MH) 6/71; withdrawn by 12/76.
832 CRX (C402): FJ Miller (Bristol) Ltd (dealer), Bristol 11/68; D Pow {F Pow & Sons / Berkeley Coaches},
Paulton (SO) 2/69; Berkeley, Paulton (SO) 11/72; withdrawn 2/78.
833 CRX (C403): FJ Miller (Bristol) Ltd (dealer), Bristol 12/68; AW & MK Spiller {Arleen Coach Tours},
Peasedown St John (SO) 2/69; withdrawn 10/73; Morris, Cardiff (GG) 2/74; Phillips, Cardiff
(SG) at an unknown date; Westbourne Motors (St Austell) Ltd, St Austell (CO) 10/76;
withdrawn 4/77.

Vehicle transferred from Thames Valley Traction Co Ltd 7/63:

674	HBL 76	Bristol LS6G	89.109	ECW		6213	C39F	10/52	11/66

Previous history:

HBL 76 (674): New to Thames Valley Traction Co Ltd 674.

Disposal:

HBL 76 (674): W Norths (PV) Ltd (dealer), Sherburn in Elmet 11/66; George's Coaches, Kirkburton (WR)
12/66; W Norths (PV) Ltd (dealer), Sherburn in Elmet 6/67; Business Vehicles, York (XYK)
7/67; unidentified contractor, Ashton-under-Lyne (not licensed) by 2/68; noted Oldham 9/69
and Corby 1970.

1964

New Vehicles:

C404	834 CRX	Bristol RELH6G	212.021	ECW	13731	C47F	1/64	12/70
C405	835 CRX	Bristol RELH6G	212.022	ECW	13732	C47F	1/64	12/70
C407	837 CRX	Bedford SB13	93540	Duple	1170/156	C37F	1/64	9/70
C408	838 CRX	Bedford SB13	93607	Duple	1170/157	C37F	1/64	7/70
C409	842 CRX	Bedford SB13	93526	Duple	1170/158	C37F	1/64	9/70
C410	EMO 551C	Bedford SB13	95349	Harrington	3008	C37F	10/64	12/70
C411	EMO 552C	Bedford SB13	95354	Harrington	3009	C37F	10/64	12/70
C412	EMO 553C	Bedford SB13	95359	Harrington	3010	C37F	10/64	12/70

Notes:

834-835 CRX (C404-405): Fitted with Gardner 6HLX engines; renumbered 404-405 2/69.

837 CRX (C407): Did not enter service until 5/64; renumbered 407 2/69.

838 CRX (C408): Did not enter service until 4/64 renumbered 408 2/69.

842 CRX (C409): Did not enter service until 5/64; hired to City of Oxford Motor Services Ltd, Oxford (OX) during 11/68; renumbered 409 2/69.

EMO 551C (C410): Delivered un-registered; registered and entered service 4/65; renumbered 410 2/69; hired to City of Oxford Motor Services Ltd, Oxford (OX) at various times in 1/70.

EMO 552C (C411): Delivered un-registered; registered and entered service 4/65; hired to City of Oxford Motor Services Ltd, Oxford (OX) at various times in 11/68; renumbered 411 2/69; hired to City of Oxford Motor Services Ltd, Oxford (OX) at various times in 1/70.

EMO 553C (C412): Delivered un-registered; registered and entered service 4/65; renumbered 412 2/69; hired to City of Oxford Motor Services Ltd, Oxford (OX) at various times in 1/70.

Disposals:

834 CRX (404): City of Oxford Motor Services Ltd, Oxford (OX) 404 1/71; renumbered 4 2/71; withdrawn 12/73; P Sykes (dealer), Barnsley for scrap 3/74.

835 CRX (405): City of Oxford Motor Services Ltd, Oxford (OX) 405 1/71; renumbered 5 2/71; being cannibalised for spares 11/76; A Barraclough (dealer), Carlton for scrap 3/77.

837 CRX (407): FJ Miller (Bristol) Ltd (dealer), Whitchurch 11/70; FJ Miller (Bristol) Ltd {Rambling Rose}, Whitchurch (SO) 2/71; Owen, Barry (GG) 9/71; LG Potter, Skewen (GG) 6/72.

838 CRX (408): Thames Valley Traction Co Ltd 408 7/70 (qv).

842 CRX (409): FJ Miller (Bristol) Ltd (dealer), Bristol 10/70; FJ Miller (Bristol) Ltd {Rambling Rose}, Whitchurch (SO) 4/71; JN & J Nutley, Parkwall (MH) 9/71; scrapped 6/81.

EMO 551C (410): City of Oxford Motor Services Ltd, Oxford (OX) 410 1/71; renumbered 10 2/71; withdrawn 2/74; W Norths (PV) Ltd (dealer), Sherburn in Elmet 7/74; Yorkshire Engineering Supplies, Leeds (XWR) 9/74; W Norths (PV) Ltd (dealer), Sherburn in Elmet 8/79; Nacap Ltd (contractor), Doncaster as a site hut at Fordoun by 5/81.

EMO 552C (411): City of Oxford Motor Services Ltd, Oxford (OX) 411 1/71; renumbered 11 2/71; withdrawn 3/74; W Norths (PV) Ltd (dealer), Sherburn in Elmet 7/74; Christian Schools, Ormskirk (XMY) 8/74; W Norths (PV) Ltd (dealer), Sherburn in Elmet for scrap 9/76.

EMO 553C (412): City of Oxford Motor Services Ltd, Oxford (OX) 412 1/71; renumbered 12 2/71; W Norths (PV) Ltd (dealer), Sherburn in Elmet 7/74; unidentified owner, Lancashire 10/74; Liverpool Community Transport (XMY) c9/78; Rayshelles Jazz Band, Stoke-on-Trent (XST) 7/79.

1965

New Vehicles:

C413	GRX 413D	Bedford VAM14	6807175	Duple	1205/94	C41F	1/66	12/70
C414	GRX 414D	Bedford VAM14	6804745	Duple	1205/95	C41F	2/66	12/70

Notes:

GRX 413D (C413): Delivered unregistered in 12/65; registered and entered service 3/66; renumbered 413 2/69.

GRX 414D (C414): Delivered unregistered in 12/65; registered and entered service 3/66; renumbered 414 2/69.

Disposals:

GRX 413D (413): City of Oxford Motor Services Ltd, Oxford (OX) 413 1/71; renumbered 13 2/71; withdrawn 3/74; W Norths (PV) Ltd (dealer), Sherburn in Elmet 7/74; Garforth Coachways, Allerton Bywater (WY) 9/74; unidentified dealer, Barnsley for scrap 2/75.

GRX 414D (414): City of Oxford Motor Services Ltd, Oxford (OX) 414 1/71; renumbered 14 2/71; W Norths (PV) Ltd (dealer), Sherburn in Elmet 7/74; Costain (contractor), London (X) 11/74; Westminster Plant Ltd (contractor), Boston Spa (XWY) 11/74.

Vehicle transferred from Thames Valley Traction Co Ltd 4/65:

672	HBL 74	Bristol LS6G	89.037	ECW	6211	C39F	7/52	8/66

Previous history:
    HBL 74 (672): New to Thames Valley Traction Co Ltd 672.

Disposal:
    HBL 74 (672): W Norths (PV) Ltd (dealer), Sherburn in Elmet 8/66; Allenways Ltd, Birmingham (WK) 8/66; W Norths (PV) Ltd (dealer), Sherburn in Elmet 11/68; A Barraclough (dealer), Carlton 5/70.

1966

New Vehicles:

C415	GRX 415D	Bedford VAM14	6823686	Duple	1205/96	C41F	3/66	12/70
C416	GRX 416D	Bedford VAM14	6823908	Duple	1205/97	C41F	3/66	12/70

Notes:
    GRX 415D (C415): Did not enter service until 3/66; renumbered 415 2/69.
    GRX 416D (C416): Did not enter service until 3/66; hired to A Timpson & Sons Ltd, London SE6 (LN) during 8/66 (in exchange for JJJ 568D (qv)); renumbered 416 2/69.

Disposals:
    GRX 415D (415): City of Oxford Motor Services Ltd, Oxford (OX) 415 1/71; renumbered 15 1/71; W Norths (PV) Ltd (dealer), Sherburn in Elmet 7/74; Brentwood Coaches (Brentwood) Ltd, Brentwood (EX) 10/74; Farrow, Potter Street (EX) ?4/76?; Eyres-Scott, Hutton (LN) 10/77; LJ Smith {Moulsham Transport Services}, Terling (EX) 7/79; Wacton Trading / Coach Sales (dealer), Bromyard 8/84; Salopia Starlets Jazz Band, Shrewsbury (XSH) 1985; itinerants as a mobile caravan 2/87.
    GRX 416D (416): City of Oxford Motor Services Ltd, Oxford (OX) 416 1/71; renumbered 16 1/71; W Norths (PV) Ltd (dealer), Sherburn in Elmet 7/74; unidentified owner, West Yorkshire 11/74; noted London 12/74.

Vehicles transferred from Thames Valley Traction Co Ltd 5-12/66:

675	HBL 77	Bristol LS6G	89.110	ECW	6214	C39F	10/52	10/67
866	520 ABL	Bristol MW6G	195.008	ECW	12839	C39F	5/62	12/66

Previous histories:
    HBL 77 (675): New to Thames Valley Traction Co Ltd 675; transferred 12/66.
    520 ABL (866): New to Thames Valley Traction Co Ltd 866; transferred 5/66.

Disposals:
    HBL 77 (675): Winlon Autos Ltd, Harrow (LN) 12/67; withdrawn by 2/71.
    520 ABL (866): Thames Valley Traction Co Ltd 866 12/66 (qv).

1967

New Vehicles:

C421	LJB 421E	Bristol RELH6G	238.081	ECW	16579	C47F	4/67	12/70
C422	LJB 422E	Bristol RELH6G	238.082	ECW	16580	C47F	5/67	12/70
C423	LJB 423E	Bristol RELH6G	238.083	ECW	16581	C47F	5/67	12/70

Notes:
    LJB 421-423E (C421-423): Renumbered 421-423 2/69.

Disposals:
    LJB 421E (421): City of Oxford Motor Services Ltd, Oxford (OX) 421 1/71; renumbered 21 2/71; Ensign Bus Co Ltd (dealer), Grays 12/78; JM Lewington {Lewington's Hire Services}, Harold Hill (EX) 2/79; JM & AA Lewington {Lewington's Hire Services}, Harold Hill (EX) 7/80; withdrawn 3/82; RW Denyer {Denyer Bros}, Stondon Massey (EX) by 2/89.
    LJB 422E (422): City of Oxford Motor Services Ltd, Oxford (OX) 422 1/71; renumbered 22 2/71; Ensign Bus Co Ltd (dealer), Grays 12/78; GEW Dack {Rosemary Coaches}, Terrington St Clement (NK) 6/79; last licensed 10/85; Passenger Vehicle Spares (Barnsley) Ltd (dealer), Carlton for scrap 11/85.

LJB 423E (423): City of Oxford Motor Services Ltd, Oxford (OX) 423 1/71; renumbered 23 1/71; Ensign Bus
Co Ltd (dealer), Grays 12/78; JM Lewington {Lewington's Hire Services}, Harold Hill (EX) 7/79;
JM & AA Lewington {Lewington's Hire Services}, Harold Hill (EX) 7/80; Bordabus Ltd, Abridge
(EX) 3/82.

1968

New Vehicles:

C428	RJB 428F	Bristol LH6L	LH-115	Duple	193/1	C41F	5/68	12/70
C429	RJB 429F	Bristol LH6L	LH-116	Duple	193/2	C41F	5/68	12/70
C430	RJB 430F	Bristol LH6L	LH-117	Duple	193/3	C41F	5/68	12/70
C431	RJB 431F	Bristol LH6L	LH-118	Duple	193/4	C41F	5/68	12/70

Notes:

RJB 428-431F (C428-431): Renumbered 428-431 2/69.

Disposals:

RJB 428F (428): City of Oxford Motor Services Ltd, Oxford (OX) 428 1/71; renumbered 28 2/71; H Cowley
(dealer), Heywood 6/75; George Wimpey & Co Ltd (contractor), London W6 (XLN) 11/75.
RJB 429F (429): City of Oxford Motor Services Ltd, Oxford (OX) 429 1/71; renumbered 29 2/71; H Cowley
(dealer), Heywood 6/75; Paul Sykes Organisation Ltd (dealer), Barnsley 1975; D Arnold,
Bristol (XGL) 10/78.
RJB 430F (430): City of Oxford Motor Services Ltd, Oxford (OX) 430 1/71; renumbered 30 2/71; H Cowley
(dealer), Heywood 7/75; George Wimpey & Co Ltd (contractor), London W6 (XLN) 11/75;
Hounslow Commercials (dealer), Hounslow 3/79.
RJB 431F (431): City of Oxford Motor Services Ltd, Oxford (OX) 431 1/71; renumbered 31 2/71; H Cowley
(dealer), Heywood 7/75; George Wimpey & Co Ltd (contractor), London W6 (XLN) 2/76;
Newham Joint Community Centre, London E12 (XLN) 3/79.

Vehicles acquired from Eastern National Omnibus Co Ltd, Chelmsford (EX) 3/68:

432	613 JPU	Bristol LS6G	119.037	ECW	9916	C34F	3/57	12/70
433	614 JPU	Bristol LS6G	119.038	ECW	9920	C34F	3/57	12/70
434	618 JPU	Bristol MW6G	135.001	ECW	9915	C34F	3/58	12/70

Previous histories:

613-614 JPU (432-433): New to Eastern National Omnibus Co Ltd 428-429 [reseated to C39F 1963;
renumbered 320-321 8/64; reseated C34F c12/65]; entering service 5/68.
618 JPU (434): New to Eastern National Omnibus Co Ltd 433 [renumbered 328 8/64]; entering service 5/68.

Notes:

613 JPU (432): Renumbered 440 1/69.
614 JPU (433): Renumbered 441 2/69.
618 JPU (434): Renumbered 442 4/69.

Disposals:

613 JPU (440): City of Oxford Motor Services Ltd, Oxford (OX) 440 1/71; renumbered 40 2/71; withdrawn
10/71; South Wales Transport Co Ltd, Swansea (GG) 281 11/71; reseated to DP45F and
equipped for one-man-operation during 1972; K Askin (dealer), Barnsley for scrap 6/74.
614 JPU (441): City of Oxford Motor Services Ltd, Oxford (OX) 441 1/71; renumbered 41 2/71; withdrawn
9/71; South Wales Transport Co Ltd, Swansea (GG) 282 11/71; reseated to DP45F and
equipped for one-man-operation during 1972; Paul Sykes Organisation Ltd (dealer), Barnsley
6/74; J & J Car Dismantlers (dealer), Carlton for scrap 7/74.
618 JPU (442): City of Oxford Motor Services Ltd, Oxford (OX) 442 1/71; renumbered 42 2/71; renumbered
20 10/73; withdrawn 12/73; Transport (Passenger Equipment) Ltd (dealer), Macclesfield 1/74;
Rennies Lion & Comfort Coaches Ltd, Dunfermline (FE) 1/74 (as DP45F); Loudon
(contractor), Newmains (XSC) by 8/74.

Vehicles transferred from Thames Valley Traction Co Ltd 5/68:

| C417 | LJB 417E | Bedford VAM14 | 6875393 | Duple | 1208/159 | C41F | 3/67 | 5/68 | 11/70 |
| C418 | LJB 418E | Bedford VAM14 | 6875051 | Duple | 1208/160 | C41F | 3/67 | 5/68 | 9/69 |

Previous histories:

LJB 417-418E (C417-418): New to Thames Valley Traction Co Ltd C417-418.

Notes:
> LJB 417-418E (C417-418): Renumbered 417-418 2/69.

Disposals:
> LJB 417E (417): Thames Valley Traction Co Ltd C417 11/70.
> LJB 418E (418): Thames Valley Traction Co Ltd C418 9/69.

Vehicle on hire from A Timpson & Sons Ltd, London SE6 (LN):

JJJ 568D	AEC Reliance	2MU4RA6037	Duple Northern	170/3	C41F	4/66	8/66	8/66

Notes:
> JJJ 568D: On hire for comparative trials (in exchange for GRX 416D (C416).

1969

New Vehicles:

432	UMO 688G	Bristol LH6L	LH-186	Duple Northern	208/1	C41F	5/69	12/70
433	UMO 689G	Bristol LH6L	LH-187	Duple Northern	208/2	C41F	5/69	12/70
434	UMO 690G	Bristol LH6L	LH-188	Duple Northern	208/3	C41F	5/69	12/70
435	UMO 691G	Bristol LH6L	LH-189	Duple Northern	208/4	C41F	5/69	12/70

Disposals:
> UMO 688G (432): City of Oxford Motor Services Ltd, Oxford (OX) 432 1/71; renumbered 32 2/71; Martin (dealer), Middlewich 6/78; Buckley, Northwich (XCH) 2/79; Lew-Ways Ltd, Norton Canes (XST) 3/80; last licensed 12/85.
> UMO 689G (433): City of Oxford Motor Services Ltd, Oxford (OX) 433 1/71; renumbered 33 2/71; Paul Sykes Organisation Ltd (dealer), Barnsley 7/78; Harris Coaches (Pengam) Ltd, Fleur-de-Lis (GT) 1/79.
> UMO 690G (434): City of Oxford Motor Services Ltd, Oxford (OX) 434 1/71; renumbered 34 2/71; Paul Sykes Organisation Ltd (dealer), Barnsley 7/78; Harris Coaches (Pengam) Ltd, Fleur-de-Lis (GT) 1/79; withdrawn by 7/86; unidentified dealer for scrap 12/86; last licensed 3/87.
> UMO 691G (435): City of Oxford Motor Services Ltd, Oxford (OX) 435 1/71; renumbered 35 2/71; Martin (dealer), Middlewich 10/78; Bryn Alyn Community, Wrexham (CL) 11/78; Clarke, Hangton, Tarporley (XCH) as a driver training vehicle c4/83; K Smedley, Crewe (CH) 3/84; St Peters High School, Penkhull (XST) 6/84; last licensed 6/89.

1970

New Vehicles:

436	YBL 925H	Bristol LH6L	LH-410	Duple	224/13	C41F	5/70	12/70
437	YBL 926H	Bristol LH6L	LH-424	Duple	224/14	C41F	5/70	12/70
438	YBL 927H	Bristol LH6L	LH-452	Duple	224/15	C41F	7/70	12/70
439	YBL 928H	Bristol LH6L	LH-463	Duple	224/16	C41F	9/70	12/70

Disposals:
> YBL 925H (436): City of Oxford Motor Services Ltd, Oxford (OX) 436 1/71; renumbered 36 2/71; Martins Bus & Coach Sales Ltd (dealer), Middlewich 10/78; Harrison-Meyer Ltd, Meir (XST) 2/79; last licensed 1/84; T Goodwin (dealer), Carlton for scrap 5/84.
> YBL 926H (437): City of Oxford Motor Services Ltd, Oxford (OX) 437 1/71; renumbered 37 2/71; Paul Sykes Organisation Ltd (dealer), Barnsley 7/78; Harris Coaches (Pengam) Ltd, Fleur-de-Lis (GT) 1/79; last licensed 4/86; unidentified dealer for scrap 12/86.
> YBL 927H (438): City of Oxford Motor Services Ltd, Oxford (OX) 438 1/71; renumbered 38 2/71; Martins Bus & Coach Sales Ltd (dealer), Middlewich 10/78; P Kavanagh, Urlingford (EI) re-registered 37 JIP 11/81; Kenneally, Dungarvan (EI) 5/83; unidentified dealer probably for scrap by 3/89.
> YBL 928H (439): City of Oxford Motor Services Ltd, Oxford (OX) 439 1/71; renumbered 39 2/71; Martins Bus & Coach Sales Ltd (dealer), Middlewich 10/78; S Leavy {Southern Coaches}, Botley (OX) 10/78; last licensed 5/84; stolen from the depot (not recovered) 6/84.

Vehicle on hire from Worth's Motor Services, Enstone (OX) 2-3/70:

MBW 159E	Ford R226	BC04ER14189	Strachan		DP53F	-/67	2/70	3/70

Notes:
> MBW 159E: On hire as cover for the accident damaged EMO 552C (411).

ANCILLARY VEHICLES

New & acquired vehicles:

	?	Hallford	lorry	-/--	-/--	by-/24
	FC 7333	Thornycroft J	lorry	-/--	10/24	-/--
	?	Thornycroft J	lorry	-/--	-/26	-/--
	EUW 584	Austin	van	-/38	-/--	7/51
35	RWL 71	Bedford 10/12 cwt	van	6/51	6/51	10/65
ED59	GBL 227C	Austin Gypsy	recovery vehicle	10/65	10/65	12/70

Notes:

The unidentified lorries were ex-War Department (GOV) and probably used in an associated haulage business. The Hallford may have been acquired as early as 1919.

RWL 71 (35): Renumbered 27 c1957.

Disposals:

Only those vehicles listed below have a known disposal:

RWL 71 (27): Taylor, Botley c10/65, MD Shaw, Oxford for preservation 3/73.
GBL 227C (ED59): City of Oxford Motor Services Ltd, Oxford (OX) 1/71; renumbered 6 3/72; withdrawn 1/76.

REGISTRATION CROSS REFERENCE

Reg	No.	Reg	No.	Reg	No.	Reg	No.	Reg	No.
X 8161	136	DP 1756	12	DX 2174	18	GN 5139	125	JB 5843	42
		DP 1757	12	DX 2175	18	GN 5145	41	JB 5843	62
AE 3792	186	DP 1759	12	DX 2175	123	GN 5145	125	JB 5843	179
AF 1344	186	DP 1794	12	EF 3469	39	GN 5150	41	JB 5844	42
AN 6452	27	DP 1795	12	EF 3469	137	GP 5139	139	JB 5844	125
BH 0311	143	DP 1798	12	EL 3769	188	GP 5140	139	JB 5845	42
BH 5951	143	DP 1801	12	EM 2723	205	GP 5141	139	JB 5846	42
BH 9063	144	DP 1826	12	EM 2730	176	GP 5142	139	JB 5847	42
BH 9409	143	DP 1827	12	EM 2735	176	GP 5143	139	JB 5848	42
BH 9638	144	DP 2032	12	EM 2736	176	GP 5144	139	JB 5849	42
BH 9991	143	DP 2033	12	EM 2741	176	GP 5145	139	JB 5850	42
BL 027	191	DP 2064	12	EM 2743	205	GT 9199	47	JB 5851	42
BL 0336	188	DP 2111	12	EV 5909	165	GT 9199	133	JB 5852	42
BL 884	195	DP 2112	12	EX 2861	171	GT 9324	47	JB 5853	42
BL 946	195	DP 2113	12	FC 3902	201	GT 9324	133	JB 5854	42
BL 1351	201	DP 2114 (1)	12	FC 4010	201	GU 7544	37	JB 5855	42
BL 3415	191	DP 2114 (2)	16	FC 4501	201	GU 7544	145	JB 5856	42
BL 3850	192	DP 2115	12	FC 8130	201	GU 7545	153	JB 6834	154
BL 5420	193	DP 2116	13	FG 4104	133	GU 7545	190	JB 7289	70
BL 6490	149	DP 2117	13	FG 4427	154	GW 540	41	JB 7494	42
BL 6490	184	DP 2118	13	FJ 9581	160	GW 540	145	JB 7494	141
BL 7936	186	DP 2119	13	FL 1561	11	GX 5327	165	JB 7495	42
BL 7936	188	DP 2120	13	FL 1562	11	HA 7493	203	JB 7496	42
BL 8006	186	DP 2121	13	FM 6486	154	HC 2833	30	JB 7497	42
BL 8278	195	DP 2122	13	FM 6487	154	HC 2837	30	JB 7498	42
BL 8684	191	DP 2123	13	FM 6488	154	HD 4368	164	JB 7499	42
BL 8804	188	DP 2124	13	FM 7455	54	HD 4369	164	JB 8341	45
BL 9316	193	DP 2125	13	FN 9001	54	HD 4370	164	JB 8342	45
BL 9316	195	DP 2126	13	FN 9009	54	HD 4371	164	JB 8343	45
BL 9713	193	DP 2127 (1)	13	FN 9011	54	HE 8	11	JB 8344	45
BL 9751	18	DP 2127 (2)	13	FS 8560	174	HE 9	11	JB 8345	45
BL 9752	18	DP 2128 (1)	13	FS 8562	174	HE 10	11	JB 8346	45
BL 9861	136	DP 2128 (2)	13	FS 8565	174	HE 11	11	JB 8346	141
BL 9861	186	DP 2129	13	FS 8566	174	HE 12	11	JB 8347	46
BL 9886	191	DP 2130 (1)	13	FS 8567	174	HE 2323	32	JB 8348	46
BL 9892	18	DP 2130 (2)	13	FS 8572	174	HE 2325	32	JB 8348	141
BU 5690	149	DP 2377	13	FS 8574	174	HE 2326	32	JB 8349	46
BU 5690	186	DP 2377	120	FS 8575	174	HE 2327	32	JB 8349	141
CC 5083	188	DP 2378	13	FS 8576	174	HE 2331	32	JB 8350	46
CC 9415	154	DP 2597	16	FS 8582	174	HE 2336	32	JB 8350	141
CD 5379	22	DP 2598	16	FV 3795	137	HE 2339	32	JB 9860	70
CD 6353	22	DP 2599	16	FV 8971	55	HE 5229	169	JD 1220	162
CG 1724	160	DP 2600	16	FX 4922	136	HF 6041	55	JG 1417	54
CG 1724	192	DP 2601	16	GC 1866	139	HG 1221	175	JG 1431	54
CH 9864	135	DP 2602	16	GC 1867	139	HJ 8718	153	JG 1447	54
CK 3951	168	DP 2603	16	GC 1868	139	HJ 8718	190	JG 1451	54
CK 4312	169	DP 2604	16	GC 1869	139	HL 5228	166	JG 1624	54
CK 4518	171	DP 2604	120	GC 1870	139	HO 6306	181	JG 7010	55
CK 4573	167	DP 2605	13	GC 1871	139	HO 6335	138	JG 8205	55
CR 4021	188	DP 2606	16	GC 8783	133	HX 1059	149	JG 8206	55
CW 6802	181	DP 3590	139	GC 9901	49	HX 1059	186	JG 8207	55
CW 6802	188	DP 3633	17	GF 6676	139	HX 1855	157	JG 8208	55
DF 7841	168	DP 3647	17	GF 6677	139	HX 7560	159	JG 8209	55
DG 9516	161	DP 4400	21	GF 6677	165	JB 437	160	JG 8210	55
DL 2122	188	DP 4400	145	GF 6678	139	JB 437	193	JG 8979	54
DL 9011	171	DP 4919	28	GF 6679	139	JB 3354	168	JG 9933	54
DP 1655	11	DP 5628	28	GJ 1331	139	JB 5701	160	JG 9939	54
DP 1656	11	DP 7669	139	GJ 1332	139	JB 5701	193	JG 9940	54
DP 1657	11	DR 9636	58	GJ 7973	153	JB 5841	42	JG 9942	54
DP 1658	11	DR 9846	58	GJ 7973	185	JB 5841	56	JG 9943	54
DP 1659	11	DW 7353	137	GJ 8024	139	JB 5841	179	JG 9944	54
DP 1660	11	DX 2173	18	GN 5139	41	JB 5842	42	JG 9946	54

Reg	No	Reg	No	Reg	No	Reg	No	Reg	No
JG 9948	54	KX 5010	135	MO 1573	194	MO 5443	146	MO 9328	28
JG 9949	54	KX 5733	44	MO 1625	20	MO 5620	196	MO 9329	28
JG 9964	54	KX 5733	143	MO 1626	20	MO 5899	193	MS 8438	163
JH 492	158	KX 6094	47	MO 1627	20	MO 6078	145	MS 8834	169
JJ 8873	159	KX 6094	134	MO 1647	146	MO 6184	24	MS 9336	157
JK 1911	155	KX 6094	141	MO 1714	184	MO 6184	146	MT 1330	47
JN 9541	54	KX 6376	49	MO 1714	186	MO 6416	194	MT 1330	134
JN 9542	54	KX 7157	47	MO 1715	20	MO 6416	196	MT 1330	141
JN 9543	54	KX 7157	134	MO 1716	20	MO 6744	151	MT 1842	158
JO 200	202	KX 7157	141	MO 1717	20	MO 6744	195	MW 825	149
JO 1593	202	KX 7382	44	MO 1763	188	MO 6842	24	MW 825	186
JO 1595	202	KX 7382	143	MO 1797	186	MO 6843	24	MW 4028	156
JO 1597	202	KX 7575	49	MO 1803	20	MO 6844	24	MW 6161	154
JO 1599	202	KX 7843	44	MO 1803	123	MO 6845	24	MW 6161	196
JO 4789	203	KX 7843	143	MO 1846	194	MO 6846	24	MY 346	158
JT 9354	86	KX 8092	44	MO 2059	185	MO 6847	24	MY 639	47
JT 9355	86	KX 8092	143	MO 2059	193	MO 6848	24	MY 639	134
JT 9360	86	KX 8481	40	MO 2213	24	MO 6849	24	MY 639	141
JU 4374	170	KX 8481	141	MO 2213	146	MO 6850	24	MY 3052	153
JY 4752	160	KX 8481	142	MO 2406	186	MO 6851	24	MY 3052	191
KE 3196	149	KX 8482	40	MO 2610	21	MO 6851	123	MY 4213	153
KE 3196	186	KX 8482	120	MO 2611	21	MO 6852	24	MY 4213	191
KM 3028	153	KX 8482	142	MO 2612	21	MO 6853	24	NB 1215	136
KN 2873	16	KX 8533	49	MO 2613	21	MO 6854	24	NK 8073	137
KN 3652	16	KX 8744	44	MO 2614	21	MO 6855	24	NW 8018	136
KO 4530	145	KX 8744	143	MO 2615	21	MO 6855	123	OR 2576	191
KP 8371	164	LC 5373	134	MO 2616	21	MO 6856	24	OR 4295	186
KP 8372	164	LF 9044	186	MO 2617	21	MO 6856	123	OT 816	158
KV 9903	166	LF 9214	15	MO 2618	21	MO 6857	24	OT 816	192
KX 498	44	LF 9219	12	MO 2619	21	MO 6858	24	OT 1333	192
KX 498	143	LK 8069	201	MO 2620	21	MO 6858	123	OT 1339	139
KX 760	135	LP 8364	15	MO 2621	21	MO 7043	195	OT 3284	192
KX 978	47	MA 2284	15	MO 2622	21	MO 7182	196	OT 4452	160
KX 978	133	MA 2569	15	MO 2850	144	MO 7517	185	OT 4452	192
KX 1312	44	MA 3128	15	MO 2851	144	MO 7520	193	OT 6861	181
KX 1312	143	MC 3937	188	MO 3343	188	MO 7526	138	OT 6862	181
KX 1523	39	MD 8213	186	MO 3514	191	MO 7924	138	OT 7672	192
KX 1523	133	MF 6914	28	MO 3530	24	MO 7924	188	OT 7923	181
KX 1541	44	MJ 4550	167	MO 3530	146	MO 7942	24	OT 9741	192
KX 1541	143	MN 8844	150	MO 3558	144	MO 7943	24	OU 2885	156
KX 1734	44	MO 51	18	MO 3565	21	MO 7944	24	OU 3317	151
KX 1734	143	MO 52	18	MO 3566	21	MO 7945	24	OU 6047	160
KX 1795	135	MO 53	188	MO 3875	187	MO 7946	24	OU 6047	192
KX 2558	47	MO 62	19	MO 3959	191	MO 8231	151	OY 2093	157
KX 2558	133	MO 62	123	MO 4154	21	MO 8231	194	OY 5807	157
KX 3159	135	MO 128	19	MO 4155	21	MO 9039	138	PE 2077	150
KX 3279	135	MO 129	19	MO 4156	23	MO 9312	28	PG 1099	159
KX 3484	44	MO 150	19	MO 4157	21	MO 9313	28	PG 2018	159
KX 3484	143	MO 151	19	MO 4158	23	MO 9314	28	PG 3236	159
KX 3638	40	MO 151	123	MO 4306	23	MO 9315	28	PG 4226	159
KX 3638	142	MO 158	19	MO 4307	23	MO 9316	28	PJ 3827	173
KX 3869	40	MO 159	19	MO 4308	23	MO 9316	143	PK 1822	135
KX 3869	142	MO 160	19	MO 4309	23	MO 9317	28	PM 581	186
KX 3870	40	MO 160	120	MO 4310	23	MO 9318	28	PP 820	143
KX 3870	142	MO 218	184	MO 4311	23	MO 9319	28	PP 1119	143
KX 3898	40	MO 307	19	MO 4610	21	MO 9320	28	PP 1194	143
KX 3898	142	MO 659	193	MO 4614	185	MO 9321	28	PP 2245	44
KX 3899	40	MO 773	18	MO 4614	194	MO 9322	28	PP 2245	143
KX 3899	142	MO 773	120	MO 4648	24	MO 9323	28	PP 2700	135
KX 3900	40	MO 774	18	MO 4648	146	MO 9324	28	PP 3133	135
KX 3900	142	MO 1196	146	MO 4695	145	MO 9325	28	PP 3005	143
KX 3901	40	MO 1197	146	MO 4984	187	MO 9326	28	PP 3006	143
KX 3901	142	MO 1503	20	MO 5313	193	MO 9327	28	PP 3343	142
KX 4530	135	MO 1504	20	MO 5443	24	MO 9327	143	PP 3344	142

PP 3649	142	RU 7559	162	RX 4348	31	RX 6264	149	RX 9971	194
PP 3811	143	RU 7560	162	RX 4349	31	RX 6264	188	SH 3380	153
PP 3940	142	RU 8058	162	RX 4350	31	RX 6401	154	SH 3380	191
PP 4107	40	RV 6259	167	RX 4351	31	RX 6401	196	SK 1505	137
PP 4107	142	RX 188	37	RX 4352	31	RX 6662	151	SY 4441	170
PP 4281	135	RX 188	141	RX 4353	31	RX 6662	195	TB 2522	181
PP 4308	142	RX 215	145	RX 4556	150	RX 6887	193	TB 2522	186
PP 4388	40	RX 1162	40	RX 4556	191	RX 6888	150	TD 5974	135
PP 4388	142	RX 1162	137	RX 4706	185	RX 6888	191	TF 4155	169
PP 4616	143	RX 1394	29	RX 5432	152	RX 7150	160	TG 1568	173
PP 4837	142	RX 1395	29	RX 5432	190	RX 7150	193	TG 1819	177
PP 4875	44	RX 1396	29	RX 5432	193	RX 7256	150	TJ 1139	42
PP 4875	143	RX 1397	29	RX 5493	154	RX 7256	195	TJ 4511	42
PP 4884	142	RX 1398	30	RX 5493	196	RX 7772	150	TK 2740	160
PP 4885	142	RX 1399	30	RX 5561	31	RX 7772	195	TK 2740	192
PP 5166	44	RX 1456	139	RX 5562	31	RX 8164	35	TM 1258	40
PP 5166	143	RX 1590	139	RX 5563	33	RX 8165	35	TM 1258	137
PP 5930	40	RX 1753	30	RX 5564	33	RX 8166	35	TM 5639	153
PP 5930	120	RX 1754	30	RX 5565	33	RX 8167	35	TM 5726	162
PP 5930	142	RX 1754	125	RX 5566	33	RX 8168	35	TM 5726	194
PP 6279	136	RX 1755	30	RX 5567	33	RX 8169	35	TM 8402	137
PP 6302	40	RX 1755	125	RX 5568	33	RX 8170	35	TO 9554	149
PP 6302	142	RX 1756	30	RX 5569	33	RX 8210	188	TO 9554	186
PP 6432	135	RX 1756	125	RX 5570	33	RX 8261	149	TP 7118	154
PP 6811	143	RX 1757	30	RX 5571	33	RX 8261	184	TP 7118	196
PP 6918	143	RX 1757	125	RX 5571	141	RX 8373	41	TP 7951	159
PP 7563	143	RX 1758	30	RX 5572	33	RX 8373	145	TP 8693	159
PP 7564	143	RX 1758	120	RX 5572	141	RX 8374	41	TP 9164	159
PP 8371	40	RX 1758	125	RX 5573	33	RX 8374	145	TR 1231	149
PP 8371	142	RX 1759	30	RX 5573	141	RX 8375	41	TR 1231	186
PP 8497	135	RX 1759	125	RX 5574	33	RX 8375	145	TR 8198	149
PP 8721	143	RX 1760	30	RX 5574	141	RX 9005	150	TR 8198	186
PP 9263	143	RX 1761	30	RX 5575	33	RX 9005	195	TV 5363	161
PP 9413	137	RX 1761	125	RX 5575	141	RX 9307	35	TV 6036	161
PP 9657	44	RX 1762	30	RX 5576	33	RX 9308	37	TW 8979	40
PP 9657	143	RX 1762	125	RX 5576	142	RX 9309	37	TW 8979	137
PP 9943	136	RX 1763	30	RX 5577	33	RX 9463	156	TX 1965	134
PR 9053	152	RX 1764	30	RX 5577	141	RX 9541	37	TX 9498	173
PY 7380	135	RX 1764	125	RX 5578	33	RX 9541	59	TY 6174	151
RA 1794	152	RX 1992	188	RX 5578	141	RX 9699	37	TY 8886	158
RA 9830	157	RX 2907	161	RX 5579	33	RX 9699	125	UC 4865	36
RD 1886	139	RX 2907	193	RX 5579	141	RX 9700	37	UL 7692	156
RD 1886	149	RX 3131	37	RX 5580	33	RX 9700	125	UL 7692	185
RD 1886	184	RX 3131	136	RX 5580	141	RX 9700	179	UN 3196	160
RD 3016	46	RX 3330	196	RX 6110	33	RX 9701	37	UN 3196	192
RD 6270	46	RX 3553	153	RX 6111	33	RX 9701	125	UN 5227	156
RD 6270	141	RX 3553	185	RX 6112	33	RX 9702	37	UN 5381	156
RD 6270	163	RX 3981	190	RX 6242	33	RX 9702	125	UO 9841	161
RF 1625	40	RX 4101	145	RX 6243	33	RX 9703	37	UR 644	133
RF 1625	142	RX 4109	193	RX 6244	33	RX 9703	125	UR 2932	164
RF 1708	40	RX 4272	150	RX 6245	33	RX 9704	37	UR 3767	47
RF 1708	142	RX 4272	195	RX 6245	141	RX 9704	125	UR 3767	134
RG 881	157	RX 4338	31	RX 6246	33	RX 9705	38	UR 3767	141
RH 2257	155	RX 4339	31	RX 6246	141	RX 9706	38	UR 7968	158
RM 3889	39	RX 4340	31	RX 6246	179	RX 9706	56	UR 9658	166
RM 3889	137	RX 4341	31	RX 6247	33	RX 9707	38	UU 5011	36
RO 9027	47	RX 4341	179	RX 6247	141	RX 9707	56	UU 5749	49
RO 9027	133	RX 4342	31	RX 6248	33	RX 9708	38	UU 7594	149
RT 4952	39	RX 4343	31	RX 6248	141	RX 9709	38	UU 7594	188
RT 4952	137	RX 4343	179	RX 6249	33	RX 9709	56	UV 4080	39
RU 5072	162	RX 4344	31	RX 6249	142	RX 9709	179	UV 4080	141
RU 5394	162	RX 4345	31	RX 6250	33	RX 9710	38	UV 6002	151
RU 5796	155	RX 4346	31	RX 6250	56	RX 9710	56	UV 7778	44
RU 5843	155	RX 4347	31	RX 6250	142	RX 9971	151	UV 7778	143

UV 7962	138	XP 4051	25	ABL 763	180	BBL 563	50	CJB 134	55
UV 7963	138	XP 4705	25	ABL 764	48	BBL 564	50	CJB 135	55
UV 7964	138	XP 4706	25	ABL 765	48	BBL 565	50	CJB 136	55
UV 7965	138	XP 5449	25	ABL 766	48	BBL 565	180	CJB 137	55
UV 7966	138	XP 5450	25	ABL 767	48	BBL 566	50	CJB 138	55
UV 7967	138	XP 5984	25	ABL 768	48	BBP 339	168	CJB 139	56
UV 9116	149	XP 5985	25	ACG 644	160	BFC 675	203	CJB 139	180
UV 9116	188	XP 6421	25	ACG 644	192	BHJ 532	54	CJB 140	56
UV 9121	36	XP 6422	25	ADF 797	137	BHJ 533	54	CJB 141	56
UV 9413	36	XP 9080	25	AFC 531	203	BJB 580	70	CKL 719	165
UV 9414	36	XP 9081	25	AGJ 929	177	BKE 720	168	CMO 523	170
UW 2615	138	XP 9325	25	AGP 841	177	BKX 431	44	CMO 624	171
UW 2616	138	XP 9831	25	AGX 455	177	BKX 431	144	CMO 653	56
UW 6646	138	XR 999	27	AHJ 401	54	BKX 696	44	CMO 654	56
UW 7597	139	XR 4559	27	AHJ 402	54	BKX 696	144	CMO 655	56
UW 7598	139	XR 4694	27	AHJ 403	54	BKX 898	44	CMO 657	171
UW 7599	139	XR 9847	27	AJB 811	48	BKX 898	144	CMO 658	171
UW 7600	139	XU 2191	25	AJB 812	48	BMG 703	49	CMO 659	171
UW 7601	139	XV 5867	134	AJB 813	48	BMO 980	51	CPA 828	166
UX 9410	156	YB 7442	150	AJB 814	48	BMO 981	51	CPP 80	49
VA 3156	149	YB 7442	188	AJB 814	180	BMO 982	51	CRR 820	137
VA 3156	184	YD 9912	165	AJB 815	48	BMO 983	51	CRX 196	57
VA 7942	152	YE 8768	150	AJB 815	180	BMO 984	51	CRX 197	57
VA 7943	152	YE 8768	188	AJB 816	48	BMO 985	51	CRX 198	57
VF 1381	134	YF 3921	36	AJB 816	180	BMO 986	51	CRX 279	172
VF 3004	40	YF 6815	39	AJB 817	48	BMO 987	51	CRX 280	172
VF 3004	137	YH 3797	36	AJB 818	48	BMO 988	51	CRX 281	172
VF 9339	164	YH 3800	36	AJB 818	180	BMO 989	51	CRX 282	172
VG 1631	47	YK 3822	36	AJB 819	48	BON 886	162	CRX 283	172
VG 1631	133	YR 1089	36	AJB 820	48	BON 887	162	CRX 333	70
VM 3669	155	YT 5420	49	AMD 47	177	BPG 531	165	CRX 540	57
VM 8638	139	YT 9565	150	APC 421	36	BPH 293	170	CRX 541	57
VM 8638	149	YT 9565	188	APP 271	44	BPP 141	49	CRX 542	57
VM 8638	184	YV 3567	135	APP 271	143	BRX 656	52	CRX 543	57
VR 9822	163	YV 5053	134	APP 272	44	BRX 908	52	CRX 544	57
VT 184	149	YV 5499	166	APP 272	143	BRX 909	52	CRX 545	57
VT 184	186	YW 1721	36	APP 273	44	BRX 910	52	CRX 546	57
VT 2653	42	YW 1721	40	APP 273	143	BRX 911	52	CRX 547	57
VX 43	149	YW 1721	142	ARA 370	166	BRX 912	52	CRX 548	58
VX 43	188	YW 5366	36	ARX 981	50	BRX 913	52	CRX 549	58
VX 6462	134	YX 5680	39	ARX 982	50	BRX 914	52	CRX 550	58
VX 6549	49			ARX 983	50	BRX 915	52	CRX 551	58
VX 6549	141			ARX 984	50	BRX 916	52	CRX 595	174
WL 2696	201	ABH 350	44	ARX 985	50	BRX 917	52	CRX 596	174
WL 4131	201	ABH 350	143	ARX 986	50	BRX 918	52	CWL 951	178
WL 5055	201	ABL 751	48	ARX 987	50	BRX 919	52	CWL 951	203
WL 7221	202	ABL 751	141	ARX 988	50	BRX 920	52	CWL 953	178
WL 7233	202	ABL 752	48	ARX 989	50	BRX 921	52	CWL 953	203
WL 7240	202	ABL 752	141	ARX 990	50	BRX 921	120	CYL 243	54
WL 7456	202	ABL 753	48	ARX 990	180	BRX 922	52	DBL 151	58
WL 9058	202	ABL 753	141	ARX 991	50	BRX 923	52	DBL 152	58
WL 9076	202	ABL 754	48	ARX 992	50	BRX 924	52	DBL 153	58
WL 9079	202	ABL 754	141	AUB 354	167	BRX 925	52	DBL 154	58
WL 9081	202	ABL 755	48	AVO 977	166	BUA 795	170	DBL 155	58
WL 9415	202	ABL 755	141	AYA 102	161	BWL 349	178	DBL 156	58
WL 9810	202	ABL 756	48	BBH 755	44	BWL 349	203	DBL 157	58
WL 9862	202	ABL 756	141	BBH 755	144	CAP 132	80	DBL 158	58
WL 9942	202	ABL 757	48	BBL 557	50	CAP 176	80	DBL 159	58
WP 6206	163	ABL 758	48	BBL 558	50	CAP 206	80	DBL 160	58
WU 9870	149	ABL 759	48	BBL 558	180	CAP 206	209	DBL 161	59
WU 9870	186	ABL 760	48	BBL 559	50	CAP 211	80	DBL 162	59
WX 7898	169	ABL 761	48	BBL 560	50	CJB 131	53	DBL 163	59
XH 8592	195	ABL 761	141	BBL 561	50	CJB 132	55	DBL 164	59
XK 7225	184	ABL 762	48	BBL 562	50	CJB 133	55	DBL 165	59
		ABL 763	48						

DBL 166	59	EJB 210	60	FBL 920	178	FMO 963	67	GJB 253	71
DBL 167	59	EJB 211	60	FBL 921	178	FMO 964	67	GJB 254	71
DMO 320	175	EJB 212	60	FLJ 978	86	FMO 965	68	GJB 255	71
DMO 321	175	EJB 213	60	FMO 7	64	FMO 966	68	GJB 256	71
DMO 322	175	EJB 214	60	FMO 8	64	FMO 967	68	GJB 257	71
DMO 323	175	EJB 215	60	FMO 9	63	FMO 968	64	GJB 258	71
DMO 324	175	EJB 216	60	FMO 10	64	FMO 969	64	GJB 259	71
DMO 325	175	EJB 217	60	FMO 11	64	FMO 970	64	GJB 260	71
DMO 326	175	EJB 218	60	FMO 12	64	FMO 971	64	GJB 261	71
DMO 327	175	EJB 219	62	FMO 13	64	FMO 972	64	GJB 262	71
DMO 328	175	EJB 220	62	FMO 14	64	FMO 973	64	GJB 263	71
DMO 329	175	EJB 221	60	FMO 15	64	FMO 974	64	GJB 264	71
DMO 330	175	EJB 222	62	FMO 16	64	FMO 975	64	GJB 265	71
DMO 331	175	EJB 223	62	FMO 17	64	FMO 976	64	GJB 266	71
DMO 332	175	EJB 224	62	FMO 18	64	FMO 977	68	GJB 267	71
DMO 333	175	EJB 225	62	FMO 19	64	FMO 978	68	GJB 268	71
DMO 664	59	EJB 226	62	FMO 20	64	FMO 979	68	GJB 269	71
DMO 665	60	EJB 227	62	FMO 20	212	FMO 980	68	GJB 270	71
DMO 666	59	EJB 228	62	FMO 21	64	FMO 981	68	GJB 271	71
DMO 667	59	EJB 229	62	FMO 22	64	FMO 982	68	GJB 272	68
DMO 668	60	EJB 230	62	FMO 23	64	FMO 983	65	GJB 273	68
DMO 669	59	EJB 231	62	FMO 23	83	FMO 984	65	GJB 274	68
DMO 670	59	EJB 232	62	FMO 23	209	FMO 985	65	GJB 275	68
DMO 671	59	EJB 233	62	FMO 24	64	FPU 509	85	GJB 276	68
DMO 672	60	EJB 234	62	FMO 25	64	FPU 510	85	GJB 277	68
DMO 673	60	EJB 235	62	FMO 25	212	FPU 510	120	GJB 278	68
DMO 674	60	EJB 236	62	FMO 26	64	FPU 511	86	GJB 279	68
DMO 675	60	EJB 237	62	FMO 26	212	FPU 513	86	GJB 280	68
DMO 676	60	EJB 238	62	FMO 515	178	FPU 515	85	GJB 281	68
DMO 677	60	EJB 239	62	FMO 516	178	FPU 517	85	GJB 282	68
DMO 678	60	EJB 240	63	FMO 517	178	FRP 832	207	GJB 283	68
DMO 679	60	EJB 241	63	FMO 934	64	FRP 833	207	GJB 284	68
DMO 680	60	EJB 242	63	FMO 934	212	FRP 834	207	GJB 285	68
DMO 681	60	EJB 521	176	FMO 935	64	FRP 835	211	GJB 286	71
DMO 682	60	EJB 649	176	FMO 935	209	FRP 836	207	GJB 287	71
DMO 683	60	EJB 649	206	FMO 936	64	FRP 837	211	GJB 288	71
DMO 684	60	EJB 650	176	FMO 936	212	FRP 838	211	GLB 887	162
DMO 685	60	EJB 650	206	FMO 937	64	FRP 839	211	GLU 645	39
DMO 686	60	EKP 140	165	FMO 937	212	FRP 840	211	GNO 688	87
DMO 687	60	ERX 937	177	FMO 938	64	FRP 841	211	GNO 698	87
DMO 688	60	ERX 937	206	FMO 939	64	FRP 842	211	HAD 745	177
DMO 689	60	EWO 454	172	FMO 940	64	FRP 843	84	HAX 657	206
DMO 690	60	EWO 476	172	FMO 941	64	FRP 844	84	HAX 828	206
DNW 359	169	EWO 479	172	FMO 942	64	FRX 313	65	HBL 53	71
DWN 258	173	EWO 480	172	FMO 943	64	FRX 314	65	HBL 54	71
DWN 295	173	EWO 481	172	FMO 944	64	FRX 315	65	HBL 55	71
DWN 298	173	EWO 484	178	FMO 945	64	FWL 795	203	HBL 56	71
DWN 299	173	EWO 490	179	FMO 946	64	FWL 797	203	HBL 57	71
DWN 379	93	EWO 492	179	FMO 947	64	GBL 871	68	HBL 58	71
DXV 741	54	EXF 878	55	FMO 948	64	GBL 872	68	HBL 59	71
DYF 184	162	FAD 253	175	FMO 949	64	GBL 872	212	HBL 60	71
EAX 647	172	FAX 349	177	FMO 950	64	GBL 873	68	HBL 61	71
EBD 234	75	FBL 23	63	FMO 951	64	GBL 873	212	HBL 62	71
EBD 234	207	FBL 24	63	FMO 952	67	GBL 874	68	HBL 63	71
EBD 235	75	FBL 25	63	FMO 953	67	GBL 874	214	HBL 64	71
EBD 235	207	FBL 26	63	FMO 954	67	GBL 875	68	HBL 65	73
EBD 236	207	FBL 27	63	FMO 955	67	GBL 876	68	HBL 66	73
EBD 237	207	FBL 28	64	FMO 956	67	GFM 881	89	HBL 67	73
EBL 736	175	FBL 29	64	FMO 957	67	GFM 882	89	HBL 68	73
EBL 967	70	FBL 30	64	FMO 958	67	GFM 884	89	HBL 69	73
EJB 146	176	FBL 31	64	FMO 959	67	GFM 887	89	HBL 70	73
EJB 147	176	FBL 32	64	FMO 960	67	GFM 888	89	HBL 71	73
EJB 148	176	FBL 33	64	FMO 961	67	GJB 251	68	HBL 72	73
EJB 209	60	FBL 919	178	FMO 962	67	GJB 252	68	HBL 73	71

Reg	No	Reg	No	Reg	No	Reg	No	Reg	No
HBL 73	214	HMO 863	75	LFW 317	115	MJO 667	205	ORX 633	209
HBL 74	71	HMO 864	76	LFW 318	115	MPU 11	86	ORX 634	106
HBL 74	216	HMO 865	76	LFW 322	113	MPU 13	87	ORX 634	209
HBL 75	71	HMO 866	76	LFW 324	113	MPU 16	87	OTT 2	75
HBL 75	213	HMO 867	76	LFW 329	111	MUR 500	179	PHN 819	102
HBL 76	71	HMO 868	76	LHY 939	70	MWL 741	205	PHN 821	102
HBL 76	215	HMO 869	78	LJO 756	67	MWL 742	205	PHN 828	102
HBL 77	71	HMO 870	78	LJO 756	178	MWL 743	205	PHN 829	102
HBL 77	216	HMO 871	78	LJO 756	204	MWL 744	205	PHW 929	102
HBL 78	71	HOT 391	179	LJO 757	67	NBE 129	111	PHW 930	102
HBL 79	71	HOT 392	179	LJO 757	178	NBE 130	113	PHW 931	102
HBL 80	71	HOT 393	179	LJO 757	205	NBE 133	111	PHW 932	102
HBL 81	73	HOT 394	179	LJO 758	204	NBL 731	79	PNN 769	118
HBL 82	73	HTT 980	84	LJO 759	204	NBL 732	79	PRX 926	82
HBL 83	73	JCY 989	96	LJO 760	204	NBL 733	79	PRX 927	82
HBL 84	73	JCY 990	96	LJO 761	205	NBL 734	81	PRX 928	83
HBL 85	73	JCY 991	100	LWL 995	178	NBL 735	81	PRX 929	83
HBL 86	73	JCY 992	100	LWL 995	204	NBL 736	81	PRX 930	107
HBL 87	73	JCY 993	99	LWL 995	210	NBL 737	81	PRX 930	210
HBL 88	73	JCY 994	99	LWL 996	204	NBL 738	81	PRX 931	107
HBL 89	73	JCY 995	99	LWL 997	204	NBL 739	81	PRX 931	210
HFC 548	204	JCY 996	99	LWL 998	204	NBL 740	81	PRX 932	107
HFC 550	204	JCY 997	96	LWL 999	204	NBL 741	81	PRX 932	210
HMO 834	73	JFC 12	204	LWN 48	95	NBL 742	81	PRX 933	110
HMO 834	93	JFC 42	204	LWN 49	95	NBL 743	81	PRX 933	210
HMO 834	213	JFC 707	204	LWN 50	95	NBL 744	82	SFC 501	208
HMO 835	73	JRX 801	76	LWN 51	95	NBL 745	82	SFC 502	208
HMO 835	91	JRX 802	76	LWN 52	96	NBL 746	82	SFC 503	208
HMO 835	210	JRX 803	76	LWN 53	96	NBL 747	82	SFC 504	208
HMO 836	73	JRX 804	76	MAX 116	104	NBL 748	82	SFC 565	206
HMO 836	91	JRX 805	76	MAX 117	104	NBL 749	82	SFC 566	206
HMO 836	210	JRX 806	76	MAX 118	104	NBL 750	82	SFC 567	206
HMO 837	75	JRX 807	76	MAX 119	104	NCY 634	103	SFC 568	206
HMO 837	91	JRX 808	76	MAX 121	104	NCY 635	103	SFC 569	206
HMO 837	214	JRX 809	76	MAX 122	104	NCY 636	103	SFC 570	206
HMO 838	75	JRX 810	76	MAX 123	104	NCY 637	103	SFC 571	206
HMO 838	93	JRX 811	76	MAX 125	104	NCY 638	103	SHN 728	102
HMO 838	210	JRX 812	76	MAX 126	104	NFC 128	205	SHN 729	102
HMO 839	75	JRX 813	76	MAX 127	104	NFC 129	205	SHN 730	102
HMO 839	93	JRX 814	76	MAX 128	104	NFC 130	205	SMO 78	83
HMO 839	210	JRX 815	76	MBL 831	79	NJO 217	205	SMO 79	83
HMO 840	73	JRX 816	76	MBL 832	79	NJO 218	205	SMO 80	83
HMO 841	73	JRX 817	76	MBL 833	79	NWL 877	205	SMO 81	83
HMO 842	73	JRX 818	76	MBL 834	79	NWL 878	205	SMO 82	83
HMO 843	73	JRX 819	76	MBL 835	79	NWL 879	205	THW 742	114
HMO 844	73	JRX 820	78	MBL 836	79	OCY 947	97	THW 743	114
HMO 845	73	JRX 821	78	MBL 837	79	OCY 948	97	THW 744	114
HMO 846	73	JRX 822	78	MBL 838	79	OCY 953	103	THW 745	114
HMO 847	73	JRX 823	78	MBL 839	79	OCY 954	107	THW 750	114
HMO 848	73	JRX 824	78	MBL 840	79	OCY 955	107	TWL 55	95
HMO 849	73	JVW 430	59	MBL 841	79	OCY 956	107	TWL 55	208
HMO 850	73	JWO 213	208	MBL 842	79	OCY 957	107	TWL 56	95
HMO 851	75	JWO 546	208	MBL 843	79	OCY 958	108	TWL 56	208
HMO 852	73	KHU 601	84	MBL 844	79	OCY 960	108	TWL 57	95
HMO 853	73	KHU 604	84	MBL 845	79	OCY 961	108	TWL 57	208
HMO 854	73	KHU 605	84	MBL 846	79	OCY 962	108	TWL 58	95
HMO 855	73	KHU 606	84	MBL 847	79	OFC 204	206	TWL 58	208
HMO 856	73	KHU 622	85	MBL 848	79	OFC 205	206	TWL 59	99
HMO 857	75	KHU 624	84	MBL 849	79	OFC 206	206	TWL 59	208
HMO 858	75	KHW 633	84	MBL 850	79	ORX 631	106	TWL 60	99
HMO 859	75	KWN 794	95	MCY 39	96	ORX 631	209	TWL 60	208
HMO 860	75	KWN 795	95	MJO 278	205	ORX 632	106	UJB 196	114
HMO 861	75	KWN 796	95	MJO 664	205	ORX 632	209	UJB 196	211
HMO 862	75	KWN 797	95	MJO 665	205	ORX 633	106	UJB 197	211

Reg	No.	Reg	No.	Reg	No.	Reg	No.	Reg	No.	Reg	No.
UJB 198	211	216 ANN	119	ABL 117B	90	LBL 852E	97	VMO 225H	105		
UJB 199	211	724 APU	78	ABL 118B	90	LBL 853E	97	VMO 226H	105		
UJB 200	85	956 ARA	111	ABL 119B	90	LJB 417E	97	VMO 227H	105		
UJB 201	85	957 ARA	114	AHW 227B	108	LJB 417E	114	VMO 228H	105		
UJB 202	85	958 ARA	114	BRX 141B	90	LJB 417E	218	VMO 229H	105		
UJB 203	85	959 ARA	111	BRX 142B	90	LJB 418E	97	VMO 230H	105		
UJB 204	85	960 ARA	114	CBL 355B	90	LJB 418E	107	VMO 231H	105		
VFM 607	111	961 ARA	111	CBL 356B	90	LJB 418E	218	VMO 232H	105		
VFM 611	112	962 ARA	114	CBL 357B	90	LJB 419E	97	VMO 233H	105		
VFM 617	112	963 ARA	114	CMO 833B	90	LJB 420E	97	VMO 234H	105		
VFM 618	112	964 ARA	118	CMO 834B	90	LJB 421E	216	VMO 235H	105		
VFM 622	112	966 ARA	118	CMO 835B	90	LJB 422E	216	XMO 541H	109		
VJB 943	85	967 ARA	118	CMO 836B	90	LJB 423E	216	XMO 542H	109		
VJB 944	85	536 BBL	88	DJB 529C	92	MBW 159E	218	XRX 819H	109		
VJB 945	85	537 BBL	88	DJB 530C	92	LJB 331F	97	XRX 820H	109		
VJB 946	85	538 BBL	88	DRX 120C	92	LJB 332F	97	YBL 925H	218		
VJB 947	85	539 BBL	88	DRX 121C	92	LJB 333F	97	YBL 926H	218		
VJB 948	85	540 BBL	88	DRX 122C	92	LJB 334F	98	YBL 927H	218		
WAL 440	118	541 BBL	88	EMO 551C	215	LJB 335F	98	YBL 928H	218		
WJB 223	87	542 BBL	88	EMO 552C	215	LJB 336F	98	YJB 521H	109		
WJB 224	87	543 BBL	89	EMO 553C	215	LJB 337F	98	YJB 522H	109		
WJB 225	87	544 BBL	89	FBL 483C	92	LJB 338F	98	YJB 523H	109		
WJB 226	87	545 BBL	89	FBL 484C	92	PBL 53F	100	ABL 121J	109		
WJB 227	87	546 BBL	89	FBL 485C	92	PBL 55F	100	ABL 122J	109		
WJB 228	87	547 BBL	89	FJB 738C	92	PBL 56F	100	AMO 233J	109		
WJB 229	87	548 BBL	89	FJB 739C	92	PBL 57F	100	AMO 234J	109		
WJB 230	87	549 BBL	89	FJB 740C	92	PBL 58F	100	AMO 235J	109		
WJB 231	87	191 BRR	119	GBL 907C	92	PBL 59F	100	AMO 236J	109		
WJB 232	87	668 COD	110	GJB 874C	92	PBL 60F	100	AMO 237J	109		
WJB 233	87	669 COD	110	GMO 827C	92	RJB 424F	100	AMO 238J	109		
WJB 234	87	831 CRX	214	GMO 828C	92	RJB 425F	100	BJB 883J	115		
WJB 235	87	832 CRX	214	GRX 129D	93	RJB 426F	100	BJB 884J	115		
WRX 773	213	833 CRX	214	GRX 130D	93	RJB 427F	100	CJB 587J	115		
WRX 774	213	834 CRX	215	GRX 131D	93	RJB 428F	217	CJB 588J	115		
WRX 775	213	835 CRX	215	GRX 132D	94	RJB 429F	217	CJB 589J	115		
WRX 776	213	836 CRX	90	GRX 133D	94	RJB 430F	217	CJB 590J	115		
XFM 186	113	837 CRX	215	GRX 134D	94	RJB 431F	217	CMO 647J	115		
XFM 187	111	838 CRX	112	GRX 135D	94	RRX 991G	100	CMO 648J	115		
XFM 190	111	838 CRX	215	GRX 136D	94	RRX 992G	100	CMO 649J	115		
XFM 192	111	839 CRX	89	GRX 137D	94	RRX 993G	100	DRX 101K	115		
XFM 193	112	840 CRX	89	GRX 138D	94	RRX 994G	100	DRX 102K	115		
XFM 195	111	841 CRX	89	GRX 139D	94	RRX 995G	100	DRX 103K	115		
XFM 196	112	842 CRX	215	GRX 140D	94	RRX 996G	100	DRX 104K	115		
XNU 415	119	14 DRB	113	GRX 141D	94	RRX 997G	100	DRX 625K	115		
XNU 416	119	16 DRB	117	GRX 142D	94	RRX 998G	100	DRX 626K	115		
		17 DRB	117	GRX 143D	94	SRX 944G	105	DRX 627K	115		
516 ABL	93	18 DRB	117	GRX 144D	94	SRX 945G	100	EBL 390K	115		
516 ABL	213	19 DRB	117	GRX 145D	94	UBL 243G	105	EBL 437K	115		
517 ABL	93	20 DRB	117	GRX 146D	94	UBL 244G	105	EBL 438K	115		
517 ABL	213	566 ERR	119	GRX 413D	215	UBL 245G	105	FBL 112K	115		
518 ABL	213	613 JPU	217	GRX 414D	215	UBL 246G	105	FBL 113K	115		
519 ABL	213	614 JPU	217	GRX 415D	216	UBL 247G	105	FBL 114K	115		
520 ABL	88	618 JPU	217	GRX 416D	216	UBL 248G	105				
520 ABL	97	515 JRA	119	JJJ 568D	218	UMO 688G	218	ZI 1810	134		
520 ABL	216	844 THY	108	LBL 847E	97	UMO 689G	218	37 JIP	218		
521 ABL	214	845 THY	110	LBL 848E	97	UMO 690G	218				
213 ANN	118	846 THY	110	LBL 849E	97	UMO 691G	218				
214 ANN	118			LBL 850E	97	VMO 223H	105				
215 ANN	119	ABL 116B	90	LBL 851E	97	VMO 224H	105				

HISTORICAL COUNTY CODES

GOV   Government Department

Code	County	Code	County
AD	Aberdeenshire	KK	Kirkcudbrightshire
AH	Armagh	KN	Kesteven division of Lincolnshire
AL	Argyllshire	KS	Kinross-shire
AM	Antrim	KT	Kent
AR	Ayrshire	LA	Lancashire
AS	Angus	LC	Lincoln (City)
AY	Isle of Anglesey	LE	Leicestershire
BC	Brecknockshire	LI	Lindsey division of Lincolnshire
BD	Bedfordshire	LK	Lanarkshire
BE	Berkshire	LN	London Postal area
BF	Banffshire	LY	Londonderry
BK	Buckinghamshire	ME	Merionethshire
BU	Buteshire	MH	Monmouthshire
BW	Berwickshire	MN	Midlothian
CG	Cardiganshire	MO	Montgomeryshire
CH	Cheshire	MR	Morayshire
CI	Channel Islands	MX	Middlesex
CK	Clackmannanshire	ND	Northumberland
CM	Cambridgeshire	NG	Nottinghamshire
CN	Caernarvonshire	NK	Norfolk
CO	Cornwall	NN	Nairnshire
CR	Carmarthenshire	NO	Northamptonshire
CS	Caithness	NR	North Riding of Yorkshire
CU	Cumberland	OK	Orkney Islands
DB	Dunbartonshire	OX	Oxfordshire
DE	Derbyshire	PB	Peebles-shire
DF	Dumfries-shire	PE	Pembrokeshire
DH	Denbighshire	PH	Perthshire
DM	County Durham	RD	Rutland
DN	Devon	RH	Roxburghshire
DO	Down	RR	Radnorshire
DT	Dorset	RW	Renfrewshire
EI	Eire	RY	Ross-shire & Cromarty
EK	East Suffolk	SD	Shetland Islands
EL	East Lothian	SH	Shropshire
ER	East Riding of Yorkshire	SI	Selkirkshire
ES	East Sussex	SN	Stirlingshire
EX	Essex	SO	Somerset
EY	Isle of Ely	SP	Soke of Peterborough
FE	Fife	SR	Surrey
FH	Fermanagh	ST	Staffordshire
FT	Flintshire	SU	Sutherland
GG	Glamorgan	TY	Tyrone
GL	Gloucestershire	WF	West Suffolk
HA	Hampshire	WI	Wiltshire
HD	Holland division of Lincolnshire	WK	Warwickshire
HN	Huntingdonshire	WL	West Lothian
HR	Herefordshire	WN	Wigtownshire
HT	Hertfordshire	WO	Worcestershire
IM	Isle of Man	WR	West Riding of Yorkshire
IV	Inverness	WS	West Sussex
IW	Isle of Wight	WT	Westmorland
KE	Kincardineshire	YK	York (City)

Note: A 'G' prefix (eg GBE) indicates the vehicle had been converted to goods (eg lorry or van) and the operator was a goods operator (in this case, in Berkshire).

OVERSEAS COUNTRY CODES

O-A	Austria
O-CDN	Canada
O-CH	Switzerland
O-CY	Cyprus
O-D	Germany
O-F	France
O-HK	Hong Kong
O-IC	Canary Islands
O-MAC	Macao
O-NL	Netherlands
O-RUS	Russia
O-USA	United States of America
O-YU	Yugoslavia

ABBREVIATIONS USED FOR MANUFACTURERS

ACB	Associated Coachbuilders Ltd
BBW	Brislington Body Works
CPT	Consolidated Pneumatic Tool Co Ltd
ECOC	Eastern Counties Omnibus Co Ltd
ECW	Eastern Coach Works Ltd
LGOC	London General Omnibus Co Ltd
NCME	Northern Counties Motor & Engineering Co Ltd
RSJ	Ransomes, Sims & Jeffries Ltd
TSM	Tilling-Stevens Motors Ltd